Operation and Control in Power Systems

Second Edition

Operation and Control in Power Systems

Second Edition

Prof. P. S. R. MURTY
B.Sc. (Engg.) (Hons.) M.E.,
Dr. - Ing (Berlin), F.I.E. (India)
Life Member – ISTE

(Formerly Principal O.U. College of Engineering &
Dean, Faculty of Engineering, O.U. Hyderabad)

Director,
School of Electrical Engineering,
Sreenidhi Institute of Science and Technology

BSP BS Publications
An Imprint of **BSP Books Pvt. Ltd.**
4-4-309/316, Giriraj Lane,
Sultan Bazar, Hyderabad - 500 095

Operation and Control in Power Systems Second Edition ***by*** **P. S. R. Murty**

Sixth Reprint 2026

Published by :

BSP BS Publications

An imprint of **BSP Books Pvt., Ltd.**

4-4-309/316, Giriraj Lane, Sultan Bazar, Hyderabad - 500 095
Phone : 040 - 23445688
e-mail : info@bspbooks.net
website: www.bspbooks.net

Printed at

Repro India Limited.

Price: Rs. 795.00
ISBN: 978-81-7800-200-2 (Paperback)

Dedicated to the

LOTUS FEET OF
BHAGWAN SRI SRI SRI SATYA SAI BABA

Acknowledgment

I wish to acknowledge the *Management and Principal of Sreenidhi Institute of Science & Technology,* for proving facilities in the preparation of the manuscript.

I wish to acknowledge the help rendered in solving some of the problems in the book with MATLAB by *T. Chandra Sekhar* of the Department of Electrical & Electronics Engineering.

I thank *R. Dinesh Kumar* for giving excellent Secretarial Assistance and *M.V.L. Narasimha Rao* for his keen interest in the processing of proofs.

P. S. R. Murty

Preface to Second Edition

It is heartening to find that the book an "*Operational and Control in Power Systems*" is welcomed by both faculty and students of Electrical engineering. The utility of the book is enhanced by addition of some useful information and by thoroughly revising the contents in the book.

All the chapters of the first edition are revised. More information has been added to chapter on Introduction to Advanced Topics, Effect of Shunt Compensators, Controllable VAR Generation, Switching Converter type VAR generators are added. The topic 'Voltage Stability' is extended with some mathematical treatment. Methods of preventing voltage collapse are mentioned. In State Estimation, Least Squares Estimation, procedure is elaborated.

It is hoped that the present edition will be welcomed and found to be quite useful by electrical engineering teaching faculty as well as students.

P. S. R. Murty

Preface to First Edition

Operation and control of interconnected power systems is a field where significant changes are taking place continuously. Energy demand is growing at the rate of nearly ten per cent per annum. Generation is added in stages along with transmission capacity. The integration of the five electrical regional grids which operate at different frequencies into a single national grid requires knowledge of various control strategies for proper inter regional exchange of power within the region and within the states proper maintenance of power quality is very important.

Further, given the system in controlled steady state, economic operation of the power system wherein the generation costs, transmission losses and the related matters become important.

Analysis of the system in operation, development of suitable models for each mode in operation and control and application of mathematical theory to obtain useful results – are all important in practice.

The aim of this book is to provide at a single place all the relevant information including the latest advanced topics that have emerged in recent years – to students of Power Systems at both under graduate and Post Graduate level.

Several problems are worked out for illustrating the results developed which the student may find very useful.

P. S. R. Murty

Contents

4 Optimal Load Flow

5 Unit Commitment

6 Load Frequency Control

7 Control of Interconnected Systems

1 INTRODUCTION

Elecrical energy is the most popular form of energy, because it can be transported easily at high efficiency and reasonable costs. Thomas Edison, established the first power station in 1882 at New York city, United States of America. The lower Manhattan area was supplied DC power from this station. Underground cables were used for distribution. At Appelton, Wisconcin the first water wheel generator was installed. Under Edison's patents several companies started functioning in USA. However, these companies could supply energy to small distances due to I^2R power loss being excessive at low voltage distribution.

In 1885, Willliam Stanley invented the transformer, which revolutionized the AC transmission. The invention of induction motor in 1888 by Nikola Tesla caused dramatic change in electrical power consumption through AC replacing many DC motor loads.

It is now an acknowledged fact that HV and EHV transmission alone can reduce substantially the losses and bulk power transmission is feasible at these voltages. Nevertheless, it is also well established that HVDC is convenient and more economical from operation and control point of view under certain circumstances such as at distances of more than 500 kms. A detailed discussion of this aspect is not within the purview of this book.

In India, two third of the electrical power generated is from coal based power stations. Of the rest, about 24% comes from hydroelectric, 8.7% from Gas fired plants, 2.4% from nuclear power plants. At the time of independence, the per capita consumption of electric energy was 1.3 units. It is now about 3 units while China's per capita consumption is about 6 units. Developed countries have per capita consumptions of as high as 8,500 units. This shows the great disparity that exists between the rich and the poor countries. However, Indian Power Sector has undergone revolutionary changes. While in 1947 the installed capacity was at 1300 MW, today it has surpassed 1,00,000 MW. In India, Nuclear Power has a target of 350 GW, and Hydro Power is estimated at 84 GW by CEA.

1.1 Structure of a Power System

The Power system consists of three subsystems which have clearly demarcated functions. But, coordinated working of all the three subsystems is absolutely essential as they are parts of the same system. The subsystems are:

(i) the generation subsystem,

(ii) the transmission subsystem and

(iii) the distribution subsystem.

The generation subsystem may be called GENCO, responsible for generating electric power as per the predicted load requirements.

The transmission subsystem may be called TRANSCO. Its essential duties are to provide facilities for transmission of the required power demand at various load centers. The transmitting grid of power lines must be suitably rated and well protected with circuit breakers and relays.

The distribution subsystem may called DISCOM which is the actual link between the system and the customers. Fig. 1.1 shows a single line representation of the total system.

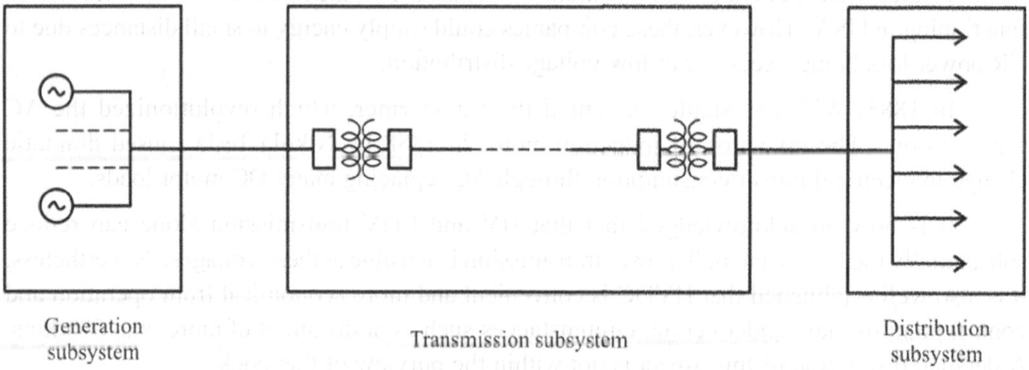

Fig. 1.1 Structure of a power system

In India regional and national power grids are established to facilitate transfer of power within and across the regions with reliability, security and economy on sound commercial principles. The Power Grid Corporation was established in August 1991 and it started its commercial operations from 1992-93. It is one of the largest transmission utilities in the world. The power grid is an ISO 9001 company with complete capability in AC transmission upto 765 kV level and HVDC transmission upto ± 500 kV. Challenging jobs in operation and maintenance of the national demand which is expected to reach a peak value of 114000 MW by 2006 are undertaken by Power Grid Corporation. Power Grid is also engaged in activities such as unified load dispatch which facilitates close monitoring of grid with real time data for economic dispatch of power between the five regional grids and states.

Planning, design, operation, control and protection of power systems requires continuous and comprehensive analysis to evaluate the current states and remedial control, if any, needed. Manual computation of power flows is extremely time consuming even for very simple networks. In 1929, AC network analyzer, an analog computer was devised. Most of the early system studies were performed on the network analyzer.

The Indian Power Grid System is divided into five regional grids. The southern region comprises of Andhra Pradesh, Tamilnadu, Karnataka, Kerala and Pondichery. All these State Electricity Boards are integrated for operation into Southern Regional Electricity Board. Likewise, other boards are formed. Each state has inter State and Inter Regional links. For example Andhra Pradesh and Maharastra have a tie-line at Ramagundam – Chandrapur 400 kV link at Chandrapur.

In a similar way Andhra Pradesh has tie-line connections with Orissa, Madhaya Pradesh, Tamilnadu and Karnataka.

The stipulated system frequency in India is 50 Hz. Since, there is deficit of generation in the southern region, the operating frequency goes to 48.5 Hz. States like, Maharastra, Madhyapradesh, and Orissa operate at 50 to 52 Hz. Andhra Pradesh imports power through HVDC back to back system at Chandrapur through the 400 kV AC double circuit line from Chandrapur-Ramagundam. In a similar way, through the HVDC back to back system at Gajuwaka power is transmitted via 400 kV Jaypore-Gajuwaka double circuit AC line from Orissa.

While, we have dealt with the frequency scenario, it is worthwhile, to look at the other performance index of electric power, the voltage profile. 400 kV lines have their voltage falling to 340.3 kV at Cuddapah, 220 kV lines reaching 160.8 kV at Sullurpet and 132 kV lines operating at 95.8 kV at Nagarkurnool.

From the above, it can be seen that there is very heavy demand for electric power in these areas seriously compromising the power quality. While more generation is needed to be added continuously a thorough knowledge of various aspects involved in the study of power system operation and control is very essential for electric power engineers. This book is dedicated to this task in a manner that students of power engineering grasp the essential concepts involved in operation and control.

The system variables are continuously changing in both magnitude and number. The system never reaches a steady state so as to permit any tests to be carried out on it, so that its dynamic behaviour can be ascertained. In practice, it requires both continuous and discrete controls. The spread of the power systems over vast geographical areas contributes to its vulnerability to environmental changes. The system's dynamics extends over a broad band width ranging from micro seconds to several minutes.

Planning operation and control of isolated or inter connected power systems present a large variety of challenging problems, the solution of which requires application of several mathematical techniques from various branches of it. Knowledge of optimization techniques and optimal control methods is very essential to understand the multi level approach that has been very successfully utilized. Various mathematical techniques that needed to be applied are explained at the appropriate places while dealing with the subject.

1.2 Models for Analysis and Control

Power system engineering is a branch where practically all the results of modern control theory can be applied. Such an application will result in economy, better quality of service and the least inconvenience under abnormal situations, both anticipated and unforeseen.

Control system design, in general, for its analytical treatment, requires the determination of a mathematical model from which the control strategy can be derived. While much of the control theory postulates that a model of the system is available. It is also necessary to have a suitable technique to determine the models for the process to be controlled. Thus, it is required to model and identify power system components using both physical relationships and experimental or normal operating data. The objective of system identification is the determination of a mathematical model characterizing the operation of a system in some form. The available information is either system outputs or some functions of outputs which may contain measurement noise. The inputs may be known functions applied for the purpose of identification, or unknown functions which it may be possible to monitor somehow, or a combination of both.

The identified model may be in the form of differential equations, difference equations, transfer functions, etc.

Even though all systems are nonlinear to some extent, the assumption of a linear model leads to simpler models which can yield meaningful results with fairly good accuracy. A system may be classified as stationary or non stationary. During the period of operation, when controls are implemented, the system is normally assumed to be stationary. The system equations may be formulated either in the continuous mode or in the discrete mode. While measurements and predicted values are available at discrete intervals, continuous representation is the most familiar mode. Transformation from continuous to discrete formulation is a straight forward process. A power system invariably, is stochastic in nature since the load demand is the most uncertain aspect in the operation of it. In addition, measurement uncertainty, errors, non availability of readings, etc. all contribute to its stochastic nature in the model. In most of the power system studies only a deterministic model is assumed, but when the situation demands the probabilistic model is also used. A modern power system requires identification of the model and optimization of the same with reference to a performance criterion with computer predictive, adaptive, non interacting, sampled-data control for efficient operation.

Various models that are needed in analysis and for control are discussed and presented through out the book.

Chapter 2 deals with load flow studies. They are performed to determine voltages, active and reactive powers, etc. at various points in the network for different operating conditions subject to the constraints on generator capacities and specified net interchange between operating systems and several other restraints. Load flow solution is essential for continuous evaluation of the performance of the power systems so that suitable control measures can be taken in case of necessity. In practice it will be required to carry out numerous load flows under a variety of conditions.

Economic system operation can be defined in a more general sense as making the best use of the resources available, subject to a variety of requirements over any desired period of time. Economic power system operation deals with the means and techniques for achieving minimum operating cost to supply a given predicted load demand. It may be pointed out that extensive research has been carried out in this field covering topics such as economy of fuel, maintenance and overhaul schedules of equipment, starting and shut-down of generating plants, scheduling of generation to different units, exchange of power between neighbouring utilities and a wide range of problems related to hydrogeneration, like water usage, policies for different types of hydro plants (reservoir, pondage, run-off river and pumped storage) and their integration with the system, both hydraulically and electrically. Different combinations of thermal and hydrogenerating plants give rise to different cost structures. Also, for a given combination of plants, the operational requirement of scheduling generating plants to supply the predicted load demand and subsequent formulation of loading pattern to be imposed on individual units committed to service to minimize the cost of supplying a given load is another important aspect of the problem. In general, the ordering or committing plant to operate on one hand and loading of plant in operation on the other are the two facets of the economic operation, both considered separately in Chapters 3 and 4.

The division is mainly from the period of time over which cost minimization is affected. The loading of plant in operation is related to cost minimization over short periods of time. This problem is called instantaneous, static or optimal point minimization. Committing of plants to service, by comparison, relates to larger periods of time and gives rise to a variational form of the problem in which the minimization required is that of the time integral of operating costs over the period for which programmes of plant (unit) commitment are formulated.

1.3 Scheduling Studies

A division of scheduling studies related to operation and control can be made as follows:

Scheduling problem	Time / Period
(a) Long-range scheduling for plant maintenance and for short term availability or resources	Month / Year
(b) Short term scheduling for unit commitment and unit hourly energy schedules	1 Day / 2 Weeks
(c) Economic allocation of generation to operating units	Minutes
(d) Tie-line interchange, system frequency control	Seconds
(e) Plant and unit control	Continuous

In Chapter 5 optimal load flow problem and certain guide lines to obtain an optimal solution are presented, but the information is only at an introductory level.

There are several problems associated with hydrothermal combined operation such as:

1. Fuel ordering, i.e., given the operating pattern over the period of interest (say two weeks), determine the station fuel requirements and the optimal fuel procurement policy.
2. Plant ordering or unit commitment, i.e., the scheduling of the start up and shut down of generating units, a dynamic optimization problem.
3. Hydrothermal scheduling, i.e., the optimal use of available water to coordinate with the thermal generation, a dynamic optimization problem, etc.

The economic objective of a schedule can be assumed either by the profit from energy sales or by the cost of energy production. If the loads are fixed, then both the criteria result in the same schedule. However, under more realistic circumstances, i.e., when load is a function of a voltage, the two criteria yield different optimal policies. Minimization of production costs is taken generally as the criterion for economic operation.

Each minimization problem is subject to a number of constraints arising from the characteristics of plants and their safe operating conditions and from the requirements of technically favourable operating conditions in the transmission system interconnecting various power stations. The requirements of security are superimposed on these constraints. Added to these are the requirements of marginal or reserve generating capacity in excess of the minimum necessary to supply a predicted load demand to complement the probabilistic nature of load predicted and to cover unforeseen operational occurrences. A wide number of formulations and analytical solution techniques have been pursued in this direction. A few important methods only are discussed in Chapters 3, 4 and 5.

The disturbances to which a power system is subjected can be roughly classified as small scale and large scale disturbances. Slowly varying small magnitude changes can be effectively controlled, using governors, exciters, etc. The control of the system frequency using speed governors and supplementary controls is discussed in detail in Chapter 6 under the title "Load frequency control".

1.4 Modes of Operation

Power systems are often interconnected to improve reliability and quality of power supply to the consumer, to reduce the spinning reserve requirements of individual systems and for similar other advantages. The operating state of a power system can be divided into four modes:

1. Normal mode
2. Preventive mode
3. Emergency mode, and
4. Restorative mode.

In the normal mode of operation, the system has to maintain scheduled voltages, frequency and load flow profile maintaining the scheduled tie line power flows. In this mode of operation control is required to

1. Maintain scheduled voltages and frequency
2. Maintain scheduled tie-line flows, and
3. Obtain economic generation

In the emergency mode of operation, i.e., when the contingency has occurred, control is required to

1. Maintain the specified frequency, and
2. Maximize the amount of load demand being met.

During the restorative mode of operation, the system is brought from emergency mode of operation into either normal mode or preventive mode.

The most important aspect in any mode of operation is the matching between load demand and generation. The frequency deviation of the system is a direct measure of the mismatch between the total generation and combined load demand. It is only when the frequency is maintained at the rated value that the generation balances the load demand. An accelerating frequency means that the generation is high while a decelerating frequency indicates insufficient generation.

1.5 Synchronizing Coefficient

A transmission line may be a connection between a generating station to a system or may be an inter-tie between two large systems.

Assuming the line losses to be negligible, it can be proved that a more or less natural way of operating a transmission line would be to seek to maintain the voltage levels through regulating the reactive power flow and to provide for the variations of the active power demand by allowing the phase angle between the two end voltages δ, to change. This is brought about by adjusting the throttle of the prime movers in the generating stations at one end or both ends of the line. The power transfer over the line is given by

$$P = \frac{V_S V_R}{X_L} \sin\delta$$

where V_S and V_R are sending end and receiving end voltage magnitudes respectively.

By slowly increasing the load, the maximum power transfer can be obtained when $\delta \approx 90^o$. Further, increase in load will not increase the power transmitted, but instead decreases it. This point is referred to as the static stability limit or static transmission capacity of the line. This capacity can, of course, be increased by increasing the voltage magnitudes, but there are limits for this increase.

The incremental increase in transmitted power ΔP caused by a small increment $\Delta\delta$ in the phase angle is a measure of the electrical stiffness of the transmission line. The quantity $\left(\frac{\Delta P}{\Delta\delta}\right)$ is also called synchronizing coefficient.

It can be seen that the transmission capacity can be increased also by reducing the effective reactance of the line. This can be achieved by paralleling the lines, using bundled conductors or inserting series capacitors.

The analysis, operation and control of inter connected power systems or simply areas are discussed comprehensively in Chapter 7. The objective of system voltage control is to maintain a satisfactory voltage profile in the system during both periods of maximum and minimum loadings. A detailed analysis of excitation control and means adopted for reactive power generation in addition to synchronous machine are presented in Chapter 8.

Various devices such as tap changers, reactors, capacitors, induction regulators static var compensators etc., are discussed in Chapter 8. The role of a power system stabilizer is also presented.

In Chapter 9, certain advanced topics that are related to operation and control are introduced. These are, state estimation, FACTS controllers, Voltage stability, Power quality, load prediction, energy control centers etc. The inclusion of the topics and the presentation of the information is by no means exhaustive.

2 LOAD FLOW ANALYSIS

Load Flow or Power Flow is the solution for the Power System under static conditions of operation. Load Flow studies are undertaken to determine :

1. The line flows
2. The bus voltages and system voltage profile
3. The effect of changes in circuit configuration, and incorporating new circuits on system loading
4. The effect of temporary loss of transmission capacity and (or) generation on system loading and accompanied effects
5. The effect of in-phase and quadrature boost voltages on system loading.
6. Economic system operation
7. system transmission loss minimization
8. Transformer tap settings for economic operation and
9. Possible improvements to an existing system by change of conductor sizes and system voltages.

For the purpose of load flow studies, a single phase representation of the power network is used since the system is generally balanced. When systems had not grown to the present size, networks were simulated on network analyzers for power flow studies. These analyzers are of analogue type, scaled down miniature models of power systems with resistances, reactances, capacitances, autotransformers, transformers, loads, and generators. The generators are just supply sources operating at a much higher frequency than 50Hz to limit the size of the components. The loads are represented by constant impedances. Meters are provided on the panel board for measuring voltages, currents, and powers. The load flow solution is obtained directly from measurements for any system simulated on the analyzer.

With the advent of the modern digital computer possessing large storage and high speed, the mode of load flow studies have changed from analog to digital simulation. A large number of algorithms are developed for digital power flow solutions. Some of the generally used methods are described in this chapter. The methods basically distinguish between themselves in the rate of convergence, storage requirement and time of computation. The loads are generally represented by constant power.

In the network at each bus or node there are four variables viz.

(i) Voltage magnitude

(ii) Voltage phase angle

(iii) Real power and

(iv) Reactive power.

Out of these four quantities two of them are specified at each bus and the remaining two are determined from the load flow solution.

2.1 Bus Classification

Generator bus: A generator bus has generators connected to it. In general, at all the generators terminal voltage is maintained constant with the help of excitation control. For this reason a generator bus is also called a voltage controlled bus. The generator prime mover is controlled in such a way that the desired real power is generated at the bus. Hence, this bus is also referred to as PV-bus. The real power to be generated P_G and the voltage magnitude to be maintained constant $| V |$ are specified at a PV-bus. The reactive power required to be supplied by the generator to maintain the voltage constant is not known in advance and therefore must be computed. The bus voltage angle δ is also not known and needs to be calculated. After computing the reactive generation at any generator bus i, Q_{Gt}, it must be verified that it is within the capability range of reactive generation source at that bus i.

Load bus: Every bus where there is load and no generation exists is called a load bus. Here, the MW demand of the load connected and also the reactive power needed for the load (MVAr) are specified. These are known either from records or from measurements. Otherwise, they are to be predicted in advance before a load flow study is undertaken. In general thc real power demand is known and then assuming a suitable power factor, the reactive power demand can be estimated. Hence, at a load bus the power demands P_{Li} and Q_{Li} are known at any load bus i. Then it is required to determine the voltage magnitude $| V_i |$ and its phase angle δ_i, at every load bus i.

Swing bus: All voltage phasors require a reference axis with respect to which the phase angles of the voltage magnitude can be measured. The reference angle itself is not important as it is the difference of angles between two voltage phasors that matters. Further, the real and reactive power losses that occur in the network lines cannot be known in advance. They will be known only at the end of the load flow solution. The line flows can be computed only after all the bus voltages are estimated or known. From them the losses in the network are estimated.

For the above two reasons, a generator bus is selected to supply all the line losses. This bus is called swing bus or slack bus. Here the voltage phase angle is assumed as zero, so that all other bus voltage phase angles are measured with reference to this bus. The voltage magnitude is also tixed at this bus. This bus is also called as reference bus. The classification is given in Table 2.1

Ta ble 2.1

Bus	Specified variables	Computed variables
Slack bus	Voltage magnitude and its phase angle	Real and reactive powers
Generator bus (PV bus or voltage controlled bus)	Magnitudes of bus voltages and real powers (limit on reactive powers)	Voltage phase angle and reactive power.
Load bus	Real and reactive powers	Magnitude and phase angle of bus voltages

The three types of buses are shown in Fig. 2.1 which illustrates a typical three bus system.

2.2 Modelling for Load Flow Studies

The bus self and mutual admittances constitite the bus admittance matrix Y_{bus}. The driving point and transfer impedances compose the bus impedance matrix Z_{Bus}. For solving the power flow problem both Y_{Bus} and Z_{Bus} can be used. However, it is more convenient to use Y_{Bus} model that will become clear as we understand the application of both the models to power (load) flow solution. Initially Y_{Bus} model is considered.

Bus admittance formation

Consider the transmission system shown in Fig. 2.1.

The line impedances joining buses 1, 2 and 3 are denoted by z_{12}, z_{22} and z_{31} respectively. The corresponding line admittances are y_{12}, y_{22} and y_{31}

The total capacitive susceptances at the buses are represented by y_{10}, y_{20} and y_{30}.

Applying Kirchoff's current law at each bus

$$I_1 = V_1 y_{10} + (V_1 - V_2) y_{12} + (V_1 - V_3) y_{13}$$
$$I_2 = V_2 y_{20} + (V_2 - V_1) y_{21} + (V_2 - V_3) y_{23}$$
$$I_3 = V_3 y_{30} + (V_3 - V_1) y_{31} + (V_3 - V_2) y_{32}$$

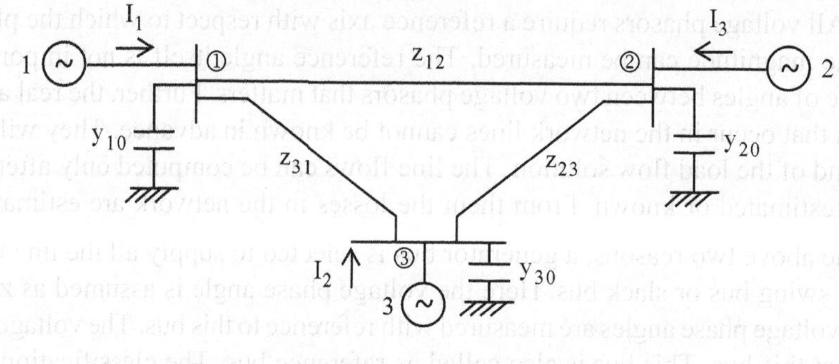

Fig. 2.1 Three bus transmission system

In matrix from

$$\begin{bmatrix} I_1 \\ I_2 \\ I_3 \end{bmatrix} = \begin{bmatrix} y_{10}+y_{12}+y_{13} & -y_{12} & -y_{13} \\ -y_{12} & y_{20}+y_{12}+y_{23} & -y_{23} \\ -y_{13} & -y_{23} & y_{30}+y_{13}+y_{23} \end{bmatrix} \times$$

$$\begin{bmatrix} V_1 \\ V_2 \\ V_3 \end{bmatrix} = \begin{bmatrix} y_{11} & y_{12} & y_{13} \\ y_{21} & y_{22} & y_{23} \\ y_{31} & y_{32} & y_{33} \end{bmatrix}, \begin{bmatrix} V_1 \\ V_2 \\ V_3 \end{bmatrix}$$

where

$$Y_{11} = y_{10} + y_{12} + y_{13}$$

$$Y_{22} = y_{20} + y_{12} + y_{23}$$

$$Y_{33} = y_{30} + y_{13} + y_{23}$$

are the self admittances forming the diagonal terms and

$$Y_{12} = Y_{21} = -y_{12}$$

$$Y_{13} = Y_{31} = -y_{13}$$

$$Y_{23} = Y_{32} = -y_{23}$$

are the mutual admittances forming the off-diagonal elements of the bus admittance matrix. For an n-bus system, the elements of the bus admittance matrix can be written down merely by inspection of the network as

diagonal terms

$$Y_{ii} = y_{i0} + \sum_{\substack{k=1 \\ k \neq i}}^{n} y_{ik}$$

off and diagonal terms

$$Y_{ik} = -y_{ik}$$

If the network elements have mutual admittance (impedance), the above formulae will not apply. For a systematic formation of the y-bus, linear graph theory with singular transformations may be used.

System Model for Load Flow Studies

The variables and parameters associated with bus i and a neighbouring bus k are presented in the usual notation as follows:

The voltage at a typical bus i of the system is given by i

$$V_i = |V_i| \exp j\delta_i = |V_i| (\cos\delta_i + j\sin\delta_i) \quad .....(2.1)$$

The bus admittance is

$$Y_{ik} = |Y_{ik}| \exp j\theta_{ik} = |Y_{ik}| (\cos\theta_{ik} + j\sin\theta_{ik})$$

$$= G_{ik} + jB_{ik} \quad .....(2.2)$$

The complex power

$$S_i = P_i + jQ_i = V_2 I_2^* \quad .....(2.3)$$

The current injected into the bus i, I_i is given by

$$I_i = Y_{i1} V_1 + Y_{i2} V_2 + ... + Y_{iN} V_N$$

$$= \sum_{k=l}^{n} Y_{ik} V_k \quad .....(2.4)$$

The bus current is given by $I_{Bus} = Y_{Bus} V_{Bus}$ .....(2.5)

Using the indices G and L for generation and load

$$P_i = P_{Gi} - P_{Li} = R_e [V_i I_i^*]$$

$$Q_i = Q_{Gi} - Q_{Li} = I_m [V_i I_i^*] \quad .....(2.6)$$

Hence, from eq. (2.3) and (2.4) for an n-bus system

$$I_i^* = \frac{P_i - jQ_i}{V_i^*} = Y_{ii} V_i + \sum_{\substack{k=1 \\ k \neq i}}^{n} Y_{ik} V_k \quad .....(2.7)$$

Solving eqn. (2.7) for V_i

$$V_i = \frac{1}{Y_{ii}} \left[\frac{P_i - jQ_i}{V_i^*} - \sum_{\substack{k=1 \\ k \neq i}}^{n} Y_{ik} V_k \right] \quad .....(2.8)$$

Further, from eqn. (2.3) substituing for I_i^*

$$P_i + jQ_i = V_i \sum_{k=1}^{n} Y_{ik}^* V_k^* \quad .....(2.9)$$

In the polar form

$$P_i + jQ_i = \sum_{k=1}^{n} |V_i \quad V_k \quad Y_{ik}| \exp j(\delta_i \quad - \delta_k \quad - \theta_{ik}) \quad .....(2.10)$$

so that

$$P_i = \sum_{k=1}^{n} |V_i \quad V_k \quad Y_{ik}| \cos(\delta_i \quad - \delta_k \quad - \theta_{ik}) \quad .....(2.11)$$

and

$$Q_i = \sum_{k=1}^{n} |V_i \quad V_k \quad Y_{ik}| \sin(\delta_i \quad - \delta_k \quad - \theta_{ik}) \quad .....(2.12)$$

$i = 1, 2, ... n; i \neq$ slack bus

The power flow eqns. (2.11) and (2.12) are nonlinear and it is required to solve 2(n-1) such equations involving $|V_i|$, δ_i, P_i and Q_i at each bus i for the load flow solution. Finally, the powers at the slack bus may be computed from which the losses and all other line flows can be ascertained. Y-matrix interactive methods are based on solution to power flow relations using their current mismatch at a bus given by

$$\Delta I_i = I_i - \sum_{k=1}^{n} Y_{ik} V_k \quad .....(2.13)$$

or using the voltage from

$$\Delta V_i = \frac{\Delta I_i}{Y_{ii}} \quad .....(2.14)$$

The convergence of the iterative methods depends on the diagonal dominance of the bus admittance matrix. The self-admittances of the buses, are usually large, relative to the mutual admittances and thus, usually convergence is obtained. Junctions of very high and low series impedances and large capacitances obtained in cable circuits long, EHV lines, series and shunt compensation are detrimental to convergence as these tend to weaken the diagonal dominance in the Y-matrix. The choice of slack bus can affect convergence considerably. In difficult cases, it is possible to obtain convergence by removing the least diagonally dominant row and column of Y. The salient features of the Y-matrix iterative methods are that the elements in the summation terms in eqn. (2.7) or (2.8) are on the average only three even for well-developed power systems. The sparsity of the Y-matrix and its symmetry reduces both the storage requirement and the computation time for iteration (sec. 4). For a large, well conditioned system of n-buses, the number of iterations required are of the order of n and total computing time varies approximately as n^2.

Instead of using eqn (2.6), one can select the impedance matrix and rewrite the equation as

$$V = Y^{-1} I = Z . I \quad .....(2.15)$$

The Z-matrix method is not usually very sensitive to the choice of the slack bus. It can easily be verified that the Z-matrix is not sparse. For problems that can be solved by both Z-matrix and Y-matrix methods, the former are rarely competitive with the Y-matrix methods.

2.3 Gauss-Seidel Iterative Method

In this method, voltages at all buses except at the slack bus are assumed. The voltage at the slack bus is specified and remains fixed at that value. The (n-1) bus voltage relations from eqn. (2.8) are:

$$V_i = \frac{1}{Y_{ii}}\left[\frac{P_i - jQ_i}{V_i^*} - \sum_{\substack{k=1 \\ k\neq 1}}^{n} Y_{ik}\ V_k\right] \qquad .....(2.16)$$

$i = 1, 2, ... n; i \neq$ slack bus

are solved simultaneously for an improved solution.

Consider a 5-bus power system shown in Fig. 2.2.

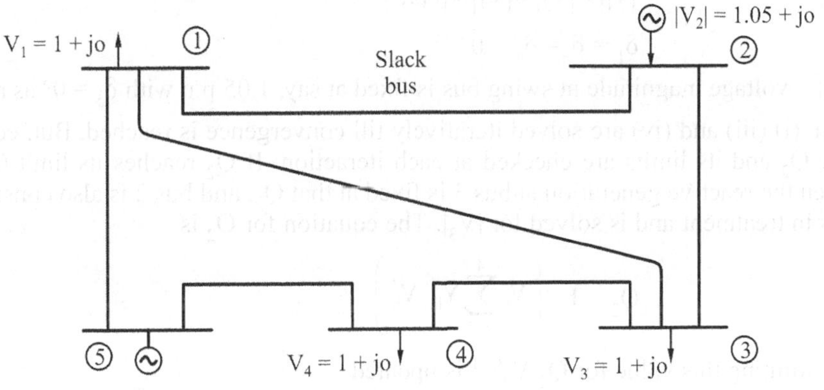

	(1)	(2)	(3)	(4)	(5)
(1)	Y_{11}	Y_{12}	Y_{13}	0	Y_{15}
(2)	Y_{21}	Y_{22}	Y_{23}	0	0
(3)	Y_{31}	Y_{32}	Y_{33}	Y_{34}	0
(4)	0	0	Y_{43}	Y_{44}	Y_{45}
(5)	Y_{31}	0	0	Y_{54}	Y_{55}

Fig. 2.2 Five bus system

Applying equation (2.8) for the five bus system, we obtain during $(k+1)^{th}$ iteraction.

$$V_1^{k+1} = \frac{1}{Y_{11}}\left[\frac{P_1 - jQ_1}{\left(V_1^k\right)^*} - Y_{12}V_2^k - Y_{13}V_3^k - Y_{15}V_5^k\right] \quad .....(i)$$

$$V_2^{k+1} = \frac{1}{Y_{22}}\left[\frac{P_2 - jQ_2}{V_2^*} - Y_{21}V_1^{k+1} - V_{23}V_3^k\right] \quad .....(ii)$$

$$V_3^{k+1} = \frac{1}{Y_{33}}\left[\frac{P_3 - jQ_3}{\left(V_3^k\right)^*} - Y_{31}V_1^{k+1} - Y_{32}V_2^{k+1} - Y_{34}V_4^k\right] \quad .....(iii)$$

and

$$V_4^{k+1} = \frac{1}{Y_{44}}\left[\frac{P_4 - jQ_4}{\left(V_4^k\right)^*} - Y_{43}V_3^{k+1} - Y_{45}V_5^k\right] \quad .....(iv)$$

Bus 5 is selected as slack bus or swing bus.

To start with all voltages at load buses are assumed (1 + jo) p.u (i.e.,)

$$|V_1| = |V_3| = |V_4| = |1 \text{ p.u}$$

and

$$\delta_1 = \delta_3 = \delta_4 = 0^o$$

$|V_5|$ = voltage magnitude at swing bus is fixed at say, 1.05 p.u with $\delta_5 = 0^o$ as reference

Eqn. (i) (iii) and (iv) are solved iteratively till convergence is reached. But, eqn. (ii) is solved for Q_2 and its limits are checked at each iteraction. If Q_2 reaches its limit (upper or lower), then the reactive generation at bus 3 is fixed at that Q_2, and bus 2 is also considered as a load bus in treatment and is solved for $|V_3|$. The equation for Q_2 is

$$Q_2 = I_m\left(V_i \sum_{k=1}^{4} Y_{ik}^* V_k^*\right) \quad .....(v)$$

Substituting this value for Q_2 V_2^{k+1} is updated

In order to accelerate the convergence, all newly-computed values of bus voltages are substituted in eqn. (2.16). The bus voltage equation for the $(m+1)^{th}$ iteration may then be written as

$$V_i^{(m+1)} = \frac{1}{Y_{ii}}\left[\frac{P_i - jQ_i}{V_i^{(m)*}} - \sum_{\substack{k=1 \\ k\neq 1}}^{i-1} Y_{ik}V_k^{(m+1)} - \sum_{k=i+1}^{n} Y_{ik}V_k^{(m)}\right] \quad .....(2.17)$$

The method converges slowly because of the loose mathematical coupling between the buses. The rate of convergence of the process can be increased by using acceleration factors to the solution obtained after each iteration.

Acceleration factor: In Gauss-Seidal method of solution to the load flow problem, the iterative process is continued until the amount of correction to voltage at every bus is less than some prespecified precision index. However, the number of iterations required can be considerably reduced, if the correction to voltage at each bus is multiplied by some constant. This increases the amount of correction thus making the process of convergence faster. The multiplier that produces the improved convergence is called acceleration factor.

Let at any bus i the voltage at the end of $(k-1)^{th}$ iteration be V_i^{k-1} and at the end of the Kth iteration be V_i^K. Them, if α is the acceleration factor,

$$V_i^{(k)} \text{ (accelerated)} = V_i^{(k-1)} + \alpha\left(V_i^{(k)} - V_i^{(k-1)}\right)$$

The accelerated value of $V_i^{(k)}$ is used for $(k+1)^{th}$ iteration. Generally, the value of α is chosen as $1 < \alpha < 2$.

A fixed acceleration factor is sometimes used, using the relation

$$\Delta V_i = \alpha \frac{\Delta S_i^*}{V_2^* Y_{ii}} \quad .....(2.18)$$

The use of acceleration factor amounts to a linear extrapolation of V_i. For a given system it is quite often found that a near optimal choice of α exists. Some researchers have suggested even a complex value for α. But, it is found convenient to use real values for α (usually 1.5 or 1.6).

Alternatively, different accleration factors may be used for real and imaginary parts of the voltage.

Treatment of a PV - bus

The method of handling a PV-bus requires rectangular coordinate representation for the voltages. Lettering

$$V_i = v_i' + jv_i'' \quad .....(2.19)$$

Where v_i' and v_i'' are the real and imaginary components of V_i. The relationship.

$$v_i'^2 + v_i''^2 = |V_i|^2_{scheduled} \quad .....(2.20)$$

must be satisfied, so that the reactive bus power required to establish the scheduled bus voltage can be computed. The estimates of voltage components, $v_i'^{(m)}$ and $v_i''^{(m)}$ after m iterations must be adjusted to satisfy eqn. (2.21). The Phase angle of the estimated bus voltage is

$$\delta_i^{(m)} = \tan^{-1}\left[\frac{v_i''^{(m)}}{v_i'^{(m)}}\right] \quad .....(2.21)$$

Assuming that the phase angles of the estimated and scheduled voltages are equal, then the adjusted estimates of $V'^{(m)}$ and $V_i''^{(m)}$ are

$$v_{i(new)}^{i(m)} = |V_i|_{scheduled} \cos\delta_i^{(m)} \quad .....(2.22)$$

and $$V''^{(m)}_{i(new)} = |V_i|_{scheduled} \sin \delta_i^{(m)} \quad .....(2.23)$$

These values are used to calculate the reactive power $Q_i^{(m)}$. Using these reactive powers $Q_i^{(m)}$ and voltages $V_{i(new)}^{(m)}$ a new estimate $V_i^{(m+1)}$ is calculated. The flowchart for computing the solution of load flow using gauss-seidel method is given in Fig. 2.3.

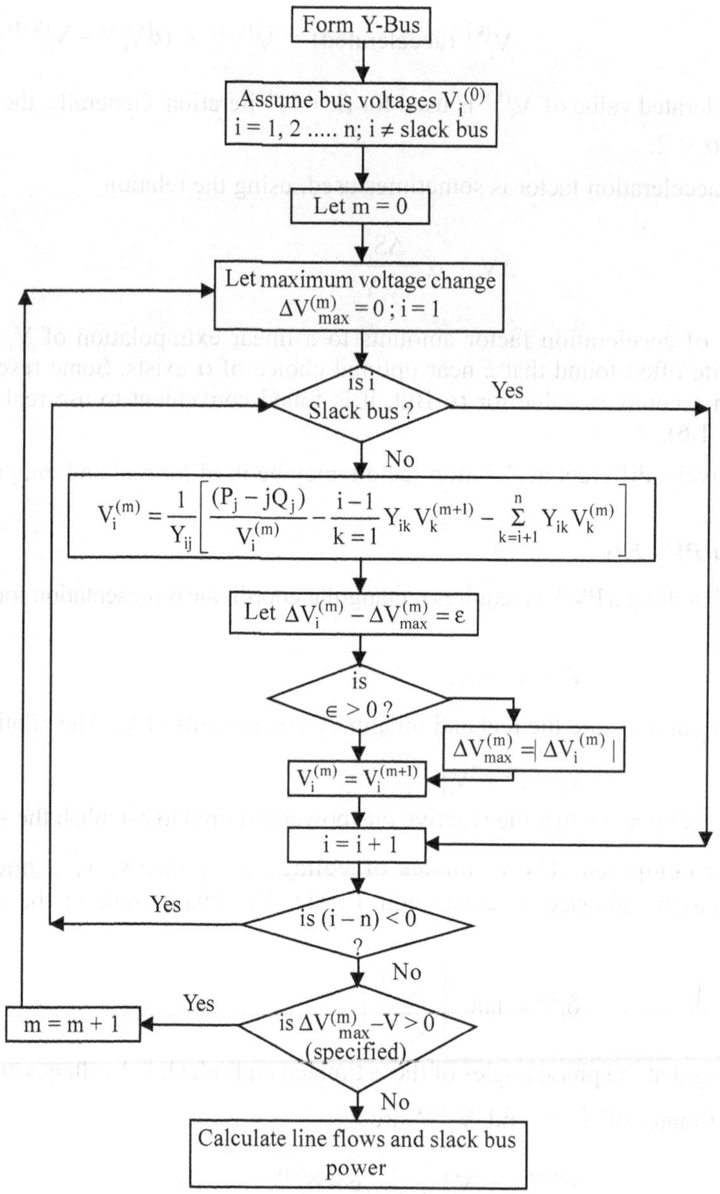

Fig. 2.3 Flowchart for Gauss-Seidel iterative method for load flow solution using Y-Bus

While computing the reactive powers, the limits on the reactive source must be taken into consideration. If the calculated value of the reactive power is beyond limits, then its value is fixed at the limit that is violated and it is no longer possible to hold the desired magnitude of the bus voltage, the bus is treated as a PQ bus or load bus.

2.4 Newton – Raphson Method

The generated Newton-Raphson method is an interactive algorithm for solving a set of simultaneous nonlinear equations in an equal number of unknowns. Consider the set of nonlinear equations.

$$f_i(x_1, x_2, \ldots\ldots, x_n) = y_i,\ i = 1, 2, \ldots., n \qquad \ldots..(2.24)$$

with initial estimates for x_i

$$x_1^{(0)}, x_2^{(0)}, \ldots\ldots, x_n^{(0)}$$

which are not far from the actual solution. Then using Taylor's series and neglecting the higher order terms, the corrected set of equations are

$$f_i\left(x_1^{(0)} + \Delta x_1, x_2^{(0)} + \Delta x_2, \ldots\ldots, x_n^{(0)} + \Delta x_n\right) = y_i \qquad \ldots..(2.25)$$

where Δx_i are the corrections to x_i = (i = 1, 2, ….., n)

A set of linear equations, which define a tangent hyperplane to the function f_i (x) at the given iteration point $\left(x_i^{(0)}\right)$ are obtained as

$$\Delta Y = J\,\Delta X \qquad \ldots..(2.26)$$

where ΔY is a column vector determined by

$$y_i - f_i\left(x_1^{(0)}, \ldots\ldots, x_n^{(0)}\right)$$

ΔX is the column vector of correction terms Δx_i, and J is the Jacobian matrix for the function f given by the first order partial derivatives evaluated at $x_i^{(0)}$ The corrected solution is obtained as

$$x_i^{(1)} = x_i^{(0)} + \Delta x_i \qquad \ldots..(2.27)$$

The square Jacobian matrix J is defined by

$$J_{ik} = \frac{\partial f_i}{\partial x_k}$$

The above method of obtaining a converging solution for a set of nonlinear equations can be used for solving the load flow problem. It may be mentioned that since the final voltage solutions are not much different from the nominal values, Newton – Raphson method is particularly suited to the load flow problem. The matrix J is highly sparse and is particularly suited to the load flow application and sparsity – programmed ordered triangulation and back substitution methods result in quick and efficient convergence to the load flow solution. This method possesses quadratic convergence and thus converges very rapidly when the solution point is close.

There are two methods of solution for the load flow using Newton – Raphson method. The first method uses rectangular coordinates for the variables, while the second method uses the polar coordinate formulation.

2.4.1 Rectangular Coordinates Method

The power entering the bus i is given by $S_i = P_i + j\,Q_i$

$$V_i\, I_i^* = V_i \sum_{k=1}^{n} Y_{ik}^*\, V_k^* , \qquad i_* = 1, 2, ..., n \qquad .....(2.28)$$

where $V_i = v_i^{'} + j\, v_i^{''}$

$Y_{ik} = G_{ik} + j\, B_{ik}$

$$(P_i + j\, Q_i) = v_i^{'} + j\, v_i^{''} \sum_{k=1}^{n} (G_{ik} - j\, B_{ik})(v_k^{'} - j\, v_k^{''}) \qquad .....(2.29)$$

Expanding the right side of the above equation and separating out the real and imaginary parts.

$$P_i = \sum_{k=1}^{n} \left[v_i^{'} (G_{ik}\, v_k^{'} - B_{ik}\, v_k^{''}) + v_i^{''} (G_{ik}\, v_k^{''} + B_{ik}\, v_k^{'}) \right] \qquad .....(2.30)$$

$$Q_i = \sum_{k=1}^{n} \left[v_i^{''} (G_{ik}\, v_k^{'} - B_{ik}\, v_k^{''}) - v_i^{'} (G_{ik}\, v_i^{''} + B_{ik}\, v_k^{'}) \right] \qquad .....(2.31)$$

These are the two power relations at each bus and the linearized equations of the form (2.27) are written as (2.33).

$$\begin{bmatrix} \Delta P_1 \\ \vdots \\ \Delta P_{n-1} \\ \Delta Q_1 \\ \vdots \\ \Delta Q_{n-1} \end{bmatrix} = \begin{bmatrix} \dfrac{\partial P_1}{\partial v_1^{'}} & \cdots & \dfrac{\partial P_1}{\partial v_{n-1}^{'}} & \dfrac{\partial P_1}{\partial v_1^{''}} & \cdots & \dfrac{\partial P_1}{\partial v_{n-1}^{''}} \\ \vdots & \cdots & & \vdots & \cdots & \vdots \\ \dfrac{\partial P_{n-1}}{\partial v_1^{'}} & \cdots & \dfrac{\partial P_{n-1}}{\partial v_{n-1}^{'}} & \dfrac{\partial P_{n-1}}{\partial v_n^{''}} & \cdots & \dfrac{\partial P_{n-1}}{\partial v_{n-1}^{''}} \\ \dfrac{\partial Q_1}{\partial v_1^{'}} & \cdots & \dfrac{\partial Q_1}{\partial v_{n-1}^{'}} & \dfrac{\partial Q_1}{\partial v_1^{''}} & \cdots & \dfrac{\partial Q_1}{\partial v_{n-1}^{''}} \\ \vdots & \cdots & & & \cdots & \vdots \\ \dfrac{\partial Q_{n-1}}{\partial v_1^{'}} & \cdots & \dfrac{\partial Q_{n-1}}{\partial v_{n-1}^{'}} & \dfrac{\partial Q_{n-1}}{\partial v_1^{''}} & \cdots & \dfrac{\partial Q_{n-1}}{\partial v_{n-1}^{''}} \end{bmatrix} \begin{bmatrix} \Delta v_1^{'} \\ \vdots \\ \Delta v_{n-1}^{'} \\ \Delta v_1^{''} \\ \vdots \\ \Delta v_{n-1}^{''} \end{bmatrix} \qquad .....(2.32)$$

Matrix equation (2.32) can be solved for the unknowns $\Delta v_i'$ and $\Delta v_i''$ $(i = 1, 2, \ldots, n-1)$, leaving the slack bus at the nth bus where the voltage is specified. Equation (2.32) may be written compactly as

$$\begin{bmatrix} \Delta P \\ \Delta Q \end{bmatrix} = \begin{bmatrix} H & N \\ M & L \end{bmatrix} \begin{bmatrix} \Delta v' \\ \Delta v'' \end{bmatrix} \qquad \text{.....(2.33)}$$

where H, N, M and L are the sub-matrices of the Jacobian. The elements of the Jacobian are obtained by differentiating Eqns. (2.30) and (2.31). The off-diagonal and diagonal elements of H matrix are given by

$$\frac{\partial P_i}{\partial v_k'} = G_{ik} v_i' + B_{ik} v_i'', \quad i \neq k \qquad \text{.....(2.34)}$$

$$\frac{\partial P}{\partial v_i'} = 2G_{ii}\, v_i' + \sum_{\substack{k=1 \\ k \neq i}}^{n} (G_{ik} v_k' - B_{ik} v_k') \qquad \text{.....(2.35)}$$

$i = 1, 2, \ldots, n, \qquad k = 1, 2, \ldots, n, \qquad k \neq i$

The off-diagonal and diagonal elements of N are :

$$\frac{\partial P_i}{\partial v_k''} = G_{ik} v_i'' - B_{ik}\, v_i', \; k \neq i \qquad \text{.....(2.36)}$$

$$\frac{\partial P_i}{\partial v_i''} = 2v_i'' G_{ii} + \sum_{\substack{k=1 \\ k \neq i}}^{n} \left(G_{ik} v_k'' + B_{ik} v_k' \right) \qquad \text{.....(2.37)}$$

$i = 1, 2, \ldots, n \qquad k = 1, 2, \ldots, n \qquad k \neq i$

The off-diagonal and diagonal elements of sub-matrix M are obtained as,

$$\frac{\partial Q_i}{\partial v_k'} = G_{ik} v_i'' - B_{ik} v_i', k \neq i \quad k \neq 1 \qquad \text{.....(2.38)}$$

$$\frac{\partial Q_i}{\partial v_i} = -2\,B_{ii}\, v_i' - \sum_{\substack{k=1 \\ k \neq i}}^{n} (v_k'' G_{ik} + v_k' B_{ik}) \qquad \text{.....(2.39)}$$

$i = 1, 2, \ldots, n \qquad k = 1, 2, \ldots, n \qquad i \neq k$

Finally, the off-diagonal and diagonal elements of L are given by

$$\frac{\partial Q_i}{\partial v_k} = -\, v_i'' B_{ik} - v_i' G_{ik} \quad (i \neq k) \qquad \text{.....(2.40)}$$

$$\frac{\partial Q_i}{\partial v_i^{"}} = 2 v_i^{"} B_{ii} + \sum_{\substack{k=1 \\ k \neq i}}^{n} \left(G_{ik} v_k^{'} - B_{ik} v_k^{"} \right) \qquad .....(2.41)$$

i = 1, 2, ..., n k = 1, 2, ...,n $i \neq k$

It can be noticed that

$$L_{ik} = -H_{ik}$$

and $N_{ik} = M_{ik}$

This property of symmetry of the elements reduces computer time and storage.

Treatment of Generator Buses

At all generator buses other than the swing bus, the voltage magnitudes are specified in addition to the real powers. At the ith generator bus

$$.....(2.42)$$

Then, at all the generator nodes, the variable ΔQ_i will have to be replaced by

$$\Delta |V_i|^2$$

But,

$$|\Delta V_i|^2 = \frac{\partial (|\Delta_i|^2)}{\partial v_i^{'}} \Delta V_i^{'} + \frac{\partial (|\Delta_i|^2)}{\partial v_i^{"}} \Delta V_i^{"}$$

$$= 2 \; v_i^{"} + \Delta v_i^{'} + 2 v_i^{'} \Delta v_i^{"} \qquad .....(2.43)$$

This is the only modification required to be introduced in eqn. (2.41)

2.4.2 The Polar Coordinates Method.

The equation for the complex power at node i in the polar form is given in eqn. (2.10) and the real and reactive powers at bus i are indicated in eqn. (2.11) and (2.12). Reproducing them here once again for convenience.

$$P_i = \sum_{k=1}^{n} \left| V_i \; V_k \; Y_{ik} \right| \cos(\delta_i \quad \delta_k - \theta_{ik})$$

and

$$Q_i = \sum_{k=1}^{n} |V_i \; V_k \; Y_{ik} \sin(\delta_i - \delta_k - \theta_{ik})$$

The Jocobian is then formulated in terms of |V| and δ instead of $V_i^{'}$ and $V_i^{"}$ in this case. Eqn. (2.26) then takes the form

$$\begin{bmatrix} \Delta P \\ \Delta Q \end{bmatrix} = \begin{bmatrix} H & N \\ M & L \end{bmatrix} \begin{bmatrix} \Delta\delta \\ \Delta|V| \end{bmatrix} \qquad .....(2.44)$$

The off-diagonal and diagonal elements of the sub-matrices H, N, M and L are determined by differentiating eqns. (2.11) and (2.12) with respect to δ and $|V|$ as before. The off-diagonal and diagonal elements of H matrix are

$$\frac{\partial P_i}{\partial \delta_k} = |V_i \; V_k \; Y_{ik}| \sin(\delta_i - \delta_k - \theta_{ik}) \qquad i \neq k \qquad .....(2.45)$$

$$\frac{\partial P_i}{\partial \delta_i} = -\sum_{\substack{k=1 \\ k \neq 1}}^{n} |V_i \; V_k \; V_{ik}| \sin(\delta_i - \delta_k - \theta_{ik}) \qquad .....(2.46)$$

The off-diagonal and diagonal elements of N matrix are

$$\frac{\partial P_i}{\partial |V_k|} = V_i \; Y_{ik} \cos(\delta_i - \delta_k - \theta_{ik}) \qquad .....(2.47)$$

$$\frac{\partial P_i}{\partial |V_i|} = 2|V_i \; Y_{ii}| \cos\theta_{ii} + \sum_{\substack{k=1 \\ k \neq i}}^{n} |V_k \; Y_{ik}| \cos(\delta_i - \delta_k - \theta_{ik}) \qquad .....(2.48)$$

The off-diagonal and diagonal elements of M matrix are

$$\frac{\partial Q_i}{\partial \delta_k} = -|V_i \quad V_k \quad Y_{ik}| \cos(\delta_i - \delta_k - \theta_{ik}) \qquad .....(2.49)$$

$$\frac{\partial Q_i}{\partial \delta_i} = \sum_{\substack{k=1 \\ k \neq i}}^{n} |V_i \quad V_k \quad Y_{ik}| \cos(\delta_i - \delta_k - \theta_{ik}) \qquad .....(2.50)$$

Finally, the off-diagonal and diagonal elements of L matrix are

$$\frac{\partial Q_i}{\partial |V_k|} = |V_i \; Y_{ik}| \sin(\delta_i - \delta_k - \theta_{ik}) \qquad .....(2.51)$$

$$\frac{\partial Q_i}{\partial |V_i|} = 2|V_i \; Y_{ii}| \sin\theta_{ii} + \sum_{\substack{k=1 \\ k \neq i}}^{n} |V_k \; Y_{ik}| \sin(\delta_i - \delta_k - \theta_{ik}) \qquad .....(2.52)$$

It is seen from the elements of the Jacobian in this case that the symmetry that existed in the rectangular coordinates case is no longer present now. By selecting the variable as $\Delta\delta$ and $\frac{\Delta|V|}{|V|}$ instead equation (2.44) will be in the form

$$\begin{bmatrix} \Delta P \\ \Delta Q \end{bmatrix} = \begin{bmatrix} H & N \\ M & L \end{bmatrix} \begin{bmatrix} \Delta\delta \\ \frac{\Delta|V|}{|V|} \end{bmatrix} \qquad .....(2.53)$$

The terms of $H_{ik} = \frac{\partial P_i}{\partial \delta_k} = |V_i \ V_k \ Y_{ik}| \sin(\delta_i - \delta_k - \theta_{ik})$, $i = k$ (eq. 2.46)

remain unchanged with the modification $\left|\frac{\Delta V}{V}\right|$ introduced. However, the terms of L_{ik},

$$\frac{\partial Q_i}{\partial |V_k|} = |V_i \quad Y_{ik}| \sin(\delta_i - \delta_k - \theta_{ik}); \qquad i \neq k$$

will get changed as

$$\frac{\partial Q_i}{\partial |V_k|} \cdot |V_k|$$

$$\frac{\partial Q}{\partial |V_k|} \text{modified} = |V_k||V_i \quad Y_{ik}| \sin(\delta_i - \delta_k - \theta_{ik})$$

$$= H_{ik} \qquad .....(2.54a)$$

Hence $\qquad L_{ik} = H_{ik}$

In a similar manner

$$M_{ik} = \frac{\partial Q_i}{\partial \delta_k} = - |V_i \quad V_k \quad Y_{ik}| \cos(\delta_i - \delta_k - \theta_{ik})$$

remains the same even with $\frac{\Delta V}{|V|}$ variable but N_{ik} changes from

$$N_{ik} = |V_i \quad Y_{ik}| \cos(\delta_i - \delta_k - \theta_{ik})$$

into

$$N_{ik}(\text{modified}) = |V_k \ V_i \ Y_{ik}| \cos(\delta_i - \delta_k - \theta_{ik}) \ i \neq k$$

$$= - M_{ik} \qquad .....(2.54b)$$

Hence $\qquad N_{ik} = - M_{ik}$

or, in other words, the symmetry is restored. The number of elements to be calculated for an n – dimensional Jacobian matrix are only $n + n^2/2$ instead of n^2, thus again saving computer time and storage. The flow chart for computer solution is given in Fig. 2.4.

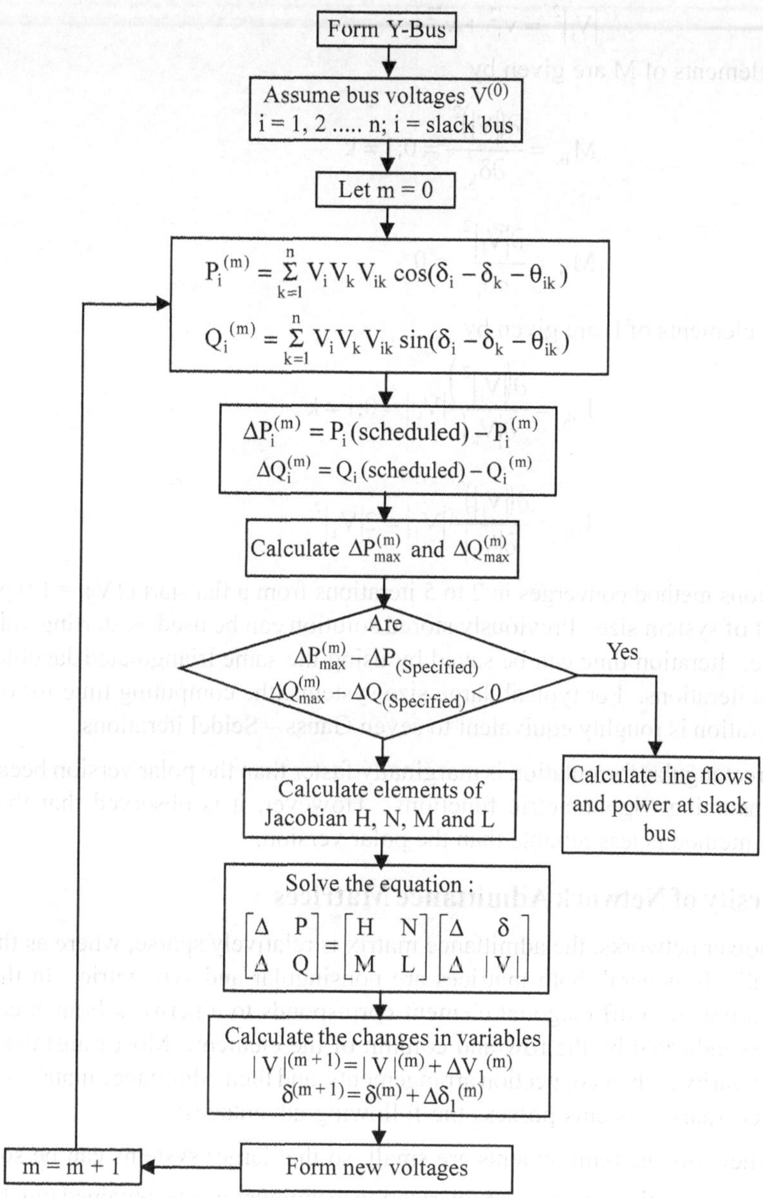

Fig. 2.4 Flow chart for Newton-Raphson method (Polar coordinates) for load flow solution

Treatment of Generator Nodes

For a PV-bus, the reactive power equations are replaced at the ith generator bus by

$$|V_i|^2 = v_i'^2 + v_i''^2$$

The elements of M are given by

$$M_{ik} = \frac{\partial(|V|)^2}{\partial \delta_k} = 0; i \neq k$$

and
$$M_{ii} = \frac{\partial |V_i|^2}{\partial \delta_i} = 0$$

Then elements of L are given by

$$L_{ik} = \frac{\partial(|V_i|^2)}{\partial |V_k|}|V_k| = 0; i \neq k$$

and
$$L_{ii} = \frac{\partial(|V_i|)^2}{\partial |V_i|}|V_i| = 2|V_i|^2$$

Newtons method converges in 2 to 5 iterations from a flat start ($\{V\} = 1.0$ p.u and $\delta = 0$) independent of system size. Previously stored solution can be used as starting values for rapid convergence. Iteration time can be saved by using the same triangulated Jacobian matrix for two or more iterations. For typical, large size systems, the computing time for one Newton – Raphson iteration is roughly equivalent to seven Gauss – Seidel iterations.

The rectangular formulation is marginally faster than the polar version because there are no time consuming trigonometric functions. However, it is observed that the rectangular coordinates method is less reliable than the polar version.

2.5 Sparsity of Network Admittance Matrices

For many power networks, the admittance matrix is relatively sparse, where as the impedance matrix is full. In general, both matrices are nonsingular and symmetric. In the admittance matrix, each non-zero off diagonal element corresponds to a network branch connecting the pair of buses indicated by the row and column of the element. Most transmission networks exhibit irregularity in their connection arrangements, and their admittance matrices are relatively sparse. Such sparse systems possess the following advantages:

1. Their storage requirements are small, so that larger systems can be solved.
2. Direct solutions using triangularization techniques can be obtained much faster unless the independent vector is extremely sparse.
3. Round off errors are very much reduced.

The exploitation of network sparsity requires sophisticated programming techniques.

2.6 Triangular Decompostion

Matrix inversion is a very inefficient process for computing direct solutions, especially for large, sparse systems. Triangular decomposition of the matrix for solution by Gussian elimination is more suited for load flow solutions. Generally, the decomposition is accomplished by elements below the main diagonal in successive columns. Elimination by successive rows is more advantageous from computer programming point of view.

Consider the system of equations

$$\mathbf{A}\,\mathbf{x} = \mathbf{b} \qquad .....(2.55)$$

where **A** is a nonsingular matrix, **b** is a known vector containing at least one non-zero element and **x** is a column vector of unknowns.

To solve eqn. (2.55) by the triangular decomposition method, matrix **A** is augmented by **b** as shown

$$\begin{bmatrix} a_{11} & a_{12} & ...... & a_{1n} & b_1 \\ a_{21} & a_{22} & ...... & a_{2n} & b_2 \\ ...... & ...... & ...... & ...... & ...... \\ a_{n1} & a_{n2} & ...... & a_{nn} & b_n \end{bmatrix}$$

The elements of the first row in the augmented matrix are divided by a_{11} as indicated by the following step with superscripts denoting the stage of the computation.

$$a_{1j}^{(1)} = \left(\frac{1}{a_{11}}\right) a_{1j}, j = 2,.........n \qquad .....(2.56)$$

$$b_1^{(1)} = \left(\frac{1}{a_{11}}\right) b_1 \qquad .....(2.57)$$

In the next stage a_{21} is eliminated from the second row using the relations

$$a_{2j}^{(1)} = a_{2j} - a_{21}\, a_{1j}^{(1)},\ j = 2,.........,n \qquad .....(2.58)$$

$$b_2^{(1)} = b_2 - a_{21}\, b_1^{(1)} \qquad .....(2.59)$$

$$a_{2j}^{(2)} = \left(\frac{1}{a_{22}^{(2)}}\right) a_{2j}^{(1)},\ j = 3,.........,n$$

$$b_2^{(2)} = \left(\frac{1}{a_{22}^{(1)}}\right) b_2^{(1)} \qquad .....(2.60)$$

The resulting matrix then becomes

$$\begin{bmatrix} 1 & 1_{12}^{(1)} & a_{13}^{(1)} & \ldots\ldots & a_{1n}^{(1)} & b_1^{(1)} \\ 0 & 1 & a_{23}^{(2)} & \ldots\ldots & a_{2n}^{(2)} & b_2^{(2)} \\ \ldots\ldots & \ldots\ldots & \ldots\ldots & \ldots\ldots & \ldots\ldots & \ldots\ldots \\ a_{n1} & a_{n2} & a_{n3} & \ldots\ldots & a_{nn} & b_n \end{bmatrix}$$

using the relations

$$b_{3j}^{(1)} = a_{3j} - a_{31}a_{1j}^{(1)} \quad j = 2,\ldots\ldots\ldots\ldots, n \qquad \ldots..(2.61)$$

$$b_{(3)}^{1} = b_3 - a_{31}b_1^{(1)} \qquad \ldots..(2.62)$$

$$a_{3j}^{(2)} = a_{3j}^{(1)} - a_{32}^{(1)}\, a_{2j}^{(2)}, j = 3,\ldots\ldots\ldots\ldots, n \qquad \ldots..(2.63)$$

$$b_3^{(2)} = b_3^{(1)} - a_{32}^{(1)} b_3^{(2)}, j = 4,\ldots\ldots, n \qquad \ldots..(2.64)$$

$$a_3^{(3)} = \left(\frac{1}{a_{33}^{(2)}}\right) a_{3j}^{(1)}, j = 4,\ldots\ldots, n \qquad \ldots..(2.65)$$

$$b_3^{(3)} = \left(\frac{1}{a_{33}^{(2)}}\right) b_3^{(2)} \qquad \ldots..(2.66)$$

The elements to the left of the diagonal in the third row are eliminated and further the diagonal element in the third row is made unity.

After n steps of computation for the nth order system of eqn. (2.55), the augmented matrix will be obtained as

$$\begin{bmatrix} 1 & a_{12}^{(1)} & \ldots\ldots & a_{1n}^{(1)} & b_1^{(1)} \\ 0 & 1 & \ldots\ldots & a_{2n}^{(2)} & b_2^{(2)} \\ \ldots\ldots & \ldots\ldots & \ldots\ldots & \ldots\ldots & \ldots\ldots \\ 0 & 0 & \ldots\ldots & 1 & b_n^{(n)} \end{bmatrix}$$

By back substitution, the solution is obtained as

$$x_n = b_n^{(n)} \qquad \ldots..(2.67)$$

$$x_{n-1} = b_{n-1}^{(n-1)} - a_{n-1}^{(n-1)}, n\ldots\ldots\ldots x_n \qquad \ldots..(2.68)$$

$$x_i = b_i^{(1)} - \sum_{j=i+1}^{n} a_{ij}^{(i)} x_j \qquad \ldots..(2.69)$$

For matrix inversion of an nth order matrix, the number of arithmetical operations required is n^3 while for the triangular decomposition it is approximately $\left(\frac{n^3}{3}\right)$.

2.7 Optimal Ordering

When the **A** matrix in eqn. (2.55) is sparse, it is necessary to see that the accumulation of non – zero elements in the upper triangle is minimized. This can be achieved by suitably ordering the equations, which is referred to as optimal ordering.

Consider the network system having five nodes as shown in Fig. 2.5

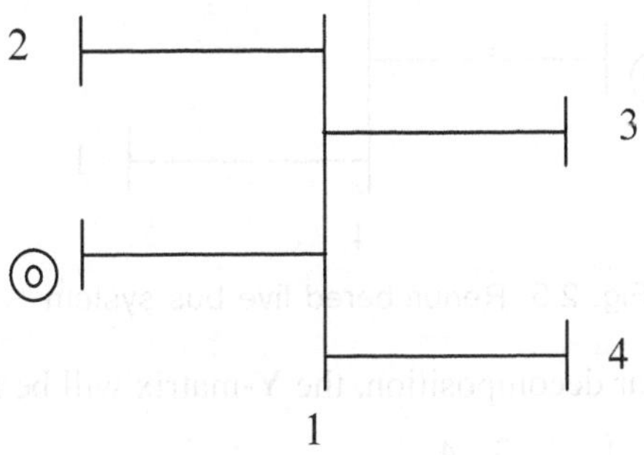

Fig. 2.5 A Five Bus system

The y-bus matrix of the network will have entries as follows

$$\begin{array}{c|cccc} & 1 & 2 & 3 & 4 \\ \hline 1 & \times & \times & \times & \times \\ 2 & \times & \times & 0 & 0 \\ 3 & \times & 0 & \times & 0 \\ 4 & \times & 0 & 0 & \times \end{array} = Y \qquad .....(2.70)$$

After triangular decomposition the matrix will be reduced to the form

$$\begin{array}{c|cccc} & 1 & 2 & 3 & 4 \\ \hline 1 & 1 & \times & \times & \times \\ 2 & 0 & 1 & \times & \times \\ 3 & 0 & 0 & 1 & \times \\ 4 & 0 & 0 & 0 & 1 \end{array} = Y \qquad .....(2.71)$$

By ordering the nodes as in Fig. 2.6 the bus admittance matrix will be of the form

$$\begin{array}{c|cccc} & 1 & 2 & 3 & 4 \\ \hline 1 & \times & 0 & 0 & \times \\ 2 & 0 & \times & 0 & \times \\ 3 & 0 & 0 & \times & \times \\ 4 & \times & \times & \times & \times \end{array} = Y \qquad \text{.....(2.72)}$$

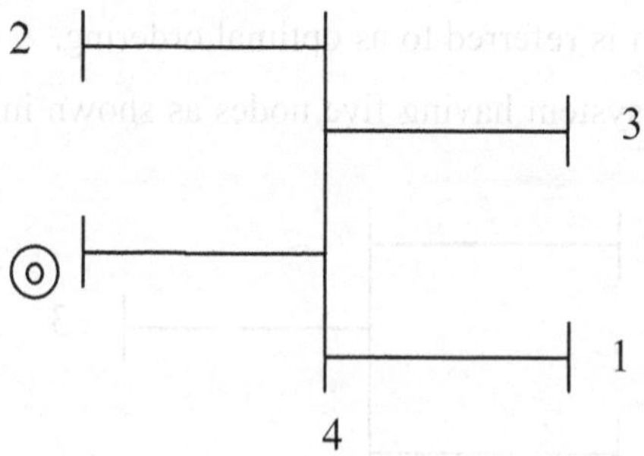

Fig. 2.6 Renumbered five bus system

As a result of triangular decomposition, the **Y**-matrix will be reduced to

$$\begin{array}{c|cccc} & 1 & 2 & 3 & 4 \\ \hline 1 & 1 & 0 & 0 & \times \\ 2 & 0 & 1 & 0 & \times \\ 3 & 0 & 0 & 1 & \times \\ 4 & 0 & 0 & 0 & 1 \end{array} = Y \qquad \text{.....(2.73)}$$

Thus, comparing the matrices in eqn. (2.71) and (2.73) the non-zero off diagonal entries are reduced from 6 to 3 by suitably numbering the nodes.

Tinney and Walker have suggested three methods for optimal ordering.

1. Number the rows according to the number of non-zero, off-diagonal elements before elimination. Thus, rows with less number of off diagonal elements are numbered first and the rows with large number last.
2. Number the rows so that at each step of elimination the next row to be eliminated is the one having fewest non-zero terms. This method required simulation of the elimination process to take into account the changes in the non-zero connections affected at each step.
3. Number the rows so that at each step of elimination, the next row to be eliminated is the one that will introduce fewest new non-zero elements. This requires simulation of every feasible alternative at each step.

Scheme 1. is simple and fast. However, for power flow solutions, scheme 2. has proved to be advantageous even with its additional computing time. If the number of iterations is large, scheme 3. may prove to be advantageous.

2.8 Decoupled Methods

All power systems exhibit in the steady state a strong interdependence between active powers and bus voltage angles and between reactive power and voltage magnitude. The coupling between real power and bus voltage magnitude and between reactive power and bus voltage phase angle are both relatively weak. This weak coupling is utilized in the development of the so called decoupled methods. Recalling equitation (2.54)

$$\begin{bmatrix} \Delta P \\ \Delta Q \end{bmatrix} = \begin{bmatrix} H & N \\ M & L \end{bmatrix} \begin{bmatrix} \Delta\delta \\ |V|/\Delta|V| \end{bmatrix}$$

by neglecting N and M sub matrices as a first step, decoupling can be obtained so that

$$|\Delta P| = |H| \, . \, |\Delta\delta| \qquad .....(2.74)$$

and

$$|\Delta Q| = |L| \, . \, |\Delta|V|/|V| \qquad .....(2.75)$$

The decoupled method converges as reliability as the original Newton method from which it is derived. However, for very high accuracy the method requires more iterations because overall quadratic convergence is lost. The decoupled Newton method saves by a factor of four on the storage for the J – matrix and its triangulation. But, the overall saving is 35 to 50% of storage when compared to the original Newton method. The computation per iteration is 10 to 20% less than for the original Newton method.

2.9 Fast Decoupled Methods

For security monitoring and outage-contingency evaluation studies, fast load flow solutions are required. A method developed for such an application is described in this section.

The elements of the sub-matrices H and L (eqn. (2.54)) are given by

$$H_{ik} = |V_i V_k Y_{ik}| \sin(\delta_i - \delta_k - \theta_{ik})$$

$$- |V_i V_k Y_{ik}| (\sin\delta_{ik} \cos\theta_{ik} - \cos\delta_{ik} \sin\theta_{ik})$$

$$= |V_i V_k| \; (G_{ik} \sin\delta_{ik} - B_{ik} \cos\delta_{ik})$$

where $\delta_i - \delta_k = \delta_{ik}$

$$H_{ii} = -\sum_{k=1}^{n} |V_i \;\; V_k \;\; Y_{ik}| \sin(\delta_i - \delta_k - \theta_{ik})$$

$$= -V_i^2 \; Y_{ii} \; \sin\theta_{ii} - \sum_{\substack{k=1 \\ k \neq i}}^{n} V_i V_k Y_{ik} \sin(\delta_i - \delta_k - \theta_{ik})$$

$$= V_i^2 \; B_{ii} - Q_i$$

In a similar manner

$$L_{ik} = |V_i \quad V_k \quad Y_{ik}| \sin(\delta_i - \delta_k - \theta_{ik})$$

$$= |V_i \quad V_k|(B_{ik} \cos\theta_{ik} - G_{ik} \operatorname{Sin}\theta_{ik})$$

$$L_{ii} = 2V_i \; Y_{ii} \sin\theta_{ii} + \sum_{\substack{k=1 \\ k\neq i}}^{n} V_k \; Y_{ik} \sin(\delta_i - \delta_k - \theta_{ik})$$

and with $\Delta|V|/|V|$ formulation on the right hand side

$$L_{ii} = 2|V_i \quad Y_{ii}| \sin\theta_{ii} + \sum_{\substack{k=1 \\ k\neq i}}^{n} V_k \; Y_{ik} \sin(\delta_i - \delta_k - \theta_{ik})$$

$$= |V_i^2| B_{ii} + Q_i$$

Assuming that

$$\cos\delta_{ik} \cong 1$$

$$\sin\delta_{ik} \cong 0$$

$$G_{ii} \sin\delta_{ik} \leq B_{ik}$$

and $\quad Q_i \leq B_{ii} |V_i|^2$

$$H_{ik} = -|V_i V_k| B_{ik}$$

$$H_{ii} = |V_i|^2 B_{ii}$$

$$L_{ik} = |V_i \quad V_k| B_{ik}$$

and $\quad L_{ll} = |V_l|^2 B_{ll}$

Rewriting eqns. (2.74) and (2.75)

$$|VP| = |V| B' |V| \Delta\delta \qquad .....(2.76)$$

$$|V| = |V| B'' |V| \frac{\Delta|V|}{|V|} \qquad .....(2.77)$$

Eq. (2.76) can be rewritten as

$$\frac{|\Delta P|}{|V|} = |V|\ |B'|\ \Delta\delta$$

$$\frac{|\Delta P|}{|V|} \sim [B']\ [\Delta\delta] \quad \text{setting } |V| \sim 1 + jo \qquad .....(2.78)$$

From eqn. (2.77)

$$\frac{|\Delta Q|}{|V|} = [B'']\ [\Delta|V|] \qquad .....(2.79)$$

Matrices B' and B" represent constant approximations to the slopes of the tangent hyper planes of the functions ΔP / |V| and ΔQ / |V| respectively. They are very close to the Jacobian sub matrices H and L evaluated at system no-load.

Shunt reactances and off-nominal in-phase transformer taps which affect the Mvar flows are to be omitted from $[B']$ and for the same reason phase shifting elements are to be omitted from $[B'']$.

Both $[B']$ and $[B'']$ are real and "sparse" and need be triangularised only once, at the beginning of the study since they contain network admittances only.

The method converges very reliably in two to five iterations with fairly good accuracy even for large systems. A good, approximate solution is obtained after the 1st or 2nd iteration. The speed per iteration is roughly five times that of the original Newton method.

2.10 Load Flow Solution Using Z Bus

2.10.1 Bus Impedance Formation

Any power network can be formed using the following possible methods of construction.

1. A line may be added to a reference point or bus.
2. A bus may be added to any existing bus in the system other than the reference bus through a new line, and
3. A line may be added joining two existing buses in the system forming a loop.

The above three modes are illustrated in Fig. 2.7

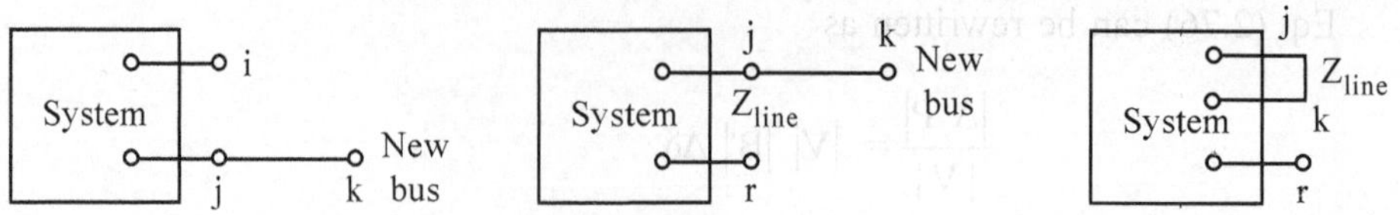

(a)
Line added to reference bus

(b)
Line added to any bus other than reference line

(c)
Line added joining two existing buses

Fig. 2.7 Building of Z - Bus

2.10.2 Addition of a Line to the Reference Bus

If unit current is injected into bus k no voltage will be produced at other buses of the systems.

$$Z_{ik} = Z_{ki} = 0, \; i \neq k \quad .....(2.80)$$

The driving point impedance of the new bus is given by

$$Z_{kk} = Z_{line} \quad .....(2.81)$$

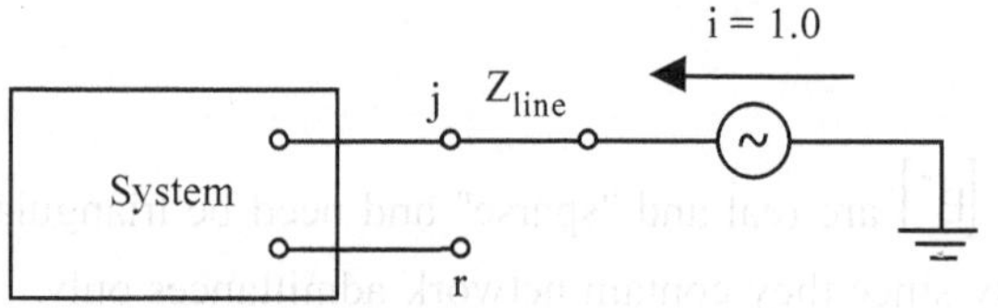

Fig. 2.8 Addition of the line to reference line

2.10.3 Addition of a Radial Line and New Bus

Injection of unit current into the system through the new bus k produces voltages at all other buses of the system as shown in Fig. 2.9

These voltages would of course, be same as that would be produced if the current were injected instead at bus i as shown.

Therefore,

$$Z_{km} = Z_{im}$$

therefore,

$$Z_{mk} = Z_{mi}, \; m \neq k \quad .....(2.82)$$

The dimension of the existing Z – Bus matrix is increased by one. The off diagonal elements of the new row and column are the same as the elements of the row and column of bus i of the existing system.

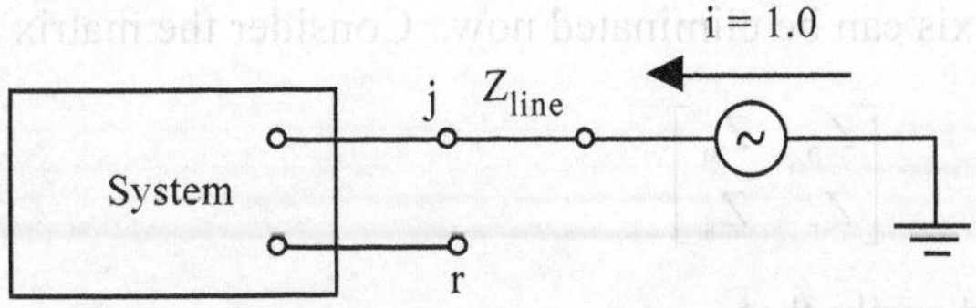

Fig. 2.9 Addition of a radial line and new bus

2.10.4 Addition of a Loop Closing Two Existing Buses in the System

Since both the buses are existing buses in the system the dimension of the bus impedance matrix will not increase in this case. However, the addition of the loop introduces a new axis which can be subsequently eliminated by Kron's reduction method.

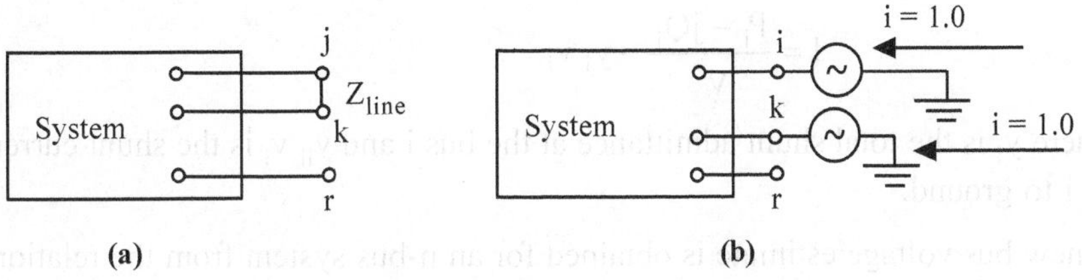

Fig. 2.10 (a) Addition of a loop (b) Equivalent representation

The systems in Fig. 2.10(a) can be represented alternatively as in Fig. 2.10(b).

The link between i and k requires a loop voltage

$$V_{loop} = 1.0\,(Z_{ii} - Z_{2k} + Z_{kk} - Z_{ik} + Z_{\,line}) \qquad .....(2.83)$$

for the circulation of unit current

The loop impedance is

$$Z_{loop} = Z_{ii} + Z_{kk} - 2Z_{ik} + Z_{line} \qquad .....(2.84)$$

The dimension of **Z** matrix is increased due to the introduction of a new axis due to the loop 1

$$Z_{\ell\ell} = Z_{loop}$$

and $$Z_{m-\ell} = Z_{mi} - Z_{mk}$$

$$Z_{\ell-m} = Z_{im} - Z_{km}\,;\, m \neq \ell$$

The new loop axis can be eliminated now. Consider the matrix

$$\begin{bmatrix} Z_p & Z_q \\ Z_r & Z_s \end{bmatrix}$$

It can be proved easily that

$$Z_p^{'} = Z_p - Z_q Z_s^{-1} Z_r \qquad .....(2.85)$$

using eqn. (2.85) all the additional elements introduced by the loop can be eliminated. The method is illustrated in example 2.3

2.10.5 Gauss – Seidel Method Using Z-bus for Load Flow Solution

An initial bus voltage vector is assumed as in the case of Y – bus method. Using these voltages, the bus currents are calculated using eqn. (2.6) or (2.7).

$$I = \frac{P_i - jQ_i}{V^*} - y_i\, v_i \qquad .....(2.86)$$

where y_i is the total shunt admittance at the bus i and $y_{ii}\, v_i$ is the shunt current flowing from bus i to ground.

A new bus voltage estimate is obtained for an n-bus system from the relation.

$$V_{bus} = Z_{bus}\, I_{bus} + V_R \qquad .....(2.87)$$

Where V_R is the (n – 1) × 1 dimensional reference voltage vector containing in each element the slack bus voltage. It may be noted that since the slack bus is the reference bus, the dimension of the Z_{bus} is (n – 1 × (n – 1).

The voltages are updated from iteration to iteration using the relation

$$V_i^{m+1} = V_S + \sum_{\substack{k=1 \\ k \neq S}}^{i-1} Z_{ik}\, I_k^{m+1} + \sum_{\substack{k=i \\ k \neq S}}^{n} Z_{ik}\, I_k^{(m)} \qquad .....(2.88)$$

Then
$$V_k^{(m)} = \frac{P_k - jQ_k}{\left(V_k^{(m)}\right)^*} - y_k\, V_k^{(m+1)}$$

i = 1, 2,........, n
S = slack bus

2.11 Load Flow Solution with Static Load Model

It can be seen that the system loads vary with both frequency and voltage. The static load model for small changes in voltages is defined by eqn. (2.89). The Newton – Rapson method in polar coordinates form is ideally suited for incorporating the load model for load flow solution. At nay bus i, with the subscript N stands for nominal values

$$\left.\begin{aligned} P_i &= P_{i(N)}\left(\frac{|V_i|}{|V_{i(N)}|}\right)^a \\ Q_i &= Q_{i(N)}\left(\frac{|V_i|}{|V_{i(N)}|}\right)^b \end{aligned}\right\} \quad .....(2.89)$$

Differentiating eqn. (2.89) with respect to V

$$\frac{\partial P_i}{\partial |V_i|} = P_{i(N)} \cdot a \cdot \left(\frac{|V_i|}{|V_{i(N)}|}\right)^{(a-1)} \frac{1}{|V_{i(N)}|} + \frac{\partial P_{i(N)}}{\partial |V_i|}\left(\frac{|V_i|}{|V_{i(N)}|}\right)^a \quad .....(2.90)$$

But from eqn. (2.49)

$$\frac{\partial P_i}{\partial |V_i|} = 2|V_i\, V_{ii}|\cos\theta_{ii} - \sum_{\substack{k=1 \\ k\neq 1}}^{n} |V_i\, Y_{ik}|\cos(\delta_i - \delta_k - \theta_{ik}) \quad .....(2.91)$$

substituting eqn. (2.91) in eqn. (2.90)

$$\frac{\partial P_i}{\partial |V_i|} = a\,\frac{P_{i(N)}}{|V_{i(N)}|} \cdot \left(\frac{|V_i|}{|V_{i(N)}|}\right)^{(a-1)} + 2|V_i\, Y_{ii}|\cos\theta_{ii}$$

$$- \sum_{\substack{k=1 \\ k\neq 1}}^{n} |V_k\, Y_{ik}|\cos(\delta_i - \delta_k - \theta_{ik})\left(\frac{|V_i|}{|V_{i(n)}|}\right)^a \quad .....(2.92)$$

Similarly,

$$\frac{\partial Q_i}{\partial V_i} - Q_{i(N)} \cdot b \cdot \left(\frac{|V_i|}{|V_{i(N)}|}\right)^{(b-1)} \frac{1}{|V_{i(N)}|} + \frac{\partial Q_{i(N)}}{\partial V_i}\left(\frac{|V_i|}{|V_{i(N)}|}\right)^{(b)} \quad .....(2.93)$$

But from eqn. (2.53)

$$\frac{\partial Q_{i(N)}}{\partial |V_i|} = -2|V_i\ V_{ii}|\sin\theta_{ii} + \sum_{\substack{k=1\\k\neq 1}}^{n}|V_i\ Y_{ik}|\ \sin(\delta_i - \delta_k - \theta_{ik}) \quad .....(2.94)$$

Substituting eqn. (2.94) into eqn. (2.93)

$$\frac{\partial Q_i}{\partial |V_i|} = b\cdot\frac{\partial Q_{i(N)}}{\partial |V_{i(N)}|}\left(\frac{|V_i|}{|V_{i(N)}|}\right) - 2|V_i\ Y_{ii}|\sin\theta_{ii} +$$

$$\sum_{\substack{k=1\\k\neq 1}}^{n}|V_i\ Y_{ik}|\sin(\delta_i - \delta_k - \theta_{ik})\left(\frac{|V_i|}{|V_{i(N)}|}\right)^b \quad .....(2.95)$$

Inclusion of static load model into load flow equations required the use of eqn. (2.92) and (2.95) in place of eqn. (2.49) and (2.53). In other words, the diagonal elements of the sub matrices **N** and **L** of eqn. (2.45) have to be modified. The advantage that is gained by the use of eqn. (2.54) is now not feasible.

2.12 Comparision of Various Methods for Power Flow Solution

The requirements of a good power flow method are - high speed, low storage, and reliability for ill-conditioned problems. No single method meets all these requirements. It may be mentioned that for regular load flow studies NR-method in polar coordinates and for special applications fast decoupled load flow solution methods have proned to be most useful than other methods. NR-method is versatile, reliable and accurate. Fast decoupled load flow method is fast and needs the least storage.

Convergence of iterative methods depends upon the dominance of the diagonal elements of the bus admittance matrix.

Advantages of Gauss-Seidel method :

1. The method is very simple in calculations and thus programing is easier.
2. The storage needed in the computer memory is relatively less.
3. In general, the method is applicable for smaller systems.

Disadvantages of Gauss-Seidel Method :

1. The number of iterations needed is generally high and is also dependent on the acceleration factor selected.

2. For large systems, use of Gauss-Seidel method is practically prohibitive.
3. The time for convergence also increases dramatically with increase of number of buses.

Advantages of Newton-Raphsan Method :

1. The method is more accurate, faster and reliable.
2. Requires less number of iteration for convergence. Infact, in three to four iterations good convergence is reached irrespective of the size of the system.
3. The number of iterations required is thus independent of the size of the system or the number of buses in the system.
4. The method is best suited for load flow solution to large size systems.
5. Decoupled and fast decoupled power flow solution can be obtained from Newton Raphsan Polar Coordinates method. Hence, it also can serve as a base for security and contingency studies.

Disadvantages of Newton-Raphsan Method :

1. The memory needed is quite large for large size systems.
2. Calculations per iteration are also much larger than Gauss-Seidel method.
3. Since, it is a gradient method, the method is quite involved and hence, programming is also comparatively difficult and complicated.

E 2.1 A three bus power system is shown in Fig. E2.1. The system parameters are given in Table E2.1 and the load and generation data in Table E2.2. The voltage at bus 2 is maintained at 1.03p.u. The maximum and minimum reactive power limits of the generation at bus 2 are 35 and 0 Mvar respectively. Taking bus 1 as slack bus obtain the load flow solution using

(a) Gauss – Seidel iterative method using Y_{Bus}

(b) Newton – Raphson polar coordinates method using Y_{Bus}

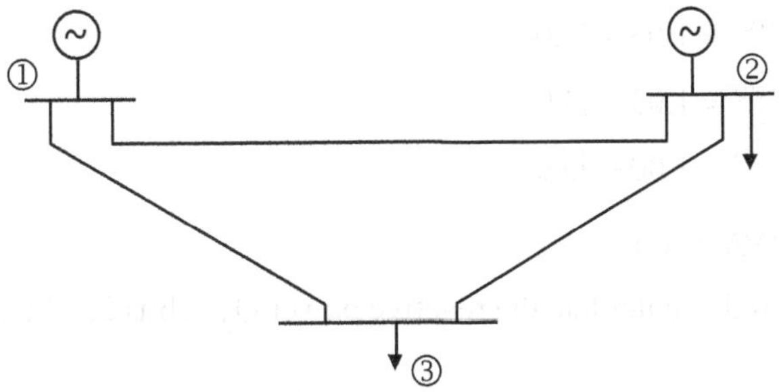

Fig. E 2.1 A three bus power system

Table E 2.1 Impedance and Line charging Admittances

Bus Code i-k	Impedance (p.u.) Z_{ik}	Line charging Admittance (p.u) y_i
1-2	0.08 + j0.24	0
1-3	0.02 + j0.06	0
2-3	0.06 + j0.018	0

Table E 2.2 Scheduled Generation, Loads and Voltages

Bus No i	Bus voltage V_i	Generation		Load	
		MW	Mvar	MW	Mvar
1	1.05+j0.0	—		0	0
2	1.03+j0.0	20	—	50	20
3	——	0	0	60	25

Solution :

The line admittance are obtained as

$$y_{12} = 1.25 - j3.75$$
$$y_{23} = 1.667 - j5.00$$
$$y_{13} = 5.00 - j15.00$$

The bus admittance matrix is formed using the procedure indicated in section 2.1 as

$$Y_{Bus} = \begin{bmatrix} 6.25 & -j18.75 & -1.25 & +j3.75 & -5.0 & +j15.0 \\ -1.25 & +j3.73 & 2.9167 & -j8.75 & -j1.6667 & +j5.0 \\ -5.0 & +j15.0 & -1.6667 & +j5.0 & 6.6667 & -j20.0 \end{bmatrix}$$

(a) Gauss – Seidel Iterative Method using Y_{BUS}

The voltage at bus 3 is assumed as 1 + j0. The initial voltages are therefore

$$V_1^{(0)} = 1.05 + j0.0$$
$$V_2^{(0)} = 1.03 + j0.0$$
$$V_3^{(0)} = 1.00 + j0.0$$

Base MVA = 100

Iteration 1 : It is required to calculate the reactive power Q_2 at bus 2, which is a P-V or voltage controlled bus

$$\delta_2^{(0)} = \tan^{-1}\left(\frac{e_2^{a}}{e_2^{'}}\right) = 0.$$

$$e'_{2(new)} = |V_2|_{sch} \cos\delta_2 = (1.03)(1.0) = 1.03$$

$$e'_{2(new)} = V_{2sch} \sin\delta_2^{(0)} = (1.03)(0.0) = 0.00$$

$$Q_2^{(0)} = \left[\left(e'_{2(new)}\right)^2 B_{22} + \left(e''_{2(new)}\right)^2 B_{22}\right] +$$

$$\sum_{\substack{k=1 \\ k\neq 2}}^{3} \left[\left(e''_{2(new)} e'_k G_{2k} + e''_k B_{2k}\right) - \left(e'_{2(new)} e''_k G_{2k} - e'_k B_{2k}\right)\right]$$

Substituting the values

$$Q_2^{(0)} = \left[(1.03.)^2 8.75 + (0)^2 8.75\right] + 0(1.05)(-1.25) + 0.(-3.75)$$

$$-1.03[(0)(-1.25) - (1.05)(-3.75)]$$

$$+(0)[(1)(-1.6667) + (0)(-5.0)]$$

$$-1.03[(0)(-1.6667) - (1)(-5)]$$

$$= 0.07725$$

Mvar generated at bus 2

= Mvar injection into bus 2 + load Mvar

= 0.077 5 + 0.2 = 0.27725 p.u.

= 27.725 Mvar

This is within the limits specified.

The voltage at bus i is

$$V_i^{(m+1)} = \frac{+1}{Y_{ii}}\left[\frac{P_1 - jQ_1}{V_i^{(m)*}} - \sum_{k=1}^{i-1} y_{ik} V_k^{(m+1)} - \sum_{k=i+1}^{n1} y_{ik} V_k^{(m)}\right]$$

$$V_2^{(1)} = \frac{1}{Y_{22}}\left[\frac{P_1 - jQ_2}{V_i^{(0)*}} - Y_{21}V_1 - Y_{23}V_3^{(0)}\right]$$

$$= \frac{1}{(2.9167 - j8.75)}$$

$$\left[\frac{-0.3 - 0.07725}{1.03 - j0.0} - (-1.25 + j3.75)(1.05 + j0.0) + (-1.6667 + j5.0)(1 + j0.0)\right]$$

$$V_2^{(1)} = 1.01915 - j0.032491$$

$$= 1.0196673\angle -1.826^0$$

An acceleration factor of 1.4 is used for both real and imaginary parts.

The accelerated voltages is obtained using

$$v_2' = 1.03 + 1.4(1.01915 - 1.03) = 1.01481$$
$$v_2'' = 0.0 + 1.4(-0.032491 - 0.0) = -0.0454874$$

$$V_2^{(1)}\,(\text{accelerated}) = 1.01481 - j0.0454874$$

$$= 1.01583\angle -2.56648^0$$

The voltage at bus 3 is given by

$$V_2^{(1)} = \frac{1}{Y_{33}}\left[\frac{P_3 - jQ_3}{V_3^{(0)*}} - Y_{31}V_1 - Y_{32}V_2^{(1)}\right]$$

$$= \frac{1}{6.6667 - j20}$$

$$\left[\left(\frac{-0.6 + j0.25}{1 - j0}\right) - (-5 + j15)(1.05 + j0) - (-1.6667 + j5)(1.01481 - j0.0454874)\right]$$

$$= 1.02093 - j0.0351381$$

The accelerated value of obtained using

$$v_3' = 1.0 + 1.4(1.02093 - 1.0) = 1.029302$$
$$v_3'' = 0 + 1.4(-0.0351384 - 0) = -0.0491933$$

$$V_3^{(1)} = 1.029302 - j0.049933$$
$$= 1.03048\angle -2.73624^0$$

The voltages at the end of the first iteration are

$$V_1 = 1.05 + j0.0$$

$$V_2^{(1)} = 1.01481 - j0.0454874$$

$$V_3^{(1)} = 1.029302 - j0.0491933$$

Check for convergence : An accuracy of 0.001 is taken for convergence

$$\left[\Delta v_2'\right]^{(0)} = \left[v_2'\right]^{(1)} - \left[v_2'\right]^{(0)} = 1.01481 - 1.03 = -0.0152$$

$$\left[\Delta v_2''\right]^{(0)} = \left[v_2''\right]^{(1)} - \left[v_2''\right]^{(0)} = -0.0454874 - 0.0 = -0.0454874$$

$$\left[\Delta v_3'\right]^{(0)} = \left[v_3'\right]^{(1)} - \left[v_3'\right]^{(0)} = 1.029302 - 1.0 = 0.029302$$

$$\left[\Delta v_2''\right]^{(0)} = \left[\Delta v_2''\right]^{(1)} - \left[\Delta v_2''\right]^{(0)} = -0.0491933 - 0.0 = -0.0491933$$

The magnitudes of all the voltage changes are greater than 0.001.

Iteration 2 : The reactive power Q_2 at bus 2 is calculated as before to give

$$\delta_2^{(1)} = \tan^{-1}\frac{\left[v_2''\right]^{(1)}}{\left[v_2'\right]^{(1)}} = \tan^{-1}\left[\frac{-0.0454874}{1.01481}\right] = -2.56648^0$$

$$\left[v_2'\right]^{(1)} = \left|V_{2sch}\right| \cdot \cos\delta_2^{(1)} = 1.03\cos(-2.56648^0) = 1.02837$$

$$\left[v_2''\right]^{(1)} = \left|V_{2sch}\right| \cdot \sin\delta_2^{(1)} = 1.03\sin(-2.56648^0) = -0.046122$$

$$\left[V_{2new}\right]^{(1)} = 1.02897 - j0.046122$$

$$\begin{aligned} Q_2^{(1)} &= (1.02897)^2(8.75) + (-0.046122)^2(8.75) \\ &+ (-0.046122)[1.05(-1.25) + (0)(-3.75)] \\ &- (1.02897)[(0)(-1.25) - (1.05)(-3.75)] + \\ &- (1.02897)[(-0.0491933)(-1.6667) - (1.029302)(-5)] \\ &= -0.0202933 \end{aligned}$$

Mvar to be generated at bus 2

= Net Mvar injection into bus 2 + load Mvar

= – 0.0202933 + 0.2 = 0.1797067 p.u. = 17.97067Mvar

This is within the specified limits. The voltages are, therefore, the same as before

$$V_1 = 1.05 + j0.0$$

$$V_2^{(1)} = 1.02897 - j0.0.46122$$

$$V_3^{(1)} = 1.029302 - j0.0491933$$

The New voltage at bus 2 is obtained as

$$V_2^{(2)} = \frac{1}{2.9167 - j8.75}\left[\frac{-0.3 + j0.0202933}{1.02827 + j0.046122}\right.$$

$$- (-1.25 + j3.75)(1 - 05 + j0)$$

$$\left. - (-1.6667 + j5) \cdot (1.029302 - j0.0491933)\right]$$

$$= 1.02486 - j0.0568268$$

The accelerated value of $V_2^{(2)}$ is obtained from

$$v_2' = 1.02897 + 1.4(1.02486 - 1.02897) = 1.023216$$

$$v_2'' = -0.046122 + 1.4(-0.0568268) - (-0.046122 = -0.0611087)$$

$$v_2^{(2)'} = 1.023216 - j0.0611087$$

The new voltage at bus 3 is calculated as

$$V_3^{(2)} = \frac{1}{6.6667 - j20}\left[\frac{-6.6 + j0.25}{1.029302 + j0.0491933}\right.$$

$$- (-5 + j15)(1.05 + j0.0)$$

$$\left. - (-1.6667 + j5.0) \cdot (1.023216 - j0.0611)\right]$$

$$= 1.0226 - j0.0368715$$

The accelerated value of $V_2^{(2)}$ obtained from

$$v_3' = 1.029302 + 1.4(1.0226 - 1.029302) = 1.02$$

$$v_3'' = (-0.0491933) + 1.4(-0.0368715) +$$

$$(0.0491933) = -0.03194278$$

$$V_3^{(2)} = 1.02 - j0.03194278$$

The voltages at the end of the second iteration are

$$V_1 = 1.05 + j0.0$$

$$V_2^{(2)} = 1.023216 - j0.0611087$$

$$V_3^{(2)} = 1.02 - j0.03194278$$

The procedure is repeated till convergence is obtained at the end of the sixth iteration. The results are tabulated in Table E2.1(a)

Table E2.1 (a) Bus Voltage

Iteration	Bus 1	Bus 2	Bus 3
0	1.05 + j0	1.03 + j0	1.0 + j0
1	1.05 + j0	1.01481 – j0.04548	1.029302 – j0.049193
2	1.05 + j0	1.023216 – j0.0611087	1.02 – j0.0319428
3	1.05 + j0	1.033476 – j0.0481383	1.027448 – j0.03508
4	1.05 + j0	1.0227564 – j0.051329	1.0124428 – j0.0341309
5	1.05 + j0	1.027726 – j0.0539141	1.0281748 – j0.0363943
6	1.05 + j0	1.029892 – j0.05062	1.020301 – j0.0338074
7	1.05 + j0	1.028478 – j0.0510117	1.02412 – j0.034802

Line flow from bus 1 to bus 2

$$S_{12} = V_1\left(V_1^* - V_2^*\right)Y_{12}^* = 0.228975 + j0.017396$$

Line flow from bus 2 to bus 1

$$S_{21} = V_2\left(V_2^* - V_1^*\right)Y_{21}^* = -0.22518 - j0.0059178$$

Similarly, the other line flows can be computed and are tabulated in Table E2.1(b). the slack bus power obtained by adding the flows in the lines terminating at the slack bus, is

$$P_1 + jQ_1 = 0.228975 + j0.017396 + 0.684006 + j0.225$$

$$= (0.912981 + j0.242396)$$

Table E2.1(b) Line Flows

Line	P	Power Flow	Q
1-2	+ 0.228975		0.017396
2-1	– 0.225183		0.0059178
1-3	0.68396		0.224
3-1	– 0.674565		–0.195845
2-3	– 0.074129		0.0554
3-2	0.07461		–0.054

(b) Newton-Raphson polar coordinates method

The bus admittance matrix is written in polar form as

$$Y_{BUS} = \begin{bmatrix} 19.7642\angle -71.6^0 & 3.95285\angle -108.4^0 & 15.8114\angle -108.4^0 \\ 3.95285\angle -108.4^0 & 9.22331\angle -71.6^0 & 5.27046\angle -108.4^0 \\ 15.8114\angle -108.4^0 & 5.27046\angle -108.4^0 & 21.0819\angle -71.6^0 \end{bmatrix}$$

Note that

$$\angle Y_{ii} = -71.6^0$$

and $\angle Y_{ik} = -180^0 - 71.6^0 = 108.4^0$

The initial bus voltages are

$$V_1 = 1.05\angle 0^0$$

$$V_2^{(0)} = 1.03\angle 0^0$$

$$V_2^{(0)} = 1.0\angle 0^0$$

The real and reactive powers at bus 2 are calculated as follows :

$$P_2 = |V_2V_1Y_{21}|\cos\left(\delta_2^{(0)} - \delta_1 - \theta_{21}\right) + \left|V_2^2 Y_{22}\right|\cos(-\theta_{22}) + |V_2V_3Y_{23}|\cos\left(\delta_2^{(0)} - \delta_3^{(0)} - \theta_{23}\right)$$

$= (1.03)\,(1.05)\,(3.95285)\cos(108^0.4) + (1.03)^2\,(9.22331)\cos(-108^0.4) + (1.03)^2\,(9.22331)\cos(71^0.6) + (1.03)(1.0)(5.27046)\cos(-108^0.4)$

$= 0.02575$

$$Q_2 = |V_2V_1Y_{21}|\sin\left(\delta_2^{(0)} - \delta_1 - \theta_{21}\right) + \left|V_2^2 Y_{22}\right|\sin(-\theta_{22}) + |V_2V_3Y_{23}|\sin\left(\delta_2^{(0)} - \delta_3^{(0)} - \theta_{23}\right)$$

$= (1.03)\,(1.05)\,(3.95285)\sin(-108^0.4) + (1.03)^2\,(9.22331)\sin(71.6^0) + (1.03)\,(1.0)\,(5.27046)\sin(108.4^0)$

$= 0.07725$

Generation of p.u Mvar at bus 2

$= 0.2 + 0.07725$

$= 0.27725 = 27.725$ Mvar

This is within the limits specified. The real and reactive powers at bus 3 are calculated in a similar way.

$$P_3 = \left|V_3^{(0)} V_1 Y_{31}\right| \cos\left(\delta_3^{(0)} - \delta_1 - \theta_{31}\right) + \left|V_3^{(0)} V_2 Y_{32}\right| \cos\left(\delta_3^{(0)} - \delta_2 - \theta_{32}\right) +$$

$$\left|V_3^{(0)2} Y_{33}\right| \cos(-\theta_{33})$$

$$= (1.0)\,(1.05)\,(15.8114) \cos(-108.4^0) +$$

$$(1.0)\,(1.03)\,(5.27046) \cos(-108.4^0)$$

$$+ (1.0)^2\,(21.0819) \cos(71.6^0)$$

$$= -0.3$$

$$Q_3 = \left|V_3^{(0)} V_1 Y_{31}\right| \sin\left(\delta_3^{(0)} - \delta_1 - \theta_{31}\right) + \left|V_3^{(0)} V_2\, Y_{32}\right| \sin\left(\delta_3^{(0)} - \delta_2 - \theta_{32}\right) +$$

$$\left|V_3^{(0)2}\, Y_{33}\right| \sin(-\theta_{33})$$

$$= (1.0)\ 1.05\ (15.8114) \sin(-108.4^0) + (1.0)\,(1.03)\,(5.27046)$$

$$\sin(-108.4^0)$$

$$+ (1.0)^2\,(21.0891) \sin(71.6^0)$$

$$= -0.9$$

The difference between scheduled and calculated powers are

$$\Delta P_2^{(0)} = -0.3 - 0.02575 = -0.32575$$

$$\Delta P_3^{(0)} = -0.6 - (-0.3) = -0.3$$

$$\Delta Q_2^{(0)} = -0.25 - (-0.9) = -0.65$$

It may be noted that ΔQ_2 has not been computed since bus 2 is voltage controlled bus.

since $\left|\Delta P_2^{(0)}\right|, \left|\Delta P_3^{(0)}\right| \text{and} \left|\Delta Q_3^{(0)}\right|$

are greater than the specified limit of 0.01, the next iteration is computed.

Iteration 1 : Elements of the Jacobian are calculated as follows.

$$\frac{\partial P_2}{\partial \delta_2} = -\left|V_2\, V_1\ Y_{21}\right| \sin\left(\delta_2^{(0)} - \delta_1^{(0)} - \theta_{21}\right) +$$

$$\left|V_2\, V_3^{(0)}\, Y_{23}\right| \sin\left(\delta_2^{(0)} - \delta_3^{(0)} - \theta_{23}\right)$$

$$= -\,(1.03)\,(1.05)\,(3.95285) \sin(108.4^0) +$$

$$(1.03)\,(1.0)\,(5.27046) \sin(-108.4^0)$$

$$-\ 9.2056266$$

$$\frac{\partial P_2}{\partial \delta_3} = \left|V_2\, V_3^{(0)}\, Y_{23}\right| \sin\left(\delta_2^{(0)} - \delta_3^{(0)} - \theta_{23}\right)$$

$$= (1.03)\,(1.0)\,(5.27046) \sin(-108.4^0) = -5.15$$

$$\frac{\partial P_3}{\partial \delta_2} = \left|V_3^{(0)} V_1 \ Y_{31}\right| \sin\left(\delta_3^{(0)} - \delta_2^{(0)} - \theta_{32}\right)$$

= (0.0) (1.03) (5.27046) sin (–108.4⁰)

= – 5.15

$$\frac{\partial P_3}{\partial \delta_3} = \left|V_3^{(0)} V_1 \ Y_{31}\right| \sin\left(\delta_3^{(0)} - \delta_1 - \theta_{31}\right) + \left|V_3^{(0)} V_2 \ Y_{32}\right| \sin\left(\delta_3^{(0)} - \delta_2^{(0)} - \theta_{32}\right)$$

= – (1.0) (1.05) (15.8114) sin (–108.4⁰) – 5.15

= 20.9

$$\frac{\partial P_2}{\partial V_3}$$

= (1.03) (5.27046) cos (108.4⁰)

= – 1.7166724

$$\frac{\partial P_3}{\partial V_3} = 2\left|V_3 \ Y_{33}\right| \cos\theta_{33} + \left|V_1 \ Y_{31}\right| \cos\left(\delta_3^{(0)} - \delta_2^{(0)} - \theta_{32}\right) +$$

$$\left|V_2 \ Y_{32}\right| \cos\left(\delta_3^{(0)} - \delta_2^{(0)} - \theta_{32}\right)$$

= 2(1.0) (21.0819) cos (71.6⁰) + (1.05) (15.8114) cos (–108.4⁰) + (1.03) (5.27046) cos (-108.4⁰)

= 6.366604

$$\frac{\partial Q_3}{\partial \delta_2} = -\left|V_3^{(0)} V_1 \ Y_{32}\right| \cos\left(\delta_3^{(0)} - \delta_2^{(0)} - \theta_{32}\right)$$

= (1.0) (1.03) (5.27046) cos (–108.4⁰)

= 1.7166724

$$\frac{\partial Q_3}{\partial \delta_3} = \left|V_3^{(0)} V_1 \ Y_{32}\right| \cos\left(\delta_3^{(0)} - \delta_1 - \theta_{31}\right) +$$

$$\left|V_3^{(0)} V_2 \ Y_{32}\right| \cos\left(\delta_2^{(0)} - \delta_3^{(0)} - \theta_{32}\right)$$

= (1.0) (1.05) (15.8114) cos (–108.4⁰) – 1.7166724

= – 6.9667

$$\frac{\partial Q_3}{\partial V_3} = 2V_3^{(o)}\, Y_{33} \sin\left(-\theta_{33}\right) \quad + \left|V_1\; Y_{31}\right| \sin\left(\delta_3^{(0)} - \delta_1 - \theta_{31}\right) +$$

$$\left|V_2\; Y_{32}\right| \sin\left(\delta_3^{(0)} - \delta_2^{(0)} - \theta_{32}\right)$$

$$= 2(1.0)\,(21.0819)\,\sin\,(71.6^0) + (1.05)\,(15.8114)\,\sin\,(-108.4^0) +$$

$$(1.03)\,(5.27046)\,\sin\,(-108.4^0)$$

$$= 19.1$$

From eqn. (2.45)

$$\begin{bmatrix} -0.32575 \\ -0.3 \\ 0.65 \end{bmatrix} = \begin{bmatrix} 9.20563 & -5.15 & -1.71667 \\ -5.15 & 20.9 & 6.36660 \\ 1.71667 & -6.9967 & 19.1 \end{bmatrix} \begin{bmatrix} |\Delta\delta_2| \\ \Delta\delta_3 \\ \Delta|V_3| \end{bmatrix}$$

Following the method of triangulation and back substations

$$\begin{bmatrix} -0.35386 \\ -0.3 \\ -0.035386 \end{bmatrix} = \begin{bmatrix} 1 & -0.55944 & -0.18648 \\ -5.15 & 20.9 & 6.36660 \\ +1.71667 & -6.9667 & 19.1 \end{bmatrix} \begin{bmatrix} \Delta\delta_2 \\ \Delta\delta_3 \\ \Delta|V_3| \end{bmatrix}$$

$$\begin{bmatrix} -0.35386 \\ -0.482237 \\ +0.710746 \end{bmatrix} = \begin{bmatrix} 1 & -0.55944 & -0.18648 \\ 0 & 18.02 & 5.40623 \\ 0 & -6.006326 & 19.42012 \end{bmatrix} \begin{bmatrix} \Delta\delta_2 \\ \Delta\delta_3 \\ \Delta|V_3| \end{bmatrix}$$

Finally,

$$\begin{bmatrix} -0.35386 \\ -0.0267613 \\ 0.55 \end{bmatrix} = \begin{bmatrix} 1 & -0.55944 & -0.18648 \\ 0 & 1 & 0.3 \\ 0 & 0 & 21.22202 \end{bmatrix} \begin{bmatrix} \Delta\delta_2 \\ \Delta\delta_3 \\ \Delta|V_3| \end{bmatrix}$$

Thus, $\quad \Delta|V_3| = (0.55)\,/(21.22202) = 0.025917$

$$\Delta\delta_3 = -\,0.0267613 - (0.3)\,(0.025917)$$

$$= -\,0.0345364 \text{ rad}$$

$$= -\,1.98^0$$

$$\Delta\delta_2 = -\,0.035286 - (-0.55944)\,(\;0.034536) - (-0.18648)\,(0.025917)$$

$$= -\,0.049874 \text{ rad}$$

$$= -\,2.8575^0$$

At the end of the firs iteration the bus voltages are

$$V_1 = 1.05 \angle 0^0$$
$$V_2 = 1.03 \angle 2.85757^0$$
$$V_3 = 1.025917 \angle -1.9788^0$$

The real and reactive powers at bus 2 are computed :

$$P_2^{(1)} = (1.03)(1.05)(3.95285)[\cos(-2.8575) - 0(-108.4^0)$$
$$+ (1.03)^2(1.025917)(5.27046)\cos[(-2.8575) - (-1.9788) - 108.4^0$$
$$= -0.30009$$
$$Q_2^{(1)} = (1.03)(1.05)(3.95285)[\sin(-2.8575) - 0(-108.4^0)$$
$$+ (1.03)^2(9.22331)\sin[(-2.85757) - (-1.9788) - 108.4^0)]$$
$$= 0.043853$$

Generation of reactive power at bus 2

$$= 0.2 + 0.043853 = 0.243856 \text{ p.u. Mvar}$$
$$= 24.3856 \text{ Mvar}$$

This is within the specified limits.

The real and reactive powers at bus 3 are computed as

$$P_3^{(1)} = (1.025917)(1.05)(15.8117)\cos[(-1.09788) - 0 - 108.4^0)]$$
$$+ (1.025917)(1.03)(5.27046)\cos[(-1.0988) - (-2.8575) - 108.4]$$
$$+ (1.025917)^2(21.0819)\cos(71.6^0)$$
$$= -0.60407$$

$$Q_3^{(1)} = (1.025917)(1.05)(15.8114)\sin[(-1.977) - 108.4^0)]$$
$$+ (1.025917)(1.03)(5.27046)\sin[(-1.9788) - (-2.8575) - 108.4^0)]$$
$$+ (1.025917)^2(21.0819)\sin(71.6^0)$$
$$= -0.224$$

The differences between scheduled powers and calculated powers are

$$\Delta P_2^{(1)} = -0.3 - (-0.30009) = 0.00009$$
$$\Delta P_3^{(1)} = -0.6 - (-0.60407) = 0.00407$$
$$\Delta Q_3^{(1)} = -0.25 - (-0.2224) = -0.0276$$

$$-(0.3) - (0.30009)$$
$$-(0.6) - (0.60407)$$
$$-(0.25) - (0.2224)$$

Even though the first two differences are within the limits the last one, $Q_2^{(1)}$ is greater than the specified limit 0.01. The next iteration is carried out in a similar manner. At the end of the second iteration even ΔQ_3 also is found to be within the specified tolerance. The results are tabulated in table E2.1.2(a) and E2.1.2(b)

Table E2.1.2(a) Bus voltages

Iteration	Bus 1	Bus 2	Bus 3
0	$1.05\angle 0^0$	$1.03\angle 0^0$	$1.\angle 0^0$
1	$1.05\angle 0^0$	$1.03\angle -2.85757$	$1.025917\angle -1.9788$
2	$1.05\angle 0^0$	$1.03\angle -2.8517$	$1.02476\angle -1.947$

Table E2.1.2(b) Line Flows

Line	P	Power Flow	Q
1-2	0.2297		0.016533
2-1	– 0.22332		– 0.0049313
1-3	0.68396		0.224
3-1	– 0.674565		– 0.0195845
2-3	– 0.074126		0.0554
3-2	0.07461		– 0.054

E2.2 Obtain the load flow solution to the system given in example E2.1 using Z-Bus. Use Gauss – Seidel method. Take accuracy for convergence as 0.0001.

Solution :

The bus impedance matrix is formed as indicated in section 2.10. The slack bus is taken as the reference bus. In this example, as in example 2.1 bus 1 is chosen as the slack bus.

(i) Add element 1-2. This is addition of a new bus to the reference bus

$$Z_{BUS} = \begin{array}{c|c} & (2) \\ (2) & 0.05 + j0.24 \end{array}$$

(ii) Add element 1-3. This is also addition of a new bus to the reference bus

$$Z_{BUS} = \begin{array}{c|cc} & (2) & (3) \\ (2) & 0.08 + j0.24 & 0.0 + j0.0 \\ (3) & 0.0 + j0.0 & 0.02 + j0.06 \end{array}$$

(iii) Add element 2-3. This is the addition of a link between two existing buses 2 and 3.

$$Z_{2\text{-loop}} = Z_{\text{loop-2}} = Z_{22} - Z_{23} = 0.08+j0.24$$

$$Z_{3\text{-loop}} = Z_{\text{loop-3}} = Z_{32} - Z_{33} = -(0.02+j0.06)$$

$$Z_{\text{loop-loop}} = Z_{22} + Z_{33} - 2\,Z_{23} + Z_{23,\,23}$$

$$= (0.08+j0.24)+(0.02+j0.06)(0.06 + j0.18)$$

$$= 0.16 + j0.48$$

Z_{BUS} =	(2)	(3)	(ℓ)
(2)	$0.08 + j0.024$	$0 + j0$	$0.08 + j0.24$
(3)	$0.0 + j0.0$	$0.02 + j0.06$	$-(0.02 + j0.06)$
ℓ	$0.08 + j0.24$	$-(0.02 + j0.006)$	$0.16 + j0.48$

The loop is now eliminated

$$Z'_{22} = Z_{22} - \frac{Z_{2-\text{loop}}\,Z_{\text{loop}-2}}{Z_{\text{loop}-\text{loop}}}$$

$$= (0.08 + j0.24) - \frac{(0.8 + j0.24)^2}{0.16 + j0.48}$$

$$= 0.04 + j0.12$$

$$Z'_{23} = Z'_{32} = \left[Z_{23} - \frac{Z_{2-\text{loop}}\,Z_{\text{loop}-3}}{Z_{\text{loop}-\text{loop}}} \right]$$

$$= (0.0 + j0.0) - \frac{(0.8 + j0.24)(-0.02 - j0.06)}{0.16 + j0.48}$$

$$= 0.01 + j0.03$$

Similarly $\quad Z'_{33} = 0.0175 + j0.0526$

The Z - Bus matrix is thus

$$Z_{Bus} = \left[\begin{array}{c|c} 0.04 + j0.12 & 0.01 + j0.03 \\ \hline 0.01 + j0.03 & 0.017 + j0.0525 \end{array} \right] =$$

$$\left[\begin{array}{c|c} 0.1265\angle 71.565^0 & 0.031623\angle 71.565^0 \\ \hline 0.031623\angle 71.565^0 & 0.05534\angle 71.565^0 \end{array} \right]$$

The voltages at bus 2 and 3 are assumed to be

$$V_2^{(0)} = 1.03 + j0.0$$

$$V_3^{(0)} = 1.0 + j0.0$$

Assuming that the reactive power injected into bys 2 is zero,

$$Q_2 = 0.0$$

The bus currents $I_2^{(0)}$ and $I_3^{(0)}$ are computed as

$$I_2^{(0)} = \frac{-0.3 + j0.0}{1.03 - j0.0} = -0.29126 - j0.0 = 0.29126\angle 180^0$$

$$I_3^{(0)} = \frac{-0.6 + j0.25}{1.0 + j0.0} = -0.6 - j0.25 = 0.65\angle 157.38^0$$

Iteration 1 : The voltage at bus 2 is computed as

$$\begin{aligned} V_2^{(1)} &= V_1 + Z_{22}\, I_2^{(0)} + Z_{23}\, I^{(0)} \\ &= 1.05\angle 0^0 + (0.1265\angle 71.565^0 (0.29126\angle 180^0 + \\ &\quad (0.031623\angle 71.565^0)(0.65\angle 157.38^0 \\ &= 1.02485 - j0.05045 \\ &= 1.02609\angle -2.8182 \end{aligned}$$

The new bus current $I_2^{(0)}$ is now calculated.

$$\Delta I_2^{(0)} = \frac{V_2^{(1)}}{Z_{22}}\left[\frac{|V_{sch}|}{|V_2^{(1)}|} - 1\right]$$

$$-\frac{1.02609\angle -2.8182}{0.1265\angle 71.565^0} \times \left(\frac{1.03}{1.02609} - 1\right) = 0.0309084\angle -74.3832^0$$

$$\begin{aligned} Q^{(0)} &= \text{Im}\left[V_2^{(1)}\, \Delta I_2^{(0)*}\right] \\ &= \text{Im}\left[1.02609\angle -2.8182^0\right](0.0309084\angle 74.383^0 \\ &= 0.03 \end{aligned}$$

$$Q_2^{(1)} = Q_2^{(0)} + \Delta Q_2^{(0)} = 0.0 + 0.03 = 0.03$$

$$I_2^{(1)} = \frac{-0.3 - j0.3}{1.02609\angle -2.8182^0} = 0.29383\angle 182.8918^0$$

Voltage at bus 3 is now calculated

$$V_3^{(1)} = V_1 + Z_{32} I_2^{(1)} + Z_{33} I_3^{(0)}$$

$$= 1.05\angle 0.0^0 + (0.031623\angle 71.565^0)(0.29383\angle 182.832^0) + (0.05534\angle 71.565^0)(0.65\angle 157.38^0)$$

$$= (1.02389 - j0.036077) = 1.0245\angle -2.018^0$$

$$I_3^{(1)} = \frac{0.65\angle 157.38^0}{1.0245\angle 2.018^0} = 0.634437\angle 155.36^0$$

The voltages at the end of the first iteration are :

$$V_1 = 1.05 \angle 0^0$$

$$V_2^{(1)} = 1.02609\angle -2.8182^0$$

$$V_3^{(1)} = 1.0245\angle -2.018^0$$

The differences in voltages are

$$\Delta V_2^{(1)} = (1.02485 - j0.05045) - (1.03 + j0.0)$$
$$= -0.00515 - j0.05045$$

$$\Delta V_3^{(1)} = (1.02389 - j0.036077) - (1.0 + j0.0)$$
$$= (0.02389 - j0.036077)$$

Both the real and imaginary parts are greater than the specified limit 0.001.

Iteration 2 :

$$V_2^{(2)} = V_1 + Z_{22} I_2^{(1)} + Z_{23} I_3^{(1)}$$

$$= 1.02 \angle 0^0 + (0.1265\angle 71.565^0)(0.29383 \angle 182.892^0) + (0.031623\angle 71.565^0)(0.63447\angle 155.36^0)$$

$$= 1.02634 - j0.050465$$

$$= 1.02758 \angle -2.81495^0$$

$$\Delta I_2^{(1)} = \frac{1.02758\angle -2.81495^0}{1.1265\angle -71.565^0}\left[\frac{1.03}{1.02758} - 1\right]$$

$$= 0.01923\angle -74.38^0$$

$$\Delta Q_2^{(1)} = \text{Im}\left[V_2^{(2)}\left(\Delta I_2^{(1)}\right)^*\right]$$

$$= \text{Im}(1.02758\angle -2.81495)(0.01913\angle 74.38^0)$$

$$= 0.0186487$$

$$Q_2^{(2)} = Q_2^{(1)} + \Delta Q_2^{(1)}$$
$$= 0.03 + 0.0186487 = 0.0486487$$

$$I_2^{(2)} = \frac{-0.3 - j0.0486487}{1.02758\angle 2.81495^0}$$

$$= 0.295763\angle 186.393^0$$

$$V_3^{(2)} = 1.05\angle 0^0 + (0.31623\angle 71.565^0(0.295763\angle 186.4^0 +$$
$$0.05534\angle 71.565^0)(0.634437\angle 155.36^0)$$

$$I_3^{(2)} = \frac{0.65\angle 157.38^0}{1.02466\angle 1.9459^0} = 0.6343567\angle 155.434^0$$

$$\Delta V_2^{(1)} = (1.02634 - j0.050465) - (1.02485 - j0.05041) = 0.00149 - j0.000015$$

$$\Delta V_3^{(1)} = (1.024 - j0.034793) - (1.02389 - j0.036077) = 0.00011 + j0.00128$$

As the accuracy is still not enough, another iteration is required.

Iteration 3 :

$$V_2^{(3)} = 1.05\angle 0^0 + (0.1265\angle 71.565^0)(0.295763\angle 186.4^0) +$$
$$(0.031623\angle 71.565^0)(0.63487\angle 155.434^0)$$
$$= 1.0285187 - j0.051262$$
$$= 1.0298\angle -2.853^0$$

$$I_2^{(2)} = \frac{1.0298\angle -2.853^0}{0.1265\angle 71.565^0}\left[\frac{1.03}{1.0298} - 1\right] = 0.001581\angle 74.418^0$$

$$\Delta Q_2^{(2)} = 0.00154456$$

$$Q_2^{(3)} = 0.0486487 + 0.001544 = 0.0502$$

$$I_2^{(3)} = \frac{-0.3 - j0.0502}{0.0298\angle 2.853^0} = 0.29537\angle 186.647^0$$

$$V_3^{(3)} = 1.05\angle 0^0 + (0.031623\angle 71.565^0) + (0.29537\angle 186.647^0) +$$
$$(0.05534\angle 71.565^0)(0.634357\angle 155.434^0)$$
$$= 1.024152 - j0.034817 = 1.02474\angle -1.9471^0$$

$$I_3^{(3)} = \frac{-0.65 - \angle 157.38^0}{1.02474\angle 1.9471^0} = 0.6343\angle 155.433^0$$

$$\Delta V_2^{(2)} = (1.0285187 - j0.051262) - (1.02634 - j0.050465)$$
$$= 0.0021787 - 0.000787$$

$$\Delta V_3^{(2)} = (1.024152 - j0.034817) - (1.024 - j0.034793)$$
$$= 0.000152 - j0.00002$$

Iteration 4 :

$$V_2^{(4)} = 1.02996\angle - 2.852^0$$
$$\Delta I_2^{(3)} = 0.0003159\angle - 74.417^0$$
$$\Delta Q_2^{(3)} = 0.0000867$$

$$Q_2^{(4)} = 0.0505$$
$$I_2^{(4)} = 0.29537\angle 186.7^0$$
$$V_2^{(4)} = 1.02416 - J0.034816 = 1.02475\angle -1.947^0$$
$$\Delta V_2^{(3)} = 0.000108 + j0.000016$$

$$\Delta V_3^{(3)} = 0.00058 + j0.000001$$

The final voltages are

$$V_1 = 1.05 + j0.0$$
$$V_2 = 1.02996\angle -2.852^0$$
$$V_3 = 1.02475\angle -1.947^0$$

The line flows may be calculated further if required.

E 2.3 Consider the bus system shown in Fig. E 2.3.

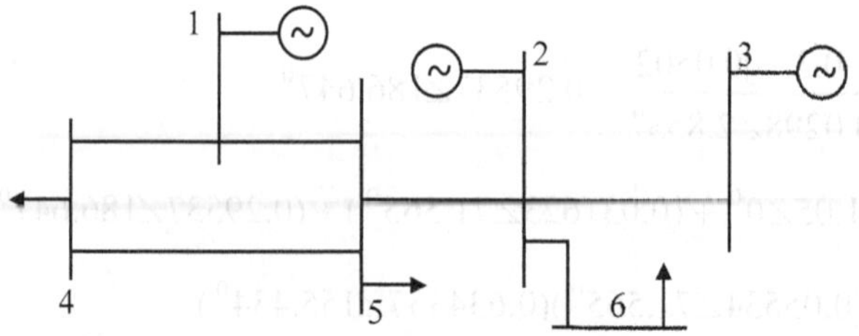

E2.3 A six bus power system

The following is the data :

Line impedance (p.u.)	Real		Imaginary	
1.4	0.57000	E-1	0.845	E-1
1-5	1.33000	E-2	3.600	E-2
2-3	3.19999	E-2	1.750	E-1
2-5	1.73000	E-2	0.560	E-1
2-6	3.00000	E-2	1.500	E-1
4-5	1.94000	E-2	0.625	E-1

Scheduled generation and bus voltages :

Bus Code P	Assumed bus voltage	Generation		Load	
		MW p.u.	Mvar p.u	MW p.u.	Mvar p.u
1	1.05 +j0.0 (specified)	---	---	---	---
2	---	1.2	0.05	---	---
3	---	1.2	0.05	---	---
4	---	---	---	1.4	0.05
5	---	---	---	0.8	0.03
6	---	---	---	0.7	0.02

Taking bus – 1 as slack bus and using an accelerating factor of 1.4, perform load flow by Gauss – Seidel method. Take precision index as 0.0001.

Solution :

The bus admittance matrix is obtained as :

Bus Code	Admittance (p.u.)	
P – Q	Real	Imaginary
1 – 1	14.516310	–32.57515
1 – 4	–5.486446	8.13342
1 – 5	–9.029870	24.44174
2 – 2	7.329113	–28.24106
2 – 3	–1.011091	5.529494
2 – 5	–5.035970	16.301400
2 – 6	–1.282051	6.410257

Contd.....

Bus Code	Admittance (p.u.)	
P – Q	Real	Imaginary
3 – 2	–1.011091	5.529404
3 – 3	1.011091	–5.529404
4 – 1	–5.486446	8.133420
4 – 4	10.016390	–22.727320
4 – 5	–4.529948	14.593900
5 – 1	–9.029870	24.441740
5 – 2	–5.035970	16.301400
5 – 4	–4.529948	14.593900
5 – 5	18.595790	–55.337050
6 – 2	–1.282051	6.410257
6 – 6	1.282051	–6.410254

All the bus voltages, $V^{(0)}$, are assumed to be 1 + j0 except the specified voltage at bus 1 which is kept fixed at 1.05 + j0. The voltage equations for the fist Gause-Seidel iteration are:

$$V_2^{(1)} = \frac{1}{Y_2}\left[\frac{P_2 - jQ_2}{V_2^{(0)*}} - Y_{23}V_3^{(0)} - Y_{25}V_5^{(0)} - Y_{26}V_6^{(0)}\right]$$

$$V_3^{(1)} = \frac{1}{Y_{33}}\left[\frac{P_3 - jQ_3}{V_3^{(0)*}} - Y_{32}V_2^{(1)}\right]$$

$$V_4^{(1)} = \frac{1}{Y_{44}}\left[\frac{P_4 - jQ_4}{V_4^{(0)*}} - Y_{41}V_1 - Y_{45}V_5^{(0)}\right]$$

$$V_5^{(1)} = \frac{1}{Y_{55}}\left[\frac{P_5 - jQ_5}{V_5^{(0)*}} - Y_{51}V_1 - Y_{51}V_2^{(1)} - Y_{54}V_4^{(1)}\right]$$

$$V_6^{(1)} = \frac{1}{Y_{66}}\left[\frac{P_6 - jQ_6}{V_6^{(0)*}} - Y_{62}V_2^{(1)}\right]$$

Substituting the values, the equation for solution are

$$V_2^{(1)} = \left(\frac{1}{7.329113} - j28.24100\right) \times \left[\frac{1.2 - j0.05}{1 - j0}\right.$$
$$- (-1.011091 + j5.529404) \times (1 + j0) - (-5.03597 + j16.3014)(1 + j0)$$
$$\left. - (1 - 282051 + j16.3014)(1 + j0)\right]$$
$$= 1.016786 + j0.0557924$$

$$V_3^{(1)} = \left(\frac{1}{1.011091} - j5.52424\right) \times \left[\frac{1.2 - j0.05}{1 - j0}\right.$$
$$\left. - (-1.011091 + j5.529404) \times (1.016786 + j0.0557924)\right]$$
$$= 1.089511 + j0.3885233$$

$$V_4^{(1)} = \left(\frac{1}{10.01639} - j22.72732\right) \times \left[\frac{-1.4 + j0.005}{1 - j0}\right.$$
$$- (-5.486446 + j8.133342) \times (1.05 + j0.)$$
$$\left. - (-4.529948 + j14.5939)(1 + j0)\right]$$
$$= 0.992808 - j0.0658069$$

$$V_5^{(1)} = \left(\frac{1}{18.59579} - j55.33705\right) \times \left[\frac{-0.8 + j0.03}{1 - j0}\right.$$
$$- (-9.02987 + j24.44174) \times (1.05 + j0)$$
$$- (-5.03597 + j16.3014)(1.016786 + j0.0557929)$$
$$\left. - (-4.529948 + j14.5939)(0.992808 - j0.0658069)\right]$$
$$- 1.028669 - j0.01879179$$

$$V_6^{(1)} = \left(\frac{1}{1.282051} - j6.410257\right) \times \left[\frac{-0.7 + j0.02}{1 - j0}\right.$$
$$\left. - (-1.282051 - j6.410257) \times (1.016786 + j0.0557924)\right]$$
$$= 0.989904 - j0.0669962$$

The results of these iterations is given in Table 2.3 (a)

In the polar form, all the voltages at the end of the 14th iteration are given in Table E2.3(b).

Table E2.3(a)

It.No	Bus 2	Bus 3	Bus 4	Bus 5	Bus 6
0	1 + j0.0	1 + j0.0	1 + j0.0	1 + j0.0	1 + j0.0
1	1.016789 + j0.0557924	1.089511 + j0.3885233	0.992808 – j0.0658069	1.02669 – j0.01879179	0.989901 – j0.0669962
2	1.05306 + j0.1018735	1.014855 + j0.2323309	1.013552 – j0.0577213	1.042189 + j0.0177322	1.041933 + j0.0192121
3	1.043568 + j0.089733	1.054321 + j0.3276035	1.021136 – j0.0352727	1.034181 + j0.00258192	1.014571 – j0.02625271
4	1.047155 + j0.101896	1.02297 + j0.02763564	1.012207 – j0.0500558	1.035391 + j0.00526437	1.02209 + j0.00643566
5	1.040005 + j0.093791	1.03515 + j0.3050814	1.61576 – j0.04258692	0.033319 + j0.003697056	1.014416 – j0.01319787
6	1.04212 + j0.0978431	1.027151 + j0.2901358	1.013044 – j0.04646546	10.33985 + j0.004504417	1.01821 – j0.001752973
7	1.040509 + j0.0963405	1.031063 + j0.2994083	1.014418 – j0.0453101	1.033845 + j0.00430454	1.016182 – j0.00770669
8	1.041414 + j0.097518	1.028816 + j0.294465	1.013687 – j0.0456101	1.033845 + j0.004558826	1.017353 – j0.0048398
9	1.040914 + j0.097002	1.030042 + j0.2973287	1-014148 – j0.04487629	1.033711 + j0.004413647	1.016743 – j0.0060342
10	1.041203 + j0.0972[illegible]18	1.02935 + j0.2973287	1.013881 – j0.04511174	1.03381 + j0.004495542	1.017089 – j0.00498989
11	1.041036 + j0.097154	1.029739 + j0.296598	1.01403 – j0.04498312	1.03374 + j0.004439559	1.016877 – j0.00558081
12	1.041127 + j0.0971[illegible]98	1.029518 + j0.2960784	1.013943 – j0.04506212	1.033761 + j0.00447096	1.016997 – j0.00524855
13	1.041075 + j0.0971451	1.029642 + j0.2963715	1.019331 – j0.04501488	1.033749 + j0.004454002	1.016927 – j0.00543323
14	1.041104 + j0.0971777	1.02571 + j0.2962084	1.0013965 – j0.04504223	1.033756 + j0.004463713	1.016967 – j0.00053283

Table E2.3(b)

Bus	Voltage magnitude (p.u.)	Phase angle (°)
1	1.05	0
2	0.045629	5.3326
3	1.071334	16.05058
4	1.014964	–2.543515
5	1.033765	2.473992
6	1.016981	–3.001928

E2.4 For the given sample find load flow solution using N-R polar coordinates, decoupled method and fast decoupled method.

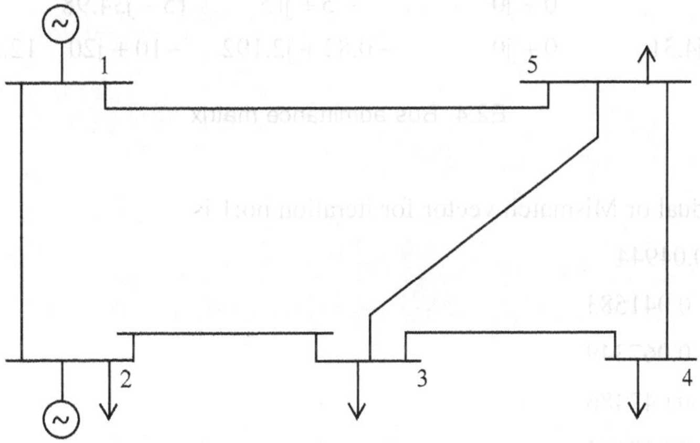

Bus Code	Line impedance Zpq	Line charging
1-2	0.02 + j0.24	j 0.02
2-3	0.04 + j0.02	j 0.02
3-5	0.15 + j0.04	j 0.025
3-4	0.02 + j0.06	j 0.01
4-5	0.02 + j0.04	j 0.01
5-1	0.08 + j0.02	j 0.2

Bus Code (Slack)	Generation		Load	
	Mw	Mvar	MW	Mvar
1	0	0	0	0
2	50	25	15	10
3	0	0	45	20
4	0	0	40	15
5	0	0	50	25

	1	2	3	4	5
1	$11.724 - j24.27$	$-10 + j20$	$0 + j0$	$0 + j0$	$-1.724 + j4.31$
2	$-10 + j20$	$10.962 - j24.768$	$-0.962 + j4.808$	$0 + j0$	$0 + j0$
3	$0 + j0$	$-0.962 + j4.808$	$6.783 - j21.944$	$-5 + j15$	$-0.822 + j2.192$
4	$0 + j0$	$0 + j0$	$-5 + j15$	$15 - j34.98$	$-10 + j20$
5	$-1.724 + j4.31$	$0 + j0$	$-0.82 + j2.192$	$-10 + j20$	$12.546 - j26.447$

E2.4 Bus admittance matrix

Solution :

The Residual or Mismatch vector for iteration no:1 is

dp[2] = 0.04944

dp[3] = –0.041583

dp[4] = –0.067349

dp[5] = –0.047486

dQ[2] = –0.038605

dQ[3] = –0.046259

dQ[4] = 0.003703

dQ[5] = –0.058334

The New voltage vector after iteration 1 is :

Bus no 1 E : 1.000000 F : 0.000000

Bus no 2 E : 1.984591 F :- 0.008285

Bus no 3 E : 0.882096 F :- 0.142226

Bus no 4 E : 0.86991 F :- 0.153423

Bus no 5 E : 0.875810 F :- 0.142707

The residual or mismatch vector for iteration no : 2 is

dp[2] = 0.002406

dp[3] = –0.001177

dp[4] = –0.004219

dp[5] = –0.000953

dQ[2] = –0.001087

dQ[3] = –0.002261

dQ[4] = –0.000502

dQ[5] = –0.002888

The New voltage vector after iteration 2 is :

Bus no 1 E : 1.000000 F : 0.000000

Bus no 2 E : 0.984357 F :- 0.008219

Bus no 3 E : 0.880951 F :- 0.142953

Bus no 4 E : 0.868709 F :- 0.154322

Bus no 5 E : 0.874651 F :- 0.143439

The residual or mismatch vector for iteration no : 3 is

dp[2] = 0.000005

dp[3] = –0.000001

dp[4] = –0.000013

dp[5] = –0.000001

dQ[2] = –0.000002

dQ[3] = –0.000005

dQ[4] = –0.000003

dQ[5] = –0.000007

The final load flow solution (for allowable error.0001) :

bus no 1 Slack P = 1.089093 Q = 0.556063 E = 1.000000 F = 0.000000

bus no 2 pq P = 0.349995 Q = 0.150002 E = 0.984357 F = –0.008219

bus no 3 pq P = –0.449999 Q = –0.199995 E = 0.880951 F = –0.1429531

bus no 4 pq P = 0.399987 Q = –0.150003 E = 0.868709 F = –0.154322

bus no 5 pq P = –0.500001 Q = –0.249993 E = 0.874651 F = –0.143439

Decoupled load flow solution (polar coordinate method)

The residual or mismatch vector for iteration no : 0 is

dp[2] = 0.350000

dp[3] = –0.450000

dp[4] = –0.400000

dp[5] = –0.500000

dQ[2] = –0.190000

dQ[3] = –0.145000

dQ[4] = –0.130000

dQ[5] = –0.195000

The new voltage vector after iteration 0 :

Bus no 1 E : 1.000000 F : 0.000000

Bus no 2 E : 0.997385 F :- 0.014700

Bus no 3 E : 0.947017 F :- 0.148655

Bus no 4 E : 0.941403 F :- 0.161282

Bus no 5 E : 0.943803 F :- 0.150753

The residual or mismatch vector for iteration no:1 is

dp [2] = 0.005323

dp[3] = –0.008207

dp[4] = –0.004139

dp[5] = –0.019702

dQ[2] = –0.067713

dQ[3] = –0.112987

dQ[4] = –0.159696

dQ[5] = –0.210557

The new voltage vector after iteration 1 :

Bus no 1 E : 1.000000 F : 0.000000

Bus no 2 E : 0.982082 F :- 0.013556

Bus no 3 E : 0.882750 F :- 0.143760

Bus no 4 E : 0.870666 F :- 0.154900

Bus no 5 E : 0.876161 F :- 0.143484

The residual or mismatch vector for iteration no:2 is

dp[2] = 0.149314

dp[3] = –0.017905

dp[4] = –0.002305

dp[5] = –0.006964

dQ[2] = –0.009525

dQ[3] = –0.009927

dQ[4] = –0.012938

dQ[5] = 0.007721

The new voltage vector after iteration 2 :

Bus no 1 E : 1.000000 F : 0.000000

Bus no 2 E : 0.981985 F :- 0.007091

Bus no 3 E : 0.880269 F :- 0.142767

Bus no 4 E : 0.868132 F :- 0.154172

Bus no 5 E : 0.874339 F :- 0.143109

The residual or mismatch vector for iteration no:3 is

dp[2] = 0.000138

dp[3] = 0.001304

dp[4] = 0.004522

dp[5] = –0.006315

dQ[2] = 0.066286

dQ[3] = 0.006182

dQ[4] = –0.001652

dQ[5] = –0.002233

The new voltage vector after iteration 3 :

Bus no 1 E : 1.000000 F : 0.000000

Bus no 2 E : 0.984866 F :- 0.007075

Bus no 3 E : 0.881111 F :- 0.142710

Bus no 4 E : 0.868848 F :- 0.154159

Bus no 5 E : 0.874862 F :- 0.143429

The residual or mismatch vector for iteration no:4 is

dp[2] = –0.031844

dp[3] = 0.002894

dp[4] = –0.000570

dp[5] = 0.001807

dQ[2] = –0.000046

dQ[3] = 0.000463

dQ[4] = 0.002409

dQ[5] = –0.003361

The new voltage vector after iteration 4 :

Bus no 1 E : 1.000000 F : 0.000000

Bus no 2 E : 0.984866 F :- 0.008460

Bus no 3 E : 0.881121 F :- 0.142985

Bus no 4 E : 0.868849 F :- 0.1546330

Bus no 5 E : 0.874717 F :- 0.143484

The residual or mismatch vector for iteration no:5 is

dp[2] = 0.006789

dp[3] = –0.000528

dp[4] = –0.000217

dp[5] = –0.0000561

dQ[2] = –0.000059

dQ[3] = –0.000059

dQ[4] = –0.000635

dQ[5] = –0.000721

The new voltage vector after iteration 5 :

Bus no 1 E : 1.000000 F : 0.000000

Bus no 2 E : 0.984246 F :- 0.008169

Bus no 3 E : 0.880907 F :- 0.142947

Bus no 4 E : 0.868671 F :- 0.154323

Bus no 5 E : 0.874633 F :- 0.143431

The residual or mismatch vector for iteration no : 6 is

dp[2] = 0.000056

dp[3] = 0.000010

dp[4] = 0.000305

dp[5] = –0.000320

dQ[2] = 0.003032

dQ[3] = –0.000186

dQ[4] = –0.000160

dQ[5] = –0.000267

The new voltage vector after iteration 6 :

Bus no 1 E : 1.000000 F : 0.000000

Bus no 2 E : 0.984379 F :- 0.008165

Bus no 3 E : 0.880954 F :- 0.142941

Bus no 4 E : 0.868710 F :- 0.154314

Bus no 5 E : 0.874655 F :- 0.143441

The residual or mismatch vector for iteration no:7 is

dp[2] = - 0.001466

dp[3] = 0.000106

dp[4] = -0.000073

dp[5] = 0.000156

dQ[2] = 0.000033

dQ[3] = 0.000005

dQ[4] = 0.000152

dQ[5] = -0.000166

The new voltage vector after iteration 7 :

Bus no 1 E : 1.000000 F : 0.000000

Bus no 2 E : 0.954381 F :- 0.008230

Bus no 3 E : 0.880958 F :- 0.142957

Bus no 4 E : 0.868714 F :- 0.154325

Bus no 5 E : 0.874651 F :- 0.143442

The residual or mismatch vector for iteration no : 8 is

dp[2] = –0.000022

dp[3] = 0.000001

dp[4] = –0.000072

dp[5] = –0.000074

dQ[2] = –0.000656

dQ[3] = 0.000037

dQ[4] = –0.000048

dQ[5] = –0.000074

The new voltage vector after iteration 8 :

Bus no 1 E : 1.000000 F : 0.000000

Bus no 2 E : 0.984352 F :- 0.008231

Bus no 3 E : 0.880947 F :- 0.142958

Bus no 4 E : 0.868706 F :- 0.154327

Bus no 5 E : 0.874647 F :- 0.143440

The residual or mismatch vector for iteration no:9 is

dp[2] = 0.000318

dp[3] = –0.000022

dp[4] = 0.000023

dp[5] = –0.000041

dQ[2] = –0.000012

dQ[3] = –0.000000

dQ[4] = 0.000036

dQ[5] = –0.000038

The new voltage vector after iteration 9 :

Bus no 1 E : 1.000000 F : 0.000000

Bus no 2 E : 0.984352 F :- 0.008217

Bus no 3 E : 0.880946 F :- 0.142954

Bus no 4 E : 0.868705 F :- 0.154324

Bus no 5 E : 0.874648 F :- 0.143440

The residual or mismatch vector for iteration no:10 is

dp[2] = 0.000001

dp[3] = –0.000001

dp[4] = 0.000017

dp[5] = –0.000017

dQ[2] = 0.000143

dQ[3] = –0.000008

dQ[4] = 0.000014

dQ[5] = –0.000020

The new voltage vector after iteration 10 :

Bus no 1 E : 1.000000 F : 0.000000

Bus no 2 E : 0.984658 F :- 0.008216

Bus no 3 E : 0.880949 F :- 0.142954

Bus no 4 E : 0.868707 F :- 0.154324

Bus no 5 E : 0.874648 F :- 0.143440

The residual or mismatch vector for iteration no:11is

dp[2] = –0.000069

dp[3] = 0.000005

dp[4] = –0.000006

dp[5] = 0.000011

dQ[2] = 0.000004

dQ[3] = –0.000000

dQ[4] = 0.000008

dQ[5] = –0.000009

The final load flow solution after 11 iterations

(for allowable arror.0001)

The final load flow solution (for allowable error.0001) :

Bus no 1	Slack	P = 1.089043	Q = 0.556088	E = 1.000000	F = 0.000000
Bus no 2	pq	P = 0.350069	Q = 0.150002	E = 0.984658	F = -0.008216
Bus no 3	pq	P = –0.450005	Q = –0.199995	E = 0.880949	F = -0.142954
Bus no 4	pq	P = –0.399994	Q = –0.150003	E = 0.868707	F = -0.154324
Bus no 5	pq	P = –0.500011	Q = –0.249991	E = 0.874648	F = –0.143440

Fast decoupled load flow solution (polar coordinate method)

The residual or mismatch vector for iteration no:0 is

dp[2] = 0.350000

dp[3] = –0.450000

dp[4] = 0.400000

dp[5] = –0.500000

dQ[2] = 0.190000

dQ[3] = –0.145000

dQ[4] = 0.130000

dQ[5] = –0.195000

The new voltage vector after iteration 0 :

Bus no 1 E : 1.000000 F : 0.000000

Bus no 2 E : 0.997563 F :- 0.015222

Bus no 3 E : 0.947912 F :- 0.151220

Bus no 4 E : 0.942331 F :- 0.163946

Bus no 5 E : 0.944696F :- 0.153327

The residual or mismatch vector for iteration no:1 is

dp[2] = 0.004466

dp[3] = –0.000751

dp[4] = 0.007299

dp[5] = –0.012407

dQ[2] = 0.072548

dQ[3] = –0.118299

dQ[4] = 0.162227

dQ[5] = –0.218309

The new voltage vector after iteration 1 :

Bus no 1 E : 1.000000 F : 0.000000

Bus no 2 E : 0.981909 F :- 0.013636

Bus no 3 E : 0.882397 F :- 0.143602

Bus no 4 E : 0.869896 F :- 0.154684

Bus no 5 E : 0.875752 F :- 0.143312

The residual or mismatch vector for iteration no: 2 is

dp[2] = 0.153661

dp[3] = –0.020063

dp[4] = 0.005460

dp[5] = –0.009505

dQ[2] = 0.011198

dQ[3] = –0.014792

dQ[4] = –0.000732

dQ[5] = –0.002874

The new voltage vector after iteration 2 :

Bus no 1 E : 1.000000 F : 0.000000

Bus no 2 E : 0.982004 F :- 0.007026

Bus no 3 E : 0.880515 F :- 0.142597

Bus no 4 E : 0.868400 F :- 0.153884

Bus no 5 E : 0.874588 F :- 0.143038

The residual or mismatch vector for iteration no: 3 is

dp[2] = –0.000850

dp[3] = –0.002093

dp[4] = 0.000155

dp[5] = –0.003219

dQ[2] = 0.067612

dQ[3] = –0.007004

dQ[4] = –0.003236

dQ[5] = –0.004296

The new voltage vector after iteration 3 :

Bus no 1 E : 1.000000 F : 0.000000

Bus no 2 E : 0.984926 F :- 0.007086

Bus no 3 E : 0.881246 F :- 0.142740

Bus no 4 E : 0.869014 F :- 0.154193

Bus no 5 E : 0.874928 F :- 0.143458

The residual or mismatch vector for iteration no: 4 is

dp[2] = –0.032384

dp[3] = 0.003011

dp[4] = –0.001336

dp[5] = –0.002671

dQ[2] = –0.000966

dQ[3] = –0.000430

dQ[4] = –0.000232

dQ[5] = –0.001698

The new voltage vector after iteration 4 :

Bus no 1 E : 1.000000 F : 0.000000

Bus no 2 E : 0.984862 F :- 0.008488

Bus no 3 E : 0.881119 F :- 0.143053

Bus no 4 E : 0.868847 F :- 0.154405

Bus no 5 E : 0.874717 F :- 0.143501

The residual or mismatch vector for iteration no: 5 is

dp[2] = 0.000433

dp[3] = 0.000006

dp[4] = –0.000288

dp[5] = 0.000450

dQ[2] = –0.014315

dQ[3] = –0.000936

dQ[4] = –0.000909

dQ[5] = –0.001265

The new voltage vector after iteration 6 :

Bus no 1 E : 1.000000 F : 0.000000

Bus no 2 E : 0.984230 F :- 0.008463

Bus no 3 E : 0.881246 F :- 0.143008

Bus no 4 E : 0.869014 F :- 0.154357

Bus no 5 E : 0.874607 F :- 0.143433

The residual or mismatch vector for iteration no: 6 is

dp[2] = 0.006981

dp[3] = –0.000528

dp[4] = 0.000384

dp[5] = –0.000792

dQ[2] = 0.000331

dQ[3] = 0.000039

dQ[4] = –0.000155

dQ[5] = 0.000247

The residual or mismatch vector for iteration no: 7 is

dp[2] = –0.000144

dp[3] = –0.000050

dp[4] = 0.000080

dp[5] = –0.000068

dQ[2] = 0.003107

dQ[3] = –0.000162

dQ[4] = –0.000255

dQ[5] = –0.000375

The new voltage vector after iteration 7 :

Bus no 1 E : 1.000000 F : 0.000000

Bus no 2 E : 0.984386 F :- 0.008166

Bus no 3 E : 0.880963 F :- 0.142943

Bus no 4 E : 0.868718 F :- 0.154316

Bus no 5 E : 0.874656F :- 0.143442

The residual or mismatch vector for iteration no: 8 is

dp[2] = –0.001523

dp[3] = –0.000105

dp[4] = –0.000115

dp[5] = –0.000215

dQ[2] = 0.000098

dQ[3] = –0.000024

dQ[4] = –0.000037

dQ[5] = –0.000038

The new voltage vector after iteration 8 :

Bus no 1 E : 1.000000 F : 0.000000

Bus no 2 E : 0.984380 F :- 0.008233

Bus no 3 E : 0.880957 F :- 0.142961

Bus no 4 E : 0.868714 F :- 0.154329

Bus no 5 E : 0.874651 F :- 0.143442

The residual or mismatch vector for iteration no: 9 is

dp[2] = –0.000045

dp[3] = 0.000015

dp[4] = –0.000017

dp[5] = 0.000008

dQ[2] = 0.000679

dQ[3] = 0.000031

dQ[4] = –0.000072

dQ[5] = –0.000105

The new voltage vector after iteration 9 :

Bus no 1 E : 1.000000 F : 0.000000

Bus no 2 E : 0.984350 F :- 0.008230

Bus no 3 E : 0.880945 F :- 0.142958

Bus no 4 E : 0.868704 F :- 0.154326

Bus no 5 E : 0.874646 F :- 0.143440

The residual or mismatch vector for iteration no: 10 is

dp[2] = 0.000334

dp[3] = –0.000022

dp[4] = 0.000033

dp[5] = –0.000056

dQ[2] = 0.000028

dQ[3] = 0.000007

dQ[4] = –0.000007

dQ[5] = 0.000005

The new voltage vector after iteration 10 :

Bus no 1 E : 1.000000 F : 0.000000

Bus no 2 E : 0.984352 F :- 0..008216

Bus no 3 E : 0.880946 F :- 0.142953

Bus no 4 E : 0.898705 F :- 0.154323

Bus no 5 E : 0.874648 F :- 0.143440

The residual or mismatch vector for iteration no: 11 is

dp[2] = –0.000013

dp[3] = –0.000004

dp[4] = 0.000003

dp[5] = –0.000000

dQ[2] = 0.000149

dQ[3] = –0.000007

dQ[4] = 0.000020

dQ[5] = –0.000027

The new voltage vector after iteration 11 :

Bus no 1 E : 1.000000 F : 0.000000

Bus no 2 E : 0.984358 F :- 0.008216

Bus no 3 E : 0.880949 F :- 0.142954

Bus no 4 E : 0.868707 F :- 0.154324

Bus no 5 E : 0.874648 F :- 0.143440

The residual or mismatch vector for iteration no: 12 is

dp[2] = –0.000074

dp[3] = 0.000005

dp[4] = –0.000009

dp[5] = –0.000014

dQ[2] = 0.000008

dQ[3] = –0.000002

dQ[4] – –0.000001

dQ[5] = –0.000000

The load flow solution

Bus no 1	Slack	P = 1.089040	Q = 0.556076	E = 1.000000	F = 0.000000
Bus no 2	pq	P = 0.350074	Q = 0.150008	E = 0.984358	F = –0.008216
Bus no 3	pq	P = –0.450005	Q = –0.199995	E = 0.880949	F = –0.142954
Bus no 4	pq	P = –0.399991	Q = –0.150001	E = 0.868707	F = 0.154324
Bus no 5	pq	P = –0.500014	Q = –0.250000	E = 0.874648	F = –0.143440

Questions

1. Explain why load flow studies are performed?
2. Discuss the classification of buses
3. With a neat flow chart explain the load flow solution by Gauss – Seidel method.
4. Explain the principle and method of solution of the load flow problem by Newton – Raphson (a) rectangular coordinates and (b) polar coordinates methods.
5. Compare Gauss – Seidel method and Newton Raphson method for load flow solution
6. Explain

   (a)

      (i) Decoupled load flow and

      (ii) Fast decoupled load flow methods

   (b) What are the application of the methods in (a)

Problems

P2.1 Obtain a load flow solution for the system shown in Fig. P2.1 use

(i) Gauss – Seidel method

(ii) N-R polar coordinator method

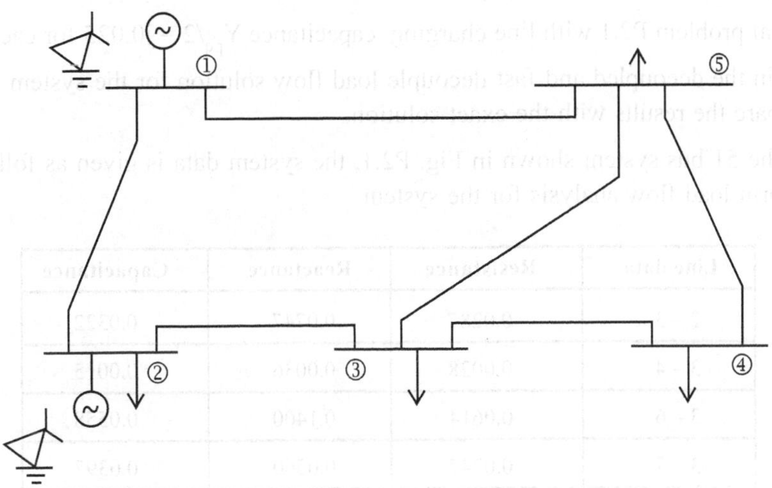

Bus code p-q	Impedance Z_{pq}	Line charges Y pq/s
1 – 2	0.02 + j0.2	0.0
2 – 3	0.01 + j0.025	0.0
3 – 4	0.02 + j0.4	0.0
3 – 5	0.02 + 0.05	0.0
4 – 5	0.015 + j0.04	0.0
1-5	0.015 + j0.04	0.0

Values are given in p.u. on a base of 100Mva.

The scheduled powers are as follows

Bus Code (P)	Generation		Load	
	Mw	Mvar	MW	Mvar
1 (slack bus)	0	0	0	0
2	80	35	25	15
3	0	0	0	0
4	0	0	45	15
5	0	0	55	20

Take voltage at bus 1 as $1\angle 0^0$ p.u.

P2.2 Repeat problem P2.1 with line charging capacitance $Y_{pq}/2 = j0.025$ for each line

P2.3 Obtain the decoupled and fast decouple load flow solution for the system in P2.1 and compare the results with the exact solution.

P2.4 For the 51 bus system shown in Fig. P2.1, the system data is given as follows in p.u. Perform load flow analysis for the system

Line data	Resistance	Reactance	Capacitance
2 – 3	0.0287	0.0747	0.0322
3 – 4	0.0028	0.0036	0.0015
3 – 6	0.0614	0.1400	0.0558
3 – 7	0.0247	0.0560	0.0397
7 – 8	0.0098	0.0224	0.0091
8 – 9	0.0190	0.0431	0.0174
9 – 10	0.0182	0.0413	0.0167
10 – 11	0.0205	0.0468	0.0190
11 – 12	0.0660	0.0150	0.0060
12 – 13	0.0455	0.0642	0.0058
13 – 14	0.1182	0.2360	0.0213
14 – 15	0.0214	0.2743	0.0267
15 – 16	0.1336	0.0525	0.0059
16 – 17	0.0580	0.3532	0.0367

Contd.....

Line data	Resistance	Reactance	Capacitance
17 – 18	0.1550	0.1532	0.0168
18 – 19	0.1550	0.3639	0.0350
19 – 20	0.1640	0.3815	0.0371
20 – 21	0.1136	0.3060	0.0300
20 – 23	0.0781	0.2000	0.0210
23 – 24	0.1033	0.2606	0.0282
12 – 25	0.0866	0.2847	0.0283
25 – 26	0.0159	0.0508	0.0060
26 – 27	0.0872	0.2870	0.0296
27 – 28	0.0136	0.0436	0.0045
28 – 29	0.0136	0.0436	0.0045
29 – 30	0.0125	0.0400	0.0041
30 – 31	0.0136	0.0436	0.0045
27 – 31	0.0136	0.0436	0.0045
30 – 32	0.0533	0.1636	0.0712
32 – 33	0.0311	0.1000	0.0420
32 – 34	0.0471	0.1511	0.0650
30 – 51	0.0667	0.1765	0.0734
51 – 33	0.0230	0.0622	0.0256
35 – 50	0.0240	0.1326	0.0954
35 – 36	0.0266	0.1418	0.1146
39 – 49	0.0168	0.0899	0.0726
36 – 38	0.0252	0.1336	0.1078
38 – 1	0.0200	0.1107	0.0794
38 – 47	0.0202	0.1076	0.0869
47 – 43	0.0250	0.1336	0.1078
42 – 43	0.0298	0.1584	0.1281
40 – 41	0.0254	0.1400	0.1008

Contd.....

Line data	Resistance	Reactance	Capacitance
41 – 43	0.0326	0.1807	0.1297
43 – 45	0.0236	0.1252	0.1011
43 – 44	0.0129	0.0715	0.0513
45 – 46	0.0054	0.0292	0.0236
44 – 1	0.0330	0.1818	0.1306
46 – 1	0.0343	0.2087	0.1686
1 – 49	0.0110	0.0597	0.1752
49 – 50	0.0071	0.0400	0.0272
37 – 38	0.0014	0.0077	0.0246
47 – 39	0.0203	0.1093	0.0879
48 – 2	0.0426	0.1100	0.0460
3 – 35	0.0000	0.0500	0.0000
7 – 36	0.0000	0.0450	0.0000
11 – 37	0.0000	0.0500	0.0000
14 – 47	0.0000	0.0900	0.0000
16 – 39	0.0000	0.0900	0.0000
18 – 40	0.0000	0.0400	0.0000
20 – 42	0.0000	0.0800	0.0000
24 – 43	0.0000	0.0900	0.0000
27 – 45	0.0000	0.0900	0.0000
26 – 44	0.0000	0.0500	0.0000
30 – 46	0.0000	0.0450	0.0000
1 – 34	0.0000	0.0630	0.0000
21 – 2	0.0000	0.2500	0.0000
4 – 5	0.0000	0.2085	0.0000
19 – 41	0.0000	0.0800	0.0000

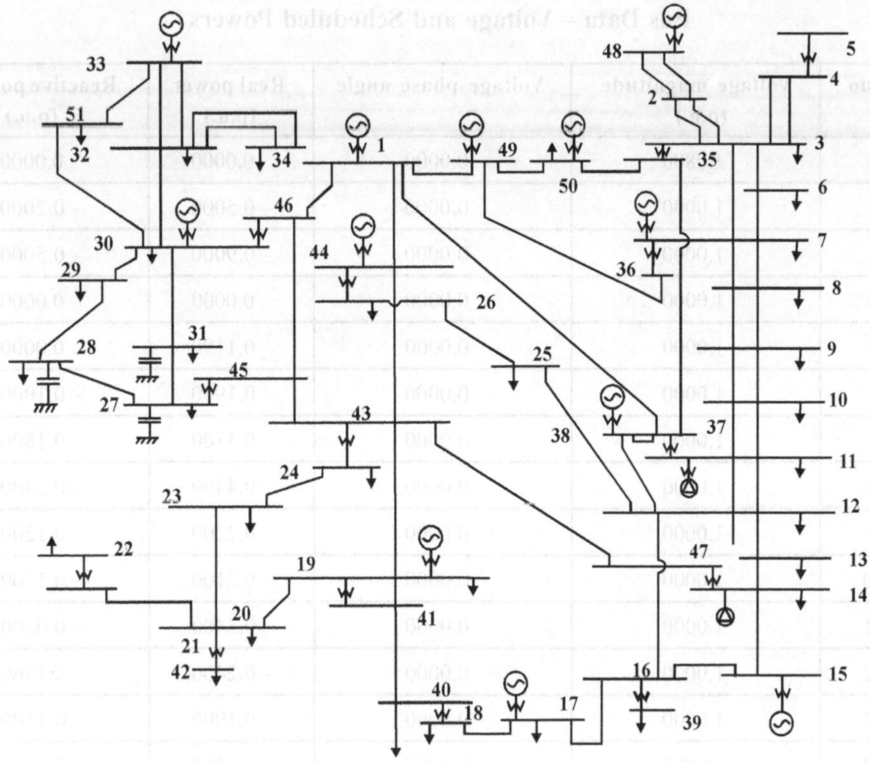

Fig. E2.1 51 Bus Power System

Bus P – Q	TAP
3 – 35	1.0450
7 – 36	1.0450
11 – 37	1.0500
14 – 47	1.0600
16 – 39	1.0600
18 – 40	1.0900
19 – 41	1.0750
20 – 42	1.0600
24 – 43	1.0750
30 – 46	1.0750
1 – 34	1.0875
21 – 22	1.0600
5 – 4	1.0800
27 – 45	1.0600
26 – 44	1.0750

Bus Data – Voltage and Scheduled Powers

Bus no	Voltage magnitude (p.u.)	Voltage phase angle	Real power (p.u.)	Reactive power (p.u.)
1	1.0800	0.0000	0.0000	0.0000
2	1.0000	0.0000	0.5000	– 0.2000
3	1.0000	0.0000	– 0.9000	– 0.5000
4	1.0000	0.0000	0.0000	0.0000
5	1.0000	0.0000	– 0.1190	0.0000
6	1.0000	0.0000	– 0.1900	– 0.1000
7	1.0000	0.0000	– 0.3300	– 0.1800
8	1.0000	0.0000	– 0.4400	– 0.2400
9	1.0000	0.0000	– 0.2200	– 0.1200
10	1.0000	0.0000	– 0.2100	– 0.1200
11	1.0000	0.0000	– 0.3400	– 0.0500
12	1.0000	0.0000	– 0.2400	– 0.1360
13	1.0000	0.0000	– 0.1900	– 0.1100
14	1.0000	0.0000	– 0.1900	– 0.0400
15	1.0000	0.0000	0.2400	0.0000
16	1.0000	0.0000	– 0.5400	– 0.3000
17	1.0000	0.0000	– 0.4600	– 0.2100
18	1.0000	0.0000	– 0.3700	– 0.2200
19	1.0000	0.0000	– 0.3100	– 0.0200
20	1.0000	0.0000	– 0.3400	– 0.1600
21	1.0000	0.0000	0.0000	0.0000
22	1.0000	0.0000	– 0.1700	– 0.0800
23	1.0000	0.0000	– 0.4200	– 0.2300
24	1.0000	0.0000	– 0.0800	– 0.0200
25	1.0000	0.0000	– 0.1100	– 0.0600
26	1.0000	0.0000	– 0.2800	– 0.1400
27	1.0000	0.0000	– 0.7600	– 0.2500
28	1.0000	0.0000	– 0.8000	– 0.3600

Contd.....

Bus no	Voltage magnitude (p.u.)	Voltage phase angle	Real power (p.u.)	Reactive power (p.u.)
29	1.0000	0.0000	– 0.2500	– 0.1300
30	1.0000	0.0000	– 0.4700	0.0000
31	1.0000	0.0000	– 0.4200	– 0.1800
32	1.0000	0.0000	– 0.3000	– 0.1700
33	1.0000	0.0000	0.5000	0.0000
34	1.0000	0.0000	– 0.5800	– 0.2600
35	1.0000	0.0000	0.0000	0.0000
36	1.0000	0.0000	0.0000	0.0000
37	1.0000	0.0000	0.0000	0.0000
38	1.0000	0.0000	1.7000	0.0000
39	1.0000	0.0000	0.0000	0.0000
40	1.0000	0.0000	0.0000	0.0000
41	1.0000	0.0000	0.0000	0.0000
42	1.0000	0.0000	0.0000	0.0000
43	1.0000	0.0000	0.0000	0.0000
44	1.0000	0.0000	1.7500	0.0000
45	1.0000	0.0000	0.0000	0.0000
46	1.0000	0.0000	0.0000	0.0000
47	1.0000	0.0000	0.0000	0.0000
48	1.0000	0.0000	0.5500	0.0000
49	1.0000	0.0000	3.5000	0.0000
50	1.0000	0.0000	1.2000	0.0000
51	1.0000	0.0000	– 0.5000	– 0.3000

Bus No.	Voltage at VCB	Reactive power limit
15	1.0300	0.1800
30	1.0000	0.0400
33	1.0000	0.4800
38	1.0600	0.9000
44	1.0500	0.4500
48	1.0600	0.2000
49	1.0700	0.5600
50	1.0700	1.500

P 2.4 The data for a 13 machine, 71 bus, 94 line system is given. Obtain the load flow solution.

Data :

No. of buses	71
No. of lines	94
Base power (MVA)	200
No. of machines	13
No. of shunt loads	23

BUS NO	GENERATION		LOAD	POWER
1	-	-	0.0	0.0
2	0.0	0.0	0.0	0.0
3	506.0	150.0	0.0	0.0
4	0.0	0.0	0.0	0.0
5	0.0	0.0	0.0	0.0
6	100.0	32.0	0.0	0.0
7	0.0	0.0	12.8	8.3
8	300.0	125.0	0.0	0.0
9	0.0	0.0	185.0	130.0
10	0.0	0.0	80.0	50.0
11	0.0	0.0	155.0	96.0
12	0.0	0.0	0.0	0.0

Contd.....

BUS NO	GENERATION		LOAD		POWER
13	0.0	0.0	100.0	62.0
14	0.0	0.0	0.0	0.0
15	180.0	110.0	0.0	0.0
16	0.0	0.0	73.0	45.5
17	0.0	0.0	36.0	22.4
18	0.0	0.0	16.0	9.0
19	0.0	0.0	32.0	19.8
20	0.0	0.0	27.0	16.8
21	0.0	0.0	32.0	19.8
22	0.0	0.0	0.0	0.0
23	0.0	0.0	75.0	46.6
24	0.0	0.0	0.0	0.0
25	0.0	0.0	133.0	82.5
26	0.0	0.0	0.0	0.0
27	300.0	75.0	0.0	0.0
28	0.0	0.0	30.0	20.0
29	260.0	70.0	0.0	0.0
30	0.0	0.0	120.0	0.0
31	0.0	0.0	160.0	74.5
32	0.0	0.0	0.0	99.4
33	0.0	0.0	0.0	0.0
34	0.0	0.0	112.0	69.5
35	0.0	0.0	0.0	0.0
36	0.0	0.0	50.0	32.0
37	0.0	0.0	147.0	92.0
38	0.0	0.0	93.5	88.0
39	25.0	30.0	0.0	0.0
40	0.0	0.0	0.0	0.0
41	0.0	0.0	225.0	123.0
42	0.0	0.0	0.0	0.0
43	0.0	0.0	0.0	0.0

Contd.....

BUS NO	GENERATION		LOAD	POWER
44	180.0	55.0	0.0	0.0
45	0.0	0.0	0.0	0.0
46	0.0	0.0	78.0	38.6
47	0.0	0.0	234.0	145.0
48	340.0	250.0	0.0	0.0
49	0.0	0.0	295.0	183.0
50	0.0	0.0	40.0	24.6
51	0.0	0.0	227.0	142.0
52	0.0	0.0	0.0	0.0
53	0.0	0.0	0.0	0.0
54	0.0	0.0	108.0	68.0
55	0.0	0.0	25.5	48.0
56	0.0	0.0	0.0	0.0
57	0.0	0.0	55.6	35.6
58	0.0	0.0	42.0	27.0
59	0.0	0.0	57.0	27.4
60	0.0	0.0	0.0	0.0
61	0.0	0.0	0.0	0.0
62	0.0	0.0	40.0	27.0
63	0.0	0.0	33.2	20.6
64	300.0	75.0	0.0	0.0
65	0.0	0.0	0.0	0.0
66	96.0	25.0	0.0	0.0
67	0.0	0.0	14.0	6.5
68	90.0	25.0	0.0	0.0
69	0.0	0.0	0.0	0.0
70	0.0	0.0	11.4	7.0
71	0.0	0.0	0.0	0.0

LINE DATA

Line No	From Bus	To Bus	Line impedance		1/2 Y charge	Turns Ratio
1	9	8	0.0000	0.0570	0.0000	1.05
2	9	7	0.3200	0.0780	0.0090	1.00
3	9	5	0.0660	0.1600	0.0047	1.00
4	9	10	0.0520	0.1270	0.0140	1.00
5	10	11	0.0660	0.1610	0.0180	1.00
6	7	10	0.2700	0.0700	0.0070	1.00
7	12	11	0.0000	0.0530	0.0000	0.95
8	11	13	0.0600	0.1480	0.0300	1.00
9	14	13	0.0000	0.0800	0.0000	1.00
10	13	16	0.9700	0.2380	0.0270	1.00
11	17	15	0.0000	0.0920	0.0000	1.05
12	7	6	0.0000	0.2220	0.0000	1.05
13	7	4	0.0000	0.0800	0.0000	1.00
14	4	3	0.0000	0.0330	0.0000	1.05
15	4	5	0.0000	0.1600	0.0000	1.00
16	4	12	0.0160	0.0790	0.0710	1.00
17	12	14	0.0160	0.0790	0.0710	1.00
18	17	16	0.0000	0.0800	0.0000	0.95
19	2	4	0.0000	0.0620	0.0000	1.00
20	4	26	0.0190	0.0950	0.1930	0.00
21	2	1	0.0000	0.0340	0.0000	1.05
22	31	26	0.0340	0.1670	0.1500	1.00
23	26	25	0.0000	0.0800	0.0000	0.95
24	25	23	0.2400	0.5200	0.1300	1.00
25	22	23	0.0000	0.0800	0.0000	0.95
26	24	22	0.0000	0.0840	0.0000	0.95
27	22	17	0.0480	0.2500	0.0505	1.00
28	2	24	0.0100	0.1020	0.3353	1.00
29	23	21	0.0366	0.1412	0.0140	1.00
30	21	20	0.7200	0.1860	0.0050	1.00
31	20	19	0.1460	0.3740	0.0100	1.00

Contd.....

Line No	From Bus	To Bus	Line impedance		1/2 Y charge	Turns Ratio
32	19	18	0.0590	0.1500	0.0040	1.00
33	18	16	0.0300	0.0755	0.0080	1.00
34	28	27	0.0000	0.0810	0.0000	1.05
35	30	29	0.0000	0.0610	0.0000	1.05
36	32	31	0.0000	0.0930	0.0000	0.95
37	31	30	0.0000	0.0800	0.0000	0.95
38	28	32	0.0051	0.0510	0.6706	1.00
39	3	33	0.0130	0.0640	0.0580	1.00
40	31	47	0.0110	0.0790	0.1770	1.00
41	2	32	0.0158	0.1570	0.5100	1.00
42	33	34	0.0000	0.0800	0.0000	0.95
43	35	33	0.0000	0.0840	0.0000	0.95
44	35	24	0.0062	0.0612	0.2120	1.00
45	34	36	0.0790	0.2010	0.0220	1.00
46	36	37	0.1690	0.4310	0.0110	1.00
47	37	38	0.0840	0.1880	0.0210	1.00
48	40	39	0.0000	0.3800	0.0000	1.05
49	40	38	0.0890	0.2170	0.0250	1.00
50	38	41	0.1090	0.1960	0.2200	1.00
51	41	51	0.2350	0.6000	0.0160	1.00
52	42	41	0.0000	0.0530	0.0000	0.95
53	45	42	0.0000	0.0840	0.0000	0.95
54	47	49	0.2100	0.1030	0.9200	1.00
55	49	48	0.0000	0.0460	0.0000	1.05
56	49	50	0.0170	0.0840	0.0760	1.00
57	49	42	0.0370	0.1950	0.0390	1.00
58	50	51	0.0000	0.0530	0.0000	0.95
59	52	50	0.0000	0.0840	0.0000	0.95
60	50	55	0.0290	0.1520	0.0300	1.00
61	50	53	0.0100	0.0520	0.0390	1.00
62	53	54	0.0000	0.0800	0.0000	0.95
63	57	54	0.0220	0.0540	0.0060	1.00

Contd.....

Line No	From Bus	To Bus	Line impedance		1/2 Y charge	Turns Ratio
64	55	56	0.0160	0.0850	0.0170	1.00
65	56	57	0.0000	0.0800	0.0000	1.00
66	57	59	0.0280	0.0720	0.0070	1.00
67	59	58	0.0480	0.1240	0.0120	1.00
68	60	59	0.0000	0.0800	0.0000	1.00
69	53	60	0.0360	0.1840	0.3700	1.00
70	45	44	0.0000	0.1200	0.0000	1.05
71	45	46	0.0370	0.0900	0.0100	1.00
72	46	41	0.0830	0.1540	0.0170	1.00
73	46	59	0.1070	0.1970	0.0210	1.00
74	60	61	0.0160	0.0830	0.0160	1.00
75	61	62	0.0000	0.0800	0.0000	0.95
76	58	62	0.0420	0.1080	0.0020	1.00
77	62	63	0.0350	0.0890	0.0090	1.00
78	69	68	0.0000	0.2220	0.0000	1.05
79	69	61	0.0230	0.1160	0.1040	1.00
80	67	66	0.0000	0.1880	0.0000	1.05
81	65	64	0.0000	0.0630	0.0000	1.05
82	65	56	0.0280	0.1440	0.0290	1.00
83	65	61	0.0230	0.1140	0.0240	1.00
84	65	67	0.0240	0.0600	0.0950	1.00
85	67	63	0.0390	0.0990	0.0100	1.00
86	61	42	0.0230	0.2293	0.0695	1.00
87	57	67	0.0550	0.2910	0.0070	1.00
88	45	70	0.1840	0.4680	0.0120	1.00
89	70	38	0.1650	0.4220	0.0110	1.00
90	33	71	0.0570	0.2960	0.0590	1.00
91	71	37	0.0000	0.0800	0.0000	0.95
92	45	41	0.1530	0.3880	0.1000	1.00
93	35	43	0.0131	0.1306	0.4293	1.00
94	52	52	0.0164	0.1632	0.5360	1.00

Shunt Load Data

S.No	Bus No	Shunt	Load
1	2	0.00	– 0.4275
2	13	0.00	0.1500
3	20	0.00	0.0800
4	24	0.00	– 0.2700
5	28	0.00	– 0.3375
6	31	0.00	0.2000
7	32	0.00	– 0.8700
8	34	0.00	0.2250
9	35	0.00	– 0.3220
10	36	0.00	0.1000
11	37	0.00	0.3500
12	38	0.00	0.2000
13	41	0.00	0.2000
14	43	0.00	– 0.2170
15	46	0.00	0.1000
16	47	0.00	0.3000
17	50	0.00	0.1000
18	51	0.00	0.1750
19	52	0.00	– 0.2700
20	54	0.00	0.1500
21	57	0.00	0.1000
22	59	0.00	0.0750
23	21	0.00	0.0500

3 ECONOMIC OPERATION OF POWER SYSTEMS

Planning operation and control of interconnected power systems presents a variety of challenging problems. An important problem in this area is the economic operation of the system, which means, that every step in planning, scheduling and operation of the system, unit-wise, plant wise and inter connection-wise must be optimal, leading to absolute economy. In this, the transmission losses too play an important role. In this chapter on economic operation of power system, both thermal and hydro systems will be dealt with using suitable analytical models that result in meaningful savings.

3.1 Characteristics of Steam Plants

In analyzing the economics of operation of thermal systems, modelling of input output characteristics assumes significance. For this purpose a single unit comprising of boiler, turbine, and generator may be considered. The unit has to supply power to the local needs for the auxiliaries in the station. This later component may be around 2-5%. The station auxiliaries includes boiler feed pumps, condenser circulating water pumps, fans etc. The total input to the unit could be either K-cal/hr in terms of heat supplied or Rs/hr in terms of the cost of the fuel such as coal, gas or fossil fuel of any other form. The net output of the unit that is supplied into the system at the generator bus will be in KW or MW. Scheduling is the process of allocation of generation among various operating generator units. Economic scheduling is the cost effective mode of generation allocation among the various units. This can also be termed as optimal operation. The analytical solution proposed in general for optimal operation depends on incremental cost concept.

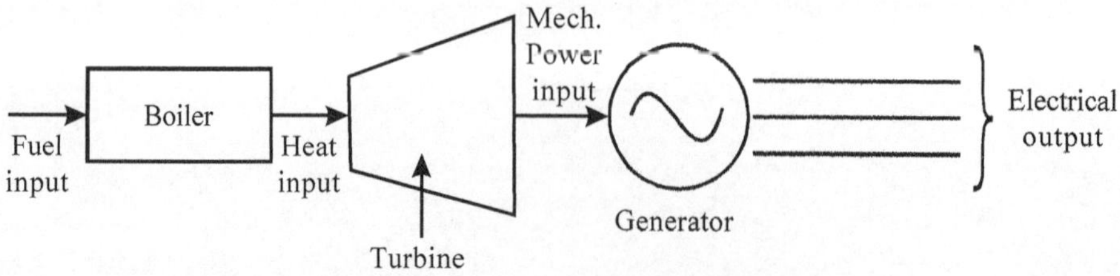

Fig. 3.1 (a) Boiler turbine generator unit

3.2 Input Output Curves

As has been already stated the input output characteristics for any thermal unit or units that comprise the plant can be obtained from the operating data. The input can be in kilo calories per hour and the output may be in kilowatts or preferably in maga watts. Typical characteristic is shown in Fig. 3.1(b) for the unit shown in Fig. 3.1(a).

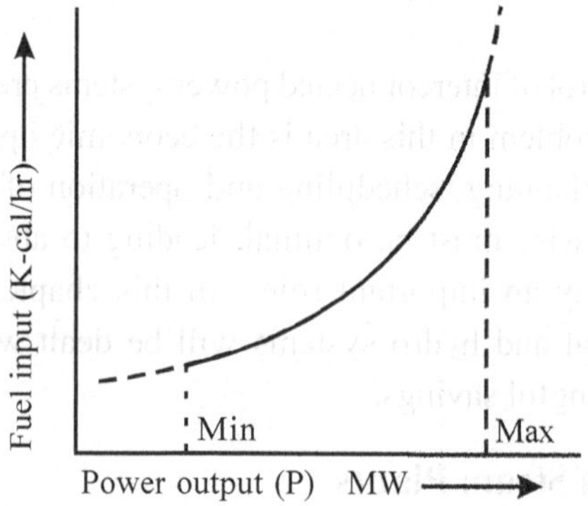

Fig. 3.1 (b) Thermal unit input-output characteristic

The characteristic in practice may not be such a smooth idealized curve and from the practical data such an idealized curve can be interpolated.

Steam turbine generating unit characteristics may have minimum and maximum limits in operation.

They may be determined by factors such as steam cycle used, operating temperatures, material thermal characteristics.

3.3 The Incremental Heat Rate Characteristic

From the input output characteristic the incremental heat rate characteristic can be obtained which is the ratio of the differentials.

$$\text{Incremental fuel rate or heat rate} = \frac{d(\text{in put})}{d(\text{out put})} \quad .....(3.1)$$

By calculating the slope of the characteristic in Fig. 3.1(b) at every point the incremental fuel rate characteristic can be plotted as shown in Fig. 3.2. This characteristic infact tells about the thermal efficacy of the unit under consideration that can be used for comparison with other units in performance.

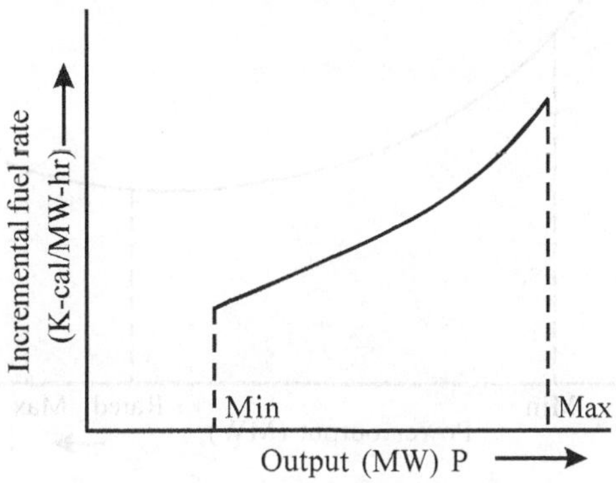

Fig. 3.2 Incremental fuel rate characteristic for thermal unit

3.4 The Incremental Fuel Cost Characteristic

The incremental fuel rate in K-cal/K-whr can be multiplied by cost of the fuel in terms of Rs per K-cal. In any case the ordinates are in Rs/Kw-hr. or Rs/MW-hr. The calorific value of the fuel is required in these calculations. This characteristic is shown in Fig. 3.3.

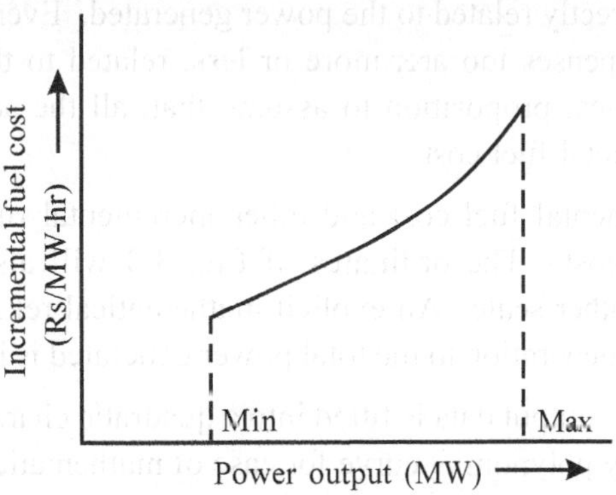

Fig. 3.3 Incremental fuel cost characteristic for thermal unit

3.5 Heat Rate Characteristic

Some times the unit net heat rate characteristic is also considered important. To obtain this characteristic the net heat rate in k.cal/K-whr is plotted against the power output (Fig. 3.4).

The thermal efficiency of the unit is influenced by factors like steam condition, reheat stages, condenser pressure and the steam cycle used. The efficiency of the units in practice is around 30%.

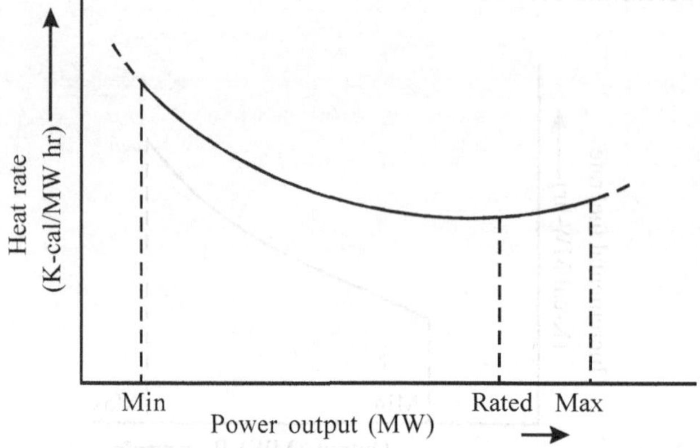

Fig. 3.4 Heat rate characteristic

3.6 Incremental Production Cost Characteristics

The production cost of the power generated actually depends on several items such as fuel cost, labour charges, cost of items such as oil, water and other supplies needed and also the cost of maintenance. It is well known that in thermal generation the fuel cost is by far the largest cost head and is directly related to the power generated. Even the other charges, that is the additional running expenses too are, more or less, related to the amount of generation. Thus, it is a simple practical proposition to assume that, all the additional costs as a fixed percentage of the incremental fuel cost.

The sum of incremental fuel cost and other incremental running expenses is called incremental production cost. The ordinates of Fig. 3.3 will also represent incremental production cost to some other scale. An explicit mathematical relationship involving all the factors involved in power generation to the total power generated is infact a very difficult task.

In general, the input-output data is fitted into a quadratic characteristic even though it is also possible to fit into any polynomial curve for ease of mathematical manipulation.

Large turbine-generator units may have several steam admission valves which are opened in a sequence to meet the increasing steam demand. The input output characteristic for such a unit with two valves may show discontinuity as shown in Fig. 3.5.

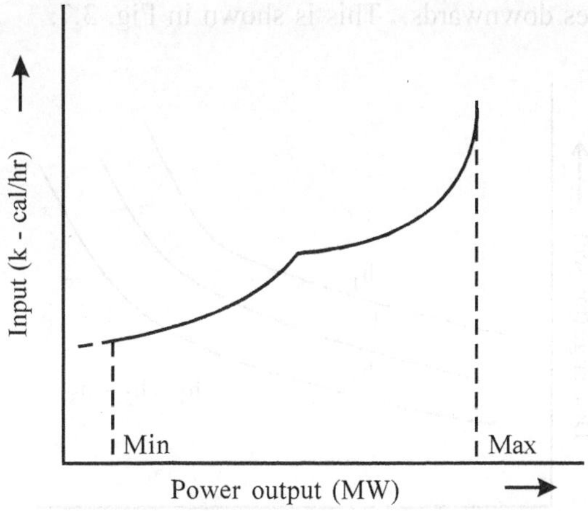

Fig. 3.5 Input-output characteristic for multiple admission valves (for two valves)

3.7 Characteristics of Hydro Plants

The input output characteristics for hydro units can be obtained in the same way as for thermal units on the assumption of constant water head. The input-output characteristic may be as shown in Fig. 3.6. The ordinates are water input or discharge in cubic meters per second shown against power output in megawatts. While the water requirement is nearly linear till rated load, after that the efficiency decreases and greater discharge is required to meet the increased load demand.

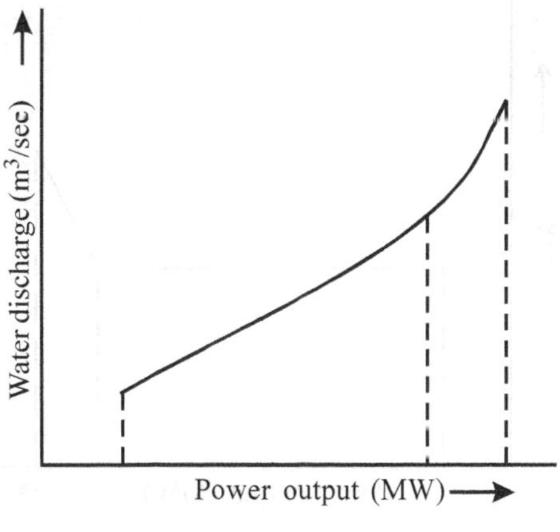

Fig. 3.6 Input-output characteristic for hydro unit

It may be noted that, if the head varies the input-output characteristics change. It will move vertically upwards, as head falls and vice versa since the hydro power generated is directly related to the head of the water level and as head falls, higher water discharge is required for the same power generation. Similarly as head rises lesser discharge is needed. The characteristic moves downwards. This is shown in Fig. 3.7.

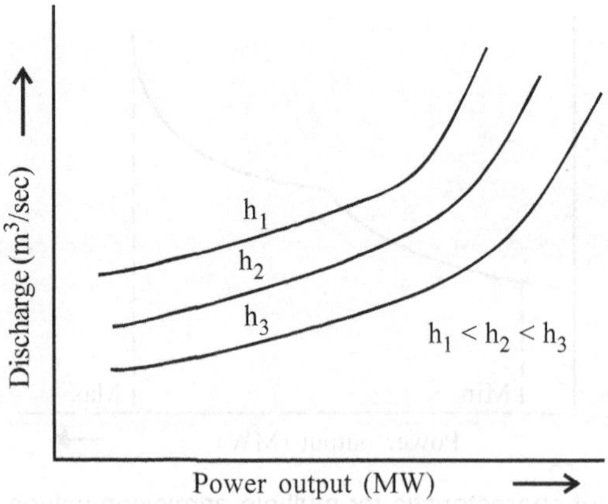

Fig. 3.7 Effect of head on discharge for hydro unit

3.8 Incremental Water Rate Characteristics

The incremental water rate curve is obtained from the water input-output characteristic in the same way as for thermal units. A typical characteristic is shown in Fig. 3.8.

As the input-output curve is linear for a greater part, the incremental water rate characteristic is a horizontal line over this region indicating constant slope, and thereafter it rises rapidly. With increase in load, more and more units will have to be brought into service.

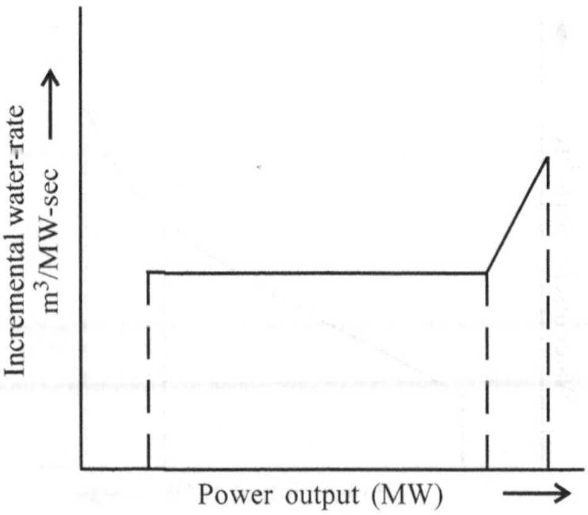

Fig. 3.8 Incremental water-rate characteristic

There will be discontinuity in the characteristics in such a case, as shown in Fig. 3.9. The discontinuity generally can be neglected so that the characteristic will still have the same shape as in Fig. 3.8.

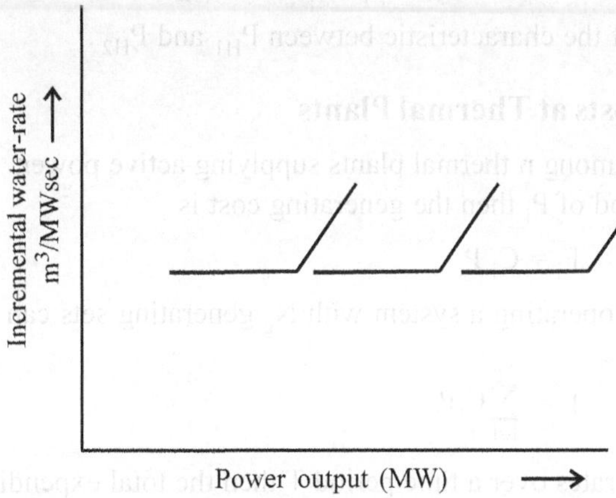

Fig. 3.9 Multiple unit operation incremental water-rate characteristic

The conversion of incremental water rate into incremental production cost requires considerations of agriculture, navigation, drinking needs of water, and other riparian rights etc. even though water is available freely in nature. Further the cost of dams, canals, conduits, gates, penstocks and other parts of hydro development are also involved.

3.9 Incremental Production Cost Characteristic

The incremental water rate characteristic can be converted into incremental production cost characteristic by multiplying the incremental water rate characteristic by water rate or cost of water in rupees per cubic meter C_w. The incremental production cost characteristic is shown in Fig. 3.10.

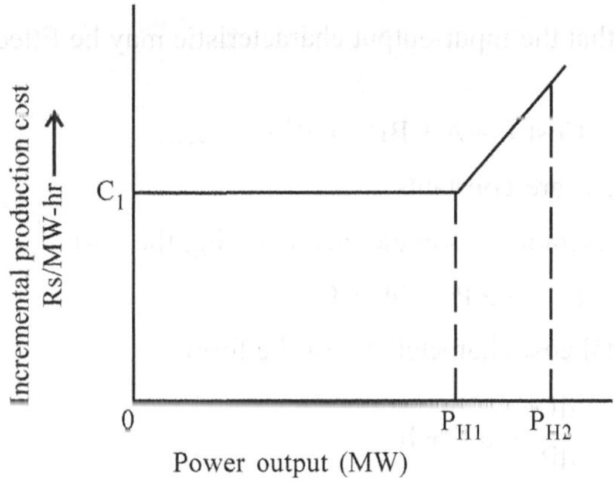

Fig. 3.10 Incremental production cost representation

The incremental production cost characteristc can be expressed analytically as follows.

$$IPC = C_1 \ (0 \le P \le P_{H1}) \qquad .....(3.2)$$

$$= a\,P_H + C_1 \ (P_{H1} \le P \le P_{H2}) \qquad .....(3.3)$$

where a is the slope of the characteristic between P_{H1} and P_{H2}.

3.10 Generating Costs at Thermal Plants

Consider any ith plant among n thermal plants supplying active power. C_i is the cost per unit of P_i in the neighborhood of P_i then the generating cost is

$$F_i = C_i\,P_i \qquad .....(3.4)$$

The total cost of operating a system with N_g generating sets can be represented by

$$F = \sum_{i=1}^{N_g} C_i P_i \qquad .....(3.5)$$

If the system operates over a time period T then the total expenditure involved will be

$$F_T = \int_0^T \sum_{i=1}^{N_g} C_i P_i(t)dt \qquad .....(3.6)$$

Steam plants with partial admission nozzle governing give better performance at partial loads since the cost coefficient increases with increasing megawatt loading. However, such units cannot be shut down, frequently, because of the complexities of steam chest. But, steam plants with throttle governing are more suitable for periodic shut down due to their simpler steam chest. Such units are more suitable for rapid starting and loading. From minimum to maximum permissible limits of operation, the cost coefficients of the units are substantially constant.

3.11 Analytical Form for Input-Output Characteristics of Thermal Units

It is already pointed out that the input-output characteristic may be fitted into a polynomial of the form

$$\text{Cost } F = A + BP + CP^2 + \ldots\ldots\ldots \qquad .....(3.7)$$

where A, B, C ...... are constants

If a quadratic representation is made then denoting the cost

$$F = \tfrac{1}{2}\,a\,P^2 + bP + C \qquad .....(3.8)$$

will lead to an incremental cost characteristic of the form

$$\frac{dF}{dP} = a\,P + b \qquad .....(3.9)$$

a linear relationship around any operating point P.

3.12 Constraints in Operation

The power system has to satisfy several constraints while in operation. These may be broadly divided into two types. The first of these arises out of the necessity for the system to satisfy load balance and are called equality constraints. At any bus i, P_{Si} and Q_{Si} correspond to the scheduled generation, P_{Di} and Q_{Di} are the load demands then the following equations must be satisfied at the bus i :

$$P_{Si} - P_{Di} - P_i = G_i = 0$$

$$Q_{Si} - Q_{Di} - Q_i = H_i = 0 \qquad .....(3.10)$$

P_i and Q_i are given by

$$P_i = \sum_{j=1}^{n} V_i V_j Y_{ij} \,\text{Cos}(\delta_i - \delta_j - \theta_{ij}) \qquad .....(3.11)$$

$$Q_i = \sum_{j=1}^{n} V_i V_j Y_{ij} \,\text{Sin}(\delta_i - \delta_j - \theta_{ij}), i = 1, 2 ....., n \qquad .....(3.12)$$

with usual notation and G_i and H_i are the residuals at bus i which should become zero at the point of solution.

In addition, a number of other constrains due to physical and operational limitations of the units and components will arise in economic scheduling. These are in the form of inequality constraints.

Each generator in operation will have a minimum and maximum permissible output and the production must be constrained to ensure that

$$P_i^{min} \le P_i \le P_i^{max}, i = 1, 2 ...., ng \qquad .....(3.13)$$

where ng is the total number of generator units

Similarly limits may also have to be considered over the range of reactive power capabilities of the generator units requiring that

$$Q_i^{min} \le Q_i \le Q_i^{max}, i = 1, 2 ...., nq \qquad .....(3.14)$$

where nq is the total number of reactive sources in the system.

Further, the constraint

$$P_i^2 + Q_i^2 \le (S_i^{rated})^2 \qquad .....(3.15)$$

must be satisfied, where S is the MVA capacity of the generating unit for limiting stator heating.

Dynamic limits may also have to be considered when fast changes in generation are envisaged for picking up or for shedding down of loads. These limits put additional constraints of the form.

$$\left|\frac{dP_i(t)}{dt}\right|^{min} \leq \left|\frac{dP_i(t)}{dt}\right| \leq \left|\frac{dP_i(t)}{dt}\right|^{max} \qquad .....(3.16)$$

The maximum and minimum operating conditions for a group of generators within a power station may be different from the respective sum of the maximum and minimum operating levels of turbines that are supplied by a single boiler. The extremes of boiler operating conditions will determine these limits. Thus, groups of generators from individual boiler units may have to be subjected to additional constraints of the nature

$$P_{kg}^{min} \leq \underset{i\varepsilon G}{P_{ki}} \leq P_{kg}^{max},\ k = 1, 2.....GR \qquad .....(3.17)$$

where GR is the total number of generator groups, the outputs of which are to be separately limited.

Spare capacity is required to account for the errors in load prediction, sudden and fast changes in load demand and the inadvertent loss of scheduled generation. Thus, the total generation G available at any time must be in excess of the total anticipated load demand and system losses by an amount not less than a specified minimum spare capacity P_{SP}.

$$G \geq \sum_{i=1}^{ng} P_i + P_{SP} \qquad .....(3.18)$$

In a similar manner, constrains may be required to be associated with groups of generators, where all plants are not equally operationally suitable for taking up additional load. If TG is the total number of groups then

$$G_k \geq \sum_{i\varepsilon G} P_{ki} + P_{SG} \qquad .....(3.19)$$

where k = 1, 2….., TG.

The summation is over the set G over which group constraints are applied.

Thermal considerations may require that the transmission lines be subjected to branch transfer constraints of the type

$$-S_i^{max} \leq S_{bi} \leq S_i^{max}, i = 1, 2,......, nb \qquad .....(3.20)$$

where nb is the number of branches and S_{bi} is the branch transfer MVA.

In addition, constraints are to be imposed for bus voltage magnitudes and for phase displacements between them for maintaining voltage profile and for limiting overloading respectively.

Thus we have

$$V_{ij}^{min} \leq V_{ij} \leq V_{ij}^{max}, i = 1, 2......, n \qquad .....(3.21)$$

$$\delta_{ij}^{min} \le \delta_{ij} \le \delta_{ij}^{max}, i = 1, 2......, n \qquad .....(3.22)$$

where $j = 1, 2......m$ and $j \ne i$

where n is the total number of nodes and m is the number of nodes neighbouring each node with interconnecting branches.

In case transformer tap positions are to be included for optimization, then the tap positions T_i must lie within the range available, i.e.

$$T_i^{min} \le T_i \le T_i^{max} \qquad .....(3.23)$$

Sometimes, phase shifting transformers are made available in the system. If such equipment exists then constraints of the type

$$PS_i^{min} \le PS_i \le PS_i^{max} \qquad .....(3.24)$$

must be reckoned where PS_i is the phase shift obtained from the ith phase shifting transformer.

If power system security is also required to be considered in the formulation for economic operation then power flows between certain important buses may also have to be considered for the final solution. It may be mentioned that consideration of each and every possible branch for outage will not be a feasible proposition.

3.13 Plant Scheduling Methods

At the plant level, several operating procedures were adopted in the past leading to efficient operation resulting in economy

(i) Base loading to capacity

The turbo generators are successively loaded to their rated capacities in the order of their efficiencies. That is to say, that the most efficient unit will get greater share in load allocation which is a natural solution to the problem.

(ii) Base loading to most efficient load

In this case the heat rate characteristics are considered and the turbo-generator units are successively loaded to their most efficient loads in increasing order of their heat rates.

In both the above methods thermodynamic considerations assumed importance and the schedules will not differ from each other much.

(iii) Proportional loading to capacity

A third method that was considered as a thumb rule in the absence of any technical data is to load the generating units in proportion to their rated capacities as stated on the name plates.

3.14 Merit Order Method

If the incremental cost characteristics are fairly constant over a wide range in operation then neglecting the transmission losses and running reserve requirements, it is possible to prepare schedules for load allocation using incremental efficiencies. Merit tables based upon incremental efficiencies are prepared and each unit is loaded to its rated capacity in order of the highest incremental efficiency. Changes in fuel costs, plant cycle efficiencies, plant availabilities etc require the merit tables to be revised regularly to reflect these factors. Then, it is possible to look at the tables so prepared and schedule the generation to different units.

3.15 Equal Incremental Cost Method : Transmission Losses Neglected

Method of Lagrange multipliers :

It is but natural that for a given load to be allocated between several generating units, the most efficient unit identified by incremental cost of production should be the one to get priority. When this is applied repeatedly to all the units the load allocation will become complete when all of them, that are involved in operation, are all working at the same incremental cost of production.

The above can be proved mathematically as follows :

Consider ng generating units supplying P_1, P_2, ..., P_{ng} active powers to supply a total load demand P_D.

The objective function for minimization is the total input to the system in rupees per hour.

$$F(P_1, P_2, ..., P_{ng}) = F(P) = \int_{i=1}^{ng} C_i(P_i) \qquad .....(3.25)$$

where $C_i(P_i)$ is the generation cost for the ith unit and ng is the total number of generating units.

The equality constraint is given by

$$G(P_1, P_2, ..., P_{ng}) = G(P) = P_D - \sum_{i=1}^{ng} P_i = 0 \qquad .....(3.26)$$

i.e., total supply = total demand neglecting losses and reserve. Using the method of Lagrange multipliers for equality constraints, the Lagrange function is defined as

$$L(P, \lambda) = F(P) + \lambda G(P) \qquad .....(3.27)$$

Where λ is a Langrange multiplier.

The necessary conditions are given by

$$\frac{\partial L}{\partial P_i} = 0 \text{, and} \quad .....(3.28)$$

$$\frac{\partial L}{\partial \lambda} = 0 \quad .....(3.29)$$

since
$$L = \sum_{i=1}^{ng} C_i(P_i) + \lambda\left(P_D - \sum_{i=1}^{ng} P_i\right) \quad .....(3.30)$$

we obtain
$$\frac{\partial L}{\partial P_i} = \frac{\partial}{\partial P_i} C_i(P_i) + \lambda(-1) = 0 \quad .....(3.31)$$

and
$$\frac{\partial L}{\partial \lambda} = P_D - \sum_{i=1}^{ng} P_i = 0 \quad .....(3.32)$$

The later equation is the load demand constraint only; while the former gives

$$\frac{\partial C_i(P_i)}{\partial P_i} = \frac{\partial C_2(P_2)}{\partial P_2} = ... = \frac{\partial C_{ng}(P_{ng})}{\partial P_{ng}} = \lambda \quad .....(3.33)$$

The above equation states that at the optimum all the generating stations operate at the same incremental cost for optimum economy and their incremental production cost is equal to the Lagrange multiplier λ at the optimum.

Eqn. (3.32) gives
$$(P_1 + P_2 + ... + P_{ng}) = P_D \quad .....(3.34)$$

The principle underlying the mathematical treatment is that load should be taken up always at the lowest incremental cost. It must be ensured that the generations so determined are within their capacities. Otherwise, the generation has to be kept constant at the capacity limit for that unit and eliminated from further optimum calculations.

It can be seen that in this method at the optimum the incremental cost of production is also the incremental cost of the power received. Eqn. (3.33) and (3.34) can be solved for economic scheduling analytically neglecting the effect of transmission losses.

The size of the power systems increased enormously, with long transmission lines connecting several power generating stations extending over large geographical areas transferring power to several load centers. With this development, it has become necessary to consider not only the incremental fuel costs but also incremental transmission losses incurred in these lines while power is transmitted. Initial attempts in this direction involved development of a comprehensive formula involving the generating powers and line parameters. The most important work has come from Kirchmayer and others in 1951. Their method is based on a set of coefficients called B. coefficients. Determination of these coefficients is based on several assumptions and is mathematically quite involved requiring transformations.

However, due to the elegance of the B-coefficient formula and simplicity in application these coefficients are widely used by a number of power companies in the past in USA and elsewhere for economic scheduling for including the effect of transmission losses.

3.16 Transmission Loss Formula – B. Coefficients

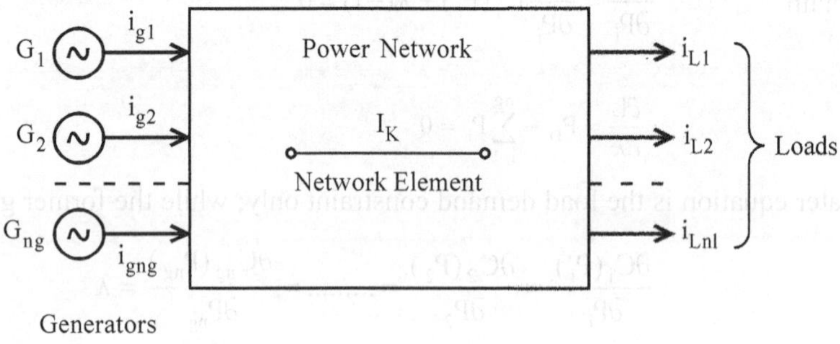

Fig. 3.11 Power system with generator and load currents

An expression for the transmission loss was derived by Kirchamayer with several assumptions made. In his derivation he used Kron's tensorial transformation. However a simplified procedure for the derivation of the B-coefficients will be presented here.

Consider a power system supplying nl loads. Let the load currents be $i_{L1}, i_{L2}, \ldots\ldots. i_{Lnl}$. These loads are supplied by ng generators. Let the generator currents be $i_{g1}, i_{g2}, \ldots\ldots. i_{gng}$. This is shown in the Fig. 3.11.

Consider a network element K (an inter connected line in the system) carrying current I_K. Let generator 1 alone supply the entire load current I_L where

$$I_L = i_{L1} + i_{L2} + \qquad + i_{Lnl}$$

$$= \sum_{j=1}^{nl} i_{Lj} \qquad \ldots..(3.35)$$

under this condition let the current in K be i_{K1}

In a similar manner if each of the ng generators operating alone also supply the total load current I_L while the rest of the generators are disconnected the current carried by the network element K changes from i_{K1} to i_{K2}, i_{K3} to i_{Kng}.

Let the ratio of i_{K1} to i_L be d_{K1}

$$d_{K1} = \frac{i_{K1}}{I_L} \quad .....(3.36)$$

Also

$$d_{K2} = \frac{i_{K2}}{I_L}$$

and so on.

Now, if all the generators are connected to the power system simultaneously to supply the same load, by the principle of super position.

$$I_K = d_{K1} i_{g1} + d_{K2} i_{g2} + ... + ... + d_{Kng} i_{gng} \quad .....(3.37)$$

Let the individual load currents remain a constant complex ratio of the total load current I_L. It is assumed that (X/R) ratio for all the line elements or branches in the network remains the same. The factors d_{Ki} will then be real and not complex.

The individual generator currents may have phase angles δ_1, δ_2, ... δ_{ng} with respect to a reference axis. The generator currents can be expressed as :

$$i_{g1} = |i_{g1}| \cos\delta_1 + |i_{g1}| \sin\delta_1$$

$$i_{g2} = |i_{g2}| \cos\delta_2 + |i_{g2}| \sin\delta_2 \quad .....(3.38)$$

$$.......................................$$

$$i_{gng} = |i_{gng}| \cos\delta_{ng} + |i_{gng}| \sin\delta_{ng}$$

For simplicity to derive the formula

Let ng = 3 so that eqn. (3.37) becomes

$$I_K = d_{k1} i_{g1} + d_{k2} i_{g2} + d_{k3} i_{g3} \quad .....(3.39)$$

$$|I_K|^2 = \left(d_{k1}|i_{g1}|\cos\delta_1 + d_{k2}|i_{g2}|\cos\delta_2 + d_{k3}|i_{g3}|\cos\delta_3\right)^2$$

$$+ \left(d_{k1}|i_{g1}|\sin\delta_1 + d_{k2}|i_{g2}|\sin\delta_2 + d_{k3}|i_{g3}|\sin\delta_3\right)^2 \quad .....(3.40)$$

$$= d_{k1}^2|i_{g1}|^2 + d_{k2}^2|i_{g2}|^2 + d_{k3}^2|i_{g3}|^2$$

$$+ 2d_{k1}d_{k2}|i_{g1}||i_{g2}|\cos\delta_1 \cos\delta_2$$

$$+ 2d_{k2}d_{k3}|i_{g2}||i_{g3}|\cos\delta_2 \cos\delta_3$$

$$+ 2d_{k3}d_{k1}|i_{g3}||i_{g1}|\cos\delta_3 \cos\delta_1 \quad .....(3.41)$$

$$+ 2d_{k1}d_{k2}|i_{g1}||i_{g2}|\sin\delta_1 \sin\delta_2$$

$$+ 2d_{k2}d_{k3}|i_{g2}||i_{g3}|\sin\delta_2 \sin\delta_3$$

$$+ 2d_{k3}d_{k1}|i_{g3}||i_{g1}|\sin\delta_3 \sin\delta_1$$

$$= d_{k1}^2|i_{g1}|^2 + d_{k2}^2|i_{g2}|^2 + d_{k3}^2|i_{g3}|^2$$

$$+ 2d_{k1}d_{k2}|i_{g1}||i_{g2}|\cos(\delta_1 - \delta_2)$$

$$+ 2d_{k2}d_{k3}|i_{g2}||i_{g3}|\cos(\delta_2 - \delta_3) \quad .....(3.42)$$

$$+ 2d_{k3}d_{k1}|i_{g3}||i_{g1}|\cos(\delta_3 - \delta_1)$$

Eliminating currents in terms of powers supplied by the generators

$$i_{g1} = \frac{P_1}{\sqrt{3}|V_1|\text{Cos}\phi_1}$$

$$i_{g2} = \frac{P_2}{\sqrt{3}|V_2|\text{Cos}\phi_2} \quad \text{and}$$

$$i_{g3} = \frac{P_3}{\sqrt{3}|V_3|\text{Cos}\phi_3}$$

where P_1, P_2 and P_3 are the active power supplied by the generators 1, 2 and 3 at voltages $|V_1|$, $|V_2|$ and $|V_3|$ and power factors at the generator buses being Cos ϕ_1, Cos ϕ_2 and Cos ϕ_3 respectively.

$$|I_K|^2 = \frac{d_{k1}^2P_1^2}{\left(\sqrt{3}|V_1|\cos\phi_1\right)^2} + \frac{d_{k2}^2P_2^2}{\left(\sqrt{3}|V_2|\cos\phi_2\right)^2} + \frac{d_{k3}^2P_3^2}{\left(\sqrt{3}|V_3|\cos\phi_3\right)^2}$$

$$+ \frac{2d_{k1}d_{k2}P_1P_2\cos(\delta_1 - \delta_2)}{3|V_1||V_2|\cos\phi_1\cos\phi_2} + \frac{2d_{k2}d_{k3}P_2P_3\cos(\delta_2 - \delta_3)}{3|V_2||V_3|\cos\phi_2\cos\phi_3}$$

$$+ \frac{2d_{k3}d_{k1}P_3P_1\cos(\delta_3 - \delta_1)}{3|V_3||V_1|\cos\phi_3\cos\phi_1}$$

The power losses in the network comprising of nb network elements or branches P_{LOSS} is given by

$$P_L = \sum_{k=1}^{nb} 3|i_K|^2 R_K$$

where R_K is the resistance of the element K.

$$P_L = \frac{P_1^2 \sum_{k=1}^{ng} d_{k1}^2 R_K}{|V_1|^2 (\cos\phi_1)^2} + \frac{P_2^2 \sum_{k=1}^{ng} d_{k2}^2 R_K}{|V_2|^2 (\cos\phi_2)^2} + \frac{P_3^2 \sum_{k=1}^{ng} d_{k3}^2 R_K}{|V_3|^2 (\cos\phi_3)^2}$$

$$+ \frac{2P_1P_2 \sum_{k=1}^{ng} d_{k1} d_{k2} R_K \cos(\delta_1 - \delta_2)}{|V_1||V_2| \cos\phi_1 \cos\phi_2}$$

$$+ \frac{2P_2P_3 \sum_{k=1}^{ng} d_{k2} d_{k3} R_K \cos(\delta_2 - \delta_3)}{|V_2||V_3| \cos\phi_2 \cos\phi_3}$$

$$+ \frac{2P_3P_1 \sum_{k=1}^{ng} d_{k3} d_{K1} R_K \cos(\delta_3 - \delta_1)}{|V_3||V_1| \cos\phi_3 \cos\phi_1} \quad .....(3.43)$$

Let

$$B_{11} = \frac{1}{|V_1|^2 (\cos\phi_1)^2} \sum d_{k1}^2 R_K \quad .....(3.44)$$

$$B_{22} = \frac{1}{|V_2|^2 (\cos\phi_2)^2} \sum d_{k2}^2 R_K \quad .....(3.45)$$

$$B_{33} = \frac{1}{|V_3|^2 (\cos\phi_3)^2} \sum d_{k3}^2 R_K \quad .....(3.46)$$

$$B_{12} = \frac{\cos(\delta_1 - \delta_2) \sum_{k=1}^{ng} d_{k1} d_{k2} R_K}{|V_1||V_2| (\cos\phi_1)(\cos\phi_2)} \quad .....(3.47)$$

$$B_{23} = \frac{\cos(\delta_2 - \delta_3)\sum_{k=1}^{ng} d_{k2} d_{k3} R_K}{|V_2||V_3|(\cos\phi_2)(\cos\phi_3)} \qquad .....(3.48)$$

$$B_{31} = \frac{\cos(\delta_3 - \delta_1)\sum_{k=1}^{ng} d_{k3} d_{k1} R_K}{|V_1||V_3|(\cos\phi_3)(\cos\phi_1)} \qquad .....(3.49)$$

$$P_{LOSS} = P_1^2 B_{11} + P_2^2 B_{22} + P_3^2 B_{33}$$

$$+ 2P_1P_2B_{12} + 2P_2P_3B_{23} + 2P_3P_1B_{31} + ... \qquad .....(3.50)$$

$$= \sum_{m=1}^{3} \sum_{m=1}^{3} P_m B_{mn} P_n$$

In general the formula for B_{mn} coefficients can be expressed as

$$B_{mn} = \frac{\cos(\delta_m - \delta_n)}{|V_m||V_n|(\cos\phi_m)(\cos\phi_n)} \sum_k d_{km} d_{kn} R_K \qquad .....(3.51)$$

In the matrix form, the loss formula is expressed for an n generator system as :

$$[P_1 \quad P_2 \quad .... \quad P_n] \begin{bmatrix} B_{11} & B_{12} & ... & B_{1n} \\ B_{21} & B_{22} & ... & B_{2n} \\ ... & ... & ... & ... \\ B_{n1} & B_{n2} & ... & B_{nn} \end{bmatrix} \begin{bmatrix} P_1 \\ P_2 \\ ... \\ P_n \end{bmatrix} \qquad .....(3.52)$$

The coefficients can be considered constant, if in addition to the assumptions already made we further assume that the generator voltages V_1, V_2..... etc remain constant in magnitude and generator bus power factors cos ϕ_1, cos ϕ_2....... also remains constant.

3.17 Active Power Scheduling

Economic scheduling of thermal plants considering effect of transmission losses :

The objective function is

$$F(P) = F(P_1, P_2, ... P_{ng})$$

$$= \sum_{i=1}^{ng} C_i(P_i) \qquad .....(3.53)$$

which has to be minimized over a given period of time. As only active power is scheduled the equality constraint G(P) is given by

$$G(P) = P_D - P_L - \sum_{i=1}^{ng} P_i = 0 \qquad .....(3.54)$$

must be satisfied at every generator bus where P_i is the generation at bus i ; P_D, the total load demand and P_L the total transmission loss in all the lines. It is desired to minimize eqn. (3.53) subject to the constraint eqn. (3.54)

The Lagrange function L is formed as

$$L(P, \lambda) = F(P) + 1\ \lambda\left[P_D + P_L - \sum_{i=1}^{ng} P_i\right] \qquad .....(3.55)$$

Applying the necessary conditions for the minimum of L

$$\frac{\partial L}{\partial P_i}(P,\lambda) = \frac{\partial}{\partial P_i}F(P_i) + \frac{\partial}{\partial P_i}\lambda\left[P_D + P_L - \sum_{i=1}^{ng} P_i\right] = 0 \qquad .....(3.56)$$

i.e.,

$$\frac{\partial}{\partial P_i}C[P1......., Pi,..Png] + \frac{\partial}{\partial P_i}\lambda\left[P_D + P_L - \sum_{i=1}^{ng} P_i\right] = 0 \qquad .....(3.57)$$

$$\therefore \qquad \frac{\partial C_i(P_i)}{\partial P_i} + \lambda\frac{\partial P_L}{\partial P_i} - \lambda = 0 \qquad .....(3.58)$$

Further,

$$\frac{\partial C_i(P_i)}{\partial P_i} = \lambda\left[1 - \frac{\partial L}{\partial P_i}\right] \ ; i = 1,2.......ng \qquad .....(3.59)$$

Also, it can be expressed as

$$\frac{\partial F_i}{\partial P_i} + \lambda\frac{\partial P_L}{\partial P_i} = \lambda \qquad .....(3.60)$$

The sum of the incremental production cost of power at any plant i and the incremental transmission losses incurred due to generation P_i at bus i charged at the rate of λ must be constant for all generators and equal to λ. This constant λ is equal to the incremental cost of the received power.

In section (3.16) the loss formula is derived as

$$P_L = \sum_i \sum_j P_i B_{ij} P_j$$

$$= B_{11}P_1^2 + B_{22}P_2^2 + ... + B_{ngng}P_{ng}^2 + 2B_{12}P_1P_2 +$$

$$2B_{13}P_1P_3 + ... + 2B_{1ng}P_{ng}^2 + ... \qquad .....(3.61)$$

Differentiating

$$\frac{\partial P_L}{\partial P_i} = \sum_j 2B_{ij}P_j \qquad .....(3.62)$$

Also

$$\frac{\partial C_i(P_i)}{\partial P_i} = \frac{dC_i(P_i)}{dP_i} \quad i = 1, 2, ... ng \qquad .....(3.63)$$

$$\frac{dC_i(P_i)}{dP_i} + \sum_{j=1}^{ng} 2B_{ij}P_j = \lambda \quad j = 1, 2, ..., ng \qquad .....(3.64)$$

If the incremental costs are represented by a linear relationship following a quadratic input-output characteristic.

Then, denoting

$$\frac{dC_i(P_i)}{dP_i} = a_i P_i + b_i \qquad .....(3.65)$$

Eqn. (3.64) will become

$$a_i P_i + b_i + \lambda \sum_{j=1}^{ng} 2B_{ij}P_j = \lambda \qquad .....(3.66)$$

Further,

$$\sum_{j=1}^{ng} 2B_{ij}P_j = 2B_{ii}P_j + \sum_{\substack{j=1 \\ j\neq i}}^{ng} 2B_{ij}P_j \qquad .....(3.67)$$

Eqn. (3.66) can be rewritten as

$$a_iP_i + b_i + \lambda 2B_{ii}P_i + \lambda \sum B_{ij}P_j = \lambda$$

$$a_iP_i + b_i + \lambda 2B_{ii}P_i + \lambda \sum_{\substack{i=1 \\ j\neq i}}^{ng} B_{ij}P_j = \lambda$$

solving for P_i

$$P_i = \frac{\lambda - b_i - \lambda \sum\limits_{\substack{i=1 \\ j\neq i}}^{ng} 2B_{ij}P_j}{a_i + 2\lambda B_{ii}} \qquad .....(3.68)$$

$$P_i = \frac{1 - \frac{b_i}{\lambda} - \sum\limits_{\substack{i=1 \\ j\neq i}}^{ng} 2B_{ij}P_j}{\frac{a_i}{\lambda} + 2B_{ii}} \; ; i = 1, 2, ..., ng \qquad .....(3.69)$$

There are ng equations to be solved for ng powers (P_i) for which Gauss's or Gauss – Seidel method is well suited. Knowing a_i, b_i, and B_{ij} coefficients for any assumed value of λ, P_i values may converge to a solution, giving the generator scheduled powers. It is very important that a suitable value is assumed for λ, so that a quick convergence of the equations is obtained.

3.18 Penalty Factor

Consider the Eqn. (3.59)

$$\frac{dC_i(P_i)}{dP_i} + \lambda \frac{\partial P_L}{\partial P_i} = \lambda$$

It can be rewritten as

$$\frac{\partial C_i(P_i)}{\partial P_i} = \lambda \left[1 - \frac{\partial P_L}{\partial P_i}\right] \qquad .....(3.70)$$

in other words

$$\frac{\partial C_i(P_i)}{\partial P_i} \left[\frac{1}{1 - \frac{\partial P_L}{\partial P_i}}\right] = \lambda \qquad .....(3.71)$$

When transmission losses are included, the incremental production cost at each plant i must be multiplied by a factor $\left(\frac{1}{1 - \frac{\partial P_L}{\partial P_i}}\right)$ which then will be equal to the incremental cost of power delivered. Hence, the factor $\left(\frac{1}{1 - \frac{\partial P_L}{\partial P_i}}\right)$ is called penalty factor :

Since $\frac{\partial P_L}{\partial P_i}$ is much less than unity some times it is approximated by 1 + $\frac{\partial P_L}{\partial P_i}$ so that

$$\frac{\partial C_i(P_i)}{\partial P_i}\left(1 + \frac{\partial P_L}{\partial P_i}\right) = \lambda \qquad .....(3.72)$$

The term 1 + $\frac{\partial P_L}{\partial P_i}$ is called approximate penalty factor.

3.19 Evaluation of λ for Computation

Consider Eqn. (3.69)

$$P_i = \frac{1 - \frac{b_i}{\lambda} - \sum_{\substack{j=1 \\ j \neq i}}^{ng} 2B_{ij}P_j}{\frac{ai}{\lambda} + 2B_{ii}P_j} ; i = 1, 2, \ldots\ldots, ng$$

solution to P_i values depends upon the value of λ chosen. The value of λ determines a set of generations for a particular received load.

It is established that for scheduling purposes it is necessary to start the computation with two different values of λ. As the arbitrarity assigned generations are improved from iteration to iteration, a new value of λ may be computed for each new iteration using the following algorithm for a specified total received load power P_R.

$$\lambda^{(i)} = \lambda^{(i-1)} + \left(P_R^d - P_R^{(i-1)}\right)\left(\frac{\lambda^{(i-1)} - \lambda^{(i-2)}}{P_R^{(i-1)} - P_R^{(i-2)}}\right) \quad \ldots\ldots(3.73)$$

where $P_R^{(i-1)}$ = received power with $\lambda^{(i-1)}$

$P_R^{(i-2)}$ = received power with $\lambda^{(i-2)}$

$\lambda^{(i)}$, $\lambda^{(i-1)}$, $\lambda^{(i-2)}$ are the values of λ during iterations (i), (i – 1) and (i – 2)

P_R^d = the desired total power to be received by the loads.

$$= \sum_{i=1}^{ng} P_i - P_L$$

When two values of P_R calculated successively during the iterations converge to a single value with reasonable accuracy, the latest value of P_R calculated will also converge to P_R^d.

E 3.1 Consider a power system with two generating stations. The incremental production cost characteristics for the two stations are

$$\frac{\partial F_1}{\partial P_1} = (27.5 + 0.15P_1)\text{Rs/MWHr}$$

$$\frac{\partial F_2}{\partial P_2} = (19.5 + 0.26P_2)\text{Rs/MWHr}$$

Given that the minimum and maximum powers are 10MW and 100MW at each plant schedule the generation at each plant to supply a system load given by the load curve shown in figure.

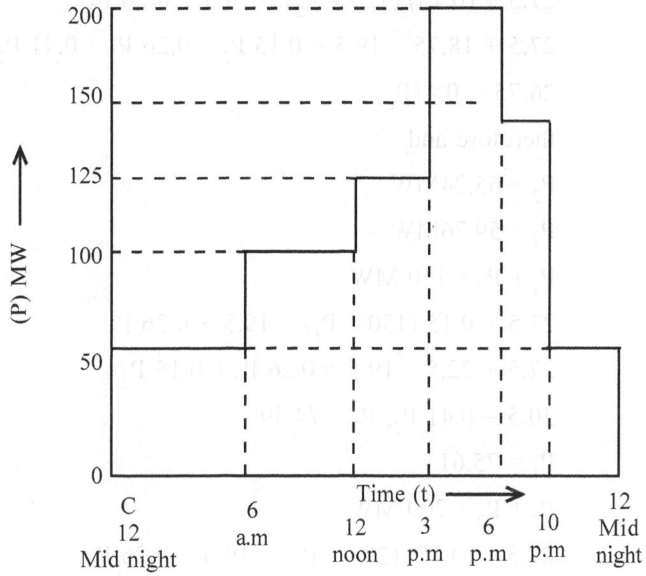

Fig. E 3.1 Load curve

Solution :

Case (i) : $P_R = P_1 + P_2$; $P_R = 50\text{MW}$; $P_1 = P_R - P_2 = 50 - P_2$

$$\frac{\partial F_1}{\partial P_1} = \frac{\partial F_2}{\partial P_2} = \lambda$$

$$27.5 + 0.15\ P_1 = 19.5 + 0.26\ P_2$$

$$27.5 + 0.15\ (50 - P_2) = 19.5 + 0.26\ P_2$$

$$27.5 - 19.5 + 7.50 = 0.26\ P_2 + 0.15P_2$$

$$15.5 = 0.41P_2;\ P_2 = 37.8$$

$$P_1 = 50 - 37.8 = 12.2\ \text{MW}$$

Case (ii) : $P_1 + P_2 = 100$ MW

$P_1 = 100 - P_2$

$27.5 + 0.15\ (100 - P_2) = 19.5 + 0.26\ P_2$

$27.5 + 15 - 19.5 = 0.26\ P_2 + 0.15\ P_2$

$23 = 0.41 P_2$

$P_2 = 23/0.41 = 56.01$MW

$P_1 = 100 - 56.1 = 43.90$ MW

Case (iii) : $P_1 + P_2 = 125$MW

$27.5 + (0.15)\ (125 - P_2) = 19.5 + 0.26\ P_2$

$27.5 + 18.75 - 19.5 = 0.15\ P_2 + 0.26\ P_2 = 0.41\ P_2$

$26.75 = 0.41 P_2$

therefore and

$P_2 = 65.24$MW

$P_1 = 59.76$MW

Case (iv) : $P_1 + P_2 = 150$ MW

$27.5 + 0.15\ (150 - P_1) = 19.5 + 0.26\ P_2$

$27.5 + 22.5 - 19.5 = 0.26\ P_2 + 0.15\ P_2$

$30.5 = 0.41\ P_2;\ P_2 = 74.39$

$P_1 = 75.61$

Case (v) : $P_1 + P_2 = 200$ MW

$27.5 + (0.15)\ (200 - P_2) = 19.5 + 0.26\ P_2$

$27.5 + 30 - 19.5 = 0.41\ P_2$

$38 = 0.41\ P_2\ ;\ P_2 = 92.68\ ;\ P_1 = 107.32$

The value of λ can be computed now. The results are tabulated.

Case	P_1	P_2	P_D	λ
Case (i)	12.2	37.8	50	29.33
Case (ii)	43.9	56.1	100	34.08
Case (iii)	59.76	65.24	125	36.55
Case (iv)	75.61	74.39	150	38.84
Case (v)	107.32	92.68	200	43.598

E3.2 The fuel input characteristics for two thermal plants are given by

$$F_1 = (8P_1 + 0.024\ P_1^2 + 80)\ 10^6\ \text{K–cal/hr}$$

$$F_2 = (6P_2 + 0.004\ P_2^2 + 120)\ 10^6\ \text{K–cal/hr}$$

Where P_1 and P_2 are in megawatts

(i) plot the input-output characteristic for each plant

(ii) plot the heat rate characteristic for each plant

(iii) assuming the cost of fuel as Rs.100/ton

calculate the incremental production cost characteristic in Rs/MWhr at each plant. Plot the same against power produced in MW.

Solution :

(i) Input-output characteristic

Consider the power in steps of 10MW

Given that

$$F_1=(8P_1+0.024+80)10^6\ \text{K-cal/hr}$$

and $$F_2=(6P_1+0.004+120)10^6\ \text{K-cal/hr}$$

Substituting P_1 and P_2 in steps of 10 MW the values of F_1 and F_2 are obtained and tabulated.

Table E 3.2.1 Input Output Calculations

P_1(MW)	$F_1 \times 10^6$ K-cal/hr	P_2(MW)	$F_2 \times 10^6$K-cal/hr
10	162.4	10	184
20	250	20	256
30	342	30	336
40	438	40	424
50	540	50	520
60	646	60	624
70	758	70	736
80	874	80	856
90	994	90	984
100	1220	100	1120

the input output characteristics are plotted as shown in figure.

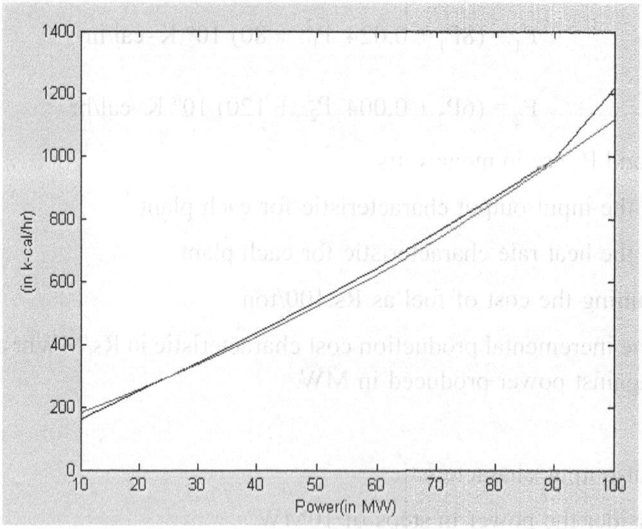

Fig. E 3.2.1 Input – Out put curves

(ii) Heat rate characteristic

Let P_1= 10 MW at plant 1

Heat rate at this P_1 is $\dfrac{162.4}{10}\times 10^6 \dfrac{\text{K}-\text{cal/hr}}{\text{MW}}$

At plant 2 for P_2 = 10 MW

$$\text{Heat rate} = \frac{184}{10}\times 10^6 = 18.4\times 10^5 \frac{\text{K}-\text{cal/hr}}{\text{MW}}$$

In a similar manner the heat rate is computed for powers in steps of 10 MW till 100 MW at both the plants. The results are tabulated and curves are plotted.

Table E 3.2.2 Heat Rate Calculations

Output MW	Heat rate × 10^6 at plant 1 K-cal/MW-hr	Heat rate × 10^6 at plant 2 K-cal/MW-hr
10	16.25	18.4
20	12.48	12.8
30	11.39	11.2
40	10.96	10.6
50	10.80	10.4
60	10.77	10.4
70	10.82	10.5
80	10.92	10.7
90	11.05	10.93
100	11.2	11.2

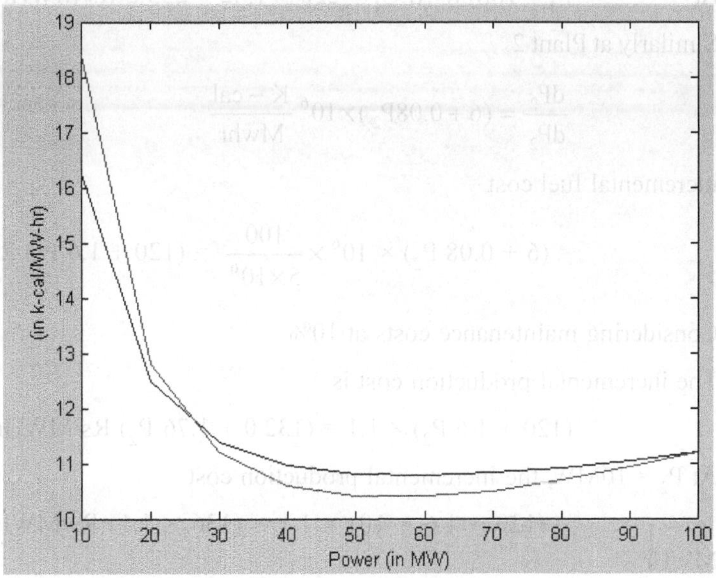

Fig. E 3.2.2 Heat rate curves

(iii) Calorific values of fuel at plant 1 = 4000 K-cal/hr

Cost of fuel = Rs.100 per ton = Rs100/1000 per kg

$$= \frac{100\,\text{Rs}}{1000\,\text{kg}} \times \frac{1}{4000}\frac{\text{kg}}{\text{k}-\text{cal}} = \frac{100}{4\times10^6}\frac{\text{Rs}}{\text{k}-\text{cal}}$$

$$\frac{dF_1}{dP_1} = (8 + 0.048P_1)10^6 \frac{\text{K}-\text{cal}}{\text{MwHr}}$$

Incremental fuel cost

$$= (8 + 0.048\ P_1)\ 10^6 \times \frac{100}{4\times10^6}\frac{\text{Rs}}{\text{MwHr}}$$

$$= (2 + 0.012\ P_1) \times 100 = (200 + 1.2\ P_1)\ \text{Rs/MWHr}$$

At 100 MW generation, the cost is

$$(200 + 12) = 212\ \text{Rs/MWHr}$$

The incremental production cost is obtained by adding the maintanance costs of 10%

Hence, the incremental production cost at plant 1

$$= (200 + 1.2\ P_1)\ 1.1 = (220 + 1.32\ P_1)$$

At $P_1 = 10MW$;$IPC_1 = 220 + 13.2 = 233.2$ Rs/MWHr

Similarly at Plant 2

$$\frac{dF_2}{dP_2} = (6 + 0.08P_2) \times 10^6 \frac{K-cal}{Mwhr}$$

incremental fuel cost

$$= (6 + 0.08\ P_2) \times\ 10^6 \times \frac{100}{5 \times 10^6} = (120 + 1.6\ P_2)\ \text{Rs/MWHr}$$

Considering maintenance costs at 10%

The incremental production cost is

$$(120 + 1.6\ P_2) \times 1.1 = (132.0 + 1.76\ P_2)\ \text{Rs/MWHr}$$

At P_2 = 10MW, the incremental production cost

$= (120 + 1.6 \times 10) \times 1.1 = (136 \times 1.1)$ Rs/MWHr = 149.6 Rs/MWHr

Like wise, the incremental production costs are calculated at all power levels and tabulated. Finally the value are plotted as shown in table (E3.2).

Table E 3.2.3 Incremental production costs

Power (P)	**IPC at plant 1 Rs/MWHr.**	**IPC at plant 2 Rs/MWHr.**
10	233.2	149.6
20	246.4	167.2
30	259.6	184.8
40	272.8	202.4
50	286.0	220.0
60	299.2	237.2
70	312.4	255.2
80	325.6	272.4
90	338.8	290.4
100	352.0	308

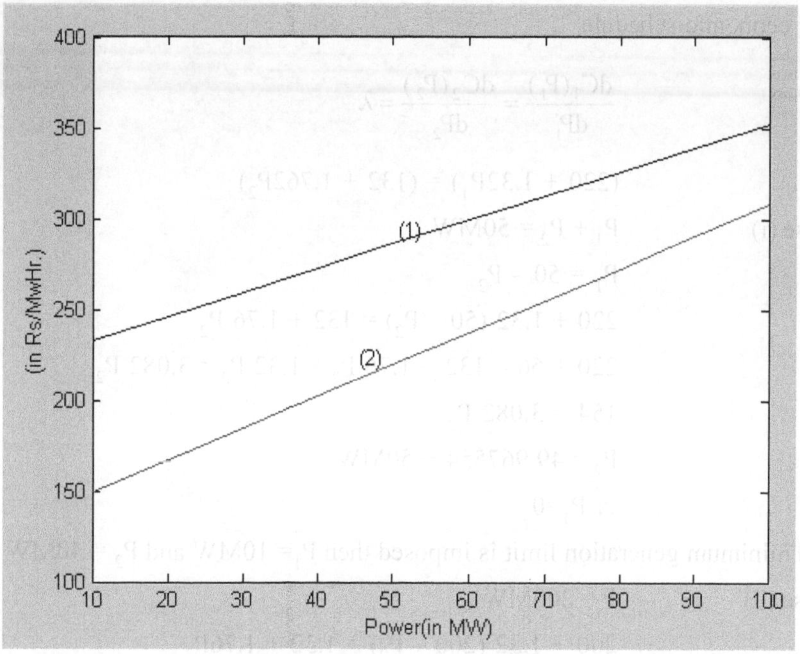

Fig. E 3.2.3 Incremental production cost curves

E 3.3 For the plants in example E3.2 obtain the economic generation schedule. The load curve is given in Fig. (E3.3)

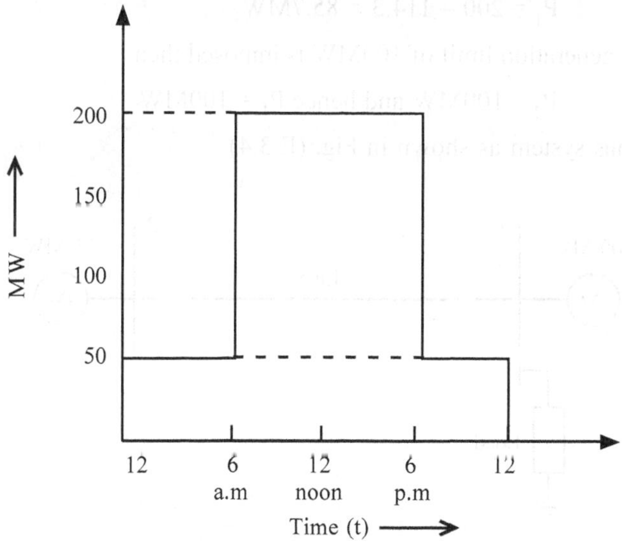

Fig. E 3.3 Load curve

Solution:

For economic schedule

$$\frac{dC_1(P_1)}{dP_1} = \frac{dC_2(P_2)}{dP_2} = \lambda$$

$$(220 + 1.32P_1) = (132 + 1.762P_2)$$

Case (i) $P_1 + P_2 = 50MW$

$$P_1 = 50 - P_2$$

$$220 + 1.32\,(50 - P_2) = 132 + 1.76\,P_2$$

$$220 + 66 - 132 = 1.76\,P_2 + 1.32\,P_2 = 3.082\,P_2$$

$$154 = 3.082\,P_2$$

$$P_2 = 49.967554 \approx 50MW$$

$$\therefore P_1 = 0$$

If a minimum generation limit is imposed then $P_1 = 10MW$ and $P_2 = 40MW$

Case (ii) $P = 200MW$

$$200 + 1.32\,(200 - P_2) = 1.32 + 1.76P_2$$

$$220 - 132 + 264 = 176\,P_2 + 1.32\,P_2 = 3.08\,P_2$$

$$352 = 3.08\,P_2$$

$$P_2 = 114.2857 \approx 114.3MW$$

$$P_1 = 200 - 114.3 = 85.7MW$$

If a maximum generation limit of 100MW is imposed then

$$P_2 = 100MW \text{ and hence } P_1 = 100MW$$

E 3.4 Given a two bus system as shown in Fig. (E 3.4)

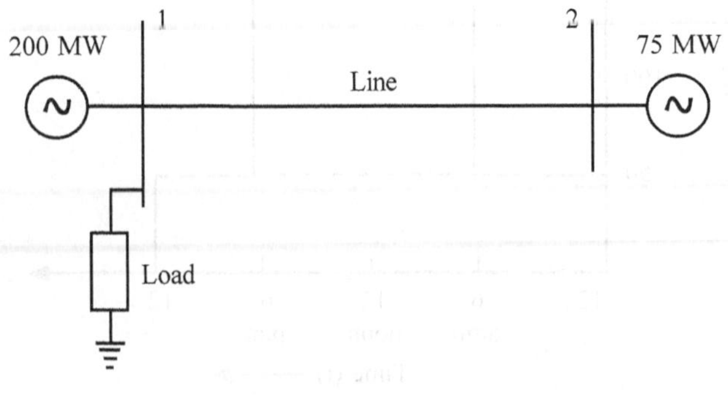

Fig. E 3.4

It is observed that when a power of 75MW is imported to bus 1, the loss amounted to 5MW. Find the generation needed from each plant and also the power received by the load, if the system λ is given by Rs.20/MWHr. The incremental fuel cost at the two plants are given by

$$\frac{dC_1(P_1)}{dP_1} = 0.03P_1 + 15\text{Rs}/\text{Mwh}$$

$$\frac{dC_2(P_2)}{dP_2} = 0.05P_2 + 18\text{Rs}/\text{Mwh}$$

Solution :

The load is at bus I. Hence, P_1 will not have any effect on the line losses

Therefore $B_{11} = B_{12} = B_{21} = 0$

$$P_L = B_{22}\,P_2^2$$

$$5 = B_{22}\,75^2$$

$$B_{22} = \frac{5}{5625} = 8.9\times10^{-4}$$

At station 1

$$\frac{C_1(P_1)}{dP_1} + \lambda\frac{\partial P_L}{dP_1} = \lambda$$

$$\frac{\partial P_L}{\partial P_1} = 0.03P_1 + 15 + \lambda.0 = \lambda; \qquad \text{(i)}$$

At station 2

$$\frac{\partial P_L}{\partial P_2} = 2B_{22}P_2;$$

$$\frac{dC_2(P_2)}{dP_2} + \lambda\frac{\partial P_L}{\partial P_2} = \lambda$$

$$0.05\,P_2 + 18 + \lambda\,(2(8.9)\times10^{-4})\,P_2 = \lambda \qquad \text{(ii)}$$

At $\lambda = 20$ from eqn. (i)

$$0.03\,P_1 + 15 = 20$$

$$0.03\,P_1 = 20 - 15 = 5$$

$$P_1 = 5/0.03 = 166.67\text{MW}$$

Again, from eqn. (ii)

$$0.05\ P_2 + 18 + 20\ (2 \times 8.9 \times 10^{-4})\ P_2 = 20$$

$$0.05\ P_2 + 0.0356\ P_2 = 20 - 18 = 2$$

$$0.0856\ P_2 = 2;\ P_2 = 23.3644\text{MW}$$

Total transmission loss $= B_{22}\ P_2^2$

$$= 8.9 \times 10^{-4} \times 23.3644^2 = 0.4858\text{MW}$$

The load demand at bus I is

$$166.67 + 23.3644 \times 0.4858 = 178.02\text{MW}$$

E 3.5 A power system with two generating stations supplied a total load of 300MW. Neglecting transmission losses the economic schedule for the plant generation is 175MW and 125MW. Find the saving in the production cost in Rs/hr. due to this economic schedule as compared to equal distribution of the same load between the two units.

The incremental cost characteristics are

$$\frac{dC_1(P_1)}{dP_1} = 30 + 0.3P_1 \text{ and}$$

$$\frac{dC_2(P_2)}{dP_2} = 32.5 + 0.4P_2$$

Solution :

The cost of generation at Plant 1

$$C_1 = \int \frac{dC_1(P_1)}{dP_1}.dP_1 = \int (0.3P_1 + 30)dP_1$$

$$= (0.3\ P_1^2 + 30P_1 + x)\ \text{Rs/Hr}$$

$$C_2 = \int \frac{dC_2(P_2)}{dP_2}.dP_2 = \int (32.5 + 0.4P_2)dP_2$$

$$= (0.4\ P_2^2 + 32.5P_2 + y)\ \text{Rs/Hr.}$$

x and y are constants of integration which need not be evaluated.

For equal distribution of generation

$$P_1 = 150\text{MW and } P_2 = 150\text{MW}$$

The increase in cost at plant 1 by generating 175MW instead of 150MW is

$$\left(0.3 \times 175^2 + 30 \times 175 + x\right) - \left(0.3 \times 150^2 + 30 \times 150 + x\right)$$

$$= 0.3(175^2\text{-}150^2) + 30(175\text{-}150)$$

$$= (30625 - 22500)0.3$$

$$= 0.3 \times 8125 + 750 = 3187.5\ \text{Rs/hr}$$

The reduction in cost at plant 2 by generating 125MW only instead of 150MW is

$$[0.4\,(150)^2 + 32.5 \times (150 + y)] - [0.4\,(125)^2 + 32.5\,(125) + y]$$

$$= 0.4\,(-15625 + 22500) + 32.5\,(-125 + 150)$$

$$= 0.4 \times 6875 + 812.5 = 2750 + 812.5 = 3562.5$$

Savings $= 3562.5 - 3187.5 = 372$Rs/hr

Annaul Savings $= 375 \times 24 \times 365 =$ Rs.32,85,000

E 3.6 Consider two steam power plants operating with incremental production costs

$$\frac{dC_1(P_1)}{dP_1} = (0.08P_1 + 16)\text{Rs/Mwhr} \quad \text{and}$$

$$\frac{dC_2(P_2)}{dP_2} = (0.08P_2 + 12)\text{Rs/Mwhr}$$

Given the loss coefficients

$B_{11} = 0.001$ per MW

$B_{12} = B_{21} = -0.0005$ per MW

$B_{22} = 0.0024$ per MW

Find the economic schedule of generation for $\lambda = 20$Rs/MWhr

Solution :

$$P_1 = \frac{1 - \frac{b_1}{\lambda} - 2B_{21}P_2}{\frac{a_1}{\lambda} + 2B_{11}} = \frac{1 - \frac{16}{20} - 2(-0.0005)P_2}{\frac{0.08}{20} + 2(0.001)} = \frac{0.2 + 0.001P_2}{0.006}$$

$$P_2 = \frac{1 - \frac{b_2}{\lambda} - 2B_{12}P_1}{\frac{a_2}{\lambda} + 2B_{22}} = \frac{1 - \frac{12}{20} - 2(-0.0005)P_1}{\frac{0.08}{20} + 2(0.0024)} = \frac{0.4 + 0.001P_2}{0.0088}$$

starting with $P_2 = 0$, $P_1 = 33.3$

then the value of P_2 is computed as 49.2

continuing the iterations the values obtained are tabulated

Iteration	P_1	P_2
1	33.3	49.2
2	41.5	50.2
3	41.7	50.2
4	41.7	50.2

The converged values are $P_1 = 41.7MW$; and $P_2 = 50.2MW$

With these generations, the total transmission losses are

$$P_L = \sum_{i=1}^{2} \sum_{j=1}^{2} P_i B_{ij} P_j$$

$$B_{11}P_1^2 + 2B_{12}P_1 P_2 + B_{22}P_2^2$$

$$= (0.001) \times (41.7)^2 + 2\,(-0.0005)\,(41.7)\,(50.2) + (0.0024)\,(50.2)^2 = 5.7MW$$

Total generation $= P_T = \sum_{i=1}^{2} P_2 = 41.7 + 50.2 = 919Mw$

Total power received

$$P_R = P_T - P_L = 91.9 - 5.7 = 86.2MW.$$

3.20 Hydro Electric Plant Models

Conventional hydroelectric plants are classified as run – of – river plants, run – of – river plants with pondage and storage type plants. In the former type water is utilized as is available in the stream, as there is no provision for storage. Where there is pondage provision, hourly fluctuations in load can be met. In the later type, where storage is provided the water stored during the excess water period can be utilized during the lean season or when power demand is high. The plant may be a single development on a river or there may be several plants constructed and cascaded on the same river (Fig. 3.13). In some cases inter connection of plants on different streams is also possible.

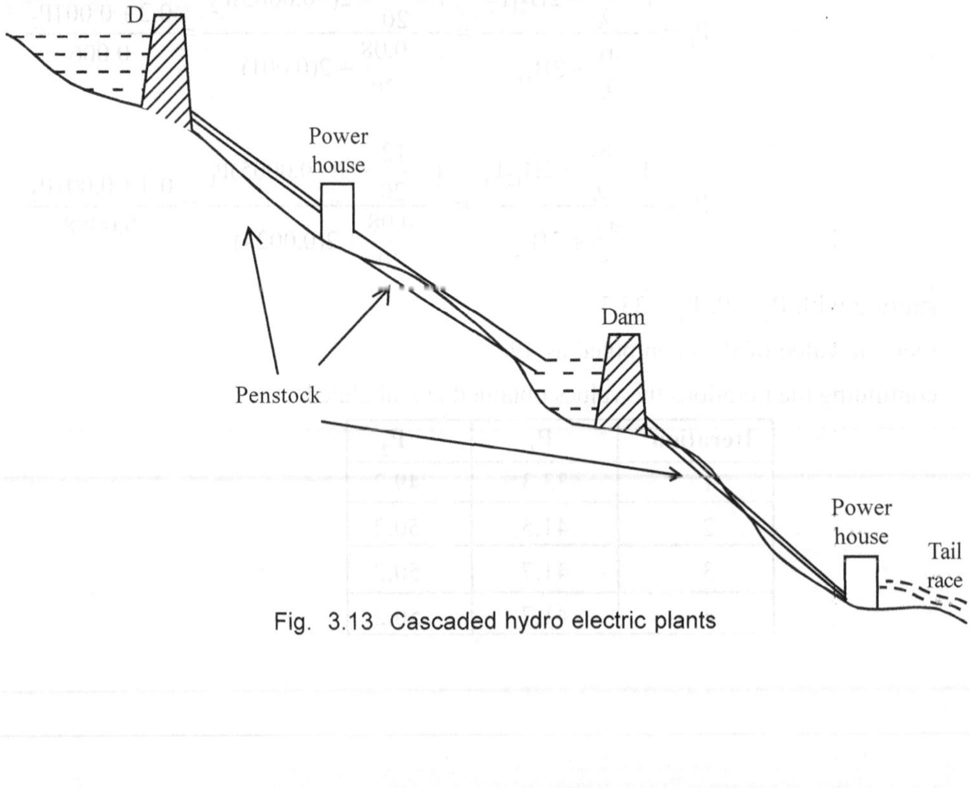

Fig. 3.13 Cascaded hydro electric plants

3.21 Pumped Storage Plant

The pumped storage hydroelectric plants generally store water to supply peak load demands, so that fuel is saved at thermal plants. For this purpose, at light load periods water is pumped to the reservoir back from the tail water pond using power from the grid. The power house may either have both turbines and pumps separately or reversible pump turbines. The operating characteristics of a pumped storage plant are shown in Fig. 3.14.

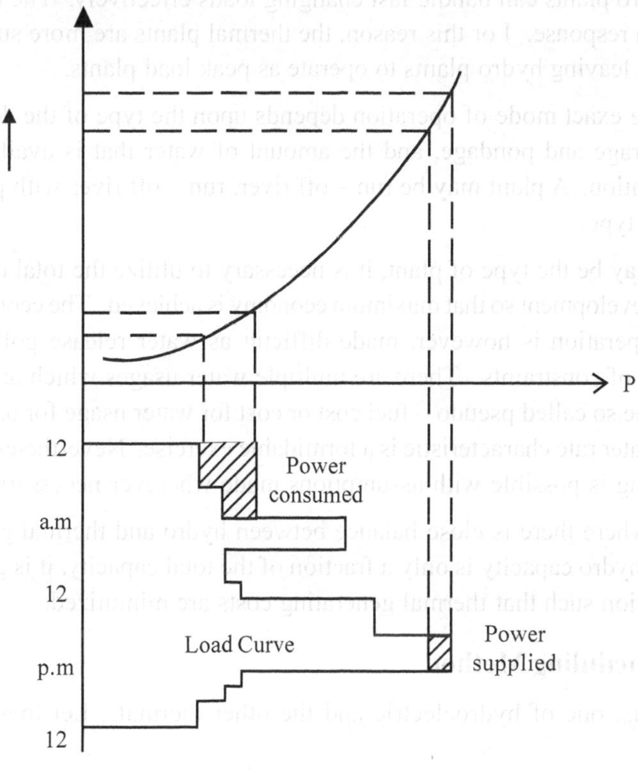

Fig. 3.14 Dumped storage plant characteristics

Let e_e be the energy spent to pump water to the reservoir. By releasing this water at peak load times the energy supplied to the load is e_S. The ratio (e_S/e_e) is usually of the order 60-70%. Pumped storage plants are to be operated in such a manner that due to the peak load chipping on the load curve, the saving in fuel cost thus achieved should exceed the pumping of water charges.

3.22 Hydro Thermal Scheduling

Most of the power systems are a mix of different modes of generating stations of which the thermal and hydro generating units are predominant. While in some systems hydro generation may be more than thermal generation in some other cases it may be the other way. The operating cost of thermal plants is high even though their capital cost is low. In case of hydro electric plants, the running costs are very low, but the capital cost is high as construction of dams, canals, penstocks, surge tanks and other elements of development are involved in addition to the power house. The hydro plants can be started easily and can be assigned load in very short time. This is not so in case of thermal plants, as it requires several hours to bring the boiler, super heater, and turbine system ready to take the load allotment. For the reason mentioned, the hydro plants can handle fast changing loads effectively. The thermal plants in contrast are slow in response. For this reason, the thermal plants are more suitable to operate as base load plants, leaving hydro plants to operate as peak load plants.

However, the exact mode of operation depends upon the type of the development, and factors such as storage and pondage, and the amount of water that is available is the most important consideration. A plant may be run – off river, run – off river with pondage, storage or pumped storage type.

Whatever, may be the type of plant, it is necessary to utilize the total quantity of water available in hydro development so that maximum economy is achieved. The economic scheduling in the integrated operation is however, made difficult as water release policy for power is subject to a variety of constraints. There are multiple water usages which are to be satisfied. Determination of the so called pseudo – fuel cost or cost for water usage for use in conjunction with incremental water rate characteristic is a formidable exercise. Nevertheless, hydro thermal economic scheduling is possible with assumptions made wherever necessary.

In systems where there is close balance between hydro and thermal generation and in systems where the hydro capacity is only a fraction of the total capacity, it is generally desired to schedule generation such that thermal generating costs are minimized.

3.23 Energy Scheduling Method

Consider two plants, one of hydroelectric and the other thermal. Let these both supply a common load.

Let for any time period K the maximum hydro power available.

$$P_{HK}^{max} \geq P_{load,k} \quad k = 1, 2, \ldots\ldots\ldots\ldots K \qquad \ldots\ldots(3.74)$$

where $P_{load,\,k}$ is the load power during the time period k. It is presumed that the energy available from the hydro plant is not sufficient to meet the load demand.

$$\sum_{k=1}^{K} P_{HK}\, n_K \leq \sum_{k=1}^{K} P_{load,k}\, n_K \qquad \ldots\ldots(3.75)$$

where n_k is the number of hours in period k

Let $$\sum_{k=1}^{K} n_K = T_{max} \qquad .....(3.76)$$

= total period of time over which energy schedule is required

It is proposed to utilize the hydro energy completely in such a way that the operating cost of the thermal plant is minimized.

Load energy to be supplied = $$\sum_{k=1}^{K} P_{load,k}\, n_K \qquad .....(3.77)$$

Hydro energy to be utilized = $$\sum_{k=1}^{K} P_{Hk}\, n_K \qquad .....(3.78)$$

Thermal energy required

$$E_S = \sum_{k=1}^{K} P_{load,k} n_k - \sum_{k=1}^{K} P_{H,k} n_k \qquad .....(3.79)$$

Let the thermal plant be operated for time period less than T_{max} and for number of intervals K_S

Hence, $$\sum_{k=1}^{K_S} P_{S,k} n_k = E_S \qquad .....(3.80)$$

where P_S denotes steam power

The problem can then, be stated as

$$\text{Min } F_T = \sum_{k=1}^{K_S} F(P_{SK}) n_k \qquad .....(3.81)$$

subject to $$\sum_{k=1}^{K_S} P_{SK} n_k - E_S = 0 \qquad .....(3.82)$$

The Lagrange function is given by

$$L = \sum_{k=1}^{K_S} F(P_{Sk}) n_k + \lambda\left(E_S - \sum_{k=1}^{K_S} P_{Sk} n_k\right) \qquad .....(3.83)$$

$$\frac{\partial L}{\partial P_{Sk}} = \frac{dF(P_{Sk})}{dP_{Sk}} - \lambda = 0 \quad \text{for } k = 1, 2, \ldots\ldots, K_S \qquad .....(3.84)$$

(i.e.) $$\frac{dF(P_{Sk})}{dP_{Sk}} = \lambda \quad \text{for } k = 1, 2, \ldots\ldots, K_S \qquad .....(3.85)$$

Eqn. (3.85) indicates that the steam plant must be run at constant incremental production cost for the entire time period of its operation. Denoting this value as P^0_{Sk}, the schedule is depicted in Fig. (3.15) graphically.

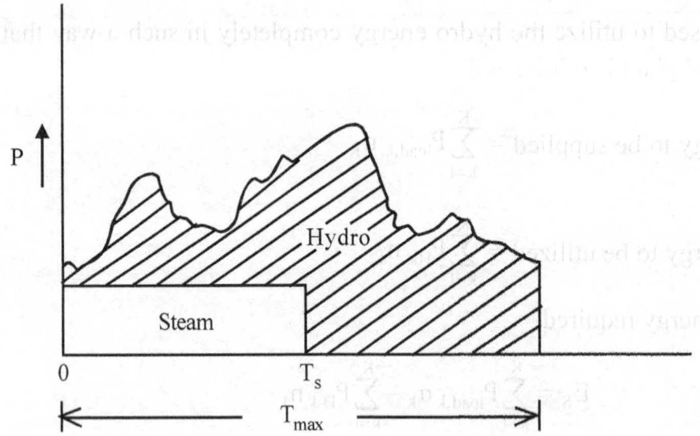

Fig. 3.15 Hydro thermal co-ordination

Let the steam plant cost characteristic be expressed by

$$F(P_S) = aP_S^2 + bP_S + C \qquad .....(3.86)$$

The total cost of running the steam plant over the interval T_S

$$F_T = \left(aP_S^{0^2} + bP_S^0 + c\right)T_S \qquad .....(3.87)$$

Infact F_T is also given by

$$F_T = \sum_{k=1}^{K_S} F(P_S^0)\,n_k$$

$$= F\left(P_S^0\right)\sum_{k=1}^{K_S} n_k$$

$$= F\left(P_S^0\right)\,T_S \qquad .....(3.88)$$

Further

$$\sum_{k=1}^{K_S} P_{Sk}n_K = \sum_{k=1}^{K_S} P_S^0 n_K = P_S^0 T_S = E_S \qquad .....(3.89)$$

Hence,

$$T_S = \frac{E_S}{P_S^0} \qquad .....(3.90)$$

So,
$$F_T = \left(aP_S^{0^2} + bP_S^0 + c\right)\left(\frac{E_S}{P_S^0}\right) \quad .....(3.91)$$

$$\frac{dF_T}{dP_S^0} = \frac{d}{dP_S^0}\left[aP_S^0 E_S + bE_S + \frac{cE_S}{P_S^0}\right]$$

$$= a\,E_S + 0 - c\,E_S\,\frac{1}{\left(P_S^0\right)^2} \quad ......(3.92)$$

$$\left(P_S^0\right)^2 = \frac{cE_S}{aE_S} = \frac{c}{a}$$

$$\left(P_S^0\right)^2 = \frac{cE_S}{aE_S} = \frac{c}{a}$$

$$P_S^0 = \sqrt{\left(\frac{c}{a}\right)} \quad .....(3.93)$$

The steam unit is operated at its maximum efficiency through out the time period T_S. This can be proved as follows:

Let f_c be the fuel cost.

$$F(P_S) = a\,P_S^2 + bP_S + c$$

$$= f_C\,H\,(P_S) \quad .....(3.94)$$

where function H denotes the heat value

The heat rate is then given by

$$\frac{H(P_S)}{P_S} = \frac{1}{fc}\left[\frac{aP_S^2 + bP_S + c}{P_S}\right] \quad .....(3.95)$$

$$\frac{d}{dP_S}\left[\frac{H(P_S)}{P_S}\right] = \frac{d}{dP_S}\left[\frac{1}{f_C}\left(aP_S + b + \frac{c}{P_S}\right)\right]$$

$$= \left[\frac{1}{f_C}a - \frac{c}{f_C}\frac{1}{P_S^2}\right] = 0 \quad .....(3.96)$$

$$P_S = \sqrt{\frac{c}{a}} = P_S^0 \quad .....(3.97)$$

3.24 Short Term Hydro Thermal Scheduling

3.24.1 Method of Lagrange Multipliers (losses neglected)

Consider a power system which contains both hydro and steam power generating stations. Consider that the entire hydro generation is equal to P_H and the total steam power is P_S. With such equivalent power generating station let a load P_L be supplied as shown in Fig. (3.16).

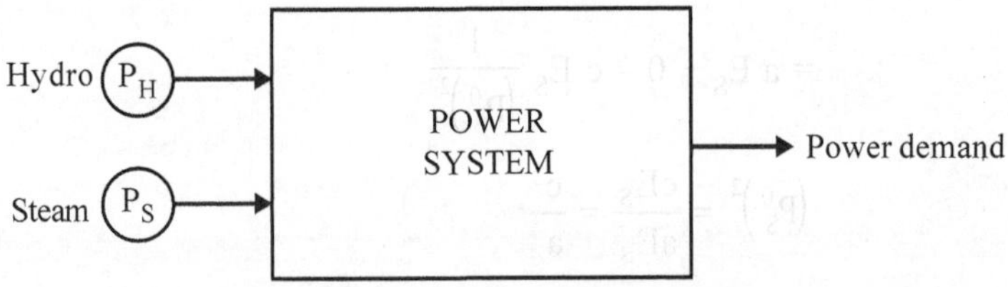

Fig. 3.16 Hydro Thermal scheduling

Let the combined operation be over a period of time T. Let this time period be divided into intervals 1, 2, ... J to suit the load curve so that

$$\sum_{j=1}^{J} n_j = T \quad .....(3.98)$$

The total volume of water available for discharge over this time period.

$$W = \sum_{j=1}^{J} n_j w_j \quad .....(3.99)$$

Where w_j is the water rate for interval j. The fuel cost required to be minimized over the time period T is given as

$$F_T = \sum_{j=1}^{J} n_j F(p_{sj}) \quad .....(3.100)$$

For load balance, the equality constraint is

$$P_{loadj} - P_{Sj} - P_{Hj} = 0 \;\; j = 1, 2, ..., J \quad .....(3.101)$$

The loads are assumed to remain constant during time intervals considered. The total value of water at the beginning and at the vend of the interval T, in the reservoir are W_i and W_f respectively.

During this period of scheduling the head of water is assumed to remain constant.

The input – output characteristic for the equivalent hydro plant is given by

$$w = w(P_H) \quad .....(3.102)$$

The Lagrange function for minimization of eqn. (3.100) subject to the constraints (3.99) and (3.101) is

$$L = \sum_{j=1}^{J} n_j F(P_{Sj}) + \lambda_j [P_{loadj} - P_{Sj} - P_{Hj}] + \gamma \left[\sum_{j=1}^{J} nj w_j (P_{Hj}) - W \right] \quad .....(3.103)$$

For any specific value of j = k, the necessary conditions are

$$\frac{\partial L}{\partial P_{Sk}} = 0 \text{ and } \frac{\partial L}{\partial P_{Hk}} = 0 \quad .....(3.104)$$

giving

$$n_k \frac{dF_{Sk}}{dP_{Sk}} = \lambda_k$$

$$\text{and} \quad \gamma n_k \frac{dw_k}{dP_{Hk}} = \lambda_k \quad .....(3.105)$$

solution to above two equations gives the economic generations at steam and hydro plants over any time interval. The incremental production cost at the steam plants must be the same as incremental production cost at the hydro plants. For simplicity n_k may be taken one unit. So that

$$\frac{dF_S}{dP_S} = \lambda$$

$$\text{and} \quad \gamma . \frac{dw}{dP_H} = \lambda \quad .....(3.106)$$

3.24.2 Lagrange Multipliers Method Transmission Losses Considered

If the transmission losses are considered then the equality constraint includes P_L, the loss terms.

$$[P_{loadj} + P_{Lj} - P_{Sj} - P_{Hj}] = 0 \quad .....(3.107)$$

The Lagrange function changes now into

$$L = \sum_{j=1}^{J} n_j F(P_{Sj}) + \lambda_j (P_{loadj} - P_{Lj} - P_{Sj} - P_{Hj}) + \gamma \sum_{j=1}^{J} [n_j w_j (P_{Hj}) - W] \quad .....(3.108)$$

For any specific j = k, we obtain the optimality conditions as before;

$$\frac{\partial L}{\partial P_{Sk}} = n_k \frac{dF(P_{Sk})}{dP_{Sk}} + \lambda_k (-1) + \lambda_k \left(\frac{-\partial P_{Lk}}{\partial P_{Sk}} \right)$$

$$\frac{\partial L}{\partial P_{Hk}} = \lambda_k (-1) + \lambda_k \frac{\partial P_{Lk})}{\partial P_{Hk}} \left[+ \gamma \frac{n_k dw_k (P_{Hk})}{dP_{Hk}} \right] = 0$$

i.e. $$n_k \frac{dF(P_{Sk})}{dP_{Hk}} + \lambda_k \frac{\partial P_{Lk}}{\partial P_{Sk}} = \lambda_k$$

and $$\gamma n_k \frac{dw_k}{dP_{Hk}}(P_{Hk}) + \gamma_k \frac{\partial P_{Lk}}{\partial P_{Hk}} = \lambda_k$$

since k is chosen arbitrarily, and by considering the time period $n_k = 1$

The equations reduce to

$$\frac{dF(P_S)}{dP_S} + \lambda \frac{\partial P_L}{\partial P_S} = \lambda \qquad .....(3.109)$$

and $$\gamma \frac{dw(P_k)}{dP_H} + \lambda \frac{\partial P_L}{\partial P_H} = \lambda \qquad .....(3.110)$$

It can be shown that the above equations are valid for any number of steam plants n_S and for any number of hydro plants n_H.

Hence

$$\frac{dF(P_{Si})}{dP_{Si}} + \lambda \frac{\partial P_L}{\partial P_{Si}} = \lambda \text{ for i – 1, 2, ..., } n_s \qquad .....(3.111)$$

and $$\gamma \frac{dw(P_{Hk})}{dP_{Hk}} + \lambda \frac{\partial P_L}{\partial P_{Hk}} = \lambda \text{ for k = 1, 2, ..., } n_H \qquad .....(3.112)$$

the above equations are called coordination equations, the solution to which will give the economic schedule for P_{si} and P_{Hk}.

3.24.3 Short Term Hydro Thermal Scheduling using B-Coefficients for Transmission losses

Let the total number of generating stations be 'n'. Out of these n stations, S stations are steam power stations and the remaining H stations are hydro electric generating stations so that

$$S + H = n \qquad .....(3.113)$$

Let the water input rate at the jth hydro plant be assumed as w_j m³/sec

The total transmission losses in the lines of the system are given by

$$P_L = \sum_{i=1}^{s} \sum_{j=1}^{s} P_{si} B_{ij} P_{sj} + \sum_{i=s+1}^{n} \sum_{j=s+1}^{n} P_{Hi} B_{ij} P_{Hj}$$

$$+2 \sum_{i=1}^{s} \sum_{j=s+1}^{n} P_{si} B_{ij} P_{Hj} \qquad .....(3.114)$$

Where the subscripts S and H refer to steam and hydro plants.

The total input hourly rate to all the thermal plants is

$$F_T = \sum_{i=1}^{s} F_i \ RS/_{hr} \qquad .....(3.115)$$

The incremental cost of production at ith steam plant

$$= \frac{dF_i}{dP_{si}} \ Rs/_{Mwhr} \qquad .....(3.116)$$

The incremental transmission losses at steam and hydro plants are given respectively by

$$\frac{\partial P_L}{\partial P_{si}} \text{ and } \frac{\partial P_L}{\partial P_{Hj}}$$

The incremental rate of water flow at j[th] hydro plant

$$= \frac{\partial w_j}{\partial P_{Hj}} \ m^3/_{sec} \qquad .....(3.117)$$

The total power received by the loads,

$$P_R = \sum_{i=1}^{s} P_{si} + \sum_{j=s+1}^{n} P_{Hj} - P_L \qquad ..... (3.118)$$

It is desired to make the total input to the system over a period T a minimum.

From Calculus of variations for F_T to be a minimum over the time period T, the first variation of eq. (3.118) must be set equal to zero.

$$\therefore \quad \sum_{i=1}^{s} \delta P_{si} + \sum_{j=s+1}^{n} \delta P_{Hj} - \sum_{i=1}^{s} \frac{\partial P_L}{\partial Psi} \delta P_{si} - \sum_{j=s+1}^{n} \frac{\delta P_L}{\partial P_{Hj}} \delta P_{Hj} = 0 \qquad .....(3.119)$$

The quantity of water available over the period T is assumed constant.

$$\text{i.e.,} \quad \int_0^T w_j dt = W \ \text{ for } j = s + 1, ..., n \qquad .....(3.120)$$

Then, it is further required to make

$$\left[\int_0^T F_T dt + \sum_{j=s+1}^{n} \gamma_j \int_0^T wjdt\right] \qquad .....(3.121)$$

a minimum; where γ_j are constant multipliers.

The first variation of the quantity in equation must vanish. Hence

$$\delta\left[\int_0^T F_T dt + \sum_{j=s+1}^{n} \gamma_j \int_0^T w_j dt\right] = 0 \qquad .....(3.122)$$

i.e., $$\sum_{i=1}^{s} \frac{\partial F_T}{\partial P_{si}} \partial P_{si} + \sum_{j=s+1}^{n} r_j \frac{\partial w_j}{\partial P_{Hj}} \partial P_{Hj} = 0 \; ...... \qquad .....(3.123)$$

Where ∂P_{si} and ∂P_{Hj} are the variations in steam power generation and hydro power generation respectively.

From equation (3.119)

$$\sum_{i=1}^{s}\left(1-\frac{\partial P_L}{\partial P_{si}}\right)\partial p_{si} + \sum_{j=s+1}^{n}\left(1-\frac{\partial P_L}{\partial P_{Hj}}\right)\partial P_{Hj} = 0 \qquad ...(3.124)$$

For a small variation of δP_{Hm} at the mth hydro plant eqn. (3.124) can be split into the following form.

$$-\left[1-\frac{\partial P_L}{\partial P_{Hm}}\right]\partial P_{Hm} = -\sum_{i=1}^{s}\left[1-\frac{\partial P_L}{\partial P_{si}}\right]\partial P_{si} - \sum_{\substack{j=s+1\\ j\neq m}}^{n}\left(1-\frac{\partial P_L}{\partial P_{Hj}}\right)\partial P_{Hj} \qquad .....(3.125)$$

Again, eqn. (3.123) can be rewritten as

$$\sum_{i=1}^{s}\frac{\partial F_T}{\partial P_{si}}\partial P_{si} + \gamma_m \frac{\partial w_m}{\partial P_{Hm}}\partial P_{Hm} + \sum_{\substack{j=s+1\\ j\neq m}}^{n}\gamma_j \frac{\partial w_j}{\partial P_{Hj}}\partial P_{Hj} = 0 \qquad .....(3.126)$$

Hence

$$\gamma_m \frac{\partial w_m}{\partial P_{Hm}}\partial P_{Hm} = -\sum_{i=1}^{\alpha}\frac{\partial F_T}{\partial P_{si}}\partial P_{si} - \gamma_j \sum_{\substack{j=s+1\\ j\neq m}}^{n}\frac{\partial w_j}{\partial P_{Hj}}\partial P_{Hj} \qquad .....(3.127)$$

Multiplying Eq. 3.127 on both sides by $\left(1-\frac{\partial P_L}{\partial P_{Hm}}\right)$

$$\gamma_m \frac{\partial w_m}{\partial P_{Hm}}\partial P_{Hm}\left(1-\frac{\partial P_L}{\partial P_{Hm}}\right) = -\sum_{i=1}^{s}\frac{\partial F_T}{\partial P_{si}}\partial P_{si}\left(1-\frac{\partial P_L}{\partial P_{Hm}}\right)$$

$$\gamma_j \sum_{\substack{i=s+1\\ j\neq m}}^{n}\frac{\partial w_j}{\partial P_{Hj}}\partial P_{Hj}\left(1-\frac{\partial P_L}{\partial P_m}\right) \qquad ......(3.128)$$

In the above eqn. (3.128) if

$\left(1-\frac{\partial P_L}{\partial P_{Hm}}\right)\partial P_{Hm}$ is replaced by the quantity on the right hand side of eqn. (3.124) we obtain.

$$\gamma_m \frac{\partial w_m}{\partial P_{Hm}}\left[-\sum_{i=1}^{s}\left(1-\frac{\partial P_L}{\partial P_{si}}\right)\delta P_{si} - \sum_{\substack{j=s+1\\ j\neq m}}^{n}\left(1-\frac{\partial P_L}{\partial P_{Hj}}\right)\partial P_{Hj}\right] \qquad ......(3.129)$$

$$= -\sum_{i=1}^{s} \frac{\partial F_T}{\partial P_{si}} \delta P_{si} \left(1 - \frac{\partial P_L}{\partial P_{Hm}}\right) - \gamma_j \sum_{\substack{j=s+1 \\ j \neq m}}^{n} \frac{\partial w_j}{\partial P_{Hj}} \delta P_H C \left(1 - \frac{\partial P_L}{\partial P_{Hj}}\right) \quad ....(3.130)$$

Rearranging the term

$$\sum_{i=1}^{s} \frac{\partial F_T}{\partial P_{si}} \left(1 - \frac{\partial P_L}{\partial P_{Hm}}\right) \delta P_{si} - \sum_{i=1}^{n} \gamma_m \frac{\partial w_m}{\partial P_{Hm}} \left(1 - \frac{\partial P_L}{\partial P_{Hm}}\right) \partial P_{si}$$

$$+ \sum_{\substack{r=s+1 \\ j \neq m}}^{n} r_j \frac{\partial w_j}{\partial P_{Hj}} \left(1 - \frac{\partial P_L}{\partial P_{Hj}}\right) \delta P_{Hj} -$$

$$\sum_{\substack{j=s+1 \\ j \neq m}}^{n} \gamma_m \frac{\partial w_m}{\partial P_{Hm}} \left(1 - \frac{\partial P_L}{\partial P_{Hj}}\right) \delta P_{Hj} = 0 \quad .....(3.131)$$

Eqn. (3.131) can be put as

$$\sum_{i=1}^{s} \frac{\partial F_T}{\partial P_{si}} \left(1 - \frac{\partial P_L}{\partial P_{Hm}}\right) - \gamma_m \frac{\partial w_m}{\partial H_m} \left(1 - \frac{\partial P_L}{\partial P_{si}}\right) \delta P_{si}$$

$$+ \sum_{\substack{j=s+1 \\ j \neq m}}^{n} \gamma_j \gamma_m \frac{\partial w_j}{\partial P_{Hj}} \left(1 - \frac{\partial P_L}{\partial P_{Hm}}\right) - \lambda_m \frac{\partial w_m}{\partial P_{Hm}} \left(1 - \frac{\partial P_L}{\partial P_{Hm}}\right) \delta P_{Hj} = 0 \quad .....(3.132)$$

Note that ∂p_{si} and ∂p_{Hj} are the variations in powers at steam and hydro plants respectively and hence are finite. Then, to make the equation (3.128) satisfied, each of the coefficients of the variations must be zero.

$$\therefore \quad \frac{\partial F_T}{\partial P_{si}} \left(1 - \frac{\partial P_L}{\partial P_{Hj}}\right) - \gamma_m \frac{\partial w_m}{\partial P_{Hm}} \left(1 - \frac{\partial P_L}{\partial P_{si}}\right) = 0 \quad .....(3.133)$$

$$\text{and} \quad \gamma_j \frac{\partial w_j}{\partial P_{Hj}} \left(1 - \frac{\partial P_L}{\partial P_{Hm}}\right) - \gamma_m \frac{\partial w_m}{\partial P_{Hm}} \left(1 - \frac{\partial P_L}{\partial P_{Hm}}\right) = 0 \quad .....(3.134)$$

In other words,

$$\frac{\dfrac{\partial F_T}{\partial P_{si}}}{\left(1 - \dfrac{\partial P_L}{\partial P_{si}}\right)} = \gamma_m \frac{\dfrac{\partial W_m}{\partial P_{Hm}}}{\left(1 - \dfrac{\partial P_L}{\partial P_{Hj}}\right)} = \gamma_i \frac{\dfrac{\partial wi}{\partial P_{Hj}}}{\left(1 - \dfrac{\partial P_L}{\partial P_{Hj}}\right)}$$

$$= \text{constant} \quad ..... (3.135)$$

The partial derivatives in the above equation are also the total derivatives. It may also be recognized that each of the term in the eq. 3.135 is also the incremental cost of the received power in Rs/ MW. If λ denotes their incremental cost, then $\frac{dF_T}{dP_{si}} = \frac{dF_i}{dP_{si}}$ is the cost of generation at each plant i and it depends on the generation at that plant only

$$\left.\begin{aligned} \frac{dF_i}{dP_{si}}\left(\frac{1}{1-\frac{\partial P_L}{\partial P_{si}}}\right) &= \lambda \\ r_j \frac{\partial w_j}{\partial P_{Hj}}\left(\frac{1}{1-\frac{\partial P_L}{\partial P_{Hj}}}\right) &= \lambda \end{aligned}\right\} \quad .....(3.136)$$

Also

$$\left.\begin{aligned} \frac{\partial F_i}{\partial P_{si}} + \lambda \frac{\lambda P_L}{\partial P_{si}} &= \lambda \\ \gamma_j \frac{dw_i}{dP_{Hj}} + \lambda \frac{\partial P_L}{\partial P_{Hj}} &= \lambda \end{aligned}\right\} \quad .....(3.137)$$

and

The above equations are called coordination equations for hydro thermal combined operation. Solution to these equations results in minimizing the input costs to supply the given load.

Let $$\frac{dF_i}{dP_{si}} = a_i P_{Si} + b_i \quad .....(3.138)$$

and $$\frac{dW_j}{dP_{Hj}} = c_j P_{Hj} + d_j \quad .....(3.139)$$

where a and c are the slopes of the incremental cost curves and b and d are the intercepts.

Further, $$P_L = \Sigma_k P_k B_{Kl} P_l \quad .....(3.140)$$

Partially differentiating P_L in eqn. (3.140)

and substituting in eqn. (3.137)

$$a_i P_{si} + b_i + 2\lambda\left(\sum_{K=1}^{s} B_{k_i} P_{sk} + \sum_{j=s+1}^{n} B_{ij} P_{Hj}\right) = \lambda \quad .....(3.141)$$

$$r_j c_j \rho_{Hj} + r_j d_j + 2\lambda\left(\sum_{k=s+1}^{n} B_{jk} P_{Hk} + \sum_{l=1}^{n} B_{jl} P_{sl}\right) = \lambda \quad .....(3.142)$$

Rewriting the third term on the left side of both the above equations, as

$$\sum_{K=1}^{s} B_{ki}P_{sk} = B_{iz'}P_{si} + \sum_{\substack{k=1\\k\neq z'}}^{s} B_{kz'}P_{sk} \qquad .....(3.143)$$

and

$$\sum_{K=s+1}^{n} B_{jk}P_{Hk} = B_{ij}P_{hj} + \sum_{\substack{K=s+1\\K\neq j}}^{n} B_{ki}P_{sk} \qquad .....(3.144)$$

combining the terms containing P_{si} and P_{Hj} for solution

$$P_{si} = \frac{1 - \frac{b_i}{\lambda} - \sum_{\substack{k=1\\k\neq z'}}^{s} 2B_{ki}P_{sk} - \sum_{l=s+1}^{n} 2B_{il}P_{Hl}}{\frac{a_i}{\lambda} + 2B_{iz'}} \qquad .....(3.145)$$

and

$$P_{Hj} = \frac{1 - \frac{d_j}{\lambda} - \sum_{k=s+1}^{n} 2B_{jk}P_{Hk} - \sum_{l=1}^{s} 2B_{jl}P_{sl}}{\gamma_j \frac{c_j}{\lambda} + 2B_{jj}} \qquad .....(3.146)$$

These two equations (3.145) and (3,146) can be solved iteratively till convergence is obtained assuming suitable values for λ and γ_j .

E 3.7 The input – output data for a particular hydro – plant is given in Fig. E 3.7.1. Find the incremental water rate characteristic and convert it into an equivalent incremental production cost characteristic taking the cost of water as 10^{-3}Rs./m^3.

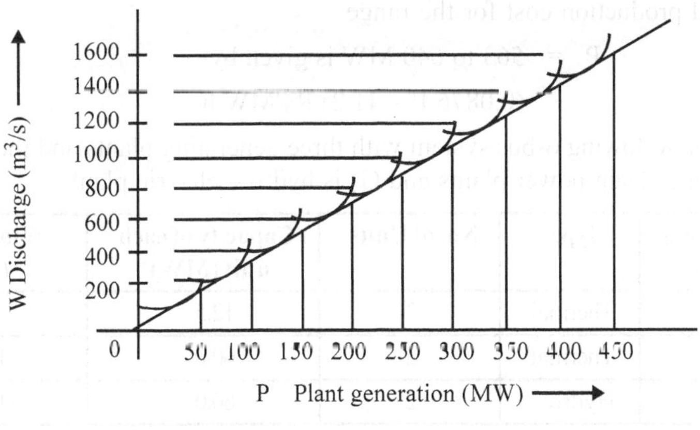

Fig. E3.7.1 Input – Output Curve

Solution : The incremental water rate is obtained by finding the slope of the given input – output curve at different points. A straight line segment approximation of incremental water rate is obtained as in Fig. E 3.7.2.

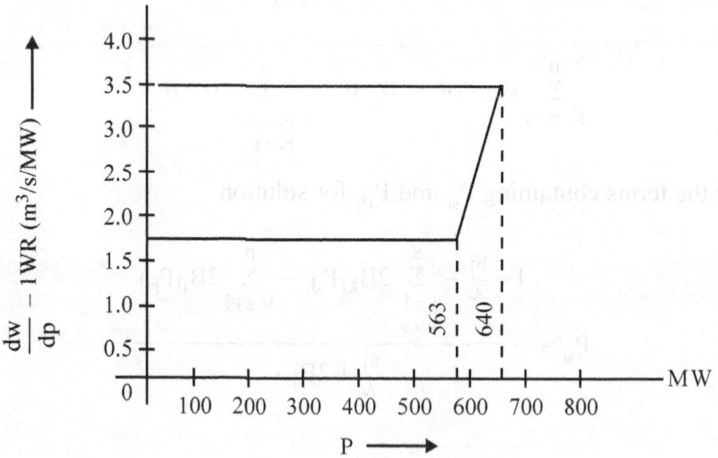

Fig. 3.7.2 Incremental Water rate

Incremental water rate

$= 1.7 m^3/s/MW$ for $P = 0$ to 563 MW

$= (0.0233P - 11.4)\ m^3/s/MW$

for $P = 563$ to 640 MW

Incremental production cost

= Incremental water rate × cost of water

$= 1.7 \times 3600 \times 10^{-3}$ Rs./MWh

= 6.2 Rs/MW h for $P = 0$ to 563 MW

Incremental production cost for the range

$P = 563$ to 640 MW is given by

$(0.0876\ P - 41.2)$ Rs/MW h

E 3.8 Consider the following 6-bus system with three generating plants and three load buses. G_1 and G_2 are steam power plants and G_3 is hydro – electric plant.

Generating Station	Type	No. of Units	Capacity of each unit (MW)	Total capacity (MW)
G_1	Thermal	3	12.5	37.5
G_2	Thermal	2	60.0	120.0
G_3	Hydro	2	60.0	120.0
	Total Capacity			277.5

Loads :

L_1 160 MW

L_2 35 MW

L_3 72.5 MW

Total Load = 267.5 MW

Base Voltage = 220kV

Base MVA = 100

The B – coefficient matrix is given as

$$B = \begin{matrix} & G_1 & G_2 & G_3 \\ G_1 & 0.0210 & 0.0034 & 0.0181 \\ G_2 & 0.0034 & 0.02497 & 0.003 \\ G_3 & 0.0181 & 0.003 & 0.050 \end{matrix}$$

Characteristics of steam and hydro plants

G_1 – thermal station :

Calorific value of coal	=	5125 kcal/kg
Cost of coal	=	Rs.45 per ton
Incremental fuel cost at near no – load	=	Rs.21/MWh
Incremental fuel cost at 40MW	=	Rs.23/MWh
Slope of incremental cost curve	=	0.05
Intercept on y-axis	=	21

$$\frac{dF_1}{dP_1} = 0.05P_{S1} + 21$$

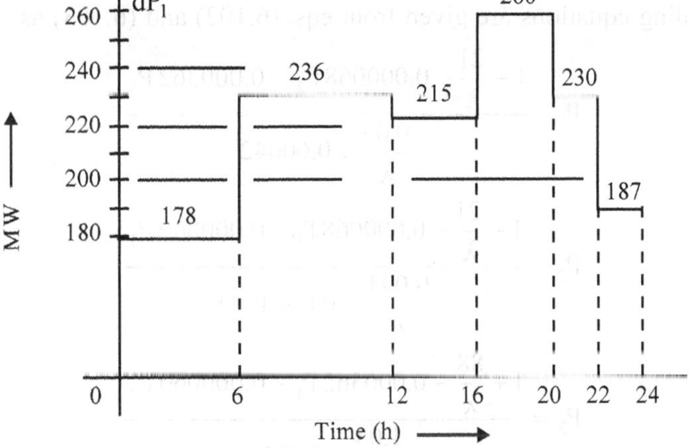

Fig. E 3.8 Load Curve

G_2 – thermal station :

Calorific value of coal	=	4600 kcal/kg
Cost of coal	=	Rs.48 per ton
Incremental fuel cost at near no – load	=	Rs.25/MWh
Incremental fuel cost at 40MW	=	Rs.31.6/MWh
Slope of incremental cost curve	=	0.094
Intercept on y-axis	=	21

$$\frac{dF_2}{dP_2} = 0.094P_{S2} + 21$$

G_3 – Hydro electric plant :

Assuming Y_3 = 1.0 paise/100 m^3 of water at 104 MW output, the incremental plant cost = Rs.19.5 per MW h and at 120 MW output the incremental plant cost = Rs.36 per MWh. Slope of the incremental cost curve

$$\gamma = \frac{16.5}{-16} = 1.03$$

Intercept on y-axis = – 88

$$\gamma_3 = \frac{dW_3}{dP_{H3}} = 19.5; 0 \le P_{H3} \le 104\text{MW}$$

$$= 1.03P_{H3} - 88;$$

$$104 \le P_{H3} \le 120\text{MW}$$

The system daily load curve is given in Fig. E 3.8 as shown. Obtain the economic schedules.

Solution :

The scheduling equations are given from eqs. (6.102) and (6.103) as

$$P_1 - \frac{1 - \dfrac{21}{\lambda} - 0.000068\,P_2 - 0.000362\,P_3}{\dfrac{0.05}{\lambda} + 0.00042}$$

$$P_2 = \frac{1 - \dfrac{21}{\lambda} - 0.000068\,P_1 - 0.000060\,P_3}{\dfrac{0.094}{\lambda} + 0.0004994}$$

$$P_3 = \frac{1 + \dfrac{88}{\lambda} - 0.000362\,P_1 - 0.000060\,P_2}{\dfrac{1.03}{\lambda} + 0.0010}$$

$$P_1 + P_2 + P_3 - (0.00021\, P_1^2 + 0.0002497\, P_2^2 + 0.0005\, P_3^2)$$
$$+ (0.000068\, P_1 P_2 + 0.000362 P_1 P_3 + 0.00006 P_2 P_3) = P_R$$

in order to schedule for a specified received load, the values of l are computed from equation as

$$\lambda^{(i)} = \lambda^{(i-1)} + \left(P_R^{(d)} - P_R^{(i-1)}\right)\left[\frac{\lambda^{(i-1)} - \lambda^{(i-2)}}{P_R^{(i-1)} - P_R^{(i-2)}}\right]$$

where the superscript i indicates the iteration being started.

P_R is the received load and $P^{(d)}{}_R$ is the desired received load.

To start the computation, two initial values for λ are assumed, namely

$$\lambda_1 = 22.0$$
$$\lambda_2 = 30.0$$

Economic schedules are then computed for different water rates over a wide range

$$\gamma_3 \frac{dw_3}{dP_3} = 0.515P_3 - 44 \text{ at } \gamma_3 = 0.5 \text{ paise}/100\text{ m}$$
$$= 0.618P_3 - 52.8 \text{ at } \gamma_3 = 0.6 \text{ paise}/100\text{ m}$$
$$= 0.742P_3 - 63.5 \text{ at } \gamma_3 = 0.7 \text{ paise}/100\text{ m}$$
$$= 0.824P_3 - 70.4 \text{ at } \gamma_3 = 0.8 \text{ paise}/100\text{ m}$$
$$= 0.927P_3 - 79.2 \text{ at } \gamma_3 = 0.9 \text{ paise}/100\text{ m}$$
$$= 1.03P_3 - 88 \text{ at } \gamma_3 = 1.0 \text{ paise}/100\text{ m}$$
$$= 1.24P_3 - 105.5 \text{ at } \gamma_3 = 1.2 \text{ paise}/100\text{ m}$$

the results of the economic schedule are shown in tables E 3.8 (a) to E 3.8 (g) corresponding to different water rates.

Table E 3.8 (a)

$\gamma - 0.5$ Ps/100m^3

$P_R^{(d)}$ (MW)	P_1 (MW)	P_2 (MW)	P_3 (MW)	P_{total} (MW)	P_{loss} (MW)	P_R (MW)	λ
178.000	34.2786	28.1089	125.870	188.168	10.2033	177.965	24.2133
187.000	37.5000	33.4225	126.731	197.674	10.6672	187.006	24.8071
215.000	37.5000	58.5480	131.085	227.133	12.1321	215.001	27.5978
230.000	37.5000	72.1076	133.447	243.055	13.0705	229.984	29.1365
236.000	37.5000	77.5726	134.404	249.477	13.4780	235.999	29.7608
260.000	37.5000	99.5099	138.274	275.284	15.2841	259.999	32.3101

Table E 3.8 (b)

$\gamma = 0.6$ Ps/100m^3

$P_R^{(d)}$ (MW)	P_1 (MW)	P_2 (MW)	P_3 (MW)	P_{total} (MW)	P_{loss} (MW)	P_R (MW)	λ
178.000	37.5000	30.4325	119.685	187.617	9.60962	178.007	24.4699
187.000	37.5000	38.6243	120.872	196.997	9.9923	187.004	25.3683
215.000	37.5000	64.2988	124.632	226.431	11.4309	215.000	28.2338
230.000	37.5000	78.1710	126.688	242.359	12.3596	229.999	29.8147
236.000	37.5000	83.7402	127.517	248.758	12.7620	235.996	30.4564
260.000	37.5000	106.168	130.888	274.556	14.5569	259.999	33.0778

Table E 3.8 (c)

$\gamma = 0.7$ Ps/100m^3

$P_R^{(d)}$ (MW)	P_1 (MW)	P_2 (MW)	P_3 (MW)	P_{total} (MW)	P_{loss} (MW)	P_R (MW)	λ
178.000	37.5000	34.7763	114.802	187.080	9.07387	172.006	24.9369
187.000	37.5000	43.1259	115.827	196.453	9.44968	187.003	25.8570
215.000	37.5000	69.3002	119.072	225.872	10.8717	215.000	28.7397
230.000	37.5000	83.4432	120.848	241-791	11.7948	229.997	30.4096
236.000	37.5000	89.1077	121.564	248.171	12.1942	235.977	31.0668
260.000	37.5000	112.001	124.484	273.985	13.9878	259.998	33.7546

Table E 3.8 (d)

$\gamma = 0.8$ Ps/100m^3

$P_R^{(d)}$ (MW)	P_1 (MW)	P_2 (MW)	P_3 (MW)	P_{total} (MW)	P_{loss} (MW)	P_R (MW)	λ
178.000	37.5000	37.1910	112.105	186.796	8.79129	178.005	25.1972
187.000	37.5000	45.6237	113.044	196.167	9.16186	187.003	26.1275
215.000	37.5000	72.0465	116.019	225.565	10.5818	214.984	29.0978
230.000	37.5000	86.4328	117.651	241.494	11.5045	229.989	30.7381
236.000	37.5000	92.0947	118.312	247.907	11.9066	236.000	31.4043
260.000	37.5000	115.205	120.994	273.699	13.7017	259.997	34.1278

Table E 3.8 (e)

$\gamma = 0.9$ Ps/100m^3

$P_R^{(d)}$ (MW)	P_1 (MW)	P_2 (MW)	P_3 (MW)	P_{total} (MW)	P_{loss} (MW)	P_R (MW)	λ
178.000	37.5000	39.5740	109.453	186.527	8.52298	178.004	25.4547
187.000	37.5000	38.0938	110.303	195.897	8.89451	187.002	26.3966
215.000	37.5000	74.8023	112.999	225.302	10.3088	214.993	29.4050
230.000	37.5000	89.2306	114.447	241.208	11.2304	229.977	31.0671
236.000	37.5000	95.0556	115.078	247.634	11.6339	236.000	31.7422
260.000	37.5000	118.416	117.513	273.429	13.4335	259.996	34.5033

Table E 3.8 (f)

$\gamma = 1.0$ Ps/100m^3

$P_R^{(d)}$ (MW)	P_1 (MW)	P_2 (MW)	P_3 (MW)	P_{total} (MW)	P_{loss} (MW)	P_R (MW)	λ
178.000	37.5000	41.5314	107.232	186.314	8.31038	178.004	25.666
187.000	35.3000	50.1235	109.682	195.682	8.68070	187.002	26.2182
215.000	37.5000	77.0672	110.525	225.048	10.0942	214.998	29.6583
230.000	35.3000	91.6397	111.878	241.018	11.0182	230.000	31.3386
236.000	37.5000	97.4943	112.426	247.421	11.4210	236.000	32.0212
260.000	37.5000	121.065	114.658	273.221	13.2262	259.995	34.8137

Table E 3.8 (g)

$\gamma = 1.2$ Ps/100m^3

$P_R^{(d)}$ (MW)	P_1 (MW)	P_2 (MW)	P_3 (MW)	P_{total} (MW)	P_{loss} (MW)	P_R (MW)	λ
178.000	37.5000	44.9039	103.559	185.963	7.96039	178.003	26.0326
187.000	37.5000	53.6119	104.220	195.332	8.33065	187.001	27.0000
215.000	37.5000	80.9275	106.321	224.749	9.74867	215.000	30.0921
230.000	37.5000	95.7020	107.476	240.678	10.6780	230.000	31.8021
236.000	37.5000	101.639	107.913	247.083	11.0835	235.999	32.4970
260.000	37.5000	125.548	109.849	272.897	12.9033	259.993	35.3412

E 3.9 A system consists of two generators with the following characteristics

$$F_1 = (7\ P_1 + 0.03\ P_1^2 + 70)\ 10^6$$

$$F_2 = (5\ P_2 + 0.05\ P_2^2 + 100)\ 10^6$$

Where F and P are fuel in put in K-cal/hr and unit output in MW respectively. The daily load cycle is given as follows.

Time	Load
12 midnight 6 am	50 MW
6 am to 6 pm	150 MW
6 pm to 12 midnight	50 MW

Give the economic schedule for the three periods of the day

Solution :

Let the cost of the fuel be the same at both the plants.

$$\frac{dF_1}{dP_1} = (7 + 0.06P_1)10^6 \text{ K-cal/MWhr}$$

If C is cost of fuel in Rs/K-cal.

The incremental production cost at plant 1

$$= \frac{dC_1}{dP_1} = (7 + 0.06P_1)10^6 \times \text{C Rs per MWhr}$$

similarly $$= \frac{dC_2}{dP_2} = (5 + 0.1P_2)10^6 \times \text{C Rs per MWhr}$$

For economy $$\frac{dC_1}{dP_1} = \frac{dC_2}{dP_2}$$

and $$P_1 + P_2 = 50 \text{ MW} \quad \text{(i)}$$

$$(7 + 0.06\ P_1)\ 10^6 \times C = (5 + 0.1\ P_2)10^6 \times C \quad \text{(ii)}$$

solving (i) and (ii) for P_1 and P_2

$$P_1 = 18.75 \text{ MW}$$

$$P_2 = 31.25 \text{ MW}$$

For $$P_1 + P_2 = 150\text{MW}$$

We obtain $(7 + 0.06\ P_1) = (5 + 0.1P_2)$

$$7 + 0.06\ P_1 = 5 + 0.1\ (150 - P_1)$$

$$0.06\ P_1 + 0.1\ P_1 = 5 - 7 + 15$$

$$0.16\ P_1 = 13$$

$$P_1 = 81.25\ MW$$

$$P_2 = 68.75\ MW$$

E3.10 The incremental production cost data of two plants are $\frac{dF_1}{dP_1} = 2 + P_1$ and $\frac{dF_2}{dP_2} = 1.5 + P_2$

where P_1 and P_2 are expressed in per unit on 100MVA base. Assume that both the units are in operation and that the maximum loading of each unit is 100MW and the minimum loading of each unit is 10MW. The loss coefficients on a 100MVA base are given by

$$B = \begin{bmatrix} 0.10 & -0.05 \\ -0.05 & 0.2 \end{bmatrix}$$

for $\lambda = 2.5$ solve the coordination equations, by the iterative method.

Solution :

$$IPC_i = a_i\ P_i + b_i$$

$$P_1 = \frac{1 - \frac{b_1}{\lambda} - 2B_{21}P_2}{\frac{a_1}{\lambda} + 2B_{11}} = \frac{1 - \frac{2}{2.5} - 2 \times (-0.05) \times P_2}{\frac{1}{2.5} + 2 \times (0.10)} =$$

$$\frac{1 - 0.8 + 0.1P_2}{0.4 + 0.2} = \frac{0.2}{0.6} = 0.333 \text{ at } P_2 = 0$$

$$P_2 = \frac{1 - \frac{b_2}{\lambda} - 2B_{12}P_2}{\frac{a_2}{\lambda} + 2B_{22}} = \frac{1 - \frac{1.5}{2.5} - 2 \times (-0.05) \times P_2}{\frac{1}{2.5} + 2 \times (0.02)} = \frac{1 - 0.6 + 0.1P_1}{0.4 + 0.4}$$

At $P_1 = 0.333$,

$$P_2 = \frac{0.4 + 0.0333}{0.8} = \frac{0.4333}{0.8} - 0.541625$$

performing iterations further

$$P_1 = \frac{0.2 + 0.1(0.5416)}{0.6} = \frac{0.2 + 0.5416}{0.6} = \frac{0.25416}{0.6} = 0.4236$$

$$P_2 = \frac{0.4 + 0.1(0.4236)}{0.8} = \frac{0.4 + 0.04236}{0.8} = 0.55295$$

$$P_3 = \frac{0.2 + 0.055295}{0.6} = 0.42549 \; P_2 = \frac{0.4 + 0.042549}{0.8} = 0.5531865$$

The results are

Iteration	P_1	P_2
1	0.333	0.541625
2	0.4236	0.55295
3	0.42546	0.55318

At the end of 3 iterations

$$P_1 = 0.4255$$

$$P_2 = 0.5532$$

If one more iteration is carried out

$$P_1 = \frac{0.2 + 0.05532}{0.6} = 0.4255$$

$$P_2 = \frac{0.4 + 0.04255}{0.5} = 0.5532$$

No change in the values.

E3.11 The following incremental costs pertain to a 2 plant system.

$$\frac{dF_1}{dP_1} = 0.03P_1 + 14 \text{ Rs/MWhr}$$

$$\frac{dF_2}{dP_2} = 0.04P_2 + 10 \text{ Rs/MWhr}$$

The loss coefficient are B_{11}=0.001 $(MW)^{-1}$

$B_{12} = B_{22} = 0$. If λ for the system is Rs.30 / MWhr compute the required generation at the 2 plants and the loss in the system.

Solution :

For economy

$$P_1 = \frac{1-\frac{b_1}{\lambda}-2B_{21}P_2}{\frac{a_1}{\lambda}+2B_{11}} = \frac{1-\frac{14}{30}-0}{\frac{0.03}{30}+2\times 0.001} = 177.78\text{MW}$$

$$P_2 = \frac{1-\frac{b_2}{\lambda}-2B_{12}P_1}{\frac{a_2}{\lambda}+2B_{22}} = \frac{1-\frac{10}{30}}{\frac{0.04}{30}} = 500\text{MW}$$

The transmission losses are

$$P_L = \sum_{i=1}^{2}\sum_{j=1}^{2} P_i B_{ij} P_j$$

$$= B_{11}P_1^2 + 2B_{12}P_1\,P_2\,B_{22}P_2^2$$

$$= B_{11}\,P_1^2 = 0.001 \times (177.78)^2 = 31.6 \text{ MW}$$

E3.12 Consider a steam station with two units the input - output characteristics being specified by

$$F_1 = 80 + 8P_1 + 0.024\ P_1^2$$

$$F_2 = 120 + 6P_2 + 0.04\ P_2^2$$

In scheduling a load of 100MW by equal incremental cost method, the incremental cost of unit 1 is specified wrongly by 10% more than the true value while that of unit 2 is specified by 6% less than the true value

Find (i) The change in generation schedules and

(ii) The change in the total cost of generation.

Solution :

The incremental production cost at plant 1 is $8 + 0.048\ P_1$

It is specified 10% more

That is $(8 + 0.048\ P_1)\ 1.1 = 8.8 + 0.0528\ P_1$.

The incremental production cost at plant 2 is $6 + 0.08\ P_2$

It is specified 6% les

That is as $(6 + 0.08P_2)\ 0.94 = 5.64 + 0.0752\ P_2$

Schedule with correct incremental production costs :

$$8 + 0.048\ P_1 = 6 + 0.08P_2$$

$$P_1 + P_2 = 100MW$$

Solving $P_1 = 46.875MW$

$$P_2 = 53.125\ MW$$

Cost of production at plant1

$$C_1 = 80 + 8 \times 46.875 + 0.024 \times 46.875^2 = 507.73438$$

Case of production at plant 2

$$C_2 = 120 + 6 \times 53.125 + 0.04 \times 53.125^2 = 551.64063$$

Total cost $C = C_1 + C_2 = 1059.375$

Schedule with incorrect specification:

$$8.8 + 0.0528P_1 = 5.64 + 0.752P_2$$

$$P_1 + P_2 = 100$$

Solving

$$P_1 = 34.0625$$

$$P_2 = 65.9375$$

Cost of production at plant 2

$$C_1^1 = 80 + 8 \times 34.0625 + 0.024 \times 34.0625^2 = 380.34609$$

Cost of production plant 1

$$C_2^1 = 120 + 6 \times 65.9375 + 6.04 \times 65.9375^2 = 569.53528$$

Total cost $C^1 = C_1^1 + C_2^1 = 949.88218$

Change in total cost of generation

$$= 1029.375 - 949.8821 = 109.49$$

E3.13 A two bus system shown in figure supplies a load at bus 2. If 50MW is transmitted from plant 1 to load at bus 2 over the line, the loss is 2.5MW. The incremental production costs at both the plants are given with usual notation by

$$\frac{dC_1}{dP_1} = 0.03P_1 + 15 \quad \text{and}$$

$$\frac{dC_2}{dP_2} = 0.05P_2 + 20$$

The value of λ is 23 Rs/MWhr

Determine the generation schedule for economy with losses coordinated. What will be the generation schedule if the losses are not coordinated but considered. What will be the savings by coordination of losses into economic schedule ?

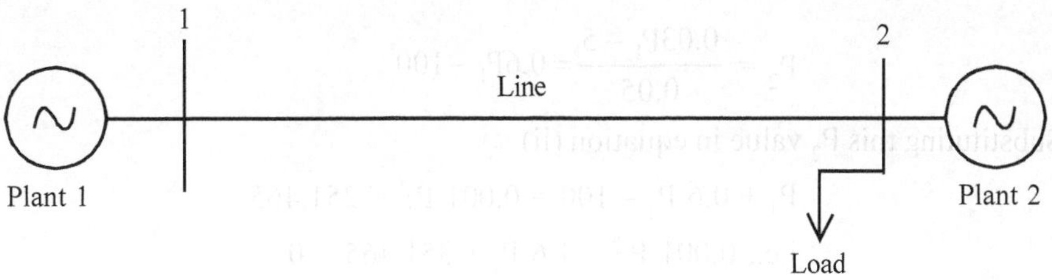

Fig. E 3.13

Solution :

The load is at bus 2 only. There is transmission loss only from the power supplied by plant 1. No power is transmitted over the line from plant 2.

Hence, $2.5\text{MW} = B_{11}P_1^2 + B_{22}.0 + 0$

$$= B_{11}50^2$$

$$B_{11} = \frac{2.5}{50 \times 50} = 0.001(\text{MW})^{-1}$$

Case (i) Losser coordinated

$$\frac{dC_1}{dP_1} + \lambda\frac{dP_L}{dP_1} = \lambda$$

$$\frac{dC_2}{dP_2} + \lambda\frac{dP_L}{dP_2} = \lambda$$

$$0.03P_1 + 15 + 2 \times 0.001P_1 = 23$$

$$P_1 = 258.06\text{MW}$$

$$0.05\ P_2 + 20 + 0 = 23$$

$$P_2 = 3/0.05 = 60\text{MW}$$

Total generation $= P_1 + P_2 = 318.06\text{MW}$

Total load demand $= P_1 + P_2 - P_{LOSS}$

$= 318.06 - 0.001 \times 258.06^2 = 60.595\text{MW}$

$P_D = 318.06 - 66.595 = 251.465\text{MW}$

Case (ii) Economic Schedule for P_D=251.465MW with losses not coordinated.

$$0.03P_1 + 15 = 0.05P_2 + 20 \quad \text{(i)}$$

$$P_1 + P_2 = B_{11}P_1^2 + 251.465 \quad \text{(ii)}$$

$$0.05\ P_2 = 0.03\ P_1 + 15 - 20$$

$$P_2 = \frac{0.03P_1 - 5}{0.05} = 0.6P_1 - 100$$

Substituting this P_2 value in equation (ii)

$$P_1 + 0.6\ P_1 - 100 = 0.001\ P_1^2 + 251.465$$

i.e., $0.001\ P_1^2 - 1.6\ P_1 + 351.465 = 0$

Solving $P_1 = 262.88$ (valid answer)

Then, $P_2 = 157.728 - 100 = 57.728$MW

Total generation $P_1 + P_2 = 320.608$MW

The savings at plant 1 due to loss coordination.

$$\int_{258.06}^{262.88} (0.03P_1 + 15)dP_1 = 0.03P_1^2 + 15P_1\Big|_{258.06}^{262.88} =$$

$$[69105.9 - 66594.9] = 2511.0\ \text{Rs / Hr}$$

The extra expenditure at plant 2 due to increased production

$$\int_{60}^{57.728} (0.05P_2 + 20)dP_2 = 0.05P_2^2 + 20P_2\Big|_{60}^{57.728} =$$

$$[180 + 1154.56] = 1334.56\ \text{Rs / Hr}$$

Net savings = 2511 – 1334.56 = 1176.44Rs/Hr

E3.14 Consider the two bus system shown in figure. The incremental production costs at the two generating stations are given by

$$\frac{dC_1}{dP_1} = 0.005P_1 + 5 \text{ and}$$

$$\frac{dC_2}{dP_2} = 0.004P_2 + 7$$

The B coefficients are given in matrix form as

$$B = \begin{bmatrix} 0.0002 & -0.00005 \\ -0.00005 & 0.0003 \end{bmatrix}$$

Determine the penalty factors at both the buses and also the approximate penalty factors. Given $\lambda = 8$

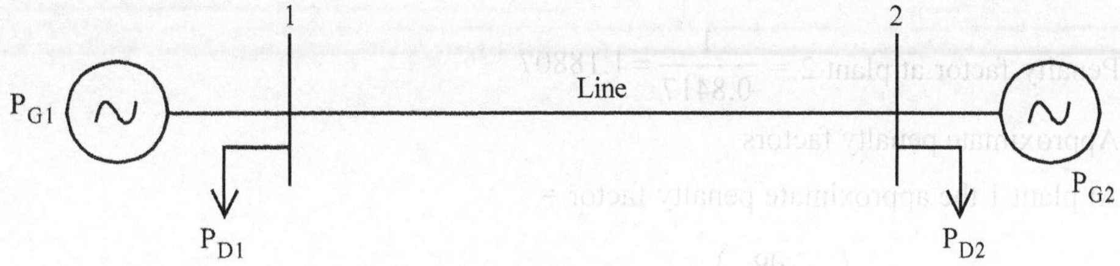

Fig. E 3.14

Solution :

$$B_{11} = 0.0002;\ B_{22} = 0.0003;\ B_{12} = B_{21} = -0.00005$$

$$P_L = P_1^2B_{11} + P_2^2B_{22} + 2P_1P_2B_{12}$$

$$\frac{\partial P_L}{\partial P_1} = 2P_1B_{11} + 2P_2B_{22} = 2\times 0.0002P_1 + 2\times 0.00005P_2$$

$$\frac{\partial P_L}{\partial P_2} = 2P_2B_{22} + 2P_1B_{21} = 2\times 0.0003P_2 + 2\times 0.00005P_1$$

The coordination equations are

$$(0.005\ P_1 + 5) + 8\ (0.0004\ P_1 + 0.0001\ P_2) = 8$$

$$(0.004\ P_2 + 6) + 8\ (0.0006\ P_2 + 0.0001P_1) = 8$$

Simplifying

$$0.005\ P_1 + 0.0032\ P_1 + 0.0008\ P_2 = 3$$

$$0.004\ P_1 + 0.0048\ P_1 + 0.0008\ P_2 = 2$$

(i.e.) $$0.0082\ P_1 + 0.0008\ P_2 = 3$$

$$0.0008\ P_1 + 0.0088\ P_2 = 2$$

Solving for P_1 and P_2

$$P_1 = 346.75 \text{ and } P_2 = 195.75$$

$$\left(1 - \frac{\partial P_L}{\partial P_1}\right) = 1 - 2\times 346.75\times 0.0002 + 0.0001\times 195.75 = 0.8417$$

$$\left(1 - \frac{\partial P_L}{\partial P_2}\right) = 1 - 2\times 0.0003\times 195.75 + 0.0001\times 346.75 = 0.847875$$

Penalty factor at plant 1 = $\dfrac{1}{0.847875} = 1.17942$

Penalty factor at plant 2 = $\dfrac{1}{0.8417} = 1.18807$

Approximate penalty factors

At plant 1 the approximate penalty factor =

$$\left(1+\frac{\partial P_L}{\partial P_1}\right) = 1 + 0.1387 + 0.019575 = 1.158275$$

At plant 2 the approximate penalty factor =

$$\left(1+\frac{\partial P_L}{\partial P_2}\right) = 1 + 0.11745 + 0.034675 = 1.152125$$

E3.15 Given the network in the figure shown along with the currents flowing in the lines and the impedances of the lines in per unit on a 100MVA base. Compute the B. coefficients for the network when the voltage at bus 1 is 1.0 $\angle 0^0$ p.u.

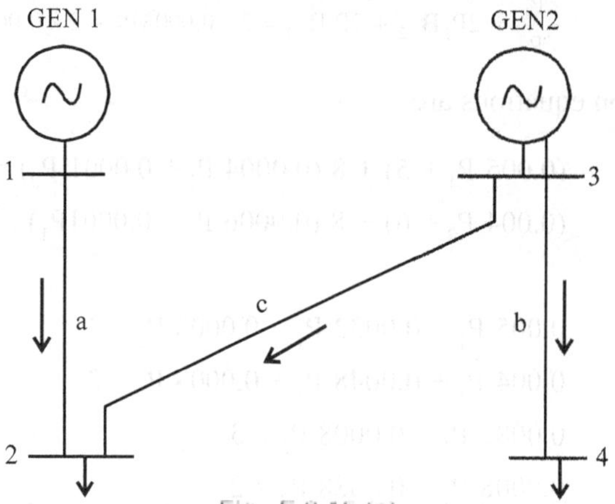

Fig. E 3.15 (a)

Current in line a = 1.5 – j0.3 p.u.

Current in line b = 2 – j0.3 p.u.

Current in line c = 1 – j0.2 p.u.

Load current at bus2 = 2.5 – j0.5 p.u.

Impedance of line a = 0.01 + j0.06 p.u.

Impedance of line b = 0.01 + j0.05 p.u.

Impedance of line c = 0.01 + j0.04 p.u.

Solution :

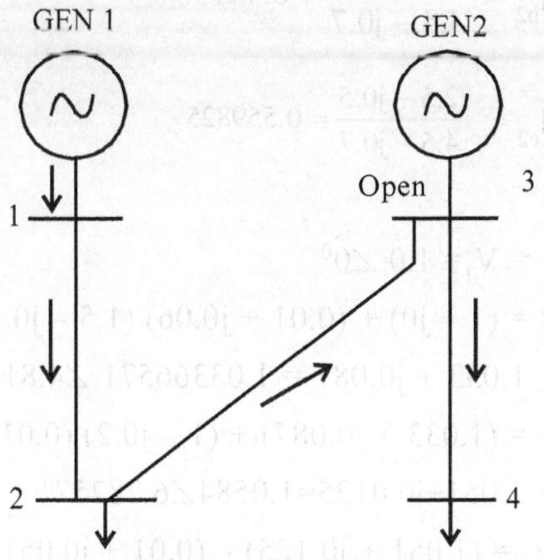

Fig. E 3.15 (b)

The current distribution factors

$$d_{a1} = 1$$

$$d_{b1} = \frac{2 - j0.2}{4.5 - j0.7} = 0.44135$$

$$d_{c1} = \frac{2 - j0.2}{4.5 - j0.7} = 0.44135$$

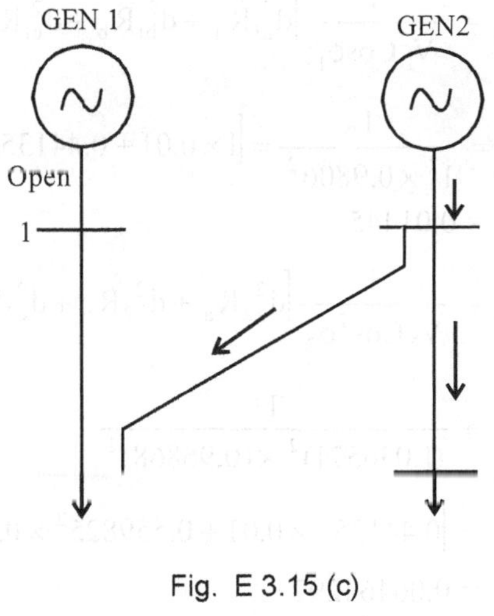

Fig. E 3.15 (c)

$$d_{a2} = 0$$

$$d_{b2} = \frac{2 - j0.2}{4.5 - j0.7} = 0.44135$$

$$d_{c2} = \frac{2.5 - j0.5}{4.5 - j0.7} = 0.559825$$

Voltages

Voltage at bus 1 = $V_1 = 1.0\ \angle 0^0$

Voltage at bus 2 = $(1 + j0) + (0.01 + j0.06)\ (1.5 - j0.3)$

$= 1.033 + j0.087 = 1.03366571\ \angle 4.814^0$

Voltage at bus 3 = $(1.033 + j0.087) + (1 - j0.2)\ (0.01 + j0.04)$

$= 1.051 + j0.0125 = 1.0584 \angle 6.78257^0$

Voltages at bus 4 $V_4 = (1.051 + j0.125) - (0.01 + j0.05)\ (2 - j0.2) =$

$1.03 + j0.027 = 1.03035\ \angle 1.50^0$

$$\delta_1 = \text{Tan}^{-1}\left(\frac{-0.3}{1.5}\right) = -11.3^0$$

$$\delta_2 = \text{Tan}^{-1}\left(\frac{-0.4}{3}\right) = -7.595^0$$

$$\text{Cos}\ (d_1 - d_2) = [-\ 11.3^0 - (-7.595^0)] = \text{Cos}\ (-3.705^0) = 0.9979$$

Power factor at plant 1 $(\text{Cos}\phi_1) = \text{Cos}\ (0^0 + 11.3^0) = 0.9806$

Power factor at plant 2 $(\text{Cos}\phi_2) = \text{Cos}\ (6.78257 + 7.595) = 0.96868$

$$B_{11} = \frac{1}{V_1^2 \text{Cos}\phi_1^2}\left[d_{a1}^2 R_a + d_{b1}^2 R_b + d_{c1}^2 R_c\right]$$

$$= \frac{1}{1^2 \times 0.9806^2} = \left[1 \times 0.01 + 0.44135^2 \times 0.01 + 0.44135^2 \times 0.01\right]$$

$$= 0.01445$$

$$B_{22} = \frac{1}{V_2^2 \text{Cos}^2\phi_2}\left[d_{a2}^2 R_a + d_{b2}^2 R_b + d_{c2}^2 R_c\right]$$

$$= \frac{1}{(1.036571)^2 \times (0.96868)^2}$$

$$= \left[0.44135^2 \times 0.01 + 0.559825^2 \times 0.01 + 0\right]$$

$$= 0.00464292$$

$$B_{12} = B_{21} = \frac{\text{Cos}(\delta_1 - \delta_2)}{|V_1||V_2|\text{Cos}\phi_1 \text{Cos}\phi_2}$$

$$[d_{a1}d_{a2}R_a + d_{b1}d_{b2}R_b + d_{c1}d_{c2}R_c]$$

$$\frac{0.9979[0 + 0.44135 \times 0.44135 \times 0.01 + 0.44135 \times 0.559825 \times 0.01]}{(1 \times 1.036657)(0.96868 \times 0.9806)}$$

$$= 0.0044778857$$

on 100 MVA base the loss coefficients are

$$B_{11} = 0.01445 \times 10^{-2}(\text{MW})^{-1}$$

$$B_{22} = 0.0046429 \times 10^{-2}(\text{MW})^{-1}$$

$$B_{12} = B_{21} = 0.00447788 \times 10^{-7}(\text{MW})^{-1}$$

Questions

3.1 Explain the following terms with reference to thermal plants

(i) heat rate curve

(ii) incremental fuel rate cure

(iii) incremental production cost curve

3.2 Explain the following terms with reference to hydro plants

(i) input out curve

(ii) incremental water rate curve

(iii) incremental production cost curve

3.3 How is generation scheduled among various generators when transmission losses are neglected in a thermal system? Explain

3.4 Derive the transmission loss formula for a system consisting of n-generating plants supplying several loads inter connected through a transmission network.

3.5 Derive expressions for economic distribution of load between generating units considering the effect of transmission losses.

3.6 What are coordination equation? Give their physical significance.

3.7 What is a penalty factor in economic scheduling. Explain its significance.

3.8 Explain how the incremental production cost of a thermal power station can be determined.

3.9 Discuss the general problem of economic operation of large inter connected areas.

3.10 State what is meant by base – load and peak – load stations. Discuss the combined operation of hydro electric and steam power stations.

3.11 Derive an expression for the hourly loss in economy due to error in the representation of input data.

3.12 What are the assumptions made in deriving transmission loss coefficients? Enumerate them.

3.13 Explain hydro thermal economic load scheduling. Derive the necessary equations.

Problems

P 3.1 (a) A power system consists of two, 120 MW units whose input cost data are represented by the equations:

$$C_1 = 0.04\,P_1^2 = +\,22\,P_1 + 800 \text{ Rupees / hour}$$

$$C_2 = 0.04\,P_2^2 = +\,22\,P_2 + 1000 \text{ Rupees / hour}$$

If the total received power $P_R = 200$MW. Determine the load sharing between units for most economic operation.

(b) Discuss the general problem of economic operation of large interconnected areas.

P 3.2 (a) Derive an expression for the hourly loss in economy due to error in the representation of input data.

(b) The incremental fuel costs for two plants are given by

$$\frac{dc_1}{dP_1} = 0.1P_1 + 20\text{Rs./Mw} - \text{Hr} \qquad \frac{dc_2}{dP_2} = 0.15P_2 + 22.5\text{Rs./Mw} - \text{Hr}$$

The system is operating at the optimum condition with $p_1 = p_2 = 100$MW and $\frac{\partial p_1}{\partial p_2} = 0.2$.

Find the penalty factor at plant 1 and the incremental cost of received power.

P 3.3 (a) The incremental fuel costs for the two plants are given by

$$\frac{dc_1}{dP_1} = 0.2P_1 + 45 \qquad \frac{dc_2}{dP_2} = 0.25P_2 + 34$$

where C is in Rs/hr and P is in MW. If both units operate at all times and maximum and minimum loads on each are 100MW and 20MW respectively, determine the economic load schedule of the plants for the loads of 80MW and 180MW. Neglect the line losses.

(b) write short notes on physical interpretation of co ordination equation.

P 3.4 (a) Derive the conditions to be satisfied for economic operation of a loss less power system.

(b) 150 MW, 220MW and 220MW are the ratings of three units located in a thermal power station. Their respective incremental costs are given by the following equations :

$$\frac{dc_1}{dP_1} = \text{Rs}(0.11P_1 + 12) \qquad \frac{dc_2}{dP_2} = \text{Rs}(0.095P_2 + 14) \qquad \frac{dc_3}{dP_3} = \text{Rs}(0.1P_3 + 13)$$

where P_1, P_2 and P_3 are the loads in MW. Determine the economical load allocation between the three units, when the total load on the station is (i) 350MW (ii) 500MW

P 3.5 The equations of the input costs of three power plants operating in conjunction and supply power to a system network are obtained as follows:

$$C_1 = 0.06 + 15P_1 + 150 \text{ Rupees / hour}$$

$$C_2 = 0.08 + 13P_2 + 180 \text{ Rupees / hour}$$

$$C_3 = 0.10 + 10P_3 + 200 \text{ Rupees / hour}$$

The incremental loss – rates of the network with respect to the plants 1,2 and 3 are 0.06, 0.09 and 1.0 per MW of generation, respectively. Determine the most economical share of a total load of 120MW which each of the plants would take up for minimum input cost of received power is Rupees per MWH.

P 3.6 (a) The incremental costs for two generating plants are

$$IC_1 = 0.1\,P_1 + 20 \text{ Rupees/MW hour}$$

$$IC_2 = 0.1\,P_2 + 15 \text{ Rupees/MW hour}$$

Where P_1 and P_2 are in MW. The loss coefficients (B_{mn}) expressed in MW^{-1} unit are

$B_{11} = 0.001$, $B_{22} = 0.0024$, $B_{12} = N_{21} = -0.0005$. Compute the economical generation scheduling corresponding to the Lagrangian multiplier 1.25 Rs/MW hr and the corresponding system load that can be met with. If the total load is 150MW, taking 5% change in the value of l, what should be the value of l in the next iteration?

(b) What are the assumptions made in deriving the loss coefficients?

P 3.7 The fuel inputs to two plants are given by

$$F_1 = 0.015 + 16P_1 + 50 \quad F_2 = 0.02 + 12P_2 + 30$$

The loss coefficients of the system are given by $B_{11} = 0.005$; $B_{12} = -0.0012$ and $B_{22} = 0.002$. The load to be met is 200MW. Determine the economic operating schedule and the corresponding cost of generation if the transmission line losses are coordinated.

P 3.8 A constant load of 300MW is supplied by two 200MW generators, 1 and 2 for which the respective incremental fuel costs are

$$\frac{dC_1}{dPG_1} = 0.10PG_1 + 20 \qquad \frac{dC_2}{dPG_2} = 0.10PG_2 + 20$$

with powers P_G in MW and costs C is Rs/h, determine

(a) The most economical division of load between the generators and

(b) The saving in Rs/day thereby obtained compared to equal load sharing between the machines.

P 3.9 A system consists of two plants connected by a tie line and a load is located at plant 2. When 100MW are transmitted from plant 1, a loss of 10MW takes place on the tie – line. Determine the generation schedule at both the plants and the power received by the load when l for the system is Rs.25 per megawatt hour and the incremental fuel costs are given by the equations :

$$\frac{dF_1}{dP_1} = 0.03P_1 + 17 Rs / MWr \qquad \frac{dF_2}{dP_2} = 0.06P_2 + 19 Rs / MWr$$

P3.10 The incremental fuel cost curves of generators A and B are shown below in the figure. How would a load (i) more than 2 P_G (ii) less than $2P_G$ and (iii) equal to $2P_G$ be shared between A and B if both generators are running.

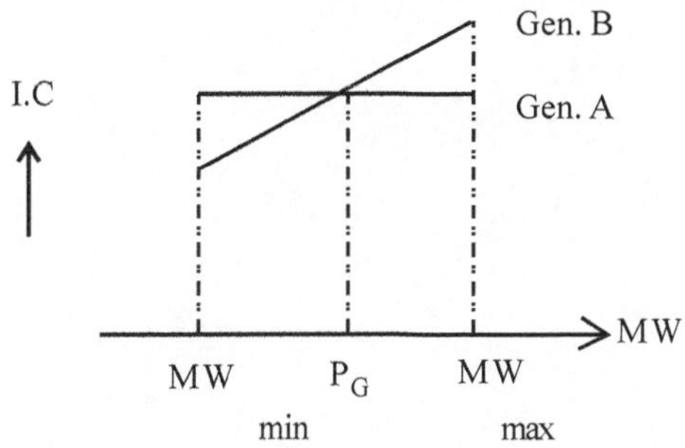

P3.11 (a) Explain heat rate curve and cost curve. Bring out the differences between them

(b) Determine the economic operating point of three units supplying a load of 800MW. The incremental fuel costs of the three units are :

$$\frac{dF_1}{dP_1} = 6.48 + 0.00256P_1 Rs./MWh \qquad \frac{dF_2}{dP_2} = 7.85 + 0.00388P_2 Rs./MWh$$

$$\frac{dF_3}{dP_3} = 7.97 + 0.00964P_3 Rs./MWh$$

4 OPTIMAL LOAD FLOW

Optimal load flow studies are concerned with economic operation of the system in all aspects. These aspects include consideration of all constraints while satisfying the load balance. The various types of inequality constraints have been already discussed in Chapter 3. Satisfying the load constraints itself is the load flow solution. Hence, in optimal operation, the cost minimization is implemented in addition to aforcesaid considerations. It may be noted that even the slack bus voltage also has to be optimized for economy while the choice of slack bus may be based on other considerations.

4.1 Reactive Power Control for Loss Minimization

Transmission losses are quadratic functions of bus-bar voltage magnitudes at all buses. With usual notation.

$$P_{LOSS} = \sum_{i=1}^{n} \sum_{j=1}^{n} |V_i||Y_{ij}||V_j| \cos(\delta_i - \delta_j - \delta_{ij}) \qquad .....(4.1)$$

At each voltage controlled bus the best voltage that minimized the loss is determined. Consider the bus impedance matrix Z_{BUS}. Let R be the real part of the Z_{BUS} matrix.

At each bus i, the current

$$I_i = A_i + jB_i = \frac{P_i - jQ_i}{|V_i|}(\text{Cos}\delta_i - j\text{Sin}\delta_i) \qquad .....(4.2)$$

The components A_i and B_i can be identified. The power loss.

$$P_{LOSS} = A^t RA + B^t RB \quad .....(4.3)$$

The necessary condition for P_{LOSS} to be a minimum is $\frac{dP_{LOSS}}{dQ} = 0$ at all the reactive generation buses. A gradient algorithm can be used for iteration

$$Q_i^{new} = Q_i^{old} + k\left(\frac{\partial P_{LOSS}}{\partial Q_i}\right)^{old} \quad .....(4.4)$$

where k is a scalar parameter.

4.2 Gradient Method for Optimal Load Flow

Dommel and Tinney (1968) proposed a method for optimal load flow based on Lagrange and Kuhn-Tucker conditions. In this method the variables are divided into two types X and Y.

$\underline{X}$ vector includes the voltage magnitudes $|V_i|$ and the phase angle of the voltage δ_i at each bus i for all P-Q type buses. At each P-V type bus δ_i is considered as X – Variable.

$\underline{Y}$ vector includes P_k and Q_k at each P, Q bus k.

At the slack bus δ_k and $|V_k|$ are also y-vector components.

It can be recognized that $\underline{Y}$ is the control vector and $\underline{X}$ is the vector of dependent variables.

At every bus the equality constraint $h(\underline{X}) = 0$ must be satisfied.

(i.e) $P_{gi} - P_{li} - P_i = 0$

$$Q_{gi} - Q_{li} - Q_i = 0 \quad ......(4.5)$$

Where the suffix g stands for generation bus and ℓ stands for load bus.

The Lagrange function is formed as :

$$L = f + \lambda^t h \quad .....(4.6)$$

The necessary conditions for minimum of L are

$$\frac{\partial L}{\partial \underline{X}} = \frac{\partial f}{\partial \underline{X}} + \frac{\partial h^t}{\partial \underline{X}}.\lambda = 0 \quad .....(4.7)$$

$$\frac{\partial L}{\partial \underline{y}} = \frac{\partial f}{\partial \underline{y}} + \frac{\partial h^t}{\partial \underline{y}}.\lambda = 0 \quad .....(4.8)$$

and

$$\frac{\partial L}{\partial \lambda} = \underline{h} = 0 \quad .....(4.9)$$

Since $\underline{X}$ vector contains |V| and δ, $\frac{\partial h}{\partial \underline{V}}$ is the Jacobian matrix of N-R method in load flow solution.

$$\lambda = -\left(\frac{\partial h^t}{\partial \underline{X}}\right)^{-1} \frac{\partial f}{\partial \underline{X}} \qquad .....(4.10)$$

where $\frac{\partial f}{\partial \underline{X}}$ is known from incremental costs. Knowing the Jacobian and incremental cost curves. λ can be computed. With λ known $\frac{\partial L}{\partial \underline{y}}$ is determined using the gradient method.

$$\underline{y}^{new} = \underline{y}^{old} + k\frac{\partial L}{\partial \underline{y}} \quad \text{where k is a scalar parameter} \qquad .....(4.11)$$

The computation is repeated till convergence is obtained. In order to consider the inequality constraints, they are set and held at their limits, in case they are violated for all control variables $\underline{y}$. If the dependent variables are violated, then the penalty function method is used to force the variables back to their limits. It is said that the method offers good convergence in general.

4.3 Non-Linear Programming

Given the objective function, that is, the function for maximization or minimization

$$f(\underline{X}) = f(x_1, x_2, ..., x_n) \qquad .....(4.12)$$

The function is subject to constraints of the type

$$h_i(\underline{X}) = 0; \qquad i = 1, 2, ... N \qquad .....(4.13)$$

and

$$g_j(\underline{X}) < 0; \qquad j = 1, 2, ... m \qquad .....(4.14)$$

If the functions f, g and h are all linear the optimization of the functional f can be achieved through linear programming methods. However, if any one of them is non-linear, then non-linear programming methods are to be applied. The general conditions for the solution of non-linear programming problem are given by Kuhn-Tucker conditions.

Forming the composite L – function

$$L = f(\underline{X}) + \alpha^t h(\underline{X}) + \beta^t g(\underline{X}) \qquad .....(4.15)$$

where α_i are arbitrary

$$\beta_i \geq 0$$

and $\beta_i\, g_i = 0$ .....(4.16)

It is to be noted that the set of active constraints is not known in advance. The variables α_I are the usual Lagrange - multiplies used in case of equality constraints and β_i are the Kuhn-Tucker multipliers. Together, they are called dual variables.

In 1962 Carpentier formulated the general problem of minimizing the instantaneous operating costs of a power system subject to both, the network constraints and inequality constraints applying Kuhn - Tucker conditions. The variables of vector $\underline{X}$ contain components of independent variables P (active power), Q (reactive power), T (in-phase transformer tap position) TS (phase shift transformer tap position) together with dependent variables voltage magnitude |V| and bus voltage phase angle δ.

$$\underline{X} = [P, Q, T, TS, V, \delta]^t \quad .....(4.17)$$

4.4 Lagrange Function for Optimal Load Flow

The general Lagrange function with all the constraints incorporated is written as

$L = f(\underline{X})$ (Scalar cost function for optimal evaluation.)

$+ \lambda^P h^P(\underline{X}) + \mu^Q h^Q(\underline{X})$ (equality constraints for load balance)

$+ \beta^P g^P(\underline{X})$ (reactive power constraints)

$+ \beta^R g^R(\underline{X})$ (generator rating constrains)

$+ \beta^B g^B(\underline{X})$ (boiler constraints, if any)

$+ \beta^{RS} g^{RS}(\underline{X})$ (running reserve constraints)

$+ \beta^{BR} g^{BR}(\underline{X})$ (branch flow constraints)

$+ \beta^V g^V(\underline{X})$ (bus voltage constraints)

$+ \beta^T g^T(\underline{X})$ (in phase tap range constraints)

$+ \beta^{TS} g^{TS}(\underline{X})$ (phase shift transformer constraints)

$+ \beta^S g^S(\underline{X})$ (line outage or security constraints) .....(4.18)

Note that the constraints h are of the type

$$h(\underline{X}) = P_{gi} - P_{\ell i} - P_i = 0 \quad .....(4.19)$$

$$Q_{gi} - Q_{\ell i} - Q_i = 0 \text{ at all buses } i = 1, 2, ... n \quad .....(4.20)$$

while constraints g, for instance g^V is of the type

$$V_i^{min} \leq V_i \leq V_i^{max} \text{ at any bus i}$$

4.5 Computational Procedures

Solution to a set of non linear equations of the form

$$\frac{\partial L}{\partial X_i} = 0 \text{ for i} = 1, 2, \ldots\ldots n \qquad \ldots\ldots(4.21)$$

is very difficult to obtain in practice. However, there are several techniques, which are iterative in nature, that can be applied to find the optimal solution around the operating point. There are sequential unconstrained minimization techniques which transform the constrained problem into an unconstrained problem. Penalty function methods are important in this category. In the next section a method that utilizes the jacobian of the Newton - Raphson method will be detailed. In this method neither the penalty functions are used nor the Kuhn - Tucker variables. No effort will be made to limit the controllable variables initially.

4.6 Conditions for Optimal Load Flow

Taking into consideration only the equality constraints, the Lagrange function becomes

$$L = F(x) + \sum_{q=1}^{n} \lambda_q g_q(x) + \sum_{q=1}^{n} \mu_q g_q(x) \qquad \ldots\ldots(4.22)$$

At the optimum $\quad \dfrac{\partial L}{\partial \delta} = 0 \qquad \ldots\ldots(4.23)$

and $\quad \dfrac{\partial L}{\partial |V|} = 0 \qquad \ldots\ldots(4.24)$

considering the voltage phase angle and its magnitude only as variables

Multiplying equations (4.23) by $d\delta_p$ and equation (4.24) by $d|V_p|$

$$\frac{\partial L}{\partial \delta} d\delta_p = \frac{\partial F_P}{\partial \delta_P} d\delta_P + \sum_{q=1}^{n} \lambda_q \frac{\partial g_q}{\partial \delta_P} \partial \delta_P + \sum_{q=1}^{n} \mu_q \frac{\partial h_q}{\partial \delta_P} \partial \delta_P \qquad \ldots\ldots(4.25)$$

and

$$\frac{\partial L}{\partial |V_p|} d|V| = \frac{\partial F_P}{\partial |V_p|} d|V_p| + \sum_{q=1}^{n} \lambda_q \frac{\partial g_q}{\partial |V_p|} \partial |V_p| + \sum_{q=1}^{n} \mu_q \frac{\partial h_q}{\partial |V_p|} \partial |V_p| \qquad \ldots\ldots(4.26)$$

Combining the two equations

$$dL = dF + \sum_{q=1}^{n} \lambda_q \frac{\partial P_{gq}}{\partial P_{gP}} d\delta_P - \sum_{q=1}^{n} \lambda_q \frac{\partial P_{lq}}{\partial P_{gP}} d\delta_P - \sum_{q=1}^{n} \lambda_q \frac{\partial P_q}{\partial P_{gP}} d\delta_P$$

$$+ + \sum_{q=1}^{n} \mu_q \frac{\partial Q_{gq}}{\partial P_{gP}} d\delta_P - \sum_{q=1}^{n} \mu_q \frac{\partial Q_{lq}}{\partial P_{gP}} d\delta_P \sum_{q=1}^{n} \mu_q \frac{\partial Q_q}{\partial P_{gP}} d\delta_P \qquad .....(4.27)$$

$$+ \sum_{q=1}^{n} \lambda_q \frac{\partial P_{gq}}{\partial |V_P|} d|V_P| - \sum_{q=1}^{n} \lambda_q \frac{\partial P_{lq}}{\partial |V_P|} d|V_P| - \sum_{q=1}^{n} \lambda_q \frac{\partial P_q}{\partial |V_P|} d|V_P|$$

$$+ \sum_{q=1}^{n} \mu_q \frac{\partial Q_{gq}}{\partial |V_P|} d|V_P| - \sum_{q=1}^{n} \mu_q \frac{\partial Q_{lq}}{\partial |V_P|} d|V_P| - \sum_{q=1}^{n} \mu_q \frac{\partial Q_q}{\partial |V_P|} d|V_P| = 0$$

The load powers are generally assumed to remain constant

Hence, $$\frac{\partial P_{lq}}{\partial \delta_P} = \frac{\partial Q_{lq}}{\partial \delta_P} = \frac{\partial P_{lq}}{\partial |V_P|} = \frac{\partial Q_{lq}}{\partial |V_P|} = 0 \qquad .....(4.28)$$

Also, the total derivatives for P_{gq} and Q_{gq} are given by

$$\sum_{q=1}^{n} \lambda_q dP_{gq} = \sum_{q=1}^{n} \lambda_q \frac{\partial P_{gq}}{\partial \delta P} d\delta P + \sum_{q=1}^{n} \lambda_q \frac{\partial P_{gq}}{\partial |V_P|} d|V_P|$$

$$\text{and} \sum_{q=1}^{n} \mu_q dQ_{gq} = \sum_{q=1}^{n} \mu_q \frac{\partial Q_{gq}}{\partial \delta P} d\delta P + \sum_{q=1}^{n} \mu_q \frac{\partial Q_{gq}}{\partial |V_P|} d|V_P| \qquad .....(4.29)$$

Hence equation (4.27) reduces to the following with the substitution of (4.28) and (4.29)

$$dL = dF + \sum_{q=1}^{n} \lambda_q dP_{gq} + \sum_{q=1}^{n} \mu_q dQ_{gq} - \sum_{q=1}^{n} \lambda_q \frac{\partial P_q}{\partial \delta_q} d\delta_q$$

$$- \sum_{q=1}^{n} \mu_q \frac{\partial Q_q}{\partial \delta_q} d\delta_q - \sum_{q=1}^{n} \lambda_q \frac{\partial P_{gq}}{\partial |V_P|} d|V_P| - \sum_{q=1}^{n} \mu_q \frac{\partial P_{gq}}{\partial |V_P|} d|V_P| = 0 \qquad .....(4.29)$$

The incremental production costs are given by

$$\frac{dF}{dP_{gq}} = \gamma_q = a_q + b_q P_{gq} \text{ for all } q = 1, 2, \text{ ..... } ng \qquad .....(4.31)$$

where ng = number of generator buses.

$$dF = -\gamma_q dP_{gq} = -(a_q + b_q P_{gq})\, d P_{gq}$$

for all dF to have a minimum. Substituting this in equation (4.30) for dF

$$\sum_{q=1}^{ng}(\lambda_q - \gamma_q)dP_{gq} + \sum_{q=1}^{ng}\mu_q dQ_{gq} - \sum_{q=1}^{ng}\lambda_q \frac{\partial P_q}{\partial \delta_p}d\delta_p$$

$$-\sum_{q=1}^{n}\mu_q \frac{\partial Q_q}{\partial \delta_P}d\delta_P - \sum_{q=1}^{n}\lambda_q \frac{\partial P_{gq}}{\partial |V_P|}d|V_P| - \sum_{q=1}^{n}\mu_q \frac{\partial Q_{gq}}{\partial |V_P|}d|V_P| = 0 \quad .....(4.32)$$

For the above equations to be zero, since, P_{gq}, Q_{gq}, δ_P and $|V_P|$ are finite changes their coefficients have to be zero.

Hence $\quad \gamma_q = \lambda_q$ .....(4.33)

$\quad \mu_q = 0$ .....(4.34)

at all generating buses

Further

$$\begin{bmatrix} \dfrac{\partial P_q}{\partial \delta_P} & \dfrac{\partial Q_q}{\partial \delta_P} \\ \dfrac{\partial P_q}{\partial |V_P|} & \dfrac{\partial Q_q}{\partial |V_P|} \end{bmatrix} \begin{bmatrix} \lambda_q \\ \mu_q \end{bmatrix} = 0$$

$$q = 1, 2 \; .... \; n \quad P = 1, 2, \; ..... \; n \quad .....(4.35)$$

The above equations are the conditions for optimal load flow.

4.7 Implementation of optimal conditions

Method of El-Abiad and Jaimes

It can be recognized that the coefficient matrix of equation (4.35) is transpose of the Jacobian of N-R method. Partitioning of this matrix is proposed to solve for the optimal solution.

Algorithm :

1. Any bus is assumed as reference bus 1. The incremental production cost at this bus from any feasible load flow solution is computed and set equal to λ_1.

   $IPC_1 = \gamma_1 = \lambda_1$

2. The coefficient matrix (4.35) is expanded and is shown in equation (4.36). Separating out the first column it has the order reduced as follows to enable the computation of all remaining λ's and μ's.

$$
\begin{bmatrix}
\frac{\partial P_1}{\partial \delta_1} & \frac{\partial P_2}{\partial \delta_2} & \cdots & \frac{\partial P_{ng}}{\partial \delta_1} & \frac{\partial P_{ng+1}}{\partial \delta_1} & \cdots & \frac{\partial P_n}{\partial \delta_1} & \cdots & \frac{\partial Q_1}{\partial \delta_1} & \cdots & \frac{\partial Q_{ng}}{\partial \delta_1} & \frac{\partial Q_{ng+1}}{\partial \delta_1} & \cdots & \frac{\partial Q_n}{\partial \delta_1} \\
\cdots & \cdots & \cdots & \cdots & \cdots & \cdots & \cdots & \cdots & \cdots & \cdots & \cdots & \cdots & \cdots & \cdots \\
\frac{\partial P_1}{\partial \delta_{ng}} & \frac{\partial P_2}{\partial \delta_{ng}} & \cdots & \frac{\partial P_{ng}}{\partial \delta_{ng}} & \frac{\partial P_{ng+1}}{\partial \delta_{ng}} & \cdots & \frac{\partial P_n}{\partial \delta_{ng}} & \cdots & \frac{\partial Q_1}{\partial \delta_{ng}} & \cdots & \frac{\partial Q_{ng}}{\partial \delta_{ng}} & \frac{\partial Q_{ng+1}}{\partial \delta_{ng}} & \cdots & \frac{\partial Q_n}{\partial \delta_{ng}} \\
\cdots & \cdots & \cdots & \cdots & \cdots & \cdots & \cdots & \cdots & \cdots & \cdots & \cdots & \cdots & \cdots & \cdots \\
\frac{\partial P_1}{\partial \delta_n} & \frac{\partial P_2}{\partial \delta_n} & \cdots & \frac{\partial P_{ng}}{\partial \delta_n} & \frac{\partial P_{ng+1}}{\partial \delta_n} & \cdots & \frac{\partial P_n}{\partial \delta_n} & \cdots & \frac{\partial Q_1}{\partial \delta_n} & \cdots & \frac{\partial Q_{ng}}{\partial \delta_n} & \frac{\partial Q_{ng+1}}{\partial \delta_n} & \cdots & \frac{\partial Q_n}{\partial \delta_n} \\
\frac{\partial P_1}{\partial |V_1|} & \frac{\partial P_2}{\partial |V_2|} & \cdots & \frac{\partial P_{ng}}{\partial |V_1|} & \frac{\partial P_{ng+1}}{\partial |V_1|} & \cdots & \frac{\partial P_n}{\partial |V_1|} & \cdots & \frac{\partial Q_1}{\partial |V_1|} & \cdots & \frac{\partial Q_{ng}}{\partial |V_1|} & \frac{\partial Q_{ng+1}}{\partial |V_1|} & \cdots & \frac{\partial Q_n}{\partial |V_1|} \\
\cdots & \cdots & \cdots & \cdots & \cdots & \cdots & \cdots & \cdots & \cdots & \cdots & \cdots & \cdots & \cdots & \cdots \\
\frac{\partial P_1}{\partial |V_{ng}|} & \frac{\partial P_2}{\partial |V_{ng}|} & \cdots & \frac{\partial P_{ng}}{\partial |V_{ng}|} & \frac{\partial P_{ng+1}}{\partial |V_{ng}|} & \cdots & \frac{\partial P_n}{\partial |V_{ng}|} & \cdots & \frac{\partial Q_1}{\partial |V_{ng}|} & \cdots & \frac{\partial Q_{ng}}{\partial |V_{ng}|} & \frac{\partial Q_{ng+1}}{\partial |V_{ng}|} & \cdots & \frac{\partial Q_n}{\partial |V_{ng}|} \\
\cdots & \cdots & \cdots & \cdots & \cdots & \cdots & \cdots & \cdots & \cdots & \cdots & \cdots & \cdots & \cdots & \cdots \\
\frac{\partial P_1}{\partial |V_n|} & \frac{\partial P_2}{\partial |V_n|} & \cdots & \frac{\partial P_{ng}}{\partial |V_n|} & \frac{\partial P_{ng+1}}{\partial |V_n|} & \cdots & \frac{\partial P_n}{\partial |V_n|} & \cdots & \frac{\partial Q_1}{\partial |V_n|} & \cdots & \frac{\partial Q_{ng}}{\partial |V_n|} & \frac{\partial Q_{ng+1}}{\partial |V_n|} & \cdots & \frac{\partial Q_n}{\partial |V_n|}
\end{bmatrix}
\bullet
\begin{bmatrix} \lambda_1 \\ \cdots \\ \lambda_{ng} \\ \cdots \\ \lambda_n \\ \mu_1 \\ \cdots \\ \mu_{ng} \\ \cdots \\ \mu_n \end{bmatrix} = 0
$$

.....(4.36)

$$
\begin{bmatrix}
\frac{\partial P_2}{\partial \delta_2} & \cdots & \frac{\partial P_n}{\partial \delta_2} & \frac{\partial Q_{ng+1}}{\partial \delta_2} & \cdots & \frac{\partial Q_n}{\partial \delta_2} \\
\cdots & \cdots & \cdots & \cdots & \cdots & \cdots \\
\frac{\partial P_n}{\partial \delta_n} & \cdots & \frac{\partial P_n}{\partial \delta_n} & \frac{\partial Q_{ng+1}}{\partial \delta_n} & \cdots & \frac{\partial Q_n}{\partial \delta_n} \\
\frac{\partial P_2}{\partial |V_{ng+1}|} & \cdots & \frac{\partial P_n}{\partial |V_{ng+1}|} & \frac{\partial Q_{ng+1}}{\partial |V_{ng+1}|} & \cdots & \frac{\partial Q_n}{\partial |V_{ng+1}|} \\
\cdots & \cdots & \cdots & \cdots & \cdots & \cdots \\
\frac{\partial P_2}{\partial |V_n|} & \cdots & \frac{\partial P_n}{\partial |V_n|} & \frac{\partial Q_{ng+1}}{\partial |V_n|} & \cdots & \frac{\partial Q_n}{\partial |V_n|}
\end{bmatrix}
\begin{bmatrix} \lambda_2 \\ \cdots \\ \lambda_n \\ \mu_{ng+1} \\ \\ \mu_n \end{bmatrix}
= (-\lambda_1)
\begin{bmatrix} \frac{\partial P_1}{\partial \delta_2} \\ \cdots \\ \frac{\partial P_1}{\partial \delta_n} \\ \frac{\partial P_1}{\partial |V_{ng+1}|} \\ \cdots \\ \frac{\partial P_1}{\partial |V_n|} \end{bmatrix}
$$

.....(4.37)

Knowing the right hand side vector the λ's and μ' s are computed for all on the left hand side.

The real power generations are computed using these λ values for γ, the incremental production cost using the relations.

$$\gamma_q = k\,\lambda_q; \quad q = 1, 2, \ldots\ ng \qquad .....(4.38)$$

$$\text{and} \quad K = \frac{\left(\sum_{q=1}^{ng} P_{gq} + \sum_{q=1}^{ng} \frac{a_q}{b_{pq}}\right)}{\sum_{q=1}^{ng}\left(\frac{\lambda_q}{b_q}\right)} \qquad .....(4.39)$$

An improved generation schedule is obtained from

$$\gamma_q = a_q + b_q P_{gq} \qquad ....(4.40)$$

At the optimum k becomes unity.

From the voltage magnitude derivatives the voltage magnitudes are computed :

$$\frac{\partial P_1}{\partial|V_P|}\lambda_1 + \frac{\partial P_2}{\partial|V_P|}\lambda_2 + ... + \frac{\partial P_n}{\partial|V_P|}\lambda_n + \frac{\partial Q_{ng+1}}{\partial|V_P|}\mu_{ng+1} + ... + \frac{\partial Q_n}{\partial|V_P|}\mu_n = 0$$

$P = 1, 2, ... ng$ .....(4.41)

The above equations do not appear in (4.37) as they are partitioned out from equn.(4.36). Separating the diagonal self terms for bus P.

$$\frac{\partial P_P}{\partial|V_P|} = 2|V_P||y_{PP}|\text{Cos}\theta_{PP} + \sum_{\substack{q=1 \\ q\neq P}}^{n}|V_q||y_{Pq}|\text{Cos}(\theta_{pq} + \delta_P - \delta_q) \qquad .....(4.42)$$

The influence of δ on reactive power can be neglected while scheduling real power. Voltages $|V_P|$ are calculated during every iteration, until convergence is obtained. Computation of real power generation and voltages is continued till the solution is obtained.

Both Q and |V| are monitored at every iteration and whichever exceeds the limit is set at that value and the node is treated as P, Q bus and that voltage equation drops from Eqn.(4.42). If both are violated, load flows are performed till they lie within the limits.

E. 4.1 For the network shown in Fig. E4.1 the following data is given :

Incremental cost curves

Generating station 1

$$\frac{dF_1}{dF_1} = (24 + 8P_1)\text{Rs./ p.u.MWh}$$

Generating station 2

$$\frac{dF_2}{dF_2} = (19.6 + 8P_2)\text{Rs./ p.u.MWh}$$

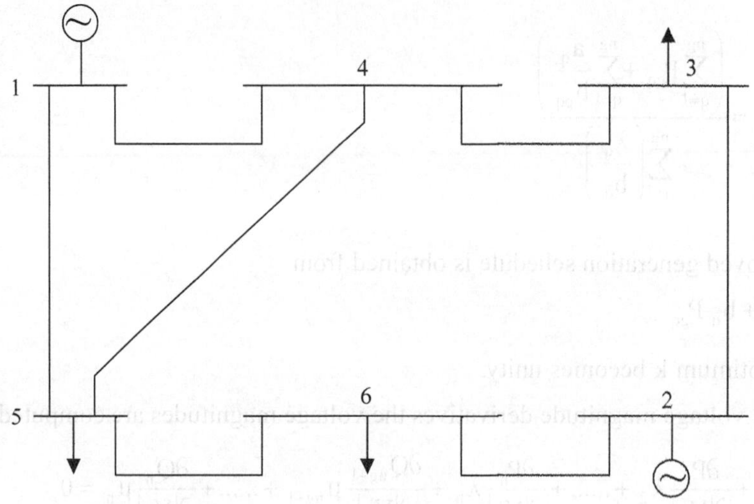

Fig. E4.1

The restrictions on real powers at the stations are

$$0.1 \leq P_1 \leq 1.0 \text{ p.u. MW}$$

$$0.1 \leq P_2 \leq 1.0 \text{ p.u. MW}$$

The load powers are given in Table E4.1.

Table E4.1

Bus	Real Power (p.u. MW)	Reactive Power (p.u. MW)
3	0.55	0.05
4	0.0	0.0
5	0.50	0.05
6	0.30	0.03

Find the most economical generation at stations 1 and 2. Find also the annual savings, if both the plants operate for 7000h in an year.

Solution :

Let bus 1 be the slack bus. Its voltage is assumed (1 + j0.0). Let the generation at bus 2 be arbitrarily assigned as

$$P = 0.80 \text{ p.u. MW and } Q = 0.05 \text{ p.u. MW}$$

Performing load flow computation following the procedure given in chapter 2, the following results are obtained.

Table E4.2 Bus Powers

Bus	Real Power (p.u. MW)	Reactive Power (p.u. MW)
1.	0.70618 (Slack bus)	0.27735 (slack bus)
2.	0.80	0.05
3.	0.55	0.05
4.	0.00	0.0
5.	0.50	0.05
6.	030	0.03
Losses	0.15618	0.19735

The voltages are given in Table E4.2.

Table E4.3

Bus	Symbol	Voltage p.u.
1.	V_1	1+j0.0
2.	V_2	1.04454+j0.18910
3.	V_3	0.95948+j0.17580
4.	V_4	0.90461+j0.12718
5.	V_5	0.88958+j0.15143
6.	V_6	0.89768+j0.1101

The production costs at plant 1 are :

$$(24 + 8 \times 0.70618) \text{ Rs./p.u. MW}$$

The production cost is Rs.5564.944h^{-1}

The load flow solution is optimized using the procedure indicated in Sec. 4.7. The following results are obtained.

$$P_1 = 0.80367 \text{ p.u. MW}$$

$$P_2 = 0.65662 \text{ p.u. MW}$$

Total real power generation = 1.46029 p.u. MW

$$Q_1 = 0.21841 \text{ p.u. MW}$$

$$Q_2 = 0.21841 \text{ p.u. MW}$$

Total reactive power generation = 0.24741 p.u. MW

Table E4.4

Iteration	λ_1	λ_2	λ_3	λ_4	λ_5	λ_6
1.	3.706	2.679	4.037	4.000	4.000	3,897
2.	3.981	3.546	4.444	4.414	4.494	4,444
3.	3.808	2.918	4.193	4.158	4.186	4,095
4.	3.850	3.099	4.244	4.213	4.252	4,173
5.	3.845	3.099	4.4232	4.201	4.239	4,160
6.	3.835	3.084	4.212	4.181	4.215	4,136
7.	3.833	3.094	4.202	4.172	4.204	4,127
8.	3.828	3.096	4.191	4.161	4.192	4,115
9.	3.824	3.098	4.180	4.152	4.180	4,105
10.	3.821	3.100	4.171	4.143	4.170	4,095
11.	3.818	3.101	4.163	4.128	4.162	4,087
12.	3.815	3.103	4.156	4.135	4.154	4,080
13.	3.812	3.104	4.150	4.122	4.146	4,073
14.	3.810	3.106	4.144	4.116	4.140	4,067
15.	3.808	3.107	4.138	4.111	4.134	4,061
16.	3.804	3.108	4.133	4.106	4.128	4,056

Table E4.5

Iteration	μ_3	μ_4	μ_5	μ_6
1.	0.0178	0.0430	0.1153	0.1433
2.	0.0315	0.0547	0.1189	0.1235
3.	0.0207	0.0501	0.1244	0.1404
4.	0.0202	0.0473	0.1162	0.1292
5.	0.1783	0.0447	0.1125	0.1260
6.	0.0150	0.0417	0.1086	0.1230
7.	0.0126	0.0390	0.1047	0.1193
8.	0.0104	0.0366	0.1013	0.1163
9..	0.0084	0.0345	0.0983	0.1137
10.	0.0068	0.0326	0.0956	0.1114
11.	0.0053	0.0310	0.0933	0.1093
12.	0.0040	0.0295	0.0912	0.1075
13.	0.0027	0.0282	0.0896	0.1058
14.	0.0016	0.0270	0.0876	0.1043
15.	0.0006	0.0260	0.0861	0.1030
16.	-0.0003	0.0249	0.0846	0.1017

Note : $\mu_1 = \mu_2 = 0.0$

Total real power losses = 0.11029 p.u. MW

Total reactive power losses = 0.24741 p.u. MW

The voltages at the buses are :

$V_1 = 1.04676 + j0.0$ p.u.

$V_2 = 1.10437 + j0.0774$ p.u.

$V_3 = 1.02699 - j0.19679$ p.u.

$V_4 = 0.95996 - j0.14310$ p.u.

$V_5 = 0.94362 - j0.17032$ p.u.

$V_6 = 0.960066 - j0.15036$ p.u.

The total production costs are Rs.5528.232h^{-1}

The savings per hour are Rs. 5564.944 – 5528-232 = Rs.36.71 h^{-1}

Annual savings with 7000 working hours is

$$7000 \times 36.71 = \text{Rs. } 258.370$$

The variation of Lagrange multipliers during iterations is shown in Tables E4.4 and E4.5.

Questions

4.1 Bring out the salient features in optimal operation of generators in thermal and hydro plants.

4.2 Discuss the various constraints to be considered for economic load dispatch problem.

4.3 What is an optimal power flow? Explain the problem in detail.

4.4 What are Kuhn – Tucker conditions? How are they employed

4.5 Explain how Kuhn – Tucker conditions are useful in optimal load flow.

4.6 Explain the non – linear programming method for optimal power flow

4.7 Explain reactive power control loss minimization

4.8 Explain gradient method for optimal power flow.

Problems

P4.1 Consider the Six bus system shown in Fig. P4.1.

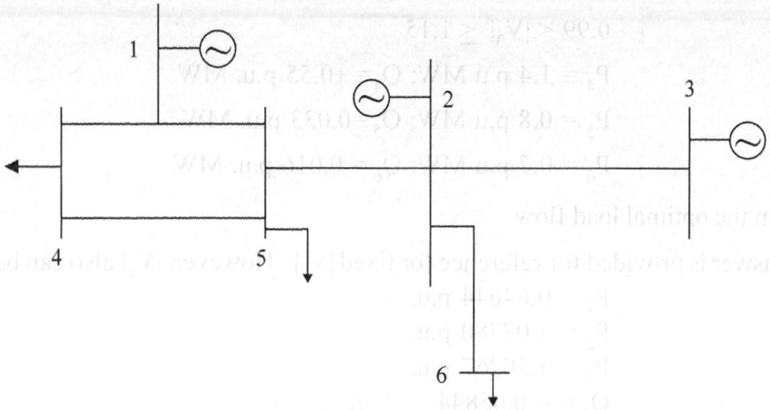

Fig. P4.1

The bus admittance matrix is given as follows

14,45 – j32,50	0,0	0,0	– 5,48 + j8,10	– 9,0 + j24,40	0,0
0,0	7,33 – j28,25	– 1,0 + 5,50	0,0	– 5,05 + j16,30	– 1,25 + j6,44
0,0	– 1,0 + j5,50	1,0 – j5,50	0,0	0,0	0,0
– 5,48 + j8,10	0,0	0,0	10,03 – j22,70	– 4,55 + j14,60	0,0
– 9,0 + j24,60	– 5,05 + j16,30	0,0	– 4,55 + j14,60	18,6 – j55,30	0,0
0,0	– 1,28 + j6,44	0,0	0,0	0,0	1,28 – j6,44

The incremental cost characteristics are given by

$$\frac{dC_1}{dP_1} = 3.85 + P_1$$

$$\frac{dC_2}{dP_2} = 3.25 + P_2$$

$$\frac{dC_3}{dP_3} = 2.75 + P_3$$

The constraints are

$$0.1 < P_1 < 1.0$$

$$0.15 < P_2 < 1.5$$

$0.15 < P_3 \leq 1.5$

$0.99 < |V_1| \leq 1.15$

$0.99 < |V_2| \leq 1.15$

$0.99 < |V_3| \leq 1.15$

$P_4 = 1.4$ p.u MW; $Q_4 = +0.55$ p.u. MW

$P_5 = 0.8$ p.u MW; $Q_5 = 0.033$ p.u. MW

$P_6 = 0.7$ p.u MW; $Q_6 = 0.016$ p.u. MW

Obtain the optimal load flow

An answer is provided for reference for fixed $|V_1|$. However, $|V_1|$ also can be optimized.

$P_1 = 0.64644$ p.u.
$P_2 = 1.07780$ p.u.
$P_3 = 1.30267$ p.u.
$Q_1 = -0.05844$
$Q_2 = -0.43422$
$Q_3 = 0.2351$
$V_1 = 1.5 + j0.0$
$V_2 = 1.08667 + j0.67867$
$V_3 = 1.10884 + j0.28434$
$V_4 = 1.02292 - j0.0475$
$V_5 = 1.04923 - j0.00235$
$V_6 = 1.06258 - j0.01875$

The Lagrange multipliers

$\lambda_1 = 4.49644$

$\lambda_2 = 4.327741$

$\lambda_3 = 4.052448$

$\lambda_4 = 4.724052$

$\lambda_5 = 4.536256$

$\lambda_6 = 4.489106$

$\mu_1 = \mu_2 = \mu_3 = 0$

$\mu_4 = 0.018764$

$\mu_5 = 0.009117$

$\mu_6 = 0.011654$

5 UNIT COMMITMENT

The life style of a modern man follows regular habits and hence the present society also follows regularly repeated cycles or pattern in daily life. Therefore, the consumption of electrical energy also follows a predictable daily, weekly and seasonal pattern. There are periods of high power consumption as well as low power consumption. It is therefore possible to commit the generating units from the available capacity into service to meet the demand. The previous discussions all deal with the computational aspects for allocating load to a plant in the most economical manner. For a given combination of plants the determination of optimal combination of plants for operation at any one time is also desired for carrying out the aforesaid task. The plant commitment and unit ordering schedules extend the period of optimization from a few minutes to several hours. From daily schedules weekly patterns can be developed. Likewise, monthly, seasonal and annual schedules can be prepared taking into consideration the repetitive nature of the load demand and seasonal variations. Unit commitment schedules are thus required for economically committing the units in plants to service with the time at which individual units should be taken out from or returned to service.

5.1 Cost Function Formulation

Let F_i be the cost of operating the ith unit when supplying an output of P_i. Then, if C_i is the running cost coefficient

$$F_i = C_i P_i$$

where C_i may vary depending on the loading condition.

We may thus define a variable cost coefficient C_{ij} for ith unit when operating at jth load for which the corresponding active power is P_{ij}. Since the level of operation is a function of time, the cost coefficient may be described with yet another index to denote the time of operation, so that it becomes C_{ijt} for the sub interval t corresponding to a power output of P_{ijt}.

If each unit is capable of operation at k discrete levels, then the running cost F_{it} of unit i in the time interval t is given by

$$F_{it} = \sum_{j=1}^{k} C_{ijt} P_{ijt}$$

If there are N units available for service in the interval t then the total running cost of N units during the period t is

$$F_{iNt} = \sum_{i=1}^{N} \sum_{j=1}^{k} C_{ijt} P_{ijt}$$

For the entire time period of optimization, having T such sub-intervals of time, the overall running cost for all the units may be put in the form

$$F_T = \sum_{t=1}^{T} \sum_{i=1}^{N} \sum_{j=1}^{k} C_{ijt} P_{ijt}$$

Suppose that for a plant to be brought into service, an additional expenditure C_{si} has to be incurred in addition to the running cost, then the start up cost of the unit i, the cost of starting X units during any subinterval is given by

$$F_{sc} = \sum_{i=1}^{X} C_{sci} \delta_{it}$$

where $\delta_{it} = 1$ if the ith unit is started in sub-interval t and is zero other wise

In a similar manner, if a plant is taken out of service during scheduling period, the cost of shutting down also must be taken into account. If Y units are to be shutdown during the sub-interval t, the shutdown cost may be represented by

$$F_{sd} = \sum_{i=1}^{Y} C_{sdi} \bullet \sigma_{it}$$

where $\sigma_{it} = 1$ when unit i is taken from service in sub-interval t and is zero otherwise.

The start up and shut down costs for X and Y units over the complete scheduling period containing T sub intervals are given respectively by

$$F_{scT} = \sum_{t=1}^{T} \sum_{i=1}^{X} C_{sct} \delta_{it}$$

and $$F_{sdT} = \sum_{t=1}^{T} \sum_{i=1}^{Y} C_{sdt} \sigma_{it}$$

The total expression for the cost function including running, start up and shut down costs will then have the form,

$$F_T = \sum_{t=1}^{T} \left[\sum_{i=1}^{Y} C_{sdi} \sigma_{it} + \sum_{i=1}^{X} C_{sci} \delta_{it} + \sum_{i=1}^{N} \sum_{j=1}^{K} C_{ijt} P_{ijt} \right] \qquad .....(5.1)$$

For each sub-interval of time t, the number of generating units to be committed to service, the generators to be shut-down and the quantized power loading levels that minimize the total cost have to be determined.

5.2 Constraints for Plant Commitment Schedules

As in the optimal point generation scheduling the output of each generator must be within the minimum and maximum value of loading

$$P_i^{min} \le P_{ijt} \le P_i^{max} \qquad .....(5.2)$$

where $i = 1, 2, ... N$

$j = 1, 2, ... k$

$t = 1, 2, ... T$

The total available plant capacity from which schedules are to be prepared must be in excess of the plant generating capacity required in meeting the predicted load demand and in satisfying the requirements for minimum running reserve capacity during the entire period of scheduling.

$$S_{TAC} \ge \sum_{i=1}^{N} P_i^{max} \alpha_{it} + S_r^{min} \qquad .....(5.3)$$

where S_{TAC} is the total available capacity in any sub-interval t and S_r^{min} is the minimum running reserve capacity.

$\alpha_{it} = 1$, if generator i is in operation during the sub-interval t and is zero otherwise.

In addition, for a predicted total load demand P_D, the total generation operated in sub-interval t must be in excess of the load demand by an amount not less than the minimum running reserve capacity S_r^{min}.

$$\sum_{i=1}^{N} \sum_{j=1}^{k} P_{ijt} \ge P_D + S_r^{min} \qquad .....(5.4)$$

Where the transmission losses P_L are also considered eqn.(5.4) then becomes

$$\sum_{i=1}^{N} \sum_{j=1}^{k} P_{ijt} \ge P_D + S_r^{min} + P_L \qquad ......(5.5)$$

The generator start-up and shut down logic indicators δ_{it} and σ_{it} respectively must be unity during the corresponding sub-intervals of operation, or

$$\alpha_{it} - \alpha_{i(t-1)} = \delta_{it} - \sigma_{it}$$

$i = 1, ... N$

$t = 1, ... T$

5.3 Priority – List Method

In this method full load average production cost is computed for every unit. Then in the order of ascending costs, the units are arranged for commitment. The method will be explained through an example. Consider three thermal plants operating with the following incremental fuel rate characteristics.

Plant 1 :

$F_1 = (7 + 0.003\ P_1)\ 10^3$ k-cal/Mw-hr

$P_1^{max} = 500$ MW and $P_1^{min} = 50$MW

Plant 2 :

$F_2 = (7.5 + 0.002\ P_2)\ 10^3$ k-cal/Mw-hr

$P_2^{max} = 400$ MW and $P_2^{min} = 40$ MW

Plant 3 :

$F_3 = (8 + 0.004\ P_3)\ 10^3$ k-cal/Mw-hr

$P_3^{max} = 200$ MW and $P_3^{min} = 20$ MW

The fuel costs at the plants are given by

$CP_1 = 1.1$ Rs/kcal

$CP_2 = 1.05$ Rs/kcal

$CP_3 = 1.2$ Rs/kcal

The full load average production cost at plant 1

$= 10^3\ (7 + 0.003 \times 500)1.1 = 10^3\ (7 + 1.5)1.1$

$= 9.35 \times 10^3$ Rs/MwHr

The full load average production cost at plant 2

$= 10^3\ (7.5 + 0.002 \times 400)1.05$

$= 10^3\ (7{+}0.8)1.05 = 8.715 \times 10^3$ Rs/MwHr

The full load average production cost at plant 3

$= 10^3\ (8 + 0.004 \times 200)1.2 = 10^3\ (8 + 0.8)1.2$

$= 10^3\ (8.8) = 10.56 \times 10^3$ Rs/MwHr

In the order of increasing costs the following table is constructed.

Unit	Rs/MwHr	Max (MW)	Min (MW)
2	8.715×10^3	400	40
1	9.35×10^3	500	50
3	10.56×10^3	200	20

The priority list for supplying a load upto 1000 Mw is prepared as follows which is self explanatory.

Units	Max (MW)	Min (MW)
2,1 and 3	1000	110
2,1	900	90
2	400	40

Table 5.1 Priority list for supply of 100MW

The general procedure can be then stated as :

1. Check at the end of every hour of operation, if the load demand has fallen. If the demand has decreased check if the last unit in the priority list is dropped, the load demand can be met, satisfying the spinning reserve requirement. Status quo is maintained if the demand cannot be met.
2. If it is possible to drop the unit in step 1, then determine the number of hours "h" before the unit is required again for service. If this "h" is less than the shut down and start up times for the unit, it has to be left in service without removal.
3. Then, calculate the cost of floating the unit within the system without supplying any generation and the cost of shut down and start up processes and if there is sufficient savings from shutting it down, and starting it again for service it can be removed.
4. The process is to be repeated for the next unit on the priority list and continued.

5.4 Dynamic Programming

This method can be applied to problems in which many sequential decisions are required to be taken in defining the optimum operation of a system or process composed of a distinct number of stages. However, it is suitable only when the decisions at the later stages do not affect the operation at the earlier stages. Dynamic programming is based on the principle of optimality enunciated by Bellman in 1957. It states that "an optimal policy has the property, that, whatever the initial state and the initial decisions are, the remaining decisions must constitute an optimal policy with regard to the state resulting from the first decision".

Hence, the method is suitable only to multistage decision processes where a decision taken at one stage does not influence the preceding events in the sequence but affect only what follows later. The principle and methodology will be explained through a routing problem.

Consider the route map shown in Fig. 5.1. The values on the routes are the cost of transport along the route. Let G be the goal to be reached from any of the locations A, B, C, D, E, F. Traffic is allowed only along the direction shown on the routes.

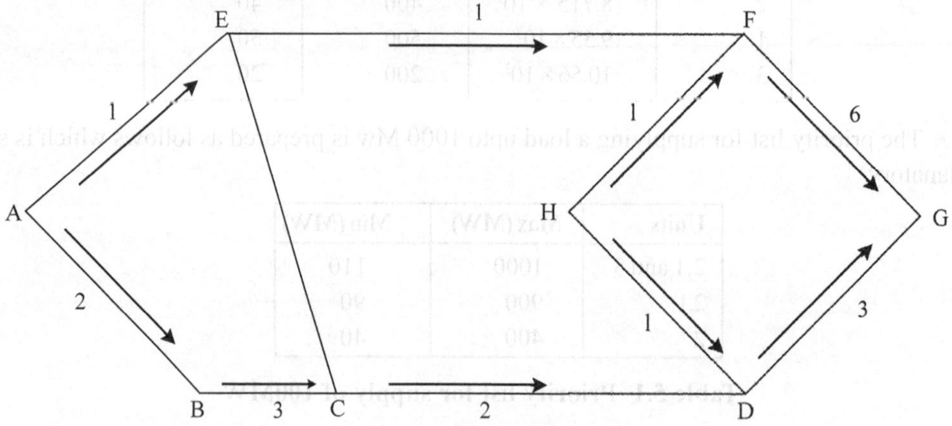

Fig. 5.1 The Routing Problem

It is desired to reach the goal G or destination G from the various locations. The costs are as indicated.

From D to reach G

$$C_{DG} = 3 = C_{DG}^0$$

From H to reach G via D

$$C_{HG}^0 = C_{HD} + C_{DG}^0 = 1 + 3 = 4$$

From C to reach G via D

$$C_{CG}^0 = C_{CD} + C_{DG}^0 = 2 + 3 = 5$$

In a similar manner

$$C_{FG}^0 = \text{Min}\left[C_{FG}, C_{FH} + C_{HG}^0\right] = \text{Min}[6, 1+4] = 5$$

$$C_{EG}^0 = \left[C_{EF} + C_{FG}^0, C_{EC} + C_{CG}^0\right] = [1+5, 4+5] = 6 \quad \text{along EFHDG}$$

$$C_{BG}^0 = \left[C_{BC} + C_{CG}^0\right] = [3+5] = 8 \quad \text{along B C D G}$$

$$C_{AG}^0 = \text{Min}\left(C_{AB} + C_{BG}^0, C_{AE} + C_{EG}^0\right) = \text{Min}[2+8, 1+6] = 7 \quad \text{along A E F H D G}$$

We can thus conclude that the minimum cost to move from one location P to another location R via Q is given by

$$C_{PR} = C_{PQ} + C_{QR}^0$$

where C_{PQ} is the cost to move from P to Q and C_{QR}^0 is the optimal cost to move from Q to R.

The optimal decision at Q is taken based on

$$C^{0}_{QR} = \text{Min}[C_{QIR}, C_{Q2R}, ..., C_{QNR}]$$

where Q1R, Q2R ..... QNR are the n alternative paths available to reach R from Q.

5.5 Unit Commitment by Dynamic Programming

In general load changes in small steps. For the complete load cycle, it is possible to apply dynamic programming method for unit commitment. For this, the number of units available, the cost characteristics of these units and the load cycle are the data required. Assuming that this information is made available, the functional recurrence relations of the method will be applied now

Let N units in service supply a total load of $\sum_{i=1}^{N} P_i$.

The total operating cost for this generation = $F_N\left(\sum_{i=1}^{N} P_i\right)$

This cost can be divided into two components as follows:

(i) The first component is the cost of operating (N-1) units to supply a reduced demand of $\sum_{i=1}^{N-1} P_i$. The operating cost for this generation is $F_{N-1}\left(\sum_{i=1}^{N} P_i\right)$

(ii) The second component is the cost of operating the Nth unit at an active power output of P_N is $f_N(P_N)$.

The cost of supplying the total load $\sum_{i=1}^{N} P_i = P_N + \sum_{i=1}^{N-1} P_i$ is given now by

$$f_N\left(P_N + \sum_{i=1}^{N-1} P_i\right) = f_N(P_N) + F_{N-1}\left(\sum_{i=1}^{N-1} P_i\right)$$

Hence

$$f_N\left(\sum_{i=1}^{N} P_i\right) = \min\left[f_N(P_N) + F_{N-1}\left(\sum_{i=1}^{N-1} P_i\right)\right]$$

subject to constraints.

Thus, the problem of unit commitment is converted into a multistage decision process. To start with the solution to the problem, consider the single stage decision process of selecting one unit that will provide the lowest cost of generation up to the maximum capacity of the unit. Once such a unit is picked up, the first stage of optimization is completed.

Let the cost of operating this first unit be $f_1(P_1)$ when supplying P_1

$$F_1(P_1) = f_1(P_1)$$

The optimal combination of this unit with a second unit can be derived next to supply a load of P_1+P_2 for which the optimal cost is

$$F_2(P_1 + P_2) = \min [f_2(P_2) + F_1(P_1)]$$

Since $F_1(P_1)$ is already the optimal value, the best unit to supply P_2 from the rest of (N-1) units will be picked up during this second stage of optimization for lowest possible cost of production.

In a similar way, the best 3 unit combination is found from

$$F_3(P_1 + P_2 + P_3) = \min [f_3(P_3) + F_2 (P_1 + P_2)]$$

Subject to constraints and so on, so that finally we arrive at

$$F_N\left(\sum_{i=1}^{N} P_i\right) = \min f_N(P_N) + F_{N-1}\left(\sum_{i=1}^{N-1} P_i\right)$$

which is the required solution.

E 5.1 Obtain the economic schedule for the two units, the production costs of which are given as follows, to supply a load of 3MW, in steps of 1MW

$$C_1 = 0.8\, p_1^2 + 25\, P_1$$

$$C_2 = 1.2\, p_2^2 + 22\, P_2$$

Use dynamic programming method.

Solution : With usual notation

$$F_1(3) = f_1(3) = 0.8 \times 3^2 + 25 \times 3 = 7.2 + 75 = 82.2$$

$$F_2(3) = \min\,[f_2(0) + f_1(3),\ f_2(1) + F_1(2),\ F_2(2) + F_1(1),\ F_2(3) + F_1(0)]$$

$$= \min\,[0 + 82.2,\ 1.2 + 22 + 3.2 + 50,\ 4.8 + 44 + 0.8 + 25,\ 10.8 + 66 + 0]$$

$$= \min\,[82.2,\ 76.4,\ 75.6,\ 76.8] = 74.6$$

The most economical combination is unit 1 supplying 1MW and unit 2 supplying 2 MW.

E 5.2 If only a load of 2MW is to be supplied, how are the units to be committed in E5.1.

Solution :

$$F_1(2) = f_1(2) = 0.8 \times 2^2 + 25 \times 2 = 53.2$$

$$F_2(2) = \mathrm{Min}\,[\,f_2(0) + F_1(2),\ f_2(1) + F_1(1),\ f_2(2) + F_1(0)]$$

$$= \min\,[\,53.2,\ 1.2 + 22 + 0.8 + 25,\ 1.2 \times 4 + 22 \times 2 + 0]$$

$$= \min\,[\,53.2,\ 49,\ 48.8]$$

$F_2(2) = f_2(2) + F_1(0)$. Unit 2 supplies the total load for economy

From the above two examples unit commitment schedule may be now prepared based on the two results.

Load range	Unit in service
1 MW	2
2 MW	2
3 MW	2 and 3

For more accuracy the step size can be reduced to 0.5 MW, 0.2Mw or even 0.1 Mw. The smaller the step, size, the larger the calculations needed.

Questions

5.1 Explain the unit commitment problem.

5.2 What are the various constraints in unit commitment problem ? List them.

5.3 Explain the priority – list method for unit commitment.

5.4 Discuss the dynamic programming method to solve unit commitment problem in a power system.

5.5 What is the cost function for unit commitment ? Explain

Problems

P 5.1 Write down the recurrence functional relation for scheduling generation among 5 units to meet a load demand of 10MW in steps of 2MW.

P5.2 Use dynamic programming method to determine the most economical units to be committed to supply a load of 6MW. There are three units with the following data

$$C_1 = 0.8P_1^2 + 22P_1$$

$$C_2 = 0.85P_2^2 + 21P_2$$

$$C_3 = 0.8P_3^2 + 20P_3$$

The maximum and minimum capacities of each unit are 5MW and 1MW respectively.

P5.3 Use dynamic programming method to determine the most economical units to be committed to supply a load of 9MW. There are four units with the following data.

$$C_1 = \frac{1}{2}0.9P_1^2 + 23P_1$$

$$C_2 = \frac{1}{2}1.0P_2^2 + 22P_2$$

$$C_3 = \frac{1}{2}1.0P_3^2 + 21P_3$$

$$C_4 = \frac{1}{2}1.0P_4^2 + 20P_4$$

The maximum and minimum limits for each unit are 6 MW and 1MW respectively.

P5.4 Given the input output cost curves

$$F_1(P_1) = 21 + 6P_1 + 0.0012P_1^2 \text{ Rs/kcal}$$

$$F_2(P_2) = 21 + 7P_2 + 0.001P_2^2 \text{ Rs/kcal}$$

$$F_3(P_3) = 17 + 8P_3 + 0.0011P_3^2 \text{ Rs/kcal}$$

The maximum and minimum values are

$$30 \leq P_1 \leq 300 \text{ MW}$$
$$40 \leq P_2 \leq 400 \text{ MW}$$
$$25 \leq P_3 \leq 250 \text{ MW}$$

Obtain unit commitment schedule for a load demand of 600MW.

6 LOAD FREQUENCY CONTROL

In a power system the load demand is continuously changing. In accordance with it the power input has also to vary. If the input – output balance is not maintained a change in frequency will occur. The control of frequency is achieved primarily through speed governor mechanism aided by supplementary means for precise control. At the outset, the speed governor mechanisms and its operation will be presented.

Governor : The power system is basically dependent upon the synchronous generator and its satisfactory performance. The important control loops in the system are :

(i) frequency control, and

(ii) automatic voltage control.

In this chapter the frequency control will be discussed. Frequency control is achieved through generator control mechanism. The governing systems for thermal and hydro generating plants are different in nature since, the inertia of water that flows into the turbine presents additional constrains which are not present with steam flow in a thermal plant. However, the basic principle is still the same; i.e. the speed of the shaft is sensed and compared with a reference, and the feed back signal is utilized to increase or decrease the power generated by controlling the inlet valve to turbine of steam or water as the case may be.

6.1 Speed Governing Mechanism

The speed governing mechanism includes the following parts.

Speed Governor : It is an error sensing device in load frequency control. It includes all the elements that are directly responsive to speed and influence other elements of the system to initiate action.

Governor Controlled Valves: They control the input to the turbine and are actuated by the speed control mechanism.

Speed Control Mechanism : It includes all equipment such as levers and linkages, servomotors, amplifying devices and relays that are placed between the speed governor and the governor controlled valves.

Speed Changer : It enables the speed governor system to adjust the speed of the turbo generator unit while in operation.

6.2 Speed Governor

A simple schematic representation of the governor is shown in Fig. 6.1.

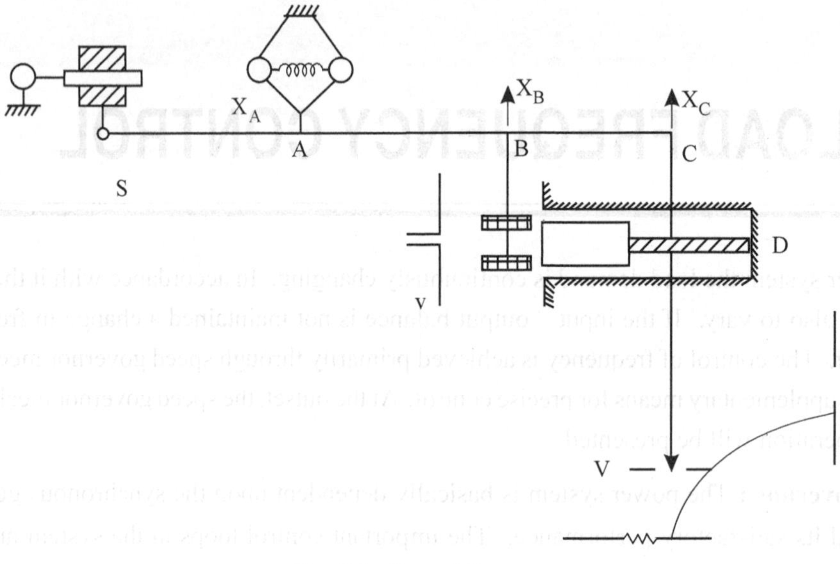

Fig. 6.1 Speed Governor

The pilot valve v operates to increase or decrease the opening of the steam inlet valve V. Let X_B and X_C be the changes in the position of the pilot valve v and control valve V responding to a change in governor position. X_A due to load.

When the pilot valve is closed $X_B = 0$ and $X_C \cong 0$, (i.e.,) the control valve is not completely closed, as the unit has to supply its no-load losses. Let ω_0 be the no-load angular speed of the turbine. As load is applied, the speed falls and through the linkages the governor operates to move the piston P downwards along with points A and B. The pilot valve v admits oil under D and lifts it up so that the input is increased and speed raised. If the link BC is removed then the pilot valve comes to rest only when the speed returns to its original value. An "isochronous" characteristic will be obtained with such an arrangement where speed is restored to its preload-disturbance value. This is shown in Fig. 6.2 and Fig. 6.3.

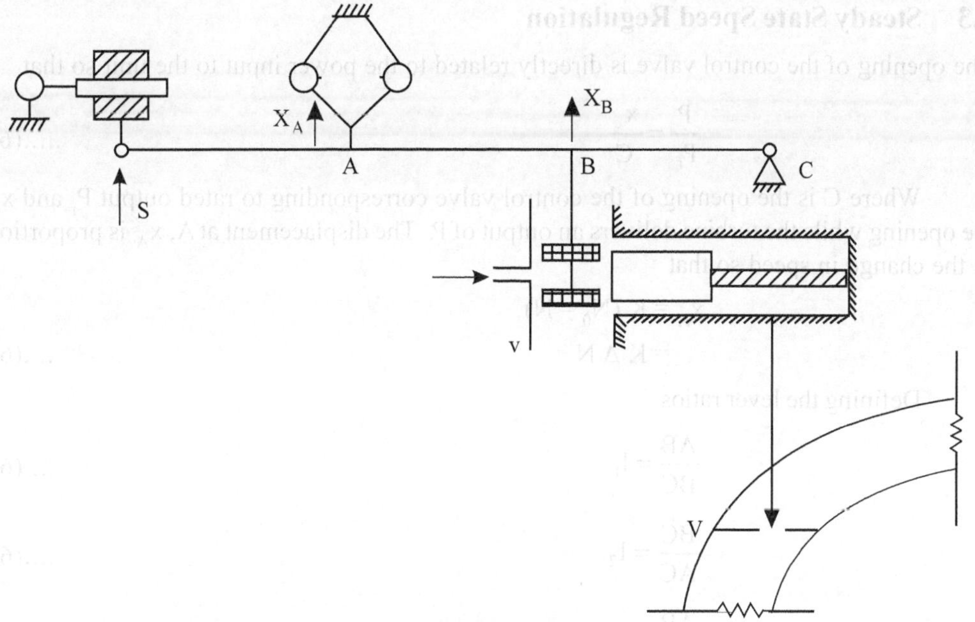

Fig. 6.2 Isochronous Governor

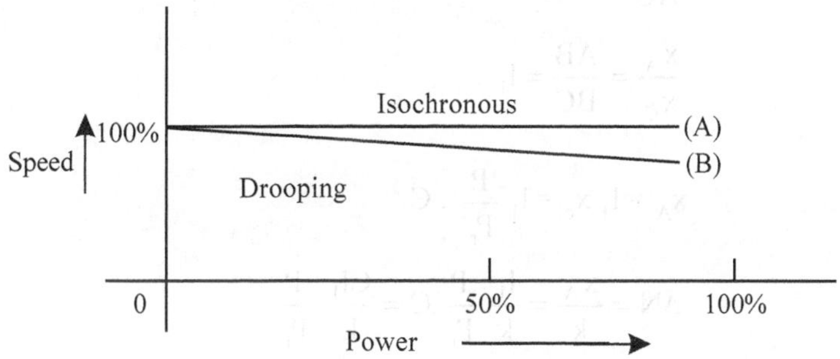

Fig. 6.3 Governor Characteristics

With the link BC, the steady state is reached at a speed slightly lower than the no load speed giving a drooping characteristic for the governor system. A finite value of the steady-state speed regulation is obtained with this arrangement. For a given speed changer position, the per unit steady state speed regulation is defined by

$$\text{Steady state speed regulation} = \frac{N_0 - N}{N_r}$$

Where N_0 = Speed at no – load
N_r = Rated speed
N = Speed at rated load

The isochronous and drooping characteristics are shown in Fig. 6.3.

6.3 Steady State Speed Regulation

The opening of the control valve is directly related to the power input to the unit so that

$$\frac{P}{P_r} = \frac{x_c}{C} \quad .....(6.1)$$

Where C is the opening of the control valve corresponding to rated output P_r and x_c is the opening while the turbine delivers an output of P. The displacement at A, x_A is proportional to the change in speed so that

$$x_A = K(N_0 - N)$$
$$= K \Delta N \quad .....(6.2)$$

Defining the lever ratios

$$\frac{AB}{BC} = l_1 \quad .....(6.3)$$

$$\frac{BC}{AC} = l_2 \quad .....(6.4)$$

and

$$\frac{AB}{AC} = l_3 \quad .....(6.5)$$

$$\frac{x_A}{x_C} = \frac{AB}{BC} = l_1 \quad .....(6.6)$$

so that

$$x_A = l_1 x_c = l_1 \frac{P}{P_r} . C$$

$$\Delta N = \frac{x_A}{k} = \frac{l_1}{k} . \frac{P}{P_r} . C = \frac{Cl_1}{k} . \frac{P}{P_r} \quad .....(6.7)$$

The steady state speed regulation

$$R = \frac{N_0 - N}{N_r} = \frac{Cl_1}{k} . \frac{P}{P_r N_r} = \left(\frac{Cl_1}{k} . \frac{1}{P_r N_r} \right) P \quad .....(6.8)$$

thus, the steady state speed regulation is directly proportional to the output power.

R has the dimension of Hz/MW.

6.4 Adjustment of Governor Characteristics

For a given governor R can be changed by varying the lever ratio l_1 and the no load speed N_0. The droop of the governor characteristics can be changed from curve B to B| as in Fig. 6.3 by changing the lever ratio l_1. Generally in order to coordinate a generating unit with the rest of the system, the lever ratio l_1 is adjusted. This is done occasionally and when the machine is cold.

When the machine is in operation the no load speed N_0 can be adjusted by varying an external force acting on the governor thrust sleeve at S so that the characteristic is shifted parallel to itself as shown by curves C and D. This is achieved by the speed changer. See Fig. 6.4.

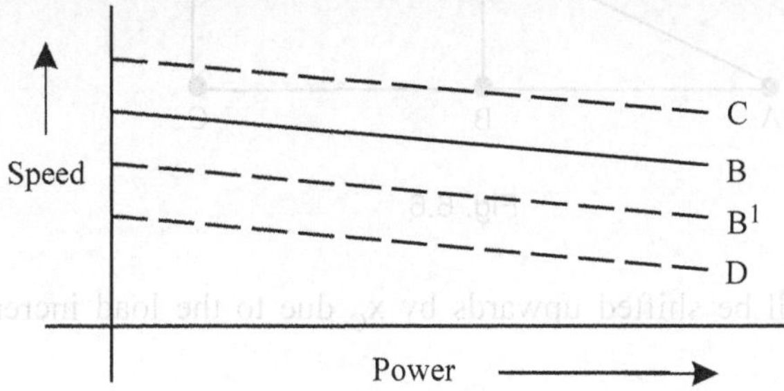

Fig. 6.4 Action of speed changer

6.5 Transfer Function of Speed Control Mechanism

From Eqn. (6.2).

$$x_A = K (N_0 - N)$$

$$= K^{\prime} (\omega_0 - \omega) = k^{\prime} \Delta\omega \qquad .....(6.9)$$

If the point C is fixed, then

$$\frac{x_B}{x_A} = \frac{BC}{AC} = l_2 \qquad .....(6.10)$$

$$x_B = l_2 x_A \qquad .....(6.11)$$

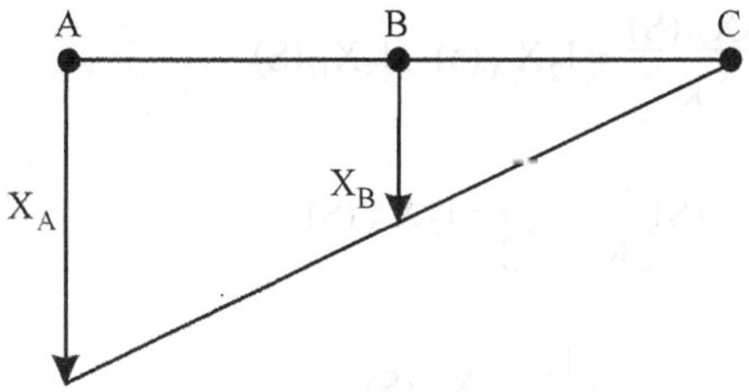

Fig. 6.5

If C were to move with A fixed then from Fig. 6.6.

$$\frac{x_B}{x_C} = \frac{AB}{AC} = l_3$$

$$x_B = l_3 \,.\, x_C\, z$$

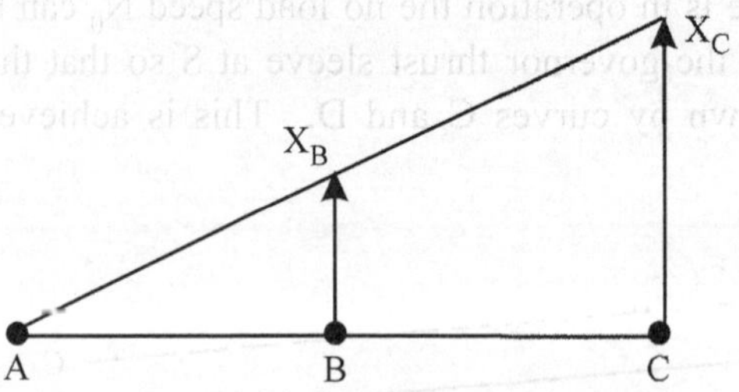

Fig. 6.6

As the point C will be shifted upwards by x_C due to the load increment, the actual movement of B would be

$$\therefore \qquad x_B = l_2\, x_A - l_3\, x_C \qquad .....(6.12)$$

The opening of the pilot valve, x_B determines the rate of oil flow into the cylinder. The movement of the control valve, x_C is proportional to the total oil admitted under the piston P.

Therefore,

$$x_C = k \int x_B \; ; \qquad \text{where k is a constant} \qquad .....(6.13)$$

Taking Laplace transform on both sides.

$$X_C(S) = \frac{k}{s} X_B(S) \qquad .....(6.14)$$

Taking Laplace transform of Eqn. (6.12),

$$X_B(S) = l_2 X_A(S) - l_3 X_C(S) \qquad .....(6.15)$$

substituting for $X_B(s)$ in (6.14),

$$\frac{sX_C(S)}{k} = l_2 X_A(s) - l_3 X_C(S) \qquad .....(6.16)$$

$$X_c(S)\left[\frac{s}{k} + l_3\right] = l_2 X_A(S) \qquad .....(6.17)$$

$$X_C(S) = \frac{\left(l_2/l_3\right) X_A(S)}{\left(\frac{s}{kl_3} + 1\right)} \qquad .....(6.18)$$

$$= \frac{k_S}{1 + T_S S} X_A(S) \qquad .....(6.19)$$

$$\frac{1}{k\,l_3} = T_S$$

is the time constant of the speed control mechanism and is of the order of several milliseconds. The transfer function of the speed control mechanism

$$G_{SC}(S) = \frac{X_C(S)}{X_A(S)} = \frac{K_S}{1 + sT_S} \quad .....(6.21)$$

6.6 Transfer Function of a Power System

Under steady state operating conditions the synchronous angular frequency

$\omega_s = 2\pi f_s$ where f_s is the synchronous frequency (i.e.) the rated frequency.

$\Delta\delta =$ Change in angular position of the generator rotor corresponding to an increased load demand ΔP_D on the generator.

$$\delta = \delta_s + \Delta\delta \text{ radians} \quad .....(6.22)$$

$$\omega = \frac{d}{dt}(\delta) = \frac{d}{dt}(\delta_s + \Delta\delta) = \omega_s + \frac{d}{dt}\Delta\delta \quad .....(6.23)$$

$$\omega = \omega_s + \Delta\omega \text{ rad/sec} \quad .....(6.24)$$

Let $f = f_s + \Delta f$ .....(6.25)

Where $\Delta f = \frac{1}{2\pi}\frac{d}{dt}\Delta\delta \text{Hz}$ .....(6.26)

The kinetic energy stored in the machine

$$W = \frac{1}{2}I\omega^2 = \frac{1}{2}I(2\pi f)^2 \text{ MJ} \quad .....(6.27)$$

The kinetic energy at synchronous speed is

$$W_s = \frac{1}{2}I(2\pi f_S)^2 \text{ MJ} \quad .....(6.28)$$

Then $W = W_S\left(\frac{f}{f_S}\right)^2 \text{ MJ}$ .....(6.29)

$$W = W_S\left(\frac{f_S + \Delta f}{f_S}\right)^2 \quad .....(6.30)$$

$$\cong W_S\left(\frac{1+2\Delta f}{f_S}\right) \text{ for smal } \frac{\Delta f}{f_S} 1 \qquad .....(6.31)$$

The rate of change of kinetic energy is the increase in power

$$\frac{d}{dt}(W) = \frac{2W_S}{f_S}\frac{d}{dt}(\Delta f) \qquad .....(6.32)$$

Defining per unit inertia constant $H = \frac{W_S}{P_r}$

$$\frac{d}{dt}(W) = \frac{2H}{f_S}\frac{d}{dt}(\Delta f)\text{p.u. taking } P_r = 1.0 \text{ pu} \qquad .....(6.33)$$

Further, all types of composite loads experience a change in power consumption with frequency. Defining the load damping factor.

$$D = \frac{\partial P_D}{\partial f} \text{ p.u. MW/Hz} \qquad .....(6.34)$$

Where P_D is the load demand in p.u.; the change in load demand in this case is then $D.\,\Delta f$ p.u.M.W

For a small step change in load demand by ΔP_D the power balance equation can be written as

$$\Delta P_G - \Delta P_D = D\Delta f + \frac{2H}{f_S}\frac{d}{dt}(\Delta f) \qquad .....(6.35)$$

Taking Laplace transform of the above equation

$$[\Delta P_G(S) - \Delta P_D(S)] = D\Delta F(S) + \frac{2H}{f_S}.S.\Delta F(S) \qquad .....(6.36)$$

$$\Delta F(S) = [\Delta P_G(S) - \Delta P_D(S)]\frac{1}{\left[D + \frac{2H}{f_S}\right]} \qquad .....(6.37)$$

$$= [\Delta P_G(s) - \Delta P_D(s)]\frac{1/D}{\left[1 + s.\frac{2H}{f_s D}\right]} \qquad .....(6.38)$$

$$\therefore \qquad \Delta F(S) = [\Delta P_G(S) - \Delta P_D(S)]\left(\frac{K_P}{1+sT_P}\right) \qquad .....(6.39)$$

where $$K_p = \frac{1}{D}\,\text{Hz/p.u.M.W.} \qquad .....(6.40)$$

and $$T_P = \frac{2H}{f_S D} \qquad .....(6.41)$$

The transfer function relating the frequency change to the change in input-output power may be then written as

$$G_P(S) = \frac{K_P}{1+ST_P} \qquad .....(6.42)$$

Fig. (6.7) shows the block schematic of Eqn. (6.39)

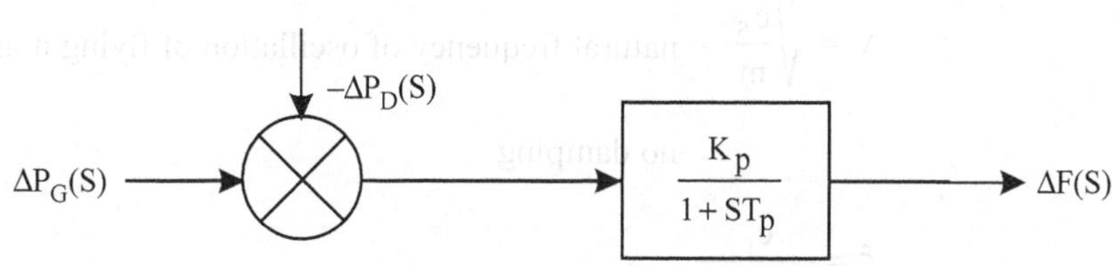

Fig. 6.7

The complete block schematic of speed governing system is shown in Fig. (6.8).

6.7 Transfer Function of the Speed Governor

Let m be the mass of the flying masses

c_f be the friction control and c_s be the spring control of the governor system.

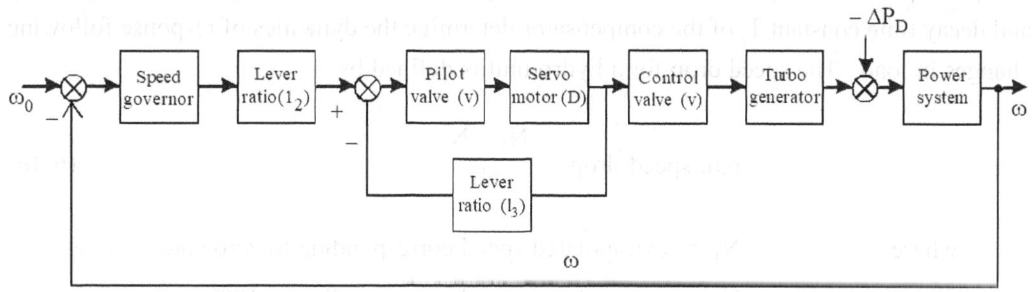

Fig. 6.8 The Block Diagram of Speed Governing System

The equation of motion of the governor is

$$m\frac{d^2x_A}{dt^2}+c_f\frac{dx_A}{dt}+c_Sx_A=k_S\Delta\omega \quad .....(6.43)$$

Taking the Laplace transform on both sides of Eqn. (6.43).

$$(mS^2 + c_fS + c_S)\, x_A(S) = k_S\Delta w(S)$$

Rearranging

$$\frac{x_A(S)}{\Delta\omega(S)}=\frac{k_S}{mS^2+c_fS+c_S}=\frac{k_S}{s^2+2\xi\nu s+\nu^2} \quad .....(6.44)$$

$$= G_g(S) \quad .....(6.44)$$

Where $G_g(S)$ is the transfer function of the speed governor.

$\nu=\sqrt{\frac{c_S}{m}}$ = natural frequency of oscillation of flying masses with no damping

$$\xi=\frac{c_f}{2\sqrt{k_s m}} = \text{damping constant} \quad .....(6.45)$$

$$X_A(S) = G(S)\,.\,\Delta\,\omega\,(S)$$

6.8 Governing of Hydro Units

The governing system of hydro turbines has to meet complex requirements because of the destabilising effect of the inertia of water. Hydro-governors are provided with temporary droop compensation to prevent over travel of the gate motion. The setting of temporary droop and decay time constant T_r of the compensator determine the dynamics of response following changes in load. The speed drop for a hydro unit is defined by

$$\text{p.u. speed drop} = \frac{N_1-N_2}{N_R} \quad .....(6.46)$$

where N_1 = extrapolated speed corresponding to zero gate opening

N_2 = extrapolated speed corresponding to 100% gate opening

and N_R = rated speed.

The temporary droop provided by a dash-pot mechanism consisting of a spring, needle valve and piston is shown in Fig. (6.9).

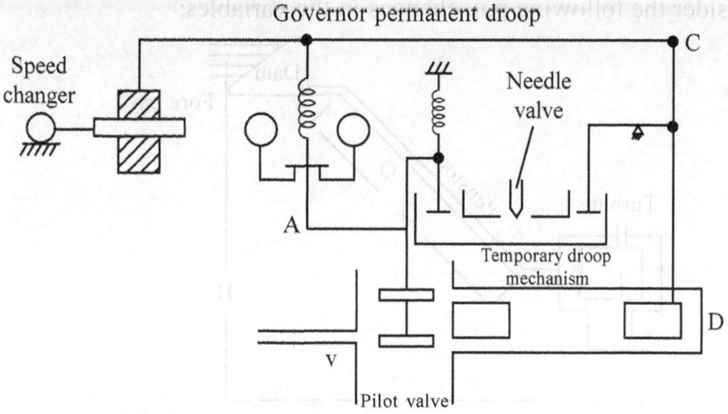

Fig. 6.9 Hydro turbine speed governing mechanism

The dash pot (temporary droop mechanism) is represented by the transfer function.

$$\left[\frac{\delta T_r S}{1+ST_r}\right] \qquad .....(6.47)$$

where s is the complex frequency $\sigma + j\omega$.

The value of the gain δ ranges from 0.2 to 1.0. The rest or decay time constant T_r lies between 2.5 and 25s. The block schematic of a typical hydro governing system is shown in Fig. 6.10. The value of k lies between 0.03 to 0.06.

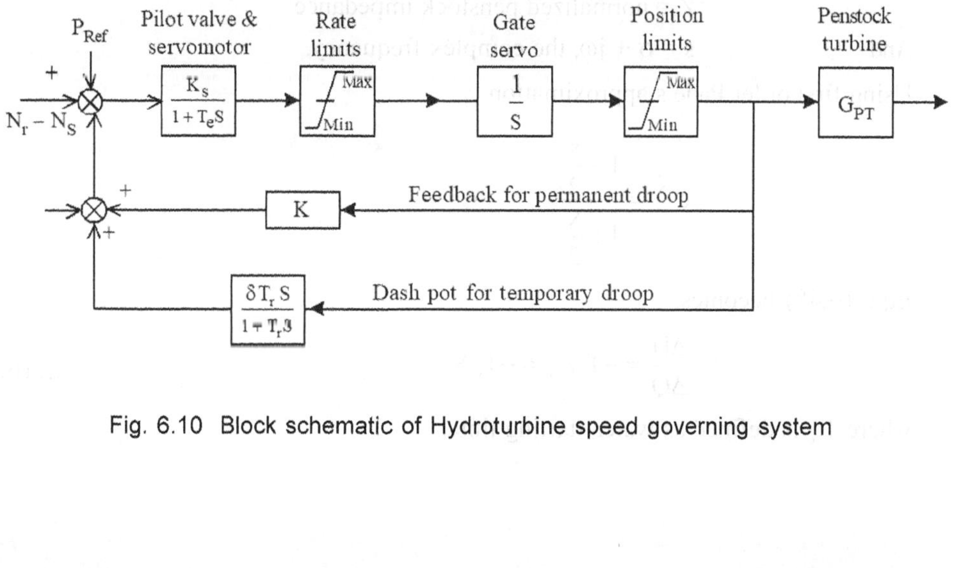

Fig. 6.10 Block schematic of Hydroturbine speed governing system

6.9 Penstock Turbine Model

Consider the penstock-turbine system shown in Fig. 6.11, having an effective length of L m discharging water to the turbine at a velocity V m/s operating at a head of H m. Following a load change, consider the following p.u. changes in the variables:

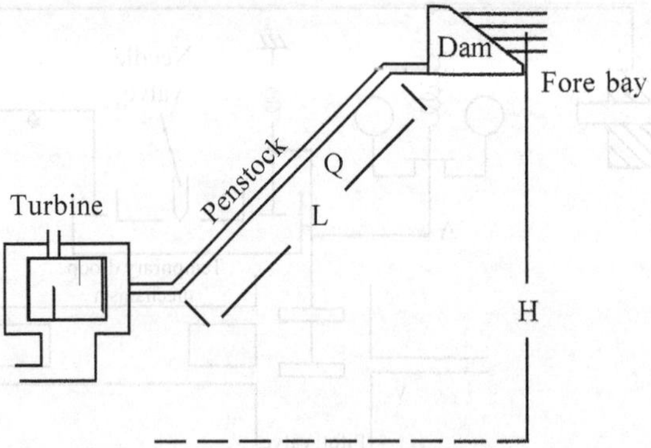

Fig. 6.11 Penstock Turbine mode

ΔH = change in head

ΔN = change in speed

ΔX = change in turbine gate opening

ΔQ = change in flow

ΔT = change in turbine torque

It can be proved that,

$$\frac{\text{p.u.change in head}(\Delta H)}{\text{p.u.change in flow}(\Delta Q)} = -Z\frac{1-\exp[-2T_e S]}{1+\exp[-2T_e S]} \qquad .....(6.48)$$

where T_e = elastic limit of the penstock

Z = normalized penstock impedance

And $s = \sigma + j\omega$, the complex frequency.

Using first order Pade's approximation

$$e^{-x} = \frac{1-\dfrac{x}{2}}{1+\dfrac{x}{2}}$$

Eqn. (6.48) becomes,

$$\frac{\Delta H}{\Delta Q} = -T_e Z_S = -T_w S \qquad .....(6.49)$$

where T_w is defined as water starting time.

The changes in flow (discharge) and torque can be represented by

$$\Delta Q = a_{11}\Delta H + a_{12}\Delta N + a_{13}\Delta X \quad .....(6.50)$$

$$\Delta T = a_{21}\Delta H + a_{22}\Delta N + a_{23}\Delta X \quad .....(6.51)$$

where a_{11}, a_{12}, a_{13}, a_{21}, a_{22} and a_{23} are constants.

The turbine torque change due to speed changes can be neglected in comparison to other changes since speed change is relatively small. Therefore, Eqn. (6.50) becomes

$$\Delta Q = a_{11}\Delta H + a_{13}\Delta X$$

$$\Delta T = a_{21}\Delta H + a_{23}\Delta X$$

Using Eqn. (6.49) and (6.50).

$$\frac{\Delta T}{\Delta X} = \frac{a_{21}\Delta H + a_{23}\Delta X}{\Delta X}$$

$$= a_{23}\frac{\left[1 - \frac{a_{13}a_{21}}{a_{23}} - a_{11}T_w s\right]3}{1 + a_{11}T_w s} \quad .....(6.52)$$

For an ideal, lossless turbine with valve opening X_0

$$a_{11} = 0.5\,X_0$$
$$a_{21} = 1.5X_0$$
$$a_{13} = 1.0$$
$$a_{23} = 1.0$$

so that $$\frac{\Delta T}{\Delta X} = \frac{1-(1.5X_0 + 0.5X_0)T_w s}{1 + 0.5X_0 T_w s} = \frac{1 - X_0 T_w s}{1 + 0.5X_0 T_w s}$$

At full load in p.u. X_0=1.0

Therefore, $$\frac{\Delta T}{\Delta X} = \frac{1 - T_w s}{1 + 0.5T_w s} = \frac{1 - T_w s}{1 + \left(\frac{T_w s}{2}\right)} = G_{PT}(S) \quad .....(6.53)$$

Eqn. (6.53), is the classical turbine penstock transfer function. The water starting time, T_w, varies from 0.5 to 4 s and can be calculated from the relation.

$$T_w = \frac{LV}{Hg} \quad .....(6.54)$$

where g is the acceleration due to gravity (6.8 m/s^2).

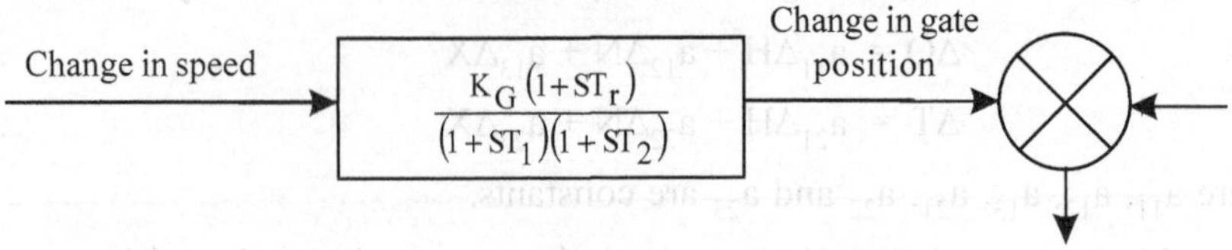

Fig. 6.12 Approximate transfer function for hydro-turbine speed governor

The block diagram in Fig. 6.10 excepting penstock turbine model can be represented by the linear approximate model shown in figure 6.12 where K_G=1/k and T_1 and T_2 are given by

$$T_1, T_2 = \frac{T_B}{2} \pm \frac{k}{\left(\frac{T_B^2}{2} - T_A\right)^{\frac{1}{2}}}$$

and
$$T_B = \left(\frac{1}{k}\right)\left[(k+\delta)T_r + T_G\right]$$

$$T_A = \frac{1}{k} T_R T_G$$

$$T_G = \frac{1}{K_S}$$

Typical values for T_r and δ can be obtained using the relations

$$T_r = 5T_W$$

and
$$\delta = \frac{2.5T_w}{2H}$$

where H is the inertia constant of the turbine-generator on the machine MVA base.

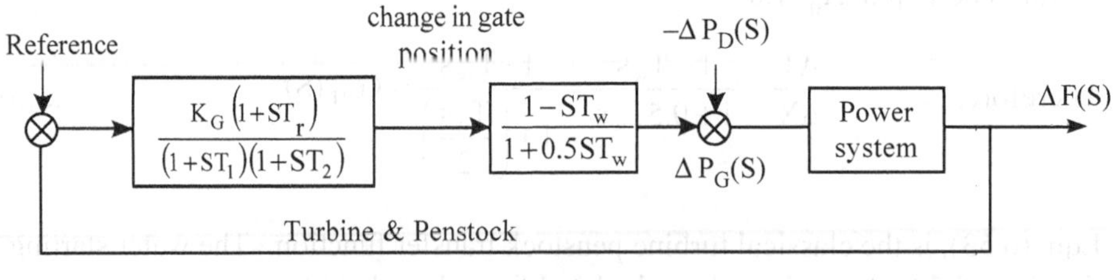

Fig. 6.13 Block diagram of a hydro turbine speed governing system

A complete block diagram for representing the speed – governing system, turbine and penstock for dynamic studies is shown in Fig. (6.13).

6.10 Modal for a Steam Vessel

Steam inlet piping or steam chest can be considered as a steam vessel with steam input and steam output Fig. 6.14.

For changes in steam valve position the dynamics can be represented by

$$\frac{dW}{dt} = Q_{in} - Q_{out}$$

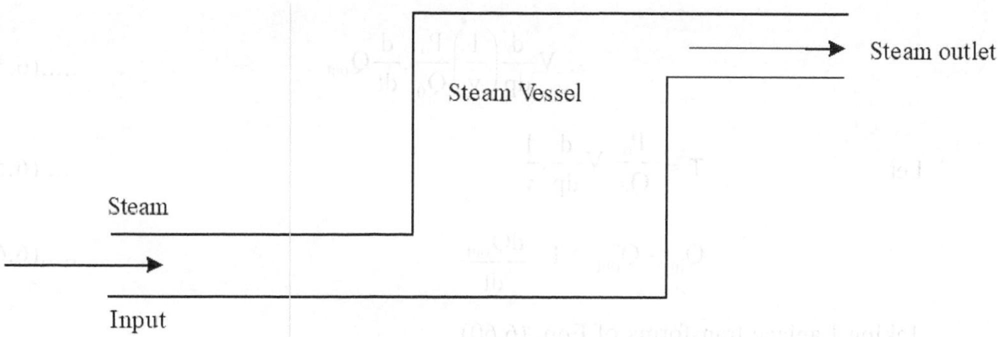

Fig. 6.14 Steam Vessel

Where W is weight of steam in kg and Q_{in} and Q_{out} are the rate of flow of steam in kg/sec at inlet and outlet of the steam vessel respectively. Assuming that the flow rate is proportional to the pressure.

$$Q_{out} = \frac{P}{P_0} Q_0 \qquad .....(6.55)$$

Where P_0 and Q_0 are the steady state pressure and rate of flow of steam in the vessel.

$$\frac{d}{dt} \cdot \frac{Q_{out}}{dt} = \frac{Q_0}{P_0} \cdot \frac{dp}{dt} \qquad .....(6.56)$$

Assuming constant temperature in the vessel

$$\frac{dW}{dt} = \frac{dW}{dp} \cdot \frac{dp}{dt} = \frac{d}{dp}\left(W . \frac{dp}{dt}\right) \qquad .....(6.57)$$

$$= \frac{d}{dp}\left(\frac{V}{v}\right)\frac{dp}{dt}$$

Where V is the volume of the vessel in m^3 and v is the specific volume of steam (m^3/kg) in the vessel.

$$Q_{in} - Q_{out} = \frac{d\omega}{dt}$$

$$= V.\frac{d}{dp}\left(\frac{1}{v}\right)\frac{dp}{dt}$$

$$= V\frac{d}{dp}\left(\frac{1}{v}\right).\frac{dQ_{out}}{dt}.\frac{P_0}{Q_0}$$

$$= V\frac{d}{dp}\left(\frac{1}{v}\right)\frac{P_0}{Q_0}.\frac{d}{dt}Q_{out} \quad .....(6.58)$$

Let

$$T = \frac{P_0}{Q_0}.V\frac{d}{dp}.\frac{1}{v} \quad .....(6.59)$$

$$Q_{in} - Q_{out} = T\ \frac{dQ_{out}}{dt} \quad .....(6.60)$$

Taking Laplace transforms of Eqn. (6.60).

$$Q_{in}(S) - Q_{out}(S) = T\,S\,Q_{out}(S)$$

$$\frac{Q_{out}(S)}{Q_{in}(S)} = \frac{1}{1+ST} \quad .....(6.61)$$

The transfer function of the steam vessel is

$$\boxed{G_{Sv}(S) = \frac{1}{1+sT}} \quad .....(6.62)$$

6.11 Steam Turbine Model

In normal steady state the turbine power P_T keeps balance with the electromechanical air-gap power P_G, resulting in zero acceleration and a constant speed or frequency. Changes in P_T or P_G i.e., ΔP_T or ΔP_G or both will upset the above balance. If the difference $\Delta P_T - \Delta P_G$ is positive the turbine generator unit will accelerate, if negative it will decelerate.

The Turbine – Generator power increment ΔP_T depends entirely upon the valve power increment ΔP_v and the response characteristics of reheat and non-reheat type of turbines are different. However, it is possible to express the turbine – generator dynamics in terms of turbine transfer function. The turbine – generator transfer function is given by

$$G_{TG}(S) = \frac{\Delta P_{TG}(S)}{\Delta P_v(S)}$$

For a simple non-reheat type turbine the model is given by a single time constant

$$G_{TG}(S) = \frac{K_{TG}}{1+sT_{TG}} \quad .....(6.63)$$

Where K_{TG} is the gain constant and T_{TG} is the time constant of turbine – generator unit.,

6.12 Reheat Type Steam Turbine Model

Reheat turbines have more than one time constant. Fig. 6.15 shows a tandem compound single reheat turbine system configuration. Its block diagram is shown in Fig. 6.16.

The time constants T_{Ch}, T_{Rh} and T_{Co} represent the delays due to the steam chest and inlet piping reheater and cross over piping respectively Fig. 6.16.

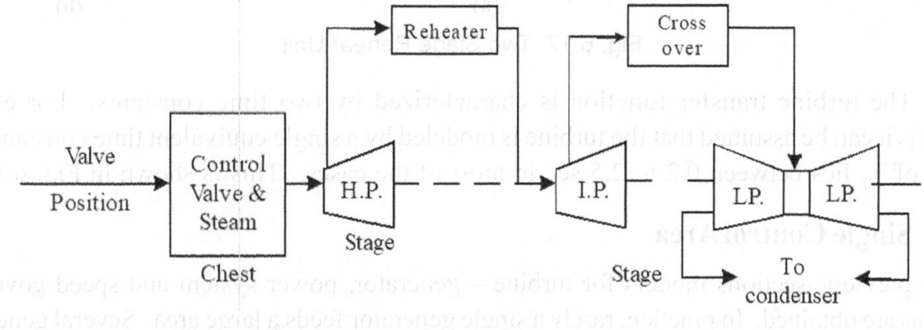

Legentd H.P. = High pressure stage turbine
I.P. = Intermediate pressure stage turbine
L.P. = Low pressure stage turbine

Fig. 6.15 Tandem Compound Single Reheat System

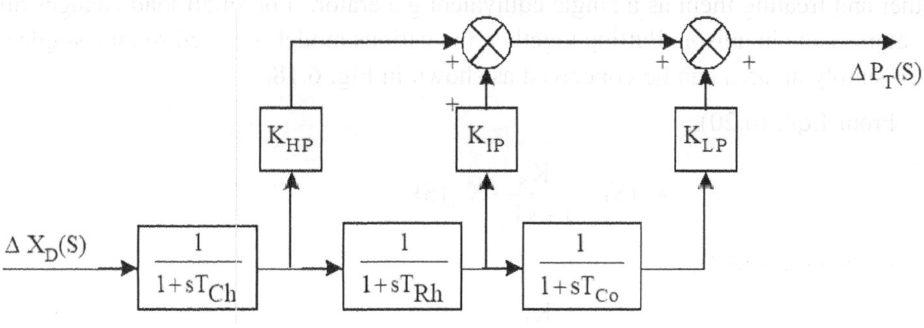

Fig. 6.16 Block Diagram Representations

K_{HP}, K_{IP} and K_{LP} are the fractions of the portions of the total turbine power developed in various stages. The steam chest and inlet piping to the first turbine cylinder, the reheater and the cross over piping down introduce time delays between valve movement and the change in steam flow. The time constants are associated with the entrained steam in the components mentioned.

If a two stage steam turbine with a reheat unit is considered then the dynamic response will be influenced by (i) the entrained steam between the steam inlet valve and first stage of turbine and (ii) the storage action in the reheater which causes the outlet of the L.P. stage to lag behind that of the H.P. stage.

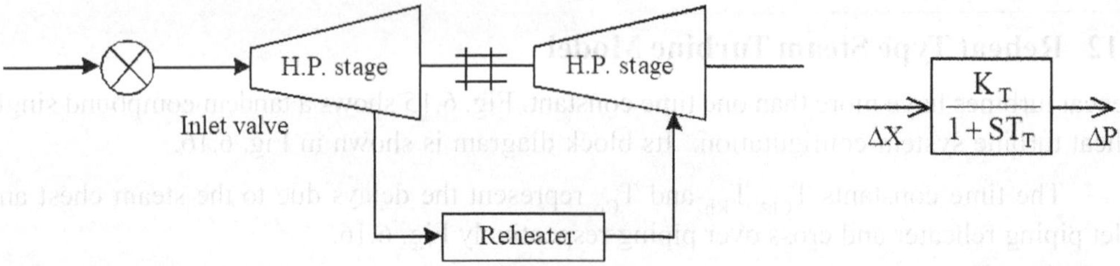

(a) (b)

Fig. 6.17 Two Stage Reheat Unit

The turbine transfer function is characterized by two time constants. For ease of analysis it can be assumed that the turbine is modeled by a single equivalent time constant. The value of T_T lies between 0.2 to 2.5 sec in most of the cases. This is shown in Fig. 6.17(b).

6.13 Single Control Area

In the previous sections models for turbine – generator, power system and speed governing systems are obtained. In practice, rarely a single generator feeds a large area. Several generators connected in parallel, located also, at different places will supply the power needs of a geographical area. Quite normally, all these generators may have the same response characteristics for changes in load demand.

In such a case, it is possible to define a control area, grouping all the generators in the area together and treating them as a single equivalent generator. For small load changes all these generators swing in unison. Putting together, the various models derived so far a single control area or simply an area can be conceived as shown in Fig. 6.18.

From Eqn. (6.20),

$$X_E(S) = \frac{K_S}{1+sT_S} X_A(S)$$

From Eqn. (6.42),

$$G_p(S) = \frac{K_P}{1+sT_P}$$

and from eqn. (6.39) $\Delta F(S) = [\Delta P_G(S) - \Delta P_D(S)] \left[\frac{K_P}{1+sT_P}\right]$

Note that $\Delta P_G(S) = \Delta P_{TG}(S)$ as generator power change which is also the turbine power change and also the turbine generator unit power change.

Also, from eqn. (6.63) $G_{TG} = K_{TG}/1 + sT_{TG}$. We obtain the block diagram of Fig. 6.18 from eqn. 6.8, 6.21, 6.39 and 6.63.

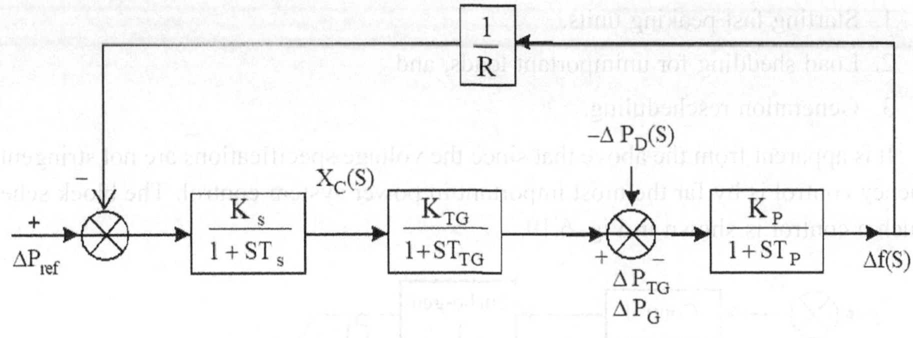

Fig. 6.18 Block diagram of a single area system

6.14 The Basics of Load Frequency Control

The following basic requirements are to be fulfilled for successful operation of the system :

1. The generation must be adequate to meet all the load demand
2. The system frequency must be maintained within narrow and rigid limits.
3. The system voltage profile must be maintained within reasonable limits and
4. In case of interconnected operation, the tie line power flows must be maintained at the specified values.

When real power balance between generation and demand is achieved the frequency specification is automatically satisfied. Similarly, with a balance between reactive power generation and demand, voltage profile is also maintained within the prescribed limits. Under steady state conditions, the total real power generation in the system equals the total MW demand plus real power losses. Any difference is immediately indicated by a change in speed or frequency. Generators are fitted with speed governors which will have varying characteristics: different sensitivities, dead bands response times and droops. They adjust the input to match the demand within their limits. Any change in local demand within permissible limits is absorbed by generators in the system in a random fashion.

An independent aim of the automatic generation control is to reschedule the generation changes to preselected machines in the system after the governors have accommodated the load change in a random manner. Thus, additional or supplementary regulation devices are needed along with governors for proper regulation.

The control of generation in this manner is termed load-frequency control. For interconnected operation, the last of the four requirements mentioned earlier is fulfilled by deriving an error signal from the deviations in the specified tie-line power flows to the neighboring utilities and adding this signal to the control signal of the load-frequency control system. This last requirement will be discussed in detail in the next chapter.

Should the generation be not adequate to balance the load demand, it is imperative that one of the following alternatives be considered for keeping the system in operating condition:

1. Starting fast peaking units.
2. Load shedding for unimportant loads, and
3. Generation rescheduling.

It is apparent from the above that since the voltage specifications are not stringent, load frequency control is by far the most important in power system control. The block schematic for such a control is shown in Fig. 6.19.

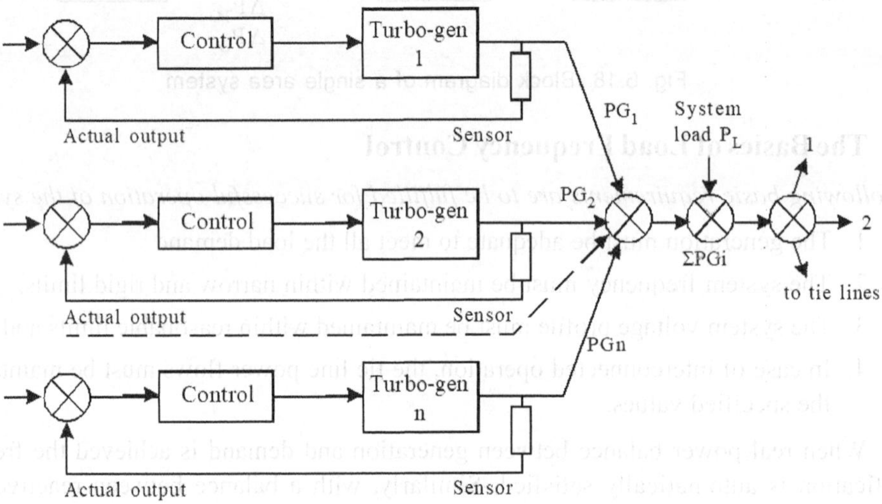

Fig. 6.19 Block diagram for load frequency control

In order to understand the mechanism of frequency control, consider a small step-increase in load. The initial distribution of the load increment is determined by the system impedance; and the instantaneous relative generator rotor positions. The energy required to supply the load increment is drawn from the kinetic energy of the rotating machines. As a result, the system frequency drops. The distribution of load during this period among the various machines is determined by the intertias of the rotors of the generators partaking in the process. This problem is studied in stability analysis of the system.

After the speed or frequency fall due to reduction in stored energy in the rotors has taken place, the drop is sensed by the governors and they divide the load increment between the machines as determined by the droops of the respective governor characteristics.

Subsequently, secondary control restores the system frequency to its normal value by readjusting the governor characteristics.

6.15 Flat Frequency Control

In this method, a master machine is charged with the task of maintaining the system frequency. All the remaining machines carry constant loads. The capacity of the machine which controls the frequency should be between 5 and 10 % of the entire generating capacity of the system for effective frequency control. In small, independent systems, old and inefficient machines may be assigned to frequency regulation leaving new and efficient machines to supply the load demand.

Modern power systems are so large that it is impossible to design a single central control system that would handle the overall control job. It is extremely useful to take into account the weak links in the system and then apply control through decomposition. The demarcation of load frequency control and Mvar voltage control characteristics is one such decomposition. Geographical and functional decomposition are successfully applied to power systems and this leads to the concept of area control. A modern power system can be divided into several areas for load frequency control. Each control area fulfils the following:

1. The area is a geographically contiguous portion of a large inter- connected area, which adjusts its own generation to accommodate load changes within its precincts.
2. Under normal conditions of operation, it exchanges bulk power with neighbouring areas.
3. Under abnormal conditions of operation, it may deviate from pre- determined schedules and provide assistance to any neighbouring control area in the system.
4. It is expected, in addition, to partake with the other areas in the system in a suitable manner in the system frequency regulation.

The rotors of all generators in a control area swing together for load changes. Thus, a coherent group of generators within a geographical region may constitute a control area which is connected to other similar areas by weak tie lines as shown in Fig. 6.20.

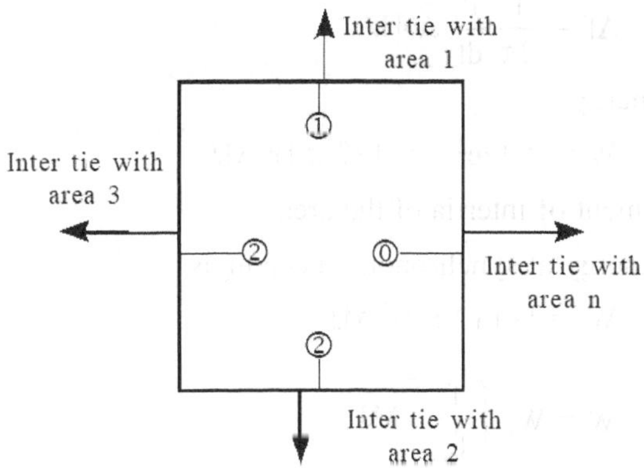

Fig. 6.20 Single control area inter ties

6.16 Real Power Balance for Load Changes

It has been already mentioned that when an imbalance occurs between real power generation and load demand, frequency deviation takes place. Consider a single area operating in steady-state and let it undergo a step change ΔP_D in load demand. Assuming that the generation changes by an amount ΔP_G following the load change due to governor action, the power imbalance is $\Delta P_G - \Delta P_D$. There are three possible modes in which this power can be absorbed. For positive power imbalance:

1. The area kinetic energy increases (i.e. the kinetic energy of all the generator rotors in the area increases),
2. The load demand increases (due to load characteristics) and
3. The power out-flow from the area to other interconnected areas increases, if such interconnections exist.

6.17 Transfer Function of a Single Area System

Under steady state operating conditions. Transfer functions for a single control area can be derived exactly in the same way as for the system in sec. (6.6).

$$\omega_S = 2\pi f_S$$

where ω_s and f_s are synchronous angular speed and rated frequency respectively.

If $\Delta\delta$ is the change in angular position of the equivalent generator representing the area corresponding to an increased load ΔP_D in the area.

Then, $\delta = \delta_S + \Delta\delta$ rad

$$\omega = \frac{d}{dt}(\delta) = \frac{d}{dt}(\delta_S + \Delta\delta) = \omega_S + \frac{d\Delta\delta}{dt}$$

$$= \omega_s + \Delta\omega \qquad .....(6.64)$$

Let $f = f_s + \Delta f$

Where $$\Delta f = \frac{1}{2\pi}\frac{d}{dt}\Delta\delta \text{Hz} \qquad .....(6.65)$$

The area kinetic energy

$$W = ½\, I\, \omega^2 = ½\, I\, (2\,\pi\, f)^2 \text{ MJ}$$

Where I is the moment of intertia of the area.

Also, the kinetic energy at synchronous speed ω_s is

$$W_s = ½\, I\, (2\,\pi\, f)^2 \text{ MJ}$$

Thus, $$W = W_S\left(\frac{f}{f_S}\right)^2 \text{MJ}$$

$$= W_S\left(\frac{f_S + \Delta f}{f_S}\right)^2$$

$$\approx W_S\left(1+2\frac{\Delta f}{f_S}\right) \text{ for small } \frac{\Delta f}{f_S} \quad \text{.....(6.66)}$$

The rate of change of kinetic energy is the increase in area power which is

$$\frac{d}{dt}(W)=\frac{2W_S}{f_S}\frac{d}{dt}(\Delta f)$$

Defining per unit inertia constant M = W_s/Pr

$$\frac{d}{dt}(W)=\frac{2M}{f_S}\frac{d}{dt}(\Delta f)\text{p.u.}$$

All types of composite loads experience a change in power consumption with frequency. Defining the load damping factor D.

$$D=\frac{\partial P_D}{\partial f} \text{ p.u. MW/HZ} \quad \text{.....(6.67)}$$

Where P_D is the load demand in p.u; the increase in load demand in this case is then D.Δf p.u. MW. For a small step change in load demand, Δf p.u. MW. For a small step change in load demand, ΔP_D the power balance equation takes the form.

$$\Delta P_G-\Delta P_D=D\,.\,\Delta f+\frac{2h}{f_S}\frac{d}{dt}(\Delta f) \quad \text{.....(6.68)}$$

Taking the Laplace transform of the above equation

$$[\Delta P_G(S)-\Delta P_D(S)]=D\Delta F(S)+\frac{2H}{fs}S\Delta F(S)$$

or

$$\Delta F(S)=[\Delta P_G(S)-\Delta P_D(S)]\frac{1}{\left[D+\frac{2HS}{f_S}\right]}$$

$$=[\Delta P_G(S)-\Delta P_D(S)]\frac{\frac{1}{D}}{\left[1+\frac{2H}{f_S D}.S\right]}$$

$$=[\Delta P_G(S)-\Delta P_D(S)]\frac{K_P}{[1+sT_P]} \quad \text{.....(6.69)}$$

Where K_P = 1/D Hz/p.u. MW

$$T_P=\frac{2H}{f_S D}$$

The transfer function relating the frequency change to the change in input/output powers may be designed by $G_P(S)$ so that

$$G_P(S) = \frac{K_P}{1+sT_P} \qquad .....(6.70)$$

The block schematic for a single area system is shown in Fig. 6.21(a) An entire control area may be represented as in Fig. 6.21(b).

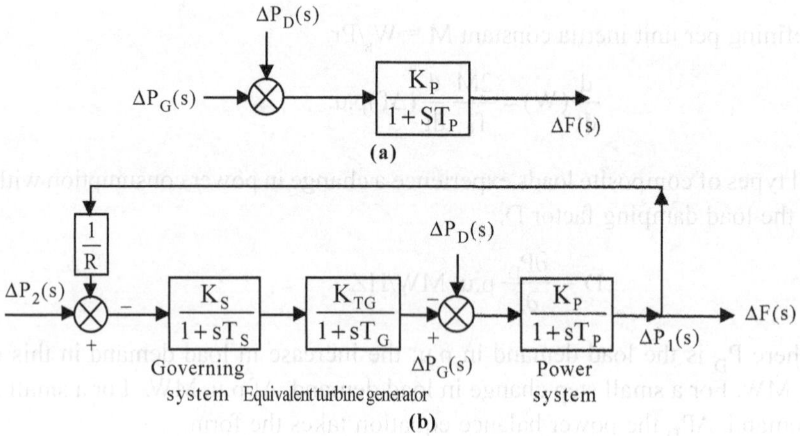

Fig. 6.21(a, b) Block diagram of a single area system

6.18 Analysis of Single Area System

Consider the single area system shown in Fig. 6.21. For a step load change in the system, the following equations can be written

$$[\Delta P_G(S) - \Delta P_G(S)]\ G_P(S) = \Delta\ F(S)$$

$$\frac{1}{RG_{ST}(S)\Delta F(S)} = \Delta P_G(S)$$

where $\quad G_{ST} = \left(\frac{K_{TG}}{1+sT_{TG}} \times \frac{K_S}{1+sT_S}\right)$

Solving for $\Delta F(S)$

$$\Delta F(S) = -\frac{G_P(S)}{1+\left(\frac{1}{R}\right)G_P(S)G_{ST}(T_S)}\Delta P_D(S) \qquad .....(6.71)$$

For a step load change, $\Delta P_D(S) = \dfrac{\Delta P_D}{s}$

Substituting the value of $\Delta P_D(S)$

$$\Delta F(S) = -\frac{G_P(S)}{1+\left(\frac{1}{R}\right)G_P(S)G_{ST}(T)} \cdot \frac{\Delta P_D(S)}{s}$$

Applying the final value theorem, the steady state error Δf_{ss} would be

$$\Delta f_{SS} = \lim_{s \to 0}[S\Delta F(S)] = -\frac{\Delta P_D}{D + \frac{K_{TG}K_S}{R}}$$

The product K_{TG} K_S can be made unity by properly selecting the units for the input-output quantities to the combined block $G_{ST}(S)$ so that

$$\Delta f_{SS} = \frac{-\Delta P_D}{D + \frac{1}{R}}$$

The quantity (D + 1/R) is defined as area frequency response characteristic or area frequency regulation characteristic (AFRC) and denoted by β. It may be noticed that as R becomes smaller Δf_{ss} approaches zero.

Reference Power Setting

In Fig. (6.18) reference power is indicated at the input summer to the system. This determines the starting point of the governor characteristic. Under static conditions setting $K_S K_{TG} = 1$. We obtain

$$\Delta P^0_{ref} - \frac{1}{R}\Delta f^0 = \Delta P^0_{TG}$$

Changing the reference power setting will also change the turbine generator output in a proportional manner. For instance if the machine connected to an infinite bus in which case $\Delta f = 0$ we have the direct relationship.

$$\Delta P_{ref} = \Delta P_{TG}$$

For a fixed setting of the speed changer the steady state increase in power output from the turbine generator ΔP_{TG} is directly proportional to the frequency drop. As in this case $\Delta P_{ref} = 0$

$$\Delta P_{TG} = -\frac{1}{R}\Delta f$$

R has the units hertz per MW or hertz pr unit MW as the case may be.

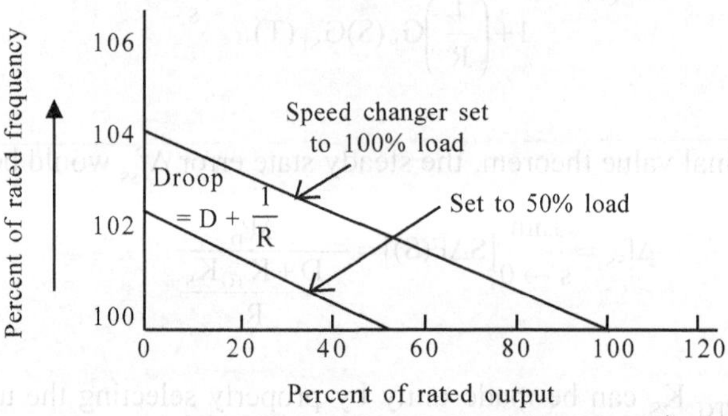

Fig. 6.22 Speed Changer Setting

If D = 0, then AFRC = $\beta = 1/R$ = the area speed regulation coefficient.

The time constants T_s and T_T are much smaller compared to T_P and as such, an approximate solution to the response of the system could be obtained by neglecting them. Then

$$\Delta F(S) = -\frac{G_P(S)}{1+\left(\frac{1}{R}\right)G_P(S)} \frac{\Delta P_D}{S}$$

$$= \frac{-\dfrac{K_P}{1+sT_P}}{1+\left(\dfrac{1}{R}\right)\dfrac{K_P}{1+sT_P}} \frac{\Delta P_D}{S}$$

$$= -\Delta P_D R K_P \left[\left(\frac{1}{s}\right)\left(\frac{1}{A+Bs}\right)\right]$$

Where $A = K_P + R$

$B = T_P R$

Partial fractions for the expression in the bracket can be obtained as follows:

$$\frac{1}{s}.\frac{1}{A+Bs} = \frac{C}{s} + \frac{D}{A+Bs}$$

At $\quad s = 0;\ C = \dfrac{1}{A}$

And at $\quad s = -\dfrac{A}{B};\ D = -\dfrac{B}{A}$

So that

$$\Delta F(S) = -\Delta P_D R K_P\left[\frac{1}{s}-\frac{1}{(K_p+R)}-\frac{T_pR}{(K_p+R)}-\frac{1}{(K_P+R)+sT_PR}\right] = -\frac{\Delta P_D R K_P}{R+K_P}\left[\frac{1}{S}-\frac{1}{\frac{K_P+R}{RT_P}+s}\right]$$

$$\Delta f(t) = L^{-1}\,[\Delta F(S)]$$

$$= L^{-1}\left[\frac{-\Delta P_D}{\beta}\left(\frac{1}{s}-\frac{1}{s+\frac{K_P\beta}{T_P}}\right)\right]$$

$$f(t) = \frac{-\Delta P_D}{\beta}\left[1-\exp\left(\beta\frac{K_P t}{T_P}\right)\right] \qquad .....(6.72)$$

The response is shown in Fig. 6.22.

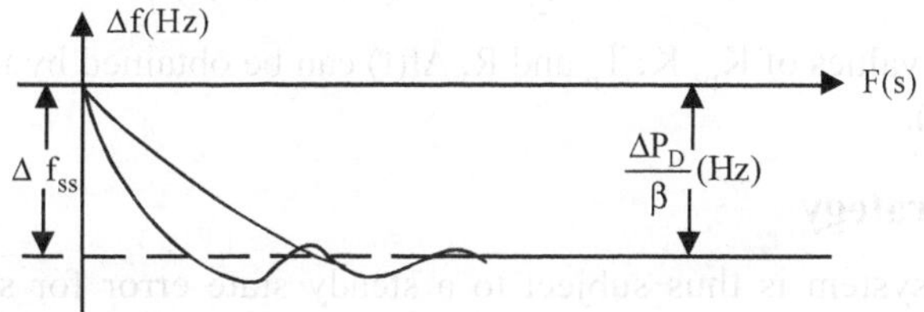

Fig. 6.23 Uncontrolled single area system-response to step load change

6.19 Dynamic Response of Load Frequency Control Loop: Uncontrolled Case

It has been shown that the load frequency control system posses inherently steady state error for a step input. Applying the usual procedure, the dynamic response of the control loop can be evaluated so that the initial response also can be seen for any overshoot.

For this purpose considering the relatively larger time constant of the power system the governor action can be neglected, treating it as instantaneous action. Further the turbine-generator dynamics also may be neglected at the first instant to derive a simple expression for the time response.

It has been proved that (eqn. 6.71)

$$\Delta F(S) = -\frac{G_P}{1+\frac{1}{R}G_S G_{TG} G_P}\Delta P_D(S)$$

For a step load change of magnitude k.

$$\Delta P_D(S) = \frac{-k}{s}$$

Neglecting the governor action and turbine dynamics

$$\Delta F(S) = -\frac{G_P}{1+\frac{1}{R}G_P}\frac{k}{s}$$

$$= -\left(\frac{K_P}{1+sT_P}\right)\frac{1}{\left(1+\frac{1}{R}\frac{K_P}{1+sT_P}\right)}\frac{k}{s}$$

Applying partial fractions

$$\Delta F(S) = -\frac{K_P k}{R+K_p}\left[\frac{1}{s}+\frac{1}{S+\left(\frac{1}{T_P}+\frac{K_p}{R\,T_p}\right)}\right] \quad .....(6.72)$$

For specific values of K_p, K, T_p and R, $\Delta f(t)$ can be obtained by taking inverse Lapalce transform of $\Delta F(s)$.

6.20 Control Strategy

The uncontrolled system is thus subject to a steady state error for step load changes. To reduce this error, consider first the introduction of a negative feedback signal from the frequency deviation ΔF (s) as shown in (Fig. 6.24).

Then, $\Delta P_{ref} = \Delta P_C = -K1\ \Delta F(s)$ .....(6.73)

For this case, the steady state frequency error has been proved in equation (6.64) as

$$\Delta f_{ss} = \frac{-\Delta P_D}{D+\frac{1}{R}} = \frac{-\Delta P_D}{\beta} \quad \text{or} \quad \frac{-\Delta P_D}{D+K_1} \quad .....(6.74)$$

If K_1 is made very large then only Δf_{ss} reduces to zero. In other words, this means that R should be made equal to zero, which is not desirable. Proportional control is not suitable for reducing the steady state error to zero.

It is a well known fact in control theory that integral control will improve the steady state performance.

Let $\quad \Delta P_C(t) = -K_2 \int \Delta f(t)dt$ .....(6.75)

So that $\quad \Delta P_C(S) = -\frac{K_2}{s}\Delta F(S)$ .....(6.76)

The negative sign signifies that the control signal ΔP_C has to be increased for reduction in frequency. The equations for the system in Fig. 6.24 are :

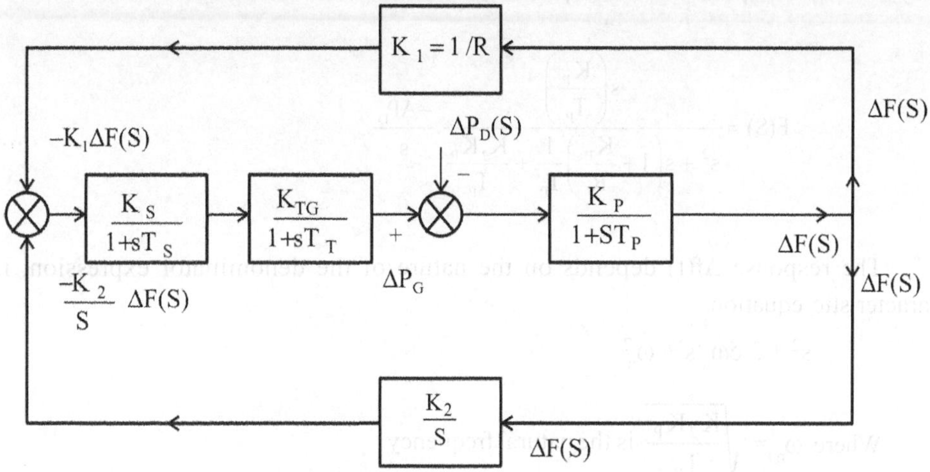

Fig. 6.24 Proportional and Intelgral Control

$$\frac{K_P}{1+sT_P}(\Delta P_G(S) - \Delta P_D(S)) = \Delta F(S) \qquad .....(6.77)$$

Also, if $K_S\, K_{TG}$ is adjusted to be unity

$$-\left(\frac{K_2}{s} + \frac{1}{R}\right)\Delta F(S)\left[\frac{1}{1+sT_S}\right]\left(\frac{1}{1+sT_T}\right) = \Delta P_G(S) \qquad .....(6.78)$$

Solving both the equations above for $\Delta F(S)$,

$$\Delta F(S) = \frac{\Delta P_D\, K_p\, (1+ST_s)(1+ST_{TG})}{S(1 + sT_p)(1+sT_S)(1+sT_T) + K_p\left(K_2 + \frac{s}{R}\right)}$$

where $\Delta P_D(S) = \frac{\Delta P_D}{S}$ (step load change) and steady state error is obtained as

$$\underset{s\to o}{Lt}\; S\,\Delta F(S) = \underset{s.\to o}{Lt}\; s.\frac{\Delta P_D\, K_p\, (1+ST_s)(1+ST_{TG})}{s(1+sT_p)(1+sT_S)(1+sT_T) + K_p\left(K_2 + \frac{s}{R}\right)}$$

$$= 0 \qquad .....(6.79)$$

By making use of integral control strategy, the steady state error can be eliminated.

For the reasons explained before, T_T and T_S cam be neglected for an approximate analysis for the response. For a step load disturbance.

$$F(S) = \frac{s\left(\frac{K_P}{T_P}\right)}{s^2 + s\left(1+\frac{K_P}{R}\right)\frac{1}{T_P} + \frac{K_2 K_P}{T_P}} \cdot \frac{-\Delta P_D}{s} \quad .....(6.80)$$

The response $\Delta f(t)$ depends on the nature of the denominator expression, i.e. the characteristic equation.

$$s^2 + 2\,\delta\omega_n\, s + \omega_n^2$$

Where $\omega_n = \sqrt{\frac{K_2 K_P}{T_P}}$ is the natural frequency

and $\delta = \frac{1+\frac{K_P}{R}}{2T_P}\sqrt{\frac{T_P}{K_2 K_P}}$ = damping ratio

The gain for critical damping can be obtained by setting δ equal to unity.

$$\left(\frac{1+\frac{K_P}{R}}{2T_P}\right)^2 \cdot \left(\frac{T_P}{K_2 T_P}\right) = 1$$

or $$K_2 = \left(\frac{1+\frac{K_P}{R}}{2T_P}\right)^2 \left(\frac{T_P}{K_P}\right) \quad .....(6.81)$$

For values of K_2 greater than that given by eqn. (6.81), the response is oscillatory due to under damping. For values of K_2 less then the critical value response is monotonically decreasing without oscillations or as in Fig. 6.24.

The selection of the gain for the controller should be such that the following specifications are satisfied.

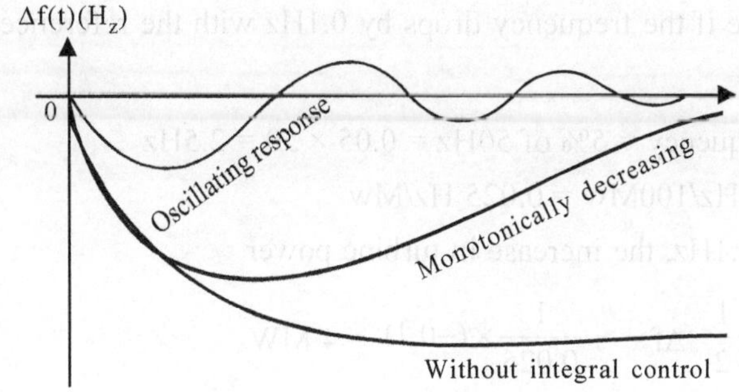

Fig. 6.25 Response to integral control with different gain settings

1. The control loop must be stable.
2. The frequency error should return to zero following a step load change. The deviation in the transient state must also be minimized.
3. The integral of the frequency error should not exceed a certain value (say 150Hz or 3 seconds)

6.21 PID Controllers

From the above analysis, it is clear that proportional integral and derivative control strategy can be applied for load frequency control. While proportional control is inherent in the feedback through the governor mechanism itself, derivative control when introduced improves transient performance and ensures better margin of stability for the system.

$$\Delta P_C(S) = -K_1 \Delta F(S) - \frac{K_2}{s}\Delta F(S) - K_3 S \Delta F(S)$$

where K_3 is the gain of derivative controller.

The response to such a control is

$$F(S) = \frac{\Delta PD(S).\dfrac{KP}{(T_P + K_P K_3)s}}{s^2 + \dfrac{1 + K_1 K_P + \dfrac{K_P}{R}}{T_P + K_P K_3} s + K_2 \dfrac{K_P}{(T_P + K_P K_3)}}$$

By proper choice of K_1, K_2 and K_3 all the specifications for the system performance can be satisfied.

E 6.1 A 100 MW generator has a regulation parameter R of 5%. By how much will the turbine power increase if the frequency drops by 0.1Hz with the reference unchanged.

Solution :

Actual change in frequency = 5% of 50Hz = 0.05 × 50 = 2.5Hz

R = 2.5Hz/100Mw = 0.025 Hz/Mw

If $\Delta f = -0.1$Hz, the increase in turbine power

$$\Delta P = -\frac{1}{2}\ \Delta f = -\frac{1}{0.025}\times(-0.1) = 4\text{ MW}$$

The turbine power increase = 4MW.

E 6.2 A 100 MW generator with R = 0.02 Hz/MW has its frequency fallen by 0.1Hz. If the turbine power remains unchanged by how much the reference power setting be changed.

Solution :

The signal to increase the generation is blocked. Thus at the input summing point the reference power setting must be changed. Such that

$$\Delta P_{ref} - \frac{1}{R}\ \Delta f = 0$$

(i.e.,) $$\Delta P_{ref} - \frac{1}{R}\ \Delta f = \frac{1}{0.025}\times 0.1 = 4\text{ Mw}$$

E 6.3 Two generators with ratings 100 MW and 300 MW operate at 50Hz frequency. The system load increases by 100 MW when both the generators are operating at about half of their capacity. The frequency then falls to 49.5Hz.

If the generators are to share the increased load in proportion to their ratings what should be the individual regulations? What should be regulations if expressed in per unit Hertz/per unit megawatt?

Solution :

$$\Delta P = -\frac{1}{R}\Delta f$$

$$\Delta P_1 = -\frac{1}{R_1}\Delta f$$

$$\Delta P_2 = -\frac{1}{R_2}\Delta f$$

$\Delta f = 0.5$ Hz

Power is shared in proportional to their ratings

$$\Delta P_1 = 100 \times \frac{100}{400} = 25 \text{ MW}$$

$$\Delta P_2 = 100 \times \frac{300}{400} = 75 \text{ MW}$$

Hence $$R_1 = -\frac{0.5}{75} = -0.00667$$

If regulation is expressed in p.u. then with f = 50Hz

$$R_1 = -\frac{0.02}{50} \times \frac{100}{1} = 0.04$$

$$R_2 = -\frac{0.00667}{50} \times \frac{300}{1} = 0.04 \text{ pu Hz/Pu MW}$$

Both have the same value, even though based on their individual ratings, they have different regulation.

E 6.4 Determine the primary load frequency control loop parameters for a control area having the following data:

Total rated area capacity P_r = 1000 Mw

Normal operating load = 500 MW

Inertia constant H = 4.0 sec

Regulation R = 2.5 Hz/pu MW

Solution :

Load damping $$D = \frac{\partial P}{\partial f} = \frac{500\text{MW}}{50\text{Hz}} = 10 \text{ MW/Hz}$$

[Here, the load damping is assumed linear and percentage change is assumed to be the same]

In per unit $$D = \frac{10}{1000} = 0.01 \text{ pu MW/Hz}$$

$$T_P = \frac{2H}{f_s D} = \frac{2 \times 4.0}{50 \times 0.01} = 16 \text{ sec}$$

$$K_p = \frac{1}{D} = \frac{1}{0.01} = 100 \text{ Hz/pu MW}$$

E 6.5 Determine the area frequency response characteristic and the static frequency error for a system with the following data, when 1% load change occurs?

$D = 0.01$ pu Mw/Hz

$R = 2.5$Hz/pu MW

$T_P = 16$ sec

$K_p = 100$ Hz/pu MW

Solution :

Area frequency response characteristic $\beta = D + \frac{1}{R}$

$$= 0.01 + \frac{1}{2.5} = 0.41 \text{ MW/Hz}$$

$$\Delta f = -\frac{M}{\beta} = -\frac{1}{100 \times 0.41} = 0.02439\text{Hz}$$

E 6.6 In the example E6.5, the governor is blocked so that it does not change the generation. In that case what would be the steady state frequency error ?

Solution :

When the governor is not acting, the feedback loop is not existing. In such a case R is infinite.

$$\beta = D + \frac{1}{R} = D = 0.01 \text{ pu MW/Hz}$$

Hence, $$\Delta f = -\frac{M}{\beta} = -\frac{0.01}{0.01} = -1\,\text{Hz}$$

Frequency falls by 1 Hz (i.e.) f = 50 – 1 = 49 Hz.

It may be noted that with the generator acting the frequency from E6.5 is

$$50 - 0.02439 = 49.9756 \text{ Hz}$$

The importance of feedback through governor mechanism can be understood from the above.

E 6.7 A 100 MVA synchronous generator operates initially at 3000 rpm, 50Hz. A 25MW load is suddenly applied to the machine and the steam valve to the turbine opens only after 0.5 sec due to the time lag in the generator action. Calculate the frequency to which the generated voltage drops before the steam flow commences to increase to meet the new load. The value of the stored energy for the machine is 5kW-sec per KVA of generator energy. Also calculate the value of H constant for the generator.

Solution :

Stored energy = 5KW per/kVA

(i.e.,) = 500 MW sec pr 100 MVA

Load increase = 25 MW

Energy required to supply this load for 0.5 sec = 25 MW sec

Frequency at 500 MW sec stored energy = 50Hz

Frequency fall = Δf

$$\frac{\Delta f}{f} = \frac{\Delta f}{50} = \frac{25 \times 0.5}{500} \text{MW sec}$$

$$\Delta f = \frac{50 \times 25 \times 0.5}{500} = 1.25\text{Hz}$$

Frequency falls to 50 – 1.25 = 48.75 Hz

$$\text{H constant} = \frac{\text{stored kinetic energy at rated frequency}}{\text{machine rating}} = \frac{5\text{MW} - \text{sec}}{\text{MVA}} \times \frac{100\text{MVA}}{100\text{MVA}} = 5\,\text{sec}$$

E 6.8 Given the following parameters, obtain the frequency error. Plot it when a step load disturbance of (i) 1% and (ii) 2% occur in the system.

$T_P = 22$ sec

$R = 2.5$

$K_P = 100$

Solution :

$$\text{The expression for } \Delta F(s) = \frac{G_P}{1 + \frac{1}{R} G_S G_{TG} G_P} \Delta P_D(S)$$

Neglecting the turbine dynamics and governor action ($G_S\, G_{TG} \approx 1.0$)

$$\Delta F(S) = -\frac{K_P}{1 + ST_P} \cdot \frac{1}{1 + \frac{1}{R} \frac{K_P}{1 + ST_P}} \cdot \frac{k}{s}$$

$$k_1 = 0.01 \text{ and } k_2 = 0.02$$

simulating the transfer functions in MATLAB the response is obtained and shown in Fig. E(6.8).

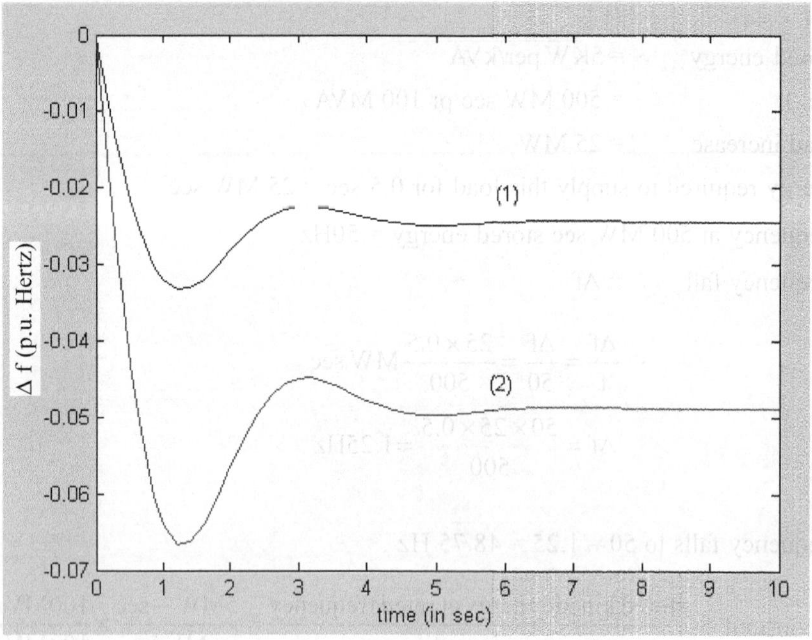

Fig. E6.8 Step load frequency error characteristic without supplementary control 1. k = 0.01 2. k = 0.02 (governor action and turbine dynamics are neglected

E 6.9 Show the effect of governor action and turbine dynamics, if they are not to be neglected in E6.8 given T_S = 100 msec and T_{TG} = 0.5 sec.

Solution :

For this the exact frequency error is used

$$\Delta F(S) = -\frac{G_P}{1+\frac{1}{R}G_S G_{TG} G_P} \cdot \Delta P_D(S)$$

$$\Delta P_D(S) = 0.01\text{pu}; \quad G_S = \frac{K_S}{1+ST_S}; \quad G_{TG} = \frac{K_{TG}}{1+ST_{TG}}$$

$$K_S K_{TG} \approx 1$$

The response is shown in Fig. E(6.9).

It can be seen that greater the step load change, larger the error and the governor action and turbine dynamics does not cause any change in the response in the steady state, except for a transient deviation at the beginning of the distribution.

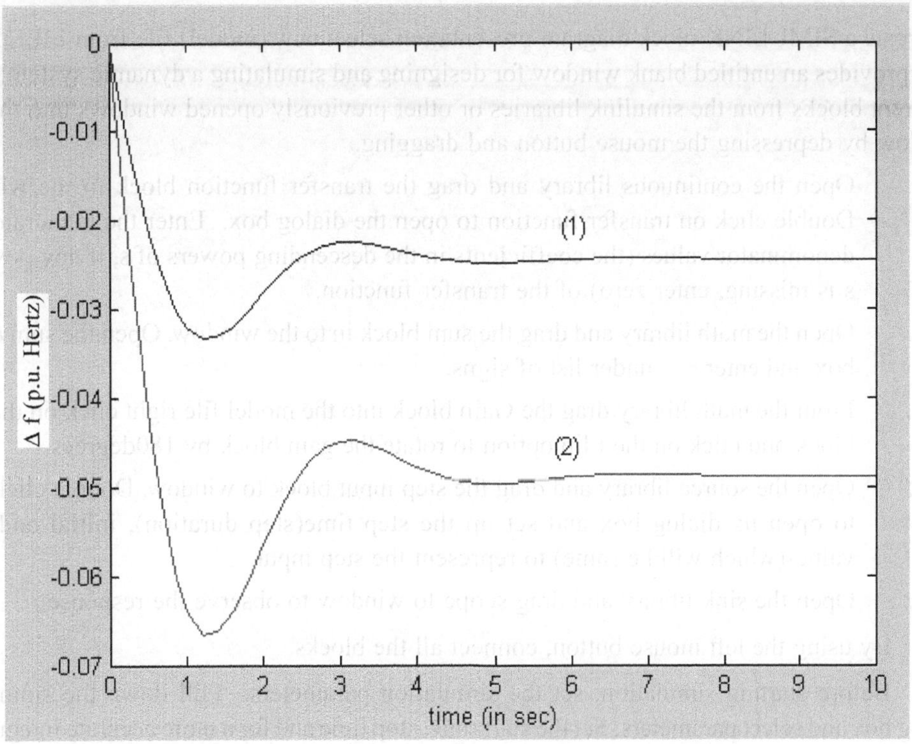

Fig. E6.9 Step load frequency error characteristic without supplementary control 1. k = 0.01 2. k = 0.02 T_S = 100 msec and T_{TG} = 0.5 sec

E 6.10 An isolated power station has the following parameters

Turbine time constant $\mathbf{T_t}$ = 0.5sec

Governor time constant $\mathbf{T_S}$ = 0.2sec

Governor inertia constant **H** = 4 sec

Governor speed regulation **R** = **R** per unit

The load varies by 0.8 percent for a 1 percent change in frequency, i.e. **D** = 0.8. The governor speed regulation is set to **R** = 0.05 pu. The turbine rated output is 250 MW at nominal frequency of 50Hz. A sudden load change of 50MW ($\mathbf{\Delta P_L}$ = 0.2 pu) occurs.

(a) Construct the SIMULINK block diagram and obtain the frequency deviation response.

(b) Set integral gain to 7 and obtain the frequency deviation response and compare both the responses.

Solution :

To create a SIMULINK block diagram presentation select new (model) file from FILE menu. This provides an untitled blank window for designing and simulating a dynamic system. Copy different blocks from the simulink libraries or other previously opened windows into the new window by depressing the mouse button and dragging.

1. Open the continuous library and drag the transfer function block to the window. Double click on transfer function to open the dialog box. Enter the numerator and denominator values (the coefficients in the descending powers of s, if any power of s is missing, enter zero) of the transfer function.
2. Open the math library and drag the sum block in to the window. Open the sum dialog box and enter + – under list of signs.
3. From the math library drag the Gain block into the model file right click on the gain block and click on the Flip option to rotate the gain block by 180degrees.
4. Open the source library and drag the step input block to window. Double click on it to open its dialog box and set up the step time(step duration), initial and final values(which will be same) to represent the step input.
5. Open the sink library and drag scope to window to observe the response.

By using the left mouse button, connect all the blocks.

Before starting simulation, set the simulation parameters. Pull down the simulation dialog box and select parameters. Set the start time, stop time and for a more accurate integration, set the maximum step size.

In this example the parameters for all the blocks for the system in the fig. are initialized. Open m-file and enter the parameter values. The following m-file has to be run prior to the simulation.(of model file)

Open new m-file and enter the parameter values as shown below.

$T_g = 0.2;$

$T_t = 0.5;$

$H = 5;$

$D = 0.6;$

$R = 0.05;$

%for integral control

$K_i = 7;$

Save the m-file under parameters and run the file. SIMULINK block diagram and results for LFC

By using above procedure construct the simulink block diagram for the load frequency control of isolated power system as shown in Fig. E 6.10(a).

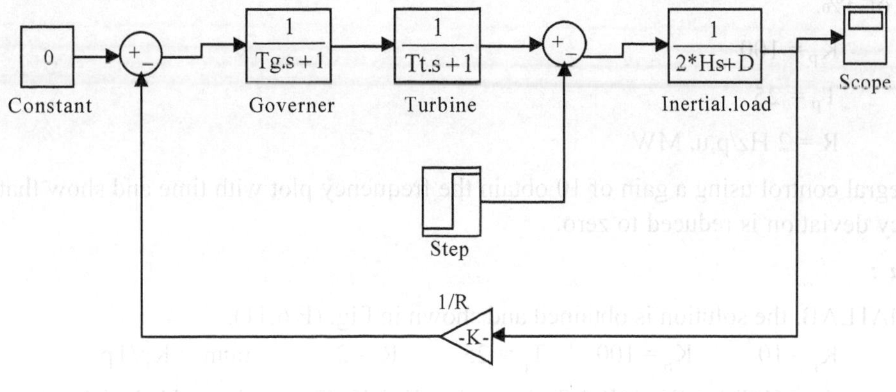

Fig. E 6.10(a) Block diagram Model of Load Frequency Control (Isolated Power System)

Pull down the file menu and use save as to save the model under AFC. Start the simulation. Double click on the scope, click on the auto scale, the result is displayed as shown in Fig. E 6.10(b).

Add integral controller block for above system and save the file under LFC1.

Start the simulation. Double click on the scope, click on the auto scale, the result is displayed as shown in figure below.

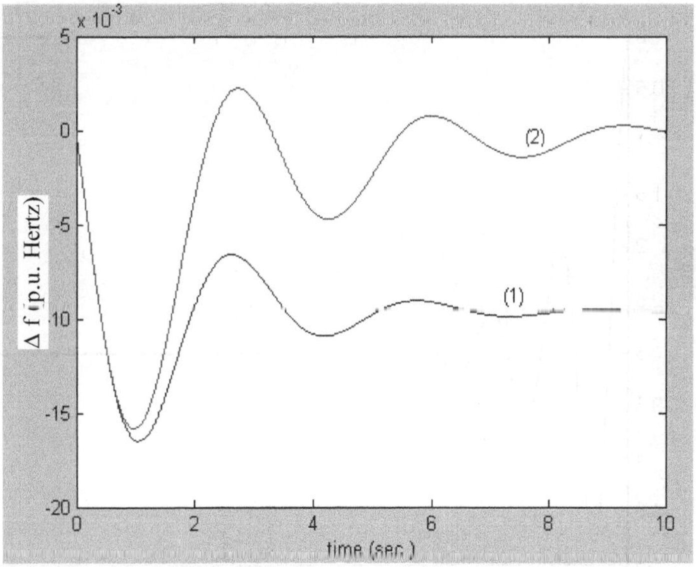

Fig. E6.10(b) Response of LFC

1. Uncontrolled response
2. Integral control response

E 6.11 A single control area system with the following data experiences a sudden load change of 3%.

$K_P = 100$

$T_P = 25$

$R = 2$ Hz/p.u. MW

with integral control using a gain of 10 obtain the frequency plot with time and show that the frequency deviation is reduced to zero.

Solution :

Using MATLAB, the solution is obtained and shown in Fig. (E 6.11).

$K_i = 10 \quad K_p = 100 \quad T_p = 25 \quad R = 2 \quad num = Kp/Tp$

$d_1 = (1/T_p) + (K_p / (R * T_p)) \quad d_2 = K_i * K_p/T_p \quad den = [1\ d_1\ d_2]$

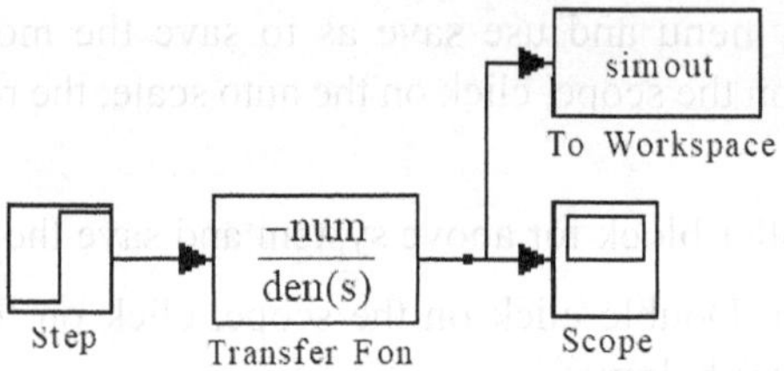

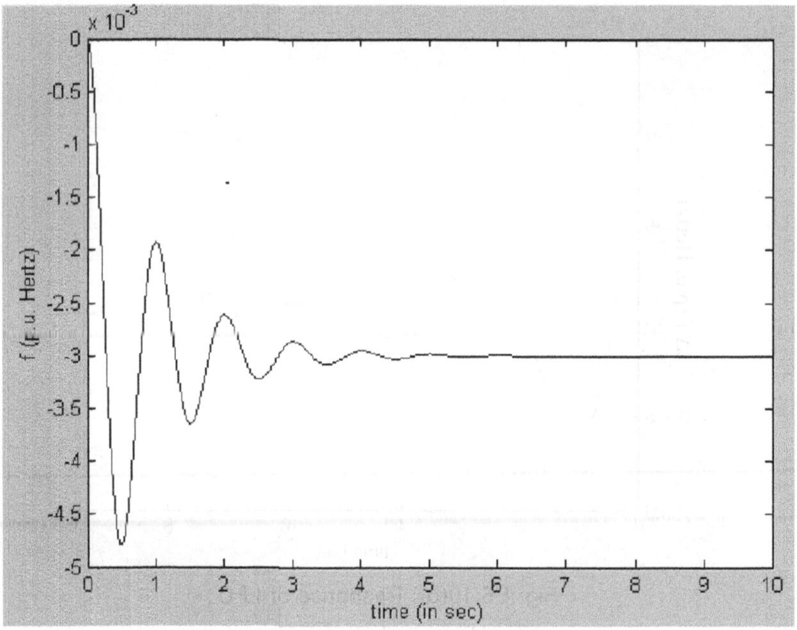

Fig. (E 6.11)

6.22 The optimal Control Problem

A dynamic system is described mathematically by

$$\dot{x} = f(\mathbf{x}, \mathbf{u}, t) \qquad .....(6.82)$$

Where x denotes the state vector and u the control vector

Let it be desired to minimize the performance index or cost functional

$$J = \int_0^t L(\mathbf{x}, \mathbf{u}, t)dt \qquad .....(6.83)$$

Pontriagyn's method for optimal control involves in creating an augmented cost function for minimization.

$$L'(\mathbf{x}, \dot{\mathbf{x}}, \mathbf{u}, t) = L(\mathbf{x}, \mathbf{u}, t) + \boldsymbol{\lambda}^t [f(\mathbf{x}, \mathbf{u}, t) - \dot{\mathbf{x}} \qquad .....(6.84)$$

Applying Euler-Lagrange equations, we obtain

$$\dot{\lambda} = -\frac{\partial \mathbf{H}}{\partial \mathbf{X}} \qquad .....(6.85)$$

$$\dot{X} = -\frac{\partial \mathbf{H}}{\partial \lambda} \qquad .....(6.86)$$

$$0 = \frac{\partial \mathbf{H}}{\partial \mathbf{u}} \qquad .....(6.87)$$

Where $\mathbf{H} = L(\mathbf{x}, \mathbf{u}, t) + \boldsymbol{\lambda}^t [f(\mathbf{x}, \mathbf{u}, t)]$ .....(6.88)

and λ denotes Lagrange multipliers. Simultaneous solution to eqn. (6.85, 6.86, 6.87) subject to boundary conditions gives optimal control U^0. But, the equations are non linear and time varying and hence even for simple systems the solution will be difficult to obtain.

6.23 The Linear Regulator Problem

Consider the linear dynamic system

$$\dot{\underline{\mathbf{X}}}(t) = [\mathbf{A}](t)\mathbf{X}(t) + [\mathbf{B}][t]\underline{u}(t) \qquad .....(6.89)$$

Let the cost functional be

$$J = \frac{1}{2}\mathbf{X}^T(t_2)\mathbf{H}\mathbf{X}(t_2) + \frac{1}{2}\int_{t_1}^{t_2} \mathbf{X}(t)\mathbf{Q}(t)\mathbf{X}(t) + \mathbf{u}^T(t)\mathbf{P}(t)\mathbf{u}(t)]dt \qquad .....(6.90)$$

Where H and Q are real symmetric positive semi definite matries and P is a real symmetric positive definite matrix. Again t_2 is fixed, but $X(t_2)$ is free. For simplicity, omitting the arguments.

$$H = \frac{1}{2}\mathbf{X}^T Q\mathbf{X} + \frac{1}{2}U^T \mathbf{P}U + \boldsymbol{\lambda}^T \Lambda \mathbf{X} + \boldsymbol{\lambda}^T \mathbf{Bu} \qquad .....(6.91)$$

For optimality $$\dot{X}^0(t) = A(t)X^0(t) + B(t)U^0(t) \quad .....(6.92)$$

$$\lambda^0(t) = -\frac{\partial H}{\partial X(t)} = -Q(t)^{\cdot} X^0(t) \; - A^T(t)\lambda^0 \; (t) \quad .....(6.93)$$

$$\frac{\partial H}{\partial U} = P(t)U^0(t) + B^T(t)\lambda^0(t) = 0 \quad .....(6.94)$$

From the above $U^0 = -P^{-1}(t)B^T(t)\lambda^0(t)$ .....(6.95)

substituting this U^0 in equation (6.92)

$$\left.\begin{aligned}\dot{X}^0(t) &= A(t)X(t) - B(t)P^{-1}(t)B^T(t)\lambda^0(t)\\ \dot{X}^0(t) &= -Q(t)X(t) - A^T(t)\lambda^0(t)\end{aligned}\right\} \quad .....(6.96)$$

Solution to equations (6.96) is given by

$$\begin{bmatrix} X^0(t_2) \\ \lambda^0(t_2) \end{bmatrix} = [\phi(t_2, t)] \begin{bmatrix} X^0(t) \\ \lambda^0(t) \end{bmatrix} \quad .....(6.97)$$

or

$$\begin{bmatrix} X^0(t_2) \\ \lambda^0(t_2) \end{bmatrix} = \begin{bmatrix} \phi_{11} & \phi_{12} \\ \phi_{21} & \phi_{22} \end{bmatrix} \begin{bmatrix} X^0(t) \\ \lambda^0(t) \end{bmatrix} \quad .....(6.98)$$

where ϕ is called state transition matrix.

$$X^0(t_2) = \phi_{11}X^0(t) + \phi_{12}\lambda^0(t) \quad .....(6.99)$$

From the boundary conditions we obtain $\lambda^0(t_2) = HX^0(t_2)$ and hence,

$$H \; X^0(t_2) \; = \phi_{21} \; X^0(t) \; + \phi_{12} \; \lambda^0(t) \quad .....(6.100)$$

It can be derived from the above that

$$\begin{aligned}\lambda^0(t) &= [\phi_{22} - H\phi_{12}]^{-1}[H\phi_{12} - \phi_{22}]X^0(t)\\ &= R(t)\; X^0\; (t)\end{aligned} \quad .....(6.101)$$

From eqn. (6.95) $U^0(t) = -P^{-1}B^T(t)\lambda^0(t)$

$$\begin{aligned}&= -P^{-1}(t)\; B^T(t)\; R(t)\; X^0(t)\\ &= -[K^t(t)\; X^0(t)]\end{aligned} \quad .....(6.102)$$

The optimal control is a time varying linear combination of system states.

6.24 Matrix Riccati Equation

Consider eqn (6.101)

$$\boldsymbol{\lambda}^0(t) = \mathbf{R}(t)\mathbf{X}^0(t)$$

Differentiating $\dot{\boldsymbol{\lambda}}^0(t) = \dot{\mathbf{R}}(t)\mathbf{X}^0(t) + \mathbf{R}(t)\dot{\mathbf{X}}^0(t)$ .....(6.103)

Substituting $\dot{\mathbf{X}}^0(t)$ and $\boldsymbol{\lambda}^0(t)$ from eqn. (6.92) and (6.93)

$$= \mathbf{Q}(t)\, \mathbf{X}(t) - \mathbf{A}^T(t)\, \boldsymbol{\lambda}^0(t)$$

$$= \mathbf{R}(t)\, \mathbf{X}(t) + \mathbf{R}(t)\, \mathbf{A}(t)\, \mathbf{X}(t) - \mathbf{R}(t)\, \mathbf{B}(t)\, \mathbf{P}^{-1}(t)\, \mathbf{B}^T(t)\, \boldsymbol{\lambda}^0(t) \quad .....(6.104)$$

Eliminating $\boldsymbol{\lambda}(t)$ and rearranging the terms

$$\mathbf{R}(t)\, \mathbf{B}(t)\, \mathbf{P}^{-1}(t)\, \mathbf{B}^T(t)\, \mathbf{R}(t)\, \mathbf{X}^0(t) - \mathbf{R}(t)\, \mathbf{A}(t)\, \mathbf{X}(t) \quad .....(6.105)$$

$$- \dot{\mathbf{R}}(t)\, \mathbf{X}^0(t) - \mathbf{Q}(t)\, \mathbf{X}^0(t) - \mathbf{A}^T(t)\, \mathbf{R}(t)\, \dot{\mathbf{X}}(t) = 0 \quad .....(6.106)$$

since the above eqn. must be satisfied for at $\mathbf{X}^0(t)$

$$\dot{\mathbf{R}}(t) + \mathbf{R}(t)\mathbf{A}(t) + \mathbf{A}^T(t)\mathbf{R}(t) - \mathbf{R}(t)\mathbf{B}(t)\mathbf{P}^{-1}(t)\mathbf{B}^T(t)\mathbf{R}(t) + \mathbf{Q}(t) \quad .....(6.107)$$

The above equation is called *matrix Riccati equation.* R is an $n \times n$ symmetric matrix.

$\frac{n(n+1)}{2}$ first order differential equations only need be solved to get the elements of R matrix, so that the elements of feed back gain **K**(t) can be computed further from equation (6.102)

For controllable dynamic systems **H** = 0, **A**, **B**, **P** and **Q** are time invariant matrices and as $t_2 \to \infty$ $\mathbf{R}(t) \to \mathbf{R}^0$, a constant matrix. The matrix Riccati equation becomes

$$\mathbf{R}^0\mathbf{A} + \mathbf{A}^T\mathbf{R}^0 + \mathbf{Q} - \mathbf{R}^0\,\mathbf{B}\mathbf{P}^{-1}\,\mathbf{B}^T\,\mathbf{R}^0 = 0 \quad .....(6.108)$$

In the steady state $\dot{\mathbf{R}}(t) \to 0$.

The gain elements from **K** matrix can be determined as constants after the elements of $\mathbf{R}^0$ matrix are determined. This involves solution to simultaneous non-linear algebraic equations. There are several methods available for the solution of which Klineman's method is simple and elegant.

6.25 Application of Modern Control Theory

The load frequency control (LFC) problem can be viewed as a dynamic optimization problem. Integral square error criterion can be applied and controllers can be designed using optimal control theory. Controller design using this theory was first proposed by Fosha and Elgerd. The results obtained by using this theory contradict the existing practice in the selection of the bias parameters and the integral controller gains

The system equations are put in the state variable form denoted compactly by

$$\dot{\mathbf{X}} = \mathbf{AX} + \mathbf{Bu} + \mathbf{Fd} \quad .....(6.109)$$

where **A.B** and **F** are the system, input distribution and disturbance distribution matrices respectively and **X**, **u** and **d** are the state, control and disturbance vectors respectively.

By a suitable transformation, eqn. (6.24) is transformed into the form.

$$\dot{X}' = A'X' + B'U' \qquad .....(6.110)$$

The LFC problem is then treated as a linear regulator problem and the solution is obtained by solving algebraic Riccatic equation.

6.26 Optimal Load Frequency Control – Single Area System

The states to be minimized are the frequency deviation Δf and the time integral of the frequency deviation $\int \Delta f.dt$. The contrl signal is to be weighted and included in the cost function so that too large a control is not required. The cost function selected is

$$J = \int_0^{\infty} \frac{1}{2}\left(\underline{x}^T Qx + u^T Pu\right)dt \qquad .....(6.111)$$

Where Q and P are the weighting matrices for the state and control vectors and X and u.

Consider the block diagram for the single area system shown in Fig. 6.26.

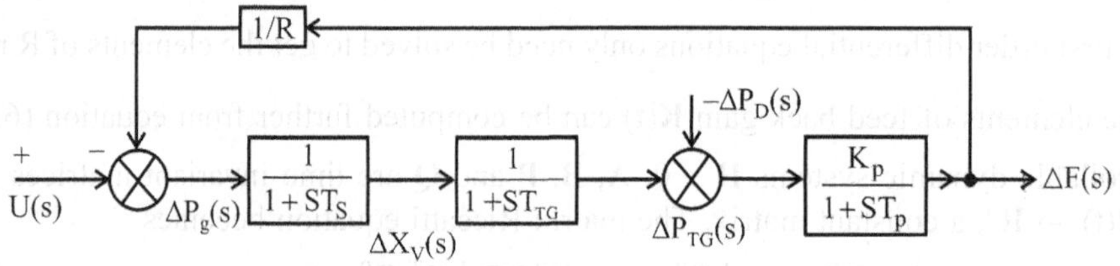

Fig. 6.26 Block diagram for single area system.

As indicated in section (6.18) K_s. K_{TG} is set equal to one.

The following states are defined

$x_1 = \int \Delta f(t)dt$ = integral of frequency error

$x_2 = \Delta f(t)$ = frequency deviation

$x_3 = \Delta P_{TG}(t)$ = change in turbo generator output

$x_4 = \Delta x_v(t)$ = valve displacement at speed governing system.

Thus, $x^T = \left[\int \Delta f \;\; \Delta f \;\; \Delta P_{TG} \;\; \Delta X_v\right]$

Let u be the control vector and $d = \Delta P_d$ be the disturbance vector.

Here, the control is a single input scalar u, and the disturbance d is the change in the load demand ΔP_d

The performance index is

$$X^T Qx = \{x_1 \, x_2\} \begin{Bmatrix} q_{11} & q_{12} \\ q_{21} & q_{22} \end{Bmatrix} \begin{Bmatrix} x_1 \\ x_2 \end{Bmatrix} \quad \text{..... (6.112)}$$

Since only Δf and $\int \Delta f \, dt$ are to be minimized.

Identifying the states and the state variable system model, we obtain

$$\dot{x}_1(t) = x_2(t) \quad \text{..... (6.113)}$$

Since $\quad x_1(t) = \int \Delta f(t) \, dt$ and $x_2(t) = \Delta f(t)$

From the block diagram

$$\Delta f(s) = \left[\Delta P_{TG}(s) - \Delta P_\rho(s)\right] \left(\frac{Kp}{1+ST_P}\right) \quad \text{.....(6.114)}$$

Cross multiplying and rearranging

$$S \Delta F(s) = -\frac{1}{T_p} \Delta F(s) + \frac{K_P}{T_P} \Delta P_{TG}(s) - \frac{K_p}{T_p} \Delta P_D(s) \quad \text{.....(6.115)}$$

In the time domain, using the state variables

$$\dot{x}_2(t) = -\frac{1}{T_p} x_2 + \frac{K_P}{T_P} x_3 - \frac{K_p}{T_P} d \quad \text{.....(6.116)}$$

Also, from the block diagram

$$\Delta P_{TG}(s) = \left(\frac{1}{1+sT_{TG}}\right) \Delta x_v(S) \quad \text{.....(6.117)}$$

As before,

$$sT_{TG} \Delta P_{TG}(s) = \Delta x_v(s) - \Delta P_{TG}(s) \quad \text{.....(6.118)}$$

and in time domain

$$\dot{x}_2(t) = \frac{1}{T_{TG}} x4(t) - \frac{1}{T_{TG}} x_3(t) \quad \text{.....(6.119)}$$

Finally, from the block diagram

$$\Delta x_v(s) = \left(\frac{1}{1+sT_s}\right) \left[U(s) - \frac{1}{R} \Delta F(s)\right] \quad \text{.....(6.120)}$$

i.e., $\quad sT_s \Delta x_v(s) = -\Delta x_v(s) + U(s) - \frac{1}{R} \Delta F(s) \quad$ .....(6.121)

In the time domain

$$\dot{x}_4(t) = -\frac{1}{RT_s} x_2(t) - \frac{1}{T_s} x_4(t) + \frac{1}{T_s} \upsilon(t) \quad \text{.....(6.122)}$$

Putting eqn. (6.113, 6.116, 6.119 and 6.122) in matrix from, the state variable model is obtained as

$$\begin{bmatrix} \dot{x}_1(t) \\ \dot{x}_2(t) \\ \dot{x}_3(t) \\ \dot{x}_4(t) \end{bmatrix} = \begin{bmatrix} 0 & 1 & 0 & 0 \\ 0 & \frac{-1}{T_P} & \frac{K_P}{T_P} & 0 \\ 0 & 0 & -\frac{1}{T_{TG}} & \frac{1}{T_{TG}} \\ 0 & -\frac{1}{RT_S} & 0 & -\frac{1}{T_S} \end{bmatrix} \begin{bmatrix} x_1 \\ x_2 \\ x_3 \\ x_4 \end{bmatrix} + \begin{bmatrix} 0 \\ 0 \\ 0 \\ \frac{1}{T_S} \end{bmatrix} + \begin{bmatrix} 0 \\ -\frac{k_P}{T_P} \\ 0 \\ 0 \end{bmatrix} d \qquad \text{.....(6.123)}$$

redefining the state and control variables.

$$x_1 = x_1'$$

$$x_2 = x_2'$$

$$x_3 = x_3' + \Delta P_D$$

$$x_4 = x_4' + \Delta P_D$$

$$u + u' + \Delta P_D \qquad \text{.....(6.124)}$$

Eqn. (6.112) can be reduced to

$$\begin{bmatrix} \dot{x}_1' \\ \dot{x}_2' \\ \dot{x}_3' \\ \dot{x}_4' \end{bmatrix} = \begin{bmatrix} 0 & 1 & 0 & 0 \\ 0 & -\frac{1}{T_P} & \frac{K_P}{1T_P} & 0 \\ 0 & 0 & -\frac{1}{T_T} & \frac{1}{T_T} \\ 0 & \frac{1}{RT_S} & 0 & -\frac{1}{T_S} \end{bmatrix} \begin{bmatrix} x_1 \\ x_2 \\ x_3 \\ x_4 \end{bmatrix} + \begin{bmatrix} 0 \\ 0 \\ 0 \\ \frac{1}{T_S} \end{bmatrix} u' \qquad \text{.....(6.125)}$$

The optimal control to minimize the performance index given in equation (6.111) can be determined using the solution technique described for the linear regulator problem. It is required to solve the algebric matrix Riccati equation.

$$\mathbf{Q + A^T R + RA - RBP^{-1} B^T R = 0} \qquad (6.126)$$

for the elements of the R matrix which is positive definite and symmetric. Kleinman's method may be used to solve the matrix Riccati equation. An initial feedback gain vector $\mathbf{K_I}$ is selected such that the matrix $\mathbf{A_i = [A - B\,K_i]}$ has eigenvalues with negative real parts. Then the matrix equations.

$$\mathbf{A_I R_I^T + R_I A_I + Q + K_I^T P K_I = 0}$$

are to be solved for the elements of $\mathbf{R_i}$. The new gains are computed using

$$\mathbf{K_i^{(1)} = P^{-1} B^T R_i}$$

The procedure is repeated till convergence is obtained for the elements of $\mathbf{R_i}$.

The optimal control

$$u^0 = -P^{-1} B^T RX(t)$$

$$= -K^T X(t) \qquad .....(6.127)$$

can be calculated.

E 6.12 For the single area system with the following data, determine the optimal control.

$T_P = 0.04s$ $\qquad R = 2Hz/p.u.\ MW$

$T_T = 0.5s$ $\qquad K_P = 100\ Hz/p.u.\ MW$

$T_S = 0.1S$ $\qquad P_D = 0.01\ p.u.$

Assume $Q\begin{bmatrix}1 & 0\\0 & 1\end{bmatrix}$

Solution :

Substituting the parameters in the algebraic matrix Riccati equation and solving the equation using, Kleinman's method with an initial vector of $K_i = [1\ 1\ 1\ 1]$

The values of K_i converge to

$$K = [1.0000 \quad 1.1368 \quad 1.7092 \quad 0.2976]$$

The optimal control is shown in Fig. E 6.12.

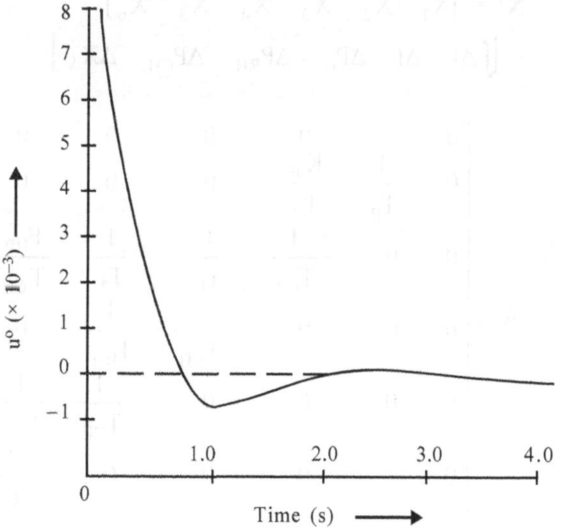

Fig. E 6.12 Optimal control

6.27 Optimal Control for Tandem Compound Single Reheat Turbine – Generator System

The model for tandem compound single reheat turbine is discussed in

Chapter 3 : The system is shown in Fig. 6.27.

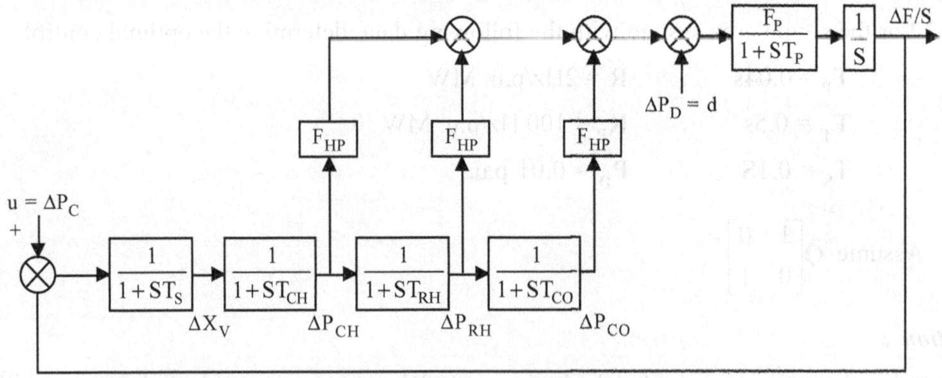

Fig. 6.27 Tandem compound single reheat turbine system

The state – variable model of this system is given by

$$X = AX + Bu + Fd$$

with the initial conditions $\mathbf{X}(0) = \mathbf{0}$

where $\mathbf{X}^T = [X_1 \quad X_2 \quad X_3 \quad X_4 \quad X_5 \quad X_6]$

$$= \left[\int \Delta f \quad \Delta f \quad \Delta P_G \quad \Delta P_{RH} \quad \Delta P_{CH} \quad \Delta X_V\right] \qquad ....(6.128)$$

$$A = \begin{bmatrix} 0 & 1 & 0 & 0 & 0 & 0 \\ 0 & -\frac{1}{T_P} & \frac{K_P}{T_P} & 0 & 0 & 0 \\ 0 & 0 & -\frac{1}{T_{CO}} & \frac{1}{T_1} & \frac{1}{T_2} & \frac{F_{HP}}{T_{CH}} \\ 0 & 0 & 0 & -\frac{1}{T_{RH}} & \frac{1}{T_{RH}} & 0 \\ 0 & 0 & 0 & 0 & -\frac{1}{T_{CH}} & \frac{1}{T_{CH}} \\ 0 & & 0 & 0 & 0 & -\frac{1}{T_S} \end{bmatrix}$$

The constant T_1 and T_2 are given in chapter 3.

$$\frac{1}{T_1} = \frac{F_{LP}}{T_{CO}} + \frac{F_{IP}}{T_{CO}} - \frac{F_{IP}}{T_{RH}}$$

$$\frac{1}{T_2} = \frac{F_{HP}}{T_{CO}} + \frac{FI_P}{T_{RH}} - \frac{F_{HP}}{T_{CH}}$$

$$B^T = \begin{bmatrix} 0 & 0 & 0 & 0 & 0 & 0 & \frac{1}{T_S} \end{bmatrix}$$

$$F^T = \begin{bmatrix} 0 & -\frac{K_P}{T_P} & 0 & 0 & 0 & 0 \end{bmatrix}$$

$$u = \Delta P_C \text{ and } d = \Delta P_D$$

The above equations are transformed into the form

$$X^{|} = AX^{|} + Bu^{|}$$

using the transformation

$$X = X' + \begin{bmatrix} 0 \\ 0 \\ d \\ d \\ d \\ d \end{bmatrix}$$

and $u = u^{|} + d$

A quadratic cost function

$$= \int_0^{\infty} \frac{1}{2}\left(X'^T.QX' + u'^T Ru'\right)dt$$

is selected and the algebraic matrix Riccati equation is solved as before to obtain the optimal gains using the equations.

$$Q - RB\,P^{-1}\,B^T\,R + R\,A + A^T R = 0$$

and $$u\text{ opt} = -\mathbf{P}^{-1}\,\mathbf{B}^T\,\mathbf{RX}$$

$$= -\mathbf{L}^T\,\mathbf{X} \qquad .....(6.129)$$

The results are plotted in Fig. E.6.

E 6.13 Compute the optimal load frequency control for a single thermal power system with tandem compound single-reheat steam turbine with the following data

$R = 20s$	$T_{RH} = 7.5s$	$K_p = 2$ p.u. Hz / p.u. MW
$T_s = 0.1s$	$T_{CO} = 0.45s$	$T_P = 20s$
$T_{CH} = 0.25s$	$F_{HP} = 0.3$	$D = 0.01$ p.u.
$F_{IP} = 0.4$	$F_{LP} = 0.3$	

Plot the variations of the controlled states with time

Solution :

Q and P matrices are selected as follows

$$Q = \begin{bmatrix} 1 & 0 & 0 & 0 & 0 & 0 \\ 0 & 1 & 0 & 0 & 0 & 0 \\ 0 & 0 & 0 & 0 & 0 & 0 \\ 0 & 0 & 0 & 0 & 0 & 0 \\ 0 & 0 & 0 & 0 & 0 & 0 \\ 0 & 0 & 0 & 0 & 0 & 0 \end{bmatrix}; \; P = 1$$

The solution is obtained using a computer program for the algorithm explained in 6.26. The feedback gains, starting from initial values of unity for each, converge to the following solution.

$$L^T = [1.0 \quad 0.6617 \quad 0.0269 \quad 0.3037 \quad 0.0047 \quad 0.0177]$$

Plots of $\int \Delta f$ and Δf, the two optimally controlled states are shown in Fig. E. 6.13 (a) and (b)

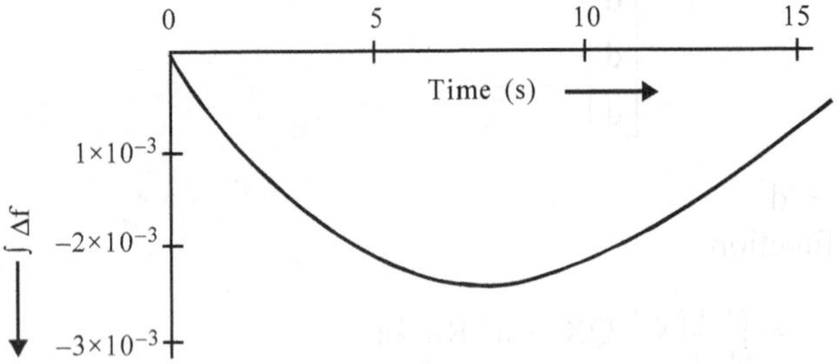

Fig. E6.13 Optimal response
(a) Optimal response of time error to step load change

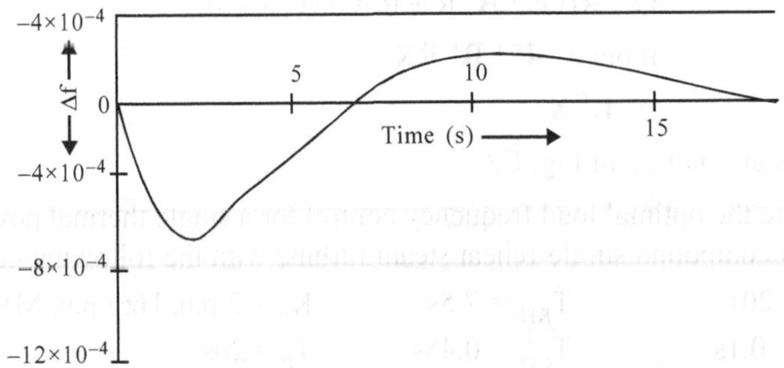

Fig. E6.13(b) optimal response of frequency error to step load change

6.28 Optimal Control of Hydro Speed Governing System

Consider the system shown in Fig. 6.20. The state variable mode for the system is

$$\dot{X} = AX + Bu + Cu + F.d \qquad .....(6.130)$$

with the initial conditions X(0) = 0

where
$$\mathbf{X}^T = [X_1 \quad X_2 \quad X_3 \quad X_4 \quad X_5 \quad X_6]$$
$$= \left[\int \Delta f \quad \Delta f \quad \Delta P_G \quad \Delta P_{GV} \quad \Delta P_{PV} \quad \Delta P_{PV}\right]$$

$$A = \begin{bmatrix} 0 & 1 & 0 & 0 & 0 & 0 \\ 0 & -\dfrac{1}{T_{PS}} & \dfrac{K_{PS}}{T_{PS}} & 0 & 0 & 0 \\ 0 & 0 & -\dfrac{1}{0.5T_W} & \dfrac{1}{0.5T_W} & \dfrac{1}{0.5T_W} & 0 \\ 0 & 0 & 0 & 0 & 1 & 0 \\ 0 & 0 & 0 & 0 & 0 & 1 \\ 0 & -K_1 & -K_2 & -K_3 & -K_4 & -K_5 \end{bmatrix}$$

$$B^T = \begin{bmatrix} 0 & 0 & 0 & 0 & 0 & \dfrac{1}{T_P T_R T_G} \end{bmatrix}$$

$$C^T = \begin{bmatrix} 0 & 0 & 0 & 0 & 0 & \dfrac{1}{T_P T_G} \end{bmatrix}$$

$$F^T = \begin{bmatrix} 0 & -\dfrac{K_{PS}}{T_{PS}} & 0 & 0 & 0 & \dfrac{K_{PS}}{T_P T_R T_{PS}} \end{bmatrix}$$

$u = \Delta P_C$ = control input

and $d = \Delta P_D$ = step-load disturbance.

The constants K_1, K_2, K_3 K_4 K_5 are given by

$$K_1 = \frac{T_{PS} - T_R}{T_P T_G T_R T_{PS}}$$

$$K_2 = \frac{K_{PS}}{T_P T_G T_{PS}}$$

$$K_3 = \frac{\sigma}{T_P T_G T_R}$$

$$K_4 = \frac{T_R(\sigma + \delta) + T_G}{T_P T_G T_R}$$

$$K_5 = \frac{1}{T_P} + \frac{1}{T_R}$$

The state and control variable are transformed using the relation,

$$\begin{bmatrix} x_1 \\ x_2 \\ x_3 \\ x_4 \\ x_5 \\ x_6 \end{bmatrix} = \begin{bmatrix} x_1' \\ x_2' \\ x_3' \\ x_4' \\ x_5' \\ x_6' \end{bmatrix} + \begin{bmatrix} 0 \\ 0 \\ d \\ d \\ 0 \\ \dfrac{u'}{T_P T_G} \end{bmatrix} \qquad .....(6.131)$$

$$u = u' + d\,\sigma$$

The transformed equations are

$$\dot{X}' = A'X' + B'.u'$$

where $A' = A$

and $B'^T = \begin{bmatrix} 0 & 0 & 0 & 0 & \dfrac{1}{T_P T_P^2} - & \dfrac{1}{T^P T_G} \end{bmatrix}$

The cost functional to be minimized is selected as

$$J = \frac{1}{2}\int_0^{\infty}\left(X'^T Q X' + u'^T P^{u'}\right)dt$$

Selecting Q and R matrices are :

$$Q = \begin{bmatrix} 1 & 0 & 0 & 0 & 0 & 0 \\ 0 & 1 & 0 & 0 & 0 & 0 \\ 0 & 0 & 0 & 0 & 0 & 0 \\ 0 & 0 & 0 & 0 & 0 & 0 \\ 0 & 0 & 0 & 0 & 0 & 0 \\ 0 & 0 & 0 & 0 & 0 & 0 \end{bmatrix}$$

and P = 1

the algebraic matrix Ricccati equation

$$\mathbf{Q = R\,B'\,P^{-1}\,B'^T\,R + R\,A' + A'^T\,R = 0}$$

is solved for the elements of R.

The optimal control is obtained using

$$\mathbf{u_{opt} = -P^{-1}\,B'^T\,R\,X'}$$

$$\mathbf{= -L^T\,X} \qquad .....(6.132)$$

The states with optimal control are determined from

$$\dot{X}' = \left(A' - B'L\right)X' \qquad .....(6.133)$$

E 6.14 For the hydro system shown in Fig. 6.14.1; using the following data, compute the optimal control

$T_G = 0.2$ s KPS = 2 p.u. Hz / p.u. MW

$T_P = 0.04$s $\Delta P_D = 0.01$ p.u.

$T_W = 0.6$ s

$T_{PS} = 20$s

$T_R = 3$s

$\sigma = 0.05$

$\delta = 0.2$ The 100 % load conditions on the plant.

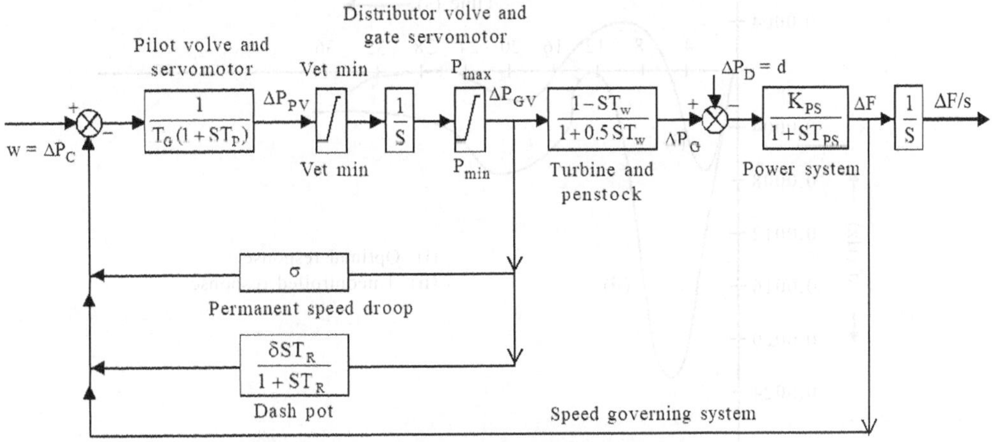

Fig. E6.14.1 Hydro speed governing system

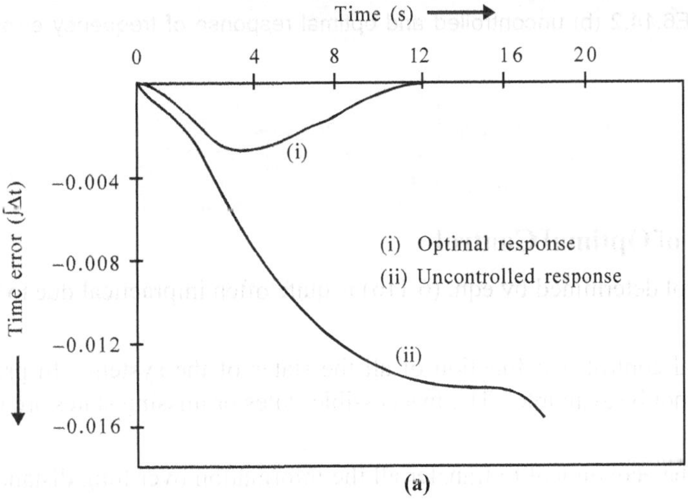

(a)

Fig. E6.14.2 Uncontrolled and optimal response of hydro speed governing system

(a) uncontrolled and optimal response of time error

Solution :

Following the procedure outlined in Sec. 6.20, the optimal feed-back gain components are computed as

$$L^T = [1.0 \quad 3.4061 \quad 0.078 \quad 0.5393 \quad 0.1656 \quad 0.0063]$$

The uncontrolled and optimal response are shown in figure E6.14.2 (a) and (b).

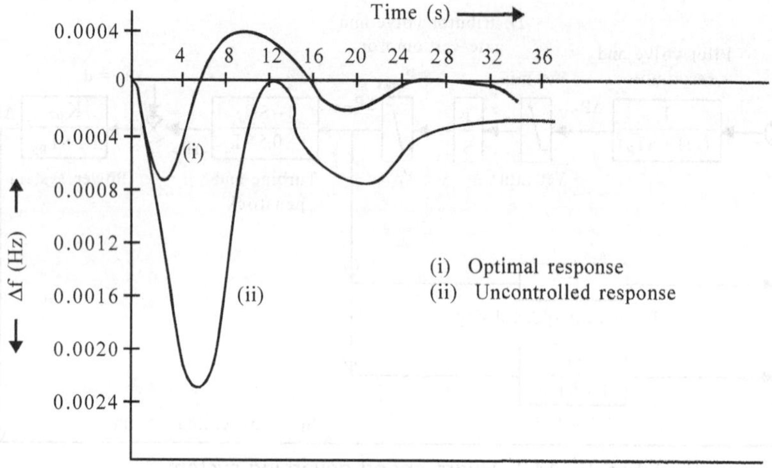

Fig. E6.14.2 (b) uncontrolled and optimal response of frequency error

6.29 A Review of Optimal Control

The optimal control determined by eqn. (6.116) is quite often impractical due to the following reasons:

1. The optimal control is a function of all the states of the system. In practice, all the states may not be available. The inaccessible states or missing states are required to be estimated.
2. It may not be economical to transfer all the information over long distances.
3. The control which is a function of the states in turn is dependent on the load demand. Accurate prediction of the load demand may be essential for realizing the optimal controller.

4. The optimal control is also dependent on the weighting matrices in equation (6.111) and is thus not unique.

6.30 Load Frequency Control with Restrictions on the Rate of Power Generation

The optimal load frequency control discussed in section 6.25 does not include the effect of the limits on the rate of change of power generation. If these limits were not included in the control, there will be a tendency for the system to chase large momentary disturbances.

This causes undue wear and tear of the controller. Even a telemetering outage may cause problems to the system in operation. Several methods are proposed to include the effect of generation rate constraints in the computation of the control.

If the generation rate constraints denoted by $\dot{P}$ are introduced into the state vector, the system order will be changed. Instead of augmenting them, it is suggested that while solving the state equations, it may be verified at each step whether or not the generation rate constraints are violated.

Another simple way of considering the generation rate constraints is dual mode control strategy. Separating the state vector **X** into those states which are to be rate limited as x_l and the rest by xr, the state space representation of the system becomes

$$\begin{bmatrix} \dot{X}_l \\ \dot{X}_r \end{bmatrix} = \begin{bmatrix} A_{ll} & A_{lr} \\ A_{rl} & A_{rr} \end{bmatrix} \begin{bmatrix} X_l \\ X_r \end{bmatrix} + \begin{bmatrix} B_l \\ B_r \end{bmatrix} u \qquad .....(6.134)$$

the generation rate constraints are given by

$$\left|\dot{X}_l\right| \leq \left|\dot{X}_l^{max}\right| = \qquad .....(6.135)$$

That is $\left|A_{ll}\ X_l\right| + A_{lr}\ X_r + Bl\ u \leq \left|\dot{X}_l^{max}\right|$

The choice of U(t) may be made using

$$B_l u(t) = K\left|\dot{X}_l^{max}\right| - A_{ll}X_l - A_{lr}X_r \qquad .....(6.136)$$

where K is a (m X m) diagonal matrix with sgn. (X_j), j = 1, 2, ... m and m is the number of rate limited state variables out of n state variables. The dual mode control may be represented by eqn. (6.134) and (6.136)

$$u^0(t) = -K_1X;\ \text{if}\ x_{1j} < \dot{x}_{ij}^{max} \quad j = 1,2,\ldots\ldots\ldots, n \qquad \ldots..(6.137)$$

$$= -B_1^{-1}\left[K\dot{x}_I^{max} - LX\right];\text{if}\ x_{ij} > \dot{x}_{Ij}^{max}\ ;j = 1,2,\ldots\ldots\ldots n \qquad \ldots..(6.138)$$

The generation rate constraints result in larger deviations in area control errors. As the rate at which generation can change in the area is constrained by the limits power import via tie lines becomes imperative. Under generation rate constrained conditions, the selection of governor speed regulation cofficient R requires careful consideration. In practice, a low value, of the order of 2 to 4%, is chosen for R. With ,a proper, supplementary control, the steady state error can be reduced to zero, whatever may be the value of R. However, it is desirable that a proper value of R be selected so as to give the best dynamic response. Improper selection of R may lead to instability whatever may be the integral controller gain settings.

In systems with hydro-thermal combination, the generation rate in the hydro area generally remains below the safe, permissible generation rate, and as such the rate constraints for generation at all the hydro plants can be omitted.

The presence of governor dead-band introduces oscillations in the dynamic response. It has been reported that the governor dead band does not influence the selection of integral controller gain settings in the presence of generation rate constraints.

6.31 Load Frequencly Control using Output Feedback

The optimal control derived in Sec. 6.22 requires the availability of all the states. However, if some of them are not available, reconstruction of those states requires either the Lueneberger observer or Kalman filter. This may not be feasible for various reasons. Controllers based on output feedback are proposed to overcome this problem. It has been pointed out later in chapter 7 that area control error for each area is used to implement the tie- line bias control strategy. Corresponding to this practice, if the area control error is taken as the output, then the load frequency control problem may be considered as an output zeroing problem in the presence of persistent disturbances.

An additional output equation

$$Y = HX$$

is required to be considered in conjunction with the system Eqn. (6.134). The design of output dependent controller is not an easy task as it leads to an equivalent parametric optimization problem. Nevertheless, making use of matrix minimum principle, the controller can be designed. To simplify the computation, minimum norm methods are proposed.

6.32 Load frequency Control and Economic Dispatch

Whenever load changes the initial frequency correction is achieved by the speed governor and this control can be treated as primary load frequency control. The adjustment of frequency by the primary control loop may take a few seconds.

After the speed governor response is over, the steady state frequency error is reduced to zero so that system frequency is maintained constant by the integral controller action. This will be after the primary control action is over and can take a time period up to one minute. This is the secondary control. The adjustment of frequency error to zero by changing the generation schedules that are determined earlier by economic criterion again requires readjustment of generation. This tertiary control can be implemented by using economic dispatch computer which works on the cost characteristics of various generating units in the area. The speed changer settings are once again operated in accordance with economic dispatch computer programme.

Questions

6.1 Explain the necessity of maintaining a constant frequency in power system operation.

6.2 With a neat diagram, explain briefly different parts of a turbine speed governing system.

6.3 Derive the model of a speed governing system and represent it by a block diagram.

6.4 With a block diagram explain the load frequency control for a single area system.

6.5 Derive the model of a speed governing system and represent it by a block diagram.

6.6 With first order approximation explain the dynamic response of an isolated area for load frequency control.

6.7 Discuss the importance of combined load frequency control and economic dispatch control with a neat block diagram

6.8 Discuss in detail the importance of load frequency problem.

6.9 Distinguish between load frequency control and economic dispatch control.

6.10 A synchronous generator supplies power to a synchronous motor via a transmission network. Find equivalent inertia constant of a machine connected to infinite bus.

6.11 Explain how modern control theory can be applied to load frequency control

6.12 Describe how optimal control can be determined in case of LFC problem.

6.13 What are the limitations of optimal control theory ?

Problems

P 6.1 Two generators rated 200MW and 400MW are operating in parallel. The droop characteristics of their governors are 4% and 5% respectively from no load to full load. Assuming that the generators are operating at 50Hz at no load, how would a load of 600Mw be shared between them? What will be the system frequency at this load? Assume free governor operation. Repeat the problem if both the governor have a droop of 4%.

P 6.2 A 100MVA asynchronous generator operates on full load at a frequency of 50Hz. The load is suddenly reduced to 50MW. Due to time lag in the governor system, the steam valve beings to close after 0.4 secs. Determine the change in frequency that occurs in this time. Given H = 5 KW –s/KVA of generator capacity.

P 6.3 Two generators rated 200Mw and 400MW are operating in parallel. The droop characteristics of their governors are 4% and 5% respectively from no load to full load. The speed changes are so set that the generators operate at 50Hz sharing the load of 600Mw in the ratio of their ratings. If the load reduces to 400Mw, how will it be shared among the generators and what will the system frequency? Assume free governor operation. The speed changers of the governors are reset so that the load of 400MW is shared among the generators at 50Hz in the ratio of their ratings. What are the no load frequencies of the generators?

P 6.4 In the single area system shown below determine

(a) The steady state frequency error with $\Delta P_C = 0$

(b) Critical gain K of the integral control of $\Delta P_C = -\int K\Delta f$

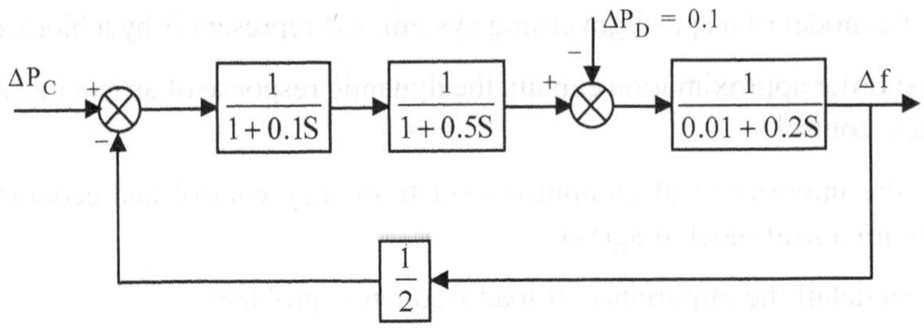

P 6.5 A 500Mw generator is operating at a load of 20Mw. A load change of 1% causes the frequency to change by 1%. If the system frequency is 50Hz determine the value of load damping factor in per unit.

7 CONTROL OF INTERCONNECTED SYSTEMS

Power Systems came into existence in 1880s and from that time onwards the systems have grown enormously in both size and complexity. For better performance and reliability of operation and control, there were many significant developments in generation, transmission and distribution. The concept of energy control centers emerged in 1970's. Computer aided analysis and computer based control have been proposed in this context.

7.1 Interconnected Operation

Power systems are interconnected for economy and continuity of power supply. For the interconnected operation incremental efficiencies, fuel costs, water availability, generation limits, tie line capacities, spinning reserve allocation and area commitments are important considerations in preparing load dispatch schedules.

In this chapter the power control of interconnected system is presented.

7.2 Flat Frequency Control of Interconnected Stations

Consider two generating stations connected by a tie line as in Fig. 7.1(a). For a load increment on station B, the kinetic energy of the generators reduces to absorb the same. Generation increases in both the stations A and B, and frequency will be less than normal at the end of the governor response period Fig. 7.1(b). The load increment will be supplied partly by

A and partly by B. The tie line power flow will change thereby. If a frequency controller is placed at B, then it will shift the governor characteristic at B parallel to itself as shown in Fig. 7.1(c) and the frequency will be restored to its normal value f_s, reducing the change in generation in A to zero.

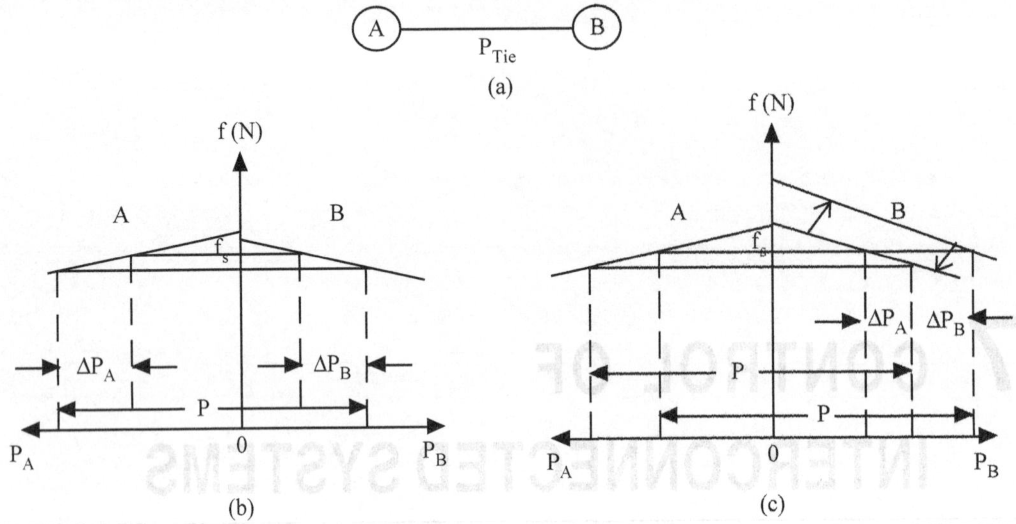

(a) Two interconnected stations

(b) Uncontrolled system with load increment on Station B

(c) Frequency controller located at Station B

Fig. 7.1 Two station system

If the load increment comes on station A, then as before, initially the generation in both A and B changes to absorb the additional load, while finally the additional load is absorbed by B only. Station A absorbs none of its load changes in the steady state. It is possible that, in interconnected operation, a given station can be made to absorb the load changes occurring elsewhere in the system so long as the controlling station has capability to absorb the change.

The same analysis can be extended to a two area system.

Assumption in Analysis :

The following assumptions are made in the analysis of the two area system:

1. The overall governing characteristic of the operating units in any area can be represented by a linear curve of frequency versus generation.
2. The governors in both the areas start acting simultaneously to changes in their respective areas.
3. Supplementary control devices act after the initial governor response is over.

The following time instants are defined to explain the control sequence :

t_o is the instant when both the areas are operating at the scheduled frequency and tie line interchange and load change takes place.

t_1 is the instant when governor action is initiated at both A and B.

t_2 is the instant when governor action ceases.

t_3 is the instant when regulator action begins.

t_4 is the instant when regulator action ceases.

Consider a load increment in area B. From Fig. 7.2(a), it is clear that at the end of the governor response, the tie-line schedule is upset and frequency is less than normal. If now a frequency controller is provided in area B, which shifts the governor characteristic upwards, parallel to itself, so as to provide the required control action, generation in B meets its own load change. Tie line schedule is maintained. Change in generation in A is also reduced to zero.

Consider now the controller action to load change in area A with the controller located in area B as before. The response is shown in Fig. 7.2(c).

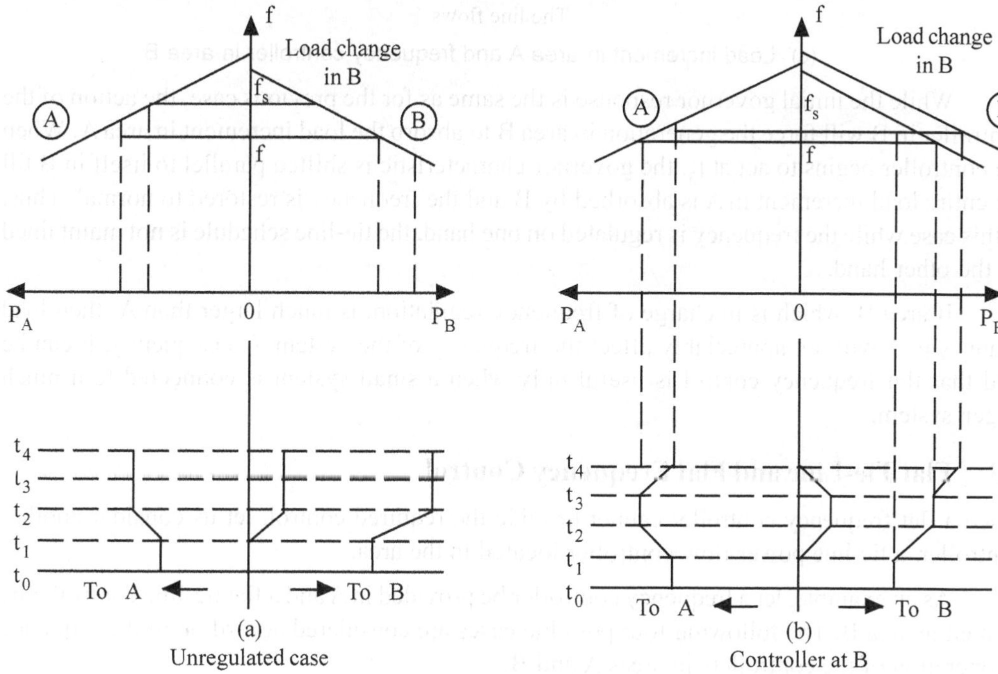

Fig. 7.2 Flat frequency control

(a) Load increment in area B – no controller

(b) Load increment in area B and frequency controller in area B

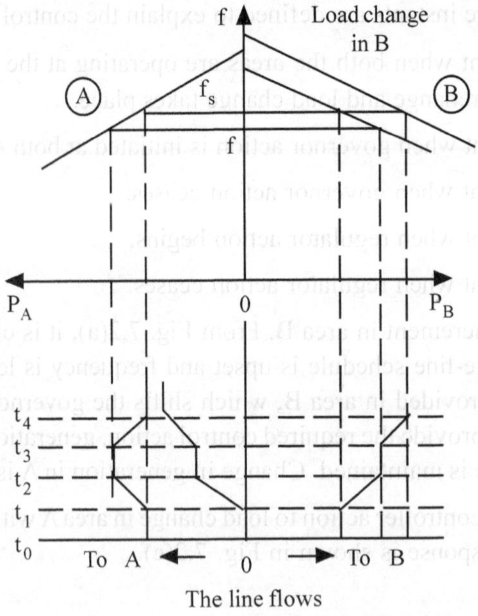

(c) Load increment in area A and frequency controller in area B

While the initial governor response is the same as for the previous case, the action of the controller in B will force the generation in area B to absorb the load increment in area A. When the controller begins to act at t_3, the governor characteristic is shifted parallel to itself in B till the entire load increment in A is absorbed by B and the frequency is restored to normal. Thus, in this case while the frequency is regulated on one hand, the tie-line schedule is not maintained on the other hand.

If area B, which is in charge of frequency regulation, is much larger than A, then load changes in A will not appreciably affect the frequency of the system. Consequently, it can be said that flat frequency control is useful only when a small system is connected to a much larger system.

7.3 Flat Tie-Line and Flat Frequency Control

Since a flat frequency controller cannot provide the required control, let us consider another controller, a tie line power flow controller located in the area.

As an example, let a frequency controller be provided in A and a flat tie-line controller be located in area B. The following four possible cases are considered according to the sequence of operation of the controllers in areas A and B.

1. Load change in A: Sequence of operation A, B, A, ...
2. Load change in B: Sequence of operation B, A, B, ...
3. Load change in A: Sequence of operation B, A, B, ...
4. Load change in B: Sequence of operation A, B, A, ...

Case 1 : Let a load increment take place in area A. It is assumed that following the initial governor response, the frequency controller in A acts first at t_3 and its control action ceases at t_4. By the time the tie-line controller at B becomes effective at t_5, it finds the system in normal condition. both frequency and tie line deviations are reduced to zero, and further regulating action is unnecessary. This action is shown in Fig. 7.3(a).

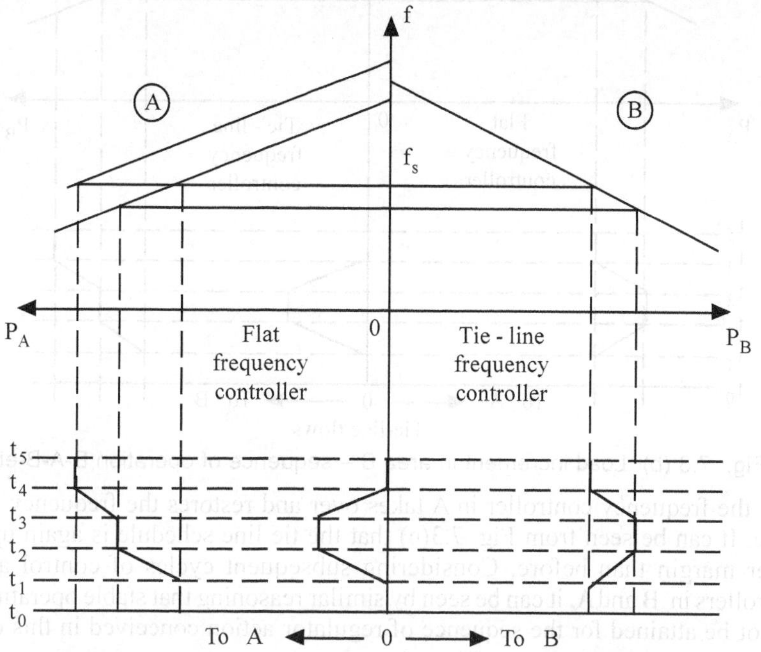

Fig. 7.3 Flat tie-line and frequency control – frequency controller in area A and tie-line controller in area B.

(a) Load increment in area A – sequence of operation A – B – A – etc.

Case 2 : Let the load increment occur in area B. The tie – line controller in B acts first following the initial governor response at t_3 and increases the generation in B till the load increment is completely absorbed. At the instant t_5, the frequency controller in A finds that the conditions are normal and no regulating action is needed. The load increment in B is absorbed by the generation in B itself. The case is illustrated in Fig. 7.3(b).

Case 3 : Load change occurs in A and the controller in B acts first. The initial governor response which begins at the instant t_1 ceases at t_2. The tie line controller in B begins and completes its action before the frequency regulator at A takes control. During this period of control action, i.e. t_3-t_4 by the tie line regulator the frequency decreases further than it was at the end of the governor action period while the tie line power schedule is maintained.

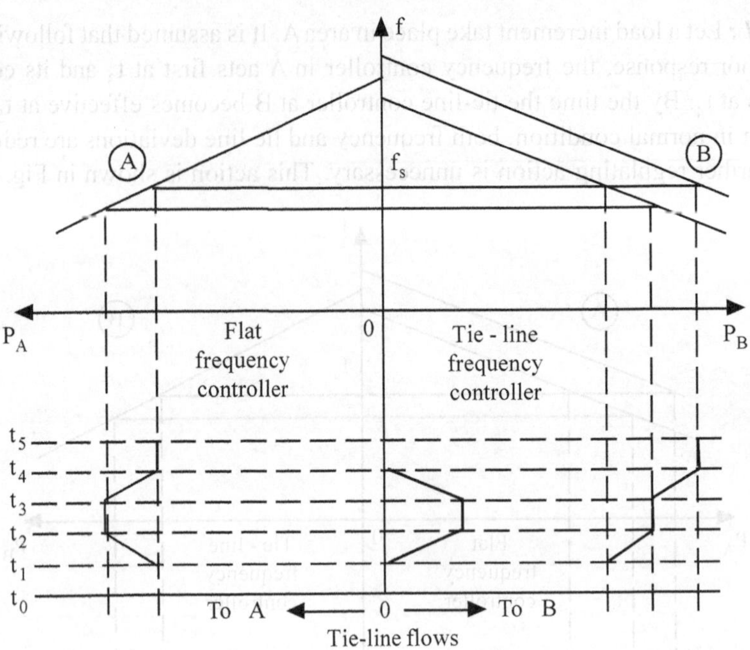

Fig. 7.3 (b) Load increment in area B – sequence of operation B-A-B-etc.

At t_5 the frequency controller in A takes over and restores the frequency to its normal value. It can be seen from Fig. 7.3(c) that the tie line schedule is again upset but by a larger margin than before. Considering subsequent cycles of control action by the controllers in B and A, it can be seen by similar reasoning that stable operating conditions cannot be attained for the sequence of regulator action conceived in this case.

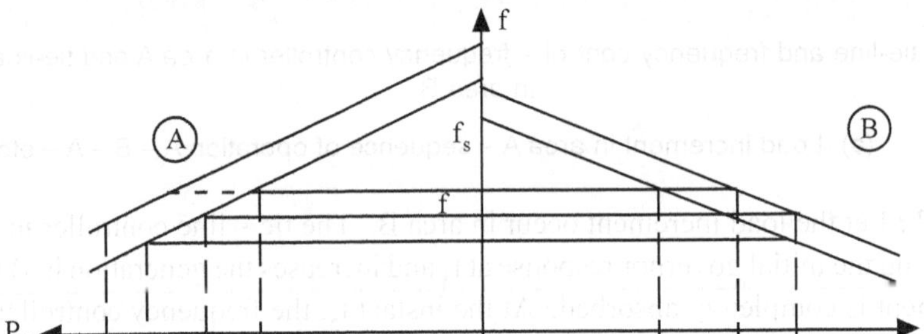

Fig. 7.3 (c) Load increment in area A – sequence of operation B-A-B-etc.

Case 4 : Finally consider the load increment to have taken place in area B. Let us assume that the frequency controller in A starts and completes its action the tie-line – controller in B starts functioning. The response to governor and controller action is shown in Fig. 7.3(d).

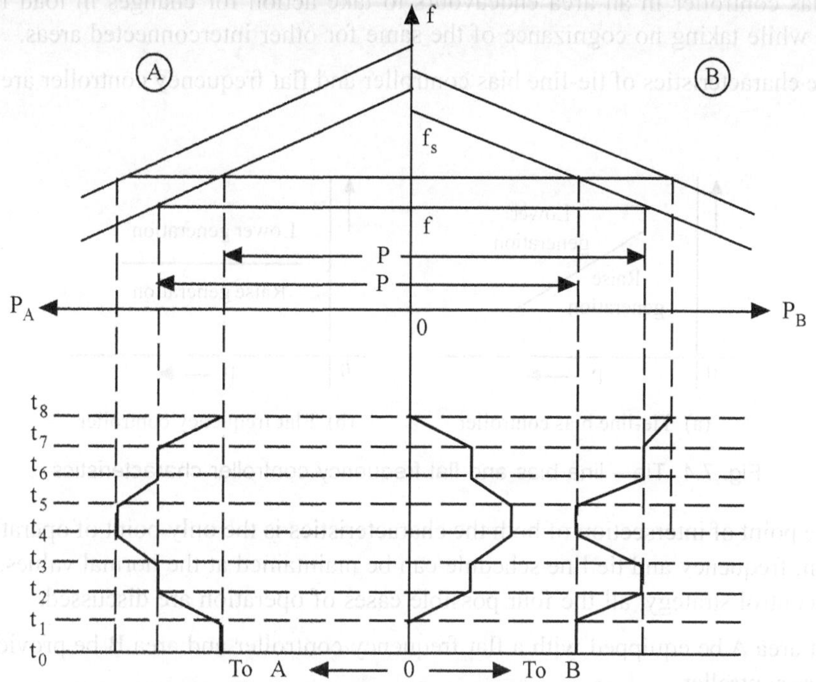

Fig. 7.3 (d) Load increment in area B – sequence of operation A-B-A etc

The flat frequency controller at A increases the generation in A to correct the frequency by shifting the characteristic parallel to itself upwards; The generation in A and hence the tie-line power from A to B increases. At t_5, when the tie-line controller takes over the control, it will find excessive power flow from A to B and to keep it at the scheduled value, it increases the generation in B. While doing so, the generation in A gets reduced and the tie line power flow to B is also reduced. Finally, when the frequency controller begins to act in A at t_8 neither the tie-line power schedule nor the frequency is normal. The system starts oscillating and no regulation is feasible.

It can be seen from the above analysis that if one of the regulators is sluggish in any area where changes in power demand take place, than other regulators, flat tie-line flat frequency regulator strategy cannot assist in getting the desired control.

7.4 Tie-Line Bias Control

The regulators described in Sec. 7.3 can attain the desired control in so far as the local load changes are considered. However, they fail to respond to changes in remote areas. One way to overcome this problem is to make the flat tie-line controller responsive to frequency changes also. That is, the flat tie-line controller is to be biased so that we obtain a tie-line bias controller.

With this type of controller, the regulator does not act to hold a constant tie-line interchange regardless of system frequency, but instead allows the tie line schedule to deviate from the normal in adjustable proportion to frequency deviations from the rated value. In principle, the tie line bias controller in an area endeavours to take action for changes in load in its own precincts, while taking no cognizance of the same for other interconnected areas.

The characteristics of tie-line bias controller and flat frequency controller are shown in Fig. 7.4.

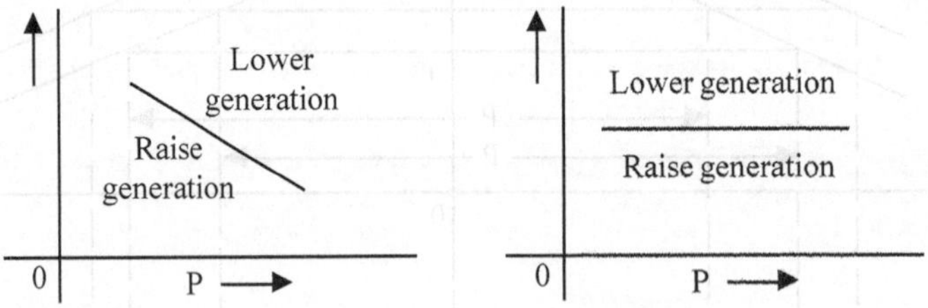

(a) Tie-line bias controller (b) Flat frequency controller

Fig. 7.4 Tie – line bias and flat frequency controller characteristics

The point of intersection of both the characteristics is the only point of operation where the system, frequency and tie line schedule can be maintained at the normal values. As in the previous control strategy, all the four possible cases of operation are discussed.

Let area A be equipped with a flat frequency controller and area B be provided with a tie-line bias controller.

Case 1 : Consider a small load increment in Area A. Let the flat frequency controller in area A act first.

The response to governor and controller action is same as that shown in Fig. 7.5(a). Following the initial governor response, the frequency controller in A begins and completes its action before the tie-line bias controller at B comes into operation. Both the frequency and tie-line power schedules are maintained at scheduled levels by the controller in A. No further corrective action is needed by the tie-line bias controller in B.

Case 2 : Let the load increment take place in B with the tie-line bias controller in B acting first. The response to governors and controllers would again be the same as given in Fig. 7.5(b). Following the initial governor response, the tie-line bias controller in B acts during t_3 - t_4 and, by shifting the governor characteristic in B, both the tie line power and frequency deviations are corrected. No further regulating action is required from the controller in A.

Case 3 : Let the load change occur in area A. The controller in area B acts first, followed by the frequency controller in area A. If the governor characteristic is prevented from being shifted by the action of the tie-line regulator in B during the interval t_3 - t_4 the frequency controller in A can restore the frequency to its normal value during the period t_5 - t_6 so that the controller at A acts for changes in load in area A only and absorbs all of them. This can happen if the slope of the tic-line bias controller in B is same as the slope of the governing characteristic at A at the point of operation under consideration. Under such a condition, the response to controller action is shown in Fig. 7.5(a).

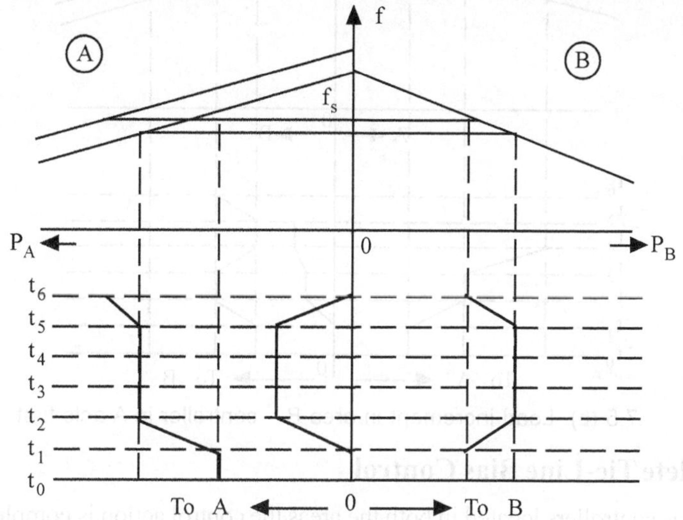

Fig. 7.5 Tie-line bias control in area A and tie-line bias controller in area B
(a) Load increment in area A – controller in A acts first

Case 4 : Finally, let the load increment occur in B while the controller in A initiates action first following the governor action. It can be seen from Fig. 7.5(b) that during the period t_1 - t_2, the governors in A act following the load increment in area B. The frequency falls and the tie line power flows from A to B. During the period t_3 - t_4, the flat frequency controller in A acts, generation in A increases and more power flows to B via the tie-line. The frequency is normal. During t_5 - t_6, the tie-line bias controller in B acts to set the tie-line deviation to zero. The governor characteristic is raised in B. Frequency increases but tie-line flow from A to B is reduced. Neither the frequency nor the tie-line schedule are normal at this stage. However, during the period t_7 - t_8, the flat frequency controller in A again takes over the control and the governor is set at a lower value in A. Generation in A is reduced until the frequency is normal and tie-line power flow deviation is zero.

From the above analysis it can be inferred that each controller operates effectively to control load changes in its own area. For load changes in other interconnected areas, the tie-line bias controller can be set to refrain from taking improper action while the frequency regulator still persists in its tendency to sacrifice the local area requirement to overall requirement.

Since the frequency controller in A responds unnecessarily to changes in load in B, it may be replaced by another tie-line bias controller. This results in complete tie-line bias control.

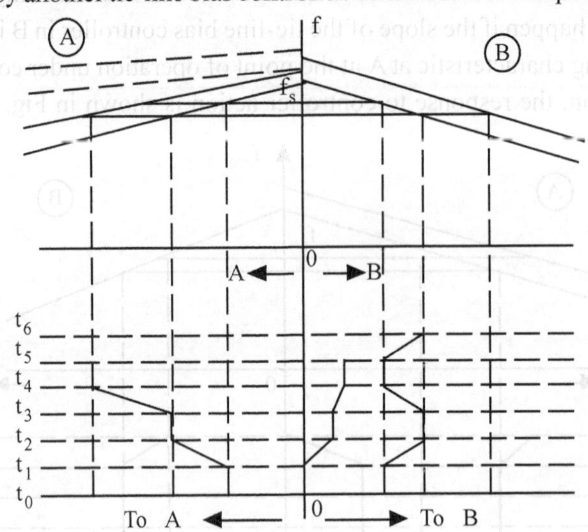

7.5 (b) Load increment in area B – controller in A acts first

7.5 Complete Tie-Line Bias Control

With tie-line bias controllers located in both the areas the control action is complete in all the cases.

For the case where the tie-line bias controller in A initiates action for local load changes, the response is shown in Fig. 7.6(a). The response to controller action is similar for load changes in B when the controller in B initiates regulating action.

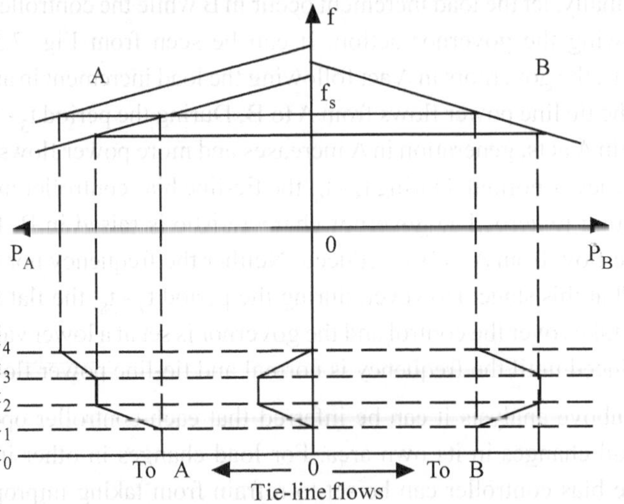

(a)

Fig. 7.6 Complete tie-line bias control – tie line controllers in both the areas A and B

(a) controller action in A for local load changes

For the case when a controller initiates action for non-local load changes the controllers will not act if the slope of the controller characteristic is matched to that of the governing characteristic. The response characteristics are illustrated for a load change in area A while the controller in B is the first to initiate action Fig. 7.6(b).

During this period the controller in B is prevented from regulating the system. The incremental changes are corrected by the controller in A only, during t_5 - t_6. The control action is quite satisfactory. From the above analysis, it is seen that the governor action in an area is not opposed by supplementary control action in the same area.

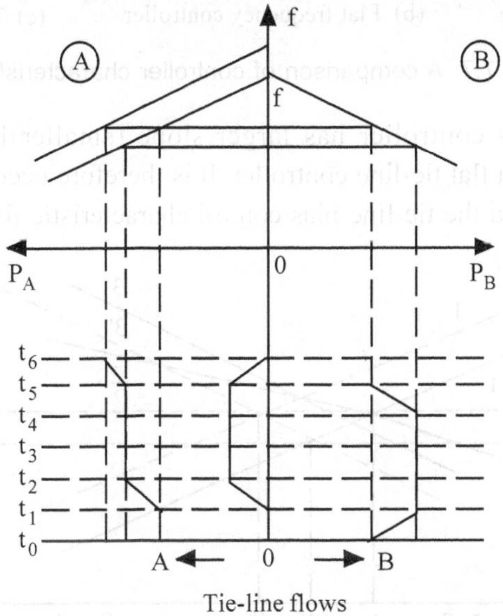

Fig. 7.6(b) Load change in A – controller in B acts first

The governor action is not changed till the controller in the area, where a load change has occurred, becomes effective. This avoids unnecessary change in generation, frequency or tie-line power. The controller in the area, where load change occurs, acts in such a manner that the area absorbs its own load change. Only a single shift is necessary to the governor characteristic to restore both frequency and tie-line power to normal. A smooth, cooperative regulation is thus achieved with a tie-line bias-tie-line bias control scheme for the two area system.

For successful operation, it is imperative that the control characteristic of each tie-line bias controller must have the same slope as the governor characteristic of its own area. Fig. 7.7 shows the three types of controller characteristics for comparison.

It can be seen from Fig. 7.7 that flat tie-line control characteristic and flat frequency control characteristic are only limiting cases of tie-line bias control characteristic with zero bias and infinite bias respectively. A tie- line bias controller with larger bias (less slope) compared to its area governor charlatanistic will be more sensitive to load changes in the outside system than the governor and acts like a flat frequency controller.

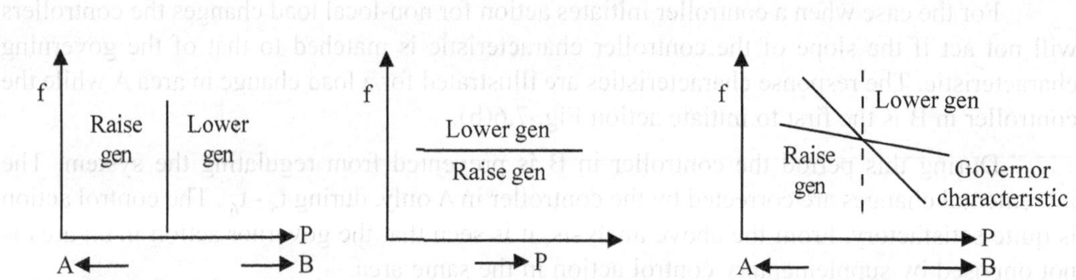

(a) Flat tie-line controller (b) Flat frequency controller (c) Tie-line bias controller

Fig. 7.7 A comparison of controller characteristics

If the tie-line bias controller has larger slope (smaller bias) than the governor characteristic, it acts like a flat tie-line controller. It is therefore necessary to match the speed governor characteristic and the tie-line bias control characteristic for satisfactory control.

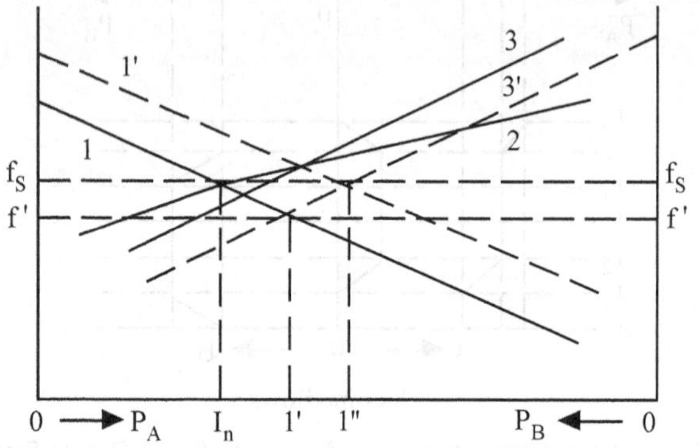

Fig. 7.8 Mismatching of tie-line bias control characteristics

Further, as the tie-line bias controller acts to correct the deviations in the tie-line power flow schedules, the tie-line interchange must be metered accurately and then a correcting strategy be applied.

If the tie-line bias controller characteristic is not matched to the concerned area governor characteristic, the effect could be seen from the following analysis.

Let the governor characteristics of areas A and B be represented by curves 1 and 2 as shown in Fig. 7.8. The tie-line bias controller characteristic is assumed to coincide with the governor characteristic in area A (i.e. curve I) but the characteristic of the controller in area B is assumed to be curve 3.I_0 is the actual tie-line power flow. Due to mismatching of the curves in B, the interchange increases to I' and the frequency falls from the synchronous frequency f_s to f '. In order to control the frequency, the characteristic I is shifted upwards to I' and the curve 3 to 3'. The inter-change increases to I" while the frequency is regulated. After this discussion mathematical analysis of the two area system will be now presented.

In chapter 6, single control area and its response to changes in load, both uncontrolled and controlled is discussed. Let us consider now two control areas connected by a tie-line. Each control area will have the same frequency and the same frequency deviations for the entire area. The tie-line is considered weak in the sense that both the areas can have frequency deviations different from each other in uncontrolled mode (i.e) Δf_1 and Δf_2 respectively.

7.6 Two Area System – Tie-Line Power Model

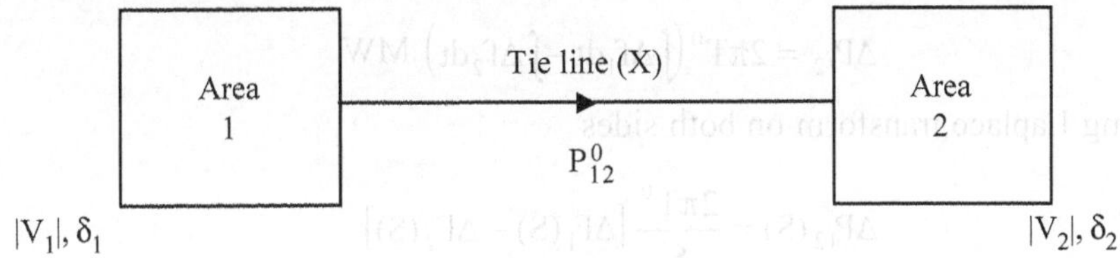

Fig. 7.9

Consider two inter connected areas as shown in figure operating at the same frequency f^0 while a power P_{12}^0 flow from area 1 to area 2 let $|V_1|$ and $|V_2|$ be the voltage magnitudes at δ_1^0 and δ_2^0 voltage phase angles at the two ends of the tie-line while P_{12}^0 flows from area 1 to area 2 then,

$$P_{12}^0 = \frac{|V_1||V_2|}{X} \operatorname{Sin}\left(\delta_1^0 - \delta_2^0\right) \qquad .....(7.1)$$

where X is the reactance of the line.

If the angles change by $\Delta\delta_1$and $\Delta\delta_2$ due to load changes in areas 1 and 2 respectively. Then, the tie-line power changes by

$$\Delta P_{12} = \frac{|V_1^0||V_2^0|}{X} \operatorname{Cos}\left(\delta_1^0 - \delta_2^0\right)(\Delta P_1 - \Delta P_2) \qquad .....(7.2)$$

Defining
$$\frac{\Delta P_{12}}{\Delta\delta_1 - \Delta\delta_2} = \frac{\Delta P_{12}}{\Delta\delta} \text{ MW/radian} \qquad .....(7.3)$$

as synchronizing coefficient of the tie-line or "stiffness coefficient" of the line, denoted by T^0

$$\Delta P_{12} = T^0 \left(\Delta\delta_1^0 - \Delta\delta_2^0\right) \qquad .....(7.4)$$

consider
$$\Delta\omega = \frac{d}{dt}\Delta\delta$$

(i.e.)
$$2\pi\Delta f = \frac{d}{dt}\Delta\delta$$

$$\Delta f = \frac{1}{2\pi}\frac{d}{dt}\Delta\delta \text{ Hz}$$

In otherwords

$$\Delta\delta = 2\pi\int \Delta f \, dt \text{ rad} \quad .....(7.5)$$

Hence $$\Delta\delta_1 = 2\pi\int \Delta f_1 \, dt \text{ rad}$$

and $$\Delta\delta_2 = 2\pi\int \Delta f_2 \, dt \text{ rad}$$

From equation (7.4)

$$\Delta P_{12} = 2\pi T^0 \left(\int \Delta f_1 dt - \int \Delta f_2 dt\right) \text{ MW} \quad .....(7.6)$$

Taking Laplace transform on both sides

$$\Delta P_{12}(S) = \frac{2\pi T^0}{S}[\Delta F_1(S) - \Delta F_2(S)] \quad .....(7.7)$$

Block schematic of the above equation is shown in Fig. (7.10)

If the two areas are rated at P_{r1} and P_{r2}

then if $$\frac{P_{r1}}{P_{r2}} = a_{12}$$

$$\Delta P_{21}(S) = \frac{2\pi T_{21}^0}{S}[\Delta F_2(S) - \Delta F_1(S)]$$

$$\frac{2\pi T_{21}^0 \cdot a_{12}}{S}[\Delta F_1(S) - \Delta F_2(S)]$$

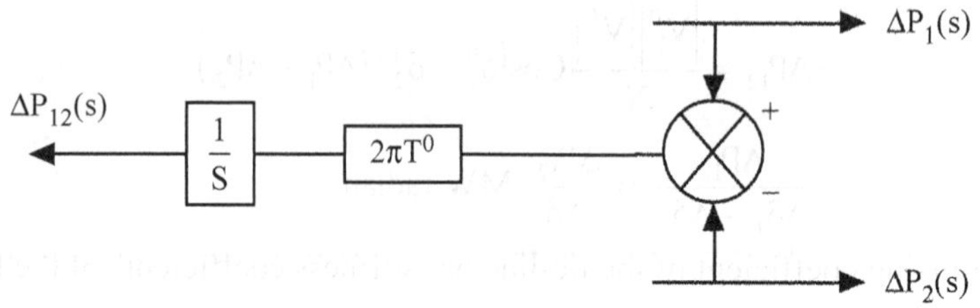

Fig. 7.10 Block diagram for tie-line power

7.7 Block Diagram for Two Area System

The block diagram for a two area system can now be developed. Each area can be represented by a block diagram as in the case of a single area system, but with suffixes 1 and 2. the block diagram for the tie-line power deviation can be used to inter connect both the areas as shown in Fig. (7.11).

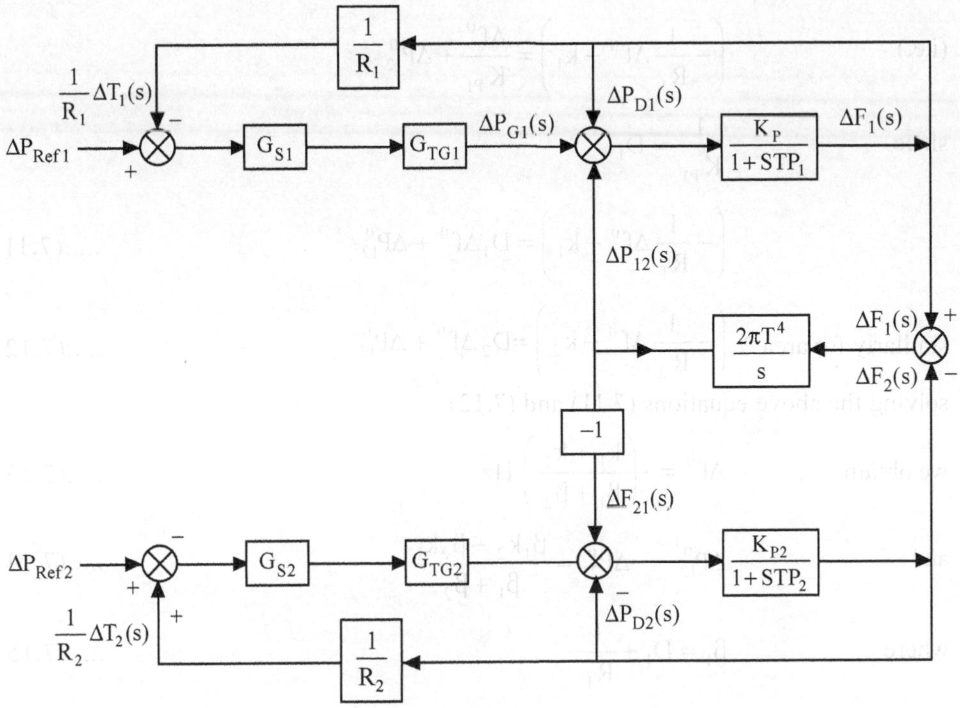

Fig. 7.11 Block diagram for 2-area systems

7.8 Analysis of Two Area System

Steady State Response :

Consider the speed changer positions as fixed so that

$$\Delta P_{ref,\,1} = \Delta P_{ref,\,2} = 0$$

let the loads in both the areas change by $\Delta P_{D1} = k_1$ and $\Delta P_{D1} = k_2$, step changes in the two area respectively. Let Δf^0 be the final or steady state frequency deviation due to load changes. Similary ΔP_{12}^0 let be the change in the tie-line power flow.

From the Fig. 7.11

$$\Delta P_{TG,1}^0 = -\frac{1}{R_1}\Delta f_0 \qquad .....(7.8)$$

$$\Delta P_{TG,2}^0 = -\frac{1}{R_2}\Delta f_0 \qquad .....(7.9)$$

where $\Delta P_{TG,1}^0$ and $\Delta P_{TG,2}^0$ are the steady state changes in turbine-generator outputs.

Also, from the same Fig. 7.11, at the summing point of load and tie-line powers, we get

$$\left(-\frac{1}{R_1}\Delta f^0 - k_1 - \Delta P_{12}^0\right)K_{P1} = \Delta f^0 \qquad .....(7.10)$$

(i.e.) $$\left(-\frac{1}{R_1}\Delta f^0 - k_1\right) = \frac{\Delta f^0}{K_{P1}} + \Delta P_{12}^0$$

since $$\frac{1}{K_{P1}} = D_1$$

$$\left(-\frac{1}{R_1}\Delta f^0 - k_1\right) = D_1\Delta f^0 + \Delta P_{12}^0 \quad .....(7.11)$$

similarly for area 2 $$\left(-\frac{1}{R_2}\Delta f^0 - k_2\right) = D_2\Delta f^0 + \Delta P_{12}^0 \quad .....(7.12)$$

solving the above equations (7.11) and (7.12)

we obtain $$\Delta f^0 = -\left(\frac{k_1 + k_2}{\beta_1 + \beta_2}\right) \text{Hz} \quad .....(7.13)$$

and $$\Delta P_{12}^0 = -\Delta P_{21}^0 = \frac{\beta_1 k_2 - \beta_2 k_1}{\beta_1 + \beta_2} \quad .....(7.14)$$

where $$\beta_1 = D_1 + \frac{1}{R_1} \quad .....(7.15)$$

and $$\beta_2 = D_2 + \frac{1}{R_2} \quad .....(7.16)$$

which are defined as the area frequency response characteristics.

Let both the areas be identical

Then, $D_1 = D_2 = D$

$R_1 = R_2 = R$

$\beta_1 = \beta_2 = \beta$

The deviations become

$$\Delta f^0 = \frac{k_1 + k_2}{2\beta} \text{ Hz} \quad ......(7.17)$$

and $$\Delta P_{12}^0 = -\Delta P_{21}^0 = \frac{k_2 - k_1}{2} \text{ p.u. MW} \quad .....(7.18)$$

If the area ratings are different and $\frac{P_{r1}}{P_{r2}} = a_{12}$ then,

$$\Delta f^0 = -\frac{k_2 + a_{12}k_1}{\beta_1 + a_{12}\beta_1}$$

and $$\Delta P_{12}^0 = -\Delta P_{21}^0 = \frac{\beta_1 k_2 - \beta_2 k_1}{\beta_2 + a_{12}\beta_1}$$

If a load disturbance occurs in only one of the areas, it is clear that with $k_1 = 0$ or $k_2 = 0$ the frequency derivation Δf^0 is only half of the steady state error that would have occurred had there been no inter connection. Thus, with several systems inter connected, the steady state frequency error would be reduced.

Also from the tie-line power derivation it can be observed that half of the load change in either area will be supplied by the other area, which demonstrates the importance of emergency assistance in inter connected or pool operation.

7.9 Dynamic Response

From the block diagram of Fig. (7.11) the following equation can be written

$$\left\{-\frac{1}{R_1}\Delta F_1(S)\left[\frac{K_{S1}}{1+sT_{S1}}\right]\left[\frac{K_{TG1}}{1+sT_{TG2}}\right]-\Delta P_{D1}(S)-\Delta P_{12}(S)\right\}\frac{K_{P1}}{1+sT_{P1}}=\Delta F_1(S) \quad .....(7.19)$$

$$\left\{-\frac{1}{R_2}\Delta F_2(S)\left[\frac{K_{S2}}{1+sT_{S2}}\right]\left[\frac{K_{TG2}}{1+sT_{TG2}}\right]-\Delta P_{D2}(S)-\Delta P_{21}(S)\right\}\frac{K_{P2}}{1+ST_{P2}}=\Delta F_2(S) \quad .....(7.20)$$

$$\Delta P_{12}(S)=\frac{2\pi T^0}{s}\left[\Delta F_1(S)-\Delta F_2(S)\right] \quad .....(7.21)$$

$$\Delta P_{21}(S)=-\Delta P_{21}(S)$$

There are four equations with four variables, Δf_1, Δf_2, Δ_{P12} and Δ_{P21} to be determined for given ΔP_{D1} and ΔP_{D2}. The dynamic response can be obtained; even though it is a little bit involved.

For simplicity assume that the two areas are equal. Neglect the governor and turbine dynamics, which means that the dynamics of the system under study is much slower than the fast acting turbine-governor system in a relative sense. Also assume that the load does not change with frequency ($D_1 = D_2 = D = 0$).

We obtain under these assumptions the following relations

$$G_{P1}=\frac{K_{P1}}{1+sT_{P1}}=G_{P2}=\frac{K_{P2}}{1+sT_{P2}}=\frac{\frac{1}{D}}{1+s\left(\frac{2H}{f^0 D}\right)}$$

since D = 0

$$G_P = \frac{1}{D + \left(\frac{2HS}{f^0}\right)} = \frac{f^0}{2HS}$$

equations (7.19) and (7.20) simplify to

$$\left[-\frac{1}{R}\Delta F_1(S) - \Delta P_{D1}(S) - \Delta P_{12}(S)\right]\frac{f^0}{2sH} = \Delta F_1(S) \quad .....(7.22a)$$

$$\left[-\frac{1}{R}\Delta F_2(S) - \Delta P_{D2}(S) - \Delta P_{21}(S)\right]\frac{f^0}{2sH} = \Delta F_2(S) \quad .....(7.22b)$$

subtracting eq. (7.22b) from (7.22a)

$$\left[-\frac{1}{R}\Delta F_1(S) + \frac{1}{R}\Delta F_2(S) - \Delta P_{D1}(S) + \Delta P_{D2}(S) - \Delta P_{12}(S) + \Delta P_{21}(S)\right]\frac{f^0}{2sH} = \Delta F_1(S) - \Delta F_2(S)$$

$$\left[\frac{1}{R}\Delta F_2(S) + \Delta F_1(S) + \Delta P_{D2}(S) - \Delta P_{D1}(S) - 2\Delta P_{12}(S)\right]\frac{f^0}{2sH} = \frac{\Delta P_{12}(S)}{2\pi T^0} \quad .....(7.23)$$

since $\quad (\Delta F_1(S) - \Delta F_2(S))\frac{2\pi T^0}{S} = \Delta P_{12}(S) = -\Delta P_{21}(S)$

Therefore,

$$\left[\frac{1}{R}\left(\frac{-\Delta P_{12}(s)s}{2\pi T^0}\right) + (\Delta P_{D2}(S) - \Delta P_{D1}(S)) - \Delta P_{12}(S)\right]\frac{f^0}{2sH} = \Delta P_{12}(S)\frac{s}{2\pi T^0}$$

$$\Delta P_{12}(S)\left[\frac{sf^0}{2\pi RT_0\, 2sH} + \frac{2f^0}{2sH} + \frac{s}{2sT^0}\right] = \left[\frac{\Delta P_{D2}(S) - \Delta P_{D1}(S)}{2sH}\right]f^0$$

$$\Delta P_{12}(S) = \frac{[\Delta P_{D2}(S) - \Delta P_{D1}(S)]\dfrac{f^0}{2sH}}{\dfrac{S}{2\pi T^0} + \dfrac{2f^0}{2\pi T^0} + \dfrac{Sf^0}{2\pi RT^0\,2SH}}$$

$$= \frac{\left[[\Delta P_{D2}(S) - \Delta P_{D1}(S)]\dfrac{\pi f^0 T^0}{sH}\right]}{s + \dfrac{2f^0\pi T^0}{SH} + \dfrac{f^0}{2RH}}$$

$$= \frac{\pi f^0 T^0}{H} \frac{[\Delta P_{D2}(S) - \Delta P_{D1}(S)]}{s^2 + \left(\dfrac{f^0}{2RH}\right)S + \left(\dfrac{2f^0\pi T^0}{H}\right)} \qquad .....(7.24)$$

The denominator is of the form

$$\left(s^2 + 2KS + \omega^2\right) = (s+K)^2 + (\omega^2 - K^2)$$

where $K = \dfrac{f^0}{4RH}$ and $\omega = \sqrt{\dfrac{2\pi f^0 T^0}{H}}$

setting $\sqrt{\omega^2 - K^2}$ as ω_0.

$$\omega_0 = \sqrt{\frac{2\pi T^0 f^0}{H} - \left(\frac{f^0}{4RH}\right)^n} \qquad .....(7.25)$$

Note that both K and ω^2 are positive. From the roots of the characteristic equation we notice that the system is stable and damped. The frequency of the damped oscillations is given by ω_0.

Since H and f^0 are constant, the frequency of oscillations depends upon the regulation parameter R. Low R gives high K and high damping and vice versa. If $R \to \alpha$; $K \to 0$ is the condition for no-governor action and there will be undamped oscillations.

We thus conclude from the preceding analysis that the two area system, just as in the case of a single area system in the uncontrolled mode, has a steady state error but to a lesser extent and the tie line power deviation and frequency deviation exhibit oscillations that are damped out later.

E 7.1 Two control areas have the following characteristics

Area 1; $R_1 = 0.011$ p.u

$D_1 = 0.85$ p.u.

Base MVA = 1000

Area 2; $R_2 = 0.018$ p.u

$D_2 = 0.95$ p.u.

Base MVA = 1000

A load change of 200 MW occurs in area 1. Determine the new steady state frequency.

Solution :

$$\Delta f^0 = \frac{k_1 + k_2}{\beta_1 + \beta_2} \text{Hz}$$

$k_1 = 0.2$pu ; $k_2 = 0$

$$\beta_1 = D_1 + \frac{1}{R_1} = 0.85 + \frac{1}{0.011} = 90.9091 + 0.85 = 91.7591$$

$$\beta_2 = D_2 + \frac{1}{R_2} = 0.95 + \frac{1}{0.018} = 55.55 + 0.95 = 56.405$$

$$\Delta f^0 = \frac{k_1}{(\beta_1 + \beta_2)} = \frac{0.2}{91.7591 + 56.405} = \frac{0.2}{148.16} = 0.0013683 \text{ p.u. Hz}$$

$f = 50 - (0.0013683 \times 50) = 49.93$Hz

E 7.2 In example E. 7.1, determine the tie-line power flow deviation.

Solution :

$$\Delta P_{\text{tie-line}} = \frac{\beta_1 k_2 - k_1 \beta_2}{\beta_1 + \beta_2} \text{puMw}$$

$k_2 = 0$

$$\Delta P_{\text{tie-line}} = \frac{-k_1 \beta_2}{\beta_1 + \beta_2}$$

$= (\Delta f^0)\, \beta_2 = -0.0013683 \times 56.405$

$= -0.0771789$ p.u MW

$= -77.1789$ MW

E 7.3 In E 7.1 if the load disturbance occurs simultaneously also in area 2 by 100 MW determine the frequency and tie-line power changes.

Solution :

$$K_2 = 0.1 \text{ pu}$$

$$\Delta f^0 = \frac{k_1 + k_2}{\beta_1 + \beta} = \frac{0.2 + 0.1}{91.7591 + 56.405} = 0.0020248 \text{ pu Hz}$$

$$\Delta f^0 = 0.10124 \text{ Hz}$$

$$f = 50 - 0.10124 = 49.89876 \cong 49.9 \text{ Hz}$$

$$\Delta P_{\text{tie-line}} = \frac{\beta_1 k_2 - k_1 \beta_2}{\beta_1 + \beta_2}$$

$$\frac{91.7591 \times 0.1 - 0.2 \times 56.405}{148.16} = \frac{9.17591 - 11.2810}{148.16}$$

$$= \frac{-2.10509}{148.16} = -0.014208 \text{ pu Mw}$$

$$= -14.2082 \text{ MW}$$

E7.4 Two interconnected areas A and B have capacities 2000 MW and 750 MW respectively. The speed regulation coefficients are 0.1 p.u. for both the areas on their own area ratings. The damping torque coefficients are 1.0 p.u. also on their own base.

Find the steady state change in system frequency when a load increment of 50 MW occurs in area A. Find also the tie line power deviation. System frequency is 50 Hz.

Solution :

$$a_{12} = \frac{P_{r1}}{P_{r2}} = \frac{2000}{750} = 2.67$$

$$D = 1.0 \text{ p.u. MW/puHz} = \frac{1}{50} \text{ p.u. MW/Hz}$$

$$R = 0.1\text{pu} = 0.1 \times 50 = 5\text{Hz/p.u. MW}$$

$$\beta_1 = \beta_2 = \beta = D + \frac{1}{R} = \frac{1}{50} + \frac{1}{5} = 0.02 + 0.02 = 0.22$$

$$\Delta f^0 = \frac{k_2 + a_{12} k_1}{\beta_2 + a_{12} \beta_1}$$

$$k_1 = \frac{50\text{Mw}}{2000\text{puMW}} = \frac{1}{40} \text{puMw}; k_2 = 0$$

$$\Delta f^0 = \frac{2.67 \times \frac{1}{40}}{0.22 + 2.67 \times 0.22} = \frac{0.06675}{0.8074} = 0.08267\text{Hz}$$

$$\Delta P_{12}^{0} = -\frac{\beta_2 K_1}{\beta_2 + a_{12}\beta_1} = \frac{-0.22\times\frac{1}{40}}{0.22 + 2.67\times 0.22} = -\frac{0.0055}{0.8074} = -0.00681 \text{puMw}$$

$$= -0.00681\times 2000 = 13.62\text{MW}$$

E7.5 In problem E 7.4, if the tie line connection is lost while it is carrying 50MW load, what will be frequency in system A.

Solution :

The system A will be now an isolated area.

The frequency drop

$$\Delta f_0 = -\frac{\Delta P_{DA}}{\beta} = \frac{-\frac{1}{40}}{0.22} = -0.113636\text{ Hz}$$

E7.6 For a two identical area system the following data is given. Determine the frequency of oscillations when a step load disturbance occurs.

Speed regulation coefficient = R = 4 Hz /p.u. MW

Damping coefficient D = 0.03 pu MW/Hz

System frequency = 50Hz

The tie – line has a capacity of 0.1 p.u.

The power angle is 30^0 just before the occurrence of the load disturbance.

Solution :

$$K = \frac{f_0}{4RH} = \frac{50}{4\times 4\times 5} = 0.625$$

$$T^0 = 0.1\cos 30^0 = 0.0866$$

$$\omega^2 = \frac{2\pi T^0 f^0}{H} = \frac{2\pi\times 0.0866\times 50}{5} = 5.443$$

$$\omega = 2.333 \qquad K^2 = 0.3906$$

$$\omega_0 = \sqrt{5.443 - 0.3906} = \sqrt{5.052375} = 2.2477489\text{rad/sec}$$

However, if the damping coefficient is not to be neglected

$$K = \frac{f_0}{4H}\left[D + \frac{1}{R}\right] = 0.625 + \frac{50}{4\times 5}\times 0.03 = 0.625 + 0.075 = 0.7;\ k^2 = 0.49$$

In this case

$$\omega = \sqrt{5.443 - 0.49} = \sqrt{0.4953} = 2.2255\text{rad/sec}$$

E7.7 A power system consists of two areas interconnected by a tie line which has a capacity of 500MW and is operating at a power angle of 35^0. If each area has a capacity of 5000MW and the speed regulation coefficients for both the areas are also the same and are equal to R = 2Hz/puMW determine the frequency of oscillation of the power for step change in load. The intertia constants are also the same for both the areas and are equal to H = 5sec.

Solution :

$$T^0 = \frac{500}{5000}\cos 35^0 = 0.819 \times 0.1 = 0.0819$$

$$\omega_0 = \sqrt{\left[\frac{2\pi \times 50 \times 0.0819}{5}\right] - \left(\frac{50}{4 \times 2 \times 5}\right)^2}$$

$$= \sqrt{5.148 - 1.5625} = \sqrt{3.5855} = 1.8935 \text{rad/sec}$$

E7.8 In the above problem, if a step load change of 85MW occurs in one of the areas determine the tie line power deviation.

Solution :

The two areas are equal, the load change will be shared equally by both the areas.

A power of 85/2 = 42.5 MW will flow from the other area into the area where a load change occurs.

E7.9 Two power stations A and B operate in parallel. They are inter connected by a short transmission line. The station capacities are 100MW and 200MW respectively. The generators at A and B have speed regulation 3% and 2% respectively. Calculate the output of each station and the load on the interconnector if,

(a) the load on each station is 125MW,

(b) the loads on respective bus bars are 60MW and 190MW and

(c) the load is 150MW at the station A bus bar only.

Solution :

Case : (a) $P_1+P_2 = 125+125 = 250\text{MW}$

$$\text{Regulation} = \frac{N_0 - N}{N_r} = \frac{f_0 - f}{f_w}$$

$$\frac{P_1}{100} = \frac{1-f}{0.03}$$

$$\frac{P_2}{200} = \frac{1-f}{0.02}$$

$$0.0003P_1 = (1 - f) = 0.0001P_2$$

that is, $3P_1 = P_2$

$$P_1 + P_2 = 250$$

Solving $P_1 = 62.5$ MW and $P_2 = 187.5$MW

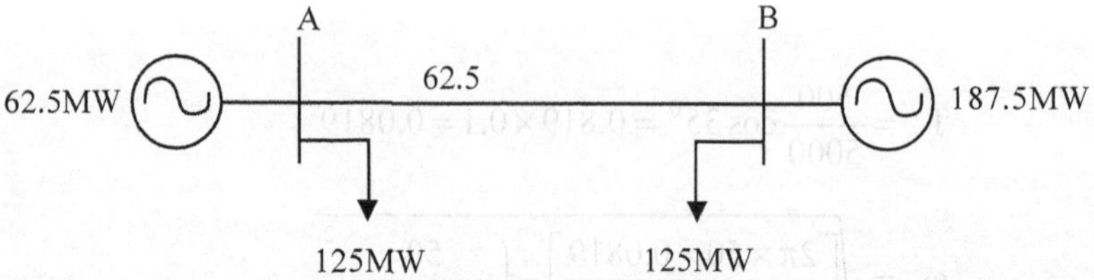

Case (b) : the loads on each bus bar is determined by the speed regulation characteristics.

$$3 P_1 = P_2$$

$$P_1 + P_2 = 60 + 190 = 250\text{MW}$$

Solving $P_1 = 62.5$ MW and $P_2 = 187.5$ MW

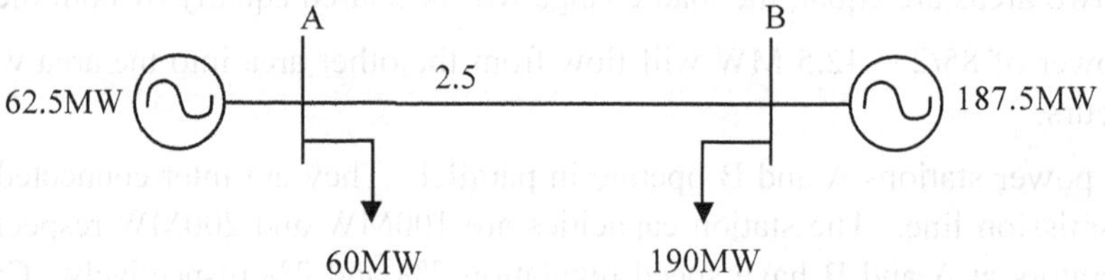

Case (c) : There is load of 150MW at A only

$$3 P_1 = P_2$$

$$P_1 + P_2 = 150$$

Solving $P_1 = 37.5$

$$P_2 = 112.5\text{MW}$$

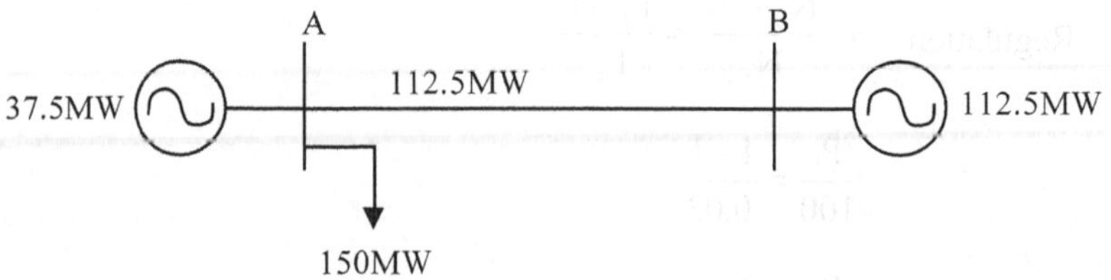

E7.10 The turbines in a power station A have a uniform speed regulation of 2.5% from no – load to full load. The rated capacity of the generators connected to the bus bars total 60MW and the frequency is 50Hz. Station B has total generating capacity of 35MW at the bus bars and has a speed regulation of 3.0% connected through an induction motor generation set rated 10MW. Which has a full load slip of 3.0%. There are loads of 32MW and 24.5MW connected to station A and B respectively. Find the load on the inter connecter cable at this operating condition.

Solution :

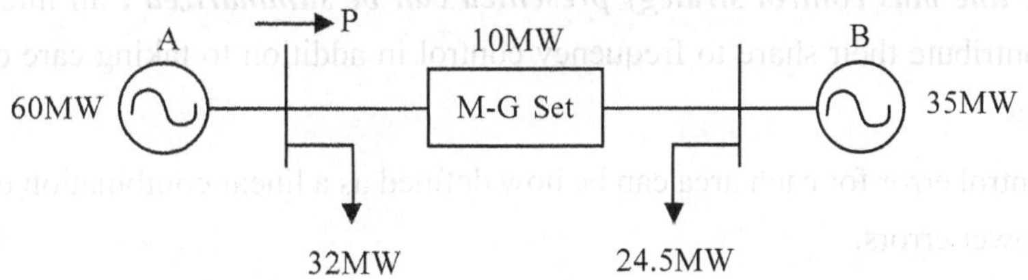

Let P MW flow from A to B

Total load on A = (32+P)MW

Total load on B = (24.5 –P)

$$\text{Percentage drop in speed at A} = 2.5\frac{(32+P)}{60}$$

$$\text{Percentage drop in speed at B} = 3.5\frac{(24.5-P)}{35}$$

$$\text{Percentage drop in speed of induction motor generator set} = \frac{3P}{100}$$

Percentage drop in speed at B - percentage drop in speed at A = percentage drop in speed of induction motor generator set

$$\frac{3.5(24.5-P)}{35} - \frac{2.5(32+P)}{60} = \frac{3P}{10}$$

$$\frac{(24.5-P)}{10} - \frac{3P}{10} = \frac{32+P}{24}$$

solving $\quad 106P = 268$

$$P = \frac{268}{106} = 2.5283\text{MW}$$

P flows from A to B

Total load as A = 32 + 2.5283 = 34.5283MW

Total load as B = 24.5 – 2.5283 = 21.9717MW

7.10 Tie-Line Bias Control – Implementation

From the preceding discussion it is clear that in interconnected operation each area in normal steady state must control the changes in such a fashion that it absorbs its own load change.

The tie line bias control strategy presented can be summarized : all inter connected areas must contribute their share to frequency control in addition to taking care of their own net interchange.

The control error for each area can be now defined as a linear combination of frequency and tie line power errors.

Area control error for area 1; $ACE_1 = \Delta P_{12} + B_1 \Delta f_1$ .....(7.26)

and area control error for area 2; $ACE_2 = \Delta P_{21} + B_2 \Delta f_2$ .....(7.27)

Hence in the block diagram of Fig. 7.11 now the ΔP_{ref} commands can be defined.

$$\Delta P_{ref,1} = -K_I' \int (\Delta P_{12} + B_1 \Delta f_1) dt \quad .....(7.28)$$

and

$$\Delta P_{ref,2} = -K_I'' \int (\Delta P_{21} + B_2 \Delta f_2) dt \quad .....(7.29)$$

where B_1 and B_2 are the frequency bias parameters for areas 1 and 2 while K_I' and K_I'' are the integral controller gain constants.

Note that under steady state conditions when ΔP_{12} and Δf_1, Δf_2 become zero, from eqn. (7.26) $\Delta P_{12} + B_1 \Delta f_1 = 0$ and $\Delta P_{21} + B_2 \Delta f_2 = 0$ convey that the controller action in the final stage is independent of B_1 and B_2.

In fact, even one of the B's, either B_1 or B_2 can be zero. It is suggested that only one B can be selected as equal to the area frequency response characteristic $\beta = D + \frac{1}{R}$ to give satisfactory performance.

The complete tie-line bias control of a two area system is shown in Fig. 7.12.

If area ratings are different (–1) block is replaced by $(-a_{12}) = \frac{P_{r1}}{P_{r2}}$

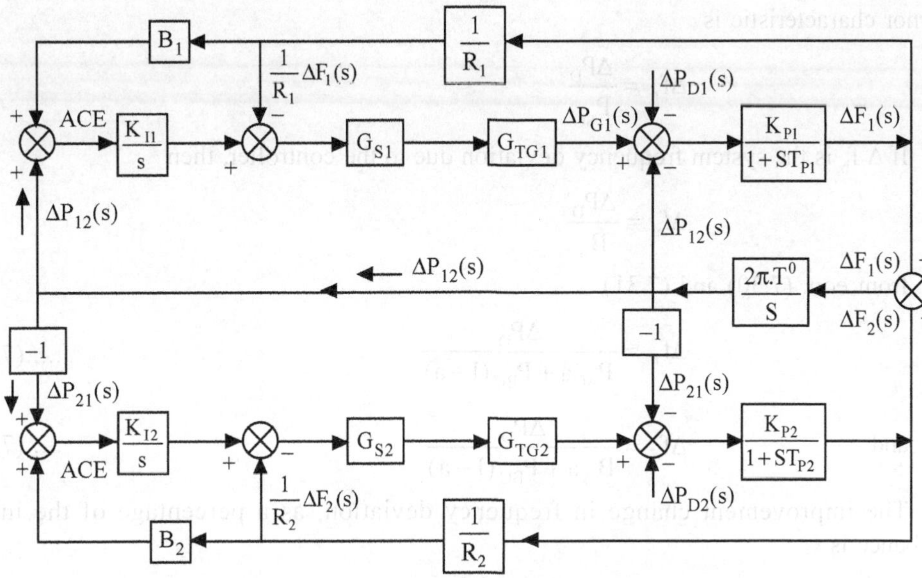

Fig. 7.12 Tie-line bias control of a two area system

The selection of integral controller gains $K_I^{'}$ and $K_I^{''}$ must be such that too large a value should not lead to chasing of minor deviations of no-consequence.

7.11 The Effect of Bias Factor on System Regulation

Let a and b be the ratios of generation of areas A and B in terms of the total generation, i.e.

$$a + b = 1 \text{ p.u.}$$

Let P_{sc} be the total system generating capacity per cycle and correspondingly, let P_{AC} and P_{BC} be the generating capacity per cycle of A and B. B_A is the tie-line bias setting at area A expressed in generation capacity / cycle and B_S is the imposed regulating characteristic for the whole system with a tie-line bias controller in A only, with no controller in B, the ratio of bias setting at A to the generation characteristic at A, r, is given by

$$r = \frac{B_A}{P_{AC}}$$

$$P_{SC} = P_{AC}\, a + P_{BC}\,(1 - a) - P_{AC} \,.\, a + P_{BC} \,.\, b \qquad .....(7.30)$$

$$B_S = B_A\, a + P_{BC}\,(1 - a) = B_A \,.\, a + P_{BC} \,.\, b \qquad .....(7.31)$$

The change in natural frequency Δf_n following the load change as dictated by the governor characteristic is

$$\Delta f_n = \frac{\Delta P_D}{P_{SC}}$$

If Δf_b is the system frequency deviation due to the controller, then

$$\Delta f_s = \frac{\Delta P_D}{B_S}$$

from eqn. (7.30) and (7.31)

$$\Delta f_n = \frac{\Delta P_D}{P_{AC}a + P_{BC}(1-a)} \qquad .....(7.32)$$

and

$$\Delta f_s = \frac{\Delta P_D}{B_A a + P_{BC}(1-a)} \qquad .....(7.33)$$

The improvement change in frequency deviation, as a percentage of the initial disturbance is

$$\Delta f = \frac{\Delta f_s - \Delta f_n}{\Delta f_n} \times 100 \qquad .....(7.34)$$

$$= \frac{\Delta P_D \left[\dfrac{1}{B_A .a + P_{BC}(1-a)} - \dfrac{1}{P_{AC}.a + P_{BC}(1-a)} \right]}{\dfrac{\Delta P_D}{P_{AC}.a + P_{BC}(1-a)}}$$

$$= \frac{(P_{AC} - B_A)a}{(B_A - P_{nc})a + P_{BC}} \times 100 \qquad .....(7.35)$$

Since, $r = B_A / P_{AC}$ and assuming $P_{AC} = P_{BC}$.

$$\Delta f = -\frac{a(r-1)}{1 + a(r-1)} \times 100\% \qquad .....(7.36)$$

or

$$\Delta f = \frac{(b-1)(r-1)}{r - b(r-1)} \times 100\% \qquad .....(7.37)$$

The percentage change in frequency is independent of ΔP_D, and depends only on a, b and r. When r = 1; $\Delta f = 0$, therefore

$$\Delta f_n = \Delta f_s$$

The initial ungoverned frequency deviation is equal to the subsequent governed frequency deviation.

7.12 Scope for Supplementary Control

During operation, the system, frequency, tie-line flows and other derived quantities will be continuously swinging with periods generally of a few seconds. Considering the time lags in measurements, the prime mover governor characteristics, etc. supplementary controllers cannot respond to rapid swings of frequency and tie-line power. Neither can they effectively regulate these changes nor is it expected of them. It is desired that supplementary controllers should regulate the frequency and tie-line deviations about a base that corresponds to the prescheduled values. In a reactive sense, the supplementary control is a steady-state control. A high speed dynamic analysis of the system and area characteristics are required only in connection with improving system stability.

7.13 State Variable Model for a Three Area System

In chapter 6 state variable mode for a single area system and application of optimal control has been discussed. Modern control theory can be applied very elegantly for multi area system.

The block diagram representation of a three area system is shown in Fig. 7.13.

The following equations are written directly from the block diagram.

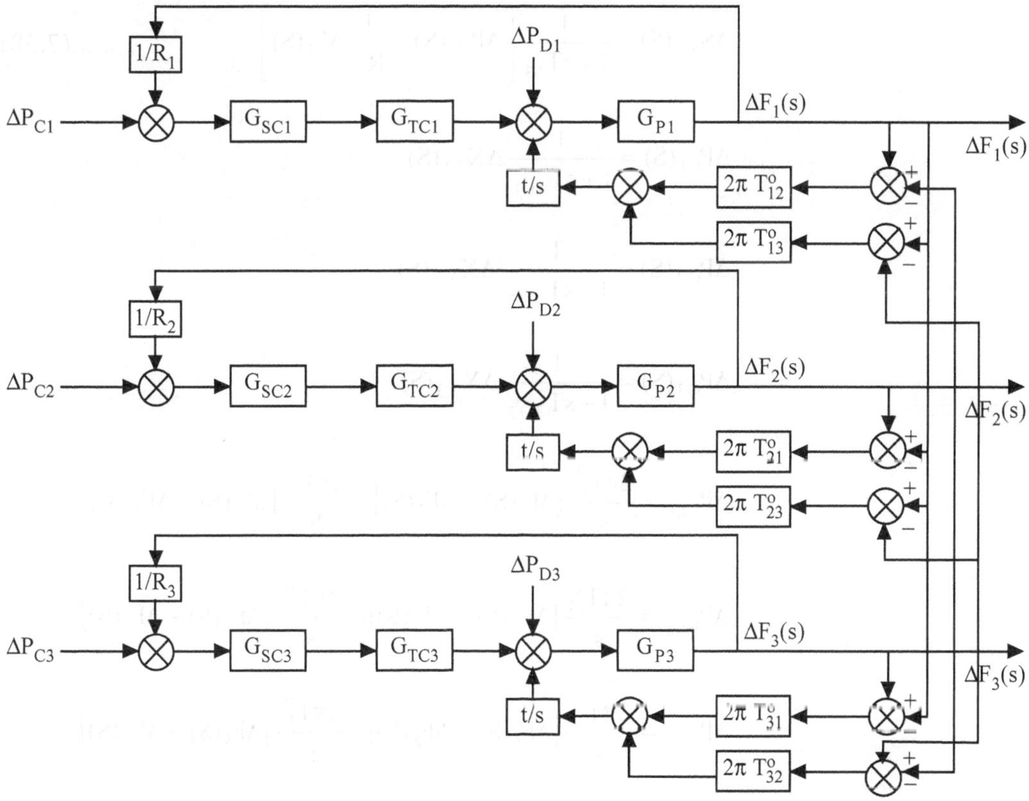

Fig. 7.13 Three area system

$$\Delta F_1(S) = \frac{K_{P1}}{1+sT_{P1}}\left[\Delta P_{G1} - \Delta P_{D1} - \Delta P_{tie,1}\right]$$

$$\Delta F_2(S) = \frac{K_{P2}}{1+sT_{P2}}\left[\Delta P_{G2} - \Delta P_{D2} - \Delta P_{tie,2}\right]$$

$$\Delta F_3(S) = \frac{K_{P3}}{1+sT_{P3}}\left[\Delta P_{G3} - \Delta P_{D3} - \Delta P_{tie,3}\right]$$

$$\Delta S_{V1}(S) = \frac{1}{1+sT_{S1}}\left[\Delta P_{C1}(S) - \frac{1}{R_1}\Delta F_1(S)\right]$$

$$\Delta S_{V2}(S) = \frac{1}{1+sT_{S2}}\left[\Delta P_{C2}(S) - \frac{1}{R_2}\Delta F_2(S)\right]$$

$$\Delta S_{V3}(S) = \frac{1}{1+sT_{S3}}\left[\Delta P_{C3}(S) - \frac{1}{R_3}\Delta F_3(S)\right] \quad .....(7.38)$$

$$\Delta P_{G1}(S) = \frac{1}{1+sT_{TG1}}\Delta X_{V1}(S)$$

$$\Delta P_{G2}(S) = \frac{1}{1+sT_{TG2}}\Delta X_{V2}(S)$$

$$\Delta P_{G3}(S) = \frac{1}{1+sT_{TG3}}\Delta X_{V3}(S)$$

$$\Delta P_{tie,1} = \frac{2\pi T_{12}^0}{s}\left[\Delta F_1(S) - \Delta F_2(S)\right] + \frac{2\pi T_{13}^0}{S}\left[\Delta F_1(S) - \Delta F_3(S)\right]$$

$$\Delta P_{tie,2} = \frac{2\pi T_{21}^0}{s}\left[\Delta F_2(S) - \Delta F_1(S)\right] + \frac{2\pi T_{23}^0}{s}\left[\Delta F_2(S) - \Delta F_3(S)\right]$$

$$\Delta P_{tie,3} = \frac{2\pi T_{31}^0}{s}\left[\Delta F_3(S) - \Delta F_2(S)\right] + \frac{2\pi T_{32}^0}{s}\left[\Delta F_3(S) - \Delta F_2(S)\right]$$

Taking the inverse Laplace transform of equation (7.38)

$$\Delta\dot{f}_1 = \frac{1}{T_{P1}}\left(-\Delta f_1 + K_{P1}\Delta P_{G1} - K_{P1}\Delta P_{D1} - K_{P1}\Delta P_{tie,1}\right)$$

$$\Delta\dot{f}_2 = \frac{1}{T_{P2}}\left(-\Delta f_2 + K_{P2}\Delta P_{G2} - K_{P2}\Delta P_{D2} - K_{P2}\Delta P_{tie,2}\right)$$

$$\Delta\dot{f}_3 = \frac{1}{T_{P3}}\left(-\Delta f_3 + K_{P3}\Delta P_{G3} - K_{P3}\Delta P_{D3} - K_{P3}\Delta P_{tie,3}\right)$$

$$\Delta\dot{P}_{G1} = \frac{1}{T_{T1}}\left(-\Delta P_{G1} + \Delta X_{V1}\right)$$

$$\Delta\dot{P}_{G2} = \frac{1}{T_{T2}}\left(-\Delta P_{G2} + \Delta X_{V2}\right) \qquad .....(7.39)$$

$$\Delta\dot{P}_{G3} = \frac{1}{T_{T3}}\left(-\Delta P_{G3} + \Delta X_{V3}\right)$$

$$\Delta\dot{X}_{V1} = \frac{1}{T_{S1}}\left(-\Delta X_{V1} + \Delta P_{C1} - \frac{1}{R_1}\Delta f_1\right)$$

$$\Delta\dot{X}_{V2} = \frac{1}{T_{S2}}\left(-\Delta X_{V2} + \Delta P_{C2} - \frac{1}{R_2}\Delta f_2\right)$$

$$\Delta\dot{X}_{V3} = \frac{1}{T_{S3}}\left(-\Delta X_{V3} + \Delta P_{C3} - \frac{1}{R_3}\Delta f_3\right)$$

$$\Delta\dot{P}_{tie,1} = 2\pi T_{12}^{0}\left(\Delta f_1 - \Delta f_2\right) + 2\pi T_{13}^{0}\left(\Delta f_1 - \Delta f_3\right)$$

$$\Delta\dot{P}_{tie,2} = 2\pi T_{21}^{0}\left(\Delta f_2 - \Delta f_1\right) + 2\pi T_{23}^{0}\left(\Delta f_2 - \Delta f_3\right)$$

$$\Delta P_{tie,3} = 2\pi T_{31}^{0}\left(\Delta f_3 - \Delta f_1\right) + 2\pi T_{32}^{0}\left(\Delta f_3 - \Delta f_2\right)$$

The above equations are put in the form

$$\dot{\mathbf{X}} = \mathbf{AX} + \mathbf{Bu} + \mathbf{Fd} \qquad .....(7.40)$$

where

$X^T = [\Delta f_1 \;\; \Delta f_2 \;\; \Delta f_3 \;\; \Delta P_{G1} \;\; \Delta P_{G2} \;\; \Delta P_{G3} \;\; \Delta P_{V1} \;\; \Delta P_{V2} \;\; \Delta P_{V3}$
$\Delta P_{tie,1} \;\; \Delta P_{tie,2} \;\; \Delta P_{tie,3}]$

$U^T = [\Delta P_{C1} \;\; \Delta P_{C2} \;\; \Delta P_{C3}]$

$d^T = (\Delta P_{D1} \;\; \Delta P_{D2} \;\; \Delta P_{D3})$

The matrices A, B and F are given by

$$A = \begin{bmatrix}
-\frac{1}{T_{P1}} & 0 & 0 & 0 & 0 & 0 & \frac{K_{P1}}{T_{P1}} & 0 & 0 & -\frac{K_{P1}}{T_{P1}} & 0 & 0 \\
0 & -\frac{1}{T_{P2}} & 0 & 0 & 0 & 0 & 0 & \frac{K_{P2}}{T_{P2}} & 0 & 0 & -\frac{K_{P2}}{T_{P2}} & 0 \\
0 & 0 & -\frac{T}{T_{P2}} & 0 & 0 & 0 & 0 & 0 & \frac{K_{P3}}{T_{P3}} & 0 & 0 & -\frac{K_{P3}}{T_{P3}} \\
0 & 0 & 0 & -\frac{1}{T_{T1}} & 0 & 0 & \frac{1}{T_{T1}} & 0 & 0 & 0 & 0 & 0 \\
0 & 0 & 0 & 0 & -\frac{1}{T_{T2}} & 0 & 0 & \frac{1}{T_{T2}} & 0 & 0 & 0 & 0 \\
0 & 0 & 0 & 0 & 0 & -\frac{1}{T_{T3}} & 0 & 0 & \frac{1}{T_{T3}} & 0 & 0 & 0 \\
-\frac{1}{R_1 T_{S1}} & 0 & 0 & 0 & 0 & 0 & -\frac{1}{T_{S1}} & 0 & 0 & 0 & 0 & 0 \\
0 & -\frac{1}{R_2 T_{S2}} & 0 & 0 & 0 & 0 & 0 & -\frac{1}{T_{S2}} & 0 & 0 & 0 & 0 \\
0 & 0 & -\frac{1}{R_3 T_{S3}} & 0 & 0 & 0 & 0 & 0 & -\frac{1}{T_{S3}} & 0 & 0 & 0 \\
\tilde{A} & \tilde{P} & \tilde{Q} & 0 & 0 & 0 & 0 & 0 & 0 & 0 & 0 & 0 \\
\tilde{R} & \tilde{B} & \tilde{S} & 0 & 0 & 0 & 0 & 0 & 0 & 0 & 0 & 0 \\
\tilde{T} & \tilde{U} & \tilde{C} & 0 & 0 & 0 & 0 & 0 & 0 & 0 & 0 & 0
\end{bmatrix} \quad .....(7.41)$$

Where,

$$\overline{A} = 2\pi\left(T_{12}^0 + T_{13}^0\right)$$

$$\overline{B} = 2\pi\left(T_{21}^0 + T_{23}^0\right)$$

$$\overline{C} = 2\pi\left(T_{31}^0 + T_{32}^0\right)$$

$$\widetilde{P} = -2\pi T_{12}^0$$

$$\widetilde{Q} = -2\pi T_{13}^0$$

$$\widetilde{R} = -2\pi T_{21}^0$$

$$\widetilde{S} = -2\pi T_{23}^0$$

$$\widetilde{T} = -2\pi T_{31}^0$$

and $$\widetilde{U} = -2\pi T_{32}^0$$

$$B = \begin{bmatrix} 0 & 0 & 0 \\ 0 & 0 & 0 \\ 0 & 0 & 0 \\ 0 & 0 & 0 \\ 0 & 0 & 0 \\ 0 & 0 & 0 \\ \frac{1}{T_{S1}} & 0 & 0 \\ 0 & \frac{1}{T_{S2}} & 0 \\ 0 & 0 & \frac{1}{T_{S3}} \\ 0 & 0 & 0 \\ 0 & 0 & 0 \\ 0 & 0 & 0 \end{bmatrix} \quad .....(7.42)$$

$$F = \begin{bmatrix} -\frac{K_{P1}}{T_{P1}} & 0 & 0 \\ 0 & -\frac{K_{P2}}{T_{P2}} & 0 \\ 0 & 0 & -\frac{K_{P3}}{T_{P3}} \\ 0 & 0 & 0 \\ 0 & 0 & 0 \\ 0 & 0 & 0 \\ 0 & 0 & 0 \\ 0 & 0 & 0 \\ 0 & 0 & 0 \\ 0 & 0 & 0 \\ 0 & 0 & 0 \\ 0 & 0 & 0 \end{bmatrix} \qquad .....(7.43)$$

The equations can be written down for any number of interconnected areas in a similar manner.

7.14 State Variable Model for a Two Area System

In the case of two area system

$$\Delta P_{tie,2} = a_{12} P_{tie,1}$$

and
$$a_{12} = -\frac{P_{t1}}{P_{r2}}$$

The system matrices will become

$$A = \begin{bmatrix} -\frac{1}{T_{P1}} & 0 & 0 & 0 & \frac{K_{P1}}{T_{P1}} & 0 & -\frac{K_{P2}}{T_{P2}} \\ 0 & \frac{1}{T_{P2}} & 0 & 0 & 0 & \frac{K_{P2}}{T_{P2}} & a_{12}\frac{K_{P2}}{T_{P2}} \\ 0 & 0 & -\frac{1}{T_{S1}} & 0 & \frac{1}{T_{S1}} & \frac{K_{P1}}{T_{P1}} & 0 \\ 0 & 0 & 0 & -\frac{1}{T_{S2}} & 0 & \frac{1}{T_{S2}} & 0 \\ -\frac{1}{R_1 T_{S1}} & 0 & 0 & 0 & -\frac{1}{T_{S1}} & 0 & 0 \\ 0 & -\frac{1}{R_2 T_{S2}} & 0 & 0 & 0 & -\frac{1}{T_{S2}} & 0 \\ 2\pi T_{12}^0 & -2\pi T_{12}^0 & 0 & 0 & 0 & 0 & 0 \end{bmatrix}$$

$$B^T = \begin{bmatrix} 0 & 0 & 0 & 0 & \frac{1}{T_{S1}} & 0 & 0 \\ 0 & 0 & 0 & 0 & 0 & \frac{1}{T_{S2}} & 0 \end{bmatrix}$$

$$F^T = \begin{bmatrix} -\frac{K_{P1}}{T_{P1}} & 0 & 0 & 0 & 0 & 0 & 0 \\ 0 & -\frac{K_{P2}}{T_{P2}} & 0 & 0 & 0 & 0 & 0 \end{bmatrix}$$

The state variables, control variables and disturbance variables reduce to

$$X^T = [\Delta f_1\ \Delta f_2\ \Delta P_{G1}\ \Delta P_{G2}\ \Delta X_{V1}\ \Delta X_{V2}\ \Delta Ptie,_1]$$

$$u = \begin{bmatrix} \Delta P_{C1} \\ \Delta P_{C2} \end{bmatrix}$$

$$d = \begin{bmatrix} \Delta P_{D1} \\ \Delta P_{D2} \end{bmatrix} \text{ respectively.}$$

7.15 State Variable Model for a Single Area System

The state variable model for the single area system is a single input, single output model with no tie-line power. The matrices of the system equations are

$$A = \begin{bmatrix} -\frac{1}{T_P} & 0 & \frac{K_P}{T_P} \\ 0 & -\frac{1}{T_S} & \frac{1}{T_S} \\ -\frac{1}{RT_S} & 0 & -\frac{1}{T_S} \end{bmatrix}$$

$$B = \begin{bmatrix} 0 \\ 0 \\ \frac{1}{T_S} \end{bmatrix}$$

$$F = \begin{bmatrix} -\frac{K_P}{T_P} \\ 0 \\ 0 \end{bmatrix}$$

$$X^T = [\Delta f\ \Delta P_G\ \Delta X_V]$$

$$u = \Delta P_C$$

$$d = \Delta P_D$$

E 7.11 Solve the state space equations for a three area system with the following parameters and plot the frequency, generation and tie-line power deviations for a step load disturbance of 0.01 p.u. in area 1.

$R_1 = R_2 = R_3 = 2.5$Hz/p.u. MW

$T_{P1} = T_{P2} = T_{P3} = 20$s

$T_{T1} = T_{T2} = T_{T3} = 0.3$s

$T_{S1} = T_{S2} = T_{S3} = 0.08$s

$K_{P1} = K_{P2} = K_{P3} = 120$Hz/p.u. MW

$T_{12} = T_{13} = T_{23} = T_{21} = T_{32} = T_{31} = 0.07$ p.u. MW/rad

$P_{D1} = 0.01$p.u. MW

$P_{D2} = P_{D3} = 0.0$

Solution :

The state variable mode for the system using eqn. (7.27) is given by

$$\Delta\dot{f}_1 = \frac{1}{20}\left[-\Delta f_1 + 120(\Delta P_{G1}) - 120(0.01) - 120(\Delta P_{tie,1})\right]$$

$$\Delta\dot{f}_2 = \frac{1}{20}\left[-\Delta f_2 + 120(\Delta P_{G2}) - 120(0.0) - 120(\Delta P_{tie,2})\right]$$

$$\Delta\dot{f}_3 = \frac{1}{20}\left[-\Delta f_3 + 120(\Delta P_{G3}) - 120(0.0) - 120(\Delta P_{tie,3})\right]$$

$$\Delta\dot{P}_{G1} = \frac{1}{0.3}(-\Delta P_{G1} + \Delta X_{V1})$$

$$\Delta\dot{P}_{G2} = \frac{1}{0.3}(-\Delta P_{G2} + \Delta X_{V2})$$

$$\Delta\dot{P}_{G3} = \frac{1}{0.3}(-\Delta P_{G3} + \Delta X_{V3})$$

$$\Delta\dot{X}_{V1} = \frac{1}{0.08}\left[-\Delta X_{V1} + 0.0 - \frac{1}{2.5}\Delta f_1\right]$$

$$\Delta\dot{X}_{V2} = \frac{1}{0.08}\left[-\Delta X_{V2} + 0.0 - \frac{1}{2.5}\Delta f_2\right]$$

$$\Delta\dot{X}_{V3} = \frac{1}{0.08}\left[-\Delta X_{V3} + 0.0 - \frac{1}{2.5}\Delta f_3\right]$$

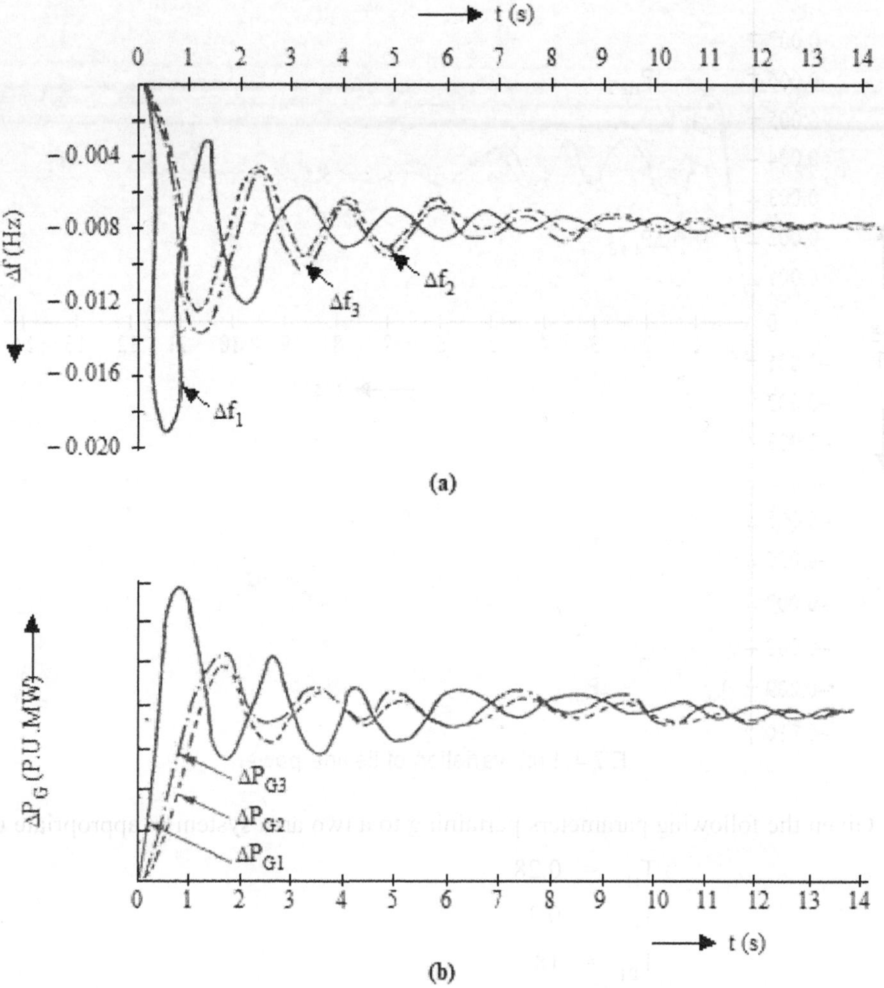

Fig. E 7.4.1 Response of a three area system to step load change in one area:
(a) variation of frequency error (b) variation of generation changes

$$\Delta P_{tie.1} = 2\pi(0.07)(\Delta f_1 - \Delta f_2) - 2\pi(0.07)(\Delta f_1 - \Delta f_2)$$

$$\Delta P_{tie.2} = 2\pi(0.07)(\Delta f_2 - \Delta f_1) - 2\pi(0.07)(\Delta f_2 - \Delta f_3)$$

$$\Delta P_{tie.3} = 2\pi(0.07)(\Delta f_3 - \Delta f_1) - 2\pi(0.07)(\Delta f_3 - \Delta f_2)$$

The equations are solved on digital computer using the Runge – Kutta method. The results are plotted: The plot is shown in Fig. E 7.4.1(c).

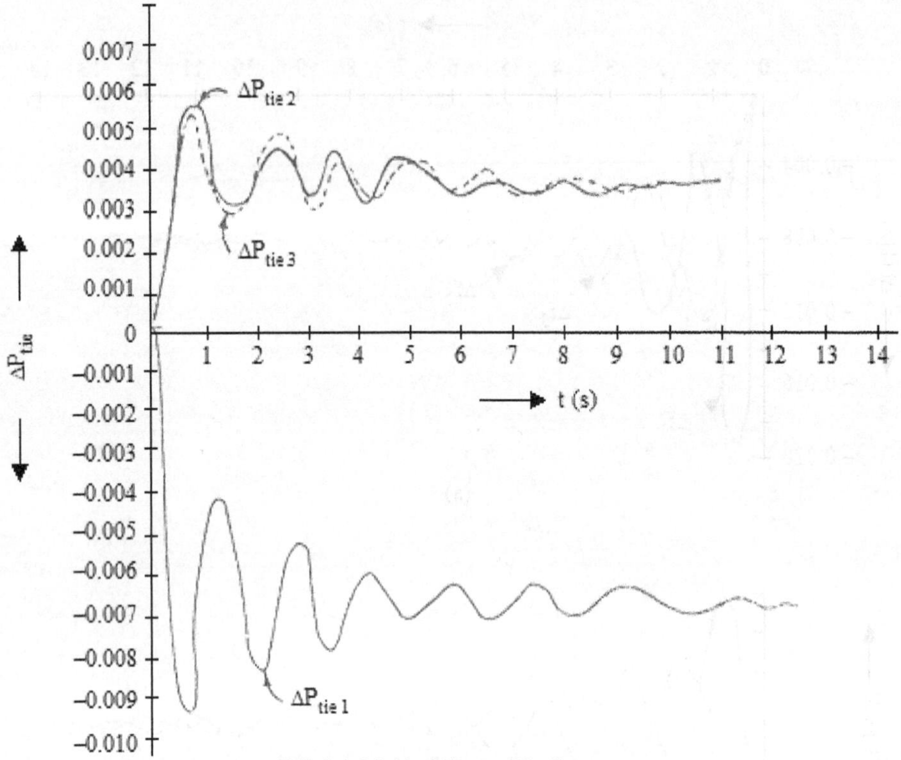

E 7.4.1 (c) Variation of tie line power

E7.12 Given the following parameters pertaining to a two area system in appropriate units

$$T_{t1} = 0.28$$
$$T_{t2} = 0.3$$
$$T_{P1} = 18$$
$$T_{P2} = 20$$
$$R_1 = 2.4$$
$$R_2 = 2.5$$
$$T_{S1} = 0.1$$
$$T_{S2} = 0.1$$
$$K_{P1} = 120$$
$$K_{P2} = 100$$
$$T_{12} = 0.06$$

Obtain the frequency deviations in both the areas and tie power deviation when a load change of $\Delta P_{D1} = 0.01$p.u. MW occurs.

Solution :

The system is simulated in MATLAB the frequency deviation is shown in Fig. E 7.5 (a) and the tie-line power deviation in Fig. E 7.5 (b).

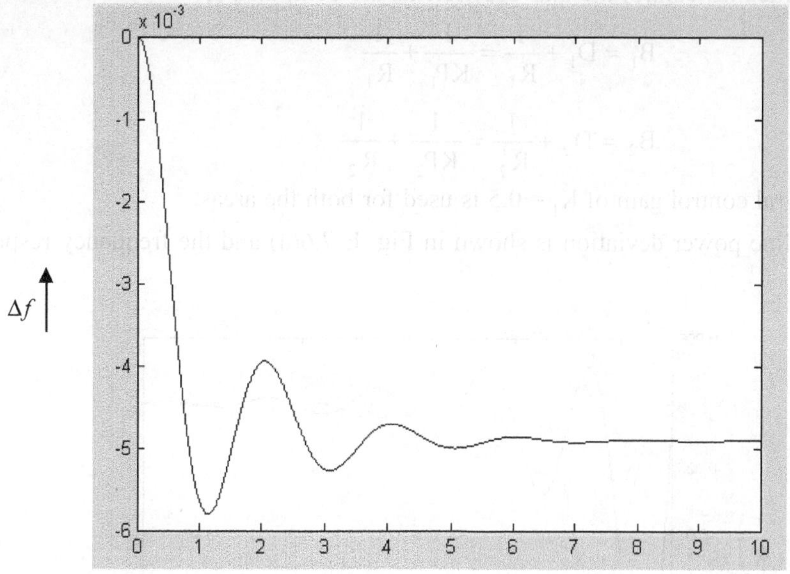

Fig. E 7.5(a)

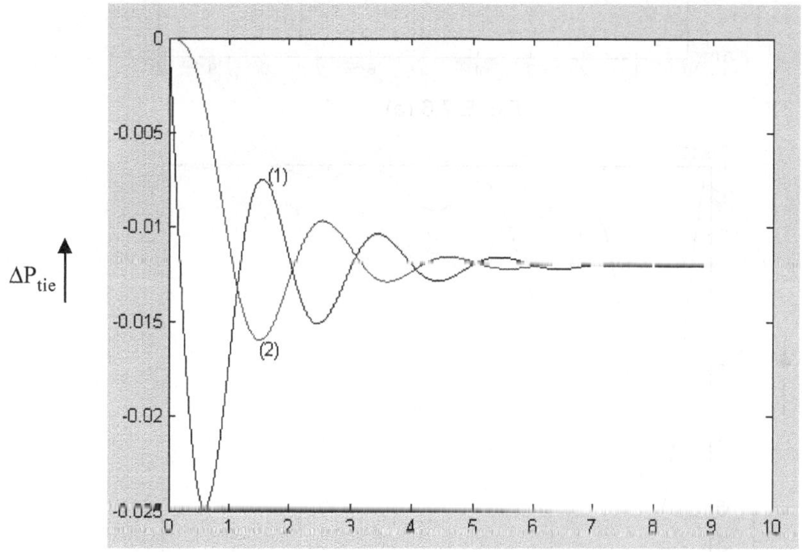

Fig. E 7.5(b)

E7.13 For the system given in E 7.5 obtain the controlled response of the system with tie-line bias control.

Solution :

For tie line bias control the bias coefficients are computed form

$$B_1 = D_1 + \frac{1}{R_1} = \frac{1}{KP_1} + \frac{1}{R_1}$$

and
$$B_2 = D_2 + \frac{1}{R_2} = \frac{1}{KP_2} + \frac{1}{R_2}$$

An integral control gain of $K_I = 0.5$ is used for both the areas.

The tie-line power deviation is shown in Fig. E 7.6(a) and the frequency response in Fig. E 7.6(b).

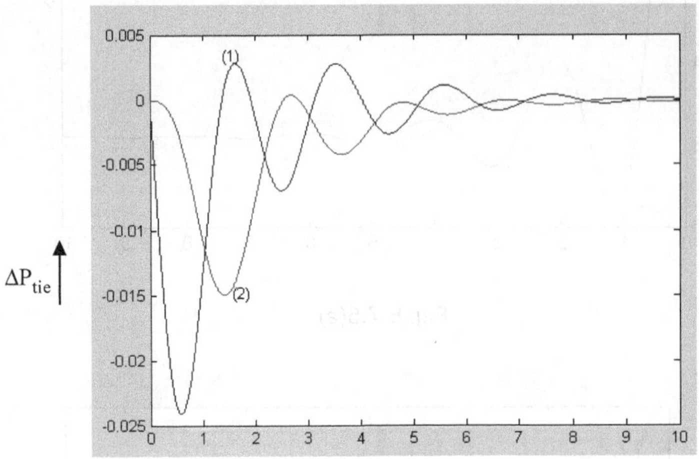

Fig. E 7.6 (a)

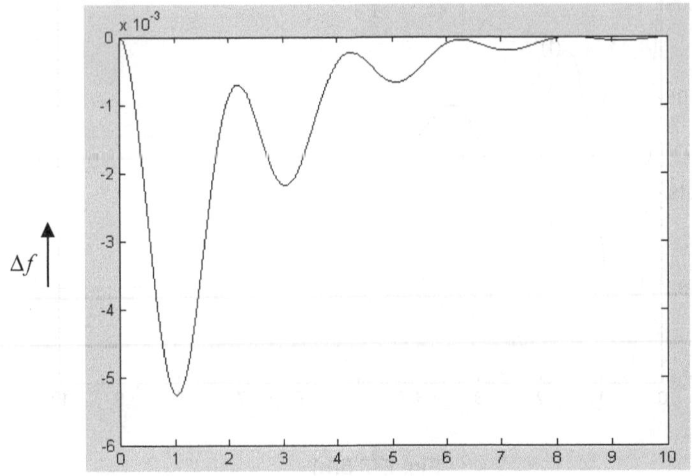

Fig. E 7.6 (b)

E7.14 In the system shown in example 7.5, if load disturbance of $\Delta P_{D1} = \Delta P_{D2} = 1$ occur simultaneously obtain the frequency response and tie line power deviation.

Solution :

The response of tie-line deviations and frequency deviation are shown in Fig. E 7.7(a) and E 7.7(b).

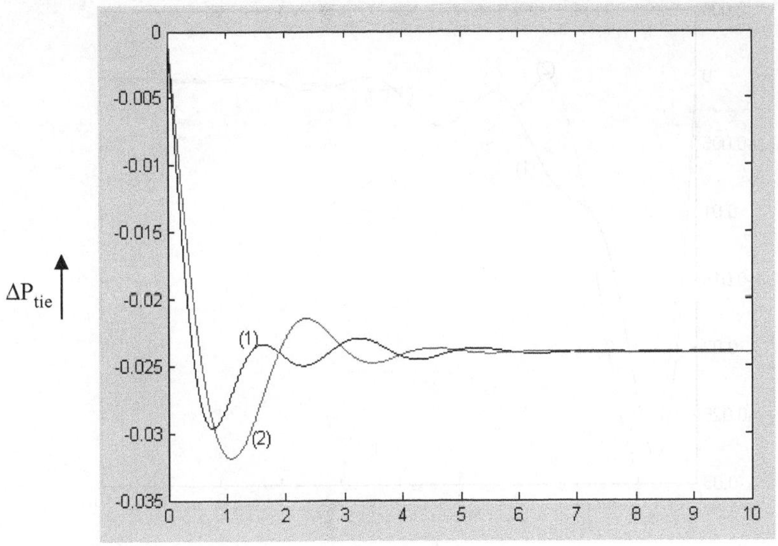

Fig. E 7.7 (a)

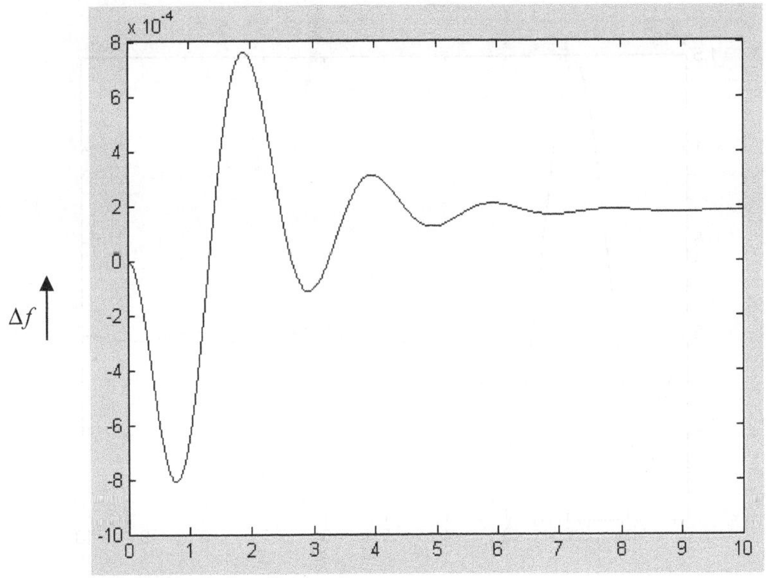

Fig. E 7.7 (b)

E7.15 For the system in E (7.5) obtain tie-line bias controlled frequency and tie-line power deviation with integral controller gains $K_{I1} = K_{I2} = 0.5$.

Solution :

The responses are shown in Fig. E 7.8(a) and E 7.8(b).

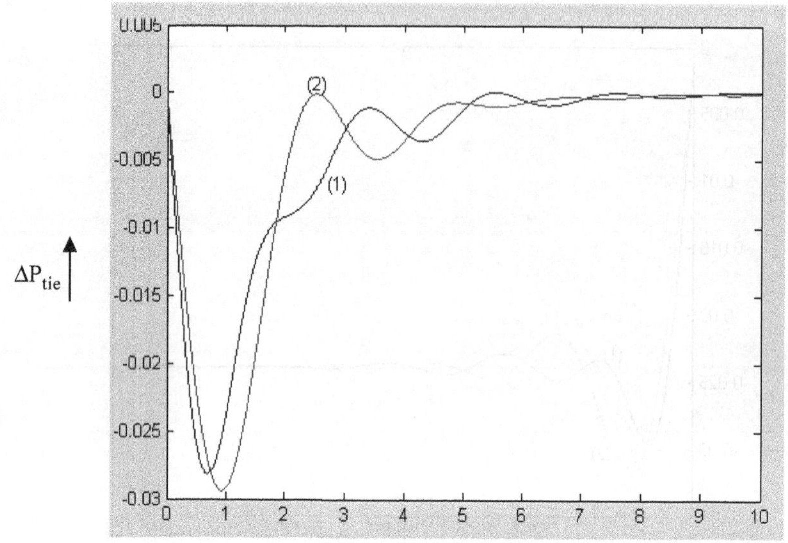

Fig. E 7.8 (a)

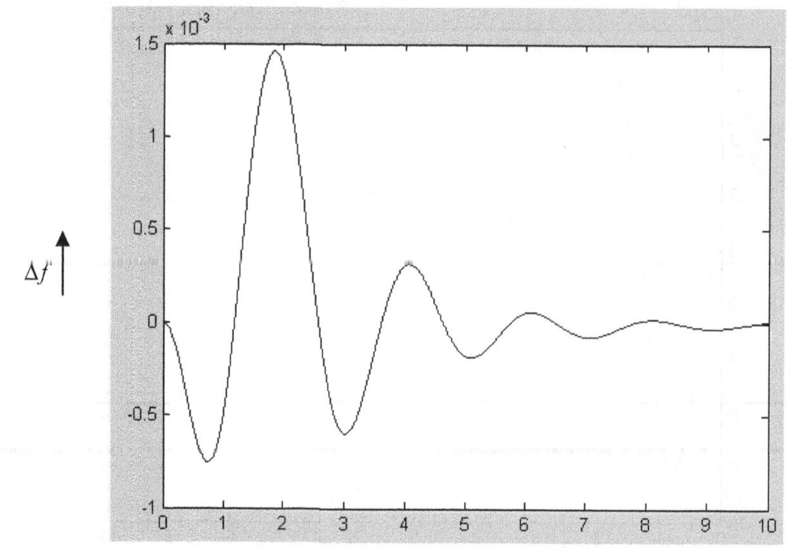

Fig. E 7.8 (b)

The MATLAB programme and the simulation setup are given below.

```
Tt1  =  0.28;
Tt2  =  0.3;
Tp1  =  18;
Tp2  =  20;
R1   =  2.4;
R2   =  2.5;
Ts1  =  0.08;
Ts2  =  0.1;
Kp1  =  120;
Kp2  =  100;
T12  =  0.06;
```

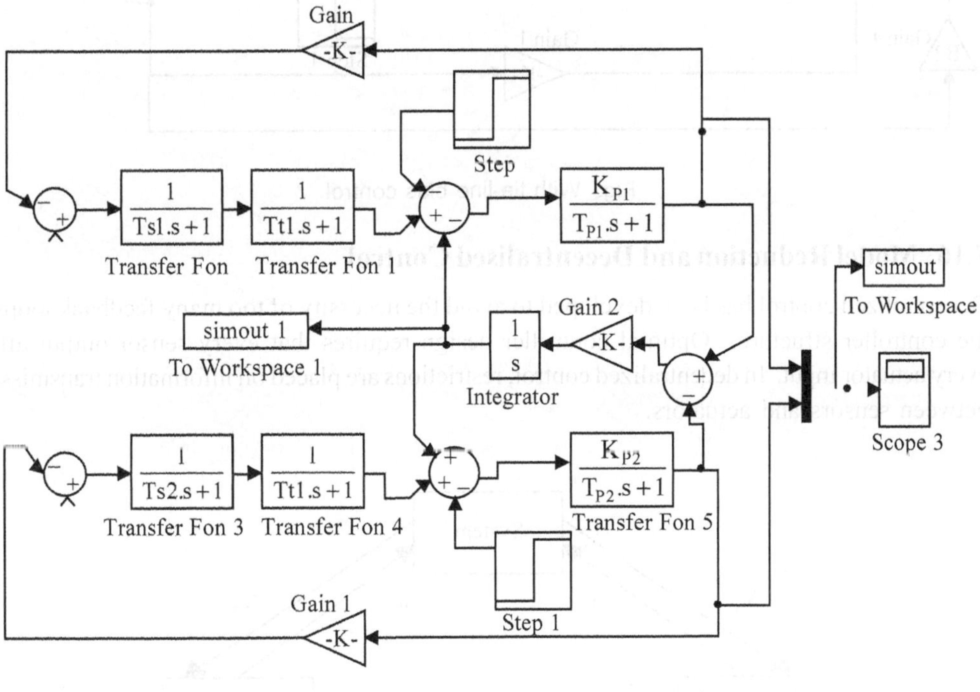

Fig. Uncontrolled Case

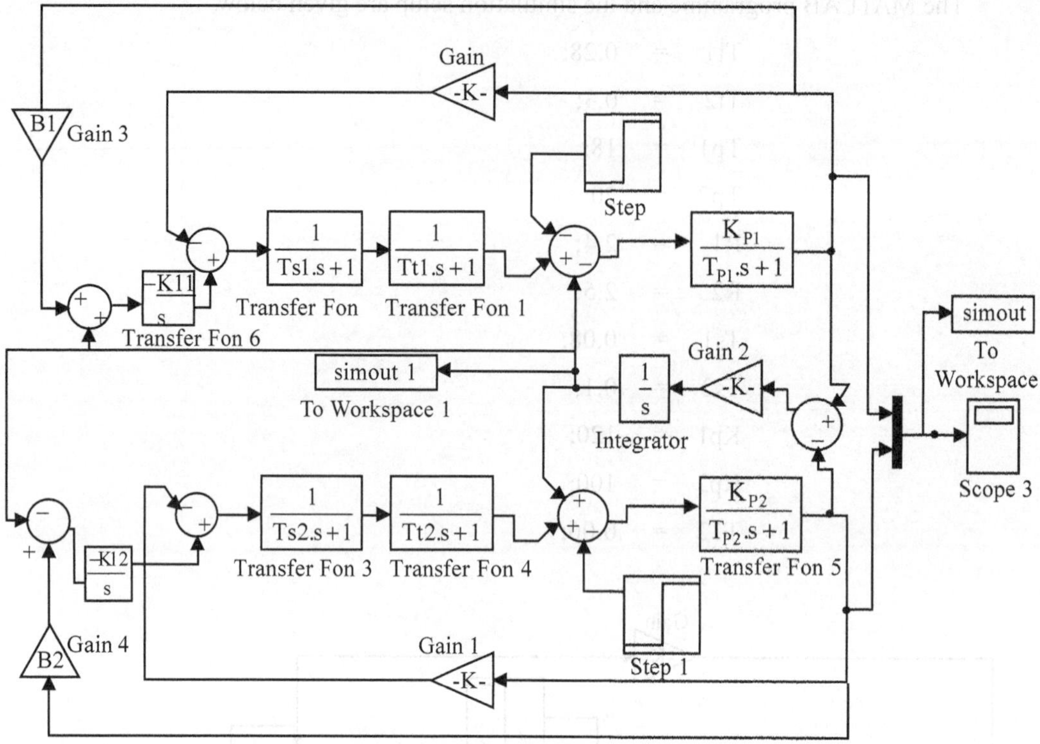

Fig. With tie-line bias control

7.16 Model Reduction and Decentralised Control

Decentralized control has been developed to avoid the necessity of too many feedback loops in the controller structure. Optimal controller design requires that every sensor output affect every actuator input. In decentralized control, restrictions are placed on information transmission between sensors and actuators.

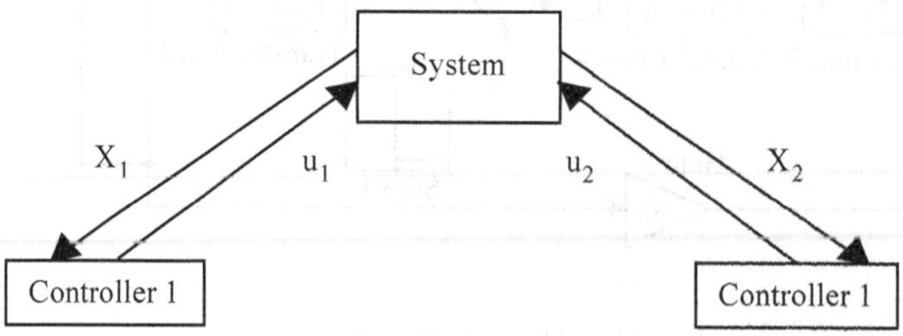

Fig. 7.14 Decentralized control

Considering Fig. (7.14) X_1 is used to determine the vector u_1 while X_2 alone is used to determine vector u_2.

This is complete decentralized control.

Model Reduction by Aggregation :

Consider

$$\dot{X}(t) = AX(t) + Bu(t) \qquad .....(7.44)$$

Let

$$\dot{Z}(t) = FZ(t) + Gu(t) \qquad .....(7.45)$$

It is required that eqn. (7.45) represent the same dynamic system represented by eqn. (7.44), given that the number of variables in Z is much less that those in X.

For dynamic exactness

$$Z(t) = CX(t) \qquad .....(7.46)$$

It is necessary then that the equations

$$FC = CA \qquad .....(7.47)$$

and

$$G = CB \qquad .....(7.48)$$

are satisfied.

The aggregate state vector Z(t) must be a linear combination of certain modes of X(t). The eigenvalues of F are the eigenvalues of A corresponding to those modes of X(t) which are retained in Z(t). In other words, a model reduction is achieved by retaining dominant modes.

Many a time, it is advantageous to define Z(t) corresponding to physical variables. Then

$$Z(t) = HX(t) \qquad .....(7.49)$$

This may be termed as modal approximation.

Eqn. (7.44) may be rewritten as

$$\begin{bmatrix} \dot{X}_1(t) \\ \dot{X}_2(t) \end{bmatrix} = \begin{bmatrix} A_{11} & \varepsilon A_{12} \\ \varepsilon A_{21} & A_{22} \end{bmatrix} \begin{bmatrix} X_1(t) \\ X_2(t) \end{bmatrix} + \begin{bmatrix} B_1 & 0 \\ 0 & B_2 \end{bmatrix} \begin{bmatrix} u_1(t) \\ u_2(t) \end{bmatrix} \qquad .....(7.50)$$

where ε is a small, positive parameter. For $\varepsilon = 0$, the system decomposes into two completely independent sub systems. The two sub stems thus obtained may be treated each separately for simulation, analysis and control design. The dimensionality of the problem is then reduced.

In multi area operation, the decision makers in each area may use a detailed model of his area and a dynamic equivalent of the remainder of the system. Thus, the same system appears in different forms to different controllers. By singular perturbation technique, it is possible to devise control strategy for fast and slow dynamic models of the system. Multi parameter perturbation method may be used for periodic coordination of all the sub-system controllers using Pareto control strategy.

Decentralized suboptimal controller

Consider a system defined by an n-dimensional state vector X. It is desired to replace it by a reduced order model with m-dimensional measurement vector Z. Then each Z may be considered to be a linear combination of the states X so that

$$Z = MX \qquad .....(7.51)$$

If U^0 is an appropriate control for the original system, it is structured from

$$U^0 = KX \qquad .....(7.52)$$

In view of the relation (7.51) U^0 must also be a linear combination of Z. Therefore

$$U^0 = FZ$$

The elements of F can be obtained using various concepts in control theory. For example, if minimum norm concept is utilized then

$$Fj = K\ M_j^T\ (M_j\ M_j^T)^{-1}\ M_j\ j = 1, 2, \ldots\ldots, m \qquad .....(7.53)$$

In eqn. (7.53) K is the full state variable feedback gain matrix.

For a two area power system each area may be controls u_1 and u_2 which depend upon the vectors Z_1 and Z_2 given by

$$Z_1^T = \left[\Delta f_1 \Delta P_{G1} \Delta X_{E1} \Delta P_{tie,1} \int ACE_1\right] \qquad .....(7.54)$$

$$Z_2^T = \left[\Delta f_2 \Delta P_{G2} \Delta X_{E2} \Delta P_{tie,2} \int ACE_2\right] \qquad .....(7.55)$$

Remote measurements are thus avoided. In fact, area controllers are influenced only a little by remote measurements.

Questions

7.1. Explain how the tie-line power deviation can be incorporated in two-area system block diagram?

7.2. What is a tie-line ? Explain

7.3. Derive the relation between steady state frequency error and tie-line derivation for step load disturbances in both areas

7.4. What is area frequency response characteristic. Explain it in the context of two area systems.

7.5. What are the advantages of inter connected operation of power systems? Explain.

7.6. Explain how state variable representation can be obtained for a two area system. Write down the equations.

7.7. Sketch and explain the block schematic of a two-area system.

7.8. What are the features of the dynamic response of a two area system for step load disturbances?

7.9. Explain tie-line bias control applied to a two-area system.

7.10. What are the considerations in selecting the frequency bias parameter.

Problems

P 7.1 Two interconnected control areas have the following characteristics

Area 1 $R_1 = 0.01$pu

$D_1 = 0.08$ p.u.

Base MVA = 500

Area 2 $R_3 = 0.02$pu

$D_2 = 1.0$ p.u.

Base MVA = 1000

A load change of 100MW occurs in area 1. Determine the new steady state frequency and tie-line power deviation.

P 7.2 In P 7.1 if a load change of 200MW occurs in area two determine the frequency derivation and tie line power deviation.

P 7.3 In P 7.1 if a load change of 150MW in area 1 and a load change of 250MW in area 2 occur simultaneously determine the frequency and tie line power deviation.

P 7.4 Given $R_1 = 2.4$Hz/pu MW

R_2 = 2.6Hz/pu MW

T_{T1} = 0.28s

T_{T2} = 0.31s

T_{S1} = 0.075 S

T_{S2} = 0.08s

K_{P1} = 100Hz / pu MW

K_{P1} = 120Hz / pu MW

T_{12} = 0.07 p.u. MW / rad

T_{21} = 0.07 p.u. MW / rad

Solve the state equations for a two area system and plot the frequency, generation and tie line power deviations for a step load disturbance.

P 7.5 Repeat problem 7.4 using MATLAB compare the result.

P 7.6 Repeat problem 7.5 with $P_{D1} = 0.01$pu MW in area 1 and $P_{D2} = 0.01$ pu MW in area 2.

P 7.7 Repeat problem 7.3 with $P_{D2} = 0.03$ p.u. MW. What are your conclusions from the study of the results of problem P7.6 and P7.7.

8 VOLTAGE AND REACTIVE POWER CONTROL

Industrial and domestic loads, both, require real and reactive power. Hence, generators have to produce both real and reactive power. Reactive power is required to excite various types of electrical equipment as well as transmission network. The reactive power requirement of consumers arises mostly from the lagging vars needed to supply magnetizing current to transformers and induction motors.

8.1 Impedance and Reactive Power

In the transmission network, requirement is the difference between that absorbed in the series inductance (I^2X) and that produced in the shunt capacitance (V^2B). There is a level of loading at which the leading vars of charging current balance the lagging vars of the inductive lines; called the natural or surge impedance loading of the system. This natural load for a transmission line is given approximately as $\left(\frac{B}{X}\right)$ p.u., In the case of cables the shunt capacitance is higher and series inductance is lower. As a consequence of which the natural loading is higher. However, this limit is generally above the thermal limit of the cable. The natural impedance loading for overhead lines is shown in Fig. 8.1 as a function of system voltage on logarithmic scale. The conductors are bundled two together for 220kV and four for 380kV. Table 8.1 shows the reactive power requirements of overhead lines, cables and transformers. The reactive power compensation of the transmission system depends on the load and its power factor. When the

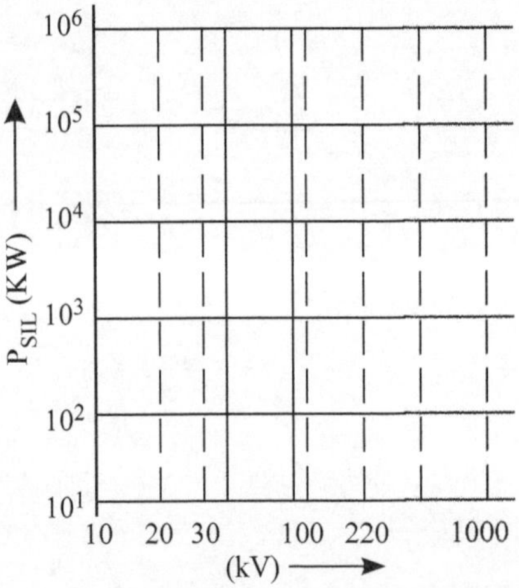

Fig. 8.1 Natural impedance loadings as a function of system voltage

line is operated at no-load, the full charging power occurs and would result in considerable increase in voltage unless some compensating device is used. With full compensation at no-load, the line may be operated at any partial load between no-load and full-load with the voltage not exceeding the permissible limits.

Table 8.1 Var requirements of overhead lines, cables and power transformers

Equipment	Mvar requirements no-load	Inductive, - Capacitive Full load
Over head lines :		
400kV, 4 × 0.4 sq. inch 100 miles	–105.0	+1251.0
275 kV. 2 × 0.4 sq. inch 50 miles	–22.0	+174.0
132 kV. 1 × 0.175 sq. inch 20 miles	–1.6	+10.0
Under taken Cables :		
400kV, 2 × 3.0 sq. inch 10 miles	–540	–487.0
275kV, 1 × 3.0 sq. inch 10 miles	–170	–155.0
132kV, 1 × 0.5 sq. inch 5 miles	–14.5	–13.6
Transformers :		
400/275kV, 750MVA	+0.5	+90.0
275/132kV, 240MVA	+0.3	+48.0
132/33kV, 90mVA	+0.2	+20.5

The loss in a line is given by,

$$P_L = K\frac{P^2 \ell}{V^2 \cos^2 \phi}$$

where P is the power transmitted at voltage V over a line of length ℓ at a power factor cosϕ. Higher voltages are selected for transmission to keep the losses in an economically justifiable relationship to the power P. In view of the inverse square relationship, reduction of reactive power becomes an essential factor for obtaining efficient operation of the high voltage lines. The reactive power requirement of overhead lines are shown in Fig. 8.2(a) & (b).

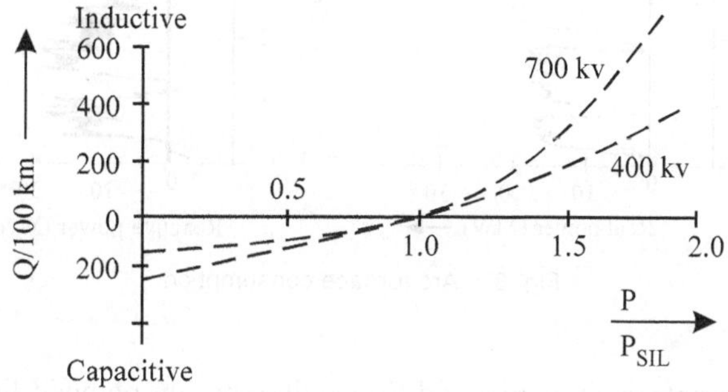

(a)

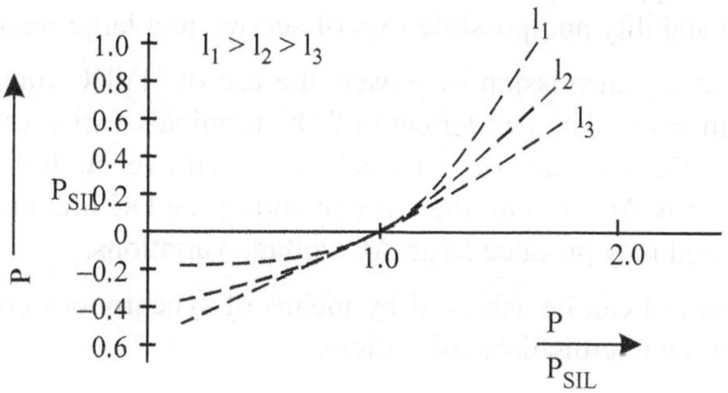

(b)

Fig. 8.2 Reactive power requirement of overhead lines (4 conductor bundle)
(a) Variation with line voltage (b) Variation with line length

In order to supply quality service to customers reliably and economically, voltage and (or) var control play (s) a leading role. Such a control has to be exercised at all the power system. i.e. right from the generating point to the consumer terminals.

Rapid changes in voltage (flicker) can result due to some industrial loads such as arc furnaces, arc welders, and wood chippers. Fig. 8.3 shows the real and reactive power demand following the daily load cycle supplying a composite system load which may create relatively large variations in voltage if control is not exercised. Also, there may be cyclic and non-cyclic loads that create voltage disturbance at both transmission and distribution levels.

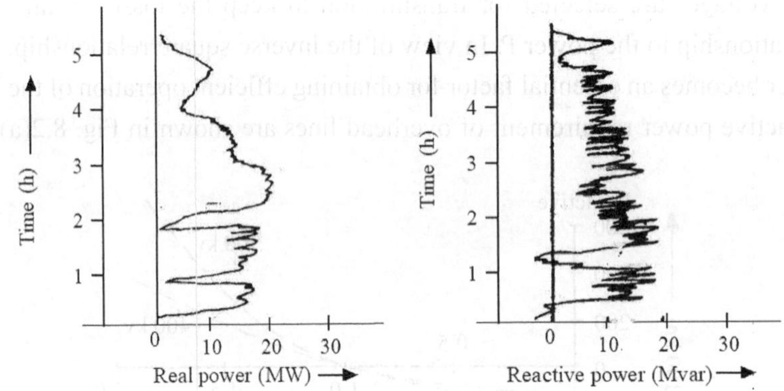

Fig. 8.3 Arc furnace consumption

In addition, events such as planned line switching, un planned line trips, planned and unforeseen generator trips and equipment failure may produce voltage and var variations. Unless proper voltage support is given at strategic locations in the system, the aforesaid events may result in loss of stability and possible loss of service to a large number of consumers.

For long distance transmission of power, the use of HVDC transmission has proved economical in certain cases. The var demand of DC terminals varies usually from 0-60% of the MW rating of the DC lines as power transfer is varied over its full range. When a fault takes place on the nearby AC system, the var demand of the DC link may reach a high value and unless compensated may produce large AC voltage variations.

Continuous control can be achieved by means of synchronous compensators installed at line ends and/or in the intermediate substations.

The use of shunt connected controllable var compensation to improve the power transfer capability and stability is an acknowledged fact. From Fig. 8.4 it can be seen that the theoretical maximum power transfer takes place at a power angle of $\delta_{12} = 90$.

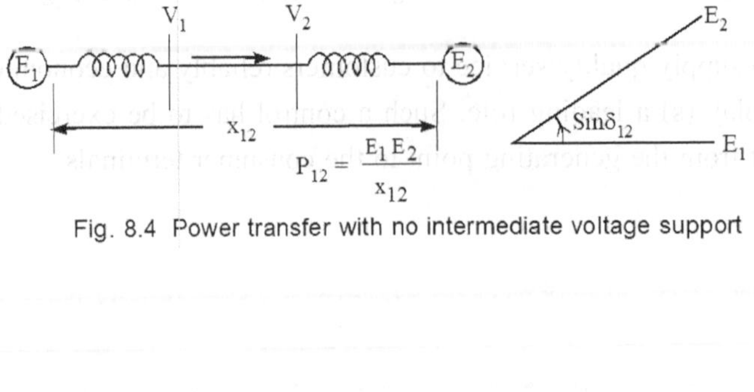

Fig. 8.4 Power transfer with no intermediate voltage support

With an intermediate, controllable, shunt var compensator, the angle could be increased, in principle to 180^0 across the line (Fig. 8.5).

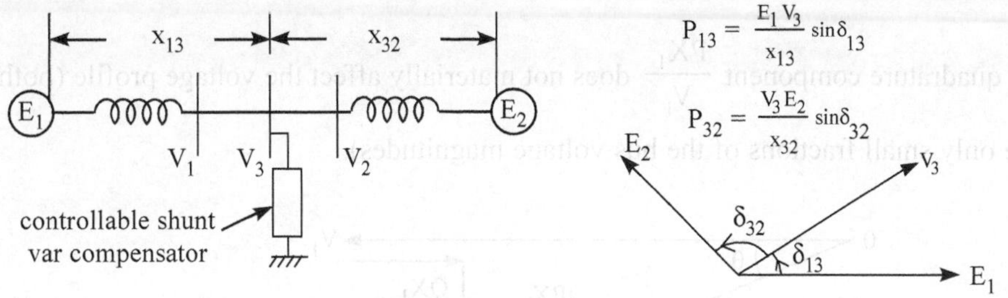

Fig. 8.5 Power transfer with intermediate var compensator

8.2 System Voltage and Reactive Power

Consider the system shown in Fig. 8.6. The voltage at bus 2 is related to the voltage at bus 1 by the relation.

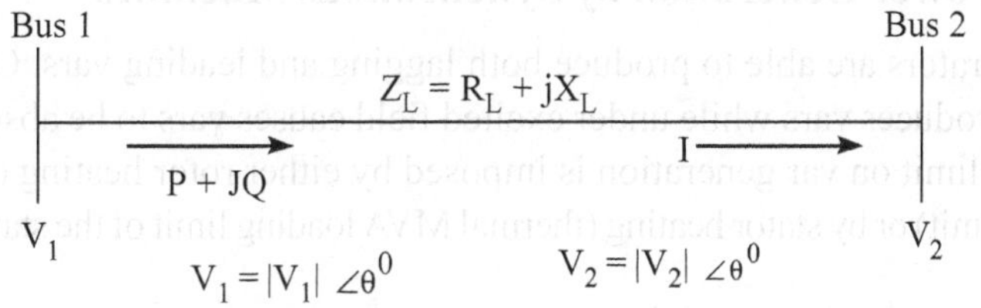

Fig. 8.6 Power flow across a short line

$$V_2 = V_1 - IZ \qquad .....(8.1)$$

Also, $$V_1 \,.\, I^* = P + jQ \qquad .....(8.2)$$

So that $$I = \frac{P - jQ}{V_1^*} = \frac{P - jQ}{V_1} \qquad .....(8.3)$$

since V_1 is the reference phasor.

From eqn. (8.1) and (8.2)

$$V_2 = V_1 - \left(\frac{P - jQ}{V_1}\right) Z$$

Neglecting the line resistance

$$V_2 = V_1 - j\,\frac{P}{V_1} X_L - \frac{Q}{V_1} X_L \qquad .....(8.4)$$

Eqn. (8.4) is illustrated by the phasor diagram in Fig. 8.7. It can be inferred from eqn. (8.3) or Fig. 8.7 the voltage level is influenced largely by the reactive power drop $\frac{QX_L}{V_1}$, since the quadrature component $\frac{PX_L}{V_1}$ does not materially affect the voltage profile (both the drops are only small fractions of the bus voltage magnitudes).

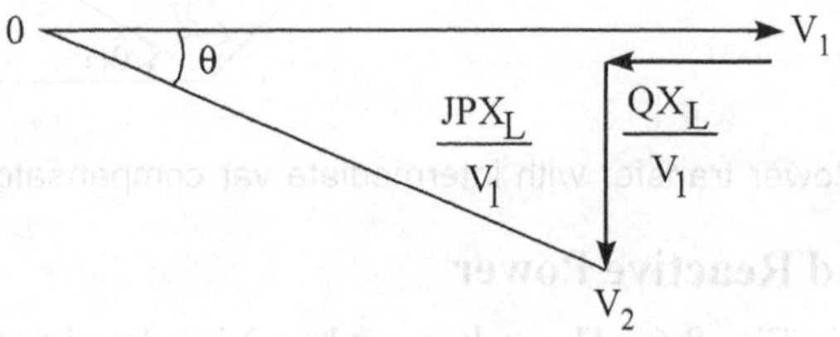

Fig. 8.7 Phasor representation of eqn. (8.3)

8.3 Reactive Power Generation by Synchronous Machines

Synchronous generators are able to produce both lagging and leading vars. Over-excitation of a generator field produces vars while under excited field causes vars to be absorbed. At lagging power factors, the limit on var generation is imposed by either rotor heating (due to maximum excitation current limit) or by stator heating (thermal MVA loading limit of the stator) consideration.

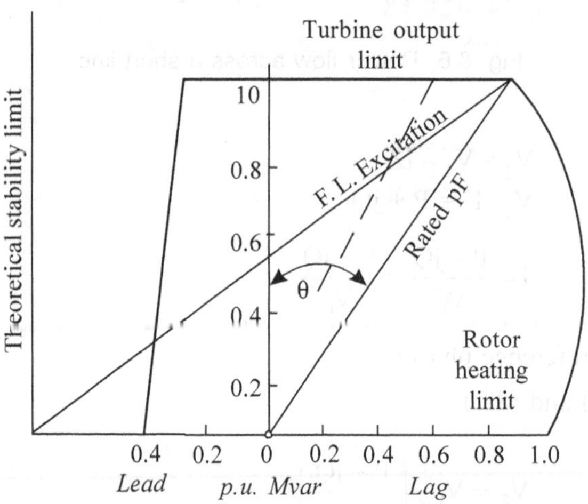

Fig. 8.8 (a) Operating chart for non-salient pole synchronous machine

Generators are invariably fitted with automatic voltage regulators which maintain the thermal voltage at its normal value by adjustment of excitation. The operating charts for salient and non salient pole synchronous machines are shown in Fig. 8.8.

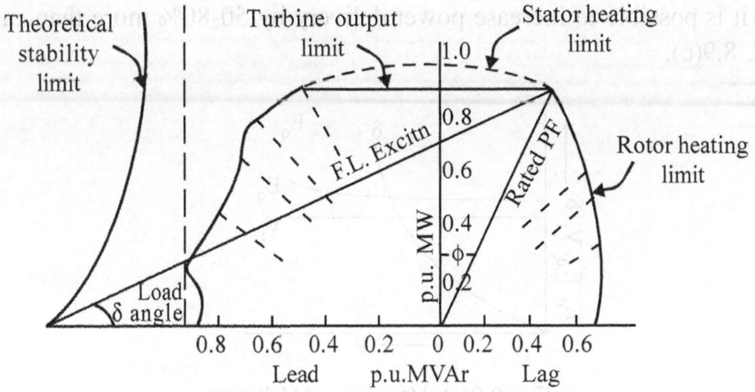

Fig. 8.8 (b) Operation chart for salient pole machine

8.4 Effect of Excitation Control

Consider a synchronous machine with terminal voltage V_t. The direct axis rotor angle with respect to a synchronously revolving axis is δ. The voltage due to excitation acting along the quadrature axis is E_q and E_q' is the transient voltage along this axis. If a load change occurs and the field current, I_f, is not changed then the various quantities mentioned change with P, the real power as shown in Fig. 8.9(a).

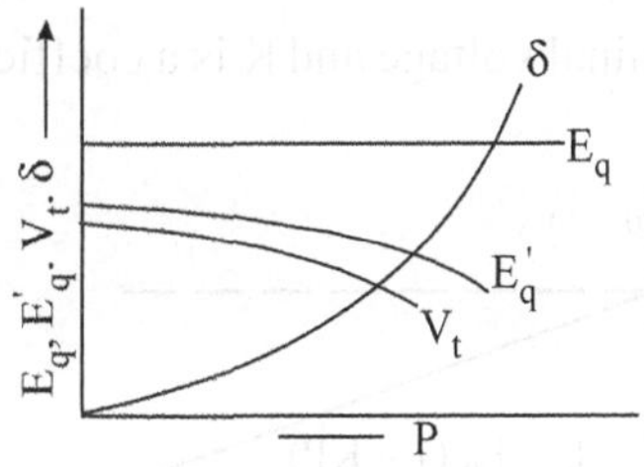

Fig. 8.9(a)

In case the field current I_f is changed such that the transient flux linkages along the q axis E_q' proportional to Ψ_f, the field flux linkages is maintained constant, the power transfer could be increased by 30-60% greater than in case (a) and the quantities are plotted for this case in Fig. 8.9(b).

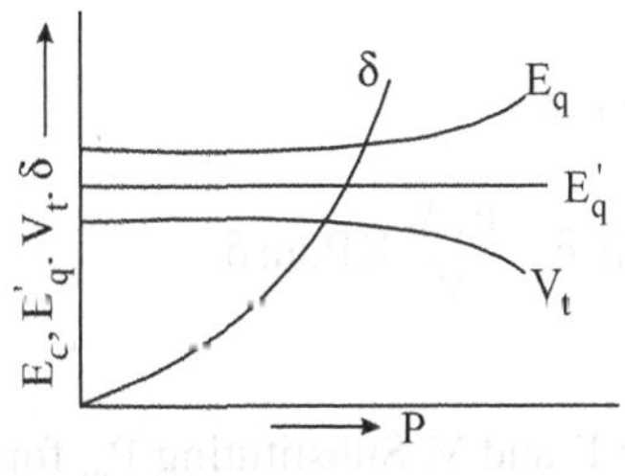

Fig. 8.9(b)

If the field current I_f is changed along with P simultaneously so that Vt is maintained constant then it is possible to increase power delivery by 50-80% more than case (a). This is shown in Fig. 8.9(c).

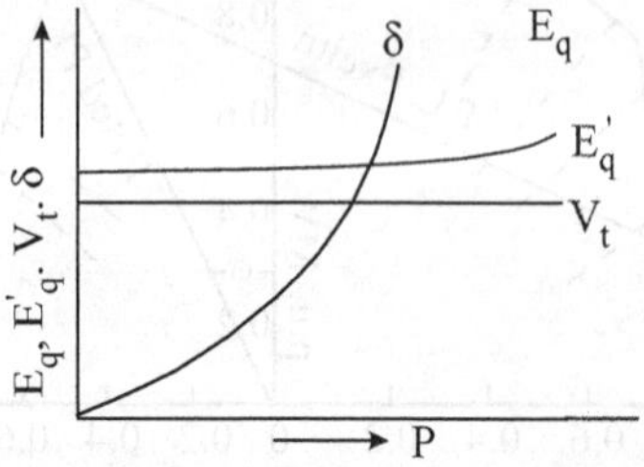

Fig. 8.9(c) Variation of Voltages

It can be concluded that excitation control has a great role to play in power system operation.

8.5 Voltage Regulation and Power Transfer

If the fall of terminal voltage is assumed to be linear, then the graphs of machine terminal voltage with load P can be represented by the relation.

$$E = E_0 (1 - KP)$$

Where E_0 is the non-load terminal voltage and K is a coefficient of regulation (Fig.8.10).

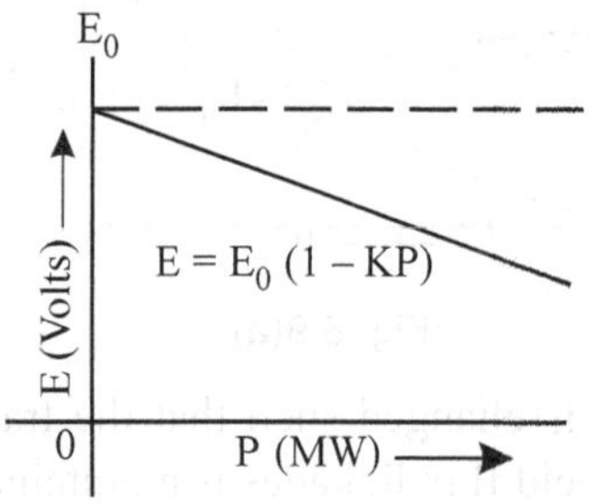

Fig. 8.10 Variation regulation

Since
$$P = \frac{EV}{X}\sin\delta$$

$$= \frac{E_0 V}{X}\sin\delta - \frac{E_0 V}{X} KP\sin\delta \qquad .....(8.5)$$

where δ is the angle between E and V. Substituting P_m for $\frac{E_0 V}{X}$ and solving for P

$$P = \frac{P_m \sin\delta}{1 + P_m K \sin\delta}$$

which is a maximum at $\delta = 90^0$ having the value

$$P_{max} = \frac{P_m}{1 + Kp_m}$$

under ideal conditions, where there is perfect control of excitation, K is zero.

If the machine is represented by a certain voltage E behind a certain reactance X_e then Fig. 8.11 illustrates the effect of various types of regulators on its performance.

It can be proved for an ideal, voltage-actuated automatic regulator that the maximum value of the gain is

$$K_{v\,max} = \frac{x_d - x_d'}{x_d'} \qquad .....(8.6)$$

where x_d and x_d' are direct axis synchronous and transient reactances of the machine respectively.

There is also a minimum value for the gain to ensure stability at large load angles. For better performance, forced regulation using the derivation of current and / or voltage is recommended.

The effect of different types of regulations is shown in Fig. 8.11.

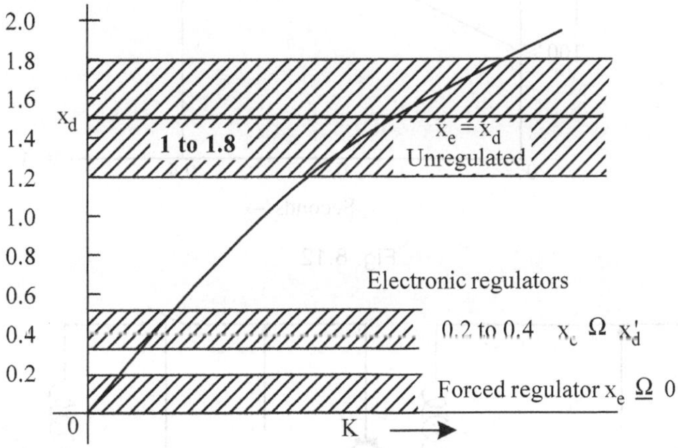

Fig. 8.11 Effect of regulators

8.6 Exciter and Voltage Regulator

The function of an exciter is to increase the excitation current for voltage drop and decrease the same for voltage rise. The voltage change is defined

$$\Delta V \triangleq (V_t - V_{ref})$$

where V_t is the terminal voltage and V_{ref} is the reference voltage.

Exciter ceiling voltage : It is defined as the maximum voltage that may be attained by an exciter with specified conditions of load.

Exciter response : It is the rate of increase or decrease of the exciter voltage. When a change in this voltage is demanded. As an example consider the response curve shown in Fig. 8.12.

$$\text{Response} = \frac{100\text{V}}{0.4\,\text{sec}} = 250\text{V/sec}$$

Exciter build up : The exciter build up depends upon the field resistance and the charging of its value by cutting or adding. The greatest possible control effort is the complete shorting of the field rheostat when maximum current value is reached in the field circuit. This can be done by closing the contactor shown in Fig. 8.13.

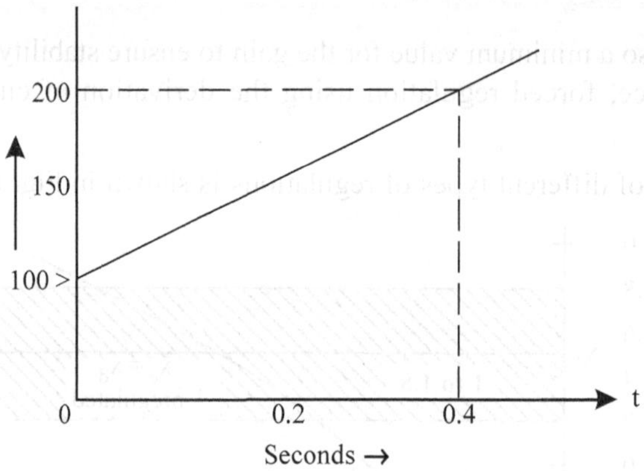

Fig. 8.12

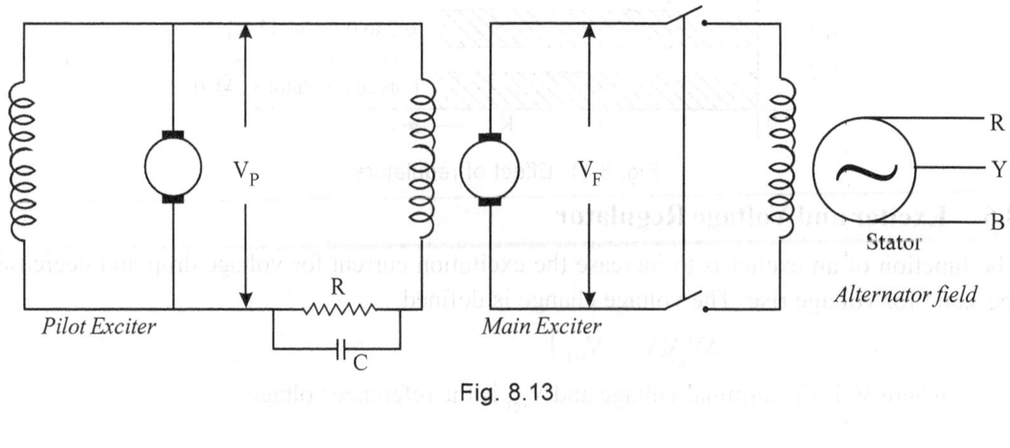

Fig. 8.13

When the exciter is operated at rated speed at no load, the record of voltage as function of time with a step change that drives the exciter to its ceiling voltage is called the exciter build up curve. Such a response curve is show in Fig. 8.14.

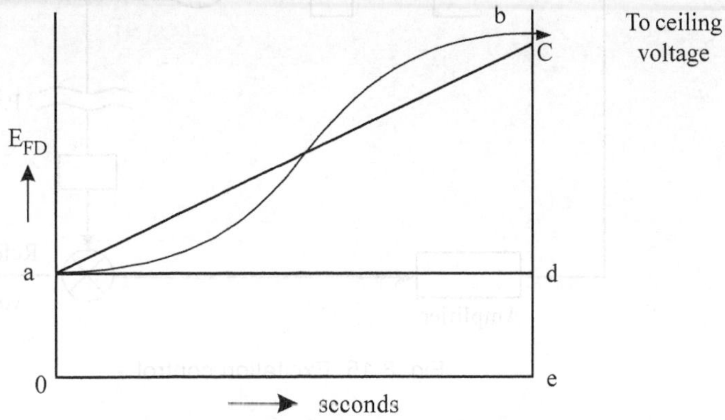

Fig. 8.14 Exciter Build-up curve

Line ac represents the excitation system voltage response.

$$\text{Response ratio} = \frac{Cd}{Oa(0.5)} \text{ p.u. V/sec} \qquad .....(8.7)$$

Table 8.2 Typical ceiling voltages

Response ratio	Conventional exciter	SCR exciter
0.5	1.25 – 1.35	1.2
1.0	1.4 – 1.5	1.2 – 1.25
1.5	1.55 – 1.65	1.3 – 1.4
2.0	1.7 – 1.8	1.45 – 1.55
4.0	. . .	2.0 – 2.1

In general the present day practice is to use 125V excitation up to 10MVA units and 250V systems up to 100MVA units. Units generating power beyond 100MVA have excitation system voltages variedly. Some use 350V and 375V system while some go up to 500V excitation system.

8.7 Block Schematic of Excitation Control

A typical excitation control system is shown in Fig. 8.15. The terminal voltage of the alternator is sampled, rectified and compared with a reference voltage, the difference is amplified and fed back to the exciter field winding to change the excitation current. An excitation system using amplidyne is shown in Fig. 8.16.

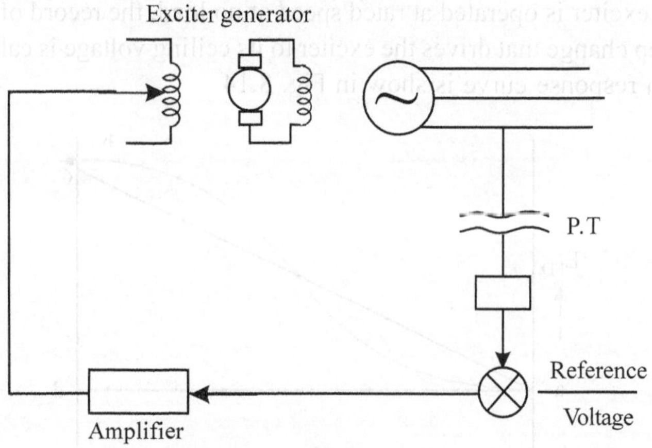

Fig. 8.15 Excitation control

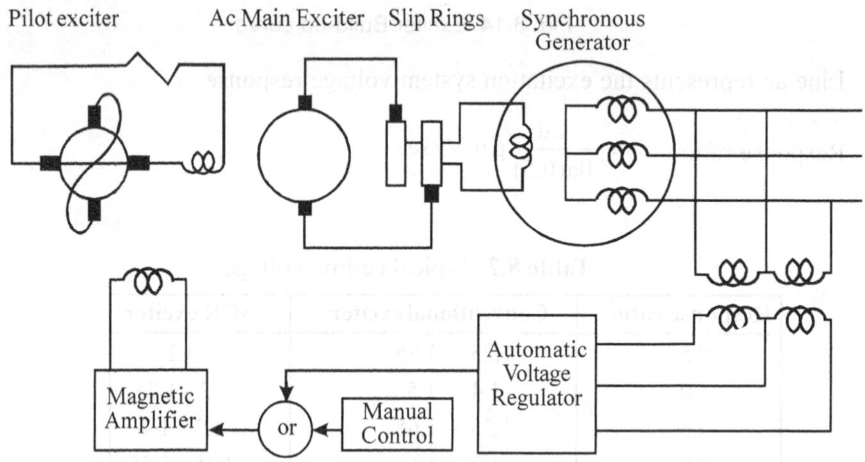

Fig. 8.16 DC-Type Excitation Systems

8.8 Static Excitation System

In the static excitation system, the generator field is fed from a thyristor network shown in Fig. 8.17. It is just sufficient to adjust the thyristor firing angle to vary the excitation level. A major advantage of such a system is that, when required the field voltage can be varied through a full range of positive to negative values very rapidly with the ultimate benefit of generator voltage regulation during transient disturbances. The thyristor network consists of either 3-phase fully controlled or semi controlled bridge rectifers. Field suppression resistor dissipates energy in the field circuit while the field breaker ensures field isolation during generator faults.

A compact AC static excitation scheme is shown in Fig. 8.18.

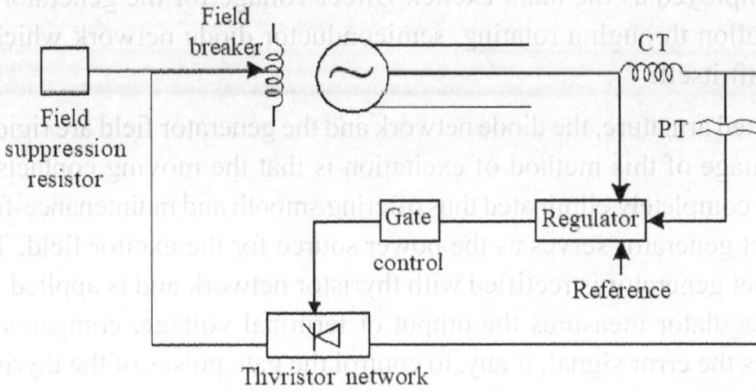

Fig. 8.17 Static Excitation Scheme

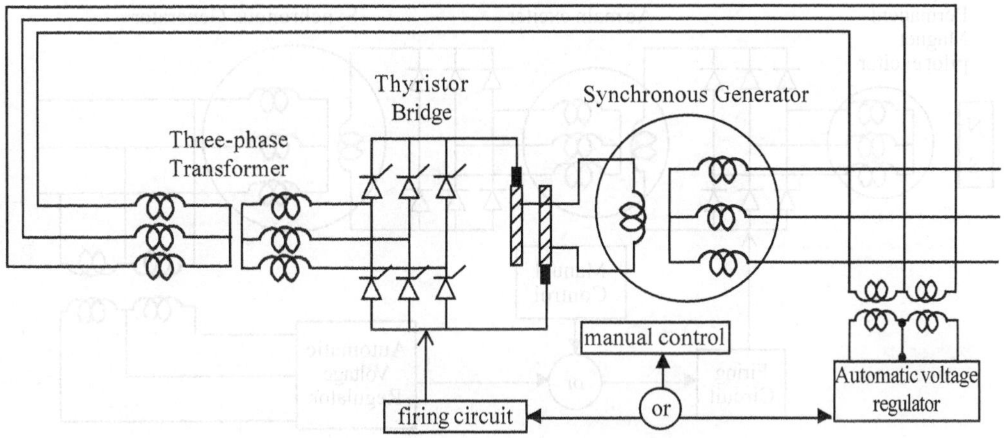

Fig. 8.18 AC Static-Type Excitation Systems

8.9 Brushless Excitation Scheme

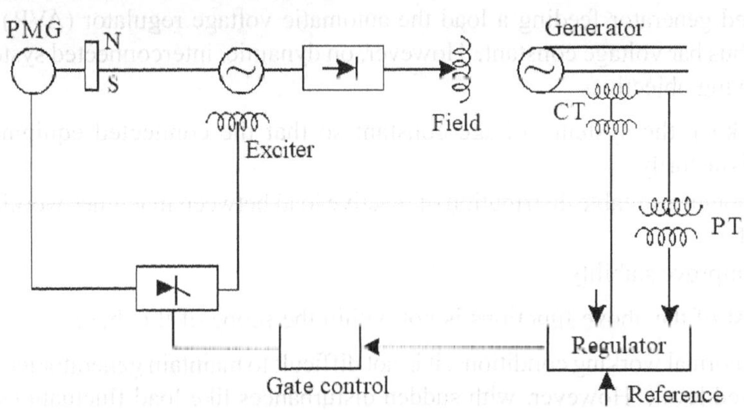

Fig. 8.19 Brushless excitation scheme

In the brushless excitation system of Fig. 8.19, an alternator with rotating armature and stationary field is employed as the main exciter. Direct voltage for the generator excitation is obtained by rectification through a rotating, semiconductor diode network which is mounted on the generator shaft itself.

Thus, the excited armature, the diode network and the generator field are rigidly connected in series. The advantage of this method of excitation is that the moving contacts such as slip rings and brushes are completely eliminated thus offering smooth and maintenance-free operation. A permanent-magnet generator serves as the power source for the excitor field. The output of the permanent magnet generator is rectified with thyristor network and is applied to the excitor field. The voltage regulator measures the output or terminal voltage, compares it with a set reference and utilizes the error signal, if any, to control the gate pulses of the thyristor network.

A detailed brushless excitation scheme is shown in Fig. 8.20.

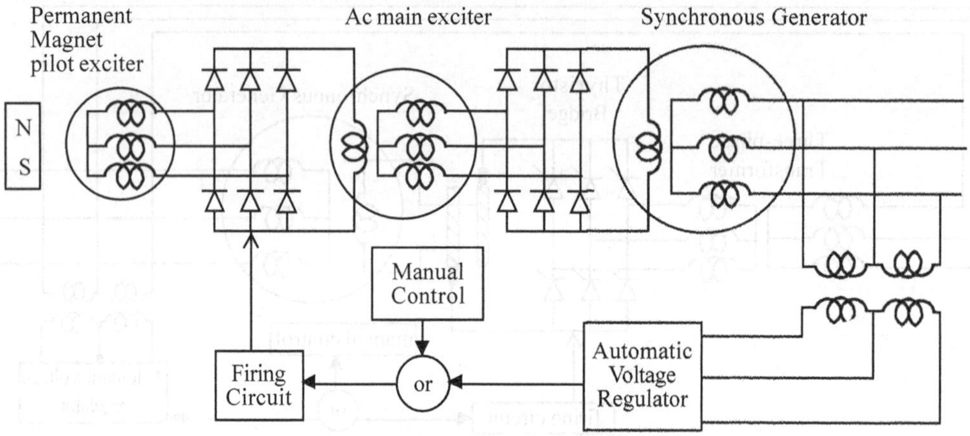

Fig. 8.20 AC Alternator–Type Excitation System

8.10 Automatic Voltage Regulators for Alternators

For an isolated generator feeding a load the automatic voltage regulator (AVR) functions to maintain the bus bar voltage constant. However, on dynamic, interconnected systems the AVR has the following objectives

1. To keep the system voltage constant so that the connected equipment operates satisfactorily
2. to obtain a suitable distribution of reactive load between machines working in parallel and
3. to improve stability.

The last of the above functions is not within the scope of this book.

Under normal working conditions, it is not difficult to maintain generator terminal voltage at any specified level. However, with sudden disturbances like load fluctuations, the AVR is required to reduce the magnitude and duration of voltage variations as effectively as possible.

The magnitude of the voltage dip is primarily determined by the transient reactance of the machine while the duration of the dip depends on the time constant of the generator and rapidity of regulation. Static regulators are more useful in this context as they have lesser time delays.

The AVR which senses the terminal voltage and adjusts the excitation to maintain a constant terminal voltage also maintains the reactive output at the required level since the latter depends on the effective voltage difference between generator terminals and its point of connection to the main system. Thus, while AVR is allowed to maintain the voltage on the low voltage side, a change in reactive output to suit a change in system conditions is obtained by tap changing a generator transformer. With several generators synchronized on a single low impedance bus section, one generator with the AVR may be permitted to maintain bus bar voltage while the excitation of the rest are used to distribute properly the vars among the generators.

8.11 Analysis of Generator Voltage Control

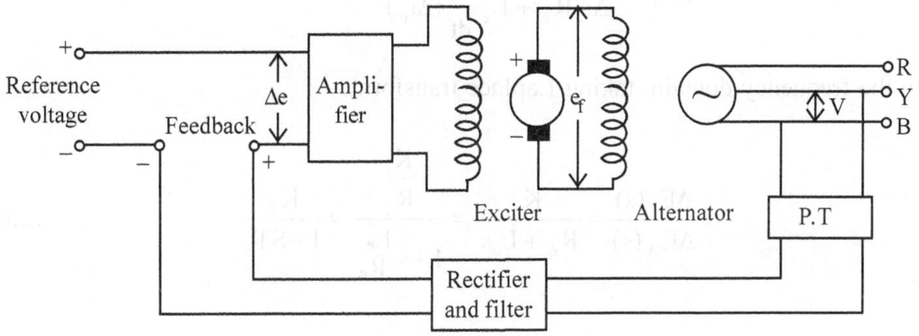

Fig. 8.21 Excitation System

Consider the excitation system shown in Fig. 8.21 the block diagram representation is given in Fig. 8.22.

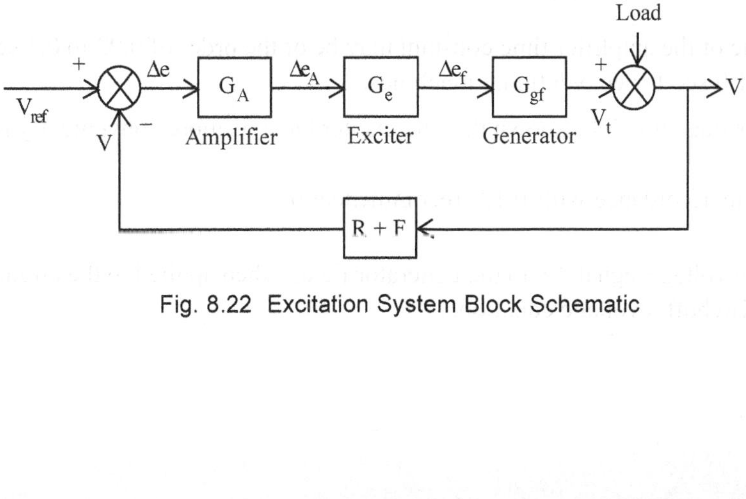

Fig. 8.22 Excitation System Block Schematic

From the block diagram

$$|V|_{ref} - |V| = \Delta e$$

The amplifier is generally assumed to be instantaneous in action so that Δe_A, the output from the amplifier is $K_A \Delta e$ where K_A, is the amplifier gain. The input to the exciter field will be absorbed by the resistance and inductance of the exciter field R_e and L_e respectively so that

$$\Delta e_A = R_e \Delta i_e + L_e \frac{d}{dt}(\Delta i_e)$$

where Δi_e is the change in exciter field current. If 1 ampere change in field current produces K_i volt change in the output, then

$$\Delta e_f = K_i \Delta i_e$$

The transfer function of the exciter can be obtained as follows :

$$\frac{\Delta e_f}{\Delta e_A} = \frac{K_i \Delta i_e}{\Delta i_e R_e + L_e \frac{d}{dt}(\Delta i_e)}$$

In the frequency domain, taking Laplace transform

$$\frac{\Delta E_f(s)}{\Delta E_A(s)} = \frac{K_i}{R_e + L_e s} = \frac{\frac{K_i}{R_e}}{1 + s\frac{Le}{Re}} = \frac{K_e}{1 + ST_e} \qquad .....(8.8)$$

Hence $G_e = \dfrac{K_e}{1 + sT_e}$ is the transfer function of the exciter with the time constant

$T_e = \left(\dfrac{L_e}{R_e}\right)$ and gain $K_e = \left(\dfrac{K_i}{R_e}\right)$.

The value of the amplifier time constant may be of the order of 0.02 to 0.1 sec while T_e may be 0.5 to 1.0 sec for conventional machines.

At a later stage it will be shown that the exciter block is more conveniently represented by $\dfrac{1}{K_E + ST_E}$ in accordance with IEEE recommendation.

The input voltage signal Δe_f to the generator field, when applied to the circuit results in the following Kirchoff's voltage equation.

$$\Delta e_f = R_f \Delta i_f + L_{ff} \frac{d}{dt} \Delta i_f$$

where R_f and L_{ff} are the alternator field resistance and self inductance respectively and Δi_f is the change in the field current. Taking Laplace transform.

$$\Delta E_f(S) = (R_f + L_{ff}s)\Delta I_f(S)$$

If the output voltage changes by $\Delta|V|$ then

$\Delta I_f(s) = \dfrac{\sqrt{2}}{\omega L_{fa}} \Delta|V|$ where L_{fa} is the mutual inductance between the field and stator phase winding. Hence, the transfer function for the generator block will be

$$\frac{\Delta V(S)}{\Delta E_f(S)} = \frac{\Delta|V|}{R_f + L_{ff}S} \frac{\sqrt{2}}{\omega L_{fa}} \Delta|V| = \frac{\sqrt{2}R_f}{\omega L_{fa}} \frac{1}{1 + S\dfrac{L_{ff}}{R_f}} = \frac{K_{gf}}{1 + ST_{gf}} \quad .....(8.9)$$

where T_{gf} is the direct axis open circuit time constant also denoted more commonly by $T_{d0} = L_{ff} / R_f$ seconds.

The voltage regulator loop can be represented by the block diagram shown in Fig. 8.23.

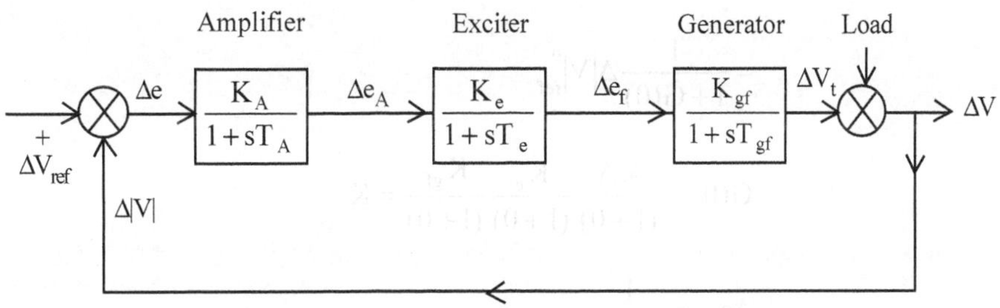

Fig. 8.23 Voltage regulator block diagram

The three cascaded transfer function blocks G_A, G_e and G_{gf} can be combined into a single block.

$$G_{VR}(S) = \left[\frac{K_A}{1+sT_A}\right]\left[\frac{K_e}{1+sT_e}\right]\left[\frac{K_{gf}}{1+sT_{gf}}\right]$$

so that the feed back control loop can be further simplified as in Fig. 8.24.

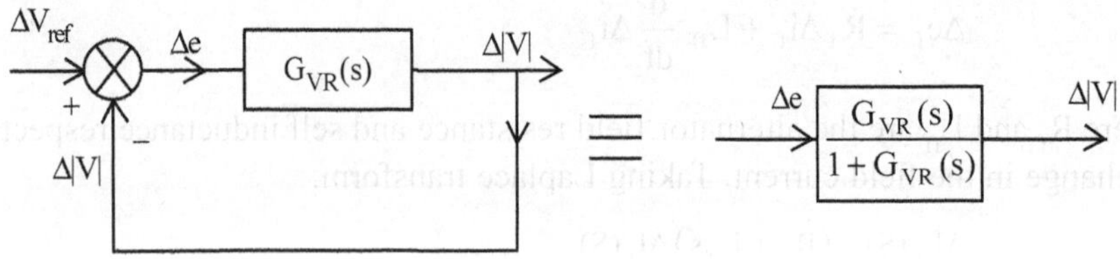

Fig. 8.24 Simplified Block Diagram

8.12 Steady State Performance Evaluation

The control loop must regulate the output voltage V_t so that the error is made equal to zero. It is also imperative that the response must be reasonably fast, yet not cause any instability problem.

The steady state voltage error Δe_{SS} is given by

$$\Delta e_{SS} = \Delta|V|^0_{ref} - \Delta V_{SS}$$

$$= \Delta|V|^0_{ref} - \frac{G(0)}{1+G(0)}\Delta|V|^0_{ref}$$

where G(0) is the value of G(s) as s → 0 (i.e.) the steady state value

$$= \frac{1+G(0)-G(0)}{1+G(0)}\Delta|V|^0_{ref}$$

$$= \frac{1}{1+G(0)}\Delta|V|^0_{ref}$$

$$G(0) = \frac{KA}{(1+0)}\frac{K_e}{(1+0)}\frac{K_{gf}}{(1+0)} = K$$

$$\Delta e_{ss} = \frac{1}{1+K} \quad .....(8.10)$$

Larger the overall gain of the forward block gain K smaller is the steady state error. But too large a gain K can cause instability.

8.13 Dynamic Response of Voltage Regulation Control

Consider

$$\Delta V(t) = L^{-1}\left[\Delta V_{ref}(S)\frac{G(S)}{1+G(S)}\right]$$

The response depends upon the roots of the characteristic eqn. 1 + G(S) = 0.

As there are three time constants, we may write the three roots as S_1, S_2 and S_3. A typical root locus plot is shown in Fig. 8.25.

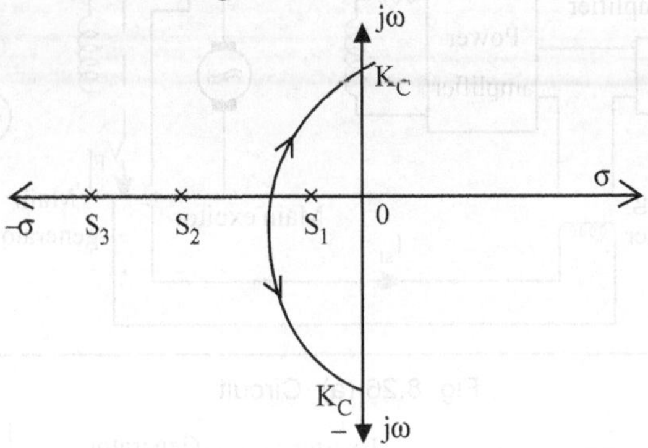

Fig. 8.25 Root - Locus Plot

From the plot, it can be observed that at gain higher than K_C the control loop becomes unstable.

8.14 Stability Compensation for Voltage Control

Since at higher gains the voltage control loop tends to oscillate and even may become unstable, it requires phase lead compensation or derivative control. As there are three time constants contributing to phase lag, a phase lead compensator with transfer function.

$$G_C(S) = 1 + sT_C$$

will alter the open loop transfer function to

$$G_{VR}(S) = \frac{K(1+ST_C)}{(1+sT_A)(1+sT_e)(1+sT_{gf})} \quad .....(8.11)$$

It will not affect the steady state accuracy as K is kept constant

8.15 Stabilizing Transformer

Consider the excitation system with a stabilizing transformer as shown in Fig. 8.26.

K_A = Error amplifier gain

K_{ST}, T_{ST} → stabilizing transformer gain and time constants.

A stabilizing transformer is introduced in the exciter circuit as shown in Fig.8.26(a, b).

The input voltage V_e causes a current $\dot{I}_{ST}$ to flow through the resistance and inductance of the feed back loop.

$$V_e = R_f \dot{I}_{ST} + L_f \frac{dI_{ST}}{dt}$$

Taking Laplace transform

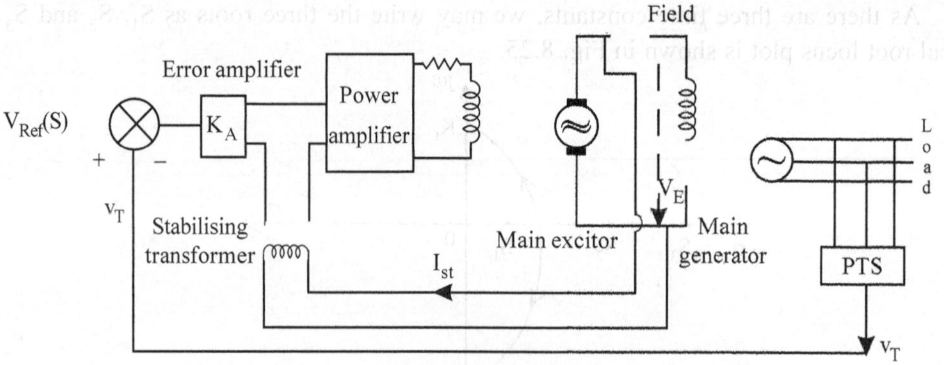

Fig. 8.26 (a) Circuit

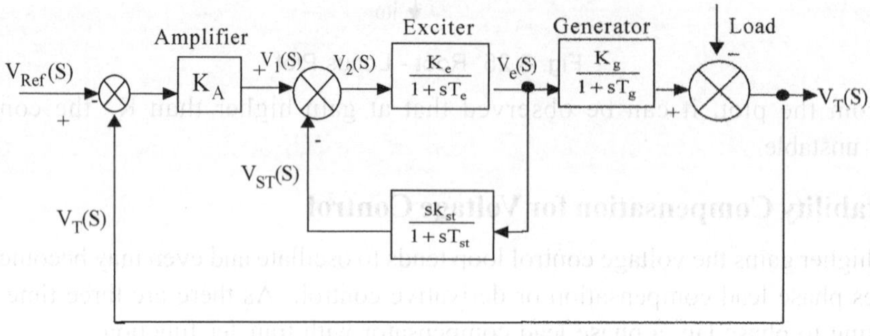

Fig. 8.26 (b) Block diagram

$$V_e(S) = R_f\, I_{ST}(S) + L_f\, S\, I_{ST}(S)$$
$$= (R_f + S\, L_f)\, I_{ST}(S)$$

If the mutual inductance is M for the stabilizing transformer then,

$$V_{ST}(t) = M \frac{d}{dt} i_{st}(t)$$

Taking Laplace transform

$$V_{ST} = MS\, I_{st}(S)$$

Hence

$$\frac{V_{ST}(S)}{V_e(s)} = \frac{sM}{R_f + L_f s} = \frac{\frac{sM}{R_f}}{1 + \frac{L_f}{R_f} s}$$

Letting $\frac{L_f}{R_f} = T_{st}$ and $\frac{M}{R_f} = K_{st}$

$$\frac{V_{st}(S)}{V_e(S)} = \frac{sK_{st}}{1 + T_{st} s} \qquad .....(8.12)$$

It may be noted that since the secondary of the stabilizing transformer is connected to the input terminals of an amplifier, it draws zero current. Thus, the stabilizing transformer improves the response of the excitation system giving derivative control.

8.16 Voltage Regulators

The heart of the excitation system lies in the voltage regulator. It is a device that serves the output voltage change (some times current or both) and provides corrective action to take place.

The early voltage regulators were all of electromechanical type. Electronic voltage regulators came in 1930's. They provide smoother and faster voltage control than the electromechanical type. Another development resulted in the use of rotating amplifiers. Magnetic amplifiers were also used for voltage regulators.

Later versions of voltage controllers used solid state active circuits. Whatever may be the hardware used, there was consistent effort to provide faster response, without dead band, backlash, and absolutely reliable. Excitation systems which include voltage regulators also are classified into continuously acting type and non continuously acting type.

All the systems have a potential transformer and rectifier to sample the output a.c. voltage and provide d.c. signal to the control loop.

Another component is a comparator that compares the d.c. signal with reference value and provides an error signal.

An amplifier amplifies the error signal and brings it to the operational level.

The exciter output is manipulated by the amplified error signal to suitably modify the output voltage of the generator.

As a simple proportional feed back results in a steady state error, a rate feedback or derivative control is proposed by Kron in 1954 and this was discussed in section (8.15).

Computer representation of excitation system

For synchronous machines, several models were developed and linear representations of the machine using state space methods needed suitable models for excitation system for computer simulation to perform dynamic studies. IEEE has suggested certain standard models for different types of excitation system.

1. *Type 1 System :* It is a continuously acting regulator and exciter system. It will be explained in detail later.
2. *Type 1 S system :* This is a special case of continuously acting system. In this system excitation is obtained through rectification of the terminal voltage while in type 1 system regulator voltage has maximum and minimum limits, in this case, the maximum regulator voltage is made proportional to V_t, the terminal voltage of the generator.

3. *Type 2 System :* In this system rotating rectifiers are used and is brushless. Alternator-exciter and diode rectifiers are rotating on the same shaft and hence has no slip rings. Being brushless, the excitation voltage (E_{FD}) is not available for feed back. In this there are two damping loops giving good performance.
4. *Type 3 System :* This type of model is evolved for systems where both current and voltage signals are used for feed back.
5. *Type 4 System :* All the previously described systems are continuously acting type with high gain and fast action. Several of the earlier systems are non continuous acting type. In such cases presence of dead zone results in open loop operation. They are also slow due to friction and inertia. Rheostat systems are examples for such an operation. In type 4 systems now there are two speeds of operation depending upon the magnitude of the voltage error. Type 4 system hence is non-linear and as such is not represented in state variable form. Westinghouse and General electric have developed such excitation systems.

8.17 IEEE Type 1 Excitation System

Consider Fig. 8.27. Let V_f be the voltage across the field winding and i_f the current through it λ_f and also the flux linkages in the field winding.

$$v_f = i_f r_f + \frac{d}{dt}\lambda_f(i_f) \qquad .....(8.13)$$

consider the non-load magnetization curve shown in Fig. 8.27 for the exciter voltage build up.

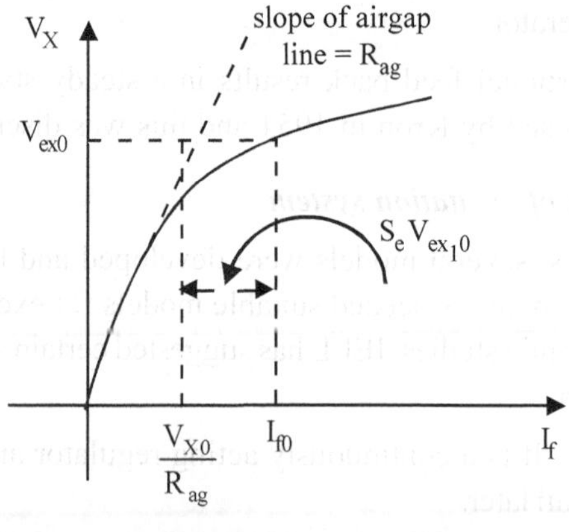

Fig. 8.27 In Engineering Units

S_e is the saturatin coefficient $\frac{A-B}{B}$

The exciter voltage $v_{ex}^0 = f(i_f, i_{ex}^0)$ .....(8.14)

$$i_f = \frac{v_{ex}^0}{R_{ag}} + S_e v_{ex}^0 \qquad .....(8.15)$$

where R_{ag} is the resistance given by air gap line.

The saturation may be represented by

$$S_e = A_{ex}^0 \, e^{B_{ex}^0} v_{ex}^0 \qquad .....(8.16)$$

an exponential relation, A and B to be determined.

$$v_f = \frac{r_f v_{ex}^0}{R_{ag}} + S_e v_{ex}^0 r_f + \frac{d}{dt}\lambda_f\left(v_{ex}^0\right) \qquad .....(8.17)$$

from eqn. (8.2)

$$= \left[\frac{r_f}{R_{ag}} + S_e(i_f)r_f\right] v_{ex}^0 + \frac{d}{dt}\lambda_f\left(v_{ex}^0\right) \qquad .....(8.18)$$

$$= \frac{r_f}{R_{ag}}\left[1 + R_{ag}S_e(i_f)\right]v_{ex}^0 + \frac{d}{dv_{ex}^0}\lambda_f\left(v_{ex}^0\right)\frac{dv_{ex}^0}{dt}$$

In per unit system (see Fig. 8.28)

$$v_f(\text{p.u.}) = \frac{r_f}{R_{ag}}\left[1 + R_{ag}S_e(i_f)\right]v_{ex}^0 \text{ p.u.} + \frac{d\lambda_f(v_{ex})}{dv_{ex}}\frac{dv_{ex}(\text{p.u.})}{dt}$$

$$= \frac{r_f}{R_{ag}}\left[1 + S_e(\text{p.u})\, v_{ex}(\text{p.u.})\right]v_{ex}(\text{p.u.}) + \tau_E \frac{d}{dt} v_{ex}(\text{p.u.})$$

Let

$$S_e(\text{p.u.}) = \frac{i_f(\text{p.u.}) - \dfrac{v_{ex}(\text{p.u.})}{R_{ag}}}{\dfrac{v_{ex}(\text{p.u.})}{R_{ag}}} = \frac{A - B}{B} \qquad .....(8.19)$$

$$\tau_E = \frac{d\lambda_f(v_{ex})}{dv_{ex}} = \frac{d\lambda_f(v_{ex}(\text{p.u.}))}{dv_{ex}(\text{p.u.})}$$

$$K_E = \frac{r_f}{R_{ag}}$$

$$S_E = \frac{r_f}{R_{ag}} S_e(\text{p.u.})\left(V_{ex}\text{p.u.}\right)$$

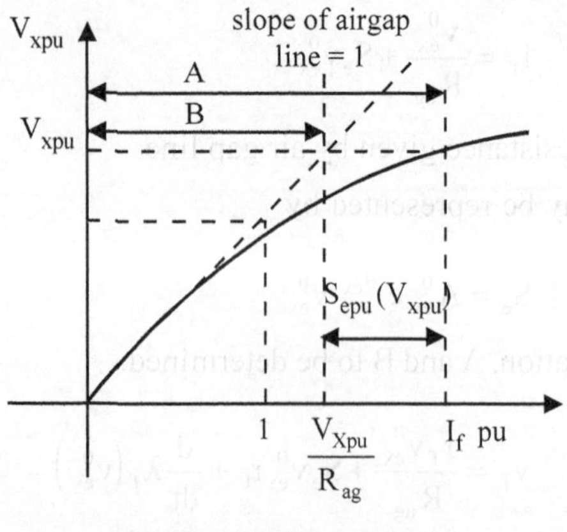

Fig. 8.28 In Per Unit

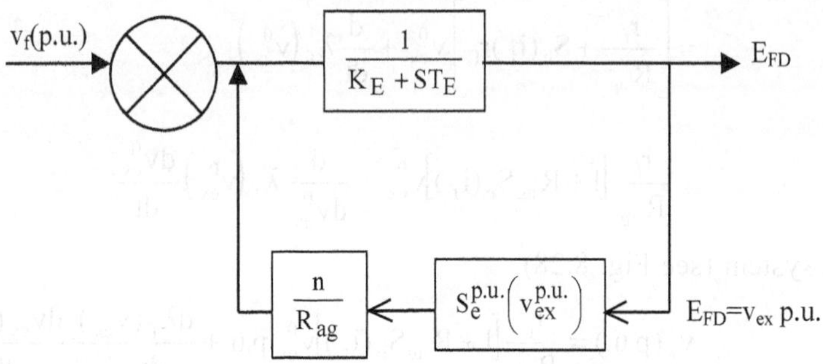

Fig. 8.29

Then the transfer function for the exciter block can be represented by Fig. (8.29).

IEEE type 1 excitation system representation is shown in Fig. 8.30.

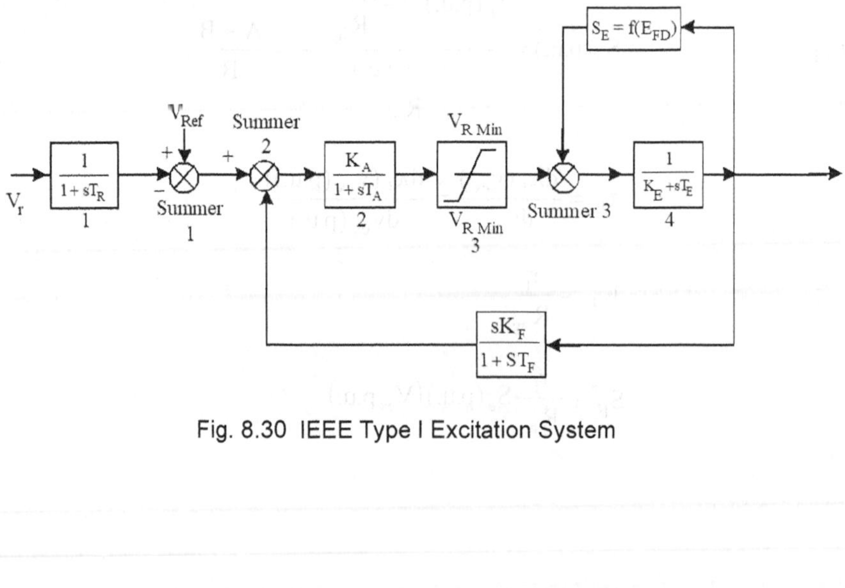

Fig. 8.30 IEEE Type I Excitation System

8.18 Power System Stabilizer

It can be proved that an voltage regulator in the forward path of the exciter generator systems will introduce a damping torque and under heavy loading conditions this damping torque becomes negative. This is a situation where dynamic instability may cause concern. Further, it has been also pointed out that in the forward path of excitation control loop, the three time constants introduce a large phase lag at low frequencies just above the natural frequency of the excitation systems. To overcome this effect and improve damping, compensating networks are introduced to produce torque in phase with the speed. Such a network is called "*power system stabilizer*" (PSS)

Fig. 8.31 shows the block schematic of PSS at the appropriate point in the control loop.

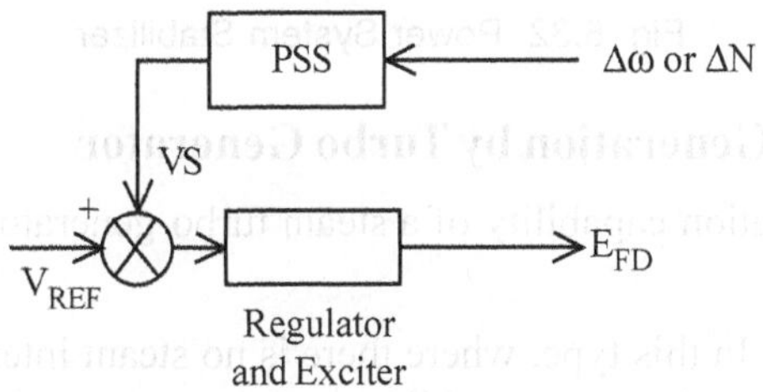

Fig. 8.31 Connecting Power System Stabilizer

Power system stabilizer is generally shown as a feedback element from the shaft speed and has a transfer function of the form

$$G_{PSS}(S) = \frac{K_0 \tau_0 S}{1+\tau_0 S}\left[\frac{[1+T_1 S][1+T_3 S]}{[1+T_2 S][1+T_4 S]}\right] \quad .....(8.20)$$

A washout circuit for reset action is used to eliminate steady effect after a time lag T_0 (4 sec to 30 sec). This control circuit ensures that there is no permanent offset in the terminal voltage due to a prolonged error in frequency. The later may occur due to prolonged over load or islanding situation. A lead compensation pair is used at two stages with center frequencies

$\frac{1}{2\pi}\sqrt{T_1 T_2}$ and $\frac{1}{2\pi}\sqrt{T_3 T_4}$. This part of the stabilizer circuit will improve the phase lag.

A filter section is generally added as shown in Fig. 8.32 so that undesirable frequency components are suppressed and thus eliminate the possibility of undesirable interaction. Limits are placed so that the output signal of the PSS is prevented from driving the excitation into heavy saturation.

The output signal of the PSS is fed as a supplementary input signal V_{PSS} for the regulation of the excitation system. Design of the PSS circuit is beyond the scope of this book.

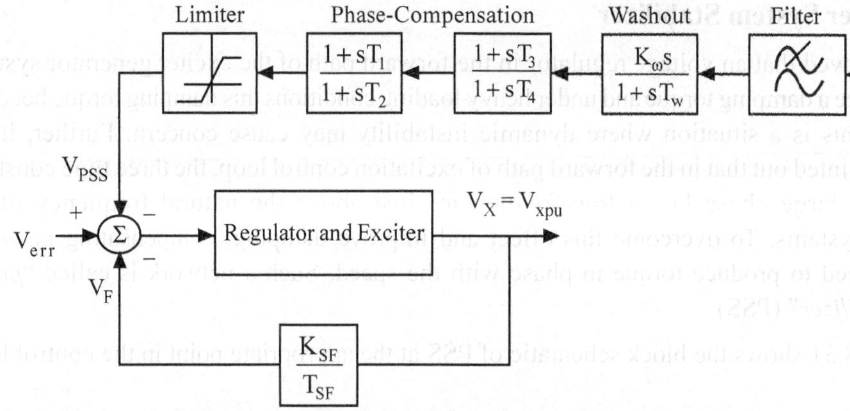

Fig. 8.32 Power System Stabilizer

8.19 Reactive Power Generation by Turbo Generator

The reactive power generation capability of a steam turbo-generator is dependent on the type of construction.

Unit construction: In this type, where there is no steam interconnection, the generator can absorb and produce reactive power while supplying the rated real power to the load. A reduction of active power load on the generator increases both its reactive absorption and production capability. However, the active power scheduling is quite often based on an optimal criterion as discussed in Chapter 6, overlooking which may add to the costs. The level to which real power loading may be reduced is mostly determined by considerations of boiler performance. Minimum permissible loadings usually fall in the range of 50 to 70% of rating.

Steam range construction: In the steam range construction having steam interconnection between generators, the minimum loading constraint imposed by the boiler is of less significance since steam from one boiler can be used to supply several generators.

As an example, if four sets are supplied by a single boiler, then with three sets drawing steam just for gland ceiling, maintaining vacuum and cooling while the fourth set at the partial load, a wide range of reactive generation or absorption capability can be obtained. However, this arrangement is not in use now.

8.20 Synchronous Compensators

There are rotating machines which are connected to the system at appropriate places only for the purpose of controlling vars. They are synchronous motors operating on load with adjustable excitation. They are normally fitted with voltage regulators which operate when the voltage deviates by a certain predetermined percentage of system voltage.

These machines are also capable of giving dynamic reactive power compensation, i.e. they make available the required reactive power within a short time. The prime consideration for installing synchronous compensator is its flexibility of operation under all load conditions.

This aspect justifies its use in certain systems even though the initial cost is high. Another important consideration for using the synchronous compensator is the occurrence of sudden voltage dips due to sudden short circuits or overloads.

Under such conditions the synchronous compensator performs better than other apparatus. With additional excitation windings through which excitation can be forced momentarily to counteract the transient effects, the synchronous compensator can even improve stability. The synchronous compensator may be supplied from the tertiary winding of the transformer as shown in Fig. 8.31, so that additional cost on transformer is not incurred.

8.21 Reactors

Inductive reactors absorb reactive power and may be used in circuits, series or shunt connected, While series connected reactors are used to limit fault currents, shunt reactors are used for var control. Reactors installed at line ends and intermediate substations can compensate upto 70% of charging power while the remaining 30% power at no-load can be provided by the under excited operation of the generator.

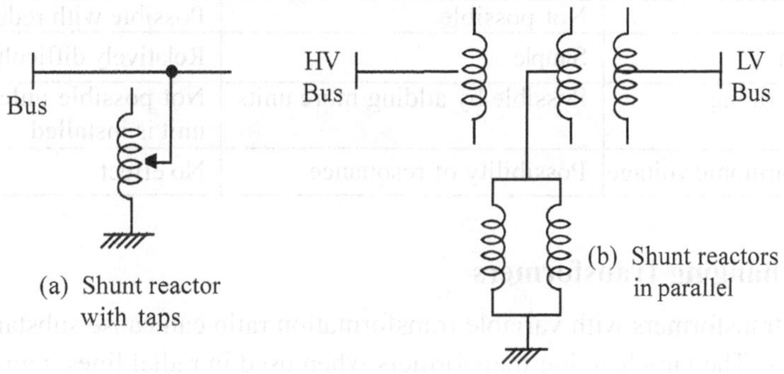

Fig. 8.33 Shunt Reactors

With increase in load, generator excitation may be increased with reactors gradually cut-out. Fig. 8.33 shows some typical shunt reactor arrangements.

8.22 Capacitors

Capacitors produce vars and may be connected in series or shunt in the system. Series capacitors compensate the line reactance in long overhead lines and thus improve the stability limit. However, they give rise to additional problems like high voltage transients, sub-synchronous resonance, etc. Shunt capacitors are used for reactive compensation. Simplicity and low cost are the chief considerations for using shunt capacitor.

Further, for expanding systems additions can be made. Fig. 8.34 shows the connected of shunt capacitors through the tertiary of a transformer.

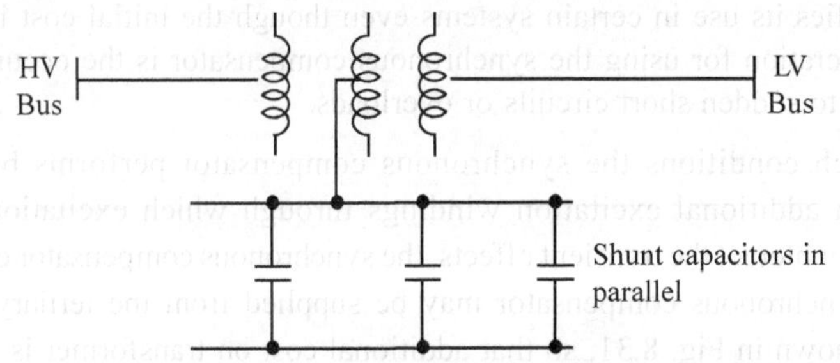

Fig. 8.34 Shunt Capacitors

Table 8.3 Comparision of Shunt Capactor and Synchronous Condensers

Criteria	Shunt capacitors	Synchronous condenser
Initial cost	1.0	1.0 to 1.2
Losses	Less than 1.5%	1.5 % to 4 %
Variation of reactive components of current	In steps only with possible surges of voltage and current	Continuous
Over load	Not possible	Possible with reduced reacting
Installation	Simple	Relatively difficult
Increase of rating	Possible by adding more units	Not possible unless another unit is installed
Effect of harmonic voltage	Possibility of resonance	No effect.

8.23 Tap–Changing Transformers

Tap-changing transformers with variable transformation ratio can cause substantial change in the flow of vars. The tap-changing transformers when used in radial lines maintain voltage at their secondary terminals or at load terminals within limits. When used in tie lines, the tap-changer can regulate vars substantially. In case of weaker tie lines, active power may also change to some extent. Lastly, when used in networks or loops, circulating vars can be controlled by tap-changing transformer.

Consider a tie line with sending end and receiving end, both having tap-changing transformer connected to them.

Let V_s and V_r be the voltages at either end at nominal conditions.

Let $t_s V_s$ = actual voltage at sending end

and $t_r V_r$ = actual voltage at receiving end

$$V_s - V_r = V_1 - V_2 \cong (IR \cos\phi_r + IX \sin\phi_r)$$

$$\Delta V \cong \frac{PR + QX}{V_r}$$

Hence $(t_s V_s - t_r V_r) \cong \dfrac{PR + QX}{V_r}$

Hence $t_s V_s \cong t_r V_r + \dfrac{PR + QX}{V_r}$

To ensure that the same overall voltage prevails allover the line minimum range of taps are used so that $t_s t_r = 1$

Substituting this condition and solving for t_s

$$t_s = \frac{1}{V_s}\left(\frac{V_r}{t_s} + \frac{Pr + QX}{\dfrac{V_r}{t_s}}\right)$$

$$t_s^2 = \frac{V_r}{t_s} + \frac{PR + QX}{V_r V_s} t_s^2$$

$$t_s^2 \left[1 - \left(\frac{PR + QX}{V_r V_s}\right)\right] = \frac{V_r}{V_s}$$

$$t_s = \frac{\dfrac{V_r}{V_s}}{\sqrt{\left[1 - \dfrac{PR + QX}{V_r V_s}\right]}} \quad \text{.....(8.21)}$$

8.24 Tap–Staggering Method

At low loads, the reactive losses in transformers are also low. The surplus generated by the system at such low loads can be absorbed by increased reactive power losses in transformers using tap staggering. Consider the pair of transformers shown in Fig. 8.35 connected between HV and LV buses.

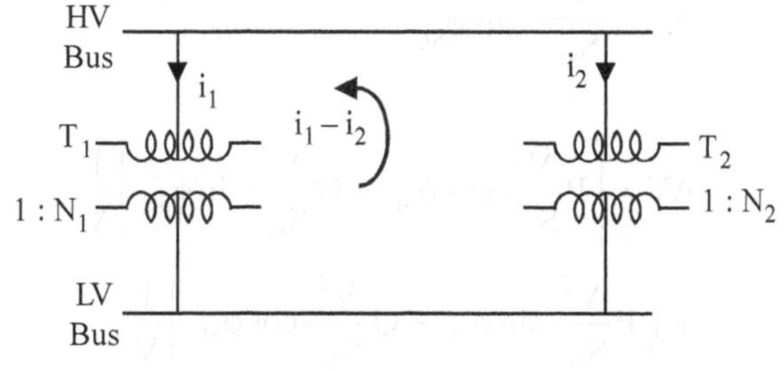

Fig. 8.35 Tap Staggering

If the taps on the transformers are staggered, a quadrature current circulates around the transformers and carries additional reactive (I^2X) losses. With more number of transformers operating, the losses could be increased by this method.

8.25 Voltage Regulation and Short Circuit Capacity

Consider the short line voltage regulation

$$\Delta V = \frac{IR}{V_r}\cos\phi_r + \frac{IX}{V_r}\sin\phi_r$$

where Vr is the receiving end voltage and ϕ_r the angle between V_r and I_r, I_r being the current in the line. This voltage drop can be obtained alternatively from the short circuit capacity of the bus. Since R + JX is the line impedance, the voltage drop is also equal to

$$\Delta V = (R + JX) \,.\, I_r$$

$$= (R + JX)\frac{P - jQ}{V}$$

$$= \left(\frac{PR + QX}{V}\right) + j\left(\frac{PX - QR}{V}\right)$$

when a three phase fault occurs at the load bus, the short circuit volt amperes into the bus

$$S_{SC} = V \,.\, I_{SC} = V \,.\, \frac{V}{Z_{SC}} = \frac{V^2}{(R + jX)}$$

$$R + jX = \frac{V^2}{S_{SC}}$$

$$R = \frac{V^2}{S_{SC}} \cos\phi_{SC}$$

and $$X = \frac{V^2}{S_{SC}} \sin\phi_{SC}$$

$$\Delta V = \left[P\frac{V^2}{S_{SC}}\cos\phi_{SC} + Q\frac{V^2}{S_{SC}}\sin\phi_{SC}\right]\frac{1}{V}$$

$$+ j\left[P\frac{V^2}{S_{SC}}\sin\phi_{SC} - Q\frac{V^2}{S_{SC}}\cos\phi_{SC}\right]\frac{1}{V}$$

It can be shown that the magnitude of voltage regulation given by $I R \cos\phi + I X \sin\phi$ or $\frac{PR + QX}{V}$ as the imaginary component gives only phase shift. Hence, the real part of equation for ΔV above gives the change in voltage magnitude

Hence,

$$\Delta V = \left[\frac{P\cos\phi_{SC}}{S_{SC}} + \frac{P\sin\phi_{SC}}{S_{SC}}\right]V$$

$$\left[\frac{P\cos\phi_{SC}}{S_{SC}} + \frac{P\sin\phi_{SC}}{S_{SC}}\right]^V$$

For small changes in P and Q

$$\frac{\Delta V}{V} = \frac{1}{S_{SC}}(\Delta P \cos\phi_{SC} + \Delta Q \cos\phi_{SC})$$

Once again, remembering that the real power does not affect the voltage magnitude much

$$\frac{\Delta V}{V} \cong \frac{1}{S_{SC}} \Delta Q \sin\phi_{SC}$$

Under short circuit conditions the current is almost lagging by 90^0 to the voltage

Hence, $\sin\phi_{SC} \cong 1.$

Thus $$\frac{\Delta V}{V} \cong \frac{\Delta Q}{S_{SC}} \quad .....(8.22)$$

Per unit change in voltage magnitude is equal to the rate of change in reactive power to the short circuit capacity of the bus.

It may be noted in this context that for a system with X >> R, the inphase voltage drop would be approximately equal to $(I \sin\phi_r)X$. An in-phase voltage compensator or booster would control the reactive power flow in the system. The quadrature voltage drop would be approximately equal to $(I \sin\phi_r)$. The quadrature voltage compensator would control the active power flow in the system.

The ratio of $\frac{X}{R}$ is very high for EHV and UHV lines.

8.26 Loading Capability of a Line

There are four kinds of limitations identified for the loading of a transmission line.

(i) thermal limit
(ii) dielectric limit
(iii) stability limit
(iv) natural loading limit.

Of all the above limits natural loading limit is the lowest limit and thermal limit is the highest.

(i) *Thermal limit :* This limit depends upon

- Atmospheric condition including ambient temperature and wind conditions
- Condition of the conductor and
- Ground clearance

Normal loading at the design and planning level is determined by loss evaluation. Any increase in line capacity with thermal consideration should also consider transformers connected at either end also.

(ii) *Dielectric limit :* Line design on the basis of insulation requirement is always on the conservative side. Line voltage can always be increased by 10% for increased power transfer. This requires proper consideration of transients and arresters in operation.

Stability limit : There are several stability considerations for increased transmission capability.

They are

- Transient stability
- Dynamic stability
- Steady state stability
- Frequency collapse
- Voltage collapse
- Sub synchronous resonance

8.27 Compensation in Power Systems

Electrical power demand is growing at a great rate day by day and the generation is, in general, not able to cope up with the demand. Several ways of increasing the power demand. Several ways of increasing the power generation are investigated including many non conventional modes. Again, transmission of increased power over the existing lines is considered to meet the increasing demand as laying of new lines and acquisition of right of way are too expentive in developed areas. This necessitated implementation of compensation in power systems. For many years series and shunt compensators are in use. Electrical energy cannot be stored in bulk quantities. There must always exist a balance between generation and demand.

8.28 Load Compensation

Utilization of reactive power to improve voltage profile and power factor is termed as load compensation. Load compensation thus refers to improving power quality. Reactive power can be injected by installing various sources such as reactors and capacitors in shunt or in series with the system at appropriate places. This has been discussed in section (8). Another aspect to be considered is that as far as possible negative sequence currents are to be avoided so that power loss is reduced. This is achieved by operating the system in balanced condition.

Line compensation : Surge impedance loading (SIL) of a line is the power delivered by a line to a purely resistive load equal to its surge impedance.

$$SIL = \frac{V_L^2}{\sqrt{\frac{L}{C}}} MW = \frac{V_L^2}{R_C}$$

Power transmitted by a line is usually expressed in terms of this power. When surge impedance is the load impedance the voltage profile of the line is flat. This is not practicable. However, it is possible to modify the characteristics of the line by using such elements as capacitors, inductors or synchronous machines. These elements can be connected in series or in parallel. Shunt compensation is similar to load compensation. Shunt connected capacitors improve the power factor, reduce the reactive power and thus increase the real power transmission. However, this method has limitations and the size of the condenser banks increase to a prohibitive level. Further they are to be switched off under light load conditions as otherwise the voltage rise may not be acceptable. Series compensations using capacitors cancel a part of the line reactance and increase the maximum power transfer. Such a compensation will reduce the power angle for a given power transfer and enables increased loading. Excessive series compensation using capacitors may result in resonance. Sub synchronous resonance at frequencies less than 50Hz occur with series compensation if care is not taken. This is discussed later in the chapter.

Line compensation results in

(i) minimization of Ferranti effect

(ii) elimination of the need for under excited operation of generators and

(iii) enhanced power transfer capability

From the receiving end power circle diagram, we have

$$P_R = \frac{|V_S||V_R|}{|B|}\cos(\beta - \delta) - \frac{|A||V_R^2|}{|B|}\cos(\beta - \alpha) \quad .....(8.23)$$

with usual notation.

P_R is a maximum when $\delta = \beta$

$$P_{R,max} = \frac{|V_S||V_R|}{|B|} - \frac{|A||V_R^2|}{|B|}\cos(\beta - \Delta) \quad .....(8.24)$$

similarly

$$P_{S,max} = \frac{|V_S||V_R|}{|B|} + \frac{D|V_S^2|}{|B|}\cos(\beta - \Delta) \quad .....(8.25)$$

For a tie-line with series impedance

$$B = Z = R + jX = \sqrt{R^2 + X^2}$$

$$D = 1.0$$

$$\alpha = 0$$

$$\Delta = 0$$

and $\beta = \text{Tan}^{-1} X/R$

$\therefore$ $$P_{R,max} = \frac{V_S V_R}{\sqrt{R^2 + X^2}} - \frac{V_R^2 R}{R^2 + X^2}$$

and $$P_{S,max} = \frac{V_S V_R}{\sqrt{R^2 + X^2}} + \frac{V_S^2 R}{R^2 + X^2}$$

differentiating $P_{R,max}$ with respective to X

$$\frac{dP_{R,max}}{dX} = -V_S V_R \left[\frac{(R^2 + X^2)}{2}\right]^{-3/2} 2X + \frac{V_R^2 R}{(R^2 + X^2)^2} 2X = 0$$

$\therefore$ $$\left(-\frac{V_S}{V_R}\right) + \frac{2R}{\sqrt{(R^2 + X^2)}} = 0$$

$$\frac{4R^2}{(R^2 + X^2)} - \left(\frac{V_S}{V_R}\right)^2 ; X = R\sqrt{4\left(\frac{V_R}{V_S}\right)^2 - 1}$$

when $V_S = V_R;\ X = \sqrt{3}\,R$ .....(8.26)

In overhead lines $\frac{X}{R}$ ratio is much greater than this optimum value needed to maintain the same voltage at both the ends. For 132kV lines $\frac{X}{R}$ ratio is from 2.5 to 3.5; for 275 kv lines it is about 8 and for 400kv lines it is as high as 16. Hence to maintain voltage profile $\frac{X}{R}$ ratio has to be decreased. This can be effectively done by series capacitor compensator so that line inductance is compensated.

Nevertheless, series capacitors are to be protected against over currents and over voltages during fault conditions.

E 8.1 Two substations A and B are interconnected by a line having an impedance of (0.03 + j0.12) p.u the substation voltages are 33 $\angle 2^0$ kv and 33 $\angle 0^0$ kv respectively. In phase and quadrature boosters are installed at A. Determine their output-voltage ratings and MVA ratings in order to supply 5MVA at 0.8p.f lagging at substation B.

Solution :

Let Base MVA = 500

Base KV = 33kv

$V_A = 1.0 \angle 2^0$ p.u and $V_B = 1.0 \angle 0^0$ p.u

Let current through the inter connector = I

Let load current at B = I_B

$$I_B = \frac{5MVA}{5MVA}(0.8 - j0.6) = (0.8 - j0.6) \text{ p.u.}$$

Without boosting voltage drop in the line

$= Z\, I_B = (0.03 + j0.12)(0.8 - j0.6)$

$= (0.096 + j0.078)$p.u.

voltage drop in the line with boosters = $V_A - V_B$

$= 1.0 \angle 2^0 - 1.0 \angle 0^0$

$= 0.99939 + j0.0348994 - 1.0$

$= (-0.00061 + j0.0348997)$ p.u.

Hence, in phase component of boosted voltage

$- + 0.096 - (-0.00061)$

$= 0.09661$ p.u.

Quadratic component of boosted voltage

$= 0.078 - 0.3349 = 0.0431$ p.u.

Rating of the in phase booster = 0.09661 x 1.00

$= 0.09661$ p.u. $= 0.09661 \times 500 = 48.3$ MVA

Rating of the quadrature booster = 0.0431 x 1.00

$= 0.0431$ p.u. $= 0.0431 \times 500 = 21.55$ MVA

E 8.2 Two substations A and B operating at 11kv 3-phase are connected by two parallel lines. 1 and 2. Each line has a 11/132 kv transformer and a 132/11kv substation. Each line has an equivalent impedance of $Z_1 = 0.2 + j0.4$ and $Z_2 = 0.2 + j0.6$ ohms per phase which includes both the transformers and the line, referred to 11kv side.

(a) If the bus bar A is at 11kv and is sending 30Mw at 0.8 p.f leading, find the individual currents into each transformer and the powers at the station A.

(b) If the transformer at A in line 2 is fitted with tappings on the 11kv side, what percentage tapping would be required to make each line carry equal reactive powers? What would be the power sent by line 2 in this case?

Solution :

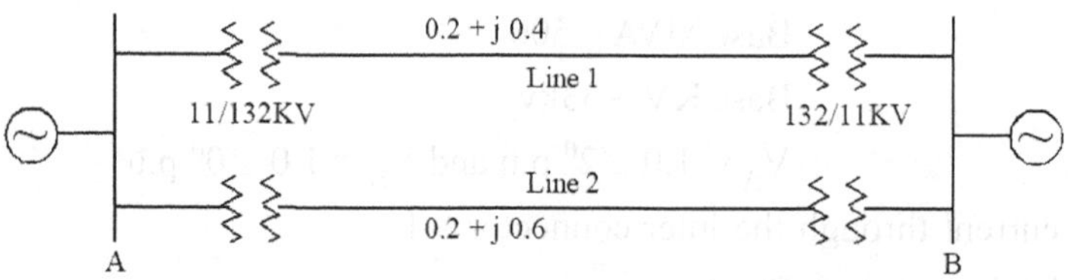

Fig. E 8.2

Let base voltage be 11kv

Let $$\text{Base MVA} = \frac{30.0}{0.8} = 37.5\text{MVA}$$

Total current flowing through both the lines

$$= \frac{37.5}{37.5}(0.8 + j0.6) - (0.8 + j0.6)\text{p.u.}$$

$$= 100 \angle 36.87^0 \text{ (since 11kv = 1p.u.)}$$

$$\dot{Z}_1\dot{I}_1 = \frac{\dot{Z}_2}{\dot{Z}_1 + \dot{Z}_2}\dot{I}_{Total}$$

Base impedance $$= \frac{11\text{kv} \times 11\text{kv}}{37.5} = 3.227\text{ohms}$$

$$\dot{Z}_1 = \frac{0.2 + j0.40}{3.227} = (0.0627)0.124dpu$$

$$= 0.1386 \angle 63^0.43$$

$$\dot{Z}_2 = \frac{0.2 + j0.60}{3.227} = 0.0627 + j0.186 = 0.1961 \quad \angle 71.56^0 \text{p.u.}$$

Hence,

$$\dot{Z}_1 + \dot{Z}_2 = \frac{0.5 + j1.0}{3227} = 0.124 + j0.310 / \text{p.u.}$$

$$= 0.334 \angle 68.20 \text{ p.u.}$$

$$\therefore \quad I_1 = \frac{0.1961 \times 1.0}{0.334} \angle \left(71^0.56 + 36^0.87 - 68^0.2\right) = 0.584 \angle 40^0.23 \text{p.u.}$$

$$I_2 = \frac{0.1386 \times 1.0}{0.334} \angle \left(68^0.43 + 36^0.87 - 68^0.2\right) = 0.415 \angle 32^0.1 \text{p.u.}$$

$$\text{Base current} \quad = \frac{37.5 \times 10^3}{\sqrt{3} \times 11} = 1968 \text{Ampers}$$

$$\therefore \quad I_1 = 1155 \angle 40.23^0 \ (1968 \times 0.587 \angle 40^0.23)$$

$$I_2 = 517 \angle 32.10^0 \ (1968 \times 0.415 \angle 32^0.10)$$

The per unit MVA line 1

$$S_1 = P_1 + jQ_1 = 1.00 \angle 0^0 \times 0.587 \angle -40.23^0 = (0.448 - j0.379) \text{ p.u.}$$

The per unit MVA from line 2

$$S_2 = P_2 + jQ_2 = 1.00 \angle 0^0 \times 0.415 \angle -32.1^0 = (0.352 - j0.2205) \text{ p.u.}$$

$P_1 = 0.448 \times 37.5 = 16.8$ MW

$P_2 = 0.352 \times 37.5 = 13.2$ MW

$Q_1 = 0.379 \times 37.5 = 14.21$ MVAR (leading)

$Q_2 = 0.2205 \times 37.5 = 8.27$ MVAR (leading)

(b) The tap changer at station A on the sending end transformer in line 2 will alter the reactive power loading.

Total load $= (P_1 + P_2 + jQ_1 + jQ_2) = (30 - j22.5)$ MVA

Equal reactive powers means

$$Q_1 = Q_2 = -\frac{22.5}{2} = -11.25 \text{MVAR}$$

$P_1 = 16.8$ MW

and $P_2 = 13.2$ MW

The change in voltage ΔV is given by the approximate expression,

$$\Delta V = ZI = \frac{PR + QX}{V}$$

$$= tV - V = \frac{PR + QX}{V}$$

where t is the tap changer setting ratio

$$(t - 1)\, V = \frac{PR + QX}{V}$$

$$(t - 1) = \frac{PR + QX}{V^2}$$

$$t = 1 + \frac{PR + QX}{V^2}$$

$P = P_2 = 0.352$ p.u. (= 13.2 MW/37.5)

$Q_2 = -0.30$ p.u. (= 11.25MVAR/37.5)

$X_2 = 0.186$ p.u.

$R_2 = 0.062$ p.u.

$$t = 1 + \frac{0.352 \times 0.062 + (-0.3)0.186}{1.00 \times 1.00} = 1 - 0.034 = 0.966$$

percentage tap change = 96.6 – 100 = –3.4 %

Power sent through line 2

$S_2 = P_2 + jQ_2 = (0.352 - j0.30)$pu

$S_1 = S - S_2 = (0.8 - j0.6) - (0.352 - j0.3)$

$= (0.448 - j0.3)$p.u.

$S_1 = P_1 + jQ_1 = 16.8 - j\,11.25$ MVA

$S_2 = P_2 + jQ_2 = 13.2 - j\,11.25$ MVA

$P_1 = 16.8$ MW

$P_2 = 13.2$ MW

$Q_1 = -11.25$ MVAR

$Q_2 = -11.25$ MVAR

E 8.3 A load of (15 + j10) MVA is supplied with power from a generating station from a line at 110kv 3-phase 50Hz. The line is of 100km length. The line is represented by π model with the parameters

$$R = 26.4 \text{ ohms}$$
$$X = 33.9 \text{ ohm}$$
$$B = 219 \times 10^{-6}$$

Voltage at the generated in 116kv. Determine the power supplied by the generating station.

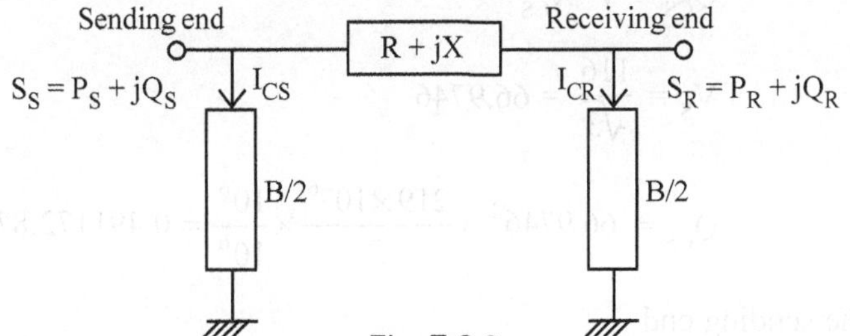

Fig. E 8.3

$$S_R = P_R + j\,Q_R = \frac{15 + j10}{3} \text{ MVA/Phase}$$

$$V_R = \frac{110}{\sqrt{3}} = 63.5\text{KV}$$

Reactive power through $\frac{B}{2}$ at receiving end

$$Q_{CR} = 63.5 \times 63.5 \times \frac{219 \times 10^{-6}}{2} \times 10^6 \text{ var}$$

$$= \frac{883062.75}{2} = 441531.37\text{VAR} = 0.44153\text{MVAR}$$

Receiving end power

$$S = P_R + Q_R = \frac{15 + j10}{3} - j0.44153$$

$$= (5 + j\,2.8918) \text{ MVA}$$

Real power loss in the line = $I^2 R$

$$I = \frac{S_R}{V_R} = \frac{(5 + j2.8918)10^6}{(63.5)^? \times 10^3}$$

$$= \frac{\sqrt{5^2 + 2.8918^2} \times 10^6}{63.5 \times 10^3} = 90.96$$

$$I^2R = (90.96)^2 \times 26.4\text{VA}$$
$$= 0.2184313\text{MW}$$

$$I^2 X = \text{reactive power loss} = \frac{5^2 + 2.89^2 \times 10^3}{63.5^2} \times 33.9 = (90.96)^2 \times 33.9\text{VA}$$

Reactive power in the sending end capacitance B/2

$$Q_{CS} = V^2 X_{CS}$$

$$V_S = \frac{116}{\sqrt{3}} = 66.9746$$

$$Q_{CS} = 66.9746^2 \times \frac{219 \times 10^{-6}}{2} \times \frac{10^6}{10^6} = 0.491172.87\text{MVAR}$$

Power at the sending end

$$S_S = S + I^2 R + I^2 X + Q_{CR} + Q_{CS}$$
$$= (5 + j2.89) + 0.218 + j0.279 - j0.04415$$
$$= (5.218 + j\ 1.9574)\ \text{MVA}$$

power consumed from the station

$$3 \times S_S = 3\ [5.218 + j1.9574]\ \text{MVA} = (15.54 + j5.8722)\text{MVA}$$

E 8.4 A short line having an impedance of (2 + j3) ohm interconnects two power stations A and B both operating at 11kv; equal in magnitude and phase. To transfer 25MW at 0.8 power factor lagging from A to B determine the voltage boost required at plant A.

Solution :

$$I = \frac{25 \times 10^3}{\sqrt{3} \times 11 \times 0.8} = 1640.2476\angle 36.87^0$$

$$= 1640.2976\ (0.8 - j0.6) = (1312 - j984.1486)\text{A}$$

voltage drop in the short line = (1312.2 – j984.1486) (2+j3)

$$= 2624.4 - j\ 1968.297 + j3936.6 + 2952\text{-}446$$
$$= 5576.8458 + j1968.3$$

This voltage drop must be compensated by the booster so that the voltages are maintain the same at both the ends

Voltage boost = (5576.85 + j1968.3) volts.

8.29 Static Compensators

In Recent years reactive compensation of charging power is made feasible with the application of 3-phase, thyristor, power controller circuits with automatic control functions

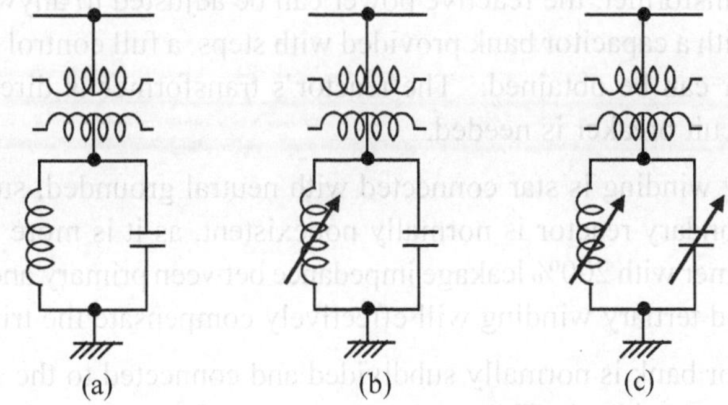

Fig. 8.36 Idealized var compensators

The term static var compensator is applied to a number of static var compensation devices for use in shunt reactive control.

These devices consist of shunt connected, static reactive element (linear or nonlinear reactors and capacitors) configured into a var compensating system. Some possible configurations are shown in Fig. 8.36.

Even though the capacitors and reactors in Fig. 8.36 are shown connected to the low voltage side of a down transformer, the capacitor banks may be distributed between high and low voltage buses.

The capacitor bank often includes, in part, harmonic filters which prevent tharmonic currents from flowing in the transformer and the high voltage system. Filters for the 5th and 7th harmonics are generally provided. Fig. 8.37 shows one type of static var compensator. The thyristor controlled reactor (TCR) is operated on the low voltage bus.

In another form of the compensator illustrated in Fig. 8.38 the reactor compensator is connected to the secondary of a transformer.

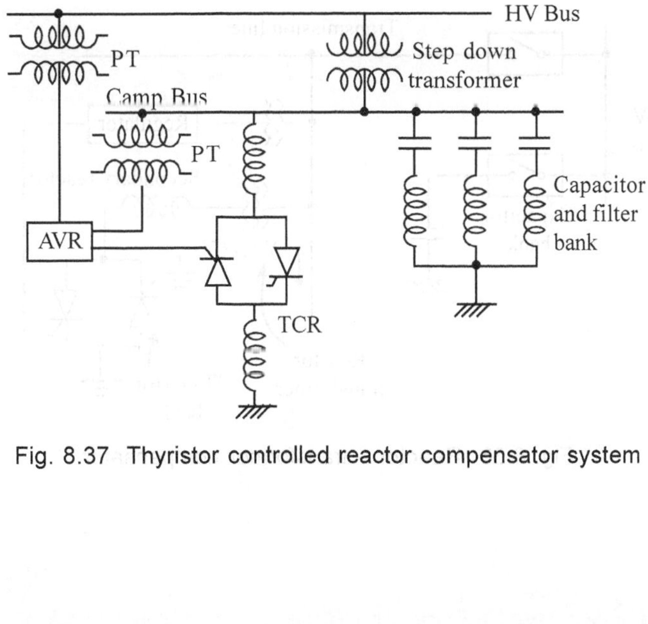

Fig. 8.37 Thyristor controlled reactor compensator system

With this transformer, the reactive power can be adjusted to anywhere between 10% to the rated value. With a capacitor bank provided with steps, a full control range from capacitive to inductive power can be obtained. The reactor's transformer is directly connected to the line, so that no circuit breaker is needed.

The primary winding is star connected with neutral grounded, suitable to the thyristor network. The secondary reactor is normally nonexistent, as it is more economical to design the reactor transformer with 200% leakage impedance between primary and secondary windings. The delta connected tertiary winding will effectively compensate the triplen harmonics.

The capacitor bank is normally subdivided and connected to the substation bus bar via one circuit breaker per subbank. The regulator generates firing pulses for the thyristor network in such a way that the reactive power required to meet the control objective at the primary side of the compensator is obtained. The reactor transformer has a practically linear characteristic from no load to full load condition. Thus, even under sustained over voltages, hardly any harmonic content is generated due to saturation. The transformer core has non ferromagnetic gaps to give the required linearity.

The following requirements are to be borne in mind while designing a compensator.

1. Reaction should be possible, fast or slow, whenever demanded. No switching of capacitor should take place at that time to avoid additional transients in the system. Commutation from capacitor to reactor and vice versa should be fast.
2. No switching of the capacitors at the high voltage bus bar, so that no higher frequency transients are produced at EHV level.
3. Elimination of higher harmonics on the secondary side and blocking them from entering the system.

In a three phase system the thyristor controlled inductors are normally delta connected as shown in Fig. 8.39 to compensate unbalanced loads and the capacitors may be star or delta connected.

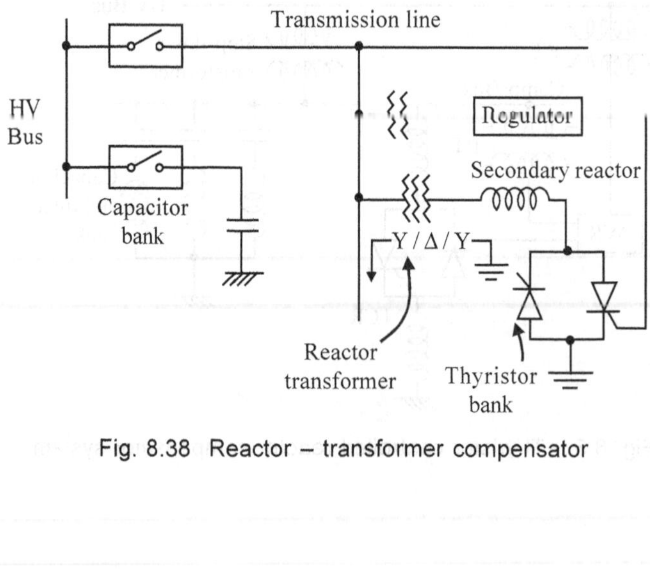

Fig. 8.38 Reactor – transformer compensator

8.30 Steady State Performance of Static var compensators

In the thyristor controlled reactor, the inductive reactance is controlled by the thyristors. For a limited range of operation the relationship between the inductive current i_L and the applied voltage V is represented in Fig. 8.40. As the inductance is varied, the susceptance varies over a range within the limits B_{Lmin} and B_{Lmax} (corresponding to X_{Lmax} and X_{Lmin}) while the voltage changes by v volts.

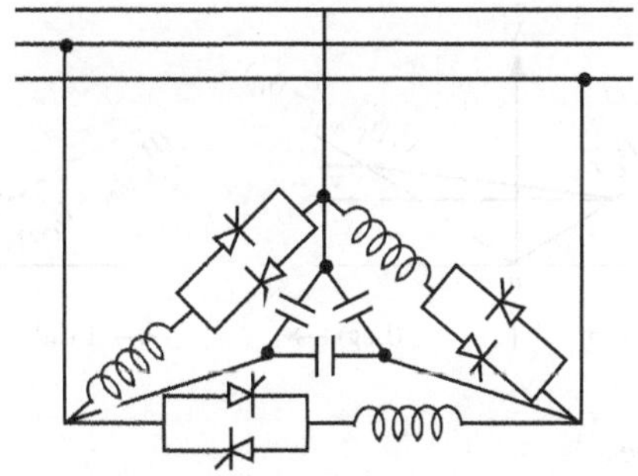

Fig. 8.39 Fixed capacitor, thyristor controlled inductor type var compensator

The use of a fixed capacitor in parallel with the controlled reactor results in the characteristics shown in Fig. 8.41. The currents can be controlled to have any desired value over the range selected from leading to lagging.

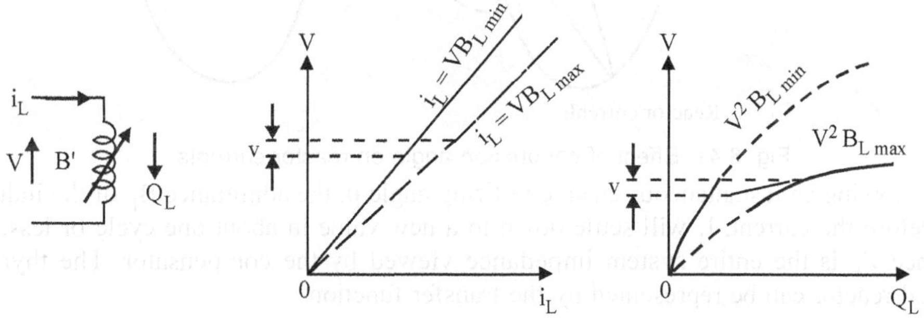

Fig. 8.40 Thyristor controlled reactor characteristics

Corresponding vars are produced or absorbed. Fig. 8.41 shows the effect of changing the conduction angle δ from 180^0 to a small value δ_C.

The current flowing in the inductance would be different in each half cycle, varying with the conduction angle such that each successive half cycle is a smaller segment of a sine wave. The fundamental component of inductor current is then reduced to each case. Quick control can be exercised within one half cycle, just by giving a proper step input to the firing angle control

Block diagram representation of a static var compensator is given in Fig. 8.42. The net change in the reactor current I_R drawn by the static var compensator supplied through the system impedance $Z_s = \frac{\Delta V_2}{\Delta I_1}$. AVR and FAR are automatic voltage and firing angle regulators.

AVR may be of the form $\frac{K(1+T_1S)}{(1+T_2S)}$ and FAR of the form $\frac{1}{1+ST_\alpha}$

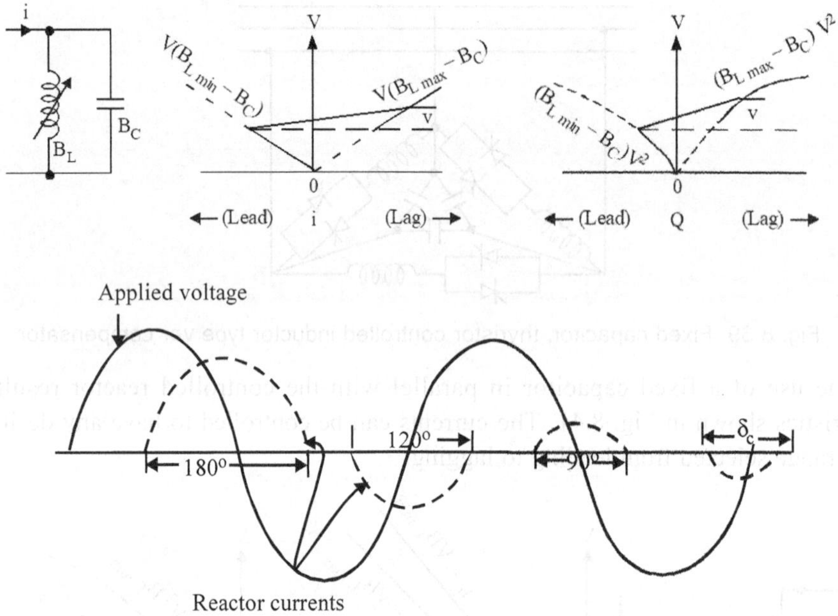

Fig. 8.41 Effect of conduction angle on reactor currents

Following an instantaneous change in firing angle θ, the admittance B_L of the inductor and therefore the current, I_1 will settle down to a new value in about one cycle or less. The impedance Z_S is the entire system impedance viewed by the compensator. The thyristor controlled reactor can be represented by the transfer function

$$G_R(S) = \frac{e^{-ST_1}}{1+T_2S}$$

where T_1 and T_2 are of the order 1 ms and 4 ms. For practical purposes, the compensator can be assumed to have a pure gain of unity with the present thyristor technology. The AVR can be represented by

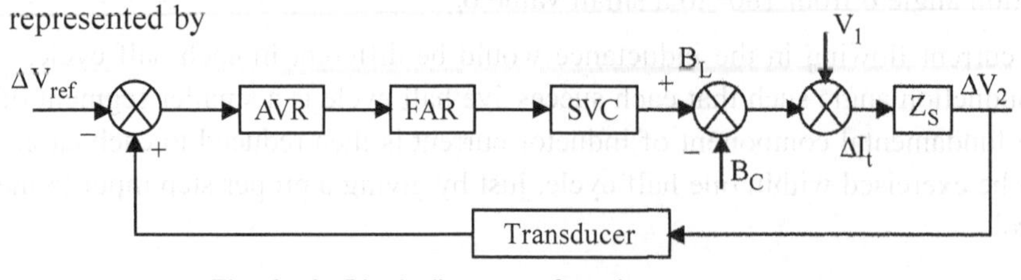

Fig. 8.42 Block diagram of static var compensator

$$G_V(S) = \frac{k}{1 + T_3 S} \frac{(1 + T_4 S)}{(1 + T_5 S)} \quad .....(8.27)$$

The time constant T_3 lies between 50 and 150 ms.

The compensator block diagram for dynamic studies is shown in Fig. 8.43.

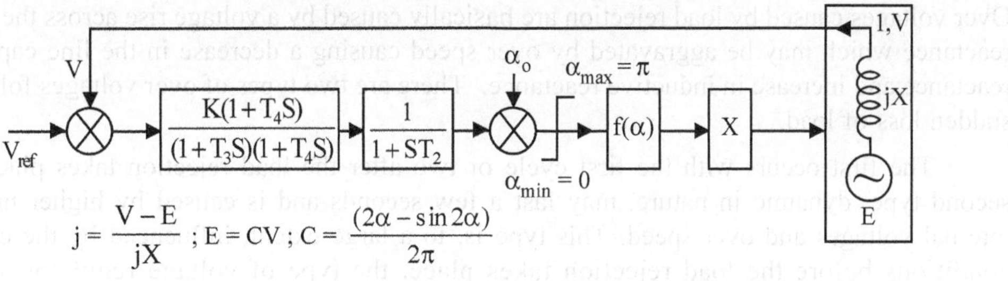

Fig. 8.43 Compensator block diagram for dynamic studies

Static var compensators when installed reduce the voltage swings at the rolling mill and power system buses in drive system applications. They compensate for the average reactive power requirements and improve power factor.

Electric arc furnaces impose extremely difficult service requirements on electrical power systems since the changes in arc furnace load impedance are rapid, random and non symmetrical.

The three phases of a static var compensator can be located independently so that it compensates for the unbalanced reactive load of the furnace and the thyristor controller will respond quickly in order to minimize the voltage fluctuations or voltage flicker seen by the system.

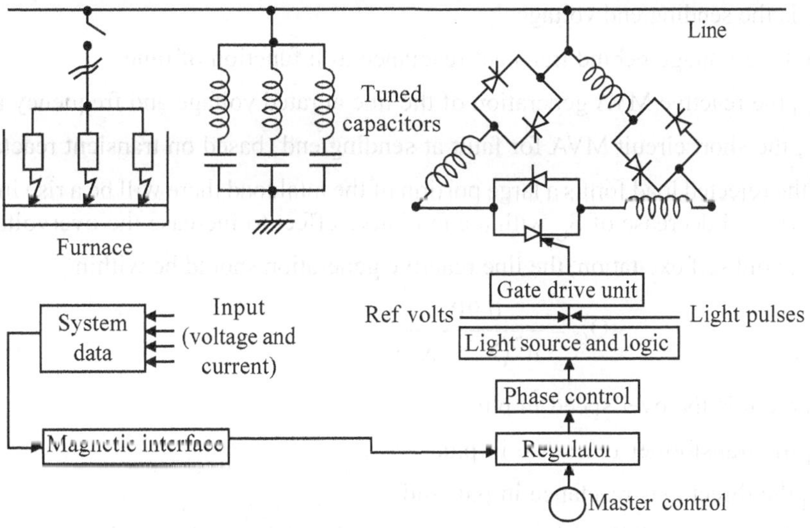

Fig. 8.44 Arc furnace applications

Thus, the furnace characteristics are made more acceptable to the power system by the static var compensator. Fig. 8.44 shows the application of the static var compensator to an arc furnace installation for reactive power compensation at the HV bus level. For more information refer to FACTS controllers of chapter 9.

8.31 Overvoltages on Sudden Loss of Load

Over voltages caused by load rejection are basically caused by a voltage rise across the source reactance which may be aggravated by over speed causing a decrease in the line capacitive reactance and increase in inductive reactance. There are two types of over voltages following sudden loss of load.

The first occurs with the first cycle or two after the load rejection takes place. The second type, dynamic in nature, may last a few seconds and is caused by higher machine internal voltages and over speed. This type is, to a large extent, influenced by the existing conditions before the load rejection takes place, the type of voltage regulator and the compensating devices. The magnitude of the first type can be determined from:

1. The constant flux linkage voltage in the equivalent circuit of the rotor direct and quadrature axes.
2. The voltage rise components across the transient reactances of the two axes due to line-charging current.

The second type of over voltage can be computed from the relation.

$$E_S = \frac{E'(t)}{1 - \frac{Q_c}{S_c}} \qquad .....(8.28)$$

where

E_S is the sending end voltage

$E'(t)$ the voltage behind transient reactance as a function of time

Q_C, the reactive MVA generation of the line at rated voltage and frequency and,

S_C, the short circuit MVA for fault at sending end (based on transient reactance).

If the rejected load forms a large portion of the total load there will be a rise in frequency, Q_C and $E'(t)$ and decrease of S_C with a cumulative effect to increase the overvoltage.

To avoid self excitation, the line reactive generation should be within

$$Q_C = \frac{0.9P_n}{n^2(X_d + X_t)} \qquad .....(8.29)$$

where n is the over speed in p.u.,

X_t the transformer reactance in p.u.

X_d the direct axis reactance in p.u. and

P_n the nominal MVA of the generating capacity at the sending end.

If the excitation system has negative field current capability and AVR is provided then

$$Q_C \leq \frac{(0.9)P_n}{n^2(X_q+X_t)}$$

where X_q is the quadrature axis reactance in p.u.

The over voltages resulting from self excitation are dangerous not only for the system but also to machines and transformers connected to the sending end. This conditions must be avoided by providing the excess of line reactive vars with shunt compensator or rapid switching off of lines. Further, over voltages caused by load rejection prove to be worse when switching is performed on the transformer secondary at the receiving end. Due to voltage increase, the transformer gets over excited and then saturated with subsequent injection of harmonic voltages into the system. Then, with some combination of system inductance and line capacitance, due to Ferro resonance, extremely high voltage will be produced for 0.5 to 1.0s, resulting in equipment damage.

Shunt reactor compensation is quite effective in limitings the over voltages due to load rejection. Such compensation has given 50% reduction in over voltages for line to ground faults.

When synchronous compensator is installed, it automatically absorbs the reactive power from the system which is a function of the compensator reactance and interval voltage.

The time constant of the machine, however, limits the rate at which the compensator inductive current can be increased. The static var compensator on the other hand can change over to its maximum current in the inductive range very rapidly since the compensator output increases as the square of the voltage. Further, the overload capacity of the static var compensator in the inductive range can be increased at additional costs much lower than those required for synchronous compensators.

8.32 Voltage Dips

Voltage dips take place either due to faults or switching in of other motors connected to the same bus. A voltage dip causes the synchronous condenser to act in accordance with its internal voltage behind the sub transient and transient reactance and immediately starts feeding the corresponding capacitive reactive power into the system. In fact, with modern excitation control equipment with an appropriate ceiling voltage, it is possible to maintain a high capacitive current for a few seconds to support the system voltage. Static var compensator, on the other hand, as it consists of passive elements only, while reacting very quickly fails to support the system voltage since the capacitive current decreases as the square of the voltage. At large voltage dips, it is observed that the synchronous compensator is superior in performance to static var compensator.

Design of Filter Circuit

The maximum harmonic content permitted in the delta connected system as per IEEE specifications are

for the 5th harmonics - 5% of fundamental

and for the 7th harmonics - 2.5% of fundamental

Since the compensator circuit is delta connected, third harmonic is not considered.

$$I_{fundamental} = 260A$$

$$I_{5th\ harmonic} = 260\left(\frac{5}{100}\right) = 13.0\ A$$

$$I_{7th\ harmonic} = 260\left(\frac{2.5}{100}\right) = 6.5\ A$$

Filter for fifth harmonic

At resonance $\omega_n = \dfrac{1}{\sqrt{L_F C_F}}$

The impedance offered by filter circuit at power frequency is

$$\frac{1-\omega^2 L_F C_F}{\omega C_F}$$

and this should be much greater than the impedance offered by C_M which is $\dfrac{1}{\omega}C_M$, i.e. we require

$$\frac{1-\omega_2 L_F C_F}{\omega C_F} \geq \frac{1}{\omega C_M}$$

Let this be greater be 20 times the value

$$C_F = \frac{1}{(n\omega)^2} L_F$$

$$\frac{1-\omega^2 L_F C_F}{C_F} = \frac{20}{C_M}$$

$$L_F = \frac{20}{1316\times10^{-6}} \times \frac{1}{314^2\times24} = 0.00643H$$

$$C_F = \frac{1}{(5\times314)^2\times6.43\times10^{-3}} = 0.00006303 = 63.03\mu F$$

Filter for seventh harmonic :

The current for 7th harmonic = 6.5A

$$nf = 350\text{Hz}$$

$$n\omega = \frac{1}{\sqrt{L_F C_F}}$$

$$C_F = \frac{1}{(n\omega)^2 L_F}$$

Again assuming a factor of 20

$$L_F = \frac{20}{1316 \times 10^{-6}(314)^2 \times 48} = 0.00016\text{H} = 0.16\text{mH}$$

Therefore,

$$C_F = \frac{1}{(7 \times 314)^2 \times 0.161 \times 10^{-3}} = 0.001284\text{F} = 1284\mu\text{F}$$

8.33 Subsynchronous Resonance

Series capacitor compensation is the most technically feasible and economically viable choice for increasing the transmission capability of EHV power systems. However, series compensation brings in certain problems related to dynamic performance of the system. One such problem is sub synchronous resonance. It is an electrical system condition where the electrical system exchanges energy with a turbine-generator at one or more frequencies below the synchronous frequency of the system. This interchange may be a little damped or undamped.

The exchange of energies takes place at the natural frequencies of the respective systems. For the electrical system, the natural frequencies are higher compared to the mechanical system. The range lies between 15Hz and 45Hz for steam turbo generator whereas it is 10Hz and below for a hydro generator. For the electrical system, the modes of oscillation depend upon the number of circuit configurations that can be made through switching. Depending on the system operating conditions and mechanical moment of inertia, the electromechanical system has a frequency of oscillation between 1 and 2 Hz.

There are three types of sub synchronous oscillations that have been identified. The apparent negative resistance (rotor resistance viewed from armature terminals) characteristic of the generator at sub synchronous frequencies causes the generator to act as an induction generator and this effect is called the induction generator effect. If this negative resistance exceeds the network resistance for a specific combination of inductance and capacitance, self excitation may result at the resonant frequency.

Resonance may take place due to the torsional interaction between electrical and mechanical systems. This may occur when the electrical resonance frequency is near the complement of the torsional resonant frequency of the turbo-generator shaft system (the difference of synchronous frequency and the turbine mechanical natural frequency is the complement of the torsional resonant frequency).

A small voltage induced in the armature by rotor oscillation under these conditions can result in large sub synchronous currents. This current will produce oscillatory component of rotor torque and if the mechanical damping is small, the electromechanical system may experience growing oscillations.

Finally, when the transmission system contains a series capacitor, the transient electrical torque, under fault or switching operations, may contain large amplitude frequency components close to resonant frequency of the shaft system. This can result in high shaft torques which may be seriously damage the turbo generator units.

Consider a series compensated transmission system, let L_l, Lg and Lt be the inductances of the line, generator and transformers respectively and let C_S be the series capacitance then the resonant frequency.

$$f_n = \frac{1}{2}\sqrt{C_S(L_1 + L_G + L_T)}$$

otherwise, $$\omega_n = 2\pi f_n = 2\pi f_s\sqrt{\frac{X_C}{X_L}}$$

$$= \omega_s\sqrt{\frac{X_C}{X_L}} \qquad .....(8.30)$$

where f_s is the rated frequency; X_C and X_L are the capacitive and inductive reactances calculated at the rated frequency. Since the compensation is generally less than 100% from eqn. (8.30) it can be seen that the resonant frequency is always less than the rated frequency.

Several methods are suggested to prevent sub synchronous resonance. One technique is the use of filtering and damping. A blocking filter may be inserted in series with the generator step-up transformer.

Otherwise, an appropriately designed reactor may be connected in parallel with an existing series capacitor to form a blocking filter. Other types of filters are also suggested in literature. Relays are also used to detect excessive mechanical system. System switching method can also be implemented to avoid sub synchronous resonance. When a system configurations occurs which can the generator can be isolated from the series capacitances that create problems. This is accomplished by switching the machine off from the compensated system and switching on to an uncompensated line. Unit tripping also can be implemented if all conditions that cause transient torques are completely predetermined.

E 8.5 A load of (66 + j60) MVA at the receiving end is being transmitted via a single circuit 220KV line having a resistance of 21 ohm and reactance of 34 ohm. The sending end voltage is maintained at 220kV. The operating conditions of power consumers require that at this load voltage drop across the line should not exceed 5%. In order to reduce voltage drop standard single phase 660V, 40 kVAR capacitors are to be switched in series in each phase of the line. Determine the required number of capacitors, and rated voltage neglect the losses.

Solution :

Three phase load $= (66 + j60)$ MVA

Per phase load $= \dfrac{66 + j60}{3} = (22 + j20)$ MVA

The impedance $Z = R + jX = (21 + j34)$ ohm

Phase voltage $V_p = \dfrac{220}{\sqrt{3}} = 127.02\text{kV}$

Without series capacitor

$$\Delta V = \frac{P_R R + Q_R X}{V_R} = \frac{22 \times 21 + 20 \times 34}{127.02} = \frac{462 + 680}{127.02} = 8.9907\text{KV}$$

Permitted drop in voltage $= 5\%$ of 127.02

$$= \frac{5}{100} \times 127.02 = 6.351\text{kV}$$

Let X_C be the capacitive reactance to bring down the drop from 8.9907kV to 6.351kV

$$6.351 = \frac{P_R R + (X - X_C)Q_R}{V_R} = \frac{22 \times 21 + 20(34 - X_C)}{127.02}$$

Solving for X_C

$$X_C = 16.65 \text{ ohm}$$

Given that 40kVAR capacitor at 0.66kV are to be switched.

$$I_C = \frac{40\text{kVAR}}{0.66\text{kV}} = 60.606\text{A}$$

$$V_R I_R = (22 + j20) \text{ MVA}$$

$$I_R = \frac{\sqrt{22^2 + 20^2} \times 10^6}{127.02 \times 10^3} = \frac{\sqrt{884} \times 10^3}{127.02} = 234.07 \text{ Amps}$$

capacitors per phase in parallel

$$n = \frac{234.07}{60.606} = 3.862$$

The number of capacitors must be either 4 or more than 4.

$$X_C = \frac{V_C}{I_C} = \frac{660\text{V}}{60.606\text{A}} = 10.89\text{ohm}$$

Each capacitor has 10.89 ohm reactance.

Four in parallel makes $X_{C\ parallel} = \frac{10.89}{4}$ ohm

Since total X_C has to be 16.65 ohm

The series units n_s will be

$$\frac{10.89}{4} \times n_s = 16.65$$

Hence $$n_s = \frac{16.65 \times 4}{10.89} = 6.1157$$

As n_s must be a whole number $n_s = 7$

Installed capacity of the capacitor bank

Q_C = Rated voltage of the capacitor bank

= 0.66 kV × 7 = 4.62 kV

E 8.6 Find the capacity of a static VAR compensator to be installed at a bus with ± 5% voltage fluctuation. The short circuit capacity = 7000MVA.

Solution :

ΔQ = capacity of the compensator

S_{SC} = Short circuit capacity

ΔV = Voltage fluctuation

$$\Delta V = \frac{\Delta Q}{S_{SC}}$$

$$\Delta Q = \Delta V \cdot S_{SC} = \pm 0.05 \times 7000 = \pm 350 \text{ MVAR}$$

Capacity of the static VAR compensator = ± 350 MVAR

E 8.8 A 400kV line is fed through a 132/400kV transformer from a constant 132kV supply. At the load end of the line another transformer of nominal ratio 400/132kV is used to reduce the voltage. The total impedance of the line and transformers at 400kV is (50+j100) ohm. Both, transformers are equipped with tap changing so arranged that the product of the off nominal setting is unity. If the load on the systems is 250MW at 0.8 p.f lagging. Calculate the settings of the tap changer required to maintain the voltage of the load bus at 132kV.

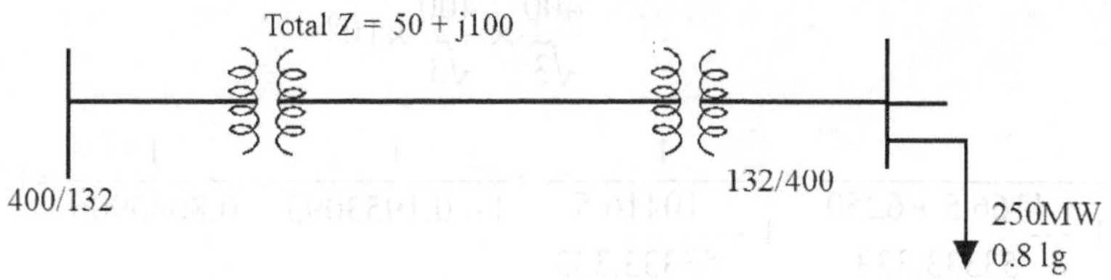

Fig. E 8.8

Solution :

$$\text{Power per phase (P)} = \frac{250}{3} = 83.33\text{MW}$$

$$\text{Reactive power per phase} = \frac{250}{0.8} \times \frac{0.6}{3} = 62.5\text{MVAR}$$

$$V_R = V_S = \frac{132}{\sqrt{3}} = 76.21247 \text{ kV} = 76.21247 \times 10^3 \text{ V}$$

we have

$$t_S^2 = \frac{\dfrac{V_R}{V_S}}{\left[1 - \left(\dfrac{PR + QX}{V_R V_S}\right)\right]}$$

$$V_R = V_S = \frac{132}{\sqrt{3}} \text{kV}$$

when the secondary is maintained at 132kV the primary is kept at 400kV.

Since total impedance is referred to 400kV side we obtain

$$t_S^2 = \left[\frac{V_R}{V_S} \frac{1}{1-\dfrac{PR+QS}{V_R V_S}}\right]$$

$$= \frac{1}{1-\dfrac{83.33\times10^6\times50+62.5\times10^6\times100}{\dfrac{400}{\sqrt{3}}\times\dfrac{400}{\sqrt{3}}\times10^6}}$$

$$= \frac{1}{1-\dfrac{4166.5+6250}{53333.333}} = \frac{1}{1-\dfrac{10416.5}{53333.333}} = \frac{1}{1-0.1953093} = \frac{1}{0.8046906} = 1.2427136$$

$$t_s = \sqrt{1.2427136} = 1.1147706$$

$$t_s = \frac{1}{1.1147706} = 0.8970455$$

Questions

1. Discuss in detail about the generation and absorption of reactive power in power system components.
2. Explain reason for variations of voltages in power systems and explain any one method to improve voltage profile.
3. Explain clearly what do you mean by compensation of line and discuss briefly different methods of compensation.
4. What is a static compensator ? Explain with diagrams working principle of various types of static compensators.
5. Explain with diagrams, the operation of a fixed capacitor and thyristor controlled reactor.
6. Discuss in detail about the generation and absorption of reactive power in power system components.
7. Discuss in detail about the generation and absorption of reactive power system components.
8. Describe the effect of connecting series capacitors in the transmission system.
9. (a) What does on mean by load compensation ?

   (b) With neat diagrams discuss shunt and series compensation

   (c) What are the specifications of load compensator ?
10. Discuss the advantages and disadvantages of different types of compensating equipment for transmission systems.
11. Discuss in detail the voltage stability problem in power systems.

Problems

P 8.1 Find the regulation and efficiency of an 80-km, 3-phase, 50-c/s transmission line delivering 24,000 kVA at a power factor of 0.8 lagging and 66kV to a balanced load. The conductors are of copper, each having resistance 0.12 ohm per km, 1.5 c, outside diameter, spaced equilaterally 2.5m between centers. Neglect leakance and use the nominal-π method.

P 8.2 A 3-phase, overhead line has resistance and reactance of 6 and 20 ohm respectively per phase. The sending end voltage is 66kV while the receiving end voltage is maintained at 66kV by a synchronous phase-modifier. Determine the kVAr of the modifier when the load at the receiving end is 75MW at power factor 0.8 lagging; also the maximum load that can be transmitted.

P 8.3 A long line from a hydroelectric station operating at 132kV feeds a 66kV system through a transformer. The load taken from the 66kV windings of the transformer is 50MVA at power factor 0.8 lagging. A tertiary winding on the transformer feeds a synchronous condenser at 11kV. If the power factor at the receiving end of the line is to be unity, calculate the rating of each of the three windings. Neglect losses.

P 8.4 Find the rating of synchronous compensator connected to the tertiary winding of a 132kV star connected, 33kV star connected, 11kV delta connected three winding transformer to supply a load of 66MW at 0.8 power factor lagging at 33kV across the secondary. Equivalent primary and tertiary winding reactances are 32 ohms and 0.16 ohm respectively while the secondary winding reactance is negligible. Assume that the primary side voltage is essentially constant at 132kV and maximum of nominal setting between transformer primary and secondary is 1:1.

P 8.5 A single circuit three phase 220kV line runs at no load. Voltage at the receiving end of the line is 210kV. Find the sending end voltage, if the line has resistance of 20.5 ohms, reactance of 81.3 ohms and the total susceptance as 5.45×10^{-4} mho. The transmission line is to be represented by π-model.

P 8.6 A power system is operating at 1000Mw, 132kV, 50Hz, with 0.8 p.f. lagging in parallel with another line at 750MW, 132kV, 50Hz with 0.707 p.f. lagging. Both are interconnected at the station and when the compensating device is on, the overall power factor is improved to 0.9 lagging. Suggest suitable capacitors, shunt and series. Individual loads and combined load are to improve power factor to 0.9 in all cases.

9 INTRODUCTION TO ADVANCED TOPICS

Modern power systems with super power plants are highly complex and sophisticated with huge capital investment. Further, advanced technologies are used in the design and operation of these systems. For efficient and reliable operation of these systems, control action is envisaged with the following organs:

1. Data acquisition and control
2. Computers,
3. Man – machine interface, and
4. Software and human operators.

During the earlier days, control action was applied to generation dispatch and supervisory control. Modern systems demand a comprehensive and integrated approach to monitoring and controlling of power flows for economic and secure operation. This brought into the picture a third and equally important aspect of control, viz, security control. The human operator is finding it more and more difficult to take instantaneous decisions in cases of serious and complex situations.

Generation control has slowly shifted from analog to digital methods during the sixties. Station and system supervisory control too has shifted to digital computer masters from hard-wired masters. The man – machine interface consisted of strip chart records, loggers, indicating lights, anunciators, console push button panels, etc. Black and white or colour CRT display is already in vogue. However, the entire control configuration has undergone a radical change with the introduction of system security requirements.

9.1 FACTS Controllers

In chapter 8 static var compensators are discussed. Subsequent developments lead to the emergence of Flexible AC Transmission System (FACTS) controller. Hingorani and Gyugi are pioneers in this area. FACTS controllers is a fast developing area with potential applications.

The basic principle of the flexibility in the transmission of power can be understood easily from the following example Fig. 9.1.

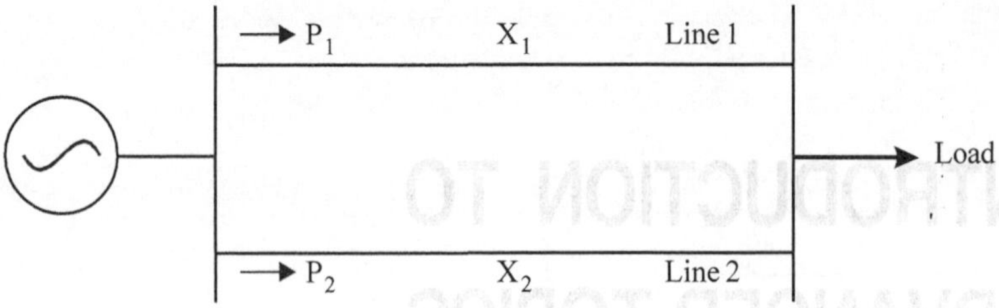

Fig. 9.1 Transfer of Power

The power flow from the generator to the load through the parallel lines is dependent upon the impedances or reactances when resistances are neglected. If $X_1 = X_2$, the transfer of power is 50% on each of the two lines. If $X_2 = 2X_1$ then the power transfer will be in the ratio of 2 : 1. Thus the higher impedance line carries less load and the lower impedance line may even get over loaded. If one of the lines, say line 1 is a HVDC line then power flow is electrically controlled and the above problem is eliminated. Further, with HVDC the stability problem also is controlled because of the speed of control. However, HVDC is expensive in a relative sense.

A FACTS controller can over come the problem discussed earlier by controlling the impedance, or phase angle. A FACTS controller can control the power flow in any manner that is desired. It is possible to inject desired voltage in series with the line.

Types of FACTS Controllers

Generally FACTS controllers are divided into four categories. They are briefly discussed.

9.1.1 Series Controllers

They are either variable reactor or capacitor or a power electronic based variable source so as to serve the need. The drop of voltage across the variable impedance can be considered as series injected voltage (Fig. 9.2).

Fig. 9.2 Series Controller

9.1.2 Shunt Controller

The shunt controller, also, may be either a variables source or a variable impedance or a combination connected in shunt as shown and they all inject current into the line (Fig. 9.3).

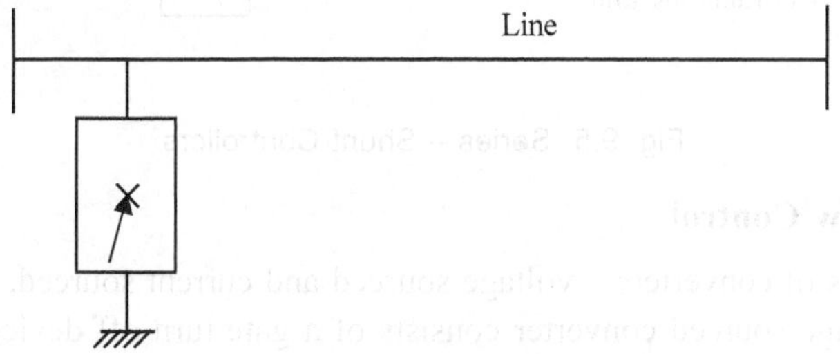

Fig. 9.3 Shunt Controller

9.1.3 Series – Series Controllers

Two different types of configurations are feasible. A combination of separate series controllers operated in a coordinated manner in the network or other wise, it could be a unified controller wherein series controllers provide independent series reactive power control as well provide real power transfer through a power link. This is shown in Fig. 9.4.

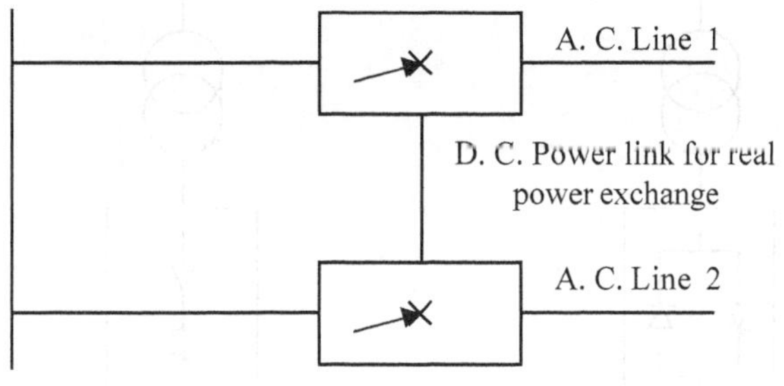

Fig. 9.4 Series – Series Controllers

In FACTS terminology the term unified is used to indicate that the D.C. terminals of all controller converters are connected together for real power transfer.

9.1.4 Series – Shunt Controllers

In the same way as series – series, this could be also a combination of separate series and shunt controller – controlled in a coordinated manner or a unified power controller with series and shunt elements. The basic scheme is shown in Fig. 9.5.

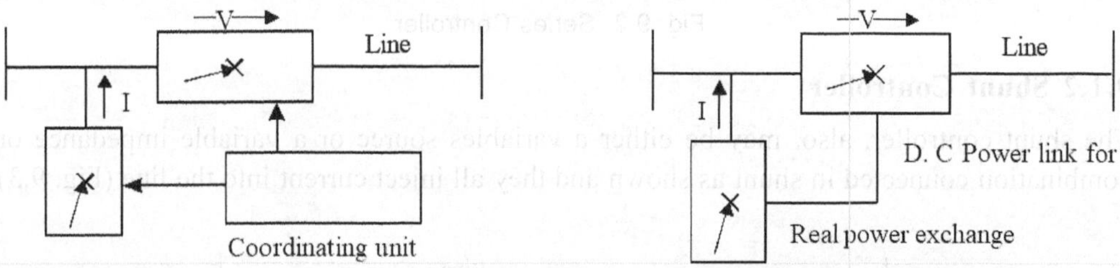

Fig. 9.5 Series – Shunt Controllers

9.1.5 Power Flow Control

There are two types of converters – voltage sourced and current sourced, using gate turn off devices. The voltage sourced converter consists of a gate turn off device paralleled with a reverse diode. A D.C. capacitor is used as a voltage source. The current sourced converter has a gate turn off device in series with a diode. It has a D.C. reactor as a current source.

Voltage sourced converters are preferred in FACTS controllers. Sequential switching of the device will give A.C. voltage from the D.C. source. They are called thus static synchronous compensator. It is operated as a shunt connected static var compensator whose output voltage can be controlled independent of A.C. system voltage. Such a device is also called STATCOM. The structure is shown in Fig. 9.6.

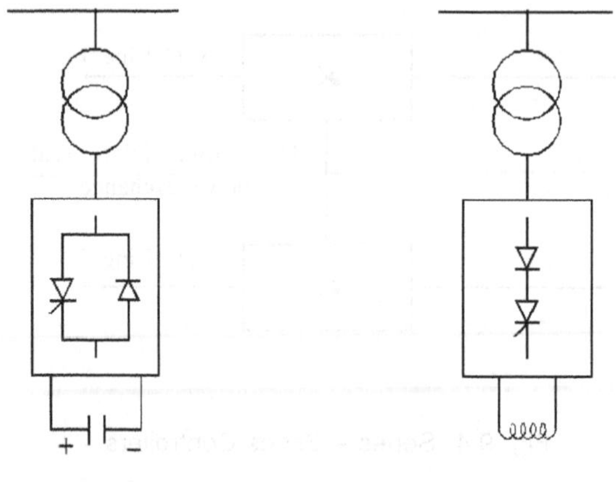

Fig. 9.6 Static Synchronous Compensator

9.1.6 Static Var Compensator(SVC)

It is a device that supplies capacitive or inductive current so as to maintain, voltage at any bus. This has been already discussed in Chapter 8. The device is shunt connected.

In a similar manner a thyristor controlled reactor (TCR), shunt connected has the effective reactance varied in a continuous manner by conduction control of the thyristor. TCR naturally belongs to the class of SVC.

If the reactance is varied in a stepped manner instead of continuous mode, the device becomes thyristor switched reactor TSR. Several shunt connected reactors may be switched in or out.

Likewise, thyristor switched capacitor (TSC) is operated such that shunt capacitor units are switched in – and out depending upon the need. It should be noted that in this case the thyristors are operated without firing angle control. They operate with full or zero conduction.

A thyristor controlled resistor (TCBR) with shunt connection can be use to brake a generator during accelerating period when a fault occurs. They are called then thyristor controlled braking resistors.

In the same way as STATCOM a static synchronous series compensator (SSSC) operates with a voltage sourced converter or current sourced converter giving output voltage in series with the line. Thyristor controlled series reactor (TCSR) thyristor controlled series capacitor (TCSC) thyristor controlled switched series reactor (TSSR) are similar devices in series mode of operation.

9.1.7 Unified Power Flow Controller

This is a combination of series and shunt connected static compensators (STATCOM and SSSC). They are coupled through a common D.C. link. The controller permits bi-directional flow of active power between both the series output terminals of the SSSC and the shunt output terminals of the STATCOM. Without any external electric energy source they provide simultaneously real and reactive series line compensation.

UPFC is also capable of providing independently controllable shunt reactive compensation. This is schematically shown in Fig. 9.7.

There are several more devices such as thyristor controlled phase shifting transformer (TCPST), inter phase power controller (IPC) Thyristor controlled voltage limiter, thyristor controlled voltage regulator etc.

9.1.8 Advantages due to FACTS devices

The following are some of the advantages that can be obtained by using FACTS controller.

1. Power in lines is controlled in any desired manner.
2. Line capacity is increased, practically upto thermal limits
3. By raising transient stability limit, system security is enhanced

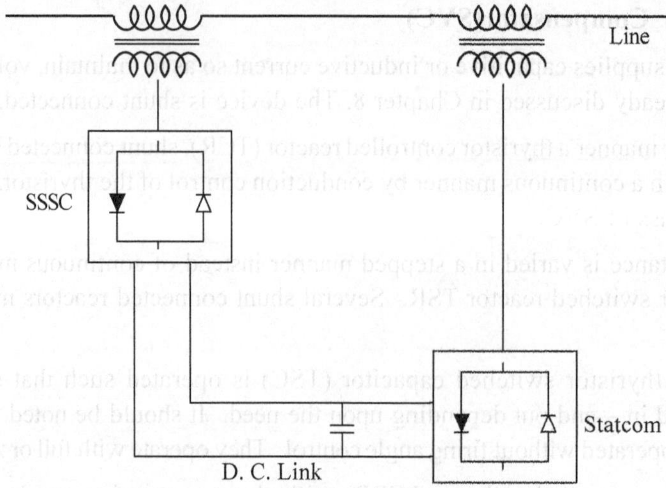

Fig. 9.7 United Power Flow Controller

4. Up gradation of lines is easier.
5. Reduced reactive power flow, thereby permitting greater active power flow.
6. Reduced cost of energy received due to enhanced line capacity.

9.2 Effect of Shunt Compensation

Consider the single line diagram of a generating station supplying load connected at the other end of a transmission line of reactance X_L with negligible resistance. Consider a reactive power source connected to the system at the mid point of the transmission line as shown. The compensator supports the line such that the sending end voltage, the receiving end voltage and the voltage at the mid point of line are all equal in magnitude ($V_R = V_S = V$). This means that no current enters the compensator branch so that $I_S = I_R = I$. Let the phase angle between V_S and V_R be δ. Then the power transferred from the sending end to the reciving end,

$$P = \frac{V_R\ V_S}{X}\sin\delta = \frac{V_R\ V_S}{X}2\sin\frac{\delta}{2}\cos\frac{\delta}{2} = \frac{2V^2}{X}\sin\frac{\delta}{2}\cos\frac{\delta}{2}$$

This is a maximum when

$$\delta = \frac{\pi}{2}; \qquad P_{max} = \frac{V^2}{X} \qquad \text{.....(i)}$$

From the phasor diagram

$$ab = \frac{IX}{4} = bc \qquad \text{and}$$

$$I = BV \qquad ac = \frac{IX}{2} = cf$$

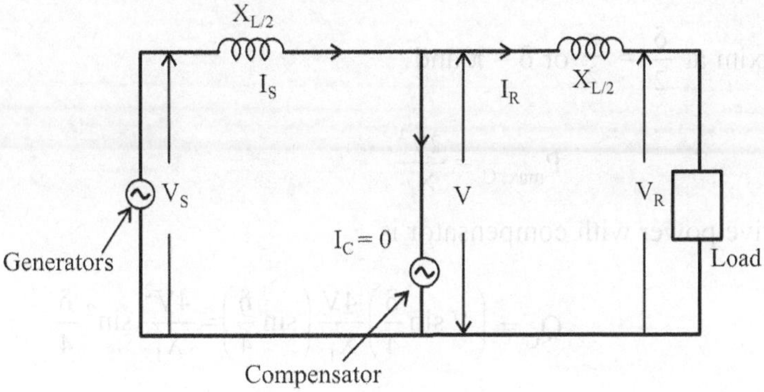

Fig. 9.8(a)

$$I_S . \frac{X}{4} = \frac{I X}{4} = V \sin \frac{\delta}{4}$$

Hence, $$I = \frac{4V}{X} \sin \frac{\delta}{4} \qquad .....(ii)$$

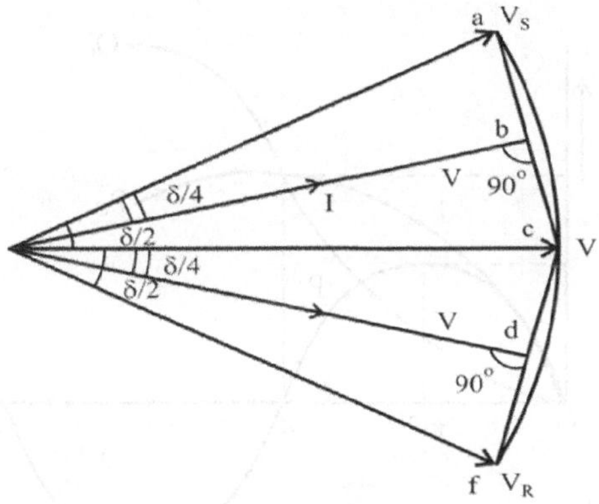

Fig. 9.8(b)

Power at sending end, mid point and receiving end will be the same since the line is lossless and the compensator is ideal.

Real power transferred $$P = \frac{V^2}{X_L} \sin \delta$$

Also, $$P = \frac{V_S . V}{\frac{X_L}{2}} \sin \frac{\delta}{2} = \frac{2V^2}{X_L} \sin \frac{\delta}{2} \qquad .....(iii)$$

It is a maxim at $\frac{\delta}{2} = \frac{\pi}{2}$ or $\delta = \pi$ and

$$P_{max,\,C} = \frac{2V^2}{X_L} \qquad .....(iv)$$

The reactive power with compensator is

$$Q_C = \left(V\sin\frac{\delta}{4}\right)\frac{4V}{X_L}\left(\sin\frac{\delta}{4}\right) = \frac{4V^2}{X_L}\sin^2\frac{\delta}{4}$$

$$= \frac{2V^2}{X_L}\left(1-\cos\frac{\delta}{2}\right) \qquad .....(v)$$

This is a maximum when $\cos\frac{\delta}{2} = 0$ or $\frac{\delta}{2} = 2\pi$

It can be observed from the curves in Fig. 9.8(c) that mid point shunt compensation significanty increases the power transmission capacity. However, the reactive power to be supplied by the compensator increases very rapidly.

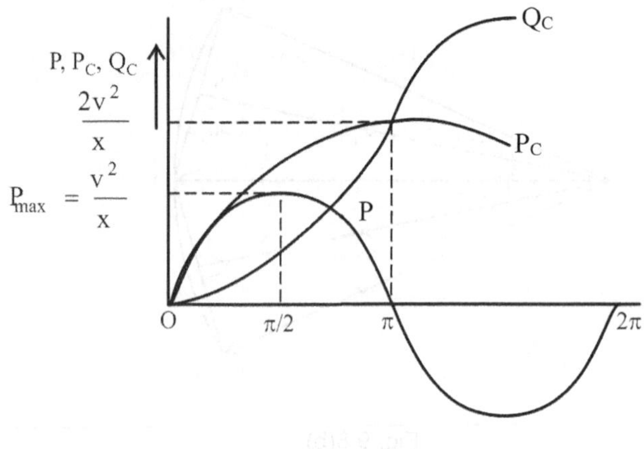

Fig. 9.8(c)

Since shunt compensators can provide effective voltage support, it can increase transmission capability for a system during transient condition, especially in post fault condition.

This can be demonstrated for a two machine system employing equal area criteria. In Fig. 9.9(a) transient stability margin is indicated for an uncompensated system with usual notation.

With shunt compensator, the area of margin in for stability is increased as shown in Fig. 9.9(b).

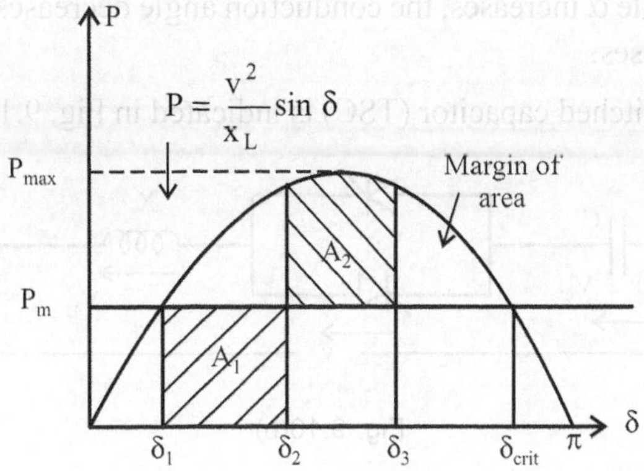

Fig. 9.9(a)

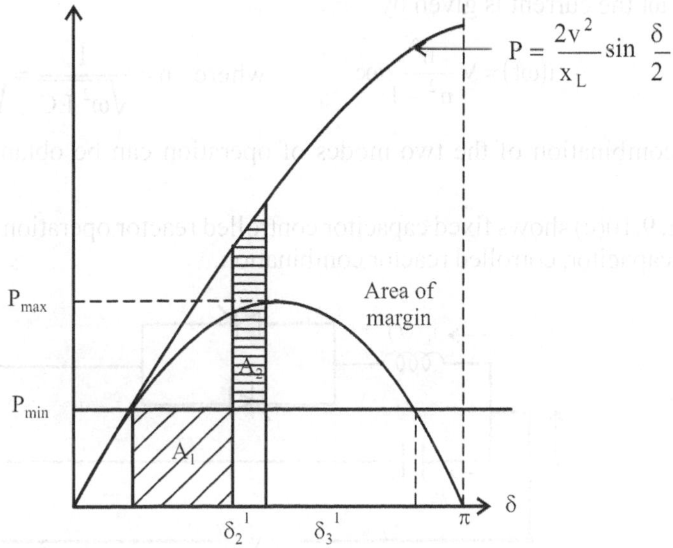

Fig. 9.9(b)

9.3 Controllable Var Generation

There are two main categories of reactive power generation.

They are thyristor controlled reactor and thyristor switched capacitor.

The thyristor controlled reactor (TCR) is schematically shown in Fig. 9.10(a).

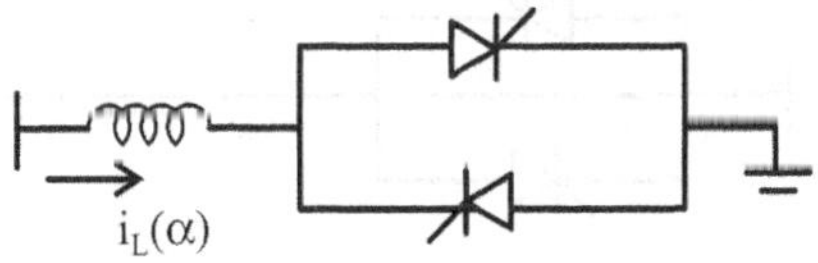

Fig. 9.10(a)

As the delay angle α increases, the conduction angle decreases and consequently the reactor current decreases.

The thyristor switched capacitor (TSC) is indicated in Fig. 9.10(b).

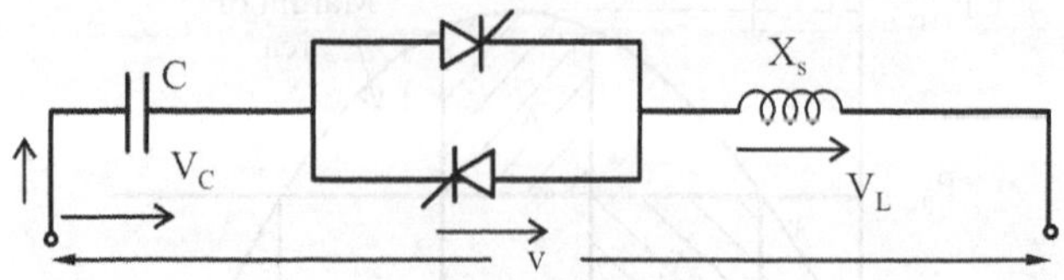

Fig. 9.10(b)

X_S is a surge limiting reactor. When connected to a sinusoidal voltage supply V = V = v sin ωt the current is given by

$$i(\omega t) = V\frac{n^2}{n^2-1}\omega c \qquad \text{where } n = \frac{1}{\sqrt{\omega^2 LC}} = \sqrt{\frac{X_C}{X_L}}$$

A combination of the two modes of operation can be obtanied as in Fig. 9.10(c) and (d)

Fig. 9.10(c) shows fixed capacitor controlled reactor operation while Fig. 9.10(d) has switched capacitor, cotrolled reactor combination.

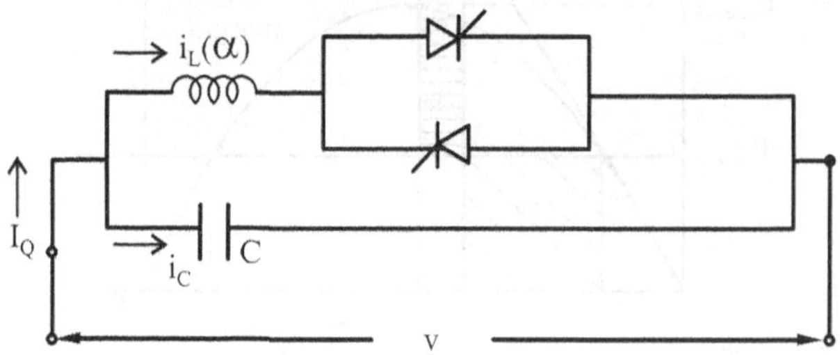

Fig. 9.10(c)

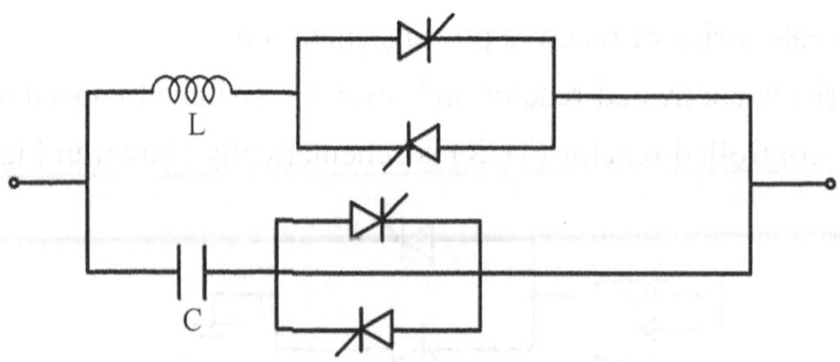

Fig. 9.10(d)

The operating V-I characteritic for TCR is shown in Fig. 9.11(a) and that of FC-TCR in Fig. 9.11(b).

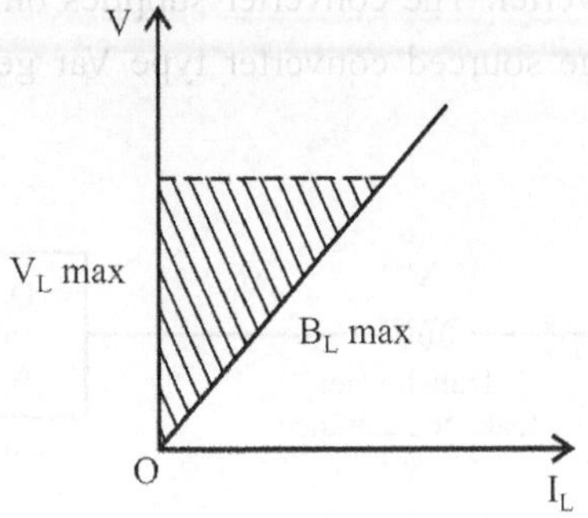

Fig. 9.11(a)

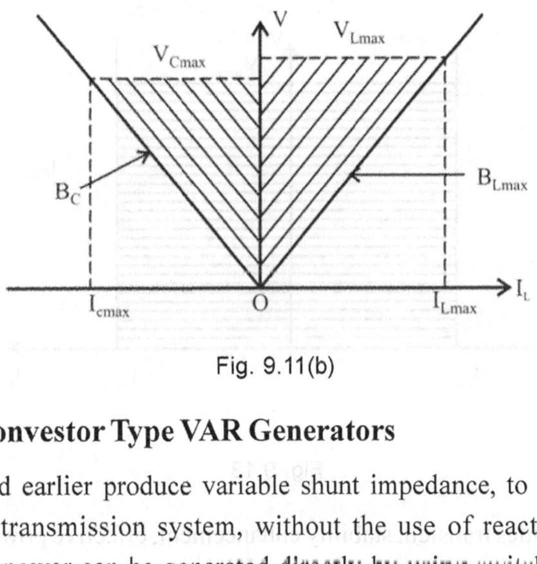

Fig. 9.11(b)

9.4 Switching Convestor Type VAR Generators

The devices discussed earlier produce variable shunt impedance, to meet the conpensation requirements of the transmission system, without the use of reactors and/or capacitors. Controllable reactive power can be generated directly by using switching power converters. The method is similar to generation by synchronous generators. They are called static synchronous generators. With appropriate controls when they are operated without an energy source, they are termed static synchronous compensators or STATCOM. Presently, they are voltage sourced converters (d.c to a.c).

A basic scheme of voltage sourced reactive power generating converter is shown in Fig. 9.12.

The charged capacitor C provides the input d.c. voltage to the converter which produces controllable three phase output voltages at the same frequency as the power system. By varying the amplitude of the output voltages the reactive power provided by the converter can be controlled. The leakage reactance of the coupling transformer acts as a tie reactance between the a.c power system and the converter. The converter supplies only reactive output power. The V-I characteristic for a voltage sourced converter type Var generator is shown in Fig. 9.13.

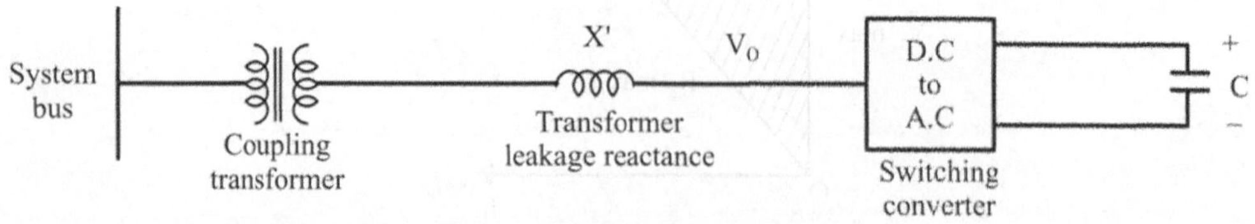

Fig. 9.12

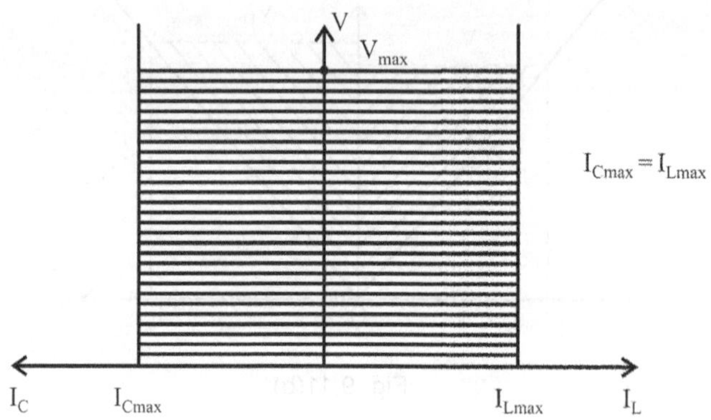

Fig. 9.13

STATCOM provides transient stability enhancement, effective power oscillation damping and sub synchronous oscillation damping.

9.5 Voltage Stability

Reactive power flow depends mainly on difference between voltage magnitudes and it flows from higher voltage to lower voltage. Reactive power, therefore, cannot be transmitted over long distances as the line regulation cannot exceed the prescribed limit. Further, if the load is suddenly disconnected at the receiving end there will a temporary over voltage in the line. Induction motors, excitation system for generators, switched capacitors and reactors, static Var compensators are some of the elements that cause fast dynamics in voltage stability along with protective relaying. On the other hand, slow changes in generation and loads, boiler dynamics are some of the factors involved in slower dynamics in voltage stability.

Voltage stability is an integral part of the power system response and is an important aspect of system stability and security. Voltage instability has been detected well before the onset of angle instability in many cases. If the problem is not corrected it can lead to voltage collapse and system wide disturbance.

The loss of synchronism of generators is called angle instability. Voltage stability also called load stability is a subset of overall stability of a power system and is a dynamic problem that occurs due to monotonically changing voltages.

In industrialized areas increase of load demand is met without a corresponding increase in transmission capacity leading to severe problem including voltage stability.

Voltage stability is the ability to maintain the voltage so that when load is increased load power will increase and so both power and voltage are controllable.

A power system at a given operating state and subjected to a given disturbance is voltage stable if voltage near loads approaches post disturbance equilibrium values. Following voltage stability, a system undergoes voltage collapse if the post disturbance equilibrium voltages near loads are below acceptance limits. Both voltage stability and collapse may occur in a time period of a fraction of a second to a few minutes.

Consider the plot of voltage V at a load bus as a function of load power P shown in Fig. 9.14 as ABCDE.

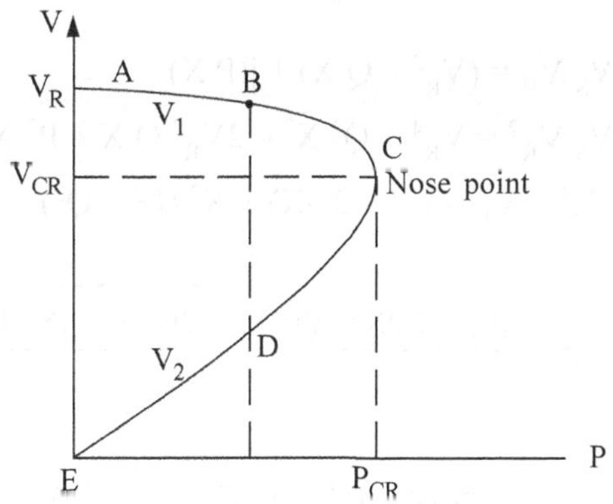

Fig. 9.14 P. V. Diagram at the Load Bus

It can be observed that there are two voltages V_1 and V_2 for a constant power load. The high voltage solution is stable while the other is unstable. The maximum loadability is determined by point C and the part CDE is uncontrollable.

Mathematically the voltage V_R can be expressed by (see Fig. 9.15).

$$V_R = \left[\frac{-2QX + V_S^2}{2} \pm \frac{1}{2}\sqrt{(2QX - V_S^2)^2 - 4X^2(P^2 + Q^2)}\right] \quad .....(9.1)$$

from which it is clear that V_R is a double valued function.

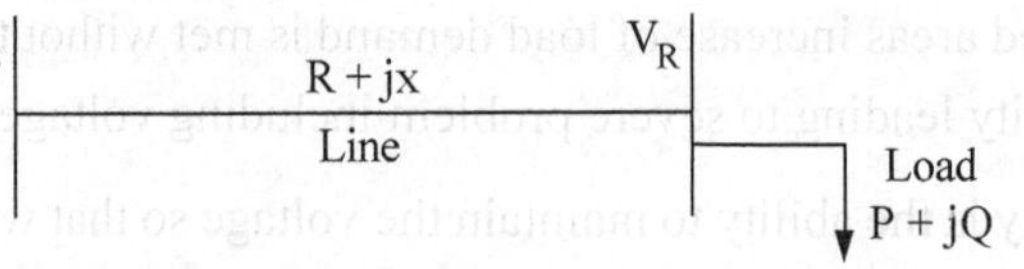

Fig. 9.15 Transmission Line with load

This can be proved as follows:

$$V_S = V_R + j\,I\,X \qquad \text{(neglecting the resistance)}$$

$$= VR + j\,\frac{(P + jQ)}{V_R}\,.\,X$$

$$V_S = V_R^2 + \frac{(-Q + jP)X}{V_R}$$

$$V_S V_R = (V_R^2 - Q\,X) + j(P\,X)$$

$$V_S V_R^2 = V_R^4 + Q^2 X^2 - 2V_R^2 Q\,X + P^2 X^2$$

$$V_R^4 - V_R^2 (V_S^2 - 2QX) + X^2 (P^2 + Q^2) = 0$$

$$V_R^2 = \frac{(V_S^2 - 2QX) \pm \sqrt{(-V_S^2 + 2QX)^2 - 4X^2(P^2 + Q^2)}}{2}$$

$$V_R = \left[\frac{-2QX + V_S^2}{2} \pm \frac{1}{2}\sqrt{(2QX - V_S^2)^2 - 4(P^2 + Q^2)X^2}\right]^{1/2}$$

Consider a line supplying only reactive power

$$Q_R = V_R \; I_R$$

$$= V_R \left(\frac{V_S - V_R}{X} \right)$$

$$Q_R = \frac{V_R \; V_S}{X} - \frac{VR^2}{X}$$

$$\frac{dQ_r}{dV_R} = 0 \qquad \text{when } \frac{1}{X} \; (V_S - 2V_R) = 0$$

The critical receiving end voltage $V_{R,crit}$

$$V_{R,crit} = \frac{V_S}{2}$$

At this critical voltage

$$Q_{R,\,crit} = \frac{V_S}{X} \cdot \frac{V_S}{2} - \frac{VS^2}{4X} = \frac{V_S^2}{4X}$$

The sending end reactive power, when no real power is transmitted

$$Q_S = Q_R + I^2 X$$

$$= Q_R + \left(\frac{Q_S}{V_S} \right)^2 X$$

Simplifying

$$Q_S{}^2 - Q_S \frac{V_S^2}{X} + Q_R \frac{V_S^2}{X} = 0$$

$$Q_S = \frac{1}{2} \left[\frac{V_S^2}{X} \pm V_S \sqrt{\left(\frac{V_S^2}{X^2} - \frac{4Q_R}{X} \right)} \right]$$

$$\frac{d\,Q_S}{d\,Q_R} = \left(\frac{1}{4X} \right) \frac{-4\,V_S}{\left(\frac{V_S^2}{X^2} - \frac{4\,Q_R}{X} \right)^{1/2}}$$

$$= \frac{1}{\left(\frac{X^2 \, V_S^2}{V_S^2 \, X^2} - \frac{4Q_R \, X^2}{V_S^2 \, X} \right)^{1/2}} = \frac{1}{\left(1 - \frac{4Q_R X}{V_S^2} \right)^{1/2}}$$

But $$Q_{R,\,crit} = \frac{V_S^2}{4X}$$

Hence $$\frac{d\,Q_S}{d\,Q_R} = \frac{1}{\left(1 - \frac{Q_R}{Q_{R,crit}}\right)^{1/2}}$$

$\frac{d\,Q_S}{d\,Q_R}$ is called voltage collapse proximity indicators. At no load it is unity, when $Q_R = Q_{R,crit}$, the voltage collapse indicator tends to infinity. Voltage may collapse in such a situation.

Voltage stability limit:

Consider the power relation

$$P_R = \frac{V_s V_R}{X} \sin\delta$$

$$\frac{dP_R}{dV_s} = \frac{V_R \sin\delta}{x} + \frac{V_s V_R}{X} \cos\delta \frac{d\delta}{dV_s}$$

If $$\frac{dP_R}{dV_s} = 0, \text{ then } \frac{d\delta}{dv_s} = -\frac{1}{V_R} \tan\delta$$

At $P_{R\,max}$, $\delta = 90^o$ so that $\frac{d\delta}{dV_s}$ tends to infinity.

Again, since

$$Q_R = \frac{V_s V_R}{X} \cos\delta - \frac{VR^2}{X}$$

$$\frac{dQ_R}{dV_R} = \frac{V_s}{X} \cos\delta - \frac{2V_R}{X} - \frac{V_S V_R}{X} \sin\delta \frac{d\delta}{dV_R}$$

$$\frac{dQ_R}{dV_R} = \frac{1}{X}\left[V_S \cos\delta + V_s \frac{\sin^2\delta}{\cos\delta} - 2V_R\right]$$

$$= \frac{1}{X}\left[\frac{V_s}{\cos\delta} - 2V_R\right]$$

If $\delta = 90^o$ for steady state power angle stability, then as cos δ tends to zero, $\frac{dQ_R}{dV_R}$ tends to infinity i.e., $\frac{dV_R}{dQ_R}$ tends to zero.

Thus, on no-load voltage instability occurs when power angle instability takes place. For different power factors the PV characteristic can have the shape shown in Fig. 9.16.

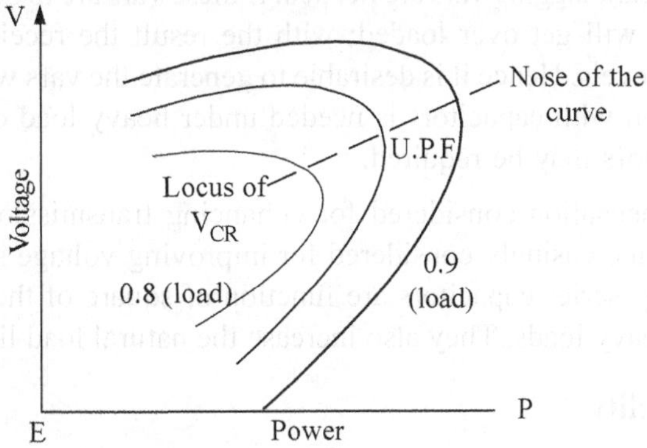

Fig. 9.16 P. V. Curves for Different Power Factors

Static analysis is sufficient to assess voltage stability, but for accurate prediction dynamic analysis must be carried out.

The probability of voltage instability increases as the system is operated close to its maximum loadability limit. Environmental and economic expansion of transmission network and for obvious reasons distant location of the generators from the load centers all result in over loading of the existing networks. The present trend is to optimally utilize the inherent margins available with flexible A.C. transmission system controllers.

Reactive power compensation close to the load centers as well as at the critical buses in the network is essential to over come voltage instability.

The location size and speed of control of FACTS controllers determine the maximum benefit that can be obtained without getting into voltage instability.

9.6 Methods for prevention of voltage collapse

1. ***Load shedding:*** Under frequency and under voltage load shedding provides protection for unusual load disturbances. This should be resorted only under extreme situations.

2. ***VAR devices:*** Use of reactive power compensating devices will generally reduce the voltage stability problem.

3. ***Transformer taps:*** By controlling the transformer taps using on-load tap changers, it is possible to some extent to overcome the voltage stability problem with proper planning, control and coordination of protective equipment. The operator at the console should not find it difficult to overcome most of the voltage stability problems.

9.7 Shunt and Series Connected Compensators

Series inductance of the lines absorbs lagging vars. Shunt capacitance of the lines absorbs leading vars. At the natural or surge impedance loading of a line, they both are equal. During heavy loads significant lagging vars are needed. If these vars are to be supplied by the generators at the station they will get over loaded; with the result the receiving end voltage may fall abnormally lower levels. Hence it is desirable to generate the vars where they are most needed. Shunt compensation with capacitors is needed under heavy load condition. But, at low load periods shunt reactors may be required.

Series compensation considered for enhancing transmission capacity and improving system stability is increasingly considered for improving voltage stability. Since the reactive power generated by series capacitors are function of square of the line current (I^2), they are very effective at heavy loads. They also increase the natural load limit.

9.8 Power Quality

Any amount of power can be drawn from and delivered to an infinite bus without affecting

(i) the magnitude of bus voltage

(ii) the frequency of bus voltage.

The short circuit ratio at a load bus (SCR) is defined as

$$SCR = \frac{\text{Short circuit current at rated voltage with load short circuited}}{\text{rated load current}}$$

It can be seen that SCR is inversely proportional to the Thevenin's impedance of the network as seen from the bus. If SCR is low the load bus is said to be connected to weak power grid and vice versa. Power quality (PQ) problem is likely to occur at that bus. One aspect of PQ can be selected in terms of phase voltages V_R, V_y and V_B as

$$\begin{bmatrix} V_R \\ V_Y \\ V_B \end{bmatrix} = \sqrt{2}\, V \begin{bmatrix} \sin \omega t \\ \sin\left(\omega t - \frac{2\pi}{3}\right) \\ \sin\left(\omega t + \frac{2\pi}{3}\right) \end{bmatrix} \quad \text{.....(9.2)}$$

under all conditions, V and ω remaining constant. Similarly the harmonic content of the bus voltage is also an indication of PQ.

Electric power quality can be loosely defined as a measure of how well electric power can be utilized by customers.

Power utilization is degraded when wave shapes are irregular, voltage regulation is poor, harmonics and flicker are present or even when there are momentary events that distort the usually sinusoidal voltage wave. All the above conditions result in degradation of power quality. The introduction and the wide spread use of high power semi conduction devices at all levels of power system operation, and utilization have made non sinusoidal load currents quite common.

9.8.1 Power Quality Index

The harmonic components of voltages and current are used as power quality indices.

Let i(t) be the load current that is periodic

I_1, I_2, ... are the fundamental and harmonics of i(t).

For all general purposes, the standard is taken as total harmonic distortion (THD) defined by

$$THD = \sum_{i=2}^{\alpha} \frac{I_i}{I_1} \qquad .....(9.3)$$

In regard to frequency, high frequency phenomenon is termed noise and the low frequency phenomenon is named flicker. As has been already mentioned rectifier loads are the main source of harmonic load current.

Different rectifier connections such as single phase bridge and 3-phase bridge rectifiers contribute to harmonic distortion and various factors such as THD, displacement factor, power factor are clearly defined. It may be noted that displacement factor is the cosine of the angle between fundamental voltage and fundamental current while, power factor is the ratio of real or active power to apparent power V_{RMS} I_{RMS}.

9.8.2 Voltage Sags

A short duration magnitude reduction in voltage is called voltage sag. The time period may be of the order of few seconds. The cause for a sag is sudden, short duration increase in current. Such an event occurs during motor starting, transformer energizing, faults etc.

For example, the transient voltage when a big motor is started will have the shape of all the phase voltages shown in Fig. 9.17. The voltage falls by a large amount with gradual recovery over a few cycles.

It can be seen that the voltage drops are practically the same in all the three phases. In case of magnetizing inrush current of transformers, the inrush current is not the same in all the phases. This is shown in Fig. 9.18 second harmonic and fourth harmonics contribute more to harmonic distortion.

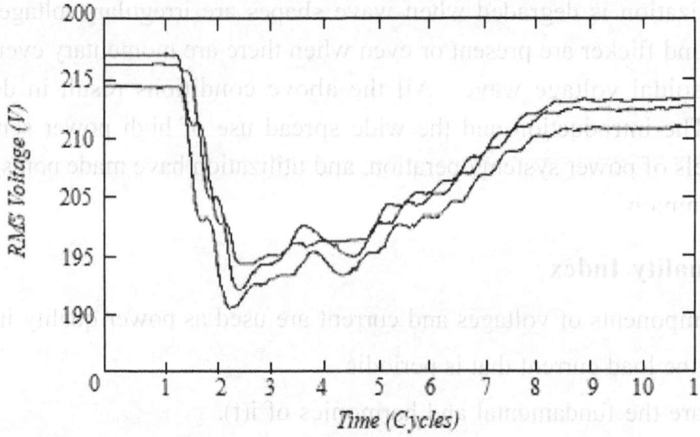

Fig. 9.18 Voltage sag due to transformer energizing

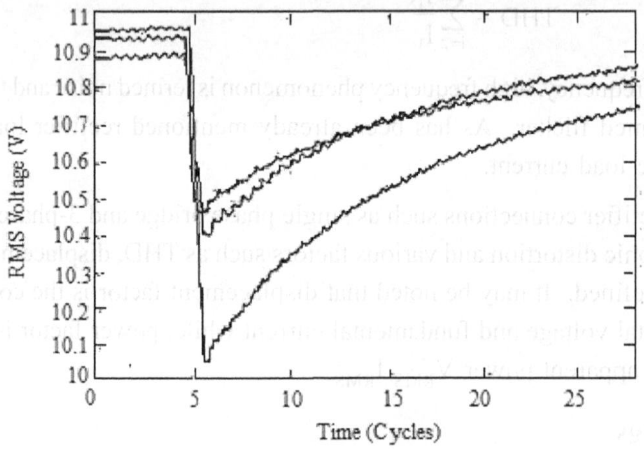

Fig. 9.17 Voltage sag due to motor starting

In case of faults, the most common type of fault is single line to ground fault. The voltage falls more in two phases and recovers sharply after a few cycles. This is shown in Fig. 9.19 the most severe faults are due to short circuits and faults involving earth.

Transformer connections affect the impedance of fault. For example a phase to phase fault for a star connected load gives a similar sag as a single-phase fault for a delta connected load.

Further a voltage sag is not exactly recorded the way it occurs at the load due to intervening components such as transformers which effect the voltage sags.

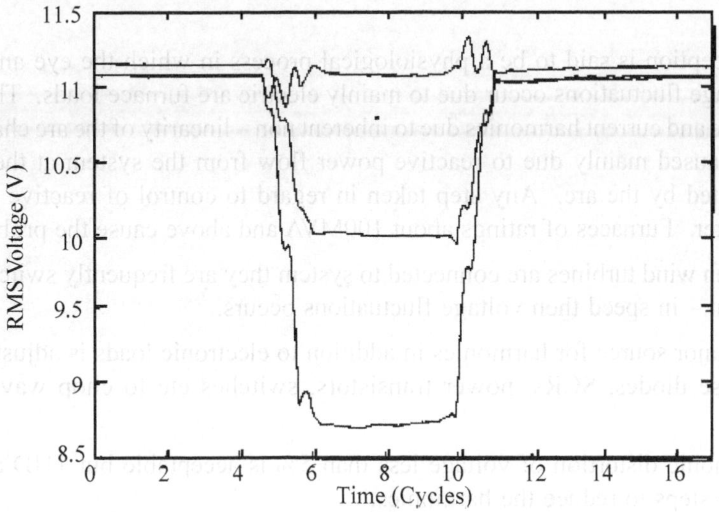

Fig. 9.19 Voltage sag due to a fault

9.8.3 Rectifier Loads

Most electronic equipment (such as personal computers) with power rating less that 1kw. Use single phase diode bridge rectifiers. The output of the bridge rectifier is filtered using a capacitor filter or an LC - filter. The diode bridge rectifiers are often followed by switch mode power supplies. The switch mode power supply converts the unregulated D.C. link voltage to a well regulated output voltage. For higher power applications (greater than 1 KW) either 3-phase bridge of six pulse type or twelve pulse type are used. The single phase case is shown in Fig. 9.20.

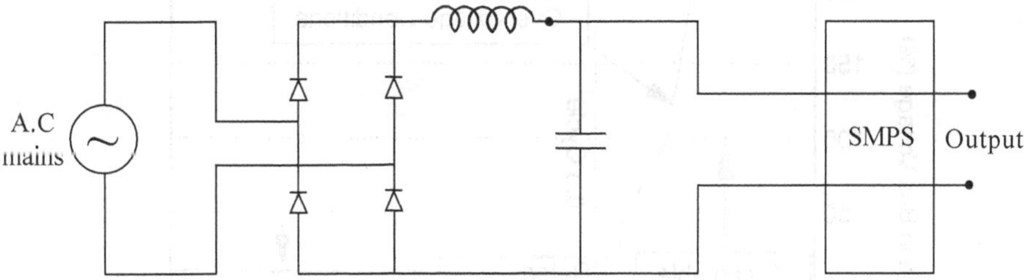

Fig. 9.20 Single phase rectifier load

The voltage sag depends upon the energy storage device used and the switch mode power supply (SMPS). If the sag in the A.C. main voltage is of considerable magnitude and duration, the D.C. link voltage may fall below the minimum value for which it is desired. This results in the shut down of the electronic load connected to the output termals of SMPS.

9.8.4 Flicker

Light flicker perception is said to be a physiological process in which the eye and the brain participate. Voltage fluctuations occur due to mainly electric arc furnace loads. These occurs because of voltage and current harmonics due to inherent non – linearity of the arc characteristic. Light flicker is caused mainly due to reactive power flow from the system at the instant of short circuit created by the arc. Any step taken in regard to control of reactive power will control light flicker. Furnaces of ratings about 100MVA and above cause the problem.

Again when wind turbines are connected to system they are frequently switched on and off around the cut – in speed then voltage fluctuations occurs.

Another major source for harmonics in addition to electronic loads is adjustable speed drives as they use diodes, SCRs, power transistors, switches etc to chop wave forms to control power.

Total harmonic distortion of voltage less than 5% is acceptable but THD above 10% requires, positive steps to reduce the harmonics.

9.8.5 Power Acceptability or Voltage Tolerance

The voltage tolerance or more commonly power acceptability curves are loci drawn in the bus voltage duration time plane. There curves indicate the tolerance of a load to withstand momentary low and high voltage events. The International Electrochemical Commission (IEC) calls the same curves as equipment immunity curves. Computer business equipment manufactures association (CBEMA) has defined its power acceptability curve but later in 1996 the Information Technology Industry Council (ITIC) announced its power acceptability curve which superceded CBEMA curve. This is shown in Fig. 9.21.

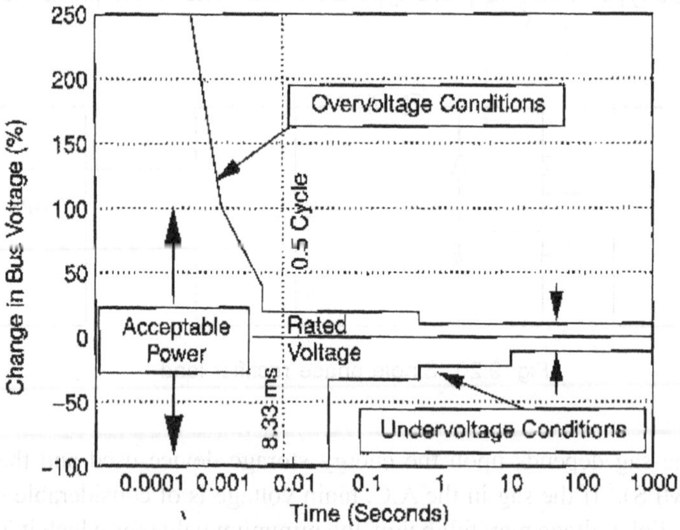

Fig. 9.21 ITIC Power acceptability curve

9.8.6 Solutions to Power Quality problem

There are several power electronic solutions to power quality problem.

A dynamic voltage restorer, which is a voltage source inverter (VSI) injects a voltage in series with the distribution line. This is shown in Fig. 9.22. Three phase voltages generated by the VSI can be injected into the line through a special coupling transformer. The terminals of each of the three primary windings are brought out individually and are connected in series with the 3-phase lines. On the secondary side the three windings are connected either in star or in delta and the three terminals of the VSI are connected to the three secondary terminals.

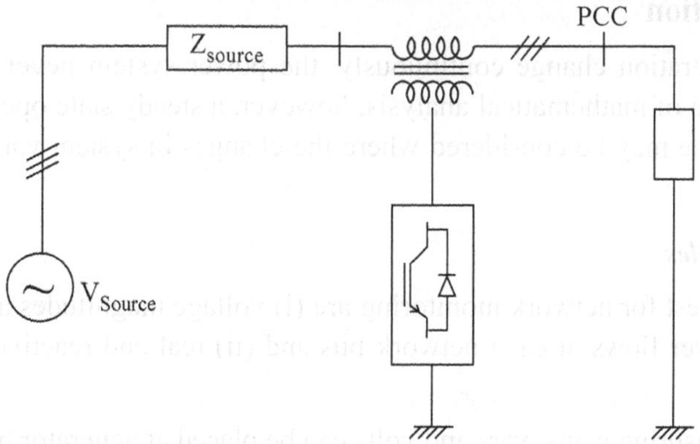

Fig. 9.22 Dynamic Voltage Restorer

Point of Common Coupling (PCC) is the point in the inter connected power system where loads are connected to the network. It is the point at which the load interacts with loads and the network itself. For example the PCC for typical residential applications is the distribution transformer secondary. Where the distribution transformer serves a single customer, the primary of the transformer is the PCC.

$$V_{PCC} = V_t(t) + V_{DVR}(t) \quad .....(9.4)$$

The DVR will maintain near perfect power quality conditions at the PCC. The DVR is useful for sags, harmonics and flicker.

There are many other devices such as unified power quality conditioner (UPQC) which is a combination of STATCOM and DVR for even better performance.

9.9 Data Base for Control

Computer control of modern power systems is proposed to improve economy, to maintain quality and for better security. Such a control is feasible, primarily if all meter readings and other information pertaining to the operating state of the system are processed in real time into a more useful form so that control decisions are made using it. For power systems in normal operating state, bus voltage magnitude and phase angles are the state variables as they completely determine the state of the system in steady-state (quasi-static state, infact). The vector of voltage magnitudes and phase angles is called the static state vector. State estimation is the mathematical process of obtaining the state vector from the variable information.

A knowledge of the state vector enables the system operator to take important decisions. The state estimator, an algorithm based on load flow and statistical estimation theory, is of immense use in calculating security and contingency evaluation. At an advanced level, it can also be used for load frequency control and economic dispatch.

9.10 State Estimation

Since loads and generation change continuously, the power system never attains a steady state. For the purpose of mathematical analysis, however, a steady state operating point over a short interval of time may be considered where the changes in system variables are within reasonable limits.

Power System Variables

The variables of interest for network monitoring are (i) voltage magnitudes and phase angles, real and reactive power flows at each network bus and (ii) real and reactive power flows in each line.

Meters for measuring watts, vars and volts can be placed at generator buses, EHV lines, tie - lines and load buses and the readings can be telemetered in real time to the control centers.

However, only some of the measurements are available immediately while the rest are either delayed as is the case of information from a neighbouring, interconnected system or not available (like data from the low voltage distribution side). Further, the available data may not be perfect due to errors in the meters. Some of the meter readings may also be missing.

Let n be the dimension of the state vector **X** and m be the dimension of the measurement vector **Z**. Since the slack bus is fixed, we have N_b voltage magnitudes and (N_b-1) voltage phase angles where N_b is the number of buses.

$$X^T = [V_1, V_2, \ldots V_{Nb}, \delta_2 \ldots \delta_{Nb}] \qquad \text{.....(9.5)}$$

Knowing **X**, all other quantities like active and reactive power flows, line flows, etc can be computed. In practice, all the values of **X** cannot be directly metered. The measurement vector **Z** and the state vector **X** are related by the nonlinear equation.

$$\mathbf{Z} = \mathbf{h(X)} + \eta \qquad \text{.....(9.6)}$$

where h is the measurement noise. By exercising option in the selection of variables for metering. Five types of measurement vectors can be identified.

Case 1 : Measuring real and reactive powers P_i and Q_i at all nodes, except P_1 at the swing bus.

$$Z^T = [P_2, P_3, \ldots P_{Nb}, Q_1 \ldots Q_{Nb}]$$

and it is a $(2\ N_b - 1)$ dimensional vector.

P_i and Q_i are given by equation (2.11) and (2.12)

Case 2 : Real and reactive powers at all buses except Pi at slack bus and voltage magnitudes at all buses may be measured in which case

$$Z^T = [P_2 \ldots P_{Nb}, Q_1 \ldots Q_{Nb}\ V_1 \ldots V_{Nb}]$$

Here Z^T is a $(3N_b - 1)$ dimensional vector.

Case 3 : Real and reactive power flow in the lines Pij and Qij at both ends of each line may be measured.

$$Z^T = [P_{ij}, Q_{ij}]$$

and it is a 4 N_ℓ dimensional vector where N_ℓ is the number of lines.

Case 4 : All the variables of case 3 and voltage magnitudes at all buses may be measured yielding.

$$Z^T = [P_{ij}, Q_{ij}, V_1, V_2 \ldots V_{Nb}]$$

an $(N_1 + N_b)$ dimensional vector.

Case 5 : All variables may be measured giving

$$Z^T = [P_i\ Q_i\ P_{ik}\ Q_{ik}\ V_j\ \delta_j]$$

Which is $(4N_b - 1 + 4\ N_\ell)$ dimensional.

Modelling of uncertainty:

Gaussian distribution is assumed for mathematical modelling of the uncertainty in measurements.

$$P(\mathbf{X}) = \frac{1}{(2\pi)^{n/2}|R|^{1/2}} \exp\left[-\frac{1}{2}(\mathbf{X} - \overline{\mathbf{X}})^T R^{-1}(\mathbf{X} - \overline{\mathbf{X}})\right] \qquad .....(9.7)$$

The uncertainty is due to :

1. Instrumentation error,
2. Operational uncertainty, and
3. Incompleteness of the model

Least Squares Estimation

Using Eqn. (9.6)

$$n = Z - h\ (X) \qquad .....(9.8)$$

The optimal estimate $\hat{X}$ is that value which minimizes the cost functional

$$J = \eta^T R^{-1} \eta = [Z - h(X)^T]\ R^{-1}\ \{Z - h(X)] \qquad .....(9.9)$$

Where R is the covariance matrix of the observation noise **n**. The minimization may be carried out using any of the standard techniques including steepest descent method, Fletcher – Powell method, etc.

The best estimate $\hat{\underline{x}}$ is the state that makes the gradient of equation (9.9) become zero

$$\frac{\partial J}{\partial X}\left(\hat{\underline{x}}\right) = 0$$

$$\frac{\partial h^t}{\partial x}\left(\hat{\underline{x}}\right) [R^{-1}] [\underline{Z} - h(\underline{x})] = 0 \qquad .....(9.10)$$

This is a set of linear equations to be solved by an iterative method. If Newton-Raphson method is selected then

$$H(\underline{x}) = \frac{\partial^2 J(\underline{x})}{\partial X^2}$$

$$\simeq -\frac{\partial h^t}{\partial x}[R^{-1}]\frac{\partial h}{\partial x} \qquad .....(9.11)$$

Neglecting higher derivatives in x. The iterative scheme to find the best state estimate for noisy measurements is

$$\underline{x}^{k+1} = \underline{x}^k + \left[\frac{dh^t}{dx} R^{-1} \frac{\partial h}{\partial x}\right]^{-1} \frac{\partial h^t}{dx} R^{-1}[\underline{z} - h(\underline{x})] \qquad .....(9.12)$$

The iterations are to be carried out until the calculated difference in states for successive iterations become less then a prespecified convergence tolerance. The inverse of the matrix in eq. (9.11) is calcualted only once.

Consider the measurements $\underline{z}$ and the non-linear state function h, separated into real and reactive parts.

$$\underline{h} = \left[\frac{P}{Q}\right] = \left[\frac{\text{Real measurements}}{\text{Reactive measurements}}\right]$$

Then,

$$\frac{\partial h}{\partial x}(\underline{x}) = \begin{bmatrix} \frac{\partial p}{\partial \delta} & \frac{\partial P}{\partial V} \\ \frac{\partial Q}{\partial \delta} & \frac{\partial Q}{\partial V} \end{bmatrix} \qquad .....(9.13)$$

The diagonal weighting matrix $[R^{-1}]$ can be separated into two parts

$$[R^{-1}] = \begin{bmatrix} R_p^{-1} & 0 \\ 0 & R_q^{-1} \end{bmatrix} \qquad .....(9.14)$$

$$J(\delta, v) = \begin{bmatrix} \frac{\partial P^t}{\partial \delta} R_P^{-1} \frac{\partial P}{\partial \delta} + \frac{\partial Q^t}{\partial \delta} R_Q^{-1} \frac{\partial Q}{\partial \delta} & \frac{\partial P^t}{\partial \delta} R_P^{-1} \frac{\partial f}{\partial v} + \frac{\partial Q^t}{\partial \delta} R_Q^{-1} \frac{\partial Q}{\partial V} \\ \frac{\partial P^t}{\partial v} R_P{}^{1} \frac{\partial P}{\partial \delta} + \frac{\partial Q^t}{\partial v} R_Q^{-1} \frac{\partial Q}{\partial \delta} & \frac{\partial Pt}{\partial v} R_P^{-1} \frac{\partial P}{\partial v} + \frac{\partial Q^t}{\partial v} R_Q^{-1} \frac{\partial Q}{\partial v} \end{bmatrix} \quad ...(9.15)$$

If we consider the phase angle differentials between directly connected buses as zero and all bus voltages as approximately 1.0 p.u, then the Jacobian becomes a constant matrix.

Generally the transmission line reactances are much larger than the resistance components. The shunt reactances from bus to ground are also large. The Jacobian can be simplified further into

$$J_{approx} = \begin{bmatrix} \frac{\partial P^t}{\partial \delta} R_P^{-1} \frac{\partial P}{\partial \delta} & 0 \\ 0 & \frac{\partial Q^t}{\partial v} R_Q^{-1} \frac{\partial Q}{\partial V} \end{bmatrix} \quad ..... (9.16)$$

This type of approximation is common in power flow studies, where the dependence of real power P on voltage magnitude and the dependence of reactive power Q on voltage phase angle are relatively negligible. Thus eq. (9.11) is of constant value. In this way a fast decoupled state estimator algorithm can be obtained. The new phase angles and voltages can be computed from

$$\delta^{(K+1)} = \delta^{(K)} + \left[\frac{\partial P^t}{\partial \delta} R_P^{-1} \frac{\partial P}{\partial \delta}\right]^{-1} \frac{\partial p^t}{\partial \delta} R_P^{-1} \left[P_m - P(x^{(k)})\right] \quad ..... (9.17)$$

$$V^{(K+1)} = V^{(K-1)} + \left[\frac{\partial Q^t}{\partial v} R_Q^{-1} \frac{\partial Q}{\partial v}\right]^{-1} \frac{\partial Q^t}{\partial v} R_Q^{-1} \left[Q_m - Q(x^{(k)})\right] \quad ..... (9.18)$$

The in-phase components of measurements are P_m and the reactive measurements are Q_m.

$$Z_m = \begin{bmatrix} P_m \\ Q_m \end{bmatrix} \quad .....(9.19)$$

Several methods are developed to calculate the state of the power network from measurements received. The various methods give different state estimators. But, basically they are all weighted least squares techniques. They find the best state vector to fit the data obtained. The data is subject to imperfect measurements of rapidly changing voltages or currents in the network. The network models may also contain errors. Within acceptable limits of error estimating the state vector is the important aspect in this task.

Linear Estimation Theory

In this case, the measured variables are assumed to be linear functions of the state variables. The measurement equation (9.1) is then written as

$$Z = AX + \eta \qquad .....(9.20)$$

where A is the m × n measurement matrix

Z is the m - dimensional vector of noise measurements comprising real and reactive powers, and voltage

X is the n-dimensional state vector and

n is the noise vector

It is desired to minimize

$$J = (Z - AX)^T R^{-1} (Z - AX) \qquad .....(9.21)$$

so that the optimal estimates $\hat{X}$ is obtained. In practice, three cases may arise.

Case 1 : m > n; the estimated equations are

$$\hat{X} = (A^T N^{-1} A)^{-1} (A^T N^{-1} Z) \qquad .....(9.22)$$

The estimate covariance matrix is

$$R_x = (A^T N^{-1} A)^{-1} \qquad .....(9.23)$$

The noise covariance matrix

$$N_x = E(\eta\eta^T) \qquad .....(9.24)$$

The number of basic arithmetic operations required for the computation of the optimum estimate area of the optimum estimate are of the order of mn'. The difficulty in this case is that the maximum $\mathbf{R_x}$ tends to be singular making inversion difficult.

Case 2 : m = n: The estimation equations are

$$X = A^{-1} Z \qquad .....(9.25)$$

$$R_x = (A^T N^{-1} A)^{-1} \qquad .....(9.26)$$

In this case, the computational problems are fewer since A is a square non singular matrix and $\mathbf{R_x}$ is determined from

$$R_x = A^{-1} N (A^T)^{-1}$$

Case 3 : m < n; while an estimate of η can be determined in principle, he estimate is neither unique nor does it have much relevance to state estimation in power systems.

9.11 Power System Security

The operating modes of a power system have already been discussed in Chapter 1. In the 'normal' mode, both the load and the operating constraints are satisfied and adequate spinning reserve is available. In the 'alert' state the load requirements are met with, but an adequate spinning reserve is not available. A system is in 'emergency' mode when the operating constraints are not completely satisfied. There may be two types of emergency modes. The system may be in 'steady state emergency' when the steady state operating constraints like bus voltage limits are violated. On the other hand, the system may reach 'dynamic emergency mode of operation when, for example, stability operating constraints are violated. In either case, the normal load requirements cannot be satisfied. In the 'restorative mode' control action is initiated, but the load constraints are not completely satisfied. Under this condition, the system may be in a completely or partially shut-down state.

The above classification of the states of the power system will facilitate in distinguishing between the different types of controls to be applied to the system. It can now be stated that the objective of system security control is to keep the power system in normal mode of operation and prevent it from entering into either emergency or restorative mode.

The system state is continuously assessed via data acquisition systems making use of telemetered data, redundant data and by predicting the missing or doubtful data whenever a metering channel becomes erroneous or its accuracy is beyond the normal specified range. This job is referred to as security monitoring.

During security assessment, a series of fast computations are made to examine the effect of various credible contingencies and those that are not so. If some of the assumed contingencies result in unsatisfactory performance from the point of view of security, a corrective strategy is called for, to determine the best corrective action either by special calculations within the computer or from results obtained from off-line studies.

Continuous monitoring for security and sending command signal for corrective action whenever necessary is referred to as security control.

Steady state security analysis is performed to determine whether there will be a new steady state operating point at which the system will settle after the post-fault oscillations have been damped out. The post contingency steady-state solution will have to be checked for violation of operational constraints. If it violates the constraints, the contingency is declared to be insecure and necessary corrective action is to be initiated.

Steady state security may be defined as the ability of the system to operate steady-state-wise within the specified limits of safety and supply, following a contingency in the time period, after the fast acting automatic Control devices have restored the system balance, but before the slow-acting controls like transformer tappings, human decisions, etc, have responded.

For steady state security analysis the following contingencies may be considered :

1. Loss of a generating unit
2. Sudden loss of a load,
3. Sudden change in flow in an inter-tie,
4. Outage of a transmission line,
5. Outage of a transformer, and
6. Outage of a shunt capacitor or reactor.

The outage may be either network outage or power outage. Fast and decoupled load flows are employed for security analysis of systems.

The purpose of contingency analysis of a power system is to alert the operator about the possibility of occuring a vulnerable condition of the system on a real time basis as load and generation change.

It determines the bus voltages that are excessively high or too low. It also calculates the power flows that are above the overload limits for generation and transmission lines.

Precalculated results of the analysis are to be used to take corrective actions such as shedding.

9.12 Steady State Security Assessment

The steady state security assessor is a computer program that uses real time data for analyzing the current state of the system for steady state security and is thus essentially an on-line process. For this, an approximate load flow algorithm is needed. Consider the input-output model given by

$$F(X, u, d) = 0 \qquad .....(9.27)$$

where X is the vector of dependent variables
u is the vector of control variables and
d is the vector of disturbance variables

For a given disturbance vector, it is required to determine the output X corresponding to a given input u as shown In Fig. 9.23.

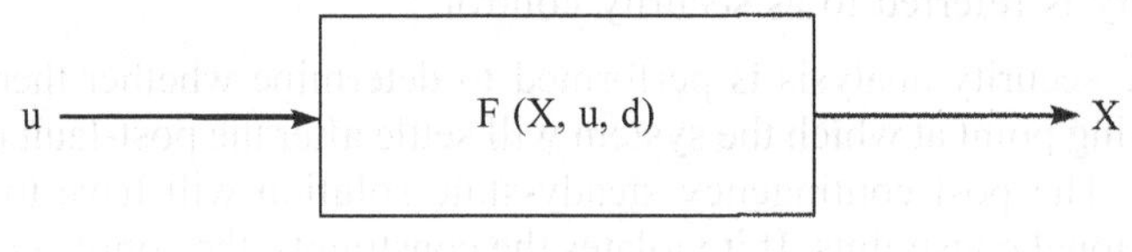

Fig. 9.23 System representation

Eqn. (9.14) and Fig. 9.17 correspond to 2n real nonlinear power equations for any n-bus system. There are 2n bus power injections (n-real power and n-reactive power) which may be denoted by the vector S. The network parameters are given by the bus admittance or bus impedance matrix, designated by P.

The steady state security assessment problem is concerned with the analysis of the system described by the vector triplet (X, S, P). Given a base triplet (X^0, s^0, P^0) along with contingency details,

$$P^i, i = 1, 2, ..., nw;$$
$$S^i, i = nw + 1, ... nw + p0$$

where nw is the number of network outages and po is the number of power outages, it is then required to determine the post-contingency states.

$$X_i, i = 1, 2, ..., (nw + po)$$

The steady state security assessor is a computer program that determines the post-contingency states. The program is also interlinked with several other programs at the computer control center.

9.13 Application to Outage Studies

Referring to the fast decoupled load flow algorithm given in chapter 2.

$$B' \Delta\delta = \frac{\Delta P}{|V|}$$

$$B'' \Delta\delta = \frac{\Delta Q}{|V|}$$

The above equations may be represented as

$$KY = C \qquad .....(9.28)$$

so that $$Y = K^{-1}C \qquad .....(9.29)$$

The outage of a line (neglecting charging capacitance) joining buses i and j can be reflected in K by modifying two elements in row i and two in row j. The new outage matrix can be presented as

$$K' = [K + BAA^T] \qquad .....(9.30)$$

where B is the line susceptance and

A is a column vector with $A_i = +1$ and $A_j = -1$ and zeroes in other locations.

It can be shown that

$$K'^{-1} = K^{-1} - hLA^T K^{-1} \qquad .....(9.31)$$

with $$h = [B^{-1} + A^T L]^{-1} \qquad .....(9.32)$$

and $$L = K^{-1}A \qquad .....(9.33)$$

The solution vector

$$Y^i = K'^{-1}C \qquad .....(9.34)$$

gives the post-outage state of the system.

Complete system security involves the following :

1. *System prediction :* This is done by computer programs that predict the system load conditions in advance for a predetermined time interval (say, an hour or day),
2. *System contingency evaluation :* This involves programs that determine the state of the system consequent to generation, line or transformer outages.
3. *System corrective strategy :* This is aimed at taking all possible decisions to keep the system in steady state secure condition. It also involves the necessary steps to be taken to overcome both unexpected and anticipated problems, either in the present state of operation or in future :
4. *Automatic control :* This eliminates the necessity of the operator taking initiative for all corrective actions.

9.14 Pattern Recognition Methods

System security can be evaluated through pattern recognition techniques also. The approach is quite different from conventional methods. Pattern recognition methods essentially involve the formation of a training set with pattern vectors, feature extraction and defining a security function.

Pattern Vector

Each operating condition of a power system is determined by real and reactive power generation, line flows, loads voltage and voltage magnitudes and phase angles. All these variables from measurements constitute the components of a pattern vector $X = (x_1, x_2 \ldots\ldots, x_n)$.

Training Set

Every conceivable operating condition of the system gives rise to a corresponding pattern vector. The set of all possible pattern vectors constitutes the training set.

Pattern Classification

Each of the patterns belonging to the training set are classified as either secure or insecure through off-line studies. Secure patterns contain all operating conditions that are secure while insecure ones contain such conditions in system operation that are insecure.

Feature Extraction

The actual number of variables used for representing an operating condition may be too many. But in practice, only a few of them may considerably influence the security of the pattern. It is desired to select a relatively small number of such variables called feature variables and the process of selection is called feature extraction. Feature extraction can be simplified by applying operational experience and engineering judgment in addition to any statistical criterion.

The feature vector is defined by

$$F = (f_1, f_2, \ldots\ldots\, f_m);\ m < n \qquad \ldots..(9.35)$$

All variables that are redundant may be removed from the pattern. Variables with high correlation coefficients may also be eliminated.

Security Function

A security function may be defined as a linear function of the feature variables,

$$S\,(F) = S_0 + S_1\, f_1 + S_2\, f_2 + \ldots.. + S_m\, f_m \qquad \ldots..(9.36)$$

The security function S (F) > 0 if F is secure and S (F) < 0 if F is insecure. Different methods are available to determine the constants $S_0, S_1, \ldots.. S_m$. For example, least squares method or optimal search method can be used successfully to determine the coefficients S_0, S_m. More sophisticated and mathematically complex functions may be defined in place of Eqn. (9.26).

After the security function is identified, its validity may be checked using patterns of known class.

Security Evaluation

Once a valid security function is determined, then any operating condition represented by the corresponding feature vector may be used, and from Eqn. (9.23) the operating state may be classified either as secure or insecure.

The success of the method depends on the proper selection of the feature variables and security function.

Pattern recognition methods may not have much relevance for steady state security evaluation. However, it appears that for transient security evaluation, pattern recognition techniques may provide the answer in future for situations where the fast acting automatic control devices have restored the system balance and the slow acting controls like transformer tappings, human decisions, etc. have not yet responded.

9.15 Power System Control Centres

Increase in unit sizes, growth of interconnections and the need to maintain the system in normal mode require sophisticated control, instrumentation and protection: The multiplicity of monitoring instruments in the control room and their distance apart make the observation of more than a few vital ones almost impossible, especially during the intense activity of plant start-up. The operators are called upon to visualize the implications of a variety of changing plant parameters and take critical decisions. These requirements led to the development and application of more advanced solid-state modular electronic instruments, computer based direct digital control and data processing systems.

A modern power system control centre has the following functions to perform :

1. Automatic generation control,
2. Economic load despatch
3. Automatic voltage (reactive power) control,
4. On-line load flow,
5. On-line short circuit.
6. State estimation,
7. Security monitoring,
8. Steady state security analysis,
9. Supervisory control,
10. Automatic trouble analysis,
11. Emergency control like load shedding, generator t ripping, and
12. Automatic circuit restoration, etc.

The computer system involves dual configuration with external interfaces to monitor the data. The first one is a process computer linked by telechannels to various generating and sub-stations for data acquisition. The second one is a larger one where major calculations are carried out and is linked to the process computer. For real-time computer control of power systems, the following basic components are needed:

1. System wide instrumentation,
2. High speed digital telemetry,
3. Central processing unit (CPU),
4. Memory and bulk storage,
5. Interactive display, and
6. Software (operating and application).

The real time computer is designed to perform data acquisition, storage and retrieval, data processing, interactive display and remote signaling and control. It consists of modems and interfaces, CPU, memory and bulk storage-and input-output devices like display devices, card reader, printer, etc. Fig. 9.23 shows a functional block diagram of a real-time computer.

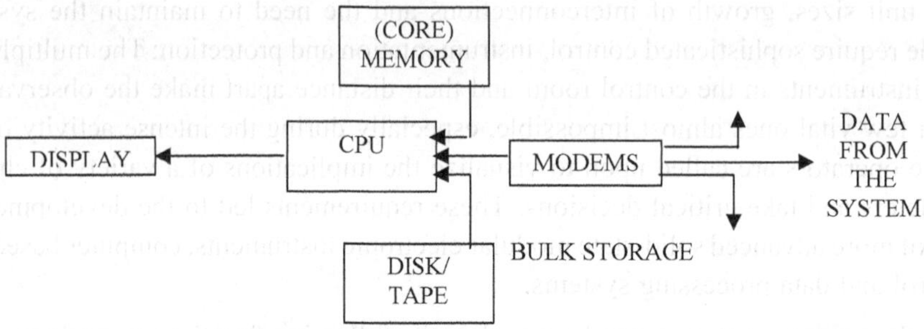

Fig. 9.23 Functional Block Diagram of a real time computer

The data base consists of static data, dynamic data and software. The static data consists of the details of lines, transformers, generators, etc. The dynamic data includes line flows, voltage levels, breaker condition, generation and demand. The software includes operating software, application software and support software.

The operating software is the system software for real time operation compiling routines, file management, etc. The application software consists of programs written for power system operation and control, which were listed earlier. The support software consists of diagnostics: debugging, maintenance and testing programs.

Computer control can take any of the following forms :

1. Off-line computer control,
2. computer-assisted control, and
3. on-line computer control.

For planning and operating computation, which are carried out at infrequent intervals, off-line computer calculations suffice. The results are to be updated at regular time intervals. ;

In the computer-assisted control scheme, necessary data is transmitted at regular intervals to the computer located in a central control station and its decisions are communicated to the human operator.

For short-time processes extending up to a few minutes, the system is under continuous control of direct acting devices. Under emergency conditions, the on-line computer which processes the data continuously sends commands to the direct acting devices according to a pre-planned strategy to prevent danger to the system.

The type of computer control, the configuration and the peripherals used are ultimately decided by the cost that the utility industry is willing to invest.

9.16 Level Decomposition in Power Systems

Power systems are characterized by strong hierarchical order. Accordingly, control strategy can be devised to fit into the hierarchical structure advantageously as indicated in table 9.1.

Table 9.1 Hierarchical Structure in Power System

Level	System	Monitoring and control
First Level	Generating stations and sub stations	Local control center
Second Level	Sub transmission and transmission networks	Area load dispatch center
Third level	Transmission system	State load dispatch center
Fourth level or top level	Interconnected power systems	Regional control centers

Local Control Centre

A number of control functions can be performed locally at power generating stations and sub-stations using local equipment and automatic devices.

Some of the typical control applications are :

1. Local monitoring and control,
2. Protection,
3. Auto reclosure,
4. Voltage regulation,
5. Capacitor switching,
6. Feeder synchronization;
7. Load shedding in the event of necessity, and
8. Network restoration.

Area Load Dispatch Centre

A group of generating stations and sub-stations, along with the associated network and loads may be considered as a unit for control under an area load dispatch centre. The area control centre receives information and processes it for appropriate control action.

State Load Dispatch Centre

The minute-to-minute operation of the power system at the state level may be carried out by the state load dispatch centre. It may have the following functions:

1. System generation and load monitoring and control,
2. System wide, state monitoring and control,
3. Circuit breaker state monitoring and control,
4. Load shedding and load restoration,
5. Supervisory control for lines and equipment states,
6. System alarm monitoring and corrective action, and
7. Planning and monitoring of system operations.

Regional Load Dispatch Centre

The regional load dispatch centre may be regarded as a coordinating and monitoring centre for state level dispatch centres with the following main objectives:

1. Integrated operation of state level dispatch centres,
2. Operation and maintenance schedules for the generating plant,
3. Operation and maintenance schedules for maximum capacity utilization,
4. Monitor and control inter-state power transactions, and
5. Monitor and control inter-regional power transactions.

9.17 NetworkAutomation

Network automation reduces the job of the human operator to some extent. It involves monitoring the process and remote control. Whatever may be the level of automation, all important emergency decisions are required to be taken by the human operator.

The input data for the network automation may be obtained from important load centres through microprocessor or computer-based remote terminal units. The remote terminal units may perform the following functions:

1. Obtain the system data in analog form,
2. Convert the analog data into digital form, and
3. Transmit the digital data to area load dispatch centre.

The data so transmitted will contain information like circuit breaker status, isolator position, etc. which will be indicated only when the condition changes as well as regularly sampled information about the network variables such as line flows (MW, Mvar), frequency (Hz), voltage levels (kV), currents (Amps), etc. The information processed will also include generator or transformer tripping, battery failure, etc. Also other functions that the remote terminal units may perform include limit or threshold value monitoring, fluid level processing, data logging, etc.

The data may be used for taking appropriate control action with the system of computer control planned.

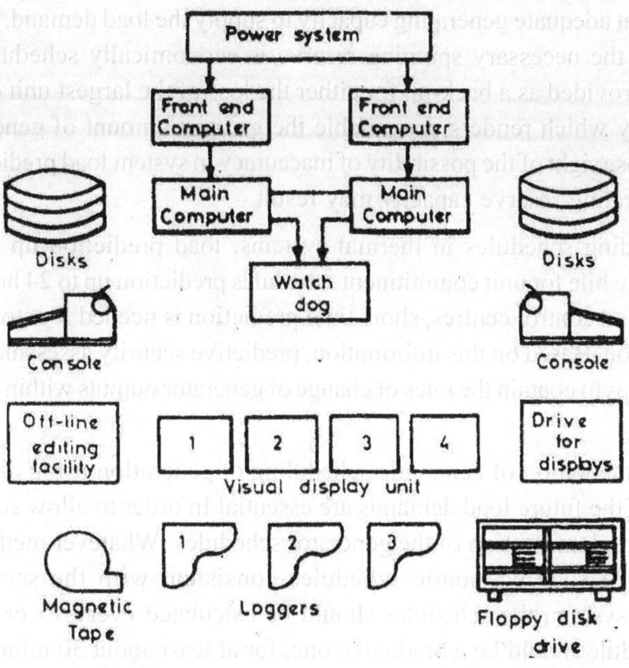

Fig. 9.24 Computer control in Power system

The data may be classified as real time, static and long term data. The real time data consists of measurands, alarms, etc and is stored in core memory. Static data consists of the background picture, text data files, etc. and is normally stored on a secondary, fast access memory.

Long term data may be stored on secondary, slow-access memory and consists of data for postmortem analysis, measurands, etc

The man-machine interface may consists of the following :

1. Alphanumeric – technological key boards.
2. Visual display units.
3. Mosaic boards
4. Digital displays
5. Loggers, and
6. Strip chart recorders

A typical computer control set up is shown in Fig. 9.19.

9.18 Load Prediction

Accurate prediction of load demand is required for service reliability and efficient operating performance of a power system. If the system is predominantly thermal, this is all the more important in order that adequate generating capacity to supply the load demand, maintain system security and supply the necessary spinning reserve is economically scheduled. In practice, spinning reserve is provided as a back-up for either the loss of the largest unit or for the loss of transmission capacity which renders unavailable the greatest amount of generating capacity. But, one should not lose sight of the possibility of inaccuracy in system load prediction consequent to which deficit operating reserve capacity may result.

For plant loading schedules in thermal systems, load prediction up to two hours in advance is necessary while for unit commitment schedules prediction up to 24 hours is sufficient. Also, at all stations and control centres, short-time prediction is needed for storage and display of advance information. Based on this information, predictive security assessment of the system is made. This also helps to contain the rates of change of generator outputs within their permissible limits.

For the implementation of economic scheduling of generation using digital computers, detailed estimates of the future load demands are essential In order to allow sufficient time for the calculation and implementation of the generator schedules. Whatever method is envisaged for the calculation of such economic schedules consistent with the security and spare requirements of the system, the schedules should be calculated every 15 or 30 minutes and each economic schedule should be a predictive one, for at least about 30 minutes ahead of the event. It is then obvious that the predictions are to be revised frequently in the light of any fresh information so as to minimize the estimation errors.

Peak load demand forecasts are useful in determining the investment required for additional generating and transmission capacities required. Forecasts for planning require data extending over several previous years. Meaningful forecasts can be obtained with lead time of 3 to 5 years.

Generally, load demand is assumed to have two salient features helpful in prediction. These are the long-term trend component dependent on economic growth, seasonal changes, etc. and the weather sensitive fluctuations in daily and hourly load demands.

Thus, the overall load demand has a predictable trend component superimposed on which is an erratic variation attributable to weather fluctuations. Summer, winter and monsoon periods will have definite patterns of load consumption. Also, the load demand varies during the day continuously, following a pattern with definite peaks at certain times of the day.

The weather sensitive component depends on the following meteorological factors :

1. Temperature,
2. cloudiness,
3. wind velocity,
4. visibility, and
5. precipitation.

9.19 Load Prediction using Matereological Data

Weather Weighting Method

In this method, the load is separated into two main components. The first component is a base load which is of fixed value and the second a variable component which is a function of the weather conditions.

Estimates can be made 24 hours ahead, using the weather, forecast. The temperature base for weighting the effect of the predicted temperature on the load is the normal, mean temperature of the month. The normal, mean temperature of the month has zero weight. Similarly the change in consumers demand due to cloudy weather may be assumed to vary in direct proportion to the degree of cloudiness. This in turn may be expressed by an illumination index with fair, clear sky corresponding to zero weight.

The base load is determined from past records, proper weighting of the elements of the weather will be attained only after several trials. The method of prediction stabilizes after this trial period. It may be noted that the base loads for week days and weekend will generally be different for any hour.

Using these base loads, a load estimate based on the best available weather forecast can be made using proper weighting of meteorological factors like temperature, cloudiness, wind, velocity; etc.

In thermal stations, a boiler may take about 3 hours of time to reach full operating condition from the cold. Thus, peak load estimates In systems with predominantly thermal generation are more critical, since they are required in time to bring any necessary generating capacity on-line. The feasibility of this method lies in the consistency of the calculations of the base load. The base loads are to be revised every year as load demand changes continuously.

Multiple Regression Methods

The meteorological information can be reduced to a number of specific factors like :

1. Temperature (T)
2. Cooling power of the wind(W),
3. Illumination index(L)
4. Rate of precipitation (P), etc

In deriving the functional relationship between the variation of demand and the specific metrological factors to which it is sensitive, it may be assumed that the weather –sensitive component of the demand may be expressed as the sum of functions of the respective meteorological factors.

Linear Regression Techniques

The first obvious approximation which can be made is to assume a linear functional relationship. It may be assumed that the basic demand curve is closely approximately by a step function with a step length of one week.

The data may be fitted into a regression equation of the form

$$Y = a + b_1 T + b_2 W + b_3 L + b_4 P + F(t) + d$$

where Y is the demand at a fixed time each day; T,W,L, P are the corresponding specific meteorological factors; a, b1, b2, b3, b4 are constants d is the day of the week correction and F(t) is a polynomial function of the ith week. The regression coefficients b1, b2, b3, b4 and d are to be estimated. In the above equation, more factors may be added or some may be removed, if necessary. In the linear regression technique the data points are fitted into a linear equation of the type.

$$Y = a_0 + a_1 X$$

where Y is the dependent and X the independent variable. In the least squares curve fitting method, we minimize the square of the deviation of the dependent variable from its actual or observed value.

Let $\quad Y_i = a_0 + a_1 X_i$

If n is the number of observations or data points

$$\sum_{i=1}^{n} Y_i = n\,a_0 + a_1 \sum_{i=1}^{n} X_i$$

Dividing throughout by n gives

$$\frac{\sum Y_i}{n} = a_0 + a_1 \frac{\sum X_i}{n}$$

since $\sum \frac{Y_i}{n}$ and $\sum \frac{X_i}{n}$ are the mean values of Y and X respectively $\overline{Y} = a_0 + a_1 \overline{X}$ and

$\overline{Y}$ and $\overline{X}$ are the average values.

$$y_i = Y_i - \overline{Y}$$

and $\quad x_i = X_i - \overline{X}$

Then, subtracting $\overline{Y}$ from the both sides of the basic equation

$$Y_i - Y = a_0 X_i - Y$$

$$= a_0 + a_1 X_i - a_0 - a_1 X_i$$

i.e. $\quad y_i = a_0 - a_0 + a_1 x_i = a_1 x_i$

i.e. a coordinate transformation is effected. The individual deviations become

$$|d_i| = |y_i - a_1 x_i|$$

and $\quad D = \sum_{i=1} d_i^2 = \sum (y_i - a_1 x_i)^2$

is the error term.

To minimize D we get the condition

$$\frac{dD}{da_1} = 0 = -2\sum x_1(y_i - a_1 x_i)$$

or $$\Sigma x_i y_i - a_1 \sum x_i^2 = 0$$

from which $$a \sum x_i^2 = \sum x_i y_i$$

i.e., $$a_1 = \frac{\sum x_i y_i}{\sum x_i^2} = \frac{\sum(X_i - \overline{X})(Y_i - \overline{Y})}{\sum(X_i - \overline{X})^2}$$

having found a_1, from the equation

$\overline{Y} = a_0 + a_1 \overline{X}$ we get a_0 as

$$a_0 = \overline{Y} - a_1 \overline{X}$$

Also $$a_1 = \frac{n\sum X_i Y_i - \sum X_i \sum Y_i}{n\sum X_i^2 - (\sum X_i)^2}$$

$$a_0 = \frac{\sum Y_i - a_1 \sum X_i}{n}$$

For the case where Y is a function of several sets of variables X_1, X_2, ..., X_k the multiple regression coefficients a_1, a_2, ... a_k can be derived.

Let $$\tilde{Y} = a_0 + a_1 X_1 + a_2 X_2 + ... + a_k Y_k$$

where $\tilde{Y}$ is the most probable value of Y.

then if, $$y = Y - \overline{Y}$$

$$x = X - \overline{X}$$

we have $\tilde{Y} = a_1 X_1 + a_2 X_2 + ... + a_k Y_k$ so that a_0 is eliminated.

Let $$D = (y - \tilde{y})^2$$

$$= \sum[y - (a_0 + a_1 X_1 + a_2 X_2 + ... + a_k x_k)]^2$$

If we differentiate this with reference to a_1, a_2, a_k

$$\frac{\partial D}{\partial a_1} = -2\sum x_1 (y - a_1 x_1 - a_2 x_2 - .... - a_k x_k) = 0$$

$$\frac{\partial D}{\partial a_2} = -2\sum x_2 (y - a_1 x_1 - a_2 x_2 - .... - a_k x_k) = 0$$

....

$$\frac{\partial D}{\partial a_{ak}} = -2\sum x_k (y - a_1 x_1 - a_2 x_2 - .... - a_k x_k) = 0$$

$$-\sum x_1 y + a_1\sum x_1^2 + a_2\sum x_1 x_2 + \dots\dots\dots + a_k\sum x_1 x_k = 0$$

$$-\sum x_2 y + a_1\sum x_1 x_2 + a_2\sum x_2^2 + \dots\dots\dots + a_k\sum x_1 x_k = 0$$

i.e.

$$\dots\dots\dots\dots\dots\dots\dots\dots\dots\dots\dots\dots$$

$$-\sum x_k y + a_1\sum x_1 x_k + a_2\sum x_2 x_k + \dots\dots\dots + a_k\sum x_k^2 = 0$$

Rewriting as

$$a_1\sum x_1^2 + a_2\sum x_1 x_2 + a_3\sum x_1 x_3 + \dots\dots\dots\dots + a_k\sum x_1 x_k = \sum x_1 y$$

$$a_1\sum x_1 x_2 + a_2\sum x_2^2 + a_3\sum x_2 x_3 + \dots\dots\dots\dots + a_k\sum x_2 x_k = \sum x_2 y$$

$$\dots\dots\dots\dots\dots\dots\dots\dots\dots\dots\dots\dots$$

$$a_1\sum x_1 x_k + a_2\sum x_2 x_k + a_3\sum x_3 x_k + \dots\dots\dots\dots + a_k\sum x_k^2 = \sum x_k y$$

or in matrix equation form

[X X] [A] = [X Y]

the matrix equation is to be solved for **A**.

Using the technique indicated above, the coefficients in eqn. (9.1) can be determined.

The terms of F(t) can be determined using the method of polynomials of least squares. It was found that a good fit to a year's data could be obtained by fitting polynomials up to the sixth degree.

Least Squares Polynomials

If we write

$$\tilde{Y} = a_0 + a_1 X + a_2 X^2 + a_3 X^3$$

for a cubic form, the individual deviations d_i can be expressed as

$$d_i = Y_i - a_0 - a_1 X_i - a_2 X_i^2 - a_3 X_i^3$$

and D the sum of the squared deviation is

$$D = \sum_{i=1}^{n} d_i^2 = \left(Y_i - a_0 - a_1 X_i - a_2 X_i^2 - a_3 X_i^3\right)^2$$

Minimizing with respect to a_0, a_1, a_2 and a_3

$$\frac{\partial D}{\partial a_0} = -2\sum\left(Y_i - a_0 - a_1 X_i - a_2 X_i^2 - a_3 X_i^3\right) = 0$$

$$\frac{\partial D}{\partial a_1} = -2\sum X_i\left(Y_i - a_0 - a_1 X_i - a_2 X_i^2 - a_3 X_i^3\right) = 0$$

$$\frac{\partial D}{\partial a_2} = -2\sum X_i^2\left(Y_i - a_0 - a_1 X_i - a_2 X_i^2 - a_3 X_i^3\right) = 0$$

$$\frac{\partial D}{\partial a_3} = -2\sum X_i^3\left(Y_i - a_0 - a_1 X_i - a_2 X_i^2 - a_3 X_i^3\right) = 0$$

which can be rewritten as

$$\sum Y_i = na_0 + a_1\sum X_i + a_2\sum X_i^2 + a_3\sum X_i^3$$

$$\sum X_i Y_i = a_0\sum X_i + a_1\sum X_i^2 + a_2\sum X_i^3 + a_3\sum X_i^4$$

$$\sum X_i^2 Y_i = a_0\sum X_i^2 + a_1\sum X_i^3 + a_2\sum X_i^4 + a_3\sum X_i^5$$

$$\sum X_i^3 Y_i = a_0\sum X_i^3 + a_1\sum X_i^4 + a_2\sum X_i^5 + a_3\sum X_i^6$$

In the matrix form

$$\begin{bmatrix} n & \sum X_i & \sum X_i^2 & \sum X_i^3 \\ \sum X_i & \sum X_i^2 & \sum X_i^3 & \sum X_i^4 \\ \sum X_i^2 & \sum X_i^3 & \sum X_i^4 & \sum X_i^5 \\ \sum X_i^3 & \sum X_i^4 & \sum X_i^5 & \sum X_i^6 \end{bmatrix} \begin{bmatrix} a_0 \\ a_1 \\ a_2 \\ a_3 \end{bmatrix} = \begin{bmatrix} \sum Y_i \\ \sum X_i Y_i \\ \sum X_i^2 Y_i \\ \sum X_i^3 Y_i \end{bmatrix}$$

from which the values of a_0, a_1, a_2 and a_3 can be calculated. Extending the equation to sixth order will yield a good fit for F(t) for an year's data.

Nonlinear Regression Methods

If the relationship between demand and the specific meteorological factors on which it depends are nonlinear, the linear functions introduced in the regression analysis earlier will give only average effects over the range covered by the data. We cannot assume any specific mathematical model for nonlinear functional relationship in advance, since its nature is not known in advance. We can write

$$S = f_1(T) + f_2(W) + f_3(L) + f_4(P) + F(t) + d$$

Where the constant a has been included in the basic demand curve F(t). As a first approximation, the form of the unspecified functional relationships $f_1(T)$, $f_2(W)$, $f_3(L)$, $f_4(P)$ can be taken as straight lines whose slopes have the values of the corresponding linear regression coefficients. First, all the weather sensitive components are completely removed.

$$F(t) + d = x - f_1(T) - f_2(W) - f_3(L) - f_4(P)$$

Plotting a graph of the above relations, we can make an estimate of F(t) +d. Grouping these estimates according to the day of the week and noting the difference between their respective means and the grand mean, approximation to the day – of the week adjustments are to be made. Then F(t) is known, giving the basic demand curve.

From this initial estimate and the data of the meteorological variables T, W etc. the linear approximations are successively replaced by curvilinear relationships and the process is carried on until no further improvement is obtained. For a daily load estimation, the basic demand for the following day can be read from the final graph of F(t) and to this can be added the day-of-the week correction. A further weather correction can be made by applying the weight determined from the meteorological response curves using the best available weather forecasts.

9.20 Spectral Expansion Method

In this method, only past load data is required. It is well – known that the pattern of load demand tends to repeat every 24 hours. The load demand curves may be divided into given ensemble of time series. The problem then becomes one of predicting a non-stationary process given by an ensemble of sample functions.

Consider the load curve for any working day, divided into three 8 hour periods or four 6 hour periods. These parts may be made to have an overlap of, say, 2 hours for continuity in prediction. Then the load on the mth working day at the nth instant of time can be denoted by P_{mn}. For example, we can have six part load curves for the time period of, say, 12 noon to 6 pm for the six working days of a week, this forms an ensemble of six functions. For Sundays a similar ensemble can be constructed. It is possible to represent the load by the relation.

$$\begin{aligned} P_{mn} &= A_{mn} + f_1(T_m)\, B_{mn} \\ &+ f_2(L_m)\, C_{mn} \\ &+ f_3(W_m)\, D_{mn} + \ldots\ldots \end{aligned} \qquad \ldots..(9.37)$$

Where $f_1(T_m)$, $f_2(L_m)$, $f_3(W_m)$ are functions of temperature T_m, illumination L_m, and wind velocity W_m respectively. B_{mn}, C_{mn} and D_{mn} are coefficients used to given weightage to the weather parameters depending on the time of the day. A_{mn} is the base load. The sample functions P_{mn} are thus assumed to belong to a linear manifold generated by the weighting functions of their linear combinations.

As a preliminary step, it is required that from the load all trend components are eliminated. Finally, the residual component can be expanded into time series using spectral theory of stochastic processes.

Equation (9.32) may be rewritten as

$$P_{mn}(t) = P_W(t) + P_d(t) + p_{mn}(t) \qquad \ldots..(9.38)$$

where $P_W(t)$ and $P_d(t)$ represent the trend components of weekly and daily patterns of load demand. $p_{mn}(t)$ is the residual load component. The component $P_W(t)$ is given by

$$P_W(t) = \frac{1}{n_d}\sum_{n=1}^{n_d} P_{mn}(t) \qquad \ldots..(9.39)$$

where n_d is the number of days in a week.

$P_d(t)$ is computed from

$$P_d(t) = \frac{1}{n_w}\sum_{n=1}^{n_w} P_{mn}(t) - P_W(t) \qquad \ldots..(9.40)$$

where n_w is the number of weeks for which data is available. The residual component

Pmn(t) can be expressed as a time series. If N is the total number of days for which data is available, the auto correlation function for the residual component is given by

$$R(t,\tau) = \frac{1}{N}\sum_{i=1}^{N} y_i(t) y_i(\tau) \qquad .....(9.41)$$

A characteristic function $f_k(t)$ is defined by the integral equation

$$\int_0^T R(t,\tau) f_k(\tau) d\tau = b_k f_k(\tau) \qquad .....(9.42)$$

where T is the total time period over which the prediction is valid.

The residual load component is then expressed as

$$P_{mn}(t) = \sum_{k=1}^{K} a_k b_k^{\frac{1}{2}} f_k(t) + e(t)$$

The coefficients a_k can be determined for the best fit using any standard criterion. The coefficients b_k are determined by eqn. (9.32) and e(t) is the error term.

The number of terms in the time series, K, can be determined using the minimum, mean - square error criterion given by

$$e^2(t) = R(t.\tau) - b_k f_k(t)$$

where e(t) is the average error.

9.21 Prediction by Scaling a Standard Load

In this method, a particular day is taken as reference and the load curve for the reference day is taken as standard. The load on the day of prediction is compared with the standard load curve. Each measured load of the day is divided by the corresponding value of the load on the standard load curve at that instant.

Consider the load curve for the previous hours. Let this be divided into four quarter – hourly periods. The load for the next one hour can be predicted as exponentially weighed average of the previous four ratios. The ratio at the (n + k)th instant is estimated from the relation

$$r_{(n+k)} = \frac{1-x}{1-x^4} \sum_{m=0}^{3} r_{n-m} x^n \qquad .....(9.43)$$

where x is a weighting parameter determined empirically, the value of which varies between zero and unity. The predicted load can be obtained by multiplying the predicted ratio $r_{(n+k)}$ by the corresponding value of the load on the standard load curve.

9.22 Short – Term Load Forecasting Using Exponential Smoothing

From the available data, the seasonal and weekly variations are removed. The remaining load may be represented as a linear combination of known functions of time and noise component.

$$\mathbf{P(t) = A^T\ F(t) + n(t)} \qquad .....(9.44)$$

The elements **A** are to be assumed constant during the period of forecasting even though they change slowly. Using known fitting functions **F**(t) and current coefficients **A**(T). forecasted loads can be computed by extrapolating equation

$$\mathbf{P(t + \tau) = A^T(T)\ F(t + t)} \qquad .....(9.45)$$

Where **P(t + τ)** is the forecast with the lead time t. The elements of **A(T)** can be computed using weighted least squires criterion. For this, the expression

$$\mathbf{J = \sum_{j=0}^{\infty} \beta^j \left[P(T-j) - A^T(T).F(T-j)\right]^2}$$

is minimized. The constant β has value between zero and unity.

As an example, the time function may be a Fourier series given by

$$\mathbf{P(t) = A +} \sum_{i=1}^{m} a_i \sin \omega_i t + b_i \sin \omega_i t$$

If the time period is taken as one week then.

$$\omega_i = \frac{2\pi}{(7)(24)} N_i$$

where N is a positive integer. The selection of the actual number of frequencies is dependent on the auto – correlation function and power spectrum for the observed hourly data. The coefficients "a_i", "b_i" and A_0 are to be revised each hour

9.23 Peak Power Demand Prediction

The fluctuating values of peak power demand may be assumed to be controlled by probabilistic laws in time. The monthly peak demand series, for example, contains three additive components, the trend P_T, seasonal P_s and noise P_N.

Thus the peak demand is given by

$$P_{M0}\ (T) = P_T\ (t) + P_S\ (t) + P_N\ (t)$$

The trend component shows a continuous change in the demand, normally an increase. The seasonal component consists of periodic variations, the pattern of which increases in amplitude year-by-year. Using the stochastic theory of stationary and nonstationary processes, the peak demand can be predicted.

9.24 State Estimation in Load Forecasting

Real time control of power systems requires accurate short term forecasting of load demand. State estimation in forecasting will be quite useful for such a purpose.

The model for forecasting demands upon the lead time. For a very short lead time, less than 10 minutes or so, the system load and the observations may be represented by

$$P(t + \Delta t) = P(t) + n(t)$$

$$Z(t) = P(t) + K(t) \qquad .....(9.46)$$

Where P(t) is the load at the instant t

n is the system noise

Z(t) is the observation at the instant t

and k(t) is the observation noise.

For short term load forecasting, with lead times of about ten minutes to an hour, the load may contain an increment $\Delta P(t)$. The weather conditions may not play any role, since in such a short time they may not vary so much as to change the consumption pattern.

The model could be represented in this case by

$$P(t + \Delta t) = P(t) + \Delta P(t) + n_1(t)$$

$$\Delta P(t + \Delta t) = P(t) + n_2(t) \qquad .....(9.47)$$

$$Z(t) = P(t) + K(t)$$

The expected or average values of the noises is zero.

$$E[n(t)] = E[n_1(t)] = E[n_2(t)] = E[K(t)] = 0$$

Further $\quad E[n(t)\,K(t)] = 0 \qquad .....(9.48)$

Rewriting eqn. (9.37) for the forecasted model $\hat{P}$

$$\hat{P}(t+\Delta t) = \hat{P}(t) + K(t)[Z(t+\Delta t) - \hat{P}(t) \qquad .....(9.49)$$

where $0 < K(t) < 1$

The value of K that minimizes the variance of forecasting error is

$$K(t + \Delta t) = R(t)\,K(t) + Q(t) \qquad .....(9.50)$$

Where R(t) and Q(t) are the variance of observation noise and system noise respectively.

The forecasted load demand is

$$\hat{P}(t+\Delta t) = \hat{P}(t) + K(t+\Delta t)[Z(t+\Delta t) - \hat{P}(t) \qquad .....(9.51)$$

for the short term model

$$\ddot{P}(t+\Delta t) = [1 - K(t+\Delta t)][\dot{P}(t)] + K(t+\Delta t)Z(t+\Delta t) \qquad .....(9.52)$$

the procedure is basically not different from the exponential smoothing method, but the correcting gain **K** can be sequentially evaluated if the noise variances are known in advance.

9.25 Generating Capacity Reliability and Outage Probabilities

The availability of enough generating capacity to meet the load demand is the foremost priority at the planning level that ensures satisfactory operation of the power system. The application of probability methods enables quantitative prediction of the system reliability. The results obtained by probability techniques will only provide a criterion for evaluation of the situation rather than give a guarantied result.

Rules for combination of event probabilities

All events such that occurrence of any one event is not influenced by the occurrence of any other event, are called independent events. The probability of occurrence of any two independent events is given by the product of the probabilities of occurrence of each event separately.

On the other hand, if two events cannot happen both at the same time, then they are said to be mutually exclusive. The probability of occurrence of mutually exclusive events is given by the sum of the probabilities of the occurrence of each event in the mutually exclusive event group.

Binomial distribution may be used to calculate the probabilities for power generation reserve capacity calculations. For any event, if s is the probability of success and f is the probability of failure, then for n trials

$$(s+f)^n = \sum_{r=0}^{n} nC_r\, S_r\, f^{n-r}$$

The binomial coefficients can be determined from Pascal's triangle

```
        1
      1 2 1
    1 3   3 1      etc.
  1 4   6   4 1
```

Application to Power Plant Capacity Calculations

Consider a power station with two units each of 60MW. Let the forced outage rate or the probability of any set being out of service be 0.05. Then the availability rate or the probability of the set being in service is obtained as (1-0.05) = 0.95. For the plant under consideration three states of operation may be listed :

1. Both the units are in services
2. only one unit is in service, and
3. both the units are out of service

The probability for the existence of each of the above states can be computed using the binomial expansion with n = 2. The results are shown in Table 9.2

Table 9.2 Two – unit System Outage Probabilities

State	Capacity Outage MW	Capacity Available MW	Probability
1	0	120	(0.95)(0.95) = 0.9029
2	60	60	2(0.95)(0.05) = 0.0950
3	120	0	(0.05)(0.05) = 0.0025
		Total	**1.0000**

It may be noted that the probabilities are computed from the relation

$$(s + f)^2 = s^2 + 2sf + f^2$$

In a similar manner, the probability of occurrence of various outages for a 3-unit power plant can be computed. Consider a power station with three identical units, each of capacity 110MW. The forced outage rate for each unit is 0.03. the availability rate, therefore, for each units is 0.97. The probability of occurrence of various states in operation are computed and listed in Table 9.3

Table 9.3 Three – Unit System Outage Probabilities

State	Capacity Outage MW	Capacity Available MW	Probability
1	0	120	(0.95)(0.95) = 0.9029
1	0	330	$(0.97)^3 = 0.912673$
2	110	220	$3(0.97)^2 (0.03) = 0.084681$
3	220	110	$3(0.97)^2 (0.03)^2 = 0.002619$
4	330	0	(0.03)3 = 0.000027
		Total	**1.000000**

The probabilities are computed from the relation

$$(s+f)^3 = s^3 + 3s^2f + 3sf^2 + f^3$$

Finally, taking the example of a 4-unit power plant, each with a rating of 65Mw and forced outage rate of 0.04, the probabilities of occurrence of the five possible states of operation are listed in Table 9.4.

$$(s+f)^4 = s^4 + 4s^3f + 6s^2f^2 + 4sf^3 + f^4$$

outage probabilities for dissimilar units in a plant or system with different forced outage rates can be calculated extending the basic principle further.

Consider a power system with two similar units, each of 60MW capacity and another generating unit and another generating unit of 110Mw. The forced outage rate for the 60Mw unit is 0.03, while the same for the 110MW unit is 0.1.

Table 9.4 Four unit System Outage Probabilities

State	Capacity Outage MW	Capacity Available MW	Probability
1	0	260	$(0.96)^4 = 0.84934000$
2	65	195	$4(0.96)^3(0.04) = 0.14155000$
3	130	130	$6(0.96)^2(0.04)^2 = 0.00884730$
4	195	65	$4(0.96)\,(0.04)^3 = 0.00024576$
5	260	0	(0.04)4 = 0.00000250
		Total	1.00000000

To begin with, the probabilities are computed separately as before. These are shown in Table 9.5

Table 9.5 Outage probabilities for different type of units

Two – 60 MW sets		One – 110MW	
Capacity out Mw	Probability	Capacity out MW	Probability
0	$(0.97)^2 = 0.9409$	0	0,90
60	2(0.97)(0.03) = 0.0582	110	0,10
120	$(0.03)^2 = 0.0009$		
Total	1.0000	Total	1,00

The results of both the calculations are combined now to find the outage probabilities for the combined system (Table 9.6)

Table 9.6 Outage Probabilities for System with Dissimilar Units

Capacity out MW	Probability
0	(0.9409) (0.9 = 0.846810
60	(0.0582) (0.9) = 0.523800
110	(0.1) (0.9409) = 0.940900
120	(0.0009) (0.9) = 0.000081
170	(0.0582) (0.1) = 0.005820
230	(0.0009) (0.1) = 0.000090
Total	1.000000

Loss of load probability

Loss of load probability can be obtained by combining the system load duration curve with the capacity outage probability. It may be pointed that capacity outage may not necessarily result in loss of load. This will be demonstrated in the example that follows.

It can be seen from Fig. 9.25 that any capacity outage less than the reserve capacity will not result in loss of load.

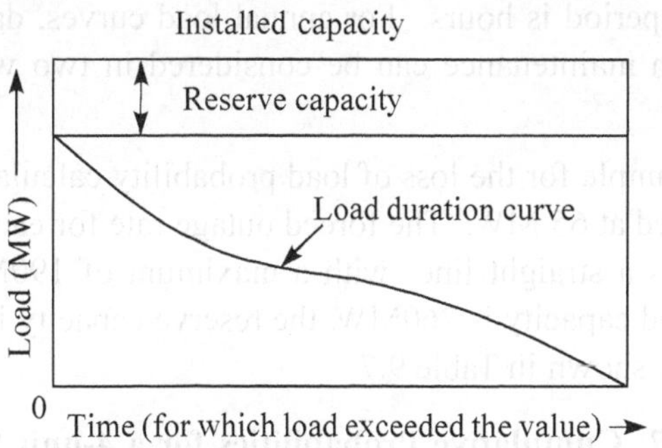

Fig. 9.25 Application of probability to loss of load

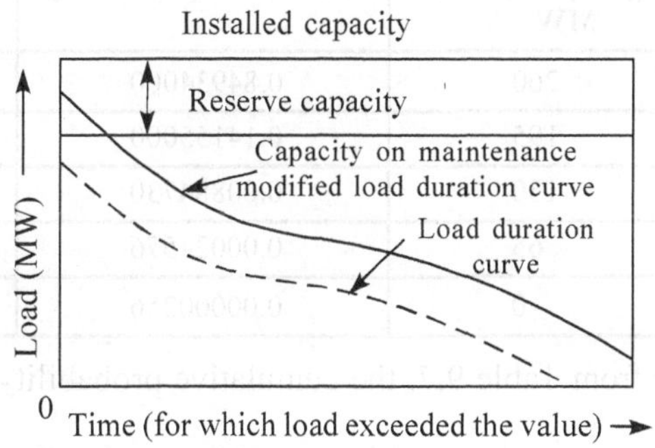

Fig. 9.26 Modified model of capacity on maintenance

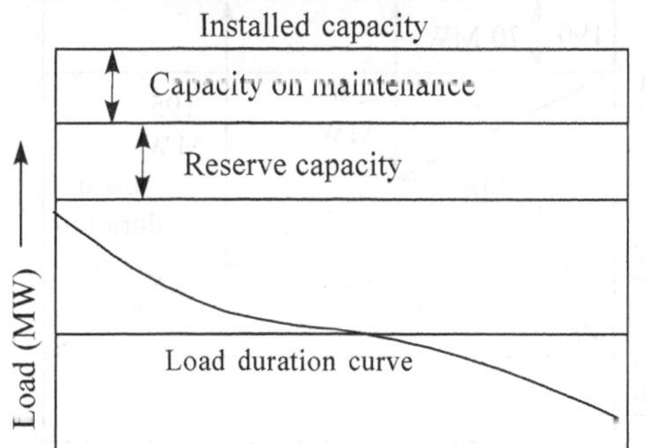

Fig. 9.27 Alternative model for capacity on maintenance

If P_k is the probability of the outage L_k and t_k is the period of time units for which the outage causes loss of load. The total expected loss of load for the time period is

$$E(t) = \sum_{k=1}^{n} P_k t_k \quad \text{time units}$$

All outages in excess of the reserve capacity will result in loss of load for different time periods and each outage P_k contributes a system load loss of $P_k t_k$ time units. For a daily load duration, curve, the time period is hours. For annual load curves, daily peaks may be used. The effect of capacity on maintenance can be considered in two ways. This is shown in Fig. 9.20 & 9.21.

Consider, as an example for the loss of load probability calculation, a system with four generating units, each rated at 65 MW. The forced outage rate for each generator unit is 0.04. the load duration curve is a straight line with a maximum of 190MW and a minimum of 40MW. Since the installed capacity is 260MW, the reserve capacity is 260-190=70MW. The outage probability table is shown in Table 9.7

Table 9.7 Cumulative Probabilities for a 4-unit System

State	Capacity MW	Capacity available MW	Individual probability	Cumulative probability
1	0	260	0.84934000	1.00000000
2	65	195	0.14155000	0.15064000
3	130	130	0.00884730	0.00909560
4	195	65	0.00024576	0.00024830
5	260	0	0.00000256	0.00000256

As may be noted from Table 9.7, the cumulative probability decreases as the capacity outage increases.

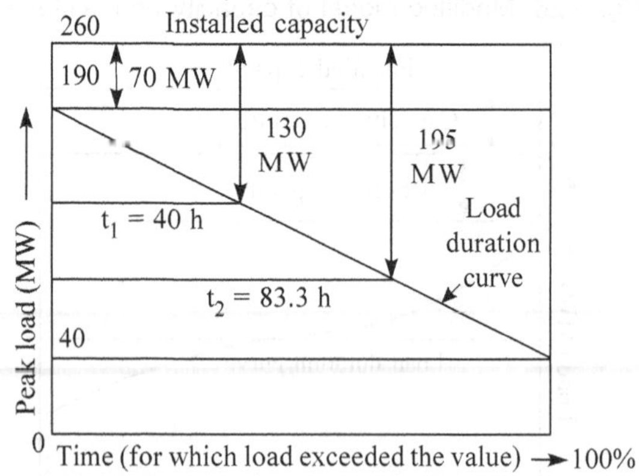

Fig. 9.28 Loss of load with time

Since the reserve capacity is 70MW, state 2 does not involve any loss of load. State 3 results in a loss of load for a period of 40% of time and state 4 has loss of load for 83.3% of time. This is shown in Fig. 9.22. The expected load calculations are shown in Table 9.8.

Table 9.8 Expected Load Loss calculations

State	Capacity MW	Capacity available MW	Individual probability	Time t_k in per cent	Cumulative probability
1.	0	260	0.84934000	0	—
2.	65	195	0.14155000	0	—
3.	130	130	0.00884730	40	0.353890
4.	195	65	0.00024576	83.3	0.020466
				Total	**0.374350**

If the load duration curve has a time period of about 261 days excluding 52 weekends (Sundays and Saturdays) from 365 days, then the expected load loss is

$$\frac{(0.37435)(261)}{100} = 0.97705 \text{ days}$$

the maintenance of the desired level of reliability on the operation of the system is dependent o the spinning capacity reserve. In the case of static reserve capacity, the available generation is the entire installation capacity; while for a spinning reserve capacity, it is generally assumed that there is sufficient installed capacity available and only the time delay in bringing in a replacement is considered. Thus, in spinning reserve capacity calculations, outage replacement rate is used in place of forced outage rate for probability evaluation. The outage replacement rate is defined as the product of unit failure rate and delay time for replacement unit. However, this is valid only if the outage replacement rate is much less than unity.

Questions

1. What are FACTS controllers? Explain
2. What are the various types of FACTS devices? Explain their working principle briefly
3. Explain the working of a dynamic voltage restorer
4. What is state estimation. What is the significance of it in power systems operation
5. Explain the various methods of load prediction
6. Why load prediction is necessary in power system operation? Explain
7. Explain the term voltage stability. How can it be over come? Discuss
8. What do you understand by the term "power quality"? Explain
9. Discuss the various factors involved in power quality problem
10. Explain any method for the computation of loss of load probability.
11. How reliability studies are important in power system operation? Explain.
12. Explain "Security" in relation to power system operation.
13. What is contingency evaluation is connection with power system security.
14. What are energy control centers? Explain.

Objective Questions

1. Consider a power system with three identical generators. The transmission losses are negligible. One generator (GI) has a speed governor which maintains its speed constant at the rated value, while the other generators (G2 and G3) have governors with a droop of 5%. If the load of the system is increased, then in steady state [ ]

   (a) generation of G2 & G3 is increased equally while generation of G1 is unchanged.

   (b) generation of G1 alone is increased while generation of G2 & G3 is unchanged

   (c) generation of G1, G2 and G3 is increased equally

   (d) generation of G1, G2 and G3 is increased in the ratio 0.5:0.25:0.25

2. Gausss – Seidel iterative method can be used for solving a set of

   (a) linear differential equations only

   (b) linear algebraic equations only

   (c) both linear and nonlinear algebraic equations

   (d) both linear and nonlinear differential equations

3. A power station consists of two synchronous generators A and B of ratings 250 MVA and 500 MVA with inertia 1.6 p.u. and 1 p.u., respectively on their own base MVA ratings. The equivalent p.u. inertia constant for the system on 100 MVA common base is

   (a) 2.6 (b) 0.615 (c) 1.625 (d) 9.0 [ ]

4. The incremental cost characteristics of two generators delivering 200MW are as follows

   $$\frac{dF_1}{dP_1} = 2.0 + 0.01P_1 \qquad \frac{dF_2}{dP_2} = 1.6 + 0.2P_2$$ [ ]

   For economic operation, the generations P_1 and P_2 should be:

   (a) $P_1 = P_2 = 100$ Mw (b) $P_1 = 80$MW, $P_2 = 120$Mw

   (c) $P_1 = 200$MW, $P_2 = 0$Mw (d) $P_1 = 120$MW, $P_2 = 80$Mw

5. A power system has two synchronous generators. The Governer - turbine characteristics corresponding to the generators are

$$P_1 = 50(50 - f),\ P_2 = 100(51 - f)$$

Where f denotes the system frequency in Hz, and P_1 and P_2 are respectively, the power outputs (in MW) of turbines 1 and 2. Assuming the generators and transmission network to be lossless, the system frequency for a total load of 400MW is [ ]

(a) 47.5Hz (b) 48.0Hz (c) 48.5Hz (d) 49.0Hz

6. The bus impedance matrix of a 4-bus power system is given by

$$Z_{BUS} = \begin{bmatrix} j0.3435 & j0.2860 & j0.2723 & j0.2277 \\ j0.2860 & j0.3408 & j0.2586 & j0.2414 \\ j0.2723 & j0.2586 & j0.2791 & j0.2209 \\ j0.2277 & j0.2414 & j0.2209 & j0.2791 \end{bmatrix}$$

A branch having an impedance of j0.2 ohm is connected between bus 1 and the reference. Then the values of $Z_{22,new}$ and $Z_{23,new}$ of the bus impedance matrix of the modified network are respectively [ ]

(a) j0.5408 ohm and j0.4586 ohm (b) j0.1260 ohm and j0.0956 ohm
(c) j0.5408 ohm and j0.0956 ohm (d) j0.1260 ohm and j0.1630 ohm

7. A power system consists of 300 buses out of which 20 buses are generator buses, 25 buses are the ones with reactive power support and 15 buses are the ones with fixed shunt capacitors. All the other buses are load buses. It is proposed to perform a load flow analysis for the system using Newton – Raphson method. The size of the Newton – Raphson Jacobian matrix is [ ]

(a) 553 × 553 (b) 540 × 540 (c) 555 × 555 (d) 554 × 554

8. If a generator of 250 MVA rating has an inertia constant of 6MJ/MVA, its inertia constant on 100MVA base is [ ]

(a) 15MJ/MVA (b) 10.5MJ/MVA (c) 6MJ/MVA (d) 2.4MJ/MVA

9. In load – flow analysis, the load at a bus is represented as [ ]

(a) a constant current drawn from the bus

(b) a constant impedance connected at the bus

(c) constant real and reactive powers drawn from the bus

(d) a voltage – dependent impedance at the bus

10. A transmission line has equal voltages at the two ends, maintained constant by two sources. A third source is to be provided to maintain constant voltage (equal to end voltages) at either the midpoint of the line or at 75% of the distance from the sending end. Then the maximum power transfer capabilities of the line in the original case and the other two cases respectively will be in the following ration. [ ]

(a) 1 : 1 : 1 (b) 1 : 2 : 1/0.75 (c) 1 : 2 : 4 (d) 1 : 4 : 16

11. The inertia constant of a 100MVA, 50Hz, 4-pole generator is 10MJ/MVA. If the mechanical input to the machine is suddenly raised from 50MW to 75MW, the rotor acceleration will be equal to [ ]

(a) 400kV (b) 260kV (c) 80kV (d) 40kV

12. Economic scheduling of generation is performed for a period of [ ]

(a) ½ hr (b) 24 hr (c) 1 sec (d) 1 week

13. The input – output characteristic is plotted [ ]

(a) Fuel input Vs power output (b) Fuel input Vs time

(c) Fuel rate Vs power output (d) Fuel rate Vs energy output

14. Hear rate curve is plotted in [ ]

(a) k-cal/kwhr Vs KW (b) K-cal/hr Vs KW

(c) k-cal/KW Vs Kw (d) K-cal Vs KW

15. Incremental production cost and incremental fuel cost are [ ]

(a) both the same (b) IPC > IFC

(c) IPC < IFC (d) They are not related

16. The incremental transmission loss for a 2-plant system is given by [ ]

(a) $B_{11}\ P_1^2 + B_{12}\ P_2^2 + 2B_{12} P_1 P_2$ (b) $B_{11}P_1 + B_{12}P_1 P_2$

(c) $2B_{22}\ P_2 + 2B_{12} P_2$ (d) $\begin{bmatrix} 2B_{11}P_1 + 2B_{12}P_2 \\ 2B_{22}P_2 + 2B_{12}P_1 \end{bmatrix}$

17. Consider the following constraints

(i) $P_G - P_D - P = 0$ (ii) $Q_G - Q_D - Q = 0$

(iii) $P^2 + Q^2 \leq (S^{rated})^2$ (iv) $P^{min} \leq P \leq P^{max}$

The equality constraints are [ ]

(a) (i) only (b) (i) (ii) and (iii) (c) (i), (iii) and (iv) (d) (i) and (ii)

18. Penalty factor is given by [ ]

(a) $\frac{dF}{dP_i}\left(1+\frac{\partial P_L}{\partial P_i}\right)$ (b) $\frac{dF}{dP_i}\left(1-\frac{\partial P_L}{\partial P_i}\right)$ (c) $\frac{1}{\left(1+\frac{\partial P_L}{\partial P_i}\right)}$ (d) $\frac{1}{\left(1-\frac{\partial P_L}{\partial P_i}\right)}$

19. If R = 0.04 Hz/Mw by how much will the turbine power decrease, if frequency rises by 0.1HZ [ ]

(a) 0.024Mw (b) 1/0.024MW (c) 0.0024Mw (d) 4.17MW

20. What is the load damping factor D for an area operated at 1000Mw, 50Hz [ ]

(a) 100 (b) 50 (c) 25 (d) 20

21. If the power system has a transfer function $\frac{K_P}{1+ST_P}$ and given that the load damping D = 25MW/Hz. What is the value of K_p [ ]

(a) 0.04Hz/MW (b) 0.4Hz/MW (c) 0.25Hz/MW (d) 25Hz/MW

22. Area frequency response characteristic is [ ]

(a) $D+\frac{1}{R}$ (b) $R+\frac{1}{D}$ (c) $\frac{D}{R}$ (d) $-\frac{D}{R}$

23. A speed governing system has D = 20MW/Hz. What is the frequency drop for 1% load increase if the area is rated for 2000MW [ ]

(a) 1 Hz (b) 1.5 Hz (c) 0.5 Hz (d) 0.2Hz

24. Steady state frequency error in a single control area can be eliminated by [ ]

(a) proportional control (b) derivative control
(c) integral control (d) proportional plus derivative control

25. In a single uncontrolled area, area control error is defined by [ ]

(a) $\int \Delta dt$ (b) $\frac{d}{dt}\Delta f$ (c) Δf (d) $-\frac{1}{R}\Delta f$

26. When integral control is applied, if the control gain K_r is greater than critical gain, the response is [ ]

(a) over damped (b) damped oscillatory
(c) un damped oscillatory (d) unstable operation

27. Which of the following statements is correct ? [ ]

(a) primary load frequency control is performed by integral control

(b) secondary load frequency control is performed by integral control

(c) speed governor action always keeps the speed constant with load changes

(d) economic load scheduling is always required to be performed before load frequency control

28. Turbine generator dynamics and speed governor actions affect the performance of the frequency response with load [ ]

(a) seriously

(b) only negligible action at $t = 0^+$

(c) may cause trouble if governor is fast in action

(d) may cause trouble if the rating of the turbine is very high

29. The time constant of the power system T_P is defined by [ ]

(a) $T_P = \dfrac{2H}{f^0 D}$ (b) $T_P = \dfrac{2f^0}{HD}$ (c) $T_P = \dfrac{2D}{f^0 H}$ (d) $\dfrac{f^0}{2HD}$

30. Which of the following correct ? [ ]

(a) load frequency control has serious affect on voltage profile

(b) if a generator is connected to an infinite bus the frequency change with load is negligible

(c) turbine power increment for load change does not depend upon the response characteristic of the turbine

(d) all the generating stations in any country can be treated as belonging to a single control area

31. Given $f^0 = 50$Hz, D = 20Mw/Hz, area rated power = 2000Mw and H = 5 sec the area time constant T_P is [ ]

(a) 5 sec (b) 10 sec (c) 15 sec (d) 20 sec

32. Unit commitment is [ ]

(a) Economic schedule among different units

(b) Planning of generating units for future load increase

(c) Optimal combination of units for operation at any one time

(d) To choose proper units from thermal, hydro and nuclear plants

33. Which of the following is valid constraint for unit commitment [ ]

(a) $V_i^{min} \le V_i \le V_i^{max}$ (b) $\delta_i^{min} \le \delta_i \le \delta_i^{max}$

(c) $P_i^{min} \le P_i \le P_i^{max}$ (d) $V_i^{min} \le \sqrt{{P_i^{max}}^2 + {Q_i^{max}}^2}$

34. Which of the following is a valid dynamic programming equation [ ]

(a) $\sum P_{Gi} - \sum P_{Di} + P_{LOSS}$ (b) $F_n\left(\sum_{i=1}^{n} P_i\right) - f_n(P_n) + F_{n-1}\left(\sum_{i=1}^{n-1} P_i\right)$

(c) $F_N(P_N) = F_{N-1}(P_{N-1}) + f_N(P_N)$ (d) $F_n\left(\sum_{i=1}^{n} P_i\right) = \min\left[f_N(P_N) + F_{n-1}\left(\sum_{i=1}^{n-1} P_i\right)\right]$

35. Dual variables are [ ]

(a) Lagrange multipliers

(b) Kuhn – Tucker multipliers

(c) both Lagrange and Kuhn – Tucker multipliers

(d) the problem variables

36. The dependent variables in optimal load flow studies are [ ]

(a) P and Q (b) |V| and δ (c) P and |V| (d) P,Q, |V| and δ

37. Given $B_{11} = 0.02$, $B_{22} = 0.04$; $B_{12} - B_{21} = 0.001$

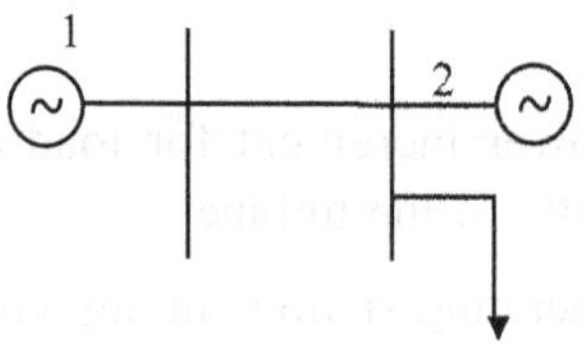

What are the transmission loss when 10Mw is supplied by plant 2 to the load [ ]

(a) 2Mw (b) 4Mw (c) 0.001MW (d) zero

38. 0.04 regulation in speed for a 100Mw rated generator means [ ]

(i) 2.0Hz drop in frequency

(ii) 40Hz drop in frequency

(iii) R = 0.02 Hz/Mw

(a) (i) is only correct (b) (i) and (ii) are both correct

(c) (ii) and (iii) are both correct (d) (i) and (iii) are both correct

39. In a power system during load flow studies

(i) there are four variables at each bus

(ii) the voltage magnitude at one bus is specified and this bus is called voltage controlled bus

(iii) at all the load buses P and Q are specified for the loads

(iv) power losses are assigned to swing bus.

Which of the above is / are correct? [ ]

(a) (i) and (ii) (b) (ii) and (iii)

(c) (i) (iii) and (iv) (d) (i) (ii) (iii) and (iv)

40. In load flow studies

(i) convergence of iterative method depends upon the diagonal dominance in Y_{BUS} matrix

(ii) sparsity of Z – bus matrix is well exploited

(iii) for large well conditioned system with n-buses the number of iteration required is approximately n^2.

(iv) Z – matrix methods is very sensitive to choice of slack bus. Which of the above is / are true. [ ]

(a) (i) and (ii) (b) (ii) and (iv)

(c) (iii) and (iv) (d) (i) and (iii)

41. In load flow solution by N-R method

(i) the rectangular coordinates method is slower compared to polar – coordinates method

(ii) the Jacobian in case of rectangular coordinates is not symmetric

(iii) the Jacobian with usual formulation in polar coordinates is symmetric

(iv) the N-R method converges in 2-5 iterations

which of the following is correct [ ]

(a) (i) and (iv) are true (b) (ii) and (iv) are true

(c) (i), (ii) and (iv) are true (d) (i), (ii) and (iii) are true

42. Economic dispatch problem is related to [ ]

(i) selection of generating units for loading

(ii) planning for generating system expansion

(iii) determine profit from energy sales

(iv) ascertain cost of energy production

(a) (i) and (iii) (b) (i) and (iv)

(c) (ii) and (iii) (d) (iii) and (iv)

43. In the emergency mode of operation [ ]

(a) only system frequency is maintained

(b) only maximal load demand is being met

(c) both (a) and (b) are maintained

(d) only system frequency and voltage are maintained

44. Electrical stiffness of the transmission line is given by [ ]

(a) $\frac{\Delta P}{\Delta \delta}$ (b) $\frac{\Delta P}{\Delta f}$ (c) $\frac{\Delta Q}{\Delta \delta}$ (d) $\frac{\Delta Q}{\Delta f}$

45. Transmission capacity can be increased by [ ]

(i) reducing the effective reactance of the line

(ii) increasing the voltage levels

(iii) by suing bundled conductors

(iv) by increasing the load angle d to some extent

(a) (i) and (iii) are the same

(b) (i) (ii) and (iii) increase the power transfer

(c) (i) and (iv) do not mean the same control

(d) bundled conductors infact decrease the transmission capacity

46. The natural load of a transmission line can be expressed by [ ]

(a) B . X (b) B / X (c) X /B (d) B + X

where B is the line susceptance and X is the line reactance of the line being considered

47. The transmission losses in a line are [ ]

(a) directly proportional to voltage V

(b) inversely proportional to voltage V

(c) directly proportional to V^2

(d) inversely proportional to V^2

48. Rapid changes in system voltage cause [ ]

(a) Flicker (b) Voltage dips

(c) corona (d) loss of synchronism

49. Shunt connected controllable var compensators will [ ]

(i) improve power transfer capability

(ii) improve stability

(iii) improve power transfer but deteriorate stability

(iv) improve stability but reduced power transfer capacity

(a) (iii) is correct (b) (iv) is correct

(c) (i) and (ii) both are correct (d) (i) is only correct all other are wrong.

50. Voltage response of an exciter expressed as [ ]

(a) Volts / sec

(b) volts / ampere

(c) field amperes per output amperes

(d) change in field voltage to change in output voltage

51. The exciter voltage for a 100MVA set is about [ ]

(a) 100V (b) 440V (c) 1KV (d) 250V

52. As per IEEE standard, the exciter block is represented by [ ]

(a) $\frac{K_e}{1+ST_e}$ (b) $\frac{1}{1+ST_e}$ (d) $\frac{1}{K_e+ST_e}$ (d) $\frac{\frac{K_e}{T_e}}{1+ST_e}$

53. The voltage regulator block diagram shows an [ ]

(i) inherent phase lag (ii) inherent phase lead

(iii) inherent steady state error (iv) inherent instability at larger gains

(a) (i) and (ii) are correct (b) (ii) and (iii) are correct

(c) (ii), (iii) and (iv) are correct (d) (i) iii) and (iv) are correct

54. Under sterdy state condition, if K is the over all forward path gain. Then, the steady state error Δe_{ss} is [ ]

(a) $\Delta e_{ss} = \frac{1}{1+K}$ (b) $\Delta e_{ss} = \frac{1}{K}$

(c) Δe_{ss} is independent of k (d) $\Delta e_{ss} = 1+\frac{1}{K}$

55. A stabilizing transformer [ ]

(i) introduces phase lead

(ii) introduces phase lag

(iii) increases stability margin

(iv) has its secondary drawing negligible current in a voltage regulator

(a) (ii) is correct (b) (i) and (ii) are both correct

(c) (ii) and (iv) are correct (d) (ii) (iii) and (iv) are correct

56. A power system stabilizer improves [ ]

(i) phase lag

(ii) improves damping

(iii) produces torque in phase with speed

(a) (i) and (ii) only are correct (b) (ii) and (iii) only are correct

(c) (i) and (iii) only are correct (d) (i) (ii) and (iii) are correct

57. Which of the following is false [ ]

(a) synchronous motors operate with adjustable excitation

(b) synchronous compensators cannot given dynamic reactive power compensation

(c) by supplying a synchronous compensator from a tertiary winding, need for separate transformer can be avoided.

(d) A synchronous compensator can even improve stability

58. Per unit change in voltage magnitude is equal to [ ]

(a) $\frac{\Delta Q}{S_{SC}}$ (b) $\frac{S_{SC}}{\Delta Q}$ (c) $S_{SC}\Delta Q$ (d) $\Delta Q + S_{SC}$

where ΔQ is the change in reactive power and S_{SC} is the short circuit capacity.

59. Which of the following are true ? [ ]

(i) the quadrature voltage compensator would control active power flow in the system

(ii) an in-phase voltage booster would control the reactive power flow in the system

(iii) the natural loading limit is the lowest limit for power transfer

(iv) thermal limit is the highest limit for power transfer

(a) (i) and (ii) are only correct (b) (ii) only is correct

(c) (i) (ii) and (iii) only are correct (d) all are correct

60. Line compensation [ ]

(i) increases Ferranti effect

(ii) requires under excited operation of generators

(iii) reduces power transfer capability

(iv) is never used in power system operation

(a) (i) and (ii) are false (b) (ii) and (iii) are false

(c) (i) (iii) and (iv) are false (d) all are false

61. When sending voltage is equal to receiving end voltage, for maximum power at receiving end [ ]

(a) $X = \sqrt{3}R$ (b) $R = \sqrt{3}X$ (c) $R = \frac{X}{2}$ (d) $X = \frac{R}{2}$

62. For a 400kv line the ratio $\frac{X}{R}$ is about [ ]

(a) 1.5 (b) 6 (c) 10 (d) 16

63. In Var compensators using thyristors [ ]

(a) filters are not necessary

(b) the dominant harmonic is second

(c) filters are needed for 5th and 7th harmonic

(d) capacitors are switched on the h.v. side only

64. Static var compensators [ ]

(i) reduce voltage swings at the rolling mills

(ii) improve power factor

(iii) compensate the unbalanced reactive load of arc furnace loads

(iv) can control the fundamental component of current flowing in an inductor

(a) (i) and (ii) are correct (b) (ii) and (iv) are correct

(c) (i), (ii) (iii) and (iv) are correct (d) all are correct

65. Series – capacitor compensation

(i) produces undamped or slightly damped oscillations

(ii) produces oscillations the frequency of which are of the order of 10^3 to 10^6 K.Hz. – which causes serious problem

(iii) may produce electromechanical oscillations of frequency 1 to 2 Hz

(iv) will not produce any self excitation.

Which of the above is true? [ ]

(a) (i) and (ii) (b) (ii) and (iv) (c) (iii) and (iv) (d) (i) and (iii)

66. The power flow from area 1 to area 2 is given by with usual notation [ ]

(a) $P_{12} = \frac{V_1 V_2}{X} \sin(\delta_1 - \delta_2)$ (b) $P_{12} = \frac{V_1 X}{V_2} \cos(\delta_1 - \delta_2)$

(c) $P_{12} = \frac{V_2 X}{V_1} \sin(\delta_1 - \delta_2)$ (d) $P_{12} = \frac{V_2 V_1}{X} \cos(\delta_1 - \delta_2)$

67. Synchronizing coefficient of a line is given by [ ]

(a) $T_S = \frac{\Delta P}{\Delta \delta}$ (b) $T_S = \Delta P\, [\Delta\delta_1 - \Delta\delta_2]$

(c) $T_S \Delta P = [\Delta\delta_1 - \Delta\delta_2]$ (d) $\Delta P = T_S + \Delta P$

68. Which of the following is correct [ ]

(i) $\Delta f = \frac{1}{2\pi}\frac{d}{dt}\Delta\delta$ Hz (ii) $\Delta f = 2\pi \int \Delta f dt$ rad

(iii) $\Delta f = \frac{1}{2\pi}\int \Delta f dt$ (iv) $\Delta f = 2\pi \int \Delta f dt$

(a) (i) and (ii) (b) (i) only (c) (i) and (iv) (d) (i) (iii) and (iv)

69. The inertia consists of two groups of machines which do not swing together are M_1 and M_2. The equivalent inertia constant of the system is : [ ]

(a) $M_1 + M_2$ (b) $M_1 - M_2$ if $M_1 > M_2$

(c) $\frac{M_1 M_2}{M_1 + M_2}$ (d) $\sqrt{M_1 M_2}$

70. If $\Delta P_{D1} = K_1$ and $\Delta P_{D2} = 0$, in a two area system, the steady state frequency error is [ ]

(a) $\frac{K_1}{\beta_1 + \beta_2}$ (b) $\frac{\beta_1}{K_1 + \beta_2}$ (c) $\frac{\beta_1 + \beta_2}{K_1}$ (d) $\frac{\beta_2}{K_1 + \beta_1}$

71. What is the tie-line power deviation if $\Delta P_{D2} = k_2$ and $\Delta P_{D1} = 0$ for a two area system [ ]

(a) $\frac{\beta_1 k_2}{\beta_1 + \beta_2}$ (b) $\frac{\beta_2 k_2}{\beta_1 + \beta_2}$ (c) $\frac{k_2}{\beta_1 + \beta_2}$ (d) $\frac{k_2(\beta_1 + \beta_2)}{\beta_2}$

72. For two equal areas, for a load disturbance of ΔP_D in an area, the steady state frequency error is [ ]

(a) $\frac{\Delta P_D}{2\beta}$ (b) $\frac{\beta}{2\Delta P_D}$ (c) $\frac{2\beta}{\Delta P_D}$ (d) $\frac{\Delta\beta P_D}{2}$

73. If two equal areas with tie line power interchange of P_{12} experience a load change ΔP_D in one of the areas, the tie line power deviation is [ ]

(a) $\frac{\Delta P_D}{2}$ (b) $\beta_1 \frac{\Delta P_D}{2}$ (c) $\beta_2 \frac{\Delta P_D}{2}$ (d) ΔP_D

74. Which of the following is true [ ]

(i) A synchronous generator at sub synchronous frequencies acts as an induction generator

(ii) At sub synchronous frequencies the rotor resistance viewed from the armature terminals is negative.

(iii) At sub synchronous frequencies resonance may occur between electrical and mechanical system

(iv) Series compensation causes sub synchronous resonance at very low frequencies

(a) (i) is true (b) (i) and (ii) are true

(c) (i), (ii) and (iii) are true (d) (i), (ii), (iii) and (iv) are true

Answers to Objective Questions

1.	(b)	26.	(b)	51.	(d)
2.	(b)	27.	(b)	52.	(c)
3.	(b)	28.	(b)	53.	(d)
4.	(d)	29.	(a)	54.	(a)
5.	(b)	30.	(b)	55.	(d)
6.	(b)	31.	(d)	56.	(d)
7.	(b)	32.	(c)	57.	(b)
8.	(a)	33.	(c)	58.	(a)
9.	(c)	34.	(d)	59.	(d)
10.	(a)	35.	(c)	60.	(d)
11.	(a)	36.	(b)	61.	(a)
12.	(a)	37.	(d)	62.	(d)
13.	(a)	38.	(d)	63.	(c)
14.	(a)	39.	(d)	64.	(d)
15.	(b)	40.	(d)	65.	(d)
16.	(d)	41.	(d)	66.	(a)
17.	(d)	42.	(d)	67.	(a)
18.	(d)	43.	(c)	68.	(a)
19.	(d)	44.	(a)	69.	(c)
20.	(d)	45.	(d)	70.	(a)
21.	(a)	46.	(b)	71.	(a)
22.	(a)	47.	(d)	72.	(a)
23.	(a)	48.	(a)	73.	(a)
24.	(c)	49.	(c)	74.	(d)
25.	(c)	50.	(a)		

References

Books

1. Beveridge G.S.G and R.S. Schechter, Optimisation: Theory and Practice, McGraw-Hill Book Co., New York, 1970.
2. Rao, S.S., Optimisation: Theory and Application, Wiley Eastern Ltd., New Delhi. 1978.
3. Kirk, Donald E., Optimal Control Theory: An Introduction, Prentice Hall Inc., Englewood Cliffs, New Jersey, 1970.
4. Elgerd, Olle I., Electric Energy Steams Theory: An Introduction, McGraw Hill Book Co., New York, 1971.
5. Kirchmayer, L.K., Economic Control of Interconnected Systems, John Wiley and Sons, New York, 1959.
6. Zaborszky L. and J. W. Rittenhouse, Electric Power Transmission, The Ronald Press Co., New York, 1954.
7. Taylor, Openshaw (Ed.), Power System Plant, George Newnes Ltd., London. 1955.
8. Stagg Glenn W., and A.H. EI-Abiad, Computer Methods in Power System Analysis McGraw-Hill Book Co. Ltd., New York, 1968.
9. Blindleistung, VDE Verlag, GmBH, Berlin 1963.
10. Handschin E. (Ed.), Real Time Control of Electric Power Systems, Elsevier Publishing Co., Amsterdam 1972.
11. P.M. Anderson, Power System Control and Stability, A.A. Fauad, The Iowa State University Press.
12. Paul.C. Krause, Analysis of Electrical Machines, McGraw Hill Book co.
13. V. Venikov, Transient Processes in Electrical Power System, Mir Publishers, Moscow
14. Hadi Saadat, Power System Analysis, McGraw Hill International Edition.
15. PSR Murty, Power System Operation and Control, Tata – McGraw Hill –1984.

Periodicals and Conference Proceedings :

1. Albert M., 'Nonlinear programming solutions for load flow-Minimum loss and Economic dispatching solutions, IEEE Trans., PAS-88, No.4. April 1969.
2. Funk, G. "Die Spannungsabhangigkeit Von Drehstrom lasten" Elektrizitats wirtschaft, 68, 1969.
3. Murty, P.S.R., "Load modelling for power flow solution," Journal of IE(India), 58, Pt. EL3, Dec., 1977.
4. IEEE Committee Report, "Dynamic Models for steam and hydro turbines in Power system studies", IEEE Trans. PAS May 1969.
5. Dsewenski, A.I., "Uber den Einfluss der spannungsenderung auf die wirk-und Blindleistung der Verbraucher", Energietechnik, 12 Nov., 1953.
6. Anschutz, H., "Frequenz-und Spannungsschwankungen in Drehstromnetz und ihre Auswirkungen," ETZ-13, Dec. 1949.
7. Woodwards J.L. "Hydraulic turbine transfer function for use in governing studies", IEEE Proc, 115 No.3, Mar. 1968 (Correspondence).
8. Ramey, R.G. and J.W. Skooglund, "Detailed hydro-governor representation for stability studies, IEEE Trans. PAS, Jan. 1970.
9. Hale, H.W. and J.W. Ward, "Digital computer solution of power flow problems", AIEE Trans. PAS, 75, June 1956.
10. Glimn A.P. and G.W. Stagg, "Automatic calculation of load flows", AIEE Trans. (PAS), 76, June 1956. '
11. Brown H.E. et al., "Power flow solution by impedance matrix iterative method", IEEE Trans (PAS), 82, Apr. 1963.
12. H.E. Brown, Z-matrix algorithms in load flow programs, IEEE Trans (PAS), 87 March 1968.
13. Hart, C.E. and W.F. Tinney, "Power flow solution by Newton's method", IEEE Trans (PAS), 86, 1967.
14. Stott. B. "Decoupled Newton-load flow", Trans (PAS), 91, Sep/Oct. 1972.
15. Peterson N.M. W.F. Tinney, and D.W. Bree, "Iterative linear ac power flow solution for fast approximate outage studies", IEEE Trans. (PAS), 91, Sep./Oct. 1972.
16. Stott, Band O. Alsac, "Fast decoupled load flow", IEEE Trans. (PAS), 93, May/ June 1974.

17. Tinney W.F. and J. W. Walker, "Direct solution of spares network equations by optimally ordered triangular factorisation", Proc. IEEE, 55, Nov. 1967.

18. Stott, B, "Load flow calculation methods", Proc. IEEE, 62, July 1974.

19. Noakes, F. and A. Arismonandar, "A Bibliography on optimum operation of power systems 1919-1959", IEEE Trans (PAS), 82,1963.

20. Baker, A.D. and S.O. Navarro "The use of cubic cost curves in the economic loading of electric power systems", IEEE Trans. (PAS), 84,1965.

21. Smith, H.M. and S. Y. Tong, "Minimizing power transmission losses by reactive volt amperes control", IEEE Trans (PAS), 82,1963.

22. Bauman, R."Power flow solution with optimal reactive flow"., Archiv fur Elektrotechnik, 48,1963.

23. Dopazo, J.F. O.A. Klitin, G.W. Stagg andM. Watson, "An optimization technique for real and reactive power allocation", Proc IEE, 45, 1967.

24. Carpentier, J. "Contribution a I'etude du dispatching economique'Bulletin de la Societe fransaise des Electriciens, 3 Aug. 1962.

25. Carpentier, J. and J. Siroux, "L'optimisation de la production a L'Electricite de France", Bulletin de la Societe Frallcaise des Electriciens,1963.

26. Pescon, J.,D.S.Piercy,W.F. Tinney and O:J. Tvelt, "Optimum control of reactive power flow," IEEE Trans. (PAS), 1968.

27. Shen, C.M. and M.A. Laughton, "Determination of optimum power system, operating conditions under constraints", Proc. IEEE, 116, Feb. 1969.

28. Dommel, H. W. and W.F.Tinney, "Optimal power flow solutions", IEEE Trans (PAS) 87, 1968.

29. El – Abiad, A.H. and F.J. Jaimes, "A method for optimum scheduling of power and voltage magnitude, IEEE Trans (PAS) 88, Apr. 1969.

30. Fletcher, R. and M.J.D. Powell, "A rapidly convergent descent method for minimization," Computer journal, June 1963.

31. Bird, J.I.,' 'Load dispatching on the CEGB System," Paper presented at Symposium on Optimal power system operation, Univ. of Manchester, Sep. 1969.

32. Lowery, P.G. "Generating unit commitment by dynamic programming," IEEE Trails (PAS) 85,1966.

33. Udo, M., "Optimisation of start-up and shut-down of thermal units", Proc. Third PSCC 1969 Rome paper O.S.7.

34. Kerr, R.H., J.L. Scheidt, A.J. Fontana and J.K. Wiley, "Unit Commitment" IEEE Trans (PAS), 85, 1966.

35. Hara, K. Kimura M. and N. Honda, "A method for planning economic unit commitment and maintenance of thermal power systems", IEEE Trans. (PAS) 85, 1966.

36. Nagrath, I.J. and S.K. Agarwal, "Optimum scheduling of hydrothermal systems", Proc. IEE, 119, Feb. 1972.

37. Nagrath, I.J., G. Dayal and D.P. Kothari, "Optimum scheduling of hydro-thermal system taking transmission loss into account", Jour. IE (India), 52. Oct. 1971.

38. Drake, J.H., L.K. Kirchmayer, R.B. Mayall, and H. Wood, "Optimum operation of a hydro-thermal system," Trans. AIEE (PAS), 82, Aug. 1962.

39. Bonaert, A.P. A-El-Abiad and Koivo "Optimum scheduling of hydro-thermal power systems", Proc. Seventh PICA Con/., Boston, 1971.

40. Murty, P.S.R., "Effect of system loads on optimal load flow solutions," Jr. IE (India), 58, Pt. EL3, Dec. 1977.

41. Hochstetter Werner, "Properties of static compensators for power supply systems", Siemens Review, Aug. 1977.

42. Achenbach, H., W. Hanke and W. Hochstetter, "Controllable static reactive power compensators in electrical supply systems", Second IEAC Symposium on Control in Power Electronics and Electrical Drive, Dusseldorf, Oct. 1977.

43. Tyll, Heinz, "'Use of static compensators in transmission system", Symp. On Reactive Power Compensation, Rio de Janeiro, Brazil, May 1979.

44. Fouad, A.A., and K. T. Khu, "Subsynchronous resonance zones in the IEEE bench mark power system, IEEE Trans. (PAS) 97, May/June 1978.

45. Kilgore, L.A., L.C. Elioh and E.R. Taylor, "The prediction and control of self excited oscillations due to series capacitors in power systems", IEEE Trans. (PAS), 90, May/June 1971.

46. Hergert, J.C. and C.W. Park, "Parameter identification and verification of low order boiler models", IEEE Trans. on PAS. PAS-75, No.4, July/Aug. 1976.

47. Cohn, Nathan "Power flow control-Basic concepts for interconnected systems", Mid West Power Conference, USA, 1950.

48. Elgerd, 0.I. "Trends and philosophies of power systems control", Alterton Conference on Circuits and Systems, Oct. 1973.

49. Cohn, Nathan, "Fundamentals for control of generation and power flow on interconnected systems", Invited Talk, North American Power Systems Interconnection Committee Meeting, Las Vegaes, Navada, USA. Sep. 1970.

50. Elgerd, 0.I. and C.E. Fosha, "Optimum megawatt-frequency control of multi- area electric energy system", IEEE Trans (PAS), 89, Apr. 1970.

51. Fosha, C.E. and 0.I. Elgerd, "The megawatt-frequency control problem: A new approach via optimal control theory", IEEE Trans (PAS) 89. Apr. 1970.

52. Murty, P.S.R. and P.V. Ramana Rao, "Optimal load frequency control and system modelling". Jour IE (India), Pt. EL4, 57, Feb. 1977.

53. Ramana Rao P. V. and P.S.R Murty, "Identification an\t verification of reduced order steam reheat turbine model", Jour. (IE), Pt. ME6, May 1981.

54. Ramana Rao, P. V. and P.S.R Murty, "Modelling, Identification and optimal control of hydro governor system", Jour. IE (India), 60, Pt. EL2, Oct. 1979.

55. Venkateswarlu K. and A.K. Mahalanabis, "Optimum load frequency control with restrictions on the rate of power generation, Jour I.E. (India) Pt. EL4, 58, Feb. 1978.

56. Venkateswarlu K. and A.K. Mahalanabis. "Load frequency control using output feedback", Jour. IE (India), Pt EL4 58, Feb. 1978.

57. Nanda, J. M.L. Kothari, and P.S. Satsanghi, "Automatic. Generation control reheat thermal system considering generation rate constraint and governor dead band'., Journal IE (India), Pt EL6, 63. June 1983.

58. Liacco Thomas E.Dy. et al., "Automation of CEI system lor security", PICA Boston, USA, 1971.

59. Bhaskaran K., "Technology trends in power plant operation", Second Symp. on Power plant dynamics and control BHEL (R&D), Hyderabad, Feb. 1979.

60. Liacco, Thomas E. Dy "Real time computer control of power systems", Proc. A IEEE, 162, July 1974.

61. Larson, R.E. et al., "State estimation in power systems", IEEE Trans. (PAS) 89,1970.

62. Kuppurajulu, A., "Digital Computers for on line control", NPSC, Electrical Engg. Dept., Osmania University, Dec. 1981.

63. Choudhari, S.H. "Turbine instrumentation and automation", NPSC, Elec. Engg., Osmania University, Dec. 1981.

64. Gupta, P.G., "Stochastic approach to peak power demand forecasting in Electric Utility systems", IEEE Trans. on PAS PAS-90 No 2, Mar./Apr. 1971.

65. Christiannse, W.R., "Short-term load forecasting using exponential smoothing", IEEE Trans on PAS PAS-90 No.2, Mar./Apr. 1971.

66. Mathewan, P.D. and H. Nicholsan, "Techniques for load prediction in the electricity supply industry", Proc. IEE (London), 115 (power) Oct. 1968.

67. Farmer, D.E. and M.J. Potton, "Development of on-line prediction techniques with results from trials in the south West Region of the CEG", Proc IEE London, 115, Oct, 1968.

68. Toyoda. J, Mo-Shing Chev and Yukiyoshi Inoue, "An application of state to estimation to short-term load forecasting part-I "Forecasting modelling Part-II, Implementation, IEEE Trans. On PAS, PAS – 89, No 7, Sept/Oct 1970.

69. Larson, Robert E, Willam, F, Tinney and John Peschan, "State estimation in power systems part-I theory and feasibility", IEEE Trans. on PAS, PAS. March 1970.

70. Larson, Robert E., W.F. Tinney, L.P. Hajdu and D.S. Piercy "State estimation in power systems Part-II: Implementation and applications", IEEE Trans on PAS 80, March 1970.

Lecture Notes and Others :

1. Real time control of power systems for security, Summer school notes, sponsored by ISTE, College of Engg. Guindy, Madras, May/June 1976.

2. General Electric's static var control, General Electric Brochure, Switchgear Business Dept. USA.

3. Advances in power systems, Winter school notes, sponsored by ISTE, Regional Engg. College, Warangal, 1967-77.

4. P.V. Ramana Rao, Parameter estimation and model reduction of power plant components using identification techniques for power system control, Ph.D. thesis, Kakatia Univ., Warangal, May 1981.

5. P.S.R. Murty., Optimal load flow studies in interconnected networks, (German), Doctoral thesis, Technical University, Berlin.

Index

R

S

T